FASHION NOW

Edited by Terry Jones & Avril Mair

FASHION NOW

i-D selects the world's 150 most important designers

EDITED BY TERRY JONES & AVRIL MAIR

TASCHEN

KÖLN LONDON LOS ANGELES MADRID PARIS TOKYO

Very special thanks to

C.P.
COMPANY

DIESEL
FOR SUCCESSFUL LIVING

GIORGIO ARMANI

HARVEY NICHOLS

i-D

MAKE-UP ART COSMETICS

Paul Smith

PRADA

Y's YOHJI YAMAMOTO

ANTONIO BERARDI SPRING-SUMMER 2003

MIGUEL ADROVER SPRING-SUMMER 2003

HUSSEIN CHALAYAN AUTUMN-WINTER 2002

CHANEL SPRING-SUMMER 2003

HELMUT LANG SPRING-SUMMER 2003

MARC BY MARC JACOBS SPRING-SUMMER 2003

STELLA MCCARTNEY AUTUMN-WINTER 2002

ANNA MOLINARI SPRING-SUMMER 2003

JURGI PERSOONS AUTUMN-WINTER 2002

NEW YORK INDUSTRIE AUTUMN-WINTER 2002

EMANUEL UNGARO AUTUMN-WINTER 2002

JEREMY SCOTT SPRING-SUMMER 2003

VERSACE SPRING-SUMMER 2003

VIVIENNE WESTWOOD SPRING-SUMMER 2003

YOHJI YAMAMOTO AUTUMN-WINTER 2002

A

TOM FORD FOR YVES SAINT LAURENT RIVE GAUCHE SPRING-SUMMER 2003

TOM FORD FOR YVES SAINT LAURENT RIVE GAUCHE SPRING-SUMMER 2003

DOLCE & GABBANA SPRING-SUMMER 2003

Fashion has always helped define the human condition and designers are the weather-men, predicting or foreseeing what the public will need, providing a wardrobe to protect, expose or purely to entertain. This is what makes the business of fashion so fascinating. We are enthralled by the theatre of everyday life. Some act but most people just enjoy to watch, and fashion today has replaced the movie business in providing us with the fantasies and glamour that feed our dreams. With fashion now, we can select our roles. And never before has there been such a choice. The market is filled up – one might argue that it has been flooded – but that doesn't stop the dream. Each year the number of students entering fashion schools around the world increases: 8,000–10,000 at the last count. So fashion today depends on ideas, individuality and authenticity; more than ever, designers look to their roots – where they began, who they are, why they do what they are doing – essentially, what are their signatures and where are their values. To survive in fashion now, these are the ingredients that the customer, voyeur or performer is looking for. Marketing, advertising and general hype won't guarantee you a repeat season. The competition has never been greater and the running has never been more diverse. To make this book, we attempted to put together a cross-section of fashion designers who continue to express themselves and, whether they run a large business or have just produced their first collection, have an identity that defines their vision. Intentionally, this is a snapshot of fashion now.

The theatre of everyday life is what inspired i-D when it started, back in 1980. At that time, we looked to the street as inspiration – to show how popular culture influenced the way we chose to dress. i-D wanted to feature the source of ideas and originality, aiming to empower each individual to confidently express themselves. We wanted to give space for the exchange of ideas to germinate and multiply. After celebrating 20 years of i-D with the 'Smile i-D' book, published by TASCHEN in Spring 2001, Angelika and Benedikt Taschen asked if we would be interested in collaborating on 'Fashion Now'. Following their successful 'Art Now' and 'Architecture Now' books, we didn't need too much persuasion. We just needed the co-operation of over 100 designers, whose work had appeared – and often been discovered – in the pages of i-D. We had our archive, generally considered the most relevant reference for all those involved with the creative side of fashion business. Next we needed to grow extra arms, bigger brains, wider

FOREWORD

eyes and change the clock to longer days. Fortunately, we have the most dedicated contributors on earth and they are the life-blood of i-D. Through them, the magazine's ethos remains the same as when we started, promoting talent and providing links in the creative and social exchange.

Fashion, by definition, is about change and has relevance to more than the clothes we wear. It has to do with illusion, contributing to our wellbeing, feeding our insecurities, boosting our confidence. But more important than any change in fashion over the last 20 years is the democratisation of style. Style is a reflection of personal choice and fashion today is a reflection of personal style. In 1980, i-D carried the byline 'A Manual of Style' and style magazines were born. Two decades later, the tag has been applied to so many consumer marketing scams that the definition of lifestyle can be anything you want it to be. But i-D means identity and personal identity is where we look for our inspiration. Fashion is much more fun than trainspotting. I love watching people, simply observing human behaviour. It's my full-time vocation. Once I was asked why I made i-D and I replied that it forced me to keep my eyes open. I feel privileged to watch the designers' shows in New York, Paris, Milan and London. Like food for the brain, they are a big part of my diet but I also love the mess of cities, the contrast of countries and the diversity of the street. That constant new soundtrack, smell, taste or visual surprise make fashion one of the best universal languages now. Let the players play on!

TERRY JONES
Creative Director & Editor In Chief, i-D magazine

Mode hat immer schon die 'conditio humana' mit definiert. Designer können voraus-ahnen oder vorhersehen, was die Menschen auf der Straße brauchen, und Mode machen, mit der sie sich schützen, produzieren oder einfach vergnügen können. Das macht die Faszination des Modebusiness aus. Das Schauspiel des täglichen Lebens zieht uns in seinen Bann. Es gibt zwar Akteure, doch die meisten gefallen sich in der Rolle des Zuschauers, und heute hat die Mode das Filmgeschäft als Traumfabrik abgelöst. Mit der Mode heute können wir uns unsere Rollen aussuchen. Und nie war die Auswahl so groß. Der Markt ist gesättigt – man könnte fast überschwemmt sagen – aber das tut dem Traum keinen Abbruch. Die Zahl der Studenten, die an die Modeschulen in aller Welt drängen, steigt von Jahr zu Jahr: 8000 bis 10 000 sind es nach letzten Schätzun-gen. Darum lebt Mode heute von Ideen, Individualität und Authentizität; mehr denn je besinnen sich Designer auf ihre Wurzeln – woher sie kommen, wer sie sind, warum sie das tun, was sie tun – kurz gesagt, was sie unverwechselbar macht und wo ihre Werte liegen. Wenn man heute in der Modewelt überleben will, sind das die Zutaten, mit denen man die Kunden, Voyeure oder Selbstdarsteller locken muss. Marketing, Werbe-kampagnen und Hype auf allen Ebenen garantieren noch lange keine zweite Saison. Die Konkurrenz war noch nie so groß, und noch nie war ein mannigfaltigeres Feld am Start. Für dieses Buch wollten wir einen Querschnitt von Modedesignern zusammenstellen, die sich selbst in ihre Mode einbringen und deren Vision von ihrer Identität definiert wird – ganz gleich, ob sie nun eine große Firma leiten oder gerade ihre ersten Kollektionen herausgebracht haben. Dies ist bewusst als Momentaufnahme der Mode heute gedacht.

Das Schauspiel des Alltagslebens inspirierte uns damals, 1980, bei der Gründung der Zeitschrift i-D. Damals suchten und fanden wir unsere Inspiration auf der Straße – um zu zeigen, wie Populärkultur unseren Kleidungsstil beeinflusste. i-D wollte die Quellen von Ideen und Originalität in den Vordergrund stellen, zielte darauf ab, jeden einzelnen zu ermutigen, sich selbstbewusst zum Ausdruck zu bringen. Wir wollten dem Austausch von Ideen Raum geben, damit sie sich gegenseitig befruchten und vermehren konnten. Nachdem wir 20 Jahre i-D mit dem Buch 'Smile i-D' gefeiert hatten, das im Frühjahr 2001 bei TASCHEN erschien, fragten mich Angelika und Benedikt Taschen, ob wir interessiert wären, an 'Fashion Now' mitzuwirken. Nach den erfolgreichen Büchern 'Art Now' und 'Architecture Now' mussten sie uns nicht lange bitten. Wir waren 'nur' noch

VORWORT

auf die Kooperation von über 100 Designern angewiesen, deren Arbeit auf den Seiten von i-D erschienen (und oftmals entdeckt worden) ist. Wir hatten unser Archiv, die anerkanntermaßen wichtigste Referenz für alle, die mit der kreativen Seite des Modebusiness zu tun haben. Abgesehen davon mussten wir uns nur noch längere Arme, größere Gehirne und wachere Augen wachsen lassen und die Uhr auf längere Tage umstellen. Glücklicherweise haben wir die engagiertesten MitarbeiterInnen der Welt, sie sind das Herzblut von i-D. Dank ihnen gilt für uns heute noch das Ethos, mit dem wir einmal angefangen haben: Talent zu fördern und Schnittstellen für den kreativen und sozialen Austausch anzubieten. In der Mode geht es per Definition um Veränderung, und sie hat Einfluss auf weit mehr als die Kleidung, die wir tragen. Sie hat mit Illusion zu tun, sie trägt zu unserem Wohlbefinden bei, nährt unsere Unsicherheiten, stärkt unser Selbstvertrauen. Aber noch wichtiger als jeder Modewandel im Verlauf der letzten 20 Jahre ist die Demokratisierung von Stil. Stil ist ein Spiegel der persönlichen Entscheidung, und Mode ist heute ein Spiegel des persönlichen Stils. 1980 trug i-D den Untertitel ‚A Manual of Style', und die Style-Zeitschriften waren geboren. Heute, zwei Jahrzehnte später, sind unter diesem Etikett so viele billige Marketingmaschen inszeniert worden, dass die Definition von ‚Lifestyle' vollkommen beliebig geworden ist. Aber i-D bedeutet Identitätsnachweis, und die persönliche Identität ist das, wovon wir uns inspirieren lassen.

Mode ist viel mehr als ein stupider Zeitvertreib. Ich sehe gern Leute an, beobachte menschliches Verhalten. Das ist vielleicht meine Hauptbeschäftigung. Ich bin einmal gefragt worden, warum ich i-D mache, und ich antwortete, dass es mich zwingt, die Augen offen zu halten. Ich schätze mich glücklich, mir die Modeschauen der großen Designer in New York, Mailand und London ansehen zu dürfen. Als 'food for the brain' lebe ich davon, aber ich liebe auch das Durcheinander der Städte, den Kontrast zwischen den Ländern und die Vielfalt der Straße. Diese unentwegten Soundtracks, Gerüche, Geschmacksrichtungen und optischen Überraschungen machen Mode heute zu einer der großartigsten Universalsprachen. 'Let the players play on!'

TERRY JONES
Creative Director & Editor In Chief, i-D magazine

La mode a toujours contribué à définir la condition humaine. Les créateurs de mode sont des météorologues qui prédisent ou prévoient ce dont le public aura besoin et lui proposent des vêtements pour le protéger, l'exposer ou simplement l'amuser. C'est ce qui rend le monde de la mode si fascinant. Nous sommes captivés par le théâtre de la vie quotidienne. Certains agissent, mais la plupart des gens préfèrent regarder ; en alimentant nos rêves de fantasmes et de glamour, la mode d'aujourd'hui a remplacé le cinéma. Elle nous laisse le choix des rôles, un choix qui n'a jamais été aussi vaste. Certes, le marché est saturé – certains le disent même inondé – mais cela n'arrête pas le rêve. Chaque année, le nombre d'étudiants qui entrent dans les écoles de stylisme du monde entier est en constante augmentation : entre 8 000 et 10 000 inscriptions au dernier recensement. La mode d'aujourd'hui repose sur les idées, l'individualité et l'authenticité. Plus que jamais, les créateurs se tournent vers leurs racines : ils s'interrogent sur leurs origines, leur identité et les raisons qui les poussent à créer, mais avant tout sur leur style signature et sur leurs valeurs. Pour survivre dans l'univers actuel de la mode, ce sont les ingrédients que le client recherche, qu'il porte les vêtements ou se contente de regarder. Les stratégies marketing, la publicité et la médiatisation ne garantissent pas le succès de la saison suivante. La concurrence n'a jamais été aussi rude et les candidats aussi diversifiés. Pour écrire ce livre, nous avons choisi de présenter les créateurs qui continuent à s'exprimer et, qu'ils dirigent une multinationale ou aient à peine produit leur première collection, possèdent une identité propre qui définit leur vision. Ce livre se veut donc avant tout un instantané de la mode d'aujourd'hui.

i-D est né en 1980, inspiré par le théâtre de la vie quotidienne. A cette époque, nous puisions notre inspiration dans la rue pour montrer comment la culture populaire influençait nos choix vestimentaires. i-D voulait remonter à la source des idées et de l'originalité afin d'insuffler à chacun la confiance requise pour s'exprimer. Nous souhaitions dédier un espace à l'échange des idées pour favoriser leur développement et leur multiplication. Après avoir célébré le 20ème anniversaire d'i-D avec le livre « Smile i-D », édité par TASCHEN au printemps 2001, Angelika et Benedikt Taschen nous ont proposé de collaborer à la rédaction de « Fashion Now ». Face au succès de leurs parutions « Art Now » et « Architecture Now », nous n'avons pas été bien difficiles à

PRÉFACE

convaincre. Nous avions simplement besoin de coopérer avec plus de 100 créateurs dont le travail avait été présenté – et souvent découvert – dans les pages d'i-D. Nous avons ressorti nos archives, souvent considérées comme une référence de choix par tous ceux qui sont impliqués dans le côté créatif de la mode. Ensuite, nous avons dû nous faire pousser quelques bras supplémentaires, élargir nos cerveaux, écarquiller grand nos yeux et ajouter quelques heures à l'horloge pour rallonger les journées. Heureusement, nous avons travaillé avec les gens les plus passionnés, ceux sans qui i-D n'existerait pas. Grâce à eux, l'éthique du magazine reste la même qu'au premier jour. Nous continuons à promouvoir le talent et à fournir des liens pour l'échange créatif et social.

Par définition, la mode n'est que changement. Elle se rapporte à bien d'autres choses que les vêtements que nous portons. Elle relève de l'illusion, contribue à notre bien-être, alimente nos insécurités mais stimule notre assurance. Toutefois, le changement le plus important de ces 20 dernières années reste sans conteste la démocratisation du style. Le style reflète les choix personnels et la mode d'aujourd'hui incarne justement le style personnel. En 1980, i-D intitule son premier numéro « Un Manuel de Style » et les magazines de lifestyle étaient nés. Vingt ans plus tard, le concept a été appliqué à tant de fumisteries marketing que l'idée de lifestyle ne veut plus dire grand chose. Pourtant, i-D signifie « identité » et c'est l'identité personnelle qui nous inspire. La mode est bien plus divertissante que le trainspotting. J'adore regarder les gens, simplement pour observer le comportement humain. C'est pour moi une occupation à temps plein. Un jour, on m'a demandé pourquoi j'avais lancé i-D. J'ai répondu que cela m'obligeait à garder les yeux ouverts. Je me sens vraiment privilégié de pouvoir assister aux défilés de New York, Paris, Milan et Londres. Nourriture pour l'esprit, les créateurs constituent une importante part de mon régime quotidien, mais j'aime aussi le désordre des villes, le contraste des pays et la diversité de la rue. Le renouvellement constant des sons, des odeurs, des saveurs et des surprises visuelles fait de la mode l'un des langages universels les plus efficaces d'aujourd'hui. Alors longue vie à la mode !

TERRY JONES
Creative Director & Editor In Chief, i-D magazine

Fashion is a constant revolution. It's an industry whose basis is aesthetic upheaval every six months: a restless search for the new, the improved or, at least, the opposite of whatever was around last season. So 'Fashion Now' doesn't try to pin down fashion now – be it fully-fledged entertainment medium, sublime artistic endeavour or siren-symbol of global capitalism – but rather focuses on the forces that drive it, those architects of continual change. Of course, the process of fashion involves many, many contributors – photographers, stylists, editors, writers, publicists, producers – an endless stream of creatives who incite the desire, translate the message, sell the product. But, fundamentally, fashion now comes down to clothes. Which is why 'Fashion Now' is about the people who design them.

Designers who stalk the boardrooms and those who proclaim themselves seditionaries. Designers with a taste for power and politics and those who shun the spotlight completely. Designers who battle for corporate domination and those whose splendid isolation is important above all else. Designers with international empires and those struggling to find enough cash to put on their next show. Designers with decades behind them and those with all the promise to come. Designers who respect and support the industry, designers who perform brave and breathtaking acts of subversion and designers who opt out of its codes and conditions entirely. Designers who use the body as a platform for cultural exploration, designers who believe in extreme provocation and riotous extravagance, designers who simply make beautiful things to wear. Designers who embrace luxurious elitism and those who strive for sartorial transgression. Designers who balance the contrary forces of art and commerce and designers who use fashion as an experimental medium for their radical vision. Designers possessing the kind of emotional intuition that led historian Eric Hobsbawm to credit them with foretelling the future. Designers who just want to make women sexy and dresses that sell.

What all these designers have in common is a passion and dedication. They do what they do, often against all the odds, because to do anything else is, quite simply, unthinkable. In the following pages you'll find a very subjective selection of those designers. 'Fashion Now' is neither a history of contemporary design (too many of those already) nor an exhaustive, comprehensive A to Z (too boring). But we like to

INTRODUCTION

see it as a pretty good guide to what's important all the same. Put together by the team who produce i-D (unfortunately at the same time as several issues of i-D), 'Fashion Now' is hopefully informed by the magazine's energetic, irreverent but fashion-infatuated spirit. It goes without saying that we owe a great deal of thanks to all those who helped make this book possible: the creative teams who allowed us to draw on their work from i-D archives, the writers, the PRs, the agents and, of course, the designers themselves, who submitted with good humour and grace to yet another of our questionnaires. 'Fashion Now' – and fashion now – exists because of them. I feel unbelievably privileged to be a part of the process. 'Vive la révolution!'

AVRIL MAIR
Editor, i-D magazine

Mode ist eine permanente Revolution. Mode ist eine Industrie, die alle sechs Monate einen Aufstand auslöst: eine rastlose Suche nach Neuem, nach Verbesserungen oder zumindest nach dem Gegenteil dessen, was in der letzten Saison angesagt war. Deshalb versucht 'Fashion Now' auch nicht nur, den Ist-Zustand der Mode heute zu fixieren – weder als Unterhaltungsmedium noch als sublimes künstlerisches Streben noch als verführerisches Symbol eines weltumspannenden Kapitalismus. Vielmehr richten wir mit diesem Buch unsere Aufmerksamkeit auf die Designer, die die Mode bestimmen, auf die Initiatoren der kontinuierlichen Veränderung. Selbstverständlich sind viele, viele Menschen an der Entstehung von Mode beteiligt: Fotografen, Stylisten, Redakteure, Autoren, Publizisten, Hersteller – eine unüberschaubare Zahl von kreativen Köpfen, die Wünsche wecken, Botschaften entschlüsseln und das fertige Produkt verkaufen. Aber im Grunde genommen lässt sich Mode immer auf die Kleider an sich reduzieren. Und deshalb geht es in 'Fashion Now' um die Menschen, die diese Kleider entwerfen:

Designer in Vorstandsetagen und solche, die sich als Unruhestifter verstehen. Designer mit Spaß an Macht und Politik und solche, die die Öffentlichkeit scheuen. Designer, die sich Einfluss in einer Firma erkämpfen, und andere, denen ihre selbstgewählte Isolation über alles geht. Designer mit internationalen Imperien und solche, die mit Mühe das Geld für ihre nächste Modenschau zusammenbringen. Designer mit jahrzehntelangen Erfolgen und vielversprechende Newcomer. Designer, die die Industrie respektieren und unterstützen, Designer, die mit atemberaubenden Aktionen gegen die Industrie opponieren, und Designer, die sich den Konventionen und Konditionen der Modebranche völlig verweigern. Designer, die den Körper als Projektionsfläche für kulturelle Untersuchungen nutzen, Designer, die an extreme Provokation und zügellose Extravaganz glauben, und Designer, die einfach wunder-schöne, tragbare Mode produzieren. Designer, die sich einer luxussüchtigen Elite verpflichtet fühlen, und diejenigen, die nach klassenloser modischer Eleganz streben. Designer, denen die Versöhnung von Kunst und Kommerz gelingt, und Designer, die Mode als experimentelles Medium ihrer radikalen Visionen betrachten. Designer mit emotionaler Intuition, denen der Historiker Eric Hobsbawm die Vorhersage der Zukunft zutraute. Designer, die schlicht und ergreifend Frauen in sexy Kleider stecken und diese gut verkaufen wollen.

EINLEITUNG

All diese Designer haben dieselbe Leidenschaft und Berufung: Sie machen – oft allen Widrigkeiten zum Trotz – Mode, weil es für sie einfach undenkbar wäre, etwas anderes zu tun. Auf den folgenden Seiten finden Sie eine sehr subjektive Auswahl dieser Designer und Modeschöpfer. 'Fashion Now' ist keine Geschichte des zeitgenössischen Modedesigns (davon gibt es schon zu viele) und auch kein umfassendes, erschöpfendes Handbuch von A bis Z (denn das wäre zu langweilig). Wir halten dieses Buch für einen ganz gut gelungenen Guide zum Thema Mode. Zusammengestellt hat ihn das Produktionsteam der Zeitschrift i-D (leider parallel zum Erscheinen mehrerer Ausgaben unseres Magazins). Wir hoffen, dass 'Fashion Now' vom selben leidenschaftlichen, respektlosen, aber modebesessenen Geist durchdrungen ist wie unsere Zeitschrift. Es versteht sich von selbst, dass wir all jenen zu großem Dank verpflichtet sind, die dieses Buch überhaupt erst möglich gemacht haben: den Kreativteams, die uns erlaubten, auf ihre Arbeiten im i-D-Archiv zurückzugreifen, den Autoren, den PR-Leuten, den Agenten und natürlich den Designern selbst, die bereitwillig und gut gelaunt Fragen über Fragen beantwortet haben. Mode heute – 'Fashion Now' – existiert dank ihnen. Es ist eine große Ehre für mich, Teil dieses Prozesses sein zu dürfen. 'Vive la révolution.'

AVRIL MAIR
Editor, i-D magazine

La mode est une révolution permanente, une industrie dont le but consiste à bouleverser les valeurs esthétiques tous les six mois à travers une quête incessante de nouveauté, de « mieux » ou au moins du contraire de ce qu'on a vu la saison précédente. 'Fashion Now' ne cherche donc pas à étiqueter la mode d'aujourd'hui – support de divertissement parfaitement assumé, sublime effort artistique ou chant des sirènes de la mondialisation capitaliste – mais se concentre plutôt sur les forces qui la font avancer, ces architectes du changement continu. Evidemment, le processus de la mode implique de très nombreux intervenants – photographes, stylistes, rédacteurs, journalistes, publicitaires, producteurs – un flot illimité de créatifs qui provoquent le désir, traduisent le message, vendent le produit. Fondamentalement, la mode d'aujourd'hui se résume aux vêtements. C'est pourquoi 'Fashion Now' parle des gens qui les créent.

Les créateurs qui se plient aux règles de l'industrie et ceux qui se proclament dissidents. Les créateurs fascinés par le pouvoir et la stratégie et ceux qui fuient totalement les feux de la rampe. Les créateurs qui veulent devenir numéro un et ceux dont le splendide isolement compte plus que toute autre chose. Les créateurs qui ont bâti des empires mondiaux et ceux qui luttent pour trouver l'argent de leur prochain défilé. Les créateurs qui comptent plusieurs dizaines d'années de métier derrière eux et ceux qui ont encore toute la vie devant eux. Les créateurs qui respectent et soutiennent l'industrie, les courageux qui osent la subversion et ceux qui s'affranchissent entièrement des codes et des contraintes de la mode. Les créateurs qui utilisent le corps comme une plate-forme d'exploration culturelle, d'autres qui croient à la provocation extrême et l'extravagance scandaleuse et ceux qui dessinent simplement des vêtements beaux à porter. Les créateurs qui adoptent le luxe élitiste à bras ouverts et ceux qui visent la transgression vestimentaire. Les créateurs qui équilibrent les forces contraires de l'art et du commerce et ceux qui se servent de la mode pour expérimenter leur vision radicale. Les créateurs qui possèdent le genre d'intuition émotionnelle qui a conduit l'historien Eric Hobsbawm à affirmer qu'ils prédisaient l'avenir. Les créateurs qui veulent juste rendre les femmes sexy et faire des robes qui se vendent.

Ce que tous ces créateurs ont en commun, c'est leur passion et leur dévotion au métier. Ils font ce qu'ils savent faire, souvent dans la souffrance, car pour eux il est tout simplement inconcevable de faire autre chose. Les pages suivantes en présentent

INTRODUCTION

une sélection très subjective. 'Fashion Now' n'est pas une histoire de la mode contemporaine (il y en a déjà trop dans les librairies), ni un dictionnaire complet de A à Z (trop ennuyeux). Toutefois, nous le considérons comme un bon guide sur ce qui compte le plus actuellement. Rédigé par l'équipe d'i-D (hélas en même temps que plusieurs numéros), 'Fashion Now' est parcouru du même esprit dynamique, irrévérencieux et obsédé de mode que le magazine. Il va sans dire que nous devons un grand merci à tous ceux sans qui ce livre n'aurait jamais vu le jour : les équipes de création qui nous ont permis d'utiliser leur travail à partir des archives d'i-D, les rédacteurs, les RP, les agents et, bien sûr, les créateurs qui ont répondu de bonne grâce à nos dizaines de questionnaires. 'Fashion Now' – comme la mode d'aujourd'hui – existe grâce à eux. C'est pour moi un immense privilège que de faire partie d'un tel projet. Vive la révolution!

AVRIL MAIR
Editor, i-D magazine

Although he's now being championed as the brightest new hope from Antwerp, Haider Ackermann has seen many more ports than the one fronting the town he now works and lives in. Born in Santa Fe de Bogotá, Colombia, in 1971, he was adopted by a French family. Due to his father's business obligations, he spent his childhood moving around the globe. After living in Ethiopia, Chad, France, Algeria and the Netherlands, he decided fashion was his true vocation. High school finished, he left home in 1994 and headed for Belgium to study at the fashion department of the Royal Academy of Antwerp. During his three-year stay (he left the four-year course prematurely because of financial difficulties) he also managed to work as an intern at John Galliano's Paris offices. Taking up a job as an assistant to his former academy teacher Wim Neels in 1998, he worked on both the men's and womenswear collections of this Belgian designer. Quietly saving money and taking in encouragement from his friends and acquaintances, among those Raf Simons, Ackermann finally took the plunge and presented his first, self-financed women's collection in Paris for Autumn-Winter 2002. His subtle, dignified and sensuous clothes immediately struck a chord with major buyers and editors, as they did with Italian leather manufacturer Ruffo. A mere two weeks after his debut show, Ackermann was hired as the Head Designer for Ruffo Research, commissioned to design two collections (Spring-Summer and Autumn-Winter 2003), while continuing to produce his own line.

Auch wenn er inzwischen als neuer Hoffnungsträger Antwerpens gefeiert wird, hat Haider Ackermann schon sehr viel mehr von der Welt gesehen als nur die belgische Mode-metropole, in der er jetzt lebt und arbeitet. Geboren wurde er 1971 im kolumbianischen Santa Fe de Bogotá, doch schon bald adoptierte ihn eine Familie aus Frankreich. Aufgrund der geschäftlichen Verpflichtungen seines Adoptivvaters verbrachte er bereits seine Kindheit an den unterschiedlichsten Orten rund um den Globus: in Äthiopien, im Tschad, in Frankreich, in Algerien und den Niederlanden. Danach kam Ackermann zu dem Schluss, Mode sei seine wahre Berufung. Als er die Schule abgeschlossen hatte, zog er 1994 von zu Hause aus, um an der Königlichen Akademie in Antwerpen zu studieren. Während der dreijährigen Ausbildung (er brach den eigentlich vierjährigen Studiengang wegen finanzieller Schwierigkeiten vorzeitig ab) arbeitete er bereits parallel als Praktikant in der Pariser Niederlassung von John Galliano. 1998 wurde er Assistent bei seinem ehe-maligen Dozenten Wim Neels und wirkte sowohl an den Herren- wie an den Damenkollektionen des belgischen Designers mit. Nachdem er etwas Geld gespart hatte und von Freunden und Bekannten wie Raf Simons dazu ermuntert worden war, wagte Ackermann schließlich den Sprung ins kalte Wasser und präsentierte in Paris seine erste, selbst finanzierte Damenkollektion für Herbst/Winter 2002. Seine raffinierten, würdevollen und sinnlichen Kreationen riefen unmittelbar ein positives Echo bei wichtigen Einkäufern, Journalisten und beim italienischen Lederwarenhersteller Ruffo hervor. Nur zwei Wochen nach seinem Debüt auf dem Laufsteg wurde Ackermann als Chefdesigner von Ruffo Research eingestellt und mit dem Entwurf von zwei Kollektionen (Frühjahr/Sommer und Herbst/Winter 2003) beauftragt. Darüber hinaus betreibt der Designer weiterhin seine eigene Linie.

Bien qu'il soit actuellement célébré comme le nouvel espoir d'Anvers, Haider Ackermann a fait étape dans bien d'autres ports que celui qui borde la ville dans laquelle il travaille et vit aujourd'hui. Adopté par une famille française, il est en fait né en 1971 à Santa Fe de Bogotá en Colombie. En raison des obligations professionnelles de son père, il passe son enfance à parcourir le monde. Après avoir vécu en Ethiopie, au Tchad, en France, en Algérie et aux Pays-Bas, il se rend compte que la mode est sa véritable vocation. En 1994, il termine le lycée et part pour la Belgique afin d'étudier la mode à l'Académie Royale d'Anvers. Pendant son cursus de trois ans (il abandonnera prématurément la quatrième année en raison de problèmes financiers), il fait un stage dans les bureaux parisiens de John Galliano. En 1998, il devient l'assistant de son ancien professeur à l'Académie, le styliste belge Wim Neels, travaillant sur les collections pour homme et pour femme. Il réussit sagement à mettre de l'argent de côté et, encouragé par ses amis et ses relations, parmi lesquelles Raf Simons, Ackermann fait finalement le grand plongeon et présente sa première collection féminine autofinancée aux défilés parisiens Automne-Hiver 2002. Grâce à leur style subtil et voluptueux néanmoins empreint de dignité, ses vêtements séduisent immédiatement les principaux acheteurs et rédacteurs de mode, ainsi que le maroquinier italien Ruffo qui, deux semaines après son premier défilé, nomme Ackermann styliste principal de Ruffo Research et lui demande de dessiner deux collections (Printemps-Eté et Automne-Hiver 2003). Aujourd'hui, Haider Ackermann continue de travailler sur sa propre collection.

"I'd like my work to let the person who wears it be whatever she is"

PORTRAIT BY TETSU

HAIDER ACKERMANN

What are your signature designs? After presenting just one collection it is a bit early to say, isn't it? **What's your favourite piece from any of your collections?** It would be the smock-trousers: something between a tuxedo pant and streetwear cotton trousers with irregular hand-smocking over it **How would you describe your work?** I would like it to be sincere, subtle, comfortable, timeless and interesting because of all the over it. Letting the person who wears it be whatever she is… **What's your ultimate goal?** To go on and still find pleasure out of it **What inspires you?** It really could be whatever **Can fashion still have a political ambition?** Sure it can, and somewhere it should be, but it wouldn't be up to me to send out messages **Who do you have in mind when you design?** The woman in the back of the bar sitting alone and searching for… we wouldn't know. She is secretive, intriguing and therefore more beautiful **Is the idea of creative collaboration important to you?** Yes, it can only bring you some steps further **What has been the greatest influence on your career?** The different countries I lived in, the different people I met. This melting of all those nationalities between my friends **Which is more important in your work: the process or the product?** The process helps you to develop yourself and that's the most important thing but, at the end of the day, I guess it is the product that counts **Is designing difficult for you and, if so, what drives you to continue?** Yes. The curiosity, the excitement and the search for… **Have you ever been influenced or moved by the reaction to your designs?** Of course! People telling you they would like to wear them – isn't it what you're doing it for? **What's your definition of beauty?** There isn't such a definition for beauty. Probably if there was, it would be less interesting. But often it comes from a certain ugliness, it isn't perfect… **What's your philosophy?** Try to dream – reality always brings you back to earth anyway **What is the most important lesson you've learned?** It's good to take your time to realise whatever you would like to achieve

Miguel Adrover is one of fashion's realists. His themed collections, always inspired by the people and cultures he sees in New York and when travelling, are unique for their authentic interpretation of everyday dress. Born in a small village in Majorca in 1965, Adrover moved to New York in 1991 and began producing a line of customised T-shirts with his friend Douglas Hobbs. Four years later, the pair opened a boutique, Horn, selling their label alongside collections by young European designers. Adrover is entirely self-taught; friends and supporters, not tutors and examinations, have shaped his career. In 1999 the first Miguel Adrover collection, 'Manaus-Chiapas-NYC' was shown at New York Fashion Week. His debut, which showed deconstructed thrift-store clothes alongside virtuoso tailoring, was met with equal amounts of bemusement and praise. Seen as an avant-garde designer by the US fashion establishment, Adrover's recycled pieces often attract the most press attention: for Spring-Summer 2001, Adrover fashioned a sharp town coat from a mattress that had been thrown out on the street by Quentin Crisp. Showpieces aside, his reinterpretations of classic tailoring and knitwear have found him accepted with open arms by major stores such as Barneys. In June 2000 he won the CFDA award for best new designer and the Pegasus Apparel Group began financing his label, a partnership that lasted until Autumn 2001. Its dissolution meant that Adrover's Autumn-Winter 2001 collection wasn't produced. Despite this, the designer has paved the way for creatively innovative young designers wishing to be taken seriously in one of the most commercially demanding fashion capitals.

Miguel Adrover gehört zu den Realisten der Branche. Seine themenbezogenen Kollektionen sind immer von den Menschen und ihren unterschiedlichen Kulturen geprägt, denen er in New York und auf Reisen begegnet. Seine ungekünstelten Interpretationen von Alltagskleidung sind einzigartig. Der 1965 in einem kleinen Dorf auf Mallorca geborene Adrover zog 1991 nach New York, wo er zusammen mit seinem Freund Douglas Hobbs eigenwillige T-Shirts zu produzieren begann. Vier Jahre danach eröffnete das Paar eine Boutique namens Horn, wo neben dem eigenen Label auch Kollektionen anderer junger europäischer Designer vertreten waren. Adrover ist absoluter Autodidakt. Freunde und Mentoren, nicht Lehrer und Dozenten, haben seine Karriere bestimmt. 1999 war seine erste Kollektion 'Manaus-Chiapas-NYC' bei der New Yorker Fashion Week zu sehen. Dieses Debüt, bei dem der Designer abgeänderte Second-Hand-Stücke, aber auch virtuose Schneiderkunst zeigte, rief viel Erstaunen und Lob hervor. Dem amerikanischen Mode-Establishment gilt Adrover als Avantgardist, und gerade seine recycelten Kreationen erregen oft die größte Aufmerksamkeit bei der Presse. So entwarf er etwa für seine Kollektion Frühjahr/Sommer 2001 einen originellen Kurzmantel aus einer Matratze, die Quentin Crisp ausgemustert hatte. Abgesehen von den Paradestücken sorgten aber auch seine Neuinterpretationen von Klassikern aus Stoff und Strick dafür, dass große Läden wie Barneys ihn mit offenen Armen in ihr Sortiment aufnahmen. Im Juni 2000 wurde Adrover mit dem Preis der CFDA als bester neuer Designer ausgezeichnet. Bis zum Herbst des darauf folgenden Jahres finanzierte der Pegasus-Apparel-Konzern sein Label. Das Ende dieser Partnerschaft hatte leider zur Folge, dass die Herbst/Winter-Kollektion 2001 nicht produziert wurde. Trotzdem wirkte Adrover als Wegbereiter für andere kreative und innovative Jungdesigner, die in einer der kommerziell anspruchsvollsten Modemetropolen ebenfalls Fuß fassen wollen.

Miguel Adrover fait partie des «réalistes» de la mode. Ses collections à thèmes, toujours inspirées par les gens et les cultures qu'il observe à New York et lors de ses voyages, sont uniques en ceci qu'elles réinterprètent avec authenticité l'habillement du quotidien. Né dans un petit village de Majorque en 1965, Adrover s'installe à New York en 1991 et commence à produire une ligne de T-shirts customisés avec son ami Douglas Hobbs. Quatre ans plus tard, le duo ouvre une boutique baptisée Horn dans laquelle ils vendent leurs vêtements aux côtés des collections de jeunes créateurs européens. Adrover est entièrement autodidacte ; il ne doit donc pas sa carrière aux professeurs ni aux examens, mais à ses amis et à ses fans. En 1999, la première collection Miguel Adrover, «Manaus-Chiapas-NYC», est présentée à la New York Fashion Week. Des vêtements d'occasion déconstruits côtoyant des pièces à la coupe virtuose, ses débuts suscitent autant de stupéfaction que de louanges. Considéré comme un designer d'avant-garde par l'univers de la mode américaine, les vêtements recyclés d'Adrover attirent souvent l'attention de la presse : pour le Printemps-Eté 2001, Adrover façonne un manteau de ville aux lignes sévères à partir d'un vieux matelas trouvé sur le trottoir par Quentin Crisp. En dehors des pièces de défilé, son interprétation des coupes classiques et de la maille a été accueillie à bras ouverts par des magasins aussi prestigieux que Barneys. En juin 2000, la CFDA le consacre Best New Designer of the Year. Le groupe Pegasus Apparel commence alors à financer sa griffe, un partenariat qui ne tient que jusqu'à l'automne 2001, empêchant la production de la collection Automne-Hiver 2001. Néanmoins, le designer a «essuyé les plâtres» pour les jeunes créateurs d'avant-garde qui souhaitent être pris au sérieux dans l'une des capitales de la mode les plus exigeantes sur le plan commercial.

"I won't do fashion if it doesn't have political vision. If you can express some sort of political or social awareness and also produce beautiful clothes, that for me is an achievement"

PORTRAIT COURTESY OF MIGUEL ADROVER

MIGUEL ADROVER

What are your signature designs? I believe at this point I do not have so much a signature design but signature elements that have become characteristic within my collections and will continue to be important elements. These elements are: simplicity, elegance, classicism, tailoring, craftsmanship, timelessness, with a multicultural language consistently flowing through. We work on handmade and antiquated things a lot: we try to give life to new clothes. That's very important **What's your favourite piece from any of your collections?** I don't have a favourite piece because I always do the collections in a different way; it's more like characters where everybody has their role that's important to my work. Each one is an individual, as important as the others **How would you describe your work?** My work is a learning process of life, what I've learned in life up until now, and I express that with clothing. I try and take things from around the world and present it. My work is my expression, my observation of what I experience and what I feel about the world around me at a particular time. I use clothing as a venue to exhibit my interpretations and expressions **What's your ultimate goal?** My ultimate goal is living one day after the other. For my work, I guess just to continue doing it and expressing myself **What inspires you?** Life. What happens in the world; that's how I really inspire myself. Going every day through life and seeing what happens around the world **Can fashion still have a political ambition?** I won't do fashion if it doesn't have political vision. Because for me, it's very important how you see society and the world and the problems that there are, rather than it just being about fashionable clothes. If you can express some sort of political or social awareness and also produce beautiful clothes, that for me is an achievement. I think that's what I do **Who do you have in mind when you design?** A lot of people. It's not about one person and you just design clothes for that person – most of the time I don't see sex when I design clothing. I don't mind if it's a character who's a man and then I make clothes for a woman, I just put the characters and their clothes where they look the most simple and elegant, depending on the person. I challenge myself with how best I can express the story or idea, while at the same time creating a wearable item for a customer. I'm not a fantastical designer and I don't create characterised outfits only meant for the dreamworld of the catwalk. I like to think that I transport people somewhere during the show and then take it further by creating a garment they can wear in everyday life. The transport doesn't end on the runway **What has been the greatest influence on your career?** Life. My life **How have your own experiences affected your work as a designer?** My life is attached to my work, I'm inspired by everyday life and so that's my work, too. This is the inspiration: the situation of the planet, everyday living. I'm not a fantastical designer who makes a balloon to go on the catwalk; for me it's more based on reality **What's your definition of beauty?** I don't think there should be a definition of beauty because when you define you exclude the rest – so what are the other things meant to be? **What's your philosophy?** My philosophy combines several things, particularly designing clothes based on observations seen in the present. My expression is directly affected by today, what I see now. My representation has no distinction between poor and rich. I aim to put everyone on the same level. My philosophy also includes a constant interest in representing different cultures. This is important to me as it pushes me to learn about other places and people so that I can in turn present to others what I've seen **What is the most important lesson that you've learned?** To be honest with yourself and those around you. I've also learned a lot being in business with a big company, and about creativity. I think having your close friends around you is important and you also need to have an open eye to what is going on in the world

Azzedine Alaïa's place in the design hall of fame is guaranteed – his signature being the second skin that he creates when challenging the boundaries of flesh and fabric. Alaïa was born in Tunisia in the 1940s to wheat farming parents. A French friend of his mother's fed Alaïa's instinctive creativity with copies of Vogue and lied about his age to get him into the local Ecole des Beaux-Arts to study sculpture – a discipline in which he didn't excel, but that he would put to good use in the future. After spotting an ad for a vacancy at a dressmaker's, Alaïa's sister taught him to sew and he started making copies of couture dresses for neighbours. Soon afterwards, he went to Paris to work for Christian Dior, but managed only five days of sewing labels before being fired. Alaïa moved to Guy Laroche, where for two seasons he learned his craft while earning his keep as housekeeper to the Marquise de Mazan. In 1960, the Blegiers family snapped up Alaïa, and for the next five years he was both housekeeper and dressmaker to the Countess and her friends, mixing with glamorous Paris society; a clientele that followed him when he started out on his own. His first prêt-à-porter collection for Charles Jourdan in the 1970s was not well received, but eventually fashion editors tuned into Alaïa's modern elegance – something that would eventually come to define body conscious aesthetics a decade later. Worldwide success followed with exhibitions, awards, supermodel disciples and the power to command an audience outside of the catwalk schedule: Alaïa shows when he wants, regardless of the round of timetabled international fashion weeks, and editors never miss it. In 2000, Alaïa joined forces with the Prada group. The same year, a solo exhibition at the New York Guggenheim confirmed his status as a major influence that goes beyond fashion.

Ein Platz im Designer-Olymp ist Azzedine Alaïa auf alle Fälle schon sicher – wegen seines Markenzeichens, der von ihm kreierten zweiten Haut, die die Grenze zwischen Körper und Stoff aufzuheben scheint. Alaïa wurde in den 1940er Jahren als Sohn einer Bauernfamilie in Tunesien geboren. Eine französische Freundin seiner Mutter förderte die natürliche Kreativität des Jungen mit Ausgaben der Vogue und schwindelte bei der Angabe seines Alters, um ihm in die Ecole des Beaux-Arts in Tunis zu verhelfen, wo er Bildhauerei studierte. Er erwies sich dort zwar nicht unbedingt als brillant, sollte jedoch später noch von diesen Grundlagen profitieren. Weil ihn die Anzeige für eine Stelle bei einer Schneiderin interessierte, ließ er sich von seiner Schwester das Nähen beibringen und kopierte schon bald Haute-Couture-Kleider aus Zeitschriften für die Frauen der Nachbarschaft. 1957 ging er nach Paris, um bei Christian Dior zu arbeiten. Nach nur fünf Tagen, die er vor allem mit dem Annähen von Etiketten verbrachte, feuerte man ihn jedoch. Daraufhin versuchte Alaïa es bei Guy Laroche, wo er zwei Saisons lang das Couturier-Handwerk lernte und sich nebenbei seinen Lebensunterhalt als Haushälter der Marquise de Mazan verdiente. 1960 engagierte ihn die Familie Blegiers, bei der er in den folgenden fünf Jahren als Haushälter und Hausschneider der Comtesse und ihrer Freundinnen tätig war und gleichzeitig in die glamouröse Pariser Gesellschaft eingeführt wurde. Diese Klientel hielt ihm auch die Treue, als er sich schließlich selbstständig machte. Seine erste Prêt-à-Porter-Kollektion für Charles Jourdan in den 1970er Jahren wurde nicht besonders positiv aufgenommen, doch mit der Zeit fanden die Moderedaktionen Geschmack an Alaïas moderner Eleganz. Sein Stil nahm die körperbetonte Ästhetik des darauf folgenden Jahrzehnts vorweg. Der weltweite Erfolg des Designers wurde von Ausstellungen, Auszeichnungen und ihm treu ergebenen Supermodels begleitet. Außerdem besitzt Alaïa die Macht, den üblichen Zyklus der Modenschauen zu ignorieren: Er zeigt seine Kollektionen, wann es ihm gefällt, ohne sich um die fixen Termine der internationalen Modewochen zu scheren – und die Journalisten kommen immer. Im Jahr 2000 fusionierte Alaïa mit dem Prada-Konzern. Eine Einzelausstellung im New Yorker Guggenheim Museum unterstrich im selben Jahr die weit über die Grenzen der Mode hinausreichende Bedeutung des Designers.

Défiant les frontières qui séparent la chair du tissu, les créations «seconde peau» qui distinguent le travail d'Azzedine Alaïa lui garantissent une place de choix dans l'Olympe de la mode. Alaïa est né dans les années 1940 en Tunisie de parents cultivateurs de blé. Sa créativité instinctive se nourrit des exemplaires de Vogue d'une amie française de sa mère, qui mentira sur son âge pour le faire entrer à l'Ecole des Beaux-Arts de la région. Il y étudie la sculpture, discipline dans laquelle il n'excelle pas particulièrement mais qu'il utilisera à bon escient par la suite. Après avoir repéré une offre d'emploi chez un couturier, la sœur d'Alaïa lui apprend à coudre et il commence à copier les robes haute couture pour ses voisines. Peu de temps après, il s'installe à Paris pour travailler chez Christian Dior, mais se fait mettre à la porte après cinq jours passés à coudre des étiquettes. Alaïa travaille ensuite pour Guy Laroche, chez qui il se forme au métier pendant deux saisons tout en gagnant sa vie en tant qu'intendant de la Marquise de Mazan. En 1960, la famille Blegiers embauche Alaïa et pendant cinq ans, il est à la fois l'intendant et le couturier de la Comtesse et de ses amis, se mêlant à la haute société parisienne, une clientèle qui le suivra lorsqu'il lancera sa propre griffe. Dans les années 70, sa première collection de prêt-à-porter pour Charles Jourdan n'est pas bien accueillie, mais les rédacteurs de mode s'intéressent tout de même à l'élégance moderne d'Alaïa, qui finira par définir l'esthétique du «body-consciousness» une décennie plus tard. Le succès mondial suit grâce à des expositions, des récompenses, le soutien des plus grands top models et le pouvoir de séduire le public même en dehors du calendrier officiel: Alaïa présente ses collections quand ça lui chante, sans se soucier de l'agenda mondial des semaines de la mode, et la presse ne rate pas un seul de ses défilés. En l'an 2000, Alaïa s'associe au groupe Prada. La même année, le Musée Guggenheim de New York lui consacre une exposition qui confirme son statut d'influence artistique majeure, bien au-delà des cercles de la mode.

"A woman's not going to buy a little skirt for a lot of money if it's not for seduction. What else are clothes made for?"

PORTRAIT BY MAX VADUKUL

AZZEDINE ALAÏA

"I have no favourite women at all. You can't love one in particular. I work for women in general"

What is your favourite piece from any of your collections? I'm still waiting for that feeling. I always doubt **How would you describe your work?** It's not me but only journalists that can describe my work **What's your ultimate goal?** Only the future will tell us **What inspires you?** Women **What do you have in mind when you design?** How and when shall I finish it **Is the idea of creative collaboration important to you?** Always **What has been the greatest influence on your career?** Art, sculpture, design, paintings **Which is more important in your work: the process or the product?** The process **Have you ever been influenced or moved by the reaction to your designs?** Always – emotion is very important **What's your philosophy?** Overall integrity

Without question Giorgio Armani is one of the most important and influential fashion designers of the 20th Century. But he nearly didn't enter fashion at all. Born in 1934 in Piacenza, Armani trained to be a doctor for two years, completed national service in 1957, and then worked as a window dresser at Milan's La Rinascente department store. In 1961 he made his first big step into the fashion world, joining Nino Cerruti as a designer. Crucially it was here, over nine years, that Armani was allowed to experiment with the cut and cloth of menswear. In 1970, Armani went freelance, assisted by business partner Sergio Galeotti. Five years later he launched his own menswear label. It was the following year, when Armani launched his first womenswear collection, that his talents were fully realised. Adapting menswear to suit women, his unstructured yet tailored style, loose yet toying with proportion, always in the softest of fabrics, was hailed as the most influential look in womenswear since Dior's ground-breaking New Look of 1947, winning him endless CFDA awards. But the Milan-based designer has also been about more than the 1980s power dressing his look came to epitomise. Armani was the first designer to utilise Hollywood as an invaluable marketing asset. He famously dressed Richard Gere for 'American Gigolo' (1980), Diane Keaton in 'Annie Hall' (1977), the cast of 'The Untouchables' (1987) and 'Shaft' (2000). And Armani also helped invent today's essential approach of any global fashion business: lifestyle. Now spanning homewares, diffusion lines such as Emporio (launched 1981), cosmetics (2000) and an extremely successful fragrance business (certainly making him the world's richest designer and the most powerful independent), the very name Armani has become a byword for the high life of designer fashion. Giorgio Armani was the subject of a major retrospective at the Solomon R. Guggenheim Museum in New York (2000) and Bilbao (2001). In 2001 Armani collaborated with Japanese architect Tadao Ando on new company headquarters in Milan, which include a gallery and a theatre where he now shows all his collections.

Zweifellos ist Giorgio Armani einer der bedeutendsten und einflussreichsten Modeschöpfer des 20. Jahrhunderts. Doch beinahe wäre er gar nicht ins Modebusiness gekommen. 1934 in Piacenza geboren, studierte Armani zunächst zwei Jahre lang Medizin, absolvierte dann 1957 seinen Wehrdienst und arbeitete danach als Schaufensterdekorateur für das Mailänder Kaufhaus La Rinascente. 1961 tat er dann schließlich doch seinen ersten großen Schritt in die Welt der Mode und wurde Designer bei Nino Cerruti. Dann folgten neun entscheidende Jahre, in denen Armani die Möglichkeit hatte, mit Schnitten und Materialien der Herrenmode zu experimentieren. 1970 machte er sich mit Unterstützung seines Geschäftspartners Sergio Galeotti selbstständig. Nach weiteren fünf Jahren folgte die Gründung seines Herrenmodelabels. Schon ein Jahr später, als er auch seine erste Damenkollektion herausbrachte, wurde Armani die ihm gebührende Aufmerksamkeit zuteil. Seine für Frauen adaptierte Herrenmode, der informelle und doch tadellos sitzende Stil, locker und zugleich mit den Proportionen spielend, und all das aus den weichsten Stoffen: Diese Neuerungen wurden als einflussreichster Trend in der Damenmode seit Diors bahnbrechendem New Look von 1947 gepriesen und brachten ihm zahllose Preise des Council of Fashion Designers of America (CFDA) ein. Doch der in Mailand lebende und arbeitende Designer hat mehr geleistet als das Power Dressing der 1980er Jahre zu erfinden, das seinen Look so perfekt verkörperte. Armani war der erste Modeschöpfer, der Hollywood als unbezahlbares Marketing-Instrument nutzte. Berühmt sind seine Ausstattung von Richard Gere in 'American Gigolo' (1980), Diane Keaton in 'Annie Hall' (1977), seine Kostüme für die Schauspielcrews in 'Die Unbestechlichen' (1987) und 'Shaft' (2000). Armani hat außerdem dazu beigetragen, den heute unverzichtbaren Zugang jeglicher Weltmarke des Modebusiness zu »erfinden«: den Lifestyle. Seine Produktpalette umfasst heute Homeware, Nebenlinien wie Emporio (seit 1981), Kosmetika (seit 2000) und überaus erfolgreiche Parfums. All das macht Armani mit Sicherheit zum reichsten und mächtigsten unabhängigen Designer, dessen Name allein schon als Synonym für anspruchsvolle Designermode gilt. Giorgio Armani war auch Thema einer großen Retrospektive im Guggenheim Museum in New York (2000) und Bilbao (2001). 2001 ließ der Designer in Zusammenarbeit mit dem japanischen Architekten Tadao Ando in Mailand eine neue Firmenzentrale bauen, zu der auch eine Galerie und ein Theater gehören, wo seither alle Kollektionen gezeigt werden.

Giorgio Armani est sans conteste l'un des stylistes les plus importants et les plus influents du XXᵉ siècle. Pourtant, il a bien failli ne jamais travailler dans la mode. Né en 1934 à Piacenza, Armani étudie la médecine pendant deux ans. En 1957, à son retour du service militaire, il travaille comme étalagiste au grand magasin milanais La Rinascente. En 1961, il fait ses premiers pas dans le monde de la mode en devenant styliste chez Nino Cerruti. Pendant neuf ans, il s'y forme à l'art de la coupe et aux tissus de la mode pour homme. En 1970, Armani se lance en indépendant, épaulé par son partenaire en affaires Sergio Galeotti. Cinq ans plus tard, il crée sa propre griffe pour homme. Mais ce n'est que l'année suivante, lorsque Armani lance sa première collection pour femme, que ses talents se réalisent pleinement. Adaptant la mode masculine pour les femmes, son style déstructuré mais classique, décontracté, jouant sur les proportions et toujours sur la fluidité des tissus, est acclamé comme le look féminin le plus important depuis le New Look révolutionnaire de Dior en 1947, ce qui lui vaut un nombre incalculable de récompenses de la part du CFDA. Mais le créateur de Milan est bien plus que le « power dressing » des années 1980 que son style a fini par incarner. Armani est le premier styliste à comprendre le potentiel marketing de Hollywood. Il a notamment créé les costumes de Richard Gere pour « American Gigolo » (1980), de Diane Keaton dans « Annie Hall » (1977), habillé tous les acteurs du film « Les Incorruptibles » (1987) et ceux de « Shaft » (2000). Par ailleurs, Armani a inventé l'approche actuellement utilisée par toutes les marques de mode mondiales : le lifestyle. Articles pour la maison, lignes secondaires telles qu'Emporio (lancée en 1981), maquillage (2000) et parfums à succès (qui font sans doute de lui le couturier le plus riche du monde et l'indépendant le plus puissant), le nom même d'Armani est devenu synonyme de l'absolu recherché par tout créateur de mode. Giorgio Armani a fait l'objet d'une grande rétrospective aux musées Guggenheim de New York (2000) et de Bilbao (2001). En 2001, il a collaboré avec l'architecte japonais Tadao Ando sur le nouveau siège milanais de l'entreprise, qui inclut une galerie d'art et un théâtre dans lequel Armani présente désormais toutes ses collections.

"I've tried to find a new elegance. It's not easy because people want to be shocked. They want explosive fashion. But explosions don't last, they disappear immediately and leave nothing but ashes"

PORTRAIT BY ARMIN LINKE

GIORGIO ARMANI

PHOTOGRAPHY BY CRAIG MCDEAN, STYLING BY EDWARD ENNINFUL. AUGUST 2002

PHOTOGRAPHY BY SEAN ELLIS. STYLING BY MERRYN LESLIE. APRIL 2000

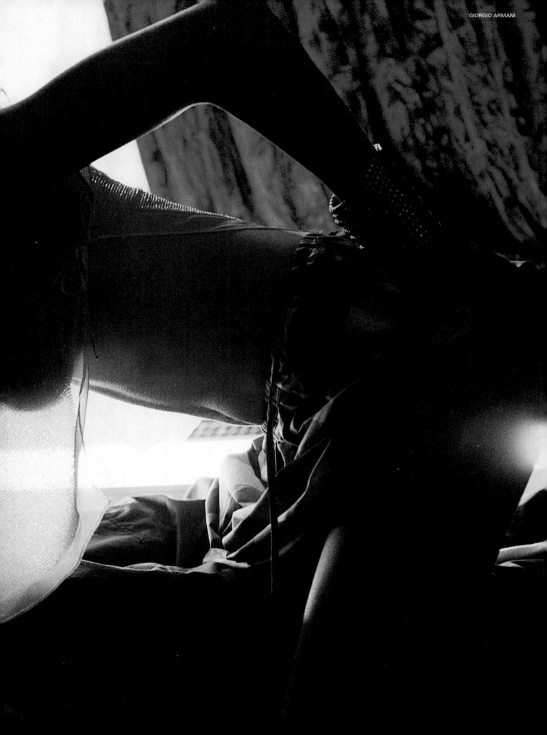

PHOTOGRAPHY BY ALASDAIR MCLELLAN, STYLING BY THOM MURPHY, MAY 2001

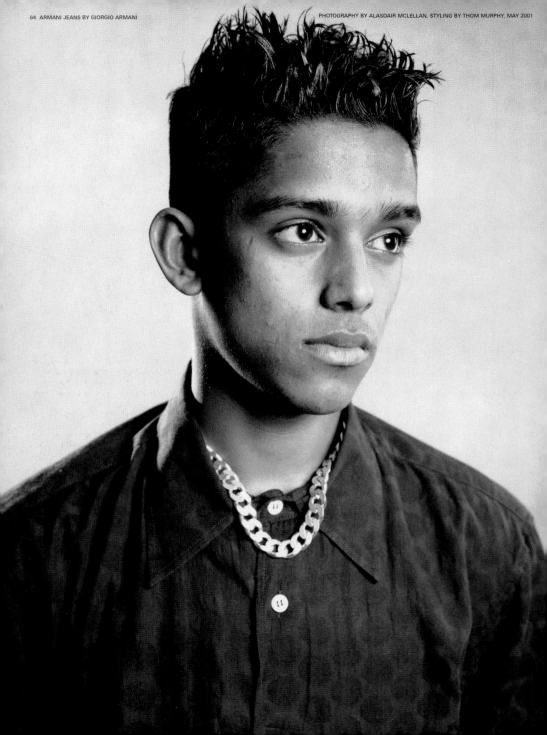

"My philosophy is evolution, not revolution"

What are your signature designs? I prefer to think about a signature philosophy rather than signature designs. I would define my fashion philosophy as understated simplicity through elimination of excess, often with an Asian influence; a certain quality of timelessness that allows a design to transcend seasons; a play on contrasts often juxtaposing the expected with the unexpected **What's your favourite piece from any of your collections?** It is impossible to nominate one particular piece. The Solomon R. Guggenheim Museum recently created a thematic exhibition based on significant influences that have linked my work over the last 25 years. Working with the Museum's curators as they selected pieces was challenging and, at the same time, evoked all kinds of memories that had been buried in the past. One collection I particularly enjoyed designing was the 'Samurai' collection I presented in 1980. It was not a great success commercially – probably the only collection I have ever produced that didn't work out at retail – but creatively it was incredibly gratifying and one of the most emotive runway shows I have done **How would you describe your work?** Even though it is all-consuming, I consider myself very fortunate because my work is extremely gratifying and fulfilling. My career has allowed me to explore many different areas that interest me such as cinema, art, music, literature and architecture. The true challenge with my work as designer has been to remain true to my identity and fashion philosophy, but at the same time continually evolve and develop. I have always considered it fundamental that my designs need to consistently meet the needs of contemporary women and men. I try to translate new inspirations and ideas into items of clothing and accessories that are modern, accessible and timeless, striving for an end result which highlights the wearer's character and identity, rather than seeking to make headlines by presenting radical but impractical designs just for the sake of the media attention **What's your ultimate goal?** To be true to myself. To be true to my customers. To be true to those who have worked with me over the years. And, in so doing, to secure the future prosperity of my company **What inspires you?** Travel. Cinema. Music. Art. Architecture. Diversity **Can fashion still have a political ambition?** As a fashion designer, I think I play a role in reflecting society rather than in changing society **What do you have in mind when you design?** As an inspiration, something different every season. As a philosophy, the customer for whom I am designing **Who or what has been the greatest influence on your career?** My mother's rigour and precision had a great formative influence on me. In my work, I suppose cinema and the Orient have been thematic touchstones throughout **How have your own experiences affected your work as a designer?** The passing of my partner Sergio Galeotti, who founded the company with me in 1975, affected my outlook completely. He had always been the one who took care of the financial aspects, while I concentrated on designing. Suddenly I found myself in a position where I was responsible for both the business and creative aspects. Although this has been very demanding, it has also undoubtedly helped the company to grow as there has been an essential connection between design and retail. In other words, a real understanding and linkage between the fashion runway and the real needs of customers **Is designing difficult for you?** I love my work and I am constantly stimulated and driven to do better. Because I have such a strongly held belief in what I am doing and the way I am doing it, I can honestly say it never feels difficult **Have you ever been influenced or moved by the reaction to your designs?** Vindicated, yes. My women's collection for Autumn-Winter 2002 provoked an interesting reaction from a number of fashion critics. There was one highly respected newspaper journalist in particular who wrote a negative review that disappointed me. I felt that this journalist did not understand what I was trying to express. A month later, this same journalist called my office to say that she had to admit that she regretted writing such a negative review because now, after seeing the Paris shows and considering everything together, she understood what I was trying to say. This delayed reaction gave me enormous satisfaction **What's your definition of beauty?** Natural, unabashed confidence **What's your philosophy?** Evolution, not revolution **What is the most important lesson you have learned?** To trust in my instincts and to be confident in my beliefs

Frequently branded a collective, As Four are in fact a group of friends who design and live together in a silver-sprayed loft in New York's Chinatown. Formed in the mid-1990s, Angela, Adi, Gabi and Kai (originally hailing from Tajikistan, Israel, Lebanon and Germany respectively) brought a variety of talents and experiences to their new identity: Adi and Angela had been stylists, Gabi had worked for Kate Spade and Kai turned up when his previous home burnt down. Working organically and intuitively, they set about creating pieces which stimulate the imagination and defy categorisation. Over the past few years, they have produced four collections along with various downtown 'events', and a show in conjunction with Seventh On Sixth in which their designs were displayed on mechanical dolls. Notable pieces have included large neon pom-poms, the now infamous (and much copied) disc-shaped bag, and rubber trousers with scale-like layers: surreal yet chic and impeccably made. While times are increasingly hard for those not toeing the corporate line, As Four have nonetheless found supporters in high places. In 2001, they were awarded a share of the $20,000 grant for innovative talent from the Ecco Domani Fashion Foundation. Their garments are to be found in stores like Colette in Paris, Via Busstop in Tokyo and Barneys in New York, and they count Björk as a fan. As children, they were the type to lie on the floor and look at the world upside down, they say. A topsy-turvy outlook that has taken them far.

Auch wenn es oft als Kollektiv bezeichnet wird, ist As Four in Wirklichkeit nur eine Gruppe von Freunden, die in einem silberfarben angesprühten Loft in New Yorks Chinatown leben und Mode entwerfen. Mitte der 1990er Jahre haben Angela, Adi, Gabi und Kai, die ursprünglich aus Tadschikistan, Israel, dem Libanon und Deutschland stammen, ihre Talente und Erfahrungen zu einer neuen gemeinsamen Identität zusammengefügt. Adi und Angela hatten zuvor als Stylisten gearbeitet, Gabi war für Kate Spade tätig gewesen, und Kai stieß zu den Dreien, nachdem seine vorherige Wohnung ausgebrannt war. Alle Beteiligten ergänzen sich instinktiv bei der Arbeit, und die Kreationen, die sie hervorbringen, inspirieren die Fantasie und sprengen alle herkömmlichen Kategorien. In den letzten Jahren sind zu verschiedenen Events in Downtown New York vier Kollektionen entstanden. Außerdem gab es zusammen mit Seventh On Sixth eine Show, bei der die Entwürfe von mechanischen Puppen präsentiert wurden. Zu den bekanntesten Stücken von As Four gehören die großen neonfarbenen Pompons, die inzwischen berüchtigten (und oft kopierten) schallplattenförmigen Taschen und Hosen mit schuppenartigen Schichten aus Gummi – lauter surreale, aber trotzdem schicke und handwerklich tadellose Produkte. Obwohl die Zeiten für Designer, die keiner Firma angehören, zunehmend härter werden, hat As Four inzwischen einflussreiche Förderer für sich gewonnen. So erhielt das Designerteam 2001 einen Teil des 20 000-Dollar-Stipendiums der Ecco Domani Fashion Foundation für innovative Talente. Prominente wie die Sängerin Björk zählen zu den Fans des Labels. Die Produkte findet man inzwischen in Läden wie Colette in Paris, Via Busstop in Tokio und Barneys in New York. Als Kinder hätten sie auf dem Boden herumgelegen und sich die Welt von unten angesehen, sagen die vier. Bis jetzt hat diese eigenwillige Perspektive sie jedenfalls schon ganz schön weit gebracht.

Souvent présenté comme un collectif, As Four est en fait un groupe d'amis qui vivent et travaillent ensemble à New York dans un loft de Chinatown peint à la bombe argentée. Formé au milieu des années 1990 par Angela, Adi, Gabi et Kai (respectivement originaires du Tadjikistan, d'Israël, du Liban et d'Allemagne), As Four réunit des talents et des expériences variés au sein d'une nouvelle identité : Adi et Angela étaient stylistes et Gabi travaillait pour Kate Spade ; quant à Kai, il les a rejoint après l'incendie de sa maison. Travaillant à l'instinct et à l'intuition, ils décident de créer des pièces capables de stimuler l'imagination et de défier toute catégorisation. Ces dernières années, ils ont produit quatre collections et différents « événements urbains », ainsi qu'un défilé en collaboration avec Seventh On Sixth à l'occasion duquel leurs créations étaient présentées sur des poupées mécaniques. Parmi les pièces les plus remarquables, on peut citer les gros pompons fluorescents, le sac en forme de disque aujourd'hui trop vu et largement copié, ainsi que le pantalon en caoutchouc aux superpositions en forme d'écailles : des créations surréalistes mais néanmoins chic et d'une facture irréprochable. En ces temps de plus en plus difficiles pour ceux qui refusent l'idée de l'entreprise, As Four a pourtant trouvé des supporters en haut lieu. En 2001, ils ont reçu une partie de la bourse de 20 000 dollars décernée aux jeunes talents par la fondation Ecco Domani Fashion. On peut trouver leurs vêtements dans des boutiques telles que Colette à Paris, Via Busstop à Tokyo et Barneys à New York, et Björk est l'une de leurs fans. Quand ils étaient enfants, les membres d'As Four étaient du genre à se coucher sur le sol pour regarder le monde à l'envers, une perspective décalée qui leur a permis d'aller loin.

"We are our work and our work is our life. We don't design, we live"

PORTRAIT BY SCHOHAJA

AS FOUR

What are your signature designs? We always eliminate every reference to something we have seen before, so everything we are left with is our original ideas. So we consider every piece our signature piece, the perfect flow of our shapes. Any shape that we make ours, call it a silhouette. Some say it's the As Four circle bag – let them say what they say, hooray! **What's your favourite piece from any of your collections?** There is no favourite, we must love it all. We do not really have a collection – it just happens to be. We four play fashion and create the most beautiful and brilliant clothes and sell to interested people in the world. Our work is an evolutionary outcome of our life and a mirror to us ourselves and the world surrounding us **How would you describe your work?** You describe for us – words don't come easy to us. Beautiful, perfect, genius… blah, blah, blah, blah is not a four letter word **What's your ultimate goal?** To find the real us **What inspires you?** Our moods **Can fashion still have a political ambition?** If it ever had one, it still has one **Who do you have in mind when you design?** When we design there is no mind the gap **Is the idea of creative collaboration important to you?** To us it came and comes naturally. We are four: that means we somehow collaborate. We are all creative and each of us has ideas all the time **Who has been the greatest influence on your career?** Adi, Ange, Kai, Gabi… As Four and more **How have your own experiences affected your work as designers?** We guess it must be everything, all our experiences; it's the mix of everything. For us it's to work on a balance between all those experiences. We are our work and our work is our life **Is designing difficult for you and, if so, what drives you to continue?** We don't design, we live and it's not always easy as you gotta get over… or you are gonna get under. Never stuck in the middle **Have you ever been influenced or moved by the reaction to your designs?** Always, we live for that **What's your definition of beauty?** Look at us baby, look at us now **What's your philosophy?** As Fourever, As Four and more if there is any **What is the most important lesson you've learned?** Love is a four letter word

Christopher Bailey is Design Director of the largest British luxury goods brand, Burberry. Born in 1971, Bailey attended London's Royal College of Art, graduating with a Masters in Fashion in 1994. Moving to New York, he worked for Donna Karan before becoming Senior Designer for Gucci womenswear in 1996. When he arrived at Burberry in 2001, he set about abandoning the eponymous check from the company's design-led range, Prorsum. Not only a message about his intentions for the design of the brand, it also proved his concern for its longevity. Although with only a couple of seasons under his belt, he has already received great applause for his work on both the men's and women's collections. A fanatic about quality and detail, he sees each design through to its conclusion, down to the size and colour of the stitching. This, combined with an interest in and a knowledge of practical wear, has been crucial to the developments he has put in place at Burberry. Although essentially contemporary, his designs have one steady foot in the company's past; with women's as well as menswear, he manages to bring these subtle influences into his own, more personal vision. Prorsum, the company's motto, is Latin for forward — something which seems particularly fitting for this relatively young designer, already a key player in British fashion's future.

Christopher Bailey ist Design Director von Burberry, der größten britischen Luxusmarke. 1971 geboren, studierte er am Royal College of Art in London Mode und schloss diese Ausbildung 1994 mit einem Mastertitel ab. Danach zog es ihn nach New York, wo er für Donna Karan arbeitete, bevor er 1996 Senior Designer für die Damenkollektionen bei Gucci wurde. Als er 2001 zu Burberry kam, widmete er sich dem typischen Karomuster der designorientierten Linie Prorsum. Das war nicht nur ein Signal hinsichtlich seiner designerischen Absichten mit der Marke, sondern auch ein Beleg für seine längerfristigen Überlegungen. Und auch wenn er erst wenige Kollektionen verantwortet hat, wurde Bailey sowohl für die Herren- wie für die Damenlinien bereits reichlich Lob zuteil. Als detailbesessener Qualitätsfanatiker schenkt er jedem Entwurf größte Aufmerksamkeit — bis zur Stichlänge und Farbe der Nähte. Dies sowie seine Begeisterung für und seine Kenntnisse über praktische Kleidung waren entscheidend für die Entwicklungen, die er bei Burberry angeregt hat. Denn auch wenn sie absolut zeitgemäß sind, wurzeln seine Entwürfe auch in der Geschichte seines Hauses. In der Damen- wie in der Herrenmode gelingt es ihm, diese subtilen Einflüsse mit seiner ganz individuellen Vision in Einklang zu bringen. Prorsum (lat. vorwärts) lautet der Wahlspruch des Unternehmens, und er scheint ziemlich gut zu diesem relativ jungen Designer zu passen, der schon jetzt eine Schlüsselfigur der britischen Modeszene ist.

Christopher Bailey est le styliste de la plus grande marque de luxe britannique: Burberry. Né en 1971, Bailey étudie la mode au Royal College of Art de Londres dont il sort diplômé d'un Master en mode en 1994. Il part ensuite pour New York et travaille pour Donna Karan avant de devenir styliste senior des collections pour femme de Gucci en 1996. Lorsqu'il arrive chez Burberry en 2001, il commence à dépouiller Prorsum, la gamme «design» de l'entreprise, des carreaux synonymes de la marque. Il fait ainsi passer un message clair sur ses intentions concernant l'orientation de la marque tout en prouvant son engagement à la faire durer. Bien qu'il n'ait aujourd'hui que deux saisons à son actif, le travail de Bailey a déjà suscité beaucoup d'enthousiasme, tant pour les collections féminines que masculines. Fanatique de la qualité et du détail, il supervise la création de chaque pièce jusqu'à sa finition, s'intéressant à toutes ces petites choses telles que la dimension et la couleur des coutures. Cette rigueur, associée à son intérêt et sa connaissance pratique de la mode, a joué un rôle crucial dans les nouvelles orientations qu'il a mises en œuvre chez Burberry. Bien qu'avant tout contemporains, ses vêtements gardent un pied dans le passé de l'entreprise; tant pour les femmes que les hommes, il réussit à mêler ces influences subtiles à sa vision personnelle de la mode. Prorsum, devise de l'entreprise, est un terme latin qui signifie «en avant»: un concept qui va comme un gant à ce créateur encore jeune, déjà considéré comme un acteur clé de la mode britannique de demain.

"Anything that I've designed
I'm bored of; anything that is
a trenchcoat is good for me"

CHRISTOPHER BAILEY

What are your signature designs? I'm a very down-to-earth designer in the sense that I love that mix of really classic, traditional, historical design with real fashion. I love fashion for its throwaway of-the-moment value, but I enjoy mixing it with something that's really thought about. That's what makes my role at Burberry particularly exciting **What's your favourite piece from any of your collections?** In terms of this company, without it sounding clichéd, I really love the trenchcoat. Obviously it's not something I designed, but it's an incredible piece: completely genderless, crossing all the different age groups and inspiring so many people and designers. It's a classic staple. Anything that I have designed I'm bored of; anything that is a trenchcoat for me is good **How would you describe your work?** It's very considered. I hate anything slapdash **What's your ultimate goal?** To always enjoy my work. I dread boredom. If I ever sensed that I was getting bored of my job, it would just be the end for me **What inspires you?** It comes in so many guises that it's impossible to say. I love architecture, I love design, I love art, I love people and I love eating. For me, inspiration is really about keeping your mind open and never getting jaded **Who do you have in mind when you design?** I don't have one particular person. It's much more about an attitude and a spirit and character than an actual person. It's nice if you can find somebody – it's my dream to discover a muse. I would love an ideal person who personifies everything I'm thinking, but I don't think that person will ever exist **Is the idea of creative collaboration important to you?** I love working with people who share my sense of passion – I'm a very upbeat person and my natural spirit is cheerful. For me it's a pleasure working with enthusiastic, passionate, happy people. I also like working with people who have a very strong will and strong mind, because it's a challenge – but it's a huge frustration as well **Who has been the greatest influence on your career?** The little person inside my body who tells me what to do. Whenever I've made any major decisions, I've always completely relied on that little voice. Even when I decided to leave Gucci and everybody without fail told me I was crazy, that little voice kept saying 'it's time, you need to move on'. I was going to nothing and I certainly didn't have this role here, but I did it anyway **Which is more important in your work: the process or the product?** The process – once you've got to the product, you're kind of over it **Is designing difficult for you and, if so, what drives you to continue?** The actual process of designing isn't difficult, but the process of designing something that fulfils all the criteria it needs to fulfil is very difficult. Fashion is functional, practical, emotional, commercial and aesthetic: there are so many things to take into consideration. Also, I have two agendas – my personal agenda when designing and then the company's one as well **Have you ever been influenced or moved by the reaction to your designs?** I guess every time and never. It's always a great feeling when someone tells you that they love it and it's always depressing when someone doesn't like what you've done. It's important in both instances to say okay, that was then and now we're on other things **What's your definition of beauty?** It's got nothing to do with fashion or clothes. It's really somebody's inner self. For me, a beautiful person is someone with kindness and happiness, a good spirit and a good soul **What's your philosophy?** Enjoy everything that you do. It's important to be happy. If tomorrow I became jaded and bored in this job and wanted to go back to filling shelves in a supermarket, which I used to do and loved, then I would do that... Listen to me sounding like I want to work at Tesco! **What is the most important lesson you've learned?** Listen to your heart. It's never wrong

PHOTOGRAPHY BY NICOLE TREVILLIAN, STYLING BY DAVID LAMB. FEBRUARY 2002

Neil Barrett's calm nature could stem from his Devon upbringing – although today he divides his time between London and Milan, where his business is based. Born in 1965, Barrett studied fashion at Central Saint Martins before completing an MA at the Royal College of Art. After graduating in 1989, he was immediately appointed Senior Menswear Designer at Gucci, where he worked for the next five years, a crucial time in the renaissance of the Italian brand. Next he moved to Prada, where he worked as Menswear Design Director, having initially approached the company with the idea of starting a menswear line. These pivotal roles gave him the confidence to finally set up his own label in 1999. Just one year later, he was invited to open Pitti Immagine Uomo Fair (the most important fair in menswear) with a catwalk show that also debuted his womenswear. Barrett's rapid success has, in part, been due to his extensive work with fabric development and research, as well as his excruciating attention to detail: a simple shirt can have as many as 30 of his adjustments. Barrett's clothing is typically simple in design with a strong emphasis on the cut, fabric and detailing. His overriding strength is that he builds desirability into clothes, reworking classic pieces in his signature palette of muted colours. Proving his understanding of the wants of a man's wardrobe, he already sells to over 160 stores worldwide.

Neil Barretts Gelassenheit könnte mit seiner Kindheit in Devon zusammenhängen – selbst wenn er sein Leben heute abwechselnd in London und Mailand verbringt, wo sich sein Firmensitz befindet. Barrett, Jahrgang 1965, studierte am Central Saint Martins Mode, bevor er 1989 seinen Magister am Royal College of Art machte. Direkt im Anschluss an seine Ausbildung wurde Barrett Senior Menswear Designer bei Gucci und füllte diese Position fünf Jahre lang aus – eine entscheidende Phase für die Wiederbelebung der italienischen Traditionsmarke. Als nächstes wechselte Barrett als Menswear Design Director zu Prada, nachdem er das Unternehmen von der Einführung einer Herrenlinie überzeugt hatte. Diese beiden einflussreichen Positionen gaben dem Designer letztlich das nötige Vertrauen, um 1999 sein eigenes Label zu gründen. Schon ein Jahr später wurde er zur Pitti Immagine Uomo Fair (der wichtigsten Herrenmode-Messe) eingeladen, und zwar mit einer Catwalk-Show, die zugleich das Debüt seiner Damenkollektion war. Barretts rascher Erfolg wurzelt zum Teil sicher in seiner intensiven Beschäftigung mit Materialentwicklung und -forschung sowie in seiner Detailbesessenheit: So schafft er es etwa, an einem simplen Hemd bis zu dreißig Änderungen vorzunehmen. Barretts Entwürfe sind typischerweise schlicht im Design, aber raffiniert, was Schnitt, Material und Details betrifft. Seine überragende Stärke ist die für ihn typische Palette gedämpfter Farben für seine klassischen Stücke. Dass er genau weiß, was Männer anziehen wollen, hat Barrett jedenfalls bewiesen: Mittlerweile verkauft er seine Kreationen an über 160 Läden auf der ganzen Welt.

Neil Barrett doit peut-être son calme légendaire à une enfance passée dans le Devon, bien qu'il partage aujourd'hui son temps entre Londres et Milan, où il a établi son entreprise. Né en 1965, Barrett étudie la mode à Central Saint Martins avant d'obtenir un MA au Royal College of Art. Une fois diplômé en 1989, il est immédiatement nommé styliste senior de la ligne masculine de Gucci, chez qui il travaillera pendant cinq ans, période cruciale dans la renaissance de la marque italienne. Il travaille ensuite pour Prada en tant que directeur de la création pour homme après avoir proposé à la griffe de lancer une ligne masculine. Ces postes à responsabilité lui confèrent l'assurance requise pour créer finalement sa propre griffe en 1999. Exactement un an plus tard, il est invité à faire l'ouverture de la Pitti Immagine Uomo Fair (le plus important salon de mode pour homme) avec un défilé qui marque également ses débuts dans la mode féminine. Le succès rapide de Barrett repose en partie sur un travail acharné dans le développement et la recherche de tissus, ainsi que sur l'incroyable attention qu'il porte aux détails : une simple chemise peut subir jusqu'à 30 remaniements de sa part. La mode de Barrett se distingue avant tout par sa simplicité et l'accent porté sur la coupe, les tissus et les détails. Sa force réside dans le fait qu'il arrive à rendre les vêtements plus désirables en revisitant les classiques à travers sa palette typique de couleurs sourdes. Comme il comprend parfaitement les attentes vestimentaires des hommes, ses collections sont actuellement vendues dans plus de 160 boutiques à travers le monde.

"What I'm trying to work out is knowing where to stop"

PORTRAIT BY ARMIN LINKE

NEIL BARRETT

What are your signature designs? Masculine cuts, simple shapes **What's your favourite piece from any of your collections?** It's like a dark brown soft shirt jacket, leather being treated like jeans **How would you describe your work?** A balance between trend and wearability. I think subtle is a good word. What I'm trying to do is not at all simple. It can be full of details, but it's clean. What I'm trying to work out is knowing where to stop **What's your ultimate goal?** Be happy **What inspires you?** Sex. Intrigue. Obscure details everywhere **Can fashion still have a political ambition?** Maybe for others, yes. But not for me. I'm just designing clothes **Who do you have in mind when you design?** Me and my friends **Is the idea of creative collaboration important to you?** I appreciate my team's opinions. But I always follow my own instincts because if I believe in something, I'm not worried by what anybody else says **Who has been the greatest influence on your career?** For personal inspiration, I think it's my mother. Then Rei Kawakubo, who is a creative genius. She encouraged me to do whatever I enjoyed, which is essential. She's just got a fabulous mind **How have your own experiences affected your work as a designer?** Elevated learning curve, basically. All your personal experiences, good or bad, contribute to it. What happens around you inspires you and drives you on **Which is more important in your work: the process or the product?** Definitely the product, because whenever I design something, I want it now. And if as a designer I don't really want it, then forget it. Throw it out. I find the process is just how you get to that **Is designing difficult for you?** I think it's straightforward. You know instinctively if something's right and, if it's not, you keep on going until it is **Have you ever been influenced or moved by the reaction to your designs?** Of course, that's the thrill of what I do. Seeing somebody wearing your clothes on the street is incredible **What's your definition of beauty?** Positive thinking **What's your philosophy?** Just do my best. Can't be doing anything else. Do your best and that's enough. It's corny, but real **What is the most important lesson you've learned?** Never take anything for granted. Never. No matter what you do. Learn from the past, live for the present and dream of the future

Born in Columbus, Ohio in 1963, a love of self-expression led John Bartlett to invest in vintage military uniforms, procured from neighbourhood Salvation Army stores. These, teamed with an Adam Ant hairstyle and more eyeliner than Dusty Springfield, thwarted his parents' dream of an investment banking future. And despite the distractions of a Harvard University degree in sociology, Bartlett continued to remain true to his obsessions: clubbing and clothing. Moving to London in 1985, he blew his postgraduate fees in King's Road boutiques, stockpiling outfits for the nightclub Taboo. Back in New York a year later, he undertook evening classes at the Fashion Institute of Technology and finally began learning the intricacies of pattern cutting, combining 'proper' techniques with an instinctive flair. Since the late 1980s, Bartlett has become an increasingly formidable force within the industry. He has held positions as menswear designer for Williwear (incredibly, his first job in 1988); menswear Design Director for Ronaldus Shamask; and, from 1998, as Creative Director for Byblos men's and womenswear. With an outlook that skilfully blends creativity with commercial nous, his eponymous label (founded in 1992) has far surpassed its origins in a West Village walk-up; prestigious awards have been bestowed from the likes of Woolmark and the CDFA (Bartlett was the first menswear designer to win its Perry Ellis Award for New Fashion Talent in 1994). In 2000, Bartlett showed his menswear collection for the first time in Italy as a guest of Pitti Immagine Uomo Fair. In 2001 he brought operations back to New York, focusing exclusively on menswear and launching a diffusion range, John Bartlett Uniform, in 2002.

Sein Hang zur Selbstinszenierung motivierte den 1963 in Columbus, Ohio, geborenen John Bartlett, sich gebrauchte Militäruniformen zuzulegen, die er über die Läden der Heilsarmee in seiner Nachbarschaft bezog. Dazu kamen noch eine Frisur wie die von Adam Ant und mehr Eyeliner als bei Dusty Springfield – zusammengenommen genügte das, um den Traum seiner Eltern von einem zukünftigen Investmentbanker in der Familie platzen zu lassen. Trotz der gewissen Ablenkung, die das Soziologiestudium in Harvard darstellte, blieb Bartlett seiner wahren Berufung treu: Mode und Clubbing. 1985 zog er nach London, verprasste das Geld für sein Postgraduierten-Studium in den Boutiquen der King's Road und hortete Outfits für Events im Londoner Night Club Taboo. Im folgenden Jahr zurück in New York, belegte er Abendkurse am Fashion Institute of Technology und lernte endlich die Feinheiten des Zuschneidens und wie er am besten klassische Schneidertechniken mit seinem Modeinstinkt kombinieren konnte. Seit den späten 1980er Jahren macht Bartlett in immer stärkerem Maße als ernstzunehmende Größe in der Textilbranche von sich reden. Erste Berufserfahrung sammelte er 1988 erstaunlicherweise gleich als Herrenmodedesigner für Williwear. Darauf folgte die Position des Design Directors bei Ronaldus Shamask. Ab 1998 war Bartlett als Creative Director für die Damen- und Herrenmode bei Byblos verantwortlich. Da John Bartlett Kreativität und kommerzielle Notwendigkeiten verbinden kann, ist sein 1992 gegründetes Label inzwischen weit über die Anfänge in einem Haus ohne Fahrstuhl im West Village hinausgewachsen. Bartlett bekam dafür angesehene Preise verliehen, etwa von Woolmark und dem Council of Fashion Designers of America (CDFA) das ihn als ersten Herrenmodedesigner 1994 mit dem Perry Ellis Award for New Fashion Talent auszeichnete. Im Jahr 2000 präsentierte der Amerikaner erstmals eine Herrenkollektion in Italien, und zwar als Gast auf der Messe Pitti Immagine Uomo Fair. 2001 kehrte er mit seiner Schau wieder nach New York zurück und widmete sich exklusiv seiner Herrenmode. Eine neue Zweitlinie namens John Bartlett Uniform wurde 2002 dem Publikum vorgestellt.

Né en 1963 à Columbus dans l'Ohio, John Bartlett se passionne pour les tenues militaires qu'il récupère à l'Armée du Salut de son quartier. Cet intérêt, associé à une coupe de cheveux digne d'Adam Ant et plus d'eyeliner que n'aurait osé en porter Dusty Springfield, vient briser le rêve de ses parents qui espéraient le voir faire carrière dans l'investissement bancaire. Et malgré un diplôme de Harvard en sociologie, Bartlett reste fidèle à ses obsessions : clubbing et mode. En 1985, il s'installe à Londres et dépense sa bourse de troisième cycle dans les boutiques de King's Road, accumulant les tenues pour des événements tels que le night club Taboo. De retour à New York un an plus tard, il prend des cours du soir au Fashion Institute of Technology et finit par s'initier aux complexités de la coupe de patrons, combinant techniques « classiques » et flair instinctif. Depuis la fin des années 1980, Bartlett s'est imposé comme une force toujours plus redoutable au sein de l'industrie. Il a occupé divers postes de styliste pour homme chez Williwear (en 1988, son premier boulot !), a été directeur de la création pour homme chez Ronaldus Shamask et, depuis 1998, occupe le même poste chez Byblos, mais cette fois également pour la ligne féminine. Dans une perspective qui mêle habilement créativité et savoir-faire commercial, sa griffe éponyme (créée en 1992) a largement dépassé les murs de son petit appartement du West Village ; il a reçu des récompenses prestigieuses, notamment de Woolmark et du CDFA (en 1994, Bartlett est le tout premier créateur pour homme à recevoir le prix Perry Ellis décerné aux jeunes talents). En l'an 2000, Bartlett présente pour la première fois sa collection masculine en Italie en tant qu'invité de la Pitti Immagine Uomo Fair. En 2001, il délocalise son entreprise à New York et décide de se consacrer exclusivement à la mode pour homme. En 2002, il lance une nouvelle gamme, John Bartlett Uniform.

"Growing up gay in Middle America provided a very specific twisted perspective on how clothing can inform and educate"

PORTRAIT COURTESY OF JOHN BARTLETT

JOHN BARTLETT

What are your signature designs? Butch uniform-inspired menswear **What's your favourite piece from any of your collections?** A chocolate brown military shirt and pant inspired by my local UPS man **How would you describe your work?** Archetypal, sociological, psychosexual **What's your ultimate goal?** To merge masculinity and fashion **What inspires you?** Fassbinder, Bacon, Genet, Mapplethorpe, Hemingway **Can fashion still have a political ambition?** Absolutely **Who do you have in mind when you design?** A young Burt Reynolds **Is the idea of creative collaboration important to you?** Yes, you cannot design in a bubble. Creativity is a dialogue, a wrestling match between reality and fantasy **Who has been the greatest influence on your career?** The late Richard Martin **How have your own experiences affected your work as a designer?** Growing up gay in Middle America provided a very specific, twisted perspective on how clothing can inform and educate **Which is more important in your work: the process or the product?** The process. The research, the weaving of the story, the dreaming is always more satisfying than the ultimate product, which is never as good as its inception **Is designing difficult for you and, if so, what drives you to continue?** Designing is like working on a puzzle with missing pieces. I continue because nothing else tortures me as much **Have you ever been influenced or moved by the reaction to your designs?** In the early days I was influenced heavily by the comments of others. Now I do what feels good to me **What's your definition of beauty?** A face lined with experience and a body taut with hard labour **What's your philosophy?** Sex sells **What is the most important lesson you've learned?** Do not run away from tests and trials

With a shared history of creative design that stretches from biological equipment to sportswear, the collaborative team Richard Edwards now work together to create sharply modern American classics. Born in Sweden in 1962, Richard Bengtsson studied fashion design at the Beckmans School of Design in Stockholm. Finishing his first womenswear collection on graduation, Richard designed for European retailers before packing two suitcases and making the move to New York in 1989. While working as a freelance menswear designer, he met his future collaborator Edward Pavlick. Born across the Hudson in New Jersey in 1966, Edward had studied industrial design in Philadelphia and begun his career as a freelance designer, creating clinical, pharmaceutical equipment. Determined to capitalise on the differences and nuances of their different cultural backgrounds and education, Richard and Edward formed a design team, following Richards' discipline in fashion. The duo's working bond was based on a shared aesthetic: forward thinking with a functional sophistication. Their clothes are simple, classic and well tailored, twisting the all-American boy into a sexy, preppy young man. Their first collaboration was the playful Holiday Shirt line in 1993 and their own complete line for an inaugural runway presentation in 1995. After a second show, they won the CFDA Perry Ellis award for New Fashion Talent in Menswear. Presenting regularly since 1999, Richard Edwards launched their first women's collection in 2001. An American sensibility as seen through sceptical European eyes, the Richard Edwards lines remain sophisticated and modern.

Von der Forschungsausrüstung für Biologen bis hin zu Sportswear reicht der kreative Erfahrungshintergrund des Designerteams Richard Edwards, die jetzt gemeinsam supermoderne amerikanische Modeklassiker entwerfen. Der 1962 geborene Schwede Richard Bengtsson absolvierte sein Modestudium an der Beckmans School of Design in Stockholm. Nachdem er zum Studienabschluss seine erste Damenkollektion vorgelegt hatte, entwarf er eine Zeit lang für verschiedene europäische Einzelhandelsketten. 1989 packte er dann zwei Koffer und zog nach New York. Als freischaffender Designer für Herrenmode lernte er dort seinen zukünftigen Partner Edward Pavlick kennen. Der war 1966 jenseits des Hudson River in New Jersey geboren worden und hatte in Philadelphia Industriedesign studiert. Anschließend begann er seine Berufskarriere mit dem Entwerfen von klinischem und pharmazeutischem Gerät. Fest entschlossen, die kleinen und großen Unterschiede zwischen ihren soziokulturellen Hintergründen und Ausbildungen zu nutzen, bildeten Richard und Edward ein Designteam, das sich fortan Richards Fach, also der Mode, zuwandte. Ihre Arbeit basiert auf einer gemeinsamen Ästhetik: vorausschauende, funktionale Raffinesse. Ihre Kreationen sind schlicht, klassisch und gut geschnitten, so dass sie den typisch amerikanischen Durchschnittsjungen in einen distinguierten, verführerischen jungen Mann verwandeln. Das erste Projekt der beiden war die verspielte Kollektion Holiday Shirt von 1993. Darauf folgte 1995 eine komplette eigene Linie für die Laufstegpremiere. Nach ihrer zweiten Schau gewannen sie den Perry Ellis Award for New Fashion Talent in Menswear des Council of Fashion Designers of America. Seit 1999 präsentiert das Label regelmäßig neue Kollektionen; die erste Damenkollektion kam 2001 hinzu. Amerikanische Empfindsamkeit, gemäßigt durch den kritischen europäischen Blick – dank dieses Konzepts präsentiert sich die Mode von Richard Edwards nach wie vor anspruchsvoll und zeitgemäß.

Grâce à une expérience de la création qui s'étend de l'équipement biologique au sportswear, l'équipe Richard Edwards modernise aujourd'hui les classiques américains avec un sens très aigu de la mode. Né en 1962 en Suède, Richard Bengtsson étudie la mode à la Beckmans School of Design de Stockholm. Après une première collection pour femme présentée pour son diplôme de fin d'études, Richard dessine pour divers distributeurs européens puis fait ses valises en 1989, direction New York. Il y travaille comme styliste pour homme en free-lance et rencontre son futur collaborateur, Edward Pavlick. Né en 1966 sur l'autre rive de l'Hudson dans le New Jersey, Edward étudie le design industriel à Philadelphie et entame une carrière de designer indépendant spécialisé dans l'équipement clinique et pharmaceutique. Bien décidés à exploiter les spécificités et les nuances de leurs différentes formations et origines culturelles, Richard et Edward forment une équipe qui suivra le chemin de Richard, c'est-à-dire la mode. Le lien professionnel qui unit le duo repose sur une esthétique commune : pensée visionnaire et sophistication fonctionnelle. Leurs vêtements simples, classiques et bien coupés transforment l'Américain de base en jeune homme sexy et BCBG. En 1993, leur première collaboration donne naissance à une ligne turbulente baptisée Holiday Shirt, suivie en 1995 d'une première ligne complète pour un défilé inaugural à l'issue duquel le CFDA leur décerne le Perry Ellis Award qui récompense les nouveaux talents en mode masculine. Rendez-vous régulier du calendrier des défilés depuis 1999, la griffe Richard Edwards a lancé sa première ligne pour femme en 2001. Résolument sophistiquées et modernes, les créations Richard Edwards présentent une vision sceptique européenne atténuée par la sensibilité américaine.

"Clothing should not mask a person, but enhance one"

PORTRAIT COURTESY OF RICHARD BENGTSSON & EDWARD PAVLICK

RICHARD BENGTSSON & EDWARD PAVLICK

What are your signature designs? Each piece is designed with the integrity of a signature **What's your favourite piece from any of your collections?** We always seem to favour the one that we are currently working on **How would you describe your work?** We design our collections to be clear enough to speak for themselves **What's your ultimate goal?** The privilege to continue to design clothes that people want and enjoy to wear **What inspires you?** Everything **Can fashion still have a political ambition?** If it wants to **Who do you have in mind when you design?** It begins with ourselves, branches out to the people closest to us, and then ultimately to any person who is intriguing to us **Is the idea of creative collaboration important to you?** Yes **Who has been the greatest influence on your career?** Each other **How have your own experiences affected your work as designers?** Everything that affects us as people, affects us as designers **Which is more important in your work: the process or the product?** Both, you have to enjoy the process in order to respect the product **Is designing difficult for you and, if so, what drives you to continue?** For us, designing is organic. There are times when it is easy and times when it is difficult. Ultimately, it is the process of discovery that motivates us to continue **Have you ever been influenced or moved by the reaction to your designs?** Yes, we are always inspired by how people incorporate our designs into their everyday life **What's your definition of beauty?** A self-confident, happy person **What's your philosophy?** Clothing should not mask a person, but enhance one **What is the most important lesson you've learned?** Design for one's self while maintaining a sense of openness

When Antonio Berardi commissioned his own perfume as a gift to the audience of his 1994 graduation show, it was clear this was a fashion student with sights set skyhigh. Born in Grantham, England, in 1968 to Sicilian parents, Berardi credits many design influences to his Italian roots: hourglass figures are his preferred silhouette and he constantly references Catholic symbolism. A job assisting at John Galliano's studio was a solid training ground while he tried to land a place on the fashion BA course at Central Saint Martins; he was finally accepted in 1990, after his third application. On leaving college, Berardi quickly rose to fame. His degree collection was bought by Liberty and A La Mode in London, Kylie Minogue modelled for his first official show and Philip Treacy and Manolo Blahnik designed accessories. His signature tailored leather trouser suits and sheer chiffon dresses, often embellished with crystals, punchwork or hand-painted flowers, were shown at spectacular themed presentations. By his fourth collection for Autumn-Winter 1997, Berardi had found a heavyweight Italian backer, Givuesse. In 1996 he moved from the London catwalks to Milan. The following year, Extè appointed Berardi as their head designer, also becoming producers of his own collection. The partnership ended in Autumn 2001 and a new Italian backer, Gibo, stepped in to provide Berardi with financial security. Berardi is a designer fascinated by technical achievement and his showstopping pieces – a coat decorated with dozens of tiny lightbulbs that illuminate to form a crucifix – support his opinion that, in the pursuit of glamour, nothing is impossible.

Als Antonio Berardi ein eigenes Parfum als Geschenk für die Zuschauer seiner Abschlussmodenschau 1994 in Auftrag gab, war klar, dass es sich bei ihm um einen Studenten mit himmelhohen Ambitionen handelte. Berardi kam 1968 als Sohn sizilianischer Eltern im englischen Grantham zur Welt, und der Einfluss der italienischen Wurzeln auf seinen Stil ist unverkennbar: So ist die Sanduhrform seine Lieblingssilhouette, und Bezüge zur katholischen Symbolik sind unverkennbar. Ein Assistenzjob im Atelier von John Galliano bildete die solide Basis für Berardis Ausbildung, während er sich um einen Studienplatz am Central Saint Martins bewarb. 1990 wurde er dort schließlich im dritten Anlauf aufgenommen. Nach Beendigung seines Studiums gelangte der junge Designer schnell zu Ruhm. Liberty und A La Mode in London erwarben seine Abschlusskollektion; Kylie Minogue modelte bei seiner ersten offiziellen Modenschau, Philip Treacy und Manolo Blahnik steuerten die Accessoires bei. Die für Berardi so typischen maßgeschneiderten Hosenanzüge aus Leder und die hauchdünnen, oft mit Kristallen, Lochstickereien oder handgemalten Blumen verzierten Chiffonkleider wurden bei spektakulären Schauen präsentiert. Als er für Herbst/Winter 1997 seine insgesamt vierte Kollektion herausbrachte, hatte Berardi in der Firma Givuesse einen starken italienischen Partner gefunden. 1999 verlegte er auch seine Shows von den Londoner Catwalks nach Mailand. Im darauf folgenden Jahr wurde Berardi Chefdesigner bei Extè, wo er fortan auch seine eigene Kollektion produzieren ließ. Diese Partnerschaft endete im Herbst 2001. Danach sorgte die italienische Firma Gibo für den nötigen finanziellen Rückhalt. Berardi ist ein Designer, den technische Neuerungen faszinieren. Außerdem erregt er immer wieder Aufsehen mit Stücken wie dem Mantel, den Dutzende kleiner Glühbirnen zieren, die in der Form eines Kreuzes leuchten. Nichts sollte unmöglich sein, wenn es darum geht, Glamour zu erzeugen, so das Credo des Exzentrikers.

Quand en 1994 Antonio Berardi commande un parfum à son nom pour l'offrir au public de son défilé de fin d'études, tout le monde s'accorde à dire que cet étudiant-là ne manque pas d'ambition. Né en 1968 de parents siciliens à Grantham en Angleterre, Berardi est largement influencé par ses racines italiennes : il affectionne particulièrement les silhouettes en forme de sablier et fait constamment référence aux symboles du catholicisme. Son expérience en tant qu'assistant dans l'atelier de John Galliano lui offre une solide base de formation tandis qu'il tente d'obtenir une place au cours de mode de Central Saint Martins, où il est finalement accepté en 1990 au bout d'une troisième candidature. Une fois diplômé, Berardi rencontre vite la célébrité : sa collection de fin d'études est achetée à Londres par Liberty et la boutique de luxe A La Mode, Kylie Minogue défile pour sa première collection officielle tandis que Philip Treacy et Manolo Blahnik dessinent ses accessoires. Son célèbre tailleur-pantalon en cuir et ses robes en mousseline de soie ultra-fine, souvent ornées de cristaux, de perforations ou de fleurs peintes à la main, sont présentés à l'occasion de défilés thématiques spectaculaires. Pour sa quatrième collection Automne-Hiver 1997, Berardi fait appel à un important financier italien, Givuesse. En 1999, il délaisse les podiums londoniens pour Milan et devient l'année suivante directeur de la création chez Extè, qui produit également ses collections. Ce partenariat prend fin à l'automne 2001 et Berardi retrouve un soutien financier auprès d'un autre Italien, Gibo. Berardi est fasciné par les exploits techniques, comme le prouve notamment son manteau décoré de dizaines d'ampoules minuscules qui s'illuminent pour former un crucifix… autant de pièces extravagantes qui viennent étayer sa vision selon laquelle dans la poursuite du glamour, tout est permis.

"My work is really a celebration of the female form. I like visible sexiness. I like tits and ass"

PORTRAIT BY SIMON FLAMIGNI

ANTONIO BERARDI

What are your signature designs? The tailoring, I guess. People come back for the tailoring every time. They love the trousers and the jackets because they fit so well **What's your favourite piece from any of your collections?** We did a show in London at the Roundhouse and there was a dress which was tulle, it was huge, completely sheer and embroidered with flowers so it looked like they were growing around the body. Stephen Jones had designed a hat with burning candles and I remember as the model was walking, the wax was pouring on her and she didn't flinch. That's one thing that sticks in my mind. In a sense the dress was nothing, but the whole effect – I always remember that **How would you describe your work?** My work is really a celebration of the female form. I like visible sexiness **What's your ultimate goal?** I'm very content with what I'm doing. For once, I feel like I'm on the right track and I have a great manufacturer now. Apart from that, it depends what comes along. I'm optimistic and that's always kept me going **What inspires you?** Anything and everything. It's not obvious. I might be inspired by a Latino club in New York, but maybe it's not directly about what I see there; it's much more about the spirit of something. I love taking things that are poles apart and then putting them together **Can fashion still have a political ambition?** When you look at it now, we're never going to change anybody's lives with fashion – it might get a line in a newspaper or in a magazine, but at the end of the day, who really gives a shit? It's clothes and I think half the time that's what we forget. I make frocks, no different from the seamstress who might be working anywhere, making dresses for people **Who do you have in mind when you design?** I like tits and ass. I like curves because I think that's what sets men apart from women. To me, someone like the actress Monica Bellucci is amazing **Who has been the greatest influence on your career?** Possibly my sister, Piera. Simply because she tells it like it is. Sometimes she's very hard: I might show her the catwalk video and she'll say 'That one's great… that's hideous… don't do that again!' She's honest. Sometimes I say to her, 'You know, I find your comments really upsetting.' But she's doing it for me, she doesn't stand to gain anything. She treats me as her brother, but also as a colleague and a friend. And I do listen to her **How have your own experiences affected your work as a designer?** I was brought up in England with very strict parents, who had a view of life that was set in '50s Sicily where certain things are a complete taboo. So the mix of the two cultures has affected me a lot. Sometimes people are interested in a designer because he might go out onto the catwalk and show his bum, but I'm not really like that. I'm told that I have to go out and play the game, but it's not my cup of tea. I always just thought of myself as a designer. Unfortunately, we live in a time where it's all about celebrity **Which is more important in your work: the process or the product?** The process. Obviously the final product has to be important, too, because otherwise it reflects badly on you. But to me, it's actually putting together a collection, choosing the fabrics, that is my be-all and end-all **Is designing difficult for you?** No, it's not difficult for me. And in fact, I'm always told to not put too many ideas in something. I'm not the kind of person who has one idea and then you have to create 200 garments that work around that idea **What's your definition of beauty?** I find beauty much more on the inside than on the outside **What's your philosophy?** To push things very slowly. It's about never being fooled by what you initially see. Give things a chance, give them time. The more you do that, the more you find in someone or something **What is the most important lesson you've learned?** Be true to yourself and don't listen too much to what other people want

'I am married to fashion and I will remain faithful,' Dirk Bikkembergs solemnly declared in the February 1991 issue of i-D. And so it is that the German-born designer (born 1959) has stayed true to his perfectly masculine, brutally erotic other half; an aesthetic vision continually reworked since graduating from Belgium's Royal Academy of Fine Arts in 1982. Bikkembergs was later recognised as one of the original 'Antwerp Six'. The son of army parents (an influence that surely bears witness to his penchant for leather and severe tailoring), Bikkembergs gained valuable early experience working for a variety of Belgian fashion companies before being awarded the coveted Golden Spindle Award for Best Young Designer in 1985. With the launch of his first collection of men's shoes a year later, the designer established his name and set out a strict, militaristic blueprint. In 1987 he introduced his menswear line, with the focus on knitwear, and the following year presented his first full collection of Dirk Bikkembergs Men in Paris. Responding to a growing appreciation of his work, 1993 saw the first Dirk Bikkembergs Women line, presenting severely tailored capes, long skirts and reefer jackets. In the years since, a flurry of additional lines have been introduced, including the White Labels for men and women and the Red Label Bikkembergs Jeans Collection in 2000. The same year also saw the designer winning the Moët & Chandon Esprit du Siècle award, a fitting testament to his continued attention to structure, sex and detail.

'Ich bin mit der Mode verheiratet und werde ihr treu bleiben', erklärte Dirk Bikkembergs 1991 feierlich in der Februarausgabe der Zeitschrift i-D. Und so hat es der 1959 in Deutschland geborene Designer seither auch gehalten; er ist bei seiner durch und durch maskulinen, brutal erotischen Linie geblieben. An dieser ästhetischen Vision arbeitet er kontinuierlich seit seinem Abschluss an der belgischen Königlichen Akademie der Schönen Künste 1982. Später zählte man Bikkembergs zu den ursprünglichen 'Antwerp Six'. Seine Vorliebe für Leder und strenge Schnitte könnte damit zusammenhängen, dass seine Eltern beide Armeeangehörige waren. Bikkembergs sammelte bei seiner Arbeit für verschiedene belgische Modefirmen eine Menge wertvoller Erfahrungen, bevor man ihm 1985 den begehrten Golden Spindle Award als bester Jungdesigner verlieh. Mit seiner ersten Schuhkollektion für Herren ein Jahr danach hatte er sich endgültig etabliert und die Weichen für seinen strengen, militaristischen Stil gestellt. 1987 präsentierte er eine Herrenmodelinie mit Schwerpunkt Strickwaren und ein Jahr später in Paris mit Dirk Bikkembergs Men seine erste komplette Herrenkollektion. Als Reaktion auf die zunehmende Wertschätzung seiner Arbeit folgte 1993 die erste Kollektion von Dirk Bikkembergs Women mit streng geschnittenen Capes, langen Röcken und Matrosenjacken. Seither hat der Designer eine Vielzahl weiterer Linien eingeführt, darunter White Labels für Damen und Herren und 2000 eine Bikkembergs Jeanskollektion unter dem Namen Red Label. Im selben Jahr gewann er auch den Preis Esprit du Siècle von Moët & Chandon – ein angemessener Beweis seiner ungebrochenen Begeisterung für Strukturen, Sex und Details.

«Je suis marié à la mode et lui resterai fidèle», déclarait solennellement Dirk Bikkembergs dans le numéro de février 1991 du magazine i-D. Et c'est ainsi que ce créateur allemand (né en 1959) ne s'est jamais départi de son côté 100% masculin à l'érotisme brutal, une vision esthétique qu'il remet continuellement en question depuis l'obtention de son diplôme à l'Académie Royale des Beaux-Arts de Belgique en 1982. Plus tard, Bikkembergs fera partie des premiers «Antwerp Six». Fils de parents militaires (une influence qui apparaît de façon évidente à travers son penchant pour le cuir et les coupes sévères), le précoce Bikkembergs acquiert une précieuse expérience en travaillant pour diverses maisons belges avant de recevoir le tant convoité Golden Spindle de Meilleur Jeune Créateur en 1985. Un an plus tard, il impose son nom en lançant sa première collection de chaussures pour homme, proposant un style sévère d'inspiration militaire. En 1987, il crée une ligne pour homme qui fait la part belle à la maille, puis l'année suivante il présente la première collection complète Dirk Bikkembergs Men à Paris. Face au succès croissant de ses créations, il présente Dirk Bikkembergs Women en 1993, première ligne féminine composée de capes aux coupes strictes, de longues chemises et de cabans. Depuis, il a lancé de nombreuses collections, notamment White Labels pour homme et pour femme, ainsi que la ligne de jeans Red Label Bikkembergs en l'an 2000. La même année, il remporte le prix Esprit du Siècle de Moët & Chandon, un hommage approprié qui vient récompenser son attention constante à la structure, au sexe et au détail.

"I am married to fashion and I will remain faithful"

DIRK BIKKEMBERGS

What are your signature designs? From the first day I designed clothes, I always wanted them to look strong. And this is why all my garments are finished with big double stitching to give the feeling that they won't fall apart. This is something I can move in, I can run in, I can roll on the ground in and it will not fall apart. For men and women, the same thing. So this would be my signature **What's your favourite piece from any of your collections?** When I started in fashion 15 years ago, what I loved more than anything in the world were a white T-shirt, Converse Allstars and a pair of Levi's 501s. And I swore to myself that I would only touch the fabric of denim the day I could do something which I could be proud of when put next to Levi's. Then a few years ago, when the fashion world was all in black, I looked at 16-year-olds and saw they were not wearing this. They had their trainers, they had their tracksuits. And I thought to myself, if young people are interested in being healthy and looking healthy, in football, in sports and all this, then you should try to make blue trousers which are healthy. And I thought, technology can do anything, so why don't I try to make fabric remember the shape of a body? So I found the healthiest football player around and took him to my pattern cutter and made haute couture second-skin trousers with my double stitching on his body shape. That was the start of my jeans trouser **How would you describe your work?** Very intense, very sexy, very healthy, very modern, very sporty. But not sportswear **What's your ultimate goal?** I don't want to be an artist who makes something for the Guggenheim Museum. My goal in designing is to express what I feel and what I think **What inspires you?** Everything that is real; normal things. I always go for more banal things, more common things. I don't need a nice interior to be inspired **Who do you have in mind when you design?** It's him and it's her and it's you and it's the bartender. It's not that I look for Tom Cruise or Brad Pitt. It's just reality **How have your own experiences affected your work?** They have absolutely affected my work in the way that for ten years, every season, I have been making a new film that I put for 20 minutes on the catwalk. And, at the end of the day, I don't know if people really understood what it was all about. And I went into this big depression. I was saying to myself in the mirror, 'Hey, you are good at making films but if you want to make films, then do it at the movies. Start making clothes.' Because giving so many different ideas every season just meant that people didn't make any sense of the whole thing. So I decided to bring it down, make it much smaller. And I bring it down to double stitching and to healthy trousers. And from now on, everybody I talk to, I talk about the healthy trousers! **What has been the greatest influence on your career?** I make a difference between what I did two years ago and, after my year of thinking, what I now stand for. In the first ten years, it would probably have been fashion in general. Now, I would say the football player. He is genuine, not touched at all. He has completely helped a natural view. Because I know that he doesn't think in terms of labels. And this is probably what gave me a complete overview on it. The moment he had the jeans trousers on his body, I could see him look in the mirror, I could see the sun in his eye. I could see he was happy. And it was not for the trousers. It was for the feeling these trousers gave to him. It felt like he had had his tracksuit on, but he didn't. He never, ever put any other jeans on afterwards **Is designing difficult for you?** No. It's my wife, it's my wedding **What's your definition of beauty?** A healthy-looking, smiling sun-tanned face **What is the most important lesson you've learned?** Don't try to impress somebody else because it's not worth it. You have to be faithful to yourself

'My shoes have something other shoes don't – personality.' Perhaps this explains why Manolo Blahnik's work has such a seductive power and how, with a career spanning over 25 years, he has become the world's most famous footwear designer. Born in the Canary Islands in 1943, Blahnik spent his childhood crafting tinfoil shoes for the family's cats. After studying languages and art in Geneva, he moved to Paris in 1968 with the intention of becoming a set designer. But on a trip to New York in 1970, Paloma Picasso took him to meet Diana Vreeland, then editor-in-chief of American Vogue, who insisted his talent lay in shoe design. A year later, based in London, he began making footwear for Ossie Clark. Midas, a UK fashion chain, asked Blahnik to create shoes for them too, and the rollercoaster ride of success began in earnest. In 1973 Blahnik opened a tiny flagship shop in Chelsea; he now has boutiques in New York, Hong Kong and the Philippines, plus concessions in some of the world's most exclusive stores. Manolo Blahnik's creations are sexy, luxurious and exquisitely crafted – he still perfects designs by hand while permanently keeping four Italian factories busy with production. Always the celebrity footwear of choice, 'Manolos' have become a household name thanks to the US television series 'Sex and the City'. Manolo Blahnik also collaborates with numerous designers, from John Galliano to Michael Kors. He has collected tributes like women collect his shoes: over 14 fashion honours since 1987, when the Council of Fashion Designers of America conferred their 'Special Award' for the first time. In 1999, the Houston Museum of Fine Art presented the Silver Slipper to Blahnik; in 2001, London's Royal College of Art awarded him an honorary Doctorate of Arts.

'Meine Schuhe besitzen etwas, das andere nicht haben – Persönlichkeit.' Vielleicht erklärt das zum einen, warum Manolo Blahniks Kreationen eine solche Anziehungskraft ausüben, und zum anderen, wie man es im Laufe einer mehr als 25-jährigen Karriere zum berühmtesten Schuhdesigner der Welt bringt. Geboren wurde Blahnik 1943 auf den Kanarischen Inseln. Als Kind bastelte er den Katzen der Familie Schühchen aus Alufolie. Nach dem Studium in Genf – Sprachen und Kunst – ging er 1968 mit dem festen Vorsatz nach Paris, Bühnenbildner zu werden. Bei einem Kurzaufenthalt in New York 1970 machte Paloma Picasso ihn jedoch mit Diana Vreeland, der damaligen Chefredakteurin der amerikanischen Vogue, bekannt. Sie beharrte darauf, dass seine Begabung im Entwerfen von Schuhen liege. Ein Jahr später, Blahnik lebte inzwischen in London, begann er, Schuhe für Ossie Clark zu kreieren. Daraufhin gab die britische Modekette Midas ebenfalls Schuhe bei ihm in Auftrag, und die Achterbahnfahrt zum Erfolg nahm ihren Anfang. 1973 eröffnete der Designer einen winzigen Flagship Store in Chelsea. Heute gehören ihm Boutiquen in New York, Hongkong und auf den Philippinen; dazu kommen noch Konzessionen in einigen der exklusivsten Läden der Welt. Die Kreationen von Manolo Blahnik sind sexy, luxuriös und handwerklich perfekt verarbeitet. Bis heute legt er selbst Hand an, um seinen Entwürfen den letzten Schliff zu geben, auch wenn inzwischen vier Fabriken in Italien mit der Produktion seiner Modelle völlig ausgelastet sind. 'Manolos' waren schon immer das Lieblingsschuhwerk der Promis, doch durch die amerikanische TV-Serie 'Sex and the City' sind sie inzwischen allgemein bekannt. Blahnik arbeitet von John Galliano bis Michael Kors mit vielen Designern zusammen. Und er scheint Preise zu sammeln wie manche Frauen seine Schuhe: über 14 Auszeichnungen seit 1987, als das Council of Fashion Designers of America ihm erstmals den Special Award verlieh. 1999 erhielt Blahnik vom Houston Museum of Fine Art den Silver Slipper. Das Royal College of Art in London verlieh ihm 2001 sogar die Ehrendoktorwürde.

«Mes chaussures ont quelque chose que les autres n'ont pas : de la personnalité», a déclaré Manolo Blahnik. Cette affirmation explique peut-être pourquoi son travail exerce un tel pouvoir d'attraction et comment, après plus de 25 ans de carrière, il est devenu le créateur de chaussures le plus célèbre au monde. Né en 1943 aux îles Canaries, Blahnik passe son enfance à confectionner des chaussures en papier alu pour les chats de la maison. Après des études artistiques et de langues à Genève, il s'installe à Paris en 1968 dans l'intention de devenir chef décorateur. Lors d'un voyage à New York en 1970, Paloma Picasso lui présente Diana Vreeland, alors rédactrice en chef du Vogue américain, qui le persuade que son talent réside en fait dans la création de chaussures. Un an plus tard, installé à Londres, il commence à dessiner des chaussures pour Ossie Clark. Midas, une chaîne britannique de magasins de vêtements, lui commande également des modèles et Blahnik se lance pour de bon dans les montagnes russes du succès. En 1973, il ouvre une minuscule boutique à Chelsea ; aujourd'hui, il compte plusieurs boutiques à New York, Hong Kong et aux Philippines ainsi que des points de vente dans les grands magasins les plus luxueux du monde. Les créations de Manolo Blahnik sont sexy, exclusives et d'une facture exquise : il finalise tous ses modèles à la main tout en remplissant les carnets de commandes de quatre usines italiennes. Chouchou des célébrités, les «Manolos» sont aujourd'hui connues de tous grâce à la série américaine «Sex and the City». De John Galliano à Michael Kors, Manolo Blahnik collabore avec de nombreux couturiers. Il accumule les récompenses comme les femmes collectionnent ses chaussures : le monde de la mode lui a décerné plus de 14 distinctions depuis 1987, lorsque le Council of Fashion Designers of America (CFDA) lui a pour la première fois remis son Special Award. En 1999, le Museum of Fine Art de Houston l'a décoré du Silver Slipper et en 2001, le Royal College of Art de Londres l'a consacré Doctor honoris causa en beaux-arts.

"My goal is to always be a challenge to myself"

PORTRAIT BY KEVIN DAVIES

MANOLO BLAHNIK

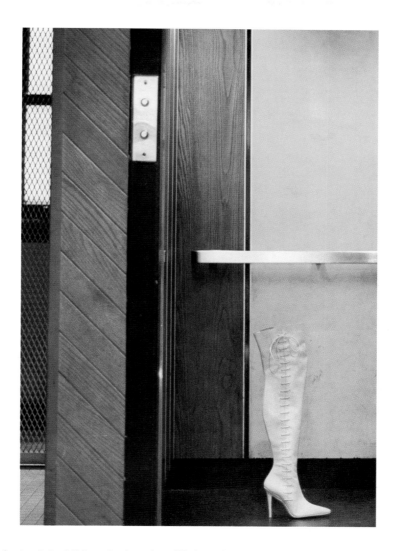

What are your signature designs? High, sexy but always elegant **What's your favourite piece from any of your collections?** There are so many, although the beaded up the leg sandals I did for John Galliano for his Dior couture 'Massai Warrior' collection are a particular favourite. And I still adore my futuristic collection from 1986 **How would you describe your work?** It is one of the most satisfying parts of my life **What's your ultimate goal?** To always be a challenge to myself **What inspires you?** That changes from day to day. It even surprises me… movies, books, painting, architecture, landscapes and certain women that I see sometimes in the streets **Can fashion still have a political ambition?** I know nothing about ambition and even less about politics, but fashion often reflects the times **What do you have in mind when you design?** So many things of totally different natures **Is the idea of creative collaboration important to you?** Sometimes **Who or what has been the greatest influence on your career?** Mr Luchino Visconti comes to mind right away and great fashion icons like Diana Vreeland, of course Balenciaga, and my homeland Spain **How have your own experiences affected your work as a designer?** Don't you think all of our experiences influence our loves and our work? At least for me, I can say yes! **Which is more important in your work: the process or the product?** Both envelop us, but I love the process because I know little by little it will determine the product **Is designing difficult for you and, if so, what drives you to continue?** I have a passion for work and all passions can have their difficulties **Have you ever been influenced or moved by the reaction to your designs?** Always **What's your definition of beauty?** Beauty is captured in fleeting moments and reflected in one's eyes **What's your philosophy?** Work hard **What is the most important lesson you've learned?** Whatever you do… always do your best

A non-designer designer with no formal training, Hardy Blechman has had an indisputable impact upon British – and international – streetwear. Best known for his technical 'Snopant' trousers, his signature use of camouflage patterns and his elaborate and instantly recognisable embroidery work, Blechman's Maharishi label embraces the notion of collaboration on a creative level: he has worked in conjunction with a number of artists including Kaws, Futura 2000 and Stash. Born in Bournemouth in 1963, Blechman established his Maharishi label in 1994 after years spent importing surplus clothing into the UK. The name of the label is indicative of Blechman's own spiritual beliefs: Maharishi is derived from Sanskrit, 'maha' meaning great and 'rishi' meaning seer or guru. Striving to create an environmentally sound company, Maharishi began life specialising in the production of hemp and natural fibre clothing, and in recycling workwear and military surplus. Maharishi's growth has been largely due to the success of Blechman's 1995 'Snopant', a design that was copied on every high street in Britain. Blechman has spent much time developing groundbreaking fabrics such as Loro Piana 3-ply weatherproof cashmeres and wools, successfully marrying luxury with utility, a Blechman trademark. In 2000 Blechman launched a second line, Mhi, and he recently introduced a capsule denim range into his mainline collection, proving himself to be a designer as adaptable and committed to the development of new ideas as he is consistent.

Als Anti-Designer ohne traditionelle Ausbildung hat Hardy Blechman die britische – wie auch die internationale – Streetwear unbestreitbar beeinflusst. Am bekanntesten sind seine technisch ausgefeilten 'Snopant'-Hosen, seine Liebe zu Camouflagemustern und seine kunstvollen, unverwechselbaren Stickereien. Blechmans Label Maharishi setzt im kreativen Bereich auf Zusammenarbeit: Zu den Künstlern, mit denen der Designer bisher gemeinsame Projekte realisiert hat, zählen unter anderem Kaws, Futura 2000 und Stash. Der 1963 in Bournemouth geborene Blechman gründete 1994 das Label Maharishi, nachdem er jahrelang Kleiderüberschüsse nach Großbritannien importiert hatte. Der Name der Marke ist ein Hinweis auf Blechmans eigene spirituelle Überzeugungen. Maharishi ist ein zusammengesetztes Wort aus dem Sanskrit, wo 'maha' groß und 'rishi' Seher oder Guru bedeutet. In dem Bemühen um eine umweltverträgliche Firma war Maharishi zunächst auf die Produktion von Kleidern aus Hanf und anderen Naturfasern spezialisiert; außerdem recycelte er Arbeitskleidung und Überbestände der Armee. Maharishis Wachstum kam hauptsächlich mit dem Erfolg von Blechmans 'Snopant' im Jahr 1995 – einem Design, das damals überall kopiert wurde. Blechman hat viel Zeit in die Entwicklung revolutionärer Stoffe gesteckt, so entstand etwa der dreifädige wetterfeste Kaschmir- und Wollstoff Loro Piana. Die erfolgreiche Verbindung von Luxus und Nützlichkeit ist ein Markenzeichen des Firmengründers. 2000 brachte Blechman mit Mhi eine zweite Linie heraus. Vor kurzem hat er in seine Hauptlinie eine Jeanskollektion integriert und sich damit wieder einmal als Designer erwiesen, der einerseits für neue Ideen aufgeschlossen, andererseits aber ebenso beständig ist.

Hardy Blechman est un «anti-créateur» qui, sans avoir suivi la moindre formation, a néanmoins exercé un impact indiscutable sur le streetwear britannique et international. Surtout connue pour le pantalon techno «Snopant», une utilisation caractéristique des motifs camouflage et un travail de broderie élaboré immédiatement reconnaissable, sa griffe Maharishi incarne le renouveau des collaborations créatives: en effet, Blechman a travaillé avec de nombreux artistes, parmi lesquels Kaws, Futura 2000 et Stash. Né en 1963 à Bournemouth, il fonde sa griffe Maharishi en 1994 après plusieurs années passées dans l'importation de vêtements de surplus au Royaume-Uni. Le nom de la griffe reflète ses croyances spirituelles: Maharishi est un terme dérivé du sanskrit, «maha», qui signifie «grand» et «rishi», qui veut dire «voyant» ou «gourou». En tant qu'entreprise sensible aux problèmes d'environnement, Maharishi se spécialise d'abord dans la production de vêtements en chanvre et en fibres naturelles, ainsi que dans le recyclage des vêtements de travail et des uniformes militaires. Le développement de la griffe repose en grande partie sur le succès du «Snopant» de Blechman en 1995, une création copiée depuis par toutes les boutiques de Grande-Bretagne. Blechman a consacré beaucoup de temps à l'invention de nouveaux tissus, notamment les cachemires et les laines Loro Piana à 3 brins qui résistent aux intempéries, combinant avec succès le luxe à l'utilitaire, aujourd'hui sa véritable marque de fabrique. En l'an 2000, il a lancé une deuxième ligne, Mhi. Plus récemment, il a ajouté une petite collection plus expérimentale à sa gamme principale, prouvant ainsi qu'il était un créateur aussi cohérent que flexible et engagé au développement des idées nouvelles.

"I take consideration of Mrs Ghandi's warning: 'There is no beauty in the finest cloth if it makes hunger and unhappiness'"

PORTRAIT BY MARK LEBON

HARDY BLECHMAN

What are your signature designs? Technical hemp, symbolic reclamation of camouflage pattern, Snobutton and cord system, dragon-embroidered Snopants and tour jackets **How would you describe your work?** Developmental, collaborative, (r?)evolutionary **What's your ultimate goal?** To become one with what I do. Not to check myself when I claim that Zen Buddhism is closest to my idea of truth when asked if I have any religion **What inspires you?** Dichotomical mixing: nature and technology, East and West, utility and beauty **Can fashion still have a political ambition?** Fashion has a great opportunity to express any view and with the right attention to intention could help shape aspects of political thought. Maharishi make efforts to use positive imagery and therefore invoke positive thought **Is the idea of creative collaboration important to you?** Collaboration has fuelled Maharishi's development and is imperative to my process. The skills I bring are questionable but somehow a myriad of unseen creative and technical forces come into play in the mix **How have your own experiences affected your work as a designer?** Travel may have had the greatest effect on my mindset and therefore design ethic, allowing another view to come into perspective **Have you ever been influenced or moved by the reaction to your designs?** People jacking your shit drives you to improve upon it. Occasional offence taken by soldiers to our use of camouflage in non-military context has influenced me to perpetuate the mission **What's your definition of beauty?** Full consideration of Mrs Ghandi's warning: 'There is no beauty in the finest cloth if it makes hunger and unhappiness' **What's your philosophy?** Still under construction **What is the most important lesson you've learned?** You can't choose who you fall in love with

When she was little, Véronique Branquinho (born 1973) wanted to be a ballerina. Years later at art school, she discovered David Bowie and the Velvet Underground. The light and angelic, plus the dark and transgressive – or Branquinho in a nutshell. Female duality is a major theme in the work of this Belgian designer. While studying fashion at the Royal Academy of Antwerp (1991–1995), she researched the many aspects of womanhood, but nailed the subject when she started to show her own collections in Paris, from Spring-Summer 1998 on. Subtly referencing ambiguous heroines like 'Twin Peaks' Laura Palmer, movie avenger Carrie or the sensuous girls of David Hamilton's photographs, Branquinho's work often focuses on the transition from girl to woman and all the contradictory emotions and desires that go with it. She translates this theme into highly personal and seductive looks that trade frivolity for dignity: pleated floor-length skirts, smoking jackets, herringbone dresses, draped gauze tops and flowing pants. Attracting loyal followers from the early stage, Véronique Branquinho climbed the stage at NYC's Madison Square Garden to receive the VH1 Fashion Award for best new designer in October 1998. For Italian leather company Ruffo's Research line, she designed the women's collection (Spring-Summer and Autumn-Winter 1999). She has participated in many exhibitions, including Biennale Della Moda in Florence in 1998, Colette in Paris in 1999 and 'Flemish Fashion: Design From Belgium' at the Fashion Institute of Technology in New York in 2001. For the 'Documenta 11' exhibition in Kassel, Germany in 2002, Véronique Branquinho created a white raincoat in a limited edition of 300.

Als kleines Mädchen wollte die 1973 geborene Véronique Branquinho noch Ballerina werden. Jahre später entdeckte sie während des Studiums David Bowie und Velvet Underground für sich. Das Leichte, Engelsgleiche und das Düstere, Grenzüberschreitende – so lässt sich das Wesen dieser Designerin vielleicht in wenigen Worten beschreiben. Weibliche Ambiguität ist ein wichtiges Thema in der Arbeit dieser belgischen Designerin. Während ihres Modestudiums an der Königlichen Akademie von Antwerpen (1991–1995), erforschte sie die vielen Aspekte des Frauseins. Als sie ab Frühjahr/Sommer 1998 begann, ihre eigenen Kollektionen in Paris zu zeigen, war zu erkennen, wie exakt sie bei diesem Thema den Nagel auf den Kopf traf. Feinsinnig bezieht sie sich auf ambivalente Heldinnen wie Laura Palmer aus 'Twin Peaks', die Kino-Rächerin Carrie oder die sinnlichen Mädchen der Fotografien von David Hamilton. Im Blickpunkt stehen oft der Übergang vom Mädchen zur Frau und all die widersprüchlichen Gefühle und Wünsche, die mit ihm einhergehen. Branquinho gelingt es, dieses komplexe Sujet in absolut persönliche und verführerische Kreationen umzusetzen, die zugunsten von Würde auf frivole Effekte verzichten: bodenlange Faltenröcke, Smokingjacken, Kleider im Fischgrätdessin, drapierte Oberteile aus Gaze und Hosen mit fließendem Schnitt. Schon sehr früh konnte Branquinho auf eine treue Fangemeinde bauen, und bereits im Oktober 1998 nahm sie im New Yorker Madison Square Garden den VH1 Fashion Award als beste neue Designerin entgegen. Für den italienischen Lederwarenhersteller Ruffo Research entwarf sie die Frühjahr/Sommer- und die Herbst/Winter-Kollektion 1999. Außerdem hat sie bereits an vielen Ausstellungen teilgenommen: 1998 an der Biennale Della Moda in Florenz, 1999 bei Colette in Paris und 2001 an der Schau 'Flemish Fashion: Design From Belgium' am Fashion Institute of Technology in New York. Für die 'Documenta 11' in Kassel entwarf Branquinho 2002 einen weißen Regenmantel in einer limitierten Auflage von 300 Stück.

Quand elle était petite, Véronique Branquinho (née en 1973) voulait devenir ballerine. Des années plus tard, alors étudiante en art, elle découvre David Bowie et le Velvet Underground. Légère et angélique, mais aussi sombre et transgressive, telle est Véronique Branquinho. La dualité féminine représente un thème majeur dans le travail de la créatrice belge. Alors qu'elle étudie la mode à l'Académie Royale d'Anvers (de 1991 à 1995), elle effectue des recherches sur les nombreuses facettes de la féminité, mais referme ce dossier au Printemps-Eté 1998 lorsqu'elle commence à présenter ses propres collections à Paris. Parsemé de références subtiles à des héroïnes ambiguës telles que la Laura Palmer de « Twin Peaks », Carrie la vengeresse du grand écran ou les filles sensuelles des photos de David Hamilton, le travail de Véronique Branquinho parle souvent de la métamorphose des jeunes filles en femmes, prenant en compte toutes les émotions et tous les désirs contradictoires qui l'accompagnent. Elle réussit à traduire ce thème universel dans des looks très personnels et séduisants qui privilégient la dignité sur la frivolité : jupes plissées tombant jusqu'au sol, vestons d'intérieur, robes à chevrons, tops drapés en gaze et pantalons fluides. Soutenue par ses fidèles de la première heure, Véronique Branquinho monte sur la scène du Madison Square Garden de New York en octobre 1998 pour recevoir le prix de Best New Designer décerné par la chaîne VH1. Par ailleurs, elle a dessiné une collection féminine pour le maroquinier italien Ruffo Research (Printemps-Eté et Automne-Hiver 1999). Elle a participé à de nombreuses expositions, notamment la Biennale Della Moda de Florence en 1998, à la boutique Colette de Paris en 1999 et « Flemish Fashion : Design From Belgium » au Fashion Institute of Technology de New York en 2001. Pour l'exposition « Documenta 11 », organisée dans la ville allemande de Kassel en 2002, Véronique Branquinho a créé un imperméable blanc disponible en édition limitée à 300 exemplaires.

"I'm inspired by the inner complexity of a woman. About the struggle she has with ambiguous feelings. About the attraction and rejection of those feelings, looking for harmony between them"

PORTRAIT BY WILLY VANDERPERRE

VÉRONIQUE BRANQUINHO

PHOTOGRAPHY BY WILLY VANDEPERRE, STYLING BY OLIVIER RIZZO. FEBRUARY 2001

"I see my collections as a personal diary"

What are your signature designs? Pants, skirt, blazer, shirt, turtleneck, leggings. Some designs have been in all the collections since my very first. For me they are pure. And I don't see the point of changing them every six months just because there is a new fashion season **What's your favourite piece from any of your collections?** The pants called 'Poison'. They have been in the collection since I started. They never changed and they are a bestseller since then **What's your ultimate goal?** To have the liberty to decide what I will be doing next **Who do you have in mind when you design?** I do not have a particular person in mind when I design. It's not about physique or features, like being tall, having blonde hair or green eyes... but it is more abstract. I'm inspired by the inner complexity of a woman. About the struggle she has with ambiguous feelings. About the attraction and rejection of those feelings, looking for harmony between them **How have your own experiences affected your work as a designer?** I see my collections as a personal diary. They are very close to me. In a way, they reflect my feelings **Which is more important in your work: the process or the product?** I cannot see process apart from product. You need them to make a collection. It's about continuity. That makes them both equally important. It's a circle **Is designing difficult for you?** I design very intuitively. It comes very naturally to express myself through my collection, so in a way it's not difficult **Have you ever been influenced or moved by the reaction to your designs?** Yes, it already happened that I have felt threatened by the way people put conventions on my work. So I made a reaction collection. But it's also part of my work, this duality-fight **What's your definition of beauty?** I don't want to define beauty. It's part of beauty that it can move you where you wouldn't expect it **What is the most important lesson you've learned?** That life and work become more interesting and satisfying when you have caring people around you

Zowie Broach and Brian Kirby work (and live) together as Boudicca. A fashion label and regular fixture on the London show calendar since Spring-Summer 1998, Boudicca is also the name of the rebel Iceni queen who rose up against the Romans in Britain. A similarly rebellious streak permeates Boudicca's design and has led to Broach and Kirby gaining a non-conformist reputation within the fashion industry. Although they don't see themselves as 'fashion rebels', the aesthetics of revolution and change together with the 'uniforms' of global capitalism have been frequent reference points within Boudicca's womenswear collections. There is also a sense of breaking the rules in terms of the amount of time and effort spent on each ready-to-wear garment, making their clothes a kind of politico couture. At home on the catwalk and in the gallery, Boudicca's work has included a collaboration with Turner Prize winning artist Gillian Wearing in 2000. Their backgrounds are just as unconventional as their fashion: Brian Kirby grew up in Manchester, where he trained to be a mechanic, later studying fashion and completing an MA at the Royal College of Art, London, in 1994. Zowie Broach grew up between various seaside towns in the West Country, studied at Middlesex (graduating 1989), then became a stylist and video director. They met on a windswept beach in Rimini in 1996. In the near future, Boudicca plan to launch their own fragrance, Wode, and a shoe range.

Sowohl beruflich als auch privat sind Zowie Broach und Brian Kirby von Boudicca ein Team. Das Label, das seit Frühjahr/Sommer 1998 fester Bestandteil des alljährlichen Londoner Modenschau-Kalenders ist, hat seinen Namen nach der keltischen Iceni-Königin Boudicca, die Widerstand gegen die Römer in Britannien leistete. Eine gewisse Aufmüpfigkeit findet man denn auch in den Kreationen von Boudicca, was Broach und Kirby in der Modebranche den Ruf von Nonkonformisten eingebracht hat. Auch wenn die beiden sich nicht als 'Moderebellen' betrachten, so sind die Ästhetik von Revolution und Veränderung sowie die 'Uniformen' des weltweit regierenden Kapitalismus doch häufig Bezugspunkte in den Damenkollektionen ihres Labels. Einen Regelbruch stellen auch die viele Zeit und Mühe, die auf jedes Prêt-à-Porter-Stück verwendet werden, dar. So gesehen ist diese Mode eine Art Politico Couture, die genauso gut auf den Laufsteg wie in eine Kunstgalerie passt. Letzteres traf vor allem auf das Jahr 2000 zu, als man mit dem Künstler Gillian Wearing, der bereits mit dem Turner-Preis ausgezeichnet wurde, zusammenarbeitete. Die Lebensgeschichten der beiden Designer sind ebenso unkonventionell wie ihre Mode. Brian Kirby wuchs in Manchester auf, wo er eine Mechanikerlehre absolvierte. Später studierte er Mode und machte 1994 seinen Magister am Royal College of Art in London. Zowie Broach wuchs in verschiedenen Küstenorten im Westen Großbritanniens auf, studierte bis zu ihrem Abschluss 1989 in Middlesex und arbeitete anschließend zunächst als Stylistin und Videoregisseurin. Kennen gelernt haben sich die beiden 1996 an einem sturmgepeitschten Strand bei Rimini. Als nächstes plant Boudicca einen eigenen Duft mit dem Namen Wode und eine Schuhkollektion herauszubringen.

Zowie Broach et Brian Kirby travaillent (et vivent) ensemble sous le nom de Boudicca. Griffe de mode et rendez-vous régulier des défilés londoniens depuis le Printemps-Eté 1998, Boudicca est également le nom d'une reine de la tribu des Iceni qui s'était rebellée contre les Romains en Grande-Bretagne. Une rébellion similaire habite les créations de Boudicca, conduisant Zowie Broach et Brian Kirby à se forger une réputation d'anticonformistes au sein du monde de la mode. Bien qu'ils ne se considèrent pas comme des « rebelles de la mode », l'esthétique de la révolution et du changement, associée à leurs « uniformes » du capitalisme mondial, revient souvent sous forme de référence dans les collections pour femme de Boudicca. Dans une certaine mesure, Boudicca ne respecte pas les règles du jeu car le duo investit beaucoup de temps et d'efforts dans chaque pièce de prêt-à-porter, ce qui fait de leur mode une sorte de « couture politique ». Tout aussi à l'aise sur les podiums que dans les galeries d'art, Boudicca a collaboré en l'an 2000 avec l'artiste Gillian Wearing, lauréat du Turner Prize. Le parcours du duo est aussi inattendu que leurs créations : Brian Kirby a grandi à Manchester, où il a suivi une formation de mécanicien avant d'étudier la mode et d'obtenir un MA du Royal College of Art de Londres en 1994. Zowie Broach a grandi entre plusieurs villes de la côte du sud-ouest de l'Angleterre, a étudié à Middlesex (diplômée en 1989), puis est devenue styliste et vidéaste. Ils se sont rencontrés en 1996 à Rimini sur une plage balayée par le vent. Boudicca lancera prochainement un parfum, Wode, ainsi qu'une ligne de chaussures.

"An artist is the sum of his own risks"

PORTRAIT BY DONALD MILNE

ZOWIE BROACH & BRIAN KIRBY

What are your signature designs? To try and define yourself draws the journey to a close sooner rather than later **What's your favourite piece from any of your collections?** 'Do not try to capture life, they say. It is impossible' (Julia Ain-Krupa) **How would you describe your work?** 'A certificate of presence' (Roland Barthes) **What's your ultimate goal?** 'If we take people simply as they are, we make them worse; if we treat them as if they were what they ought to be, then we bring them to a point to which they were meant to be brought' (Goethe) **What inspires you?** 'And it isn't enough for us to identify with ourselves, it is necessary to do so passionately, to the point of life and death' (Milan Kundera) **Can fashion still have a political ambition?** 'The universalisation of the preferred priorities of a very small part of human society will destroy creativity, not encourage it' (Verdana Shiva) **Who do you have in mind when you design?** I dress for something I dreamed of all my life. 'She the timid, the sociopath, the aviator navigator' (Julia Ain-Krupa) **Is the idea of creative collaboration important to you?** 'Hand in glove I stake my claim, I'll fight to the last breath. If they dare touch a hair on your head, I'll fight to the last breath' (Morrissey) **What has been the greatest influence on your career?** 'Let there be Fashion. Down with Art' (Max Ernst) **How have your own experiences affected your work as designers?** 'An artist is the sum of his own risks' (Dorothea Tanning) **Which is more important in your work: the process or the product?** 'Desires are the premonitions of abilities' (Goethe) **Is designing difficult for you and, if so, what drives you to continue?** 'If you wish to gain much, you must sacrifice much more' (New York street graffiti) **Have you ever been influenced or moved by the reaction to your designs?** 'Beauty will be convulsive or not at all' (André Breton) **What's your definition of beauty?** 'And what I am to love, if not the enigma' (Giorgio De Chirico) **What's your philosophy?** 'To compromise an idea is to soften it, to make an excuse for it, to betray it' (John Cassavetes) **What is the most important lesson you've learned?** 'Only the dream leaves man with all his rights to liberty' (André Breton)

Barbara Bui (born Paris, 1957) entered the world of fashion in 1983 when she opened a boutique, Kabuki, with her business partner William Halimi. The name gives an insight into her former life as an actor and comedian, with a particular interest in Asian theatre. Within this environment, Bui began to introduce some of her own designs; four years later she presented her first full collection to international press and buyers. In 1988, the first Barbara Bui shop opened on Rue Etienne Marcel in Paris. From the beginning, Bui's clothes have represented a strong and elegant woman, mixing more severe pieces such as leather jackets with voluminous, bias-cut skirts. She tends to favour black or tonal colours, and traditional fabrics such as wool and leathers, which give her designs a richness and timeless quality. In 1998 Bui started a diffusion line, Barbara Bui Initials, a line of classic daywear separates that perfectly compliment the ethos of her main line. In 1999, Barbara Bui switched from Paris to New York in order to show her collection, but since then has shied away from the catwalk shows, presenting her work in a less formal way. So far this has taken the form of imagery and collaboration, currently with the photographer David Bailey, someone she believes perfectly captures the strength and spirit of the Barbara Bui woman. Today she has stores in New York and Milan, as well as Paris, and a best-selling range of shoes and bags.

Die 1957 in Paris geborene Barbara Bui trat erstmals 1983 in der Modewelt in Erscheinung, als sie zusammen mit ihrem Geschäftspartner William Halimi eine Boutique namens Kabuki eröffnete. Der Name ist ein Verweis auf ihre vorangegangene Karriere als Schauspielerin und Komikerin und ihr Faible für asiatisches Theater. In diesem Umfeld begann Bui einige ihrer eigenen Kreationen zu präsentieren; vier Jahre später stellte sie der internationalen Presse und dem Publikum ihre erste komplette Kollektion vor. Die Eröffnung des ersten Barbara Bui Shops fand 1988 in der Pariser Rue Etienne-Marcel statt. Von Anfang an entwarf Bui Mode für die starke, elegante Frau, die strengere Stücke, etwa eine Lederjacke, mit weiten, diagonal geschnittenen Röcken kombiniert. Die Designerin bevorzugt Schwarz oder gedämpfte Farben und traditionelle Materialien wie Wolle und Leder, die ihren Kreationen Wert und eine zeitlose Qualität verleihen. 1998 rief sie die Nebenlinie Barbara Bui Initials ins Leben – klassische Seperates für tagsüber, die dem Ethos ihrer Hauptlinie perfekt entsprechen. Ein Jahr später wechselte die Designerin von Paris nach New York, um ihre Kollektion zu zeigen, doch inzwischen scheut sie Catwalk-Shows und bevorzugt einen weniger formellen Rahmen, um ihre Arbeiten zu präsentieren. Momentan genügen ihr dafür auch Bilder, etwa die des Fotografen David Bailey, dem sie zutraut, Kraft und Geist der Frau, die Barbara Bui trägt, perfekt einzufangen. Neben Shops in Paris gibt es mittlerweile auch eigene Läden in New York und Mailand. Heute macht Bui zudem mit höchst erfolgreichen Schuh- und Taschenkollektionen von sich reden.

Née en 1957 à Paris, Barbara Bui débarque dans le monde de la mode en 1983 lorsqu'elle ouvre la boutique Kabuki avec son partenaire en affaires William Halimi. Elle choisit ce nom en souvenir de sa carrière de comédienne et en hommage au théâtre asiatique. Dans cette boutique, Barbara Bui commence à vendre ses propres créations ; quatre ans plus tard, elle présente sa première collection complète à la presse internationale et aux acheteurs. En 1988, la première boutique Barbara Bui ouvre ses portes rue Etienne Marcel à Paris. Dès le départ, ses vêtements s'adressent à une femme sûre d'elle et élégante, coordonnant des pièces plutôt sévères comme les vestes en cuir à des jupes asymétriques et volumineuses. Elle tend à privilégier le noir ou les couleurs sourdes, ainsi que les tissus classiques comme la laine et le cuir pour conférer à ses créations une richesse et une qualité intemporelles. En 1998, elle lance une autre ligne, Barbara Bui Initials, composée de séparés classiques pour le jour qui complètent à merveille l'esprit de sa ligne principale. En 1999, Barbara Bui quitte Paris pour New York afin de présenter sa collection, mais depuis elle fuit les défilés, préférant présenter son travail de façon moins formelle. Jusqu'à présent, elle a privilégié l'image et collaboré à cette fin avec divers artistes : elle travaille actuellement avec le photographe David Bailey car elle estime qu'il capte parfaitement toute la force et l'esprit de la femme Barbara Bui. Aujourd'hui, elle possède des boutiques à New York, Milan et Paris, ainsi qu'une gamme de chaussures et de sacs qui se vend très bien.

"In fashion, a designer
must be open-minded,
not withdraw into oneself"

PORTRAIT BY DAVID BAILEY

BARBARA BUI

What are your signature designs? The quality and the cutting, the elegance and the dynamism of the shapes **What are your favourite pieces from any of your collections?** Pants and leather pieces **How would you describe your work?** The expression of a sensitivity and a rock 'n' roll attitude revealing the character, the freedom and the self-confidence of a contemporary woman. A neat style with incisive, simple and qualitative cuts, accessorised with strong and creative details for an active and mobile woman **What's your ultimate goal?** One cannot give oneself an 'ultimate goal'. It is an evolutionary research without a final point diktat **What inspires you?** Evolution of women in general and my own evolution as a woman. Contemporary movements of music. Imaginary journeys. Cultural expansion of the large capitals **Can fashion still have a political ambition?** Of course. Fashion can convey declared or subliminal messages. It can be a sign of respect or of non-respect towards society. Fashion is a large vehicle of communication **Who do you have in mind when you design?** My close friends, touching actresses with an exacerbated duality (Romy Schneider, Emma Thompson) **Is the idea of creative collaboration important to you?** Of course, with my staff as well as in meeting with other people from other universes, like the one of music. In fashion, a designer must be open-minded, not withdraw into oneself **What has been the greatest influence on your career?** An Yves Saint Laurent exhibition at the very beginning of my career **How have your own experiences affected your work as a designer?** I receive the wounds or the joys as a person and they can be expressed in my work, whether they are private experiments or social experiments. There is always in my work a mixture of private and community. That can be a reaction to violence in society or a rejection of media superficiality **Which is more important in your work: the process or the product?** The process and the product but, moreover, the overall concept **Is designing difficult for you and, if so, what drives you to continue?** It is always difficult to keep pushing back the creative limits, to fight for requirement and quality, but at the same time it is my best way to exist and to communicate **What's your definition of beauty?** A simplicity of being; the innate beauty which does not depend on the glance of others **What's your philosophy?** Don't be impatient

Ennio Capasa co-founded Costume National with his brother Carlo in 1986. The first Costume National collection made its catwalk debut the following year and the label has remained an influential aspect of the Italian fashion landscape ever since. Educated at Milan's Accademia di Belle Arti di Brera, Capasa went to Japan in the early 1980s where he trained with master cutter Yohji Yamamoto. Costume National is best known for Capasa's extremely – and, at times, severely – lean and sharp silhouette, the predominant use of black throughout his work, and the quality of his fabrics. All of which combine to create a trademark confident, hard-edged, street-inspired chic. Capasa's love of fabrics led him to include an additional range, Costume National Luxe, in 2000: a limited series of garments within the women's collection constructed using rare materials. In addition to his womenswear, Capasa also produces a successful ready-to-wear range for men, Costume National Homme, which was introduced with an accompanying footwear line in 1993. Also executed predominantly in black, as with the womenswear, the signature silhouette is typically fitted and sleek, blending purity of cut and quality of fabric. Bags, lingerie and small leather goods were introduced by Costume National in 2000, with a fragrance collection, Costume National Scent, following a year later. The label now has flagship stores in Hong Kong, Los Angeles, Milan, New York, Osaka, Rome and Tokyo.

Ennio Capasa gründete 1986 zusammen mit seinem Bruder Carlo das Label Costume National. Mit ihrer ersten Kollektion gaben sie im darauf folgenden Jahr ihr Laufstegdebüt. Seither übt diese Marke einen ungebrochenen Einfluss auf die italienische Modelandschaft aus. Nach dem Studium an der Accademia di Belle Arti di Brera in Mailand ging Capasa in den frühen 1980er Jahren nach Japan, wo er beim Meister der Schnittkunst, Yohji Yamamoto, lernte. Costume National ist am berühmtesten für Capasas extrem schmale, scharf geschnittene und manchmal strenge Silhouetten, für den weitgehenden Verzicht auf Farbe zugunsten von Schwarz und für die Qualität der verwendeten Stoffe. Zusammengenommen ergibt das einen zuverlässigen, kantigen, von der Streetwear inspirierten Chic, der sich zum Markenzeichen entwickelt hat. Capasas Liebe zu Stoffen veranlasste ihn im Jahr 2000, mit Costume National Luxe eine Zweitkollektion zu entwerfen: Damenmode in limitierter Auflage und aus kostbaren Materialien. Neben der Damenkollektion produziert Capasa inzwischen auch erfolgreiche Prêt-à-Porter-Mode für Herren unter dem Label Costume National Homme, das gleichzeitig mit der dazugehörigen Schuhkollektion 1993 vorgestellt wurde. Auch hier dominiert wie bei den Damen Schwarz; die typische Silhouette ist figurbetont, fließend und bringt die Klarheit des Schnitts und die Stoffqualität optimal zur Geltung. Taschen, Dessous und kleine Lederaccessoires wurden im Jahr 2000 ins Sortiment aufgenommen; die Duftkollektion Costume National Scent folgte ein Jahr später. Flagship Stores des Labels findet man heute in Hongkong, Los Angeles, Mailand, New York, Osaka, Rom und Tokio.

Ennio Capasa a co-fondé Costume National avec son frère Carlo en 1986. La première collection Costume National débute sur les podiums l'année suivante et depuis, la griffe ne cesse d'exercer son influence sur le paysage de la mode italienne. Formé à la Accademia di Belle Arti di Brera de Milan, Capasa part au Japon au début des années 1980 pour apprendre le métier auprès du maître de la coupe Yohji Yamamoto. Costume National est surtout connu pour les silhouettes longues, angulaires, extrêmes et parfois sévères de Capasa, la prédominance du noir dans les collections et la grande qualité des tissus utilisés, une combinaison d'attributs qui donne vie à un chic inimitable, assuré, innovant et inspiré de la rue. En l'an 2000, la passion de Capasa pour les tissus le conduit à créer une ligne supplémentaire, Costume National Luxe : une série limitée de vêtements repris de la collection pour femme mais taillés dans des étoffes rares. Outre sa ligne féminine, Capasa produit également une gamme de prêt-à-porter à succès pour les hommes, Costume National Homme, lancée avec une ligne de chaussures coordonnée en 1993. Comme pour les femmes, le noir domine cette collection aux silhouettes caractéristiques cintrées et près du corps, mélangeant pureté de la coupe et qualité des tissus. En l'an 2000, Costume National lance des sacs, de la lingerie et de petits articles de maroquinerie, ainsi qu'une collection de parfums, Costume National Scent, l'année suivante. Aujourd'hui, la griffe possède des boutiques à Hong Kong, Los Angeles, Milan, New York, Osaka, Rome et Tokyo.

"Beauty is an ambiguous mix between life and death"

ENNIO CAPASA

What are your signature designs? My lean and sharp silhouette **What's your favourite piece from any of your collections?** I like most of them, but one of my favourites is Spring-Summer 2002's black coat with a jacquard peacock – a sign of dignity, immortality and beauty **How would you describe your work?** Underground chic **What's your ultimate goal?** Pleasure **What inspires you?** Electric guitars, rhythm and bodies **Can fashion still have a political ambition?** Any action is political **Who do you have in mind when you design?** Personal icons and the people who work with me **Is the idea of creative collaboration important to you?** Only if I think I will fully recognise myself in the result **Who has been the greatest influence on your career?** Too many women to be listed, rock 'n' roll, Friedrich Nietzsche, Carmelo Bene, my brother Carlo **How have your own experiences affected your work as a designer?** To such an extent that there is no distinction between who I am and what I do **Is designing difficult for you and, if so, what drives you to continue?** If it wasn't difficult I wouldn't enjoy it **Have you ever been influenced or moved by the reaction to your designs?** I like to see people wearing my clothes **What's your definition of beauty?** An ambiguous mix between life and death **What's your philosophy?** Stay true to yourself **What's the most important lesson you've learned?** Always trust your first impression

Pierrot's collections are proof that knitwear doesn't have to be fashion's plainest child. The New York-based designer's woolly wonders are too louche for your granny: a Pierrot sweater is more likely to feature a trompe l'oeil corset than a snowflake pattern. Pierre Carrilero, nicknamed 'Pierrot', was born in Lyon, France, in 1959. His mother taught him to knit at the age of nine, when a footballing accident left him temporarily housebound. After leaving school, Pierrot found work in Lyon as a weaver. At the weekends he made regular trips to punk clubs in Paris and eventually landed a job at the Magic Circle boutique, where the owner encouraged him to sell his own knitwear. After some success in Paris, he moved to New York in 1996, finding work in another hip boutique, Horn, the NoLIta store partly owned by Miguel Adrover. The Majorcan designer invited Pierrot to design knitwear for his Spring-Summer 1999 collection and he continued to contribute to Adrover's label until launching his own line in September 1999. Pierrot's all-knit debut, featuring sailor-boy sweaters, was a critical and commercial success, but in terms of design he remains something of a maverick. His Autumn-Winter 2001 collection explored the complicated relationship that Americans have with their weapons. Floppy, belted cardigans and knitted lumberjack shirts were punctuated by sweaters proclaiming 'The Right to Bear Arms': there's always a healthy dose of irony in Pierrot's collections. However, his success is mostly due to sheer inventiveness and his belief that any item of clothing can be knitted. Cropped dungarees, cheerleader dresses and Little Red Riding Hood capes: Pierrot's needles know no bounds.

Die Kollektionen von Pierrot sind der Beweis dafür, dass Strickwaren nicht zwangsläufig das Stiefkind der Mode sein müssen. Die wollenen Wunder des in New York lebenden Designers wären für Omas auch viel zu anrüchig. Auf einem Pullover von Pierrot findet man nämlich eher ein Trompe-l'œil-Korsett als ein Norwegermuster. Pierre Carrilero, Spitzname Pierrot, wurde 1959 in Lyon geboren. Mit neun Jahren brachte seine Mutter ihm das Stricken bei, als er wegen einer Verletzung beim Fußball eine Zeitlang das Haus hüten musste. Nach der Schule suchte sich Pierrot zunächst in Lyon Arbeit als Weber. An den Wochenenden fuhr er regelmäßig in die Punk-Clubs von Paris und fand schließlich auch einen Job in der Boutique Magic Circle, deren Besitzer ihn ermutigte, seine eigenen Strickkreationen anzubieten. Nach einigem Erfolg in Paris ging Carrilero 1996 nach New York, wo er wieder Arbeit in einem hippen Laden fand: bei Horn, dem NoLIta-Store, an dem auch Miguel Adrover beteiligt war. Der mallorquinische Designer lud Pierrot ein, Stricksachen für seine Kollektion Frühjahr/Sommer 1999 zu entwerfen. Der Franzose arbeitete danach weiter für Adrovers Label, bis er im September 1999 seine eigene Linie vorstellte. Pierrots Debüt aus reinem Strick, in diesem Fall Seemannspullover, war bei Kritikern und Kunden gleichermaßen erfolgreich. Was das Design betrifft, wird Carrilero allerdings wohl ein Außenseiter bleiben. Seine Kollektion Herbst/Winter 2001 hatte die komplizierte Beziehung der Amerikaner zu Waffen zum Thema. Schlabbrige, gegürtete Cardigans und gestrickte Holzfällerhemden wechselten sich mit Pullovern ab, die 'The Right to Bear Arms' proklamierten. Pierrot bewies damit erneut, dass er seinen Kollektionen immer eine gesunde Portion Ironie beimengt. Seinen Erfolg verdankt er jedoch vor allem seiner Erfindungsgabe und seinem Glauben daran, dass man einfach jedes Kleidungsstück stricken kann: kurze Arbeitshosen, Cheerleader-Kleider und Rotkäppchen-Capes – Pierrots Nadeln kennen keine Grenzen.

Les collections de Pierrot prouvent que la maille n'est pas l'enfant pauvre de la mode. Mais qu'on ne s'y trompe pas, les petites merveilles que tricote ce designer français installé à New York sont bien trop louches pour votre grand-mère : un pull Pierrot sera plus probablement orné d'un corset en trompe-l'œil que de motifs de flocon de neige. Pierre Carrilero, surnommé Pierrot, est né en 1959 à Lyon. Sa mère lui apprend à tricoter quand il a neuf ans, alors qu'il est temporairement coincé à la maison à la suite d'une blessure de football. Après avoir quitté l'école, Pierrot trouve un emploi de tisserand à Lyon. Le week-end, il monte régulièrement à Paris pour fréquenter les boîtes punk et finit par décrocher un job dans la boutique Magic Circle, dont le propriétaire l'encourage à vendre ses propres créations. Après un premier succès parisien, il part pour New York en 1996 et trouve du travail dans une autre boutique branchée, Horn, intégrée au magasin NoLIta qui appartient en partie à Miguel Adrover. Le designer de Majorque propose alors à Pierrot de dessiner des pièces en maille pour sa collection Printemps-Eté 1999. Il continue à travailler pour la griffe d'Adrover jusqu'au lancement de sa propre ligne en septembre 1999. Avec leurs pulls marins, les débuts « 100% maille » de Pierrot remportent à la fois un succès critique et commercial, mais en terme de création, il fait toujours figure de franctireur. A l'Automne-Hiver 2001, il présente une collection qui explore la relation complexe qu'entretiennent les Américains avec les armes. Des cardigans souples et ceinturés et des vestes trappeur tricotées sont coordonnés à des pulls portant l'inscription « The Right to Bear Arms » : en effet, il y a toujours une bonne dose d'ironie dans les collections de Pierrot. Pourtant, son succès repose avant tout sur sa grande inventivité et sa profonde conviction que tout vêtement peut être tricoté. Pantalons de travail coupés court, robes de pom-pom girls et capes de Petit Chaperon Rouge : les aiguilles de Pierrot tricotent sans limites.

"Designing is living. As long as I breathe and have a hard on, I will work"

PORTRAIT BY SHAWN MORTENSEN

PIERRE CARRILERO

What are your signature designs? The sailor-inspired sweater that comes back every season and, of course, the beret... to me the perfect hat **What's your favourite piece from any of your collections?** The spider sweater from Autumn-Winter 2002. I am amazed every time I look at it **How would you describe your work?** Poetic and technical **What inspires you?** My childhood, my friends... I am curious and always up to no good, so inspiration is bottomless... **Can fashion still have a political ambition?** Fashion is politics... Silhouettes developed by designers are just a reflection of the mood of the world and societies. I know this is why I am in knitwear; there is definitely opportunism in it. Whatever the situation it always fits... knit for freedom! **Who do you have in mind when you design?** So many people, so many sizes **Is the idea of creative collaboration important to you?** You can't be alone when you have this kind of job **Who or what has been the greatest influence on your career?** Sonia Rykiel, Thierry Mugler, Montana, Julia Childs, my grandmother, maple syrup, Eric's sense of style, Nikki Uberti... I am a sponge **How have your own experiences affected your work as a designer?** My whole life cannot be in one sweater, but there are hints of my present, future and past in every garment, season after season **Which is more important in your work: the process or the product?** I cannot dissociate the process and the product **Is designing difficult for you and, if so, what drives you to continue?** Designing is living. As long as I breathe and have a hard on, I will work **Have you ever been influenced or moved by the reaction to your designs?** One day in New York I saw a girl wearing one of my berets. She was pretty. I was rewarded by this vision **What's your definition of beauty?** Show me yours and I'll show you mine **What's your philosophy?** I'll show you mine if you show me yours **What is the most important lesson you've learned?** Tomorrow or another day something will happen that can and will upset what I thought I had learned before. What is to be learned anyway, except love and respect for others and yourself? And, of course, Nutella

PHOTOGRAPHY BY DONALD MILNE, STYLING BY JAMES SLEAFORD. JANUARY/FEBRUARY 1999

Britain's most successful black designer, Joe Casely-Hayford has had a training and education second to none – having served an apprenticeship on Savile Row, he attended London's Tailor and Cutter Academy before undertaking studies at Central Saint Martins, graduating in 1979 and going on to complete a History of Art course at the ICA. Casely-Hayford (born in Kent, 1956) made his London Fashion Week debut in 1991 as part of the Fifth Circle, a group of British menswear designers. Although Casely-Hayford also designs womenswear, it's understandable that he would belong to such a group – much of his work is informed by traditional men's tailoring techniques. His trademark is the use of old English fabrics and reworked classic garments, with cleverly layered pleating and darting that at once gives his work a contemporary feel, yet transcends the impermanence of seasonal fashion. Despite his low profile, Casely-Hayford has been an important figure over the last two decades, not only for the help he has offered young designers (most notably Walé Adeyemi) but by consistently working towards an informed and integrated multiracial Britain. Casely-Hayford designed costumes for Derek Jarman's film 'Edward II' (1991) and Jonathan Burrow's ballet 'Very' (1992), and has also designed outfits for numerous musicians, including U2's 'Zoo TV' world tour (1991–93). In 2002, Casely-Hayford collaborated with the Turner Prize-winning artist Chris Ofili, creating a T-shirt that not only takes the artist's work out of the gallery, but also reinforces black identity as an important part of British culture.

Die Ausbildung von Großbritanniens erfolgreichstem schwarzen Designer ist wohl nicht zu toppen: Nach einer Schneiderlehre in der Savile Row besuchte Joe Casely-Hayford die Londoner Tailor and Cutter Academy, studierte anschließend am Central Saint Martins, das er 1979 abschloss, und absolvierte danach noch einen Lehrgang in Kunstgeschichte am Institute of Contemporary Arts in London. Sein Debüt bei der Londoner Modewoche gab der 1956 in Kent geborene Casely-Hayford dann 1991 als Mitglied des Fifth Circle, einer Gruppe britischer Herrenmodedesigner. Obwohl er auch Damenmode entwirft, erstaunt es doch nicht, dass Casely-Hayford sich gerade einem solchen Kreis anschloss – wo doch ein Großteil seiner Arbeit von den Techniken der traditionellen Herrenschneiderei geprägt ist. So gilt etwa die Verwendung altenglischer Stoffe und umgearbeiteter Modeklassiker als eines seiner Markenzeichen. Dazu kommen mit Bedacht übereinander angeordnete Falten sowie Abnäher, die seinen Kreationen etwas Zeitgemäßes verleihen und doch die Unbeständigkeit von Saisonware vermeiden. Trotz seines zurückhaltenden Auftretens hat Casely-Hayford in den letzten zwei Jahrzehnten eine wichtige Rolle in der britischen Gesellschaft gespielt: Einmal durch die Unterstützung junger Designer – der bekannteste unter ihnen Walé Adeyemi –, vor allem aber durch sein ständiges Bemühen um eine offene, multikulturelle Gesellschaft. Zu seinen interessantesten Modeprojekten gehören sicher die Kostüme für Derek Jarmans Film 'Edward II' (1991) und Jonathan Burrows Ballett 'Very' (1992). Er hat aber auch schon Outfits für zahlreiche Musiker entworfen, darunter die der Gruppe U2 für ihre Welttournee 'Zoo-TV' (1991–93). Im Jahr 2002 arbeitete Casely-Hayford mit dem Träger des Turner-Preises Chris Ofili zusammen: Gemeinsam kreierten sie ein T-Shirt, das nicht nur die Arbeit des Malers aus dem gängigen Kunstbetrieb herausholt, sondern auch die schwarze Identität als wichtigen Teil der britischen Kultur betonen soll.

Joe Casely-Hayford est le styliste noir préféré de l'Angleterre. Sa formation en mode est des plus prestigieuses : après un apprentissage à Savile Row, il étudie à la Tailor and Cutter Academy de Londres avant d'entreprendre un cursus à Central Saint Martins, dont il sort diplômé en 1979 avant de suivre un cours d'histoire de l'art à l'Institute of Contemporary Arts, Londres. Casely-Hayford (né en 1956 dans le Kent) fait ses débuts à la London Fashion Week en 1991 en tant que membre du Fifth Circle, un groupe de créateurs pour homme britanniques. Bien qu'il dessine également pour les femmes, il n'est pas étonnant que Casely-Hayford fasse partie d'un tel groupe : son travail est largement marqué par ses techniques classiques de tailleur pour homme. Il se distingue par une utilisation originale des anciens tissus anglais et des pièces classiques revisitées à travers d'astucieuses superpositions de plis et de fronces qui donnent instantanément à son travail une touche de modernité tout en transcendant l'instabilité des modes éphémères. Malgré sa grande discrétion, Casely-Hayford joue depuis vingt ans un rôle influent sur la mode, non seulement en raison du soutien qu'il apporte aux jeunes créateurs (notamment Walé Adeyemi), mais aussi pour avoir constamment lutté en faveur d'une Angleterre multiraciale informée et intégrée. Casely-Hayford a dessiné les costumes du film « Edward II » de Derek Jarman (1991) et du ballet « Very » de Jonathan Burrow (1992). Il a créé les tenues de scène de nombreux musiciens, par exemple pour la tournée mondiale « Zoo TV » de U2 (1991–93). Casely-Hayford a collaboré avec le lauréat du Turner Prize, Chris Ofili, à la création d'un t-shirt (2002) qui a permis à l'artiste de se faire connaître en dehors du circuit des galeries d'art et à l'identité black de s'affirmer comme un élément incontournable de la culture britannique.

"I look beyond this period of bland, aspirational consumerism in the hope that a more meaningful alternative may emerge"

PORTRAIT COURTESY OF JOE CASELY-HAYFORD

JOE CASELY-HAYFORD

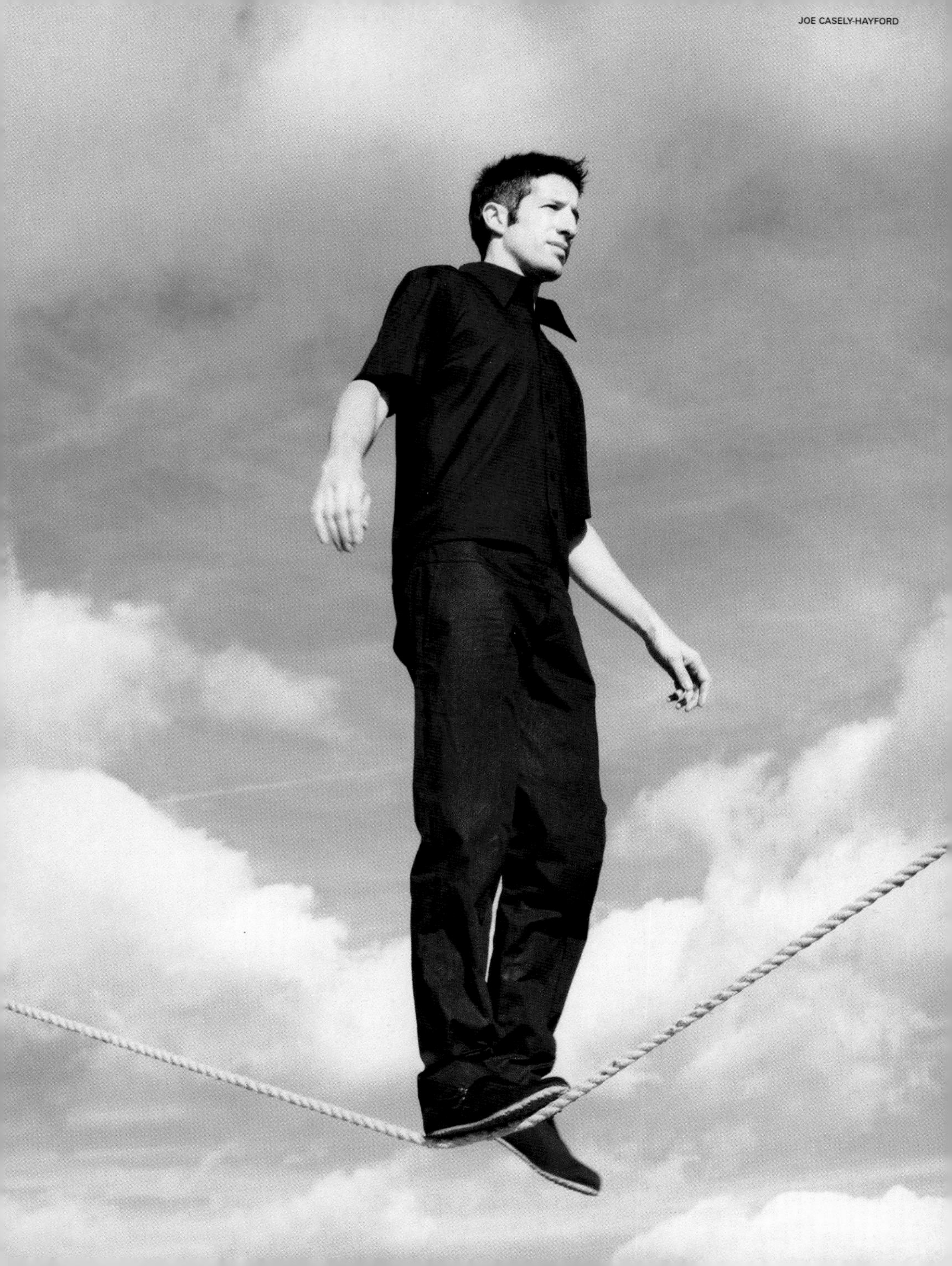

What are your signature designs? Deconstructed tailoring has been a recurring theme **What's your favourite piece from any of your collections?** One of my favourite collections was 'Excess Is More'. This was designed for Spring-Summer 2000 during my Square Period. It featured square knitwear, trousers and jeans. These were created using primitive cutting methods, extending the seams and outer edges of each garment to give the wearer freedom to adapt each design to their own personal taste **How would you describe your work?** Gemini – classic and distorted **What inspires you?** The view from the 242 bus going through Dalston **Can fashion still have a political ambition?** I sincerely hope so. I look beyond this period of bland, aspirational consumerism in the hope that a more meaningful alternative may emerge **Who do you have in mind when you design?** Someone who is outside of the mainstream, with their own agenda **Who has been the greatest influence on your career?** My wife Maria has influenced every aspect of my work **How have your own experiences affected your work as a designer?** Very much. I am a Black man living and working in London. My work reflects this **Which is more important in your work: the process or the product?** You can't have one without the other. Increasingly, the consumer is becoming less interested in process, as marketing men focus more and more on the product **Is designing difficult for you and, if so, what drives you to continue?** Designing isn't difficult for me, but some seasons flow more easily than others. This is because fashion doesn't evolve in neat six monthly cycles. I believe that a fashion revolution is imminent; the development of transeasonal and intelligent fabrics will mean designers will have to re-assess their position **Have you ever been influenced or moved by the reaction to your designs?** There have been times when I've seen my designs in other people's collections **What's your definition of beauty?** Truth **What's your philosophy?** Truth and integrity **What is the most important lesson you've learned?** That logic or pattern in this industry is down to coincidence

Consuelo Castiglioni's Marni is a cult among modern-day bohemians. Her mis-matched prints, girlish silhouettes and gently faded fabrics that recall the patina of vintage cloth have made Marni one of fashion's most sought-after labels. And the Marni effect is felt far beyond her boutiques: Castiglioni's choice of, say, ponyskin clogs or a rosette corsage have provoked popular fashion trends that arrive with the force of a flash flood. At the age of 25, she married Gianni Castiglioni, president of CiwiFurs, a prestigious Italian furrier. After raising two children, she worked as a fashion consultant for her husband's company, launching her own collection in 1994, christened Marni. The Milan-based label was produced by CiwiFurs and initially specialised in fur and leather. However, Castiglioni broke from traditional techniques; in place of bulky, rich-bitch coats she offered unlined pelts that were shaved, tailored and dyed. In 1999 her line became completely independent and fur has given up centre stage to a colourful hotchpotch of luxurious fabrics and haberdashery: eclecticism is the allure of Marni, which is often viewed by the Italian fashion establishment as an eccentric label. Castiglioni will pass over flagged trends to steer her own course; she has eschewed money-spinning license deals and heavy marketing. Instead, she has favoured a stealthier route, captivating an ever-growing audience for her show of artful decoration and neat but naïve tailoring. In October 2001 Castiglioni introduced a menswear line and Marni now has five boutiques around the world. Yet even in the serious business of retail Castiglioni is playful, hiring maverick architects Future Systems to design startling curvilinear interiors for her stores.

Consuelo Castiglionis Label Marni ist unter modernen Bohemiens Kult. Ihre sich beißenden Muster, mädchenhaften Silhouetten und leicht ausgeblichenen Stoffe, die an die Patina von Vintage-Kleidern erinnern, haben Marni zu einer der begehrtesten Modemarken gemacht. Und der Marni-Effekt reicht weit über die eigenen Läden hinaus: Castiglionis Kreationen wie beispielsweise Clogs mit Ponyfell oder eine Bandschleifen-Corsage wachsen sich oft zu Trends aus, die praktisch nichts und niemand aufhalten kann. Im Alter von 25 Jahren heiratete die Designerin Gianni Castiglioni, den Präsidenten des angesehenen italienischen Kürschnerbetriebs CiwiFurs. Nachdem sie zwei Kinder großgezogen hatte, arbeitete sie zunächst als Beraterin für die Firma ihres Mannes und stellte 1994 ihre erste eigene Kollektion unter dem Namen Marni vor. Die Kreationen des Labels mit Sitz in Mailand wurden von CiwiFurs hergestellt und beschränkten sich zunächst vornehmlich auf Pelz und Leder. Castiglioni hatte sich jedoch schon damals von den traditionellen Techniken losgesagt und bot als Alternative zum klassischen schweren Pelzmantel ungefütterte, leichte Pelze aus rasiertem, gefärbtem Fell an. 1999 wurde ihr Label vollkommen unabhängig. Seither steht auch nicht mehr Pelz im Mittelpunkt, vielmehr umfasst die Kollektion eine bunte Mischung luxuriöser Materialien und Accessoires. Eklektizismus macht den Reiz des Labels Marni aus, das innerhalb der etablierten italienischen Modeszene als ziemlich exzentrisch gilt. Castiglioni kümmert sich nicht um Mainstream-Trends, sondern steuert ihren eigenen Kurs; dabei scheut sie finanziell verlockende Lizenz-Deals und aufwändiges Marketing. Stattdessen schlägt sie weniger ausgetretene Pfade ein und begeistert ein stetig wachsendes Publikum für ihre kunstvoll dekorierten Schauen und ihre geschmackvolle, aber naive Form der Schneiderkunst. Im Oktober 2001 stellte die Designerin eine Herrenlinie vor. Marni hat inzwischen fünf eigene Läden in aller Welt. Consuelo Castiglioni nutzt ihren spielerischen Freiraum selbst im seriösen Einzelhandel, indem sie exzentrische Architekten wie die von Future Systems mit dem Design der Inneneinrichtung ihrer Boutiquen betraut.

Marni de Consuelo Castiglioni est la griffe culte des nouveaux bourgeois bohème. Grâce à ses imprimés déséquilibrés, ses silhouettes de jeune fille et ses tissus légèrement vieillis qui rappellent la patine des vêtements « vintage », Marni est aujourd'hui l'une des marques les plus recherchées. L'effet Marni agit pourtant bien au-delà des quatre murs de ses boutiques : par exemple, en optant pour les sabots en cuir de vachette ou les corsages à rosette, Consuelo Castiglioni a lancé sans le vouloir des tendances très populaires qui ont pris le monde de la mode par surprise. A 25 ans, elle épouse Gianni Castiglioni, président de CiwiFurs, un prestigieux fabricant italien de fourrures. Après avoir élevé ses deux enfants, Consuelo travaille comme consultante pour l'entreprise de son mari et lance en 1994 sa propre collection, baptisée Marni. D'abord spécialisée dans le cuir et la fourrure, la griffe milanaise est produite par CiwiFurs. Mais Consuelo Castiglioni abandonne les techniques traditionnelles ; à la place des lourds manteaux de fourrure tape-à-l'œil, elle propose des peaux sans doublure préalablement rasées, coupées et teintes. En 1999, sa ligne devient entièrement indépendante et la fourrure cède le premier rôle à un fouillis coloré de tissus et de détails luxueux : souvent considérée comme excentrique par l'establishment de la mode italienne, l'allure Marni se définit avant tout par son éclectisme. Consuelo Castiglioni ignore les tendances dominantes, préférant opter pour des chemins moins empruntés ; elle ne cède pas à l'attrait des accords de licence lucratifs ni aux stratégies de marketing. Au contraire, elle privilégie une approche moins habituelle, captivant un public toujours plus nombreux par son déballage de décorations artistiques et une coupe à la fois impeccable et naïve. En octobre 2001, Consuelo Castiglioni lance une ligne pour homme. Marni compte désormais cinq boutiques à travers le monde. Même dans l'univers impitoyable de la distribution, Consuelo ne se départit pas de son côté joueur : elle a demandé aux architectes franc-tireurs de Future Systems de dessiner les incroyables décors curvilinéaires de ses boutiques.

"It's dressing with patchworks of fragments"

PORTRAIT BY SERGIO CALATRONI

CONSUELO CASTIGLIONI

What are your signature designs? My signature characteristics are prints, combinations of fabrics, colours and lengths, details, luxury and ease **How would you describe your work?** Free from formal constraints. It's dressing with patchworks of fragments, shreds. It's conceiving a narrative wardrobe **What's your ultimate goal?** Our goal as a company is to control everything from design up to retail and distribution. My personal objective is to continue to design and produce collections in which every item receives a special attention. This, for me, has always been a focus and a privilege **What inspires you?** Memories and passions, fashions and costumes, arts and techniques **Who do you have in mind when you design?** I don't have a particular woman in mind, I merge different elements which I like. My inspiration comes from a combination of emotions in a particular moment **Is the idea of creative collaboration important to you?** At Marni, the family approach is important. I do not only work for myself, I work for them and they for me **Who has been the greatest influence on your career?** Every single person who has believed in the Marni project, giving us the chance to develop it, from the fabric companies to the editors worldwide **Which is more important in your work: the process or the product?** In my work, the product really depends on the process: at the beginning, it's always a fabric or a print which stimulates my creativity. Then I start mixing and matching, and I decide what the silhouettes will look like **What's your definition of beauty?** Beauty does not have age or sex. I see it as a combination of qualities from within, which are projected to the exterior **What's your philosophy?** Creating timeless pieces **What is the most important lesson you've learned?** I strongly believe it is important to keep an open mind towards different stimulations

Roberto Cavalli is a 24-carat gold anti-depressant. With his riotous use of colour and celebratory use of animal skins, Cavalli's baroque sexcess is as high-octane as fashion gets. Born in Florence in 1940 into a family of creative bohemians and artists (his grandfather was an illustrious painter of the Tuscan Macchiaioli movement), Cavalli attended Florence Art Academy. But it was the relationship between art and fashion that inspired him. Experiments with print produced an early income from T-shirts and eventually, in need of more money, he patented a revolutionary technique of printing on leather that was later widely adopted by the textile industry. By the 1970s, Cavalli had become something of an Italian celebrity, opening a showcase shop in St Tropez during its Bardot heyday and judging events such as the Miss Universe competition. In fact, he liked Miss Austria – Eva Düringer – so much that she not only won the Miss Universe title, but also became the second Signora Cavalli and is now his right hand in the design studio. Since his first catwalk show in 1972, the Roberto Cavalli label has become a favourite of the rock and hip hop aristocracy with its ghetto fabulous glamour and playboy chic, despite struggling through the minimalist and utilitarian dominated 1990s. Cavalli still shows his womenswear and menswear collections during Milan Fashion Week, plus his homewear range at the Milan Furniture Fair. And like many good designers, Cavalli is also his own best advertisement, owning one of Italy's finest racehorse studs, flying his own helicopter and managing to drag supermodel Cindy Crawford out of retirement for a recent catwalk extravaganza.

Roberto Cavalli ist ein hochkarätiges Antidepressivum. Sein Schwelgen in Farben und Pelzen, diese lustvolle barocke Üppigkeit reizt alle Möglichkeiten aus, die Mode zu bieten hat. Der 1940 als Sohn einer Familie von kreativen Bohemiens und Künstlern geborene Cavalli (der Großvater war ein berühmter Maler der toskanischen Gruppe der Macchiaioli) besuchte die Kunstakademie in Florenz. Inspiriert hat ihn jedoch das Verhältnis von Kunst und Mode. Sein erstes Geld verdiente er sich mit experimentellen Drucken auf T-Shirts. Als er mehr Geld benötigte, ließ Cavalli sich eine revolutionäre Technik für das Drucken auf Leder patentieren, die später von der Textilindustrie in großem Umfang übernommen wurde. In den 1970er Jahren war der Designer bereits eine italienische Berühmtheit. So eröffnete er etwa in St. Tropez während des Bardot-Booms einen Laden mit Showroom und saß bei Events wie der Wahl zur Miss Universum in der Jury. Einmal gefiel ihm die Miss Austria – Eva Düringer – sogar so gut, dass sie schließlich nicht nur die Schönheitskonkurrenz gewann, sondern auch die zweite Signora Cavalli wurde. Heute ist sie seine rechte Hand im Designatelier. Seit der ersten Modenschau im Jahr 1972 ist Roberto Cavalli mit seinem märchenhaften Ghetto-Glamour und Playboy-Chic das Lieblingslabel der Rock- und Hiphop-Elite. Nur in den vorwiegend minimalistischen, funktionalen 1990er Jahren hatte man zu kämpfen. Noch heute präsentiert Cavalli seine Damen- und Herrenkollektionen auf der Mailänder Modewoche, die Homewear bei der Mailänder Möbelmesse. Wie viele andere gute Designer ist auch er selbst seine beste Werbung: Er besitzt eines der angesehensten Gestüte für Rennpferde in ganz Italien, fliegt seinen eigenen Helikopter und schaffte es beispielsweise kürzlich, das Supermodel Cindy Crawford für einen außerplanmäßigen Auftritt auf dem Laufsteg aus dem Ruhestand zu locken.

Roberto Cavalli est ce qu'on pourrait appeler un antidépresseur en or 24 carats. Grâce à une utilisation tapageuse et festive des couleurs et des peaux d'animaux, les excès sexuels et baroques de Cavalli font de sa mode la plus explosive qui soit. Né en 1940 à Florence dans une famille de bohémiens et d'artistes (son grand-père était un célèbre peintre du mouvement toscan Macchiaioli), Cavalli suit des cours à l'Académie d'Art de Florence. Mais c'est surtout la relation entre art et mode qui l'inspire. Ses expériences d'imprimés sur T-shirts lui permettent de commencer à gagner sa vie et finalement, comme il a besoin de plus d'argent, il dépose le brevet d'une technique d'impression sur cuir révolutionnaire qui sera plus tard largement adoptée par l'industrie textile. Dans les années 1970, Cavalli devient une célébrité en Italie, ouvre une boutique à Saint-Tropez à la grande époque de Bardot et participe en tant que juge à des événements tels que le concours Miss Univers. En fait, il a tellement apprécié Miss Autriche, Eva Düringer, qu'elle a non seulement remporté le titre de Miss Univers, mais qu'elle est également devenue la seconde Signora Cavalli, aujourd'hui son bras droit dans l'atelier de création. Depuis son premier défilé en 1972, Roberto Cavalli s'est imposé comme l'un des chouchous des stars du rock et du hip hop grâce à son glamour « ghetto de luxe » et son chic de playboy, et ce malgré la domination du minimalisme et de l'utilitaire pendant les années 1990. Cavalli continue à présenter ses collections pour femme et pour homme pendant la Semaine de la Mode de Milan, ainsi que sa ligne de « homewear » au Salon du Meuble de Milan. Comme de nombreux autres designers talentueux, Cavalli est sa meilleure publicité : il possède l'un des plus beaux haras de chevaux de course d'Italie, pilote son propre hélicoptère et a récemment réussi à faire sortir le top-model Cindy Crawford de sa retraite pour un défilé extravagant qui a fait date.

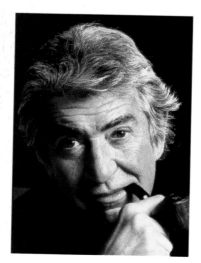

"My devotion to my job started from a personal defeat: my first girlfriend's parents rejected me because I wasn't rich. I decided I would show them what a big mistake they had made!"

PORTRAIT BY DERRICK NIMO

ROBERTO CAVALLI

PHOTOGRAPHY BY DAVIDE CERNUSHI, STYLING BY CHRISTINE FORTUNE. JANUARY/FEBRUARY 2000

What are your signature designs? My meticulous research of fabrics, continual experimenting with new technologies and bright-coloured prints **What's your favourite piece from any of your collections?** Probably the patchwork, which dates back to the beginning of my career. I still have in my mind the image of a young Brigitte Bardot walking barefoot in St Tropez in one of my creations: a pair of patchwork jeans. Thirty years later, Esther Canadas wore on my catwalk the same pair of jeans – an evergreen design that still raises enthusiasm in me **How would you describe your work?** Highly creative, elaborate… and, most of all, full of life! **What's your ultimate goal?** Even if it sounds conceited, my ultimate goal is to leave my stamp on fashion history… **What inspires you?** The great world that surrounds us: an animal coat, a starry sky, a flower's petal. Nature is a never-ending source of inspiration that continues to surprise me with its beauty and its harmony **Can fashion still have a political ambition?** Fashion has partially lost its political ambition. Just think about the difference between the folk fashion in the '70s and the ethnic trend of the last period: while in the past it meant a radical rebellion against the institution, nowadays it represents a charming journey towards unexplored territories in search of new vibes **Who do you have in mind when you design?** Sunny people that love life, nature and love; women or men who express their strong personality through my colours and prints **Is the idea of creative collaboration important to you?** It is important but difficult to reach. I thank my lucky stars because I've met my wife Eva: we have a wonderful mutual understanding in both our private and professional life **What has been the greatest influence on your career?** I come from a family with strong artistic traditions: my grandfather was a Florentine painter of the Macchiaiolo movement whose works can still be seen at the Uffizi Museum in Florence. In a sense, my way was already marked out **How have your own experiences affected your work as a designer?** My devotion to my job started from a personal defeat: my first girlfriend's parents rejected me because I was neither rich nor attending university. I was really in love with her and this breaking off hurt me deeply. Therefore I decided I would show them what a big mistake they made! **Is designing difficult for you?** Fortunately not: it comes spontaneously. At least it means that when I started this career I made the right choice **Have you ever been influenced or moved by the reaction to your designs?** No, I have never been influenced by the reaction to my designs. Fashion is my way of translating art: I cannot think of market rules directing my creative process **What's your definition of beauty?** Beauty comes from the inside; it is a reflection of the personality. This is why, unlike good looks, it does not grow old **What's your philosophy?** To live day by day **What is the most important lesson you've learned?** I have learned that somehow you have to adapt yourself to the circumstances. I am a Scorpio: if I had not been so stubborn, probably I would have been successful 20 years ago. At that time I did not feel like being a personality and attending parties all the time – maybe because I refused to wear a tuxedo… or maybe I was too shy. Afterwards, I realised that people expect a designer to be recognisable: his face, his opinions, the story of his life, are as important as his creations. Since then I have started to organise parties and have taken a liking to it. But you know what? Now I am criticised because my parties are 'too much'… Sometimes life is funny!

PHOTOGRAPHY BY PAOLO ROVERSI, STYLING BY EDWARD ENNINFUL. APRIL 2002. MODEL: ANOUCK LEPERE

Hussein Chalayan (born 1970) is one of the most original fashion designers to emerge from Britain. Yet, paradoxically, it is not fashion that interests him as such. Chalayan's designs are informed by a concentration on how the body functions within the world around it; both in terms of physical space, of volume and environment, together with the cultural and social circumstances that affect it. It is perhaps no surprise that he almost became an architect, and with its technical rigour and precision, his clothing sometimes has an architectonic feel. Yet this is not to say that what Chalayan does is 'cold'. He is also celebrated for shows that abandon the conventional catwalk, spectacular set pieces which cross the boundaries between fashion, design, performance and art, often proving very moving. From his now infamous 'buried' graduate collection at Central Saint Martins in 1993, Chalayan was already causing a stir with his presentation, although his proper London show debut was not until March 1995. Since then he has won the British Designer of the Year award twice, in 1999 and 2000. Chalayan's collections and shows have often focused on displacement and identity, isolation and oppression, and have included meditations on the Muslim veil and the dislocation of refugees. (At the same time, his life and identity has been subject to its own displacement: born in Nicosia, to Turkish-Cypriot parents, Chalayan left the divided Greek/Turkish island of Cyprus for school in England when he was 12.) After restructuring his company following financial difficulties, Chalayan started showing his collections in Paris in October 2001. In 2002 he was made Creative Director of Asprey, with a ready-to-wear line due to launch in Spring 2003. That year will also see the launch of a Hussein Chalayan fragrance.

Hussein Chalayan (Jahrgang 1970) ist einer der originellsten Modedesigner Großbritanniens. Paradoxerweise interessiert er sich jedoch gar nicht so sehr für Mode als Selbstzweck. Chalayans Entwürfe sind geprägt von seinem Interesse am Körper und dessen Funktionieren in der ihn umgebenden Welt. Dabei geht es ihm um physikalische Faktoren wie Volumen und Raum ebenso wie um prägende kulturelle und gesellschaftliche Gegebenheiten. Vor diesem Hintergrund überrascht es kaum, dass Chalayan beinahe Architekt geworden wäre. Mit ihrer technischen Exaktheit und Präzision haben seine Kreationen manchmal etwas Architektonisches an sich. Das soll jedoch nicht heißen, dass Chalayans Mode irgendwie kalt wäre. Der Designer ist auch berühmt für seine Schauen abseits des konventionellen Catwalks, für spektakuläre Inszenierungen, die die Grenzen zwischen Mode, Design, Performance und Kunst aufheben und die Zuschauer oft sehr bewegen. Schon 1993 erregte Chalayan mit seiner berüchtigten Abschlusskollektion 'buried' am Central Saint Martins Aufsehen, auch wenn sein offizielles Londondebüt mit eigener Show erst im März 1995 stattfand. Seither wurde er 1999 und 2000 zum British Designer of the Year gekürt. Chalayans Kollektionen und Schauen widmeten sich Themen wie Vertreibung, Identität, Isolation, Unterdrückung, dem muslimischen Schleier und dem Schicksal von Flüchtlingen. (Identität und Heimat spielen auch in der Biografie des Designers eine Rolle: Als Kind türkisch-zypriotischer Eltern in Nicosia geboren, verließ Chalayan im Alter von zwölf Jahren die geteilte Insel, um in England zur Schule zu gehen.) Nach finanziellen Problemen strukturierte der Modeschöpfer seine Firma neu und zeigte im Oktober 2001 seine Kollektionen erstmals in Paris. 2002 wurde er Creative Director bei Asprey, wo er im Frühjahr 2003 eine neue Prêt-à-Porter-Linie präsentieren wird. Für dasselbe Jahr ist auch die Einführung des ersten Dufts von Hussein Chalayan geplant.

Hussein Chalayan (né en 1970) compte parmi les créateurs de mode les plus originaux de Grande-Bretagne. Paradoxalement, la mode ne l'intéresse pas en tant que telle. Les créations de Chalayan se concentrent avant tout sur la façon dont fonctionne le corps au sein du monde qui l'entoure, tant en termes d'espace physique, de volume que d'environnement, sans oublier le contexte socio-culturel qui l'influence. Il n'est donc pas très surprenant d'apprendre que Chalayan a failli devenir architecte. D'ailleurs, ses vêtements sont empreints d'une telle rigueur technique et d'une telle précision qu'ils semblent parfois presque architectoniques. Pourtant, le travail de Chalayan est loin d'être froid. Il est également très apprécié pour ses défilés, qui délaissent le podium traditionnel au profit de mises en scène spectaculaires qui abolissent les frontières entre mode, design, performance et art, souvent avec une grande émotion. Chalayan fait sensation avec sa désormais célèbre collection de fin d'études « buried » à Central Saint Martins en 1993, mais ses vrais débuts londoniens n'ont lieu qu'en mars 1995. Depuis, il a remporté deux fois le prix de « British Designer of the Year », en 1999 et en l'an 2000. Les collections et les défilés de Chalayan tournent souvent autour des thèmes du déplacement et de l'identité, de l'isolement et de l'oppression. Chalayan a ainsi pu évoquer la question du voile islamique et de la diaspora des réfugiés (parallèlement, sa vie et son identité ont subi les conséquences de son propre déplacement : né à Nicosie de parents turcs-chypriotes, Chalayan a quitté l'île gréco-turque de Chypre pour venir étudier en Angleterre lorsqu'il avait 12 ans). Une fois son entreprise restructurée à la suite de problèmes financiers, Chalayan commence à présenter ses collections à Paris en octobre 2001. En 2002, il a été nommé styliste d'Asprey, pour qui il a dessiné une ligne de prêt-à-porter qui sortira au printemps 2003. Cette même année, Hussein Chalayan devrait également lancer un parfum.

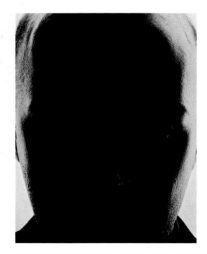

"I'm not really interested in fashion"

PORTRAIT BY SOLVE SUNDSBO

HUSSEIN CHALAYAN

PHOTOGRAPHY BY LAURENCE PASSERA. AUGUST 2002. MODEL: SHANNON PLUMB

What are your signature designs? I don't think that I have a signature design as such. My work is very much about compositions, about how mechanical shapes work with fluid shapes. What I ultimately would like is for the compositions to look like they have gone through some kind of a journey **What's your favourite piece from any of your collections?** Every collection has pieces that I like, but I can't say I really have one favourite… Maybe there are some, but they are not things that I sold. They are couture pieces really, which represent certain ideas **How would you describe your work?** I don't know how to describe my work in terms of what it looks like at the end, except that most of the time it's very abstract. I have certain cultural observations that I filter through and I try to propose new ways of looking at certain issues. A lot of the times it may have to do with cultural prejudice, it may have to do with politics, it may have to do with emotion. I'm somebody who's interested in ideas: I try to explore certain things and learn at the same time. And then share what I'm learning with people who follow my work. For me, it's the idea in a way of thinking which is as big a part of the work as the final product. So the process is really important. The shows are the last part of that process, an event where I try to capture a variety of emotions; it's not just about looking at the clothes **What's your ultimate goal?** For me, the ultimate goal is to use clothing as a medium to respond to certain things in the world. Through the events, and through the way the clothes are done. It's really to create a language for myself that is understood, or at least felt. Also, I'd like to get into other areas of design, not just clothing. Then there's other things to do with life, heart **Can fashion still have a political ambition?** Yes and no. I think you need to know what your limits are when you're designing clothes. There's only so much you can do **Who do you have in mind when you design?** I like independent women who are not too affected by fashion. Somebody who has a broad perspective on life, who enjoys other forms of design **Is the idea of creative collaboration important to you?** Yes, it is. One person can have the vision, but without a team of people you can never realise that vision. It's all about people understanding your spirit. I'm quite stubborn, however. If I believe in something really strongly, I have to do it. A few people are involved and they have a role to play. But, at the end of the day, it either represents or misrepresents me. Because I finally have my name on that garment or event **What has been the greatest influence on your career?** Essentially my childhood was in Cyprus and I think this bicultural existence has been a big influence because it opens me up to so many different things. The fact that I'm from another culture, I think, has meant that I'm more interested in other cultures and other ways of thinking **Which is more important in your work: the process or the product?** The process is as important as the product. At times more important for certain projects **Is designing difficult for you, and if so, what drives you to continue?** What's difficult for me is the lack of time you have between each collection. Sometimes you want to explore an idea to its fullest extent and you can't. And this is what really kills me. The demands of the market place are the worst part of the whole business. What drives me to continue, I suppose, is feeling that I have an evolution which I always want to take further **Have you ever been moved or influenced by the reaction to your designs?** Yes, of course **What's your definition of beauty?** Anything that is true to itself **What's your philosophy?** I think it has to do with the way I work – I feel that I'm an observer of behaviour. I filter certain ideas through and I re-propose a way of looking at things **What is the most important lesson you've learned?** That this is essentially a business that revolves around money – and I'm not in it for that

Deliciously confusing the past with the present, E2 are Michèle and Olivier Chatenet, partners in work and love. Founders of the Mariot Chanet label in the late 1980s, the pair spread their creative wings in the early 1990s to work for Azzedine Alaïa (Olivier), and Chanel and Comme des Garçons (Michèle); following this, moving together to Hermès. At the prestigious Parisian luxury goods house they developed a sense of perfectionism that would stand them in good stead when they once again launched their own label in 2000, this time called E2. A brilliant contemporary assemblage of vintage clothes – some presented as found, some reworked and others taken apart and reassembled into entirely new pieces – E2 quickly gained celebrity patronage from the likes of Madonna, Gwyneth Paltrow and Cameron Diaz. The Chatenets aim to work outside the fashion system, avoiding the distractions of seasonal shows and marketing. Their own contemporary pieces nestle seamlessly alongside thoughtfully chosen couture items by Yves Saint Laurent, Pucci, Lanvin and Grès. Meanwhile, ingeniously customised and embroidered pieces are fashioned from ethnic clothing and kilts. French house Léonard, founded in 1958 and revered for their flamboyant use of print, appointed the Chatenets as head designers in 2001 – a perfect choice thanks to the duo's own love of, and respect for, vintage prints and clothing. E2's work was exhibited alongside that of the 20th Century's greatest designers in the 'Couturier Superstar' exhibition at the Musée de la Mode in Paris in 2002.

E2, das sind Michèle und Olivier Chatenet. Die Partner im Beruf wie im Privatleben verbinden auf wunderbare Weise Vergangenheit und Gegenwart. Nachdem das Paar in den späten 1980er Jahren das Label Mariot Chanet gegründet hatte, weitete es seine kreativen Aktivitäten in den frühen 1990er Jahren auch auf andere Modemarken aus: Olivier arbeitete für Azzedine Alaïa, Michèle entwarf für Chanel und Comme des Garçons; später gingen sie beide zu Hermès. Bei diesem angesehenen Pariser Traditionsunternehmen für Luxusgüter entwickelten sie einen perfektionistischen Anspruch, der ihnen besonders zugute kommen sollte, als sie im Jahr 2000 erneut ihr eigenes Label gründeten – diesmal unter dem Namen E2. Die absolut trendgemäße Assemblage von Vintage-Mode – manche Stücke unverändert, andere umgearbeitet und wieder andere auseinander genommen und zu ganz neuen Kreationen zusammengefügt – bescherte E2 rasch prominente Kundinnen wie Madonna, Gwyneth Paltrow und Cameron Diaz. Die Chatenets haben es sich zum Ziel gesetzt, außerhalb des Modezirkus zu arbeiten, fern von den Ablenkungen saisonaler Schauen und Marketingaktivitäten. Ihre eigenen modernen Entwürfe fügen sich nahtlos an sorgsam ausgewählte Couture von Yves Saint Laurent, Pucci, Lanvin und Grès. Inzwischen sind die genial verfremdeten und verzierten Kreationen Trachten und Kilts nachempfunden. Das 1958 gegründete und für seine farbenprächtigen Druckmuster geschätzte französische Modehaus Léonard machte die Chatenets 2001 zu seinen Chefdesignern – angesichts der Liebe des Paares zu Vintage-Prints im Besonderen und Vintage-Mode im Allgemeinen eine perfekte Wahl. Im Jahr 2002 wurde Mode von E2 neben den Werken der größten Designer des 20. Jahrhunderts in der Ausstellung 'Couturier Superstar' im Musée de la Mode in Paris gezeigt.

Mêlant avec délice le passé au présent, Michèle et Olivier Chatenet, partenaires dans le travail comme dans la vie, sont les deux créateurs de la marque E2. Après avoir fondé la griffe Mariot Chanet à la fin des années 1980, le duo développe sa créativité au début des années 1990 en travaillant pour Azzedine Alaïa (Olivier), Chanel et Comme des Garçons (Michèle) avant de partir chez Hermès. Dans cette prestigieuse maison parisienne d'articles de luxe, ils aiguisent un perfectionnisme qui leur sera très utile lorsqu'ils relanceront leur propre griffe en l'an 2000, cette fois sous le nom de E2. En réussissant à assembler des pièces « vintage » dans un esprit des plus contemporains – certaines pièces sont présentées telles quelles, d'autres retravaillées, découpées puis remontées pour créer un nouveau vêtement – E2 séduit rapidement des clients célèbres tels que Madonna, Gwyneth Paltrow et Cameron Diaz. Les Chatenet essaient de travailler en dehors du système, sans se laisser distraire par le calendrier des défilés ou les contraintes marketing. Leurs créations contemporaines trouvent facilement leur place au milieu des articles haute couture qu'ils sélectionnent avec soin dans les collections passées d'Yves Saint Laurent, de Pucci, de Lanvin et de Grès. Parallèlement, leurs pièces ingénieusement customisées et brodées sont façonnées à partir de tenues ethniques et de kilts. La maison Léonard, fondée en 1958 et révérée pour son utilisation flamboyante des imprimés, nomme les Chatenet à la direction de la création en 2001 : un choix idéal au regard de l'amour et du respect des imprimés et des vêtements anciens dont fait preuve le duo. En 2002, le travail de E2 a été présenté aux côtés de celui des plus grands couturiers du XXe siècle dans le cadre de l'exposition « Couturier Superstar » du Musée de la Mode de Paris.

"We try to give new spirit to vintage clothes"

PORTRAIT COURTESY OF MICHÈLE & OLIVIER CHATENET

MICHÈLE & OLIVIER CHATENET

What are your signature designs? We try to give some new spirit to vintage clothes. Our signature designs change depending on each piece. But the application of eyelets on each garment is a typical detail of E2. They give weight to the garment and change its movement **What are your favourite pieces from any of your collections?** Kilt customised with eyelets and sequins, shirt that becomes a dress, black dress with laces **How would you describe your work?** We are a fashion guide! Our proposal is a wardrobe with customised pieces, vintage pieces as we found them changed into new creations, new shapes made out of antique fabrics **What's your ultimate goal?** To give something new to people who know about fashion **What inspires you?** Our stock of garments and fabrics, which expands every day **Can fashion still have a political ambition?** To dress up will always be a message. But nowadays the majority of people wear labels and the rich instead wear secondhand **Is the idea of creative collaboration important to you?** The idea of collaboration is the main thing of our story. E2 means 'those two' **Who has been the greatest influence on your career?** YSL, Alaïa, Rei Kawakubo, Vionnet **How have your own experiences affected your work as designers?** E2 is absolutely the result of our experiences. Because we have a strong view on our professional past and on the fashion business of today, we decided to find a new way to work in this field **Which is more important in your work: the process or the product?** The product is the goal. The way to reach the goal is always changing **Is designing difficult for you and, if so, what drives you to continue?** Each piece is unique, The most difficult part is to find the connection between the pieces to make a coherent story **Have you ever been influenced or moved by the reaction to your designs?** The client's reaction to our designs is the strongest influence. Our clothes are made to be worn **What's your definition of beauty?** Beauty is the open door to emotions **What's your philosophy?** No rules, no stress **What is the most important lesson you've learned?** Stay open-minded and be open to learn every day

Benjamin Cho is the fashion school drop-out with all of Manhattan at his feet. Born in Cambridge, Massachusetts in 1976, the son of an opera singer and scientist, Cho was raised in California but settled in New York after he began studying fashion at Parsons School of Design in 1994. He stayed there for almost two years before dropping out to concentrate on his own design work, showing a debut collection to rave reviews in 1999. Cho places much emphasis on labour-intensive techniques, which are an intrinsic aspect of his work. He takes relatively simple skills – lacing, braiding, ruching – and uses them for sensuous eveningwear, creating the complex and dramatic effects that have become a trademark of his easily recognisable work. Cho possesses more of a European rather than American aesthetic sensibility; he is at the forefront of a growing wave of less-established, avant-garde New York and Los Angeles-based designers whose clothes are directional, unconventional and stand out in the largely commercially-driven American fashion scene. Cho's distinctive work has attracted the attention of celebrities, many of whom are now loyal clients, such as actresses Jennifer Lopez and Claire Danes. In Spring 2002, following the September 11, 2001 terrorist attacks and the subsequent cancellation of Cho's New York Fashion Week show, he was invited by American Vogue to present his collection alongside ten other young designers, an invitation that helped to gain international recognition for his talent. The majority of Cho's business is now generated through private commissions.

Benjamin Cho hat sein Modestudium zwar abgebrochen, aber dennoch liegt ihm ganz Manhattan zu Füßen. Geboren wurde er 1976 in Cambridge, Massachusetts, als Sohn einer Opernsängerin und eines Wissenschaftlers. Cho wuchs in Kalifornien auf, zog jedoch 1994 nach New York, um an der Parsons School of Design zu studieren. Nach knapp zwei Jahren brach er diese Ausbildung ab, um sich ganz auf seine eigenen Entwürfe zu konzentrieren. 1999 präsentierte er seine Debütkollektion, die die Kritiker ins Schwärmen brachte. Cho legt viel Wert auf zeitaufwändige Techniken, die einen wesentlichen Teil seiner eigenen Arbeit als Designer ausmachen. Relativ einfache Dekors wie Spitzenbesatz, Borten und Rüschen verwendet er für seine sinnliche Abendmode und erzeugt so komplexe, dramatische Effekte, die bereits zum Markenzeichen seiner unverwechselbaren Kreationen avanciert sind. Chos ästhetisches Gespür wirkt eher europäisch als amerikanisch. Er steht in vorderster Linie einer wachsenden Gruppe weniger etablierter, avant-gardistischer Designer aus New York und Los Angeles, die richtungsweisende, unkonventionelle Mode machen und sich von der größtenteils kommerziell bestimmten amerikanischen Textilbranche deutlich abheben. Seine eigenwilligen Kreationen haben die Aufmerksamkeit zahlreicher Prominenter erregt, von denen viele inzwischen zu seinen treuen Kunden zählen, darunter die Schauspielerinnen Jennifer Lopez und Claire Danes. Wegen der Absage von Chos Modenschau bei der New York Fashion Week nach den Anschlägen vom 11. September 2001 lud die amerikanische Vogue im Frühjahr 2002 Cho und zehn andere junge Designer ein, ihre Kollektionen zu präsentieren. Diese Aktion brachte Cho eine Menge internationaler Anerkennung für sein Talent ein. Den Großteil seiner Arbeit machen derzeit private Aufträge aus.

Benjamin Cho a interrompu ses études de mode, il n'en a pas moins tout Manhattan à ses pieds. Né en 1976 à Cambridge dans le Massachusetts, fils d'une chanteuse d'opéra et d'un scientifique, Cho grandit en Californie mais s'installe à New York en 1994 pour étudier la mode à la Parsons School of Design. Il y passe presque deux ans avant de se consacrer à ses propres créations. En 1999, il présente une première collection saluée par une critique unanime. Cho privilégie une couture qui nécessite de nombreuses heures de travail, un aspect intrinsèque de son style. Il utilise des techniques relativement simples – dentelle, tresses, ruchés – pour créer des tenues de soirée voluptueuses aux effets complexes et théâtraux aujourd'hui immédiatement reconnaissables. La sensibilité esthétique de Cho est plus européenne qu'américaine ; il est l'une des figures de proue de cette vague croissante de créateurs d'avant-garde moins reconnus qui travaillent à New York et Los Angeles et dont les vêtements anticonformistes définissent la tendance par contraste avec le reste de la mode américaine, essentiellement motivée par la rentabilité commerciale. Le travail original de Cho attire l'attention de clients célèbres et fidèles, notamment les actrices Jennifer Lopez et Claire Danes. Au printemps 2002, alors que les attaques terroristes du 11 septembre 2001 ont entraîné l'annulation des défilés de la New York Fashion Week, le Vogue américain lui propose de présenter sa collection aux côtés de dix autres jeunes créateurs, une invitation qui lui permet de faire reconnaître son talent sur la scène internationale. Aujourd'hui, la majorité du chiffre d'affaires de Cho est issue de commandes privées.

"The designing comes easily. It's my neurosis that makes it difficult"

PORTRAIT BY MATT JONES

BENJAMIN CHO

What are your signature designs? Garments which entail extensive amounts of my hand work/Obsessive Compulsive Disorder **What's your favourite piece from any of your collections?** No favourites. Maybe only when I'm finished can I say, looking back. As for now, I'm only bored with my old clothes and engrossed with the next **How would you describe your work?** I can't **What's your ultimate goal?** Growth **What inspires you?** Everything, in a peripheral sense. But idleness drives me to inspiration. I cannot stand to be idle **Can fashion still have a political ambition?** Absolutely! I could not continue if I did not believe this **Who do you have in mind when you design?** Nobody **Is the idea of creative collaboration important to you?** At times. I am interested in a solitary and isolated creativity. A mad laboratory of sorts. But when I am able to truthfully connect with someone creatively, it is remarkable **What has been the greatest influence on your career?** Humility **How have your own experiences affected your work as a designer?** In every way they do. Not in a 'my travels to Indonesia' sort of way, but in a purely emotional way. I'm not designing to create a lifestyle. I just love to make clothes. And I feel most accomplished when I unexpectedly translate the angst, depression and the ecstasy, naïvety and happiness into something visual. The visceral into the visible **Which is more important in your work: the process or the product?** Process. (I'm really trying not to say 'both') **Is designing difficult for you and, if so, what drives you to continue?** The designing comes easily. It's my neurosis that makes it difficult. So then I guess yes, it is difficult. But it is supposed to be… I want it to be **Have you ever been influenced or moved by the reaction to your designs?** Yes, I've been very moved. There is nothing like feeling so small **What's your definition of beauty?** Never will I define this. It's impossible and confining. Sometimes beauty is pure and naïve, sometimes dark and depressed. Sometimes it is both. But it is never constant. I think defining beauty is not really human **What's your philosophy?** There must be comfort amongst all this pain **What is the most important lesson you've learned?** There is no God

It's not often a fashion designer hands you a pair of scissors, a needle and thread and a handful of safety pins and tells you to finish the job off yourself. But that's exactly what Susan Cianciolo did when she presented her Spring-Summer 2001 collection. A native of Providence, Rhode Island, Cianciolo (born 1969) founded her purposefully raw, not-quite-prêt-à-porter Run Collection in 1995 after graduating from the Parsons School of Design, New York. Cianciolo prefers to leave such details as skirt length to her clients, providing buttons, appliqués, T-shirt transfers and tattoo designs for them to customise her designs to their individual taste. This DIY postmodern punk attitude to fashion belies Cianciolo's traditional embroidery, stitching and crocheting skills, but in presenting her work in such a unique way, she is elevating it to the level of art (to the point of presenting her clothes on easels at New York's Alleged Gallery, or on sleeping models). She is also a successful film director: her film 'Pro Abortion/Anti Pink' being awarded Critics Choice at the Rotterdam Film Festival in 1997. Championed equally by designer Martin Margiela and art dealer Andrea Rosen, Cianciolo's Run Collection was a fluid collaboration between like-minded designers, artists and, of course, the buying public. After six years, however, she closed down the Run Collection studio in New York's Chinatown. Cianciolo now designs couture under her own name while continuing her parallel careers as an artist and film-maker.

Es passiert nicht oft, dass man von einem Designer eine Schere, Nadel und Faden sowie eine Handvoll Sicherheitsnadeln mit der Aufforderung in die Hand gedrückt bekommt, seine Arbeit selbst zu Ende zu führen. Doch genau das tat Susan Cianciolo bei der Präsentation ihrer Kollektion für Frühjahr/Sommer 2001. Die 1969 in Providence, Rhode Island, geborene Cianciolo gründete ihr absichtlich nicht ganz Prêt-à-Porter-Label namens Run Collection 1995, gleich nach ihrem Abschluss an der Parsons School of Design in New York. Details wie die exakte Länge eines Rocks überlässt die Designerin gern ihren Kundinnen. Außerdem stellt sie ihnen Knöpfe, Applikationen, Aufdrucke für T-Shirts und Tattoos zur Gestaltung ihrer Entwürfe nach eigenem Geschmack zur Verfügung. Diese postmoderne, punkige Do-it-yourself-Einstellung in Sachen Mode lässt zwar Cianciolos eigene Fähigkeiten in traditionellem Sticken und Häkeln außer Acht, doch indem sie ihre Arbeit auf so einzigartige Weise präsentiert, erhebt sie diese gleichzeitig zur Kunst. Dazu passt, dass sie ihre Kreationen mal wie in der New Yorker Alleged Gallery auf Staffeleien, mal an schlafenden Models zeigt. Cianciolo ist übrigens nicht nur Designerin, sondern auch erfolgreiche Regisseurin: So wurde ihr Film 'Pro Abortion/Anti Pink' 1997 beim Filmfestival in Rotterdam mit dem Kritikerpreis ausgezeichnet. Dank der Fürsprache ihres Designerkollegen Martin Margiela und der Kunsthändlerin Andrea Rosen war die Run Collection eine beständig im Fluss befindliche Koproduktion von gleichgesinnten Designern, Künstlern und natürlich dem kaufenden Publikum. Heute entwirft sie Couture unter ihrem eigenen Namen und verfolgt parallel dazu ihre Karrieren als Künstlerin und Filmemacherin.

Ce n'est pas si souvent qu'un créateur de mode vous tend une paire de ciseaux, du fil, une aiguille et quelques épingles à nourrice et vous demande de finir le travail vous-même. Pourtant, c'est exactement ce qu'a fait Susan Cianciolo lors de la présentation de sa collection Printemps-Eté 2001. Une fois diplômée de la Parsons School of Design de New York, Susan Cianciolo, née en 1969 et originaire de Providence à Rhode Island, lance Run Collection en 1995, une griffe délibérément brute et pas vraiment « prête-à-porter ». Elle préfère laisser le choix des détails à ses clientes, notamment la longueur des jupes, et leur fournit à cette fin des boutons, des appliqués, des transferts pour T-shirt et des motifs à tatouer pour qu'elles puissent personnaliser ses créations comme elles l'entendent. Cette approche « punk bricolo » post-moderne de la mode contraste avec les techniques traditionnelles de broderie, de couture et de crochet qu'affectionne tant Susan Cianciolo, mais en présentant son travail d'une façon si unique, elle parvient à le hisser au domaine de l'art (au point de présenter ses vêtements sur des chevalets à l'Alleged Gallery de New York, ou encore sur des mannequins endormis). Susan Cianciolo est également une cinéaste reconnue : son film « Pro Abortion/Anti Pink » a reçu le Prix de la Critique au Festival du Film de Rotterdam en 1997. Soutenue à la fois par Martin Margiela et la galeriste internationale Andrea Rosen, la griffe Run Collection de Susan Cianciolo est le fruit d'une collaboration fluide entre des créateurs, des artistes et, bien sûr, des acheteurs qui partagent tous le même état d'esprit. Toutefois, après six ans d'activité, elle ferme les portes de son atelier Run Collection installé dans le quartier de Chinatown à New York. Elle dessine désormais de la haute couture sous son propre nom tout en poursuivant sa carrière parallèle d'artiste et de réalisatrice.

"My goal has always been to bring back the hand-made"

PORTRAIT BY ANETTE AURELL

SUSAN CIANCIOLO

What are your signature designs? The 'Do It Yourself Denim Skirt' that I presented four years ago, then repeated with all different types of Do It Yourself kits **What's your favourite piece from any of your collections?** I thought of that denim skirt and then I also thought of all the white pieces that I did for Run Seven. I always look at Run Seven as my favourite group of work **How would you describe your work?** I would use two words: raw and innovative **What's your ultimate goal?** Just to continue working **What inspires you?** There is no difference between my life and my work – it's all the same **Who do you have in mind when you design?** Everything that I make and wear is for an exhibition or a specific order. I am directly speaking with my clients, which is how I started out – most of my early work was just customised work. Now, I've kept only a small group of clients who want to work in this way. If a store wants an order, I decide what the order's going to be, so they don't know what they're getting: they'll say 'I want ten dresses', we decide on the price, then they have to trust me. It's one of a kind. Because of the nature of my work, I feel more comfortable to be direct. It just seems more normal and human **How have your own experiences affected your work as a designer?** I think I definitely look back on my work and see that any type of tragic time is completely represented and involved in it. Or when I was married, the whole group of work with white dresses… Everything reflects, it's always very emotional **What's more important in your work: the process or the product?** The process is so intense, but the whole goal is the product, the end result. Whatever that will be I never know exactly **Is designing difficult for you and, if so, what drives you to continue?** It's very difficult and I don't know what drives me. It's my whole life, you know. Of course I think that's good and it's bad. But I don't know how I could ever do anything else **Is the idea of creative collaboration important to you?** It was everything to me before and now it seems it's almost nothing. Obviously everyone needs each other in some sense, but I was pushing this perception to an extreme level with the number of collaborators that were always involved because I felt that was the ultimate beauty. I was so obsessed with that part of life. Now I'm very interested to work alone for a period, just hear my own thoughts and work in complete silence with nothing and no-one **Can fashion still have a political ambition?** Definitely, because it's such a loud voice and you have so much opportunity to say so much. That's definitely how I've utilised it **What's your definition of beauty?** It has to do with feeling **What's your philosophy?** When I started, my main goal was to bring back the craft, the hand-made. And that's definitely still my philosophy. I realise that's my whole life too; there's nothing else. Every single aspect of my life has always been that way. Going back to having to deal with who you are, what that is **What is the most important lesson that you've learned?** I'm trying to learn to not have regrets… Actually, I also came to the realisation recently that the biggest lesson is how imperfect you'll always be

Eccentric and exuberant, Clements Ribeiro's designs are an irreverent take on traditional elegance. British-born Suzanne Clements and Brazilian Inácio Ribeiro met while studying fashion at Central Saint Martins, graduating with first class honours in 1991 and marrying a year later. After working in Brazil as design consultants, Clements Ribeiro returned to London and set up a label together in 1993, quickly becoming known for meticulous cashmere knitwear in lively stripes and maverick colour combinations. Their Union Jack sweater, worn by Naomi Campbell in the Autumn-Winter 1997 show, became a recognisable symbol of 'Cool Britannia'. In March 1995, Clements Ribeiro presented their debut catwalk show during London Fashion Week; today, the duo design everything from lingerie (from 2001) to bags, shoes (in collaboration with Manolo Blahnik) and children's cashmere knitwear (the Baby Clements range, inspired by the birth of their son Hector). Clements Ribeiro's mainline collection is a concoction of classic shapes made sophisticated and quietly playful with a bustle of unexpected detail: sequinned lace and wool, floral furnishing fabrics, checks and tweeds are twisted and turned into dressing up clothes for adults. In May 2000 Clements Ribeiro were appointed Art Directors for Parisian label Cacharel's womenswear collection; in 2001 they also took over childrenswear design. Since September 2001, Clements Ribeiro have also shown their own collection in Paris. In 1996 they won the New Generation category at the British Fashion Awards and have been nominated five times for Designer of the Year.

Die exzentrischen und überdrehten Kreationen von Clements Ribeiro sind ein unverblümter Angriff auf die traditionelle Eleganz. Die Britin Suzanne Clements und der Brasilianer Inácio Ribeiro lernten sich beim Studium am Central Saint Martins kennen, das sie beide 1991 mit Auszeichnung abschlossen. Ein Jahr später wurde geheiratet. Nachdem sie zunächst in Brasilien als Designberater gearbeitet hatten, kehrten die beiden nach London zurück, wo sie 1993 das gemeinsame Label gründeten. Hier wurden sie rasch durch ihre perfekten Kaschmirstrickwaren in kräftigem Streifendessin und eigenwilligen Farbkombinationen bekannt. Ihr Union-Jack-Pulli, den Naomi Campbell bei der Schau für Herbst/Winter 1997 trug, avancierte zum leicht wiedererkennbaren Symbol des Trends 'Cool Britannia'. Im März 1995 gab Clements Ribeiro seine Catwalk-Premiere bei der Londoner Modewoche. Heute entwirft das Designerduo praktisch alles, von Wäsche (seit 2001) über Taschen und Schuhe (in Kooperation mit Manolo Blahnik) bis hin zu Kaschmirstrick für Kinder unter dem Label Baby Clements (die Inspiration dafür lieferte der gemeinsame Sohn Hector). Die Hauptkollektion von Clements Ribeiro besteht vornehmlich aus klassischen Schnitten, die durch allerlei unerwartete Details veredelt oder aufgelockert werden: mit Pailletten bestickte Spitze und Wolle, Möbelstoffe mit floralen Mustern, Karo und Tweed. Im Mai 2000 wurden Clements und Ribeiro zu Art Directors der Damenkollektion des Pariser Labels Cacharel ernannt. 2001 übernahmen sie auch das Design der Kindermode. Die eigene Kollektion von Clements Ribeiro wird seit September 2001 in Paris gezeigt. 1996 gewann das Paar in der Kategorie New Generation bei den British Fashion Awards. Dazu kommen fünf Nominierungen als Designer of the Year.

Excentriques et exubérantes, les créations Clements Ribeiro portent un regard irrévérencieux sur l'élégance classique. La Britannique Suzanne Clements et le Brésilien Inácio Ribeiro se rencontrent pendant leurs études de mode à Central Saint Martins, dont ils sortent diplômés en 1991 avec les félicitations du jury avant de se marier un an plus tard. Après avoir travaillé au Brésil comme consultants en stylisme, le duo Clements Ribeiro revient à Londres et monte sa griffe en 1993. Leur travail est rapidement remarqué pour sa maille méticuleuse en cachemire, ses rayures joyeuses et ses combinaisons de couleurs insolites. Leur pull à l'effigie de l'Union Jack, porté par Naomi Campbell lors du défilé Automne-Hiver 1997, symbolise aujourd'hui la « Cool Britannia ». En mars 1995, Clements Ribeiro présente son premier défilé à la London Fashion Week ; aujourd'hui, le duo dessine également de la lingerie (depuis 2001), des sacs, des chaussures (en collaboration avec Manolo Blahnik) et des pulls en cachemire pour enfant (la ligne Baby Clements, inspirée par la naissance de leur fils Hector). La collection principale de Clements Ribeiro revisite les formes classiques avec sophistication et un humour tranquille à travers toute une série de détails inattendus : dentelle et laine à paillettes, tissus d'ameublement à motifs floraux, carreaux et tweeds se mélangent et se transforment en « déguisements » pour adultes. En mai 2000, les membres de Clements Ribeiro sont nommés directeurs artistiques de la collection féminine de Cacharel ; en 2001, la marque parisienne leur confie également sa ligne pour enfant. Depuis septembre 2001, Clements Ribeiro présente ses propres collection à Paris. En 1996, la griffe a remporté un prix dans la catégorie New Generation des British Fashion Awards et a été cinq fois nominée au titre de Designer of the Year.

"People think partnerships arise because of a shared vision, but we don't feel that way. We've both got strong minds and personalities, so because of that equality we fight much more. That's why it works"

PORTRAIT COURTESY OF SUZANNE CLEMENTS AND INÁCIO RIBEIRO

SUZANNE CLEMENTS & INÁCIO RIBEIRO

What are your signature designs? Striped cashmere sweaters and rugby tops, embroidered bias-cut dresses, peasant blouses **How would you describe your work?** An eclectic, colourful and heady mix of layered references. Familiar shapes, fabrics and fashion ticks revised and twisted to create pieces you would want to collect, taking possession as your own **What's your ultimate goal?** To live happily ever after **What inspires you?** The ever-changing mood swings of fashion. The people around us. Anything and everything **Can fashion still have a political ambition?** It is a bit harder now that fashion has become an entertaining industry attracting hordes craving fame and fortune, as well as being engulfed by huge industrial conglomerates. But fashion can and should be political **Who do you have in mind when you design?** A woman that loves clothes **Is the idea of creative collaboration important to you?** Yes. Teamwork is very important and creative collaborations very stimulating **Who or what has been the greatest influence on your career?** Visibly or otherwise: Yves Saint Laurent (Inácio) and Vivienne Westwood (Suzanne) **How have your own experiences affected your work as designers?** Our experiences have educated our lives and therefore shaped our influences and choices **Which is more important in your work: the process or the product?** The process is without a doubt what gives us the most pleasure but ultimately it is the result (product) that really matters **Is designing difficult for you and, if so, what drives you to continue?** Sometimes designing can be hard and frustrating, but we always feel we can do so much better and that propels us forward **Have you ever been influenced or moved by the reaction to your designs?** Inevitably, yes. Lately though we have chosen to isolate ourselves a little to protect the natural flow of inspiration from season to season **What's your definition of beauty?** Strong features on glowing surfaces backed by wit and allure **What's your philosophy?** Follow your instincts. Create a stimulating work environment. Build on the collection organically. Make sure you have fun in the process **What is the most important lesson you've learned?** There is always next season

Whenever Jean Colonna's name is mentioned, words like 'rock 'n' roll', 'underground' and 'icon' crop up. Easy press fodder or not, it's undeniably true that Jean Colonna (born 1955) proved pivotal in pushing French fashion into cutting-edge modernity. Born in Algeria and raised in France's Aix-en-Provence, Colonna moved to Paris in 1975 and enrolled at the Ecole de la Chambre Syndicale de la Couture Parisienne. After working as an assistant at Pierre Balmain, he started designing under his own name. Colonna presented his first collections from 1985, using catalogues shot by photographer friends like Bettina Rheims and Stéphane Sednaoui. When he finally organised a catwalk show in 1990, Colonna avoided the chic-and-glitz route by using big stripped-down venues and androgynous models, treating the audience to a healthy blast of rock music. His clothes reflected this outsider spirit: mostly black, sexy and hard-edged, verging on the trashy but blessed with an adventurous frisson. His aesthetics struck a chord with a new generation of artists and photographers, with whom Colonna collaborated in the coming years. When French department store Le Printemps offered him carte blanche to conceptualise their window displays and catalogues in March 1993, Colonna worked with, among others, fashion photographer David Sims. Democratic by nature, Colonna gladly accepted the invitation to produce clothes and underwear for French mail-order company La Redoute (Winter 1993–94). In December 1995, Colonna produced a calendar with photographer Glen Luchford. An ardent supporter of the Hyères Festival (where young designers compete for prestigious fashion awards), he exhibited slides made with US art photographer Jeff Burton there in May 2001.

Wann immer der Name Jean Colonna fällt, assoziiert man damit Begriffe wie Rock 'n' Roll, Underground oder Ikone. Das mögen Etiketten der Presse sein oder auch nicht – zweifellos war der 1955 geborene Colonna aber entscheidend daran beteiligt, dass die französische Mode den Anschluss an die Moderne nicht verpasste. In Algerien geboren und in Aix-en-Provence aufgewachsen, kam er 1975 nach Paris, wo er sich an der Ecole de la Chambre Syndicale de la Couture Parisienne einschrieb. Nachdem er zunächst als Assistent von Pierre Balmain Erfahrung gesammelt hatte, begann Colonna auch unter seinem Namen zu entwerfen. Ab 1985 präsentierte er eigene Kollektionen, und zwar zunächst in Form von Katalogen, zu denen befreundete Fotografen wie Bettina Rheims und Stéphane Sednaoui die Bilder beisteuerten. Als er schließlich 1990 seine erste Catwalk-Show veranstaltete, vermied Colonna die übliche Glamour-Atmosphäre, indem er sich für heruntergekommene Kulissen und androgyne Models entschied. Noch dazu musste sich das Publikum mit lauter Rockmusik beschallen lassen. Colonnas Mode spiegelt seinen Außenseitergeist wider: vornehmlich schwarz, sexy und brutal, an der Grenze zum Trash, aber zugleich mit einem Hauch von Abenteuer. Diese Ästhetik traf ziemlich genau den Geschmack einer neuen Generation von Fotografen und anderen Künstlern; mit einer Reihe von ihnen arbeitete Colonna in den folgenden Jahren zusammen. Als die französische Kaufhauskette Le Printemps ihm im März 1993 anbot, ihre Schaufenster und ihren Katalog völlig frei zu gestalten, tat sich der Designer unter anderem mit dem Modefotografen David Sims zusammen. Der von jeher demokratisch gesinnte Colonna nahm auch freudig das Angebot des französischen Versandhauses La Redoute an, Oberbekleidung und Wäsche für die Winterkollektion 1993/94 zu entwerfen. Im Dezember 1995 gestaltete er gemeinsam mit dem Fotografen Glen Luchford einen Kalender. Als engagierter Förderer des Festivals von Hyères (auf dem junge Modedesigner um angesehene Auszeichnungen ringen) zeigte er im Mai 2001 ebendort Dias, die in Zusammenarbeit mit dem amerikanischen Künstler und Fotografen Jeff Burton entstanden sind.

Il suffit de prononcer le nom de Jean Colonna pour entendre fuser des mots tels que « rock 'n' roll », « underground » et « icône ». Blabla journalistique ou pas, il est indéniable que Jean Colonna a permis à la mode française d'entrer dans la nouvelle avant-garde. Né en 1955 en Algérie, il grandit en France à Aix-en-Provence. En 1975, Colonna s'installe à Paris et suit les cours de l'Ecole de la Chambre Syndicale de la Couture Parisienne. Après un poste d'assistant chez Pierre Balmain, il commence à dessiner pour sa propre griffe. En 1985, Colonna présente ses premières collections par le biais de catalogues dont il confie les prises de vue à ses amis photographes tels que Bettina Rheims et Stéphane Sednaoui. Lorsqu'il finit par organiser son premier défilé en 1990, Colonna évite le chemin glissant des strass et des paillettes : il s'installe dans un grand lieu dépouillé et fait appel à des mannequins androgynes qui défilent sur une bande-son très rock. Ses vêtements reflètent alors son esprit d'outsider : majoritairement noirs, sexy et aux lignes acé-rées, toujours à la limite du trashy mais parcourus d'un frisson d'aventure. Son esthétique a touché une nouvelle génération d'artistes et de photographes avec lesquels Colonna collabore dans les années qui suivent. Lorsqu'en mars 1993 Le Printemps lui donne carte blanche pour conceptualiser ses vitrines et ses catalogues, Colonna travaille, entre autres, avec le photographe de mode David Sims. Démocrate par nature, Colonna accepte avec joie l'invitation de La Redoute et produit des vêtements et de la lingerie pour la saison Hiver 1993–94 du catalogue de vente par correspondance. En décembre 1995, Colonna édite un calendrier avec le photographe Glen Luchford. Fervent supporter du Festival de Hyères (où de jeunes créateurs de mode sont en compétition pour des prix prestigieux), il y présente en mai 2001 des diapositives réalisées en collaboration avec le photographe d'art américain Jeff Burton.

"Sadism and masochism, love and hate, pain and pleasure… I believe that I have something to say in fashion and it's important for me to say it. Whatever the price"

PORTRAIT COURTESY OF JEAN COLONNA

JEAN COLONNA

PHOTOGRAPHY BY NATHANIEL GOLDBERG, STYLING BY SORAYA DAYANI. JULY 2001

What are your signature designs? Above all, I work on real clothes for real people **What's your favourite piece from any of your collections?** The simplest one from each **How would you describe your work?** A tribute to the modern female consciousness **What's your ultimate goal?** The next one **What inspires you?** La Vie with a capital V **Can fashion still have a political ambition?** It should have. Today it's just could have. Can do better **Who do you have in mind when you design?** A human kaleidoscope; a jigsaw made of men and women who have inspired me since the beginning. To give names would be too limiting **Is the idea of creative collaboration important to you?** Yes, vital at all levels **How have your own experiences affected your work as a designer?** There is an intimacy between the personal and professional. Each feeds from the other. My job is to maintain the equilibrium **Which is more important in your work: the process or the product?** Both. One is the result of the other. If the product is good, my process (mind) was right, and vice-versa **Is designing difficult for you and, if so, what drives you to continue?** Sadism and masochism, love and hate, pain and pleasure... I believe that I have something to say in fashion and it's important for me to say it. Whatever the price **Have you ever been influenced or moved by the reaction to your designs?** Moved, touched, influenced and more... even sometimes by reflections in the mirror. Am I a sensitive person or just normal? **What's your definition of beauty?** Beauty is indefinable. You can see it, touch it, breathe it, but not capture it **What's your philosophy?** To be aware **What is the most important lesson you've learned?** Life is beautiful and I learn from it each day

Directional prints and designs evoking a sense of history and character are the essence of Emma Cook's work. Born in Manchester in 1975, Cook studied textiles at the University of Brighton, going on to complete an MA in Womenswear at Central Saint Martins. Her 1999 graduation collection – well received by the British press – highlighted an attention to detail that would go on to characterise her career: old pieces of brocade, gold threads and the odd tuft of recycled fur were all carefully sewn onto the clothes, instilling them with unique personality. Cook went on to work for Martine Sitbon in Paris, focusing on showpieces for the catwalk, moving later to Ghost. Finding herself torn between work in Paris and private commissions in London, she decided to start her own collection, winning a Vidal Sassoon young talent award which enabled her to produce a London Fashion Week show for Spring-Summer 2001. Titled 'Lazy Susan', all of her subsequent collections have been named around variations of the name Susan. Emma Cook's work is currently sold in London, New York, Los Angeles, Paris, Japan and Hong Kong.

Gedruckte Muster und Kreationen mit einem Hauch von Geschichte und Charakter bilden das Wesen der Arbeit von Emma Cook. 1975 in Manchester geboren, studierte die Designerin zunächst an der University of Brighton und machte schließlich ihren Abschluss in Damenmode am Central Saint Martins in London. Ihre Abschlusskollektion von 1999, die von der britischen Presse sehr wohlwollend aufgenommen wurde, unterstrich bereits diese Liebe zum Detail, die auch die weitere Karriere Cooks bestimmen sollte: Stücke von altem Brokat, Goldfäden und eigenwillige Flicken aus recyceltem Pelz waren sorgfältig auf die Kleidungsstücke genäht und verliehen diesen eine jeweils einzigartige Persönlichkeit. Zunächst arbeitete Cook für Martine Sitbon in Paris und konzentrierte sich auf Schaustücke für den Catwalk, dann wechselte sie zu Ghost. Weil sich ihr Job in Paris nur schwer mit privaten Aufträgen in London vereinbaren ließ, entschloss sich die junge Designerin zu einer eigenen Kollektion. Nachdem Sie einen von Vidal Sassoon ausgelobten Preis für junge Talente gewonnen hatte, war sie in der Lage, eine Show mit Mode für Frühjahr/Sommer 2001 zur Londoner Modewoche auf die Beine zu stellen. Diese Schau lief unter dem Titel 'Lazy Susan' wie auch alle folgenden Kollektionen mit unterschiedlichen Zusätzen den Namen Susan tragen. Gegenwärtig kann man Mode von Emma Cook in London, New York, Los Angeles, Paris, Japan und Hongkong erstehen.

Le travail d'Emma Cook se distingue avant tout par ses imprimés et ses motifs très innovants, pleins d'histoire et de caractère. Née en 1975 à Manchester, Emma Cook étudie le textile à l'Université de Brighton avant d'obtenir un Masters en mode féminine à Central Saint Martins. En 1999, sa collection de fin d'études est très bien accueillie par la presse britannique et révèle un souci du détail qui la caractérisera tout au long de sa carrière : pièces de brocart ancien, fils d'or et étranges touffes de fourrure recyclée sont tous cousus avec soin sur les vêtements, leur insufflant une personnalité vraiment unique. Ensuite, Emma Cook travaille chez Martine Sitbon à Paris, pour qui elle dessine des pièces principalement destinées aux défilés avant de partir chez Ghost. Déchirée entre son travail à Paris et ses commandes privées à Londres, elle décide finalement de lancer sa propre collection grâce au prix « Jeune Talent » de Vidal Sassoon qui lui permet de présenter son défilé Printemps-Eté 2001 lors de la London Fashion Week. Surnommée « Lazy Susan », Emma Cook baptise depuis toutes ses collections de variations autour du nom Susan. Ses créations sont actuellement vendues à Londres, New York, Los Angeles et Paris, ainsi qu'au Japon et à Hong Kong.

"My work has a sense
of history but it doesn't
look like vintage clothes"

PORTRAIT BY KENT BAKER

EMMA COOK

What are your signature designs? Girly layers of textures, colours and surface patterns **What are your favourite pieces from any of your collections?** I still like loads of things from the first one. Maybe because there was so much work in it **How would you describe your work?** It's about prints and fabrics and texture, rather than cut. Lots of layers and ideas all mixed up to create something new. It has a sense of history but it doesn't look like vintage clothes. It's not so serious, it has a sense of humour. It's also quite easy to wear **What's your ultimate goal?** To do more of what I like and less of what I don't like **What inspires you?** A mess of things mixed up together. People in the streets, stuff on TV, and fashion and history, all mixed up into something different. I also like the way you start again every six months **Can fashion still have a political ambition?** If you want to say something and you know what you are saying and you do it well, then yes **Who do you have in mind when you design?** My friends. I'll say, 'would you wear this?' and if all my friends like it, I know it will be a thing most people would buy. It's quite good to have a lot of friends who are girls when you're a designer! **Is the idea of creative collaboration important to you?** It's a good thing, yes. I work all the time with Cathy Edwards and Shona Heath; all of our best work is when we work together **Which is more important in your work: the process or the product?** The best thing is putting it all together at the end **Is designing difficult for you and, if so, what drives you to continue?** Designing is easy, but you get to do that for one week and then for the rest of the year you have to do all the other stuff. And it's all the other stuff that can be difficult **Have you ever been influenced or moved by the reaction to your designs?** When other people like what you do, it's really nice but kinda weird as well **What's your definition of beauty?** Clutter and chaos **What's your philosophy?** It's a small world, but I wouldn't want to paint it **What is the most important lesson you've learned?** Trust

Back in the early 1980s, fresh from a fashion degree at Ravensbourne College of Design and Communication, Maria Cornejo told an interviewer that what she wanted as a designer was longevity. It's a testament to her talent that, almost two decades later, she is still going strong. Now based in New York, Chilean-born Cornejo – working under the Zero womenswear moniker – creates the type of garments which fly out of Barneys, Colette, and 10 Corso Como, not to mention her own boutique in the city's NoLIta area. Having initially teamed up with designer John Richmond (the Richmond-Cornejo label was a mid-1980s London favourite), Cornejo subsequently beat an adventurous career path. Moving to France in 1988, she set up her eponymous label, showing successfully in Paris and Milan. In addition to this, she was appointed Creative Director for French company Tehen, reinvigorating their ready-to-wear label, as well as designing and consulting for Jigsaw. Such a broad CV has helped her evolve a distinctive aesthetic: highly wearable, yet still a little unconventional. Central to this are her geometric constructions – blouses are cut in a circle shape that drapes over the torso; dresses are without side seams, cut from one piece of cloth. Seasonal whims and fads are avoided, instead developing favoured themes and motifs: prints made from her own hair, for example, and the use of text upon garments. Having recently signed a production and distribution deal with Onward Kashiyama USA, Cornejo's designs look set to reach even further, always with an eye to the future.

In den frühen 1980er Jahren sagte Maria Cornejo, damals frisch gebackene Absolventin des Ravensbourne College of Design and Communication im Fach Mode, in einem Interview, sie wünsche sich als Designerin vor allem Langlebigkeit. Für ihr Talent spricht, dass sie fast zwei Jahrzehnte später nach wie vor gut im Geschäft ist. Heute lebt die in Chile geborene Cornejo in New York, wo sie für die Marke Zero Damenmode entwirft. Sie macht die Art von Kleidern, die bei Barneys, Colette und 10 Corso Como reißenden Absatz finden – von ihrer eigenen Boutique im New Yorker Szeneviertel NoLIta ganz zu schweigen. Ursprünglich hatte sich Cornejo mit ihrem Kollegen John Richmond zusammengetan – Mitte der 1980er Jahre galt das Label Richmond-Cornejo als das angesagteste von ganz London – danach entschied sich die Designerin jedoch für eine noch aufregendere Karriere. 1988 zog sie nach Frankreich, gründete dort ein Label unter ihrem Namen und präsentierte es erfolgreich in Paris und Mailand. Gleichzeitig wurde sie Creative Director des französischen Unternehmens Tehen, dessen Prêt-à-Porter-Kollektion sie neu belebte; parallel dazu war sie noch als Designerin und Beraterin für Jigsaw tätig. Dieser spannende Werdegang half Cornejo, eine unverwechselbare Ästhetik zu entwickeln: absolut tragbare, aber immer noch ein wenig unkonventionelle Mode. Die Grundlage dafür bilden ihre geometrischen Schnitte – da werden Blusen kreisrund geschnitten, so dass sie locker um den Oberkörper fallen; Kleider ohne Seitennaht sind aus einem einzigen Stück Stoff geschnitten. Spielereien und Gags, die nur eine Saison überdauern, meidet die Designerin. Stattdessen entwickelt sie wiederkehrende Lieblingsthemen und Motive: Drucke mit ihrem eigenen Haar etwa oder Texte auf den Stoffen. Nachdem sie kürzlich – und wohl wie gehabt mit dem Ziel der Langlebigkeit vor Augen – einen Produktions- und Vertriebsvertrag mit Onward Kashiyama USA abgeschlossen hat, dürften Cornejos Entwürfe bald noch mehr Verbreitung finden.

Au début des années 1980, tout juste diplômée du Ravensbourne College of Design and Communication, Maria Cornejo confie à un journaliste que ce qu'elle désire le plus en tant que créatrice de mode, c'est de durer. Le fait qu'elle soit encore là presque vingt ans après est bien la preuve de son talent. Aujourd'hui installée à New York, la Chilienne Maria Cornejo, qui dessine une ligne pour femme baptisée Zero, crée le genre de vêtements qui se trouve rapidement en rupture de stock chez Barneys, Colette et 10 Corso Como, sans parler de sa propre boutique dans le quartier NoLIta (Nord de Little Italy) de la ville. Après une première association avec le créateur John Richmond (la griffe Richmond-Cornejo était très courue à Londres au milieu des années 1980), Maria Cornejo emprunte par la suite un parcours de carrière aventureux. Lorsqu'elle s'installe en France en 1988, elle crée sa griffe éponyme et présente avec succès ses collections à Paris et à Milan. Par ailleurs, elle est nommée directrice de la création chez Tehen, redonnant vie à leur collection de prêt-à-porter tout en étant styliste et consultante pour Jigsaw. La diversité de ses expériences l'aide à faire évoluer sa propre esthétique : des vêtements très faciles à porter mais toujours un peu surprenants, comme le prouvent ses constructions géométriques, où les chemisiers sont taillés en forme de cercle puis drapés sur le torse, où ses robes dépourvues de coutures latérales sont coupées dans une seule pièce de tissu. Elle se passe des fantaisies et des petites folies de saison, préférant développer ses thèmes et ses motifs favoris : imprimés réalisés à partir de ses propres cheveux et ajout de texte sur les vêtements. Alors qu'elle vient de signer un accord de production et de distribution avec Onward Kashiyama USA, les créations de Maria Cornejo semblent bien parties pour toucher une plus large clientèle, toujours avec un œil sur l'avenir.

"I'm inspired by somebody wearing the wrong clothes"

PORTRAIT BY MARK BORTHWICK

MARIA CORNEJO

What are your signature designs? The circle top boy pants, bubble coat, manta dress, bike pants **How would you describe your work?** Very graphic, but at the same time, organic. Deceptively simple **What is your ultimate goal?** To be fulfilled and keep learning, to be successful and still have a life! **What inspires you?** It's very internal and always surprises me as it can start with a very abstract thought about shape or the way a line moves around the body. Or somebody wearing the wrong clothes **Can fashion still have a political ambition?** Fashion can provoke thought and discussion, and through uniforms provoke fear and repression **Who do you have in mind when you design?** Myself and like-minded women who don't follow trends. Architects, artists, designers, writers and mums **Is the idea of creative collaboration important to you?** Working with another creative person allows us to question and develop **Who has been the greatest influence on your career?** My greatest influence in spirit is my husband, Mark Borthwick. He has given me the confidence to find my identity as a designer **How have your own experiences affected your work as a designer?** I came from Chile with my parents as political refugees, so I am not sentimental about change **Which is more important in your work: the process or the product?** Both **Is designing difficult for you and, if so, what drives you to continue?** Designing is difficult sometimes – what drives me is the process of learning and the finished product **Have you ever been influenced or moved by the reaction to your designs?** The different reactions always interest me as they can vary from a very intellectual point to a very amusing interpretation or love of the way something fits **What's your definition of beauty?** Beauty in a person is a combination of the emotions and the superficial **What's your philosophy?** Don't sweat the small stuff – look at the big picture **What is the most important lesson you've learned?** To trust my instincts

Agent Provocateur is a lingerie label that shocks, seduces and satisfies. Since its conception in 1994, when Serena Rees and Joseph Corre opened the doors of an eponymous boutique in London's Soho, Agent Provocateur has transformed the business of upmarket underwear. The married couple set out to be retailers of choice knickers but instead ended up designing an entire range of colourful and glamorous lingerie. Neither Rees nor Corre (born in London in 1968 and 1969 respectively) had formal training – both left school at 16, Serena working as a photographic agent and Joe with his mother, Vivienne Westwood, on the retail side of her business. Instead, their creative juices flowed from a personal passion for the subject in hand. The Agent Provocateur experience is all about indulgent and mischievous sexual liberation; today they also design accessories including jewellery, shoes and stockings, and launched an award-winning perfume in 2000. Agent Provocateur directed a saucy cinema-only commercial in 1996 that debuted at the Astral Adult film-house, following it up with others featuring actress Gina Bellman and singer Kylie Minogue. In 1996 they launched a mail order catalogue and website, and have since opened two more shops in London, plus Los Angeles and New York. In 1999 they began a collaboration with UK high street chain Marks & Spencer, designing an exclusive range, Salon Rose. They have also worked with Tate Modern on products such as 'Airmail' pants which are sold in the gallery's gift shop. Agent Provocateur was included in London's Victoria & Albert Museum's 'Cutting Edge' exhibition in 1997, as well as 'The Inside Out' show at the Design Museum in 2000, which has since travelled around the world.

Agent Provocateur ist ein Dessous-Label, das schockiert und verführt. Seit seiner Gründung 1994, als Serena Rees und Joseph Corre die gleichnamige Boutique im Londoner Viertel Soho eröffneten, hat Agent Provocateur den Markt für edle Wäsche geprägt. Ursprünglich hatte sich das Ehepaar auf den Verkauf von ausgesuchten Damenslips beschränken wollen, doch schon bald entwarf man eine ganze Kollektion farbenfroher, edler Lingeriewaren. Weder Rees noch Corre, die beide aus London stammen und 1968 bzw. 1969 geboren sind, haben eine entsprechende Ausbildung. Sie verließen die Schule im Alter von 16 Jahren – Serena, um als Fotoagentin zu arbeiten, und Joe, um sich dem Vertrieb der Entwürfe seiner Mutter, Vivienne Westwood, zu widmen. Die Kreativität, die die beiden an den Tag legen, entspringt wohl ihrer persönlichen Leidenschaft für die Materie. Die Dessous von Agent Provocateur postulieren allesamt auf freche, eindeutige Weise sexuelle Freizügigkeit. Inzwischen entwirft das Designerpaar auch Accessoires wie Schmuck, Schuhe und Strumpfwaren. Im Jahr 2000 wurden sie für eine Duftkreation ausgezeichnet. Agent Provocateur inszenierte 1996 einen freizügigen Kino-Werbespot, der erstmals im berüchtigten Londoner Kino Astral Adult gezeigt wurde: weitere, unter anderem mit der Schauspielerin Gina Bellman und Popsängerin Kylie Minogue, folgten. Ebenfalls 1996 präsentierte man einen Versandkatalog und die eigene Website. Heute gibt es zwei weitere Filialen in London sowie jeweils eine in Los Angeles und New York. 1999 begann die Zusammenarbeit mit dem britischen Kaufhaus Marks & Spencer, für das man exklusive Kollektionen unter dem Label Salon Rose entwirft. Sie arbeiteten auch mit Tate Modern zusammen an Produkten, etwa an 'Airmail-Slips', die im Museums-Shop verkauft werden. Agent Provocateur war außerdem 1997 an der Ausstellung 'Cutting Edge' im Londoner Victoria & Albert Museum und an der internationalen Wanderausstellung 'The Inside Out' des Londoner Design Museum im Jahr 2000 beteiligt.

Agent Provocateur est une griffe de lingerie qui choque, qui séduit et qui comble les désirs. Depuis sa création en 1994, lorsque Serena Rees et Joseph Corre ouvrent une boutique éponyme dans Soho à Londres, Agent Provocateur a transformé le marché de la lingerie haut de gamme. Ce couple marié commence d'abord par vendre des culottes de luxe, puis finit par dessiner toute une gamme de lingerie colorée et glamour. Ni Serena Rees ni Joseph Corre (respectivement nés en 1968 et en 1969 à Londres) n'ont suivi de formation proprement dite : ils ont tous deux quitté l'école à 16 ans, Serena pour travailler en tant qu'agent de photographes et Joe pour épauler sa mère, Vivienne Westwood, dans l'activité Distribution de son entreprise. En fait, leur créativité découle de leur passion pour le sujet en question. La griffe Agent Provocateur parle d'une libération sexuelle indulgente et espiègle ; aujourd'hui, ils dessinent également des accessoires, des bijoux, des chaussures et des bas. En l'an 2000, ils lancent un parfum qui sera maintes fois primé. En 1996, Agent Provocateur réalise un spot publicitaire coquin dont la diffusion est réservée aux salles obscures, projeté en avant-première au cinéma Astral Adult. Ce spot est suivi d'autres films mettant en scène l'actrice Gina Bellman et la chanteuse Kylie Minogue. Toujours en 1996, ils lancent un catalogue de vente par correspondance et un site Web. Depuis, ils ont ouvert deux nouvelles boutiques à Londres, ainsi qu'à Los Angeles et New York. En 1999, ils entament une collaboration avec la chaîne de distribution britannique Marks & Spencer, pour laquelle ils dessinent une gamme de luxe : Salon Rose. Ils ont également travaillé avec le musée Tate Modern sur des produits tels que le pantalon « Airmail », vendu dans la boutique de souvenirs du musée. En 1997, le travail d'Agent Provocateur est présenté dans le cadre de l'exposition « Cutting Edge » du Victoria & Albert Museum de Londres, puis en l'an 2000 à l'exposition itinérante « The Inside Out » du Design Museum, qui a depuis voyagé dans le monde entier.

"Our work has been affected by previous disappointments discovering dreadful undies on various sexual escapades"

PORTRAIT BY TESH

JOSEPH CORRE & SERENA REES

What are your signature designs? Our signature is the introduction of colour and fashion fabrics into lingerie. We are constantly changing and offering new styles all year round, not just collections twice a year **What are your favourite pieces from any of your collections?** Demi fan-cup lace bra, pocket briefs **How would you describe your work?** Hard and sexy **What's your ultimate goal?** To continue working in an honest way – do only what you believe in **What inspires you?** A great arse **Can fashion still have a political ambition?** At certain points in time fashion has been about joining a gang and the gang's objective can be political **Who do you have in mind when you design?** Girls, girls, girls: sex kittens, sex bombs, seductresses, naughty girls, secretaries, schoolgirls, roly polys and Kate Moss **Is the idea of creative collaboration important to you?** In our position it is vital – we have both a male and female point of view **What has been the greatest influence on your career?** The quest for excellence in one's technique **How have your own experiences affected your work as designers?** Previous disappointments discovering dreadful undies on various different sexual escapades **Is designing difficult for you?** No **Have you ever been influenced or moved by the reaction to your designs?** At parties girls are constantly lifting their skirts and tops to show us their undies **What's your definition of beauty?** A fantastic mind. A brilliant smile. A great arse **What's your philosophy?** To only sell what we personally like and to not blab about who wears our knickers **What is the most important lesson you've learned?** It's okay to make mistakes, but don't make the same mistake twice

'Good fashion for me is like rock 'n'roll – there's always a little rebellion in it.' Eternally inspired by her friend Patti Smith, pagan poet and punk princess, Ann Demeulemeester is a designer who's not afraid to wear her heart on her sleeve. In fact, it's the essence of her approach and the reason why her work has so many loyal fans today. Born in Belgium in 1959, Demeulemeester studied fashion at Antwerp's Royal Academy, graduating in 1981 as part of the class that went on to become known as the 'Antwerp Six'. She launched her own label in 1985 with husband Patrick Robyn, showing womenswear in Paris for the first time in 1992 and combining it with menswear in 1996. The subversive austerity and uneasy romance of Demeulemeester's early designs, combined with their deliberately rough finish, soon made her one of the stars in European fashion's new wave: the deconstructionists. Demeulemeester has always eschewed the media circus, however; instead, her fashion is personal and emotional. Often working as her own fit model, as a designer she concerns herself as much with the experience of a garment as its look. Rarely adding colour to her designs, she consistently works in natural materials – particularly leathers, wools, flannels and furs – all materials that reward the tactile experience. Over the years her collections have been a constant evolution, exploring the conflict between masculine and feminine by mixing tailoring with softer wrapping layers, always retaining an easy sensuality and rock 'n' roll spirit. Ann Demeulemeester opened her own shop in Antwerp in 1999. The collection, which includes a successful range of shoes and accessories, is now sold in 30 countries worldwide.

'Gute Mode ist für mich wie Rock 'n' Roll – es steckt immer ein bisschen Rebellion drin'. Die unleugbar von ihrer Freundin, der Poetin und Punkprinzessin Patti Smith, inspirierte Designerin Ann Demeulemeester scheut sich nicht, ihr Herz auf der Zunge zu tragen. Genau genommen ist das sogar die Quintessenz ihrer Lebens- und Arbeitseinstellung sowie der Grund für die inzwischen große Zahl ihrer treuen Fans. Die 1959 geborene Belgierin studierte Mode an der Königlichen Akademie in Antwerpen. 1981 machte sie ihren Abschluss u. a. mit fünf Kollegen, die bald zusammen mit ihr als 'Antwerp Six' berühmt werden sollten. Ihr eigenes Label gründete Demeulemeester 1985 gemeinsam mit ihrem Mann Patrick Robyn; die erste Schau für Damenmode erfolgte 1992 in Paris, 1996 kam eine Herrenkollektion dazu. Die provozierende Strenge und gebrochene Romantik ihrer frühen Kreationen und ihr betont grobes Finish machten Demeulemeester rasch zu einem der Stars des neuen europäischen Modetrends: des Dekonstruktivismus. Jeglichen Medienrummel hat die Belgierin jedoch schon immer gescheut; Mode ist für sie etwas sehr Persönliches, Emotionales. Sie fungiert oft als ihr eigenes Model für die Anprobe. Wie sich ein Kleidungsstück anfühlt und trägt, ist ihr ebenso wichtig wie sein Aussehen. Farbe entdeckt man in ihren Kreationen selten, und sie verarbeitet fast ausschließlich Naturmaterialien – Leder, Wolle, Flanell und Pelz – die allesamt einen besonderen taktilen Reiz ausüben. Im Laufe der Jahre haben sich ihre Kollektionen immer weiter entwickelt. Dem Konflikt zwischen Männlichkeit und Weiblichkeit begegnet Demeulemeester mit einer Mischung aus klassischer Schneiderei und weicheren gewickelten Stofflagen. Das Resultat zeichnet nach wie vor eine gewisse Sinnlichkeit und der Geist des Rock 'n' Roll aus. 1999 eröffnete die Modemacherin einen eigenen Laden in Antwerpen. Ihre Kreationen, zu denen inzwischen auch eine erfolgreiche Schuhkollektion und Accessoires zählen, werden weltweit in dreißig Ländern verkauft.

« La mode, c'est comme le rock 'n' roll : on doit toujours y trouver un fond de rébellion ». Inspirée depuis toujours par son amie Patti Smith, poète païenne et princesse punk s'il en est, Ann Demeulemeester est une créatrice qui n'a pas peur d'exprimer ses sentiments. En fait, c'est l'essence même de son travail et la raison pour laquelle elle compte aujourd'hui de nombreux fans très fidèles. Née en 1959 en Belgique, Ann Demeulemeester étudie la mode à l'Académie Royale d'Anvers dont elle sort diplômée en 1981, membre d'une promotion qui sera plus tard connue sous le nom des « Antwerp Six ». Elle lance sa propre griffe en 1985 avec son mari Patrick Robyn. En 1992, elle présente pour la première fois sa collection pour femme à Paris, puis une collection pour homme en 1996. L'austérité subversive et le romantisme inquiet de ses premières créations, combinés à une finition délibérément brute, la hissent rapidement parmi les stars de la nouvelle vague européenne : les déconstructionnistes. Ann Demeulemeester a cependant toujours évité le grand cirque des médias, privilégiant une mode personnelle et émotionnelle. Elle coupe souvent ses vêtements sur elle car elle s'intéresse autant à la sensation du vêtement sur le corps qu'à son look. Elle ajoute rarement de la couleur à ses créations et aime travailler les matières naturelles telles que le cuir, la laine, la flanelle et la fourrure, autant d'étoffes qui mettent en avant le sens du toucher. Au fil des années, ses collections ont subi une évolution constante. Elle explore le conflit masculin/féminin en mélangeant perfection de la coupe et superpositions de tissus plus douces, toujours avec une sensualité facile et un esprit très rock 'n' roll. Ann Demeulemeester ouvre sa propre boutique à Anvers en 1999. Sa collection, qui inclut une gamme de chaussures et d'accessoires à succès, se vend aujourd'hui dans 30 pays à travers le monde.

"Good fashion for me is like rock 'n' roll – there's always a little rebellion in it"

PORTRAIT BY KEVIN DAVIES

ANN DEMEULEMEESTER

PHOTOGRAPHY BY SOPHIE DELAPORTE, STYLING BY KARL PLEWKA. MAY 2001

"Inspiration is difficult to define. I think it is given to you"

What are your signature designs? I don't like the term 'signature designs'. When I work, I pay attention to every item **What's your favourite piece from any of your collections?** This can change from day to day. Sometimes a garment is just waiting to be picked up **How would you describe your work?** Every morning I go to work and try to do 'my thing'. What comes out is what I stand for **What's your ultimate goal?** When I started my 'career' I had no fixed idea of a goal. Things have grown in a natural way and still do… **What inspires you?** Inspiration is very difficult to define. I think it is somehow given to you **Can fashion still have a political ambition?** Fashion has a reason to be because in fashion you can find new kinds of expression about human beings. It's my way to communicate **Who do you have in mind when you design?** When I design I have to start from myself but, at the same time, I try to make abstraction from myself **Is the idea of creative collaboration important to you?** Yes, there have been few but I cherish them **Who has been the greatest influence on your career?** My partner in life and work **How have your own experiences affected your work as a designer?** Everything that I have experienced in the 42 years that lie behind me has made me into the person I am now and that's my working tool **Which is more important in your work: the process or the product?** Both **Is designing difficult for you and, if so, what drives you to continue?** Yes, it is. What drives me is my never-ending will to give the best of myself **Have you ever been influenced or moved by the reaction to your designs?** Yes. It can provide me with courage after hard effort and pain **What's your definition of beauty?** Beauty is the joy that you feel when you discover it **What's your philosophy?** I don't have one **What is the most important lesson you've learned?** Learning never stops

Dolce & Gabbana are fashion's answer to Viagra, the full throbbing force of Italian style. Dolce's perfectionism and Gabbana's theatrics have been a winning combination, with a lasting impact on pop culture via Madonna (they made 1,500 outfits for her 1993 'Girlie Show' tour and created her image for 'Music') and Kylie Minogue (costumes for her 2001 'Fever' tour). Domenico Dolce was born in 1958 to a Sicilian family; his father was a tailor from Palermo who taught him to make a jacket by the age of seven. Stefano Gabbana was born in 1962, the son of a Milanese print worker. But it was Sicily, Dolce's birthplace and Gabbana's favourite childhood holiday destination, that sealed a bond between them when they first met and which has provided a reference for their aesthetic signatures ever since: the traditional Sicilian family girl (opaque black stockings, black lace, peasant skirts, shawl fringing), the Latin sex temptress (corsetry, high heels, underwear as outerwear), the Sicilian gangster (pinstripe suits, slick tailoring, fedoras). It's the friction between these polar opposites of masculine/feminine, soft/hard and innocence/corruption that makes Dolce & Gabbana so sexually exciting. Established in 1985, the label continually references Italian film legends like Fellini, Visconti, Sophia Loren and Anna Magnani; setting the stage for a love story told through the language of clothes. Although the Dolce & Gabbana empire includes childrenswear, swimwear, eyewear, fragrance and accessories, 80 percent of sales come from clothes (as opposed to perfume or accessories), and the duo maintain ownership of most of their global boutiques and a controlling stake in their manufacturer. They are, quite simply, Italian Stallions.

Dolce & Gabbana sind mit ihrer ganzen erregenden Kraft italienischer Eleganz quasi die Antwort der Mode auf Viagra. Dolces Perfektionismus und Gabbanas Theatralik erwiesen sich als gewinnbringende Kombination, die auch einen dauerhaften Einfluss auf die Popkultur ausübte. Für Madonnas 'Girlie Show'-Tour 1993 entwarf das Designer-duo 1500 Kostüme, und auch die Garderobe zum Video für 'Music' stammte von D & G. Kylie Minogue gab bei ihnen die Kostüme für ihre 'Fever'-Tour 2001 in Auftrag. Domenico Dolce wurde 1958 auf Sizilien geboren. Sein Vater war ein Schneider aus Palermo, der ihm schon im Alter von sieben Jahren beibrachte, wie man ein Jackett näht. Stefano Gabbana kam 1962 als Sohn eines Setzers in Mailand zur Welt. Es war jedoch Sizilien, Dolces Heimat und Gabbanas liebster Ferienort seiner Kindheit, das die beiden zusammenschweißte und ihre typische Ästhetik bis heute prägt. Da wäre das traditionelle sizilianische Mädchen aus strengem Hause (mit dunklen Strümpfen, schwarzer Spitze, Bauernrock und Fransentuch), der sexy Italo-Vamp (in Corsage, High Heels und deutlich sichtbar getragenen Dessous) und der sizilianische Gangster (mit schick geschnittenem Nadelstreifenanzug und Filzhut). Es sind die Brüche zwischen diesen extremen Gegensätzen von männlich und weiblich, sanft und hart, unschuldig und korrupt, die die Mode von Dolce & Gabbana so sexy und aufregend machen. Das 1985 gegründete Label zitiert immer wieder italienische Filmlegenden wie Fellini, Visconti, Sophia Loren und Anna Magnani. Diese Bezüge bilden die Bühne für eine Liebesgeschichte in der Sprache der Mode. Obwohl zum Imperium von Dolce & Gabbana auch Kinder- und Bademoden, Brillen, Düfte und Accessoires gehören, werden 80 Prozent der Umsätze mit Kleidung gemacht (der Rest entfällt auf Parfums und Accessoires). Die meisten ihrer Läden in der ganzen Welt gehören den beiden Firmengründern, die auch noch eine Kontrollmehrheit im Produktionsbereich besitzen. Sie sind eben echte Italiener.

Cœur palpitant du style italien, Dolce & Gabbana sont la réponse de la mode au Viagra. Le perfectionnisme de Dolce et le cabotinage de Gabbana ont formé une combinaison gagnante, avec un impact durable sur la culture pop grâce à Madonna (ils ont dessiné 1500 costumes pour sa tournée « Girlie Show » de 1993 et conçu son image pour l'album « Music ») et Kylie Minogue (costumes de la tournée « Fever » en 2001). Domenico Dolce est né en 1958 dans une famille sicilienne ; son père, tailleur à Palerme, lui apprend à faire une veste alors qu'il n'a que sept ans. Stefano Gabbana est né en 1962, fils d'un ouvrier d'imprimerie milanais. Patrie de Dolce et destination de vacances favorite de Gabbana lorsqu'il était enfant, c'est la Sicile qui scelle leur relation dès leur première rencontre, une référence qui transparaît continuellement dans leur esthétique : la fille de famille traditionnelle sicilienne (bas noirs opaques, dentelle noire, jupes de paysanne, franges « châle »), la séductrice latine (corseterie, talons hauts, sous-vêtements portés en vêtement du dessus) et le gangster sicilien (costumes mille-raies, coupes élégantes, chapeaux mous). Ce sont ces oppositions de masculin et de féminin, de douceur et de dureté, d'innocence et de corruption qui rendent les créations de Dolce & Gabbana si fascinantes d'un point de vue sexuel. Créée en 1985, la griffe fourmille de clins d'œil aux légendes du cinéma italien telles que Fellini, Visconti, Sophia Loren et Anna Magnani, mettant en scène une histoire d'amour racontée à travers le langage des vêtements. Bien que l'empire Dolce & Gabbana comprenne une ligne pour enfants, des maillots de bain, des lunettes, des parfums et des accessoires, 80% du chiffre d'affaires provient de la vente de vêtements (le reste allant aux parfums et aux accessoires). Le duo conserve le contrôle de la plupart de ses points de vente mondiaux et de ses fabricants. Ils sont, tout simplement, de vrais machos italiens.

"Many designers take themselves too seriously: 'I am a genius, the essence of fashion!' We just have a laugh"

PORTRAIT BY FABRIZIO FERRI

DOMENICO DOLCE & STEFANO GABBANA

PHOTOGRAPHY BY HUGER FOOTE, STYLING BY JAMIE HUCKBODY. FEBRUARY 2002

"Our job is the most beautiful one in the world!"

What are your signature designs? Guepiere dresses, pinstripe suits, Sicilian caps, tank tops **What are your favourite pieces from any of your collections?** The above-mentioned because they are classic, signature pieces that we love and that we like to show again and again, reinterpreting them according to the spirit of each collection **How would you describe your work?** Our job is the most beautiful one in the world! It is very exciting, never boring, and allows us to express our creativity and experiment **What's your ultimate goal?** As far as our private life is concerned, our goal is happiness, always and everywhere! As far as our work, to create a style that will remain throughout the years and that will be remembered **What inspires you?** We are inspired by everyday life, by the world and by the people that surround us. Besides that, there are key elements that are our constant and continuous sources of inspiration (and that represent our identity and our roots); that is to say, the Mediterranean, Sicily, black and white, and the films of Italian neo-realism. But we are also inspired by opposites that attract each other, by contrasts, by music and cinema **Can fashion still have a political ambition?** Fashion is one of the expressions of the time we live in and of all changes that happen. It can have a specific position and make statements, but for us it is essentially a way of expressing creativity **What do you have in mind when you design?** When we sketch an outfit, we are at the end of an elaborate process because the sketch is the result of many conversations between the two of us, of many deep thoughts, of many notes that we have taken, of many different experiences that we have put together. When we design we think about all these different things and about all that has led us to achieve that specific outfit **Is the idea of creative collaboration important to you?** For us it is the essence of our work. We are both creative, both in a different way because we complete each other. To have different opinions is important because it is a challenge **Who has been the greatest influence on your career?** For sure Madonna, who has been our muse and icon because of her strong personality **How have your own experiences affected your work as designers?** Our work is part of ourselves – our life. We reflect in the clothes we design all of our personal feelings **Which is more important in your work: the process or the product?** They are both important. However the final product gives more satisfaction because when you see it, you forget all the efforts you've made to achieve it! **Is designing difficult for you?** We love our work – it is our passion, our life. To design clothes is a joy for us, it is a continuous challenge but, at the same time, it allows us to express ourselves. We are lucky to be in a privileged position; that is to say, our creations have a worldwide exposure and our message is accessible to a lot of people. And this is a great support and it pushes us to go on, always and in the best possible way **Have you ever been influenced or moved by the reaction to your designs?** Of course we have, be these reactions positive or negative. If you listen to people's reactions you are challenged and led to think **What's your definition of beauty?** Beauty is something you have inside. Beauty is life. Beauty is love **What's your philosophy?** To always be ourselves and consistent **What is the most important lesson you've learned?** That you always have to be yourself, without betraying your personality and without losing your identity

The youngest of two brothers and two sisters, Alber Elbaz was born in Casablanca, Morocco. He was raised in the suburbs of Tel Aviv by his mother, a Spanish artist; his father, an Israeli barber, died when he was young. Elbaz studied at Shenkar College of Textile Technology and Fashion, Tel Aviv. Following graduation he went to New York, where for seven years he was the right-hand man of American high society designer Geoffrey Beene. In September 1996, Elbaz took over as head of prêt-à-porter design at Guy Laroche, where he successfully produced collections that remixed past house hits, but to a vibrant new beat. Elbaz was appointed Artistic Director for Yves Saint Laurent Rive Gauche womenswear in November 1998, effectively taking over design duties from Mr Saint Laurent himself. Despite attracting a new, young clientele – Chloë Sevigny wore one of his dresses to attend the Oscars – Elbaz left at the start of 2000 following the Gucci Group's purchase of the company. After a short but critically successful spell at Milanese house Krizia, in October 2001 Alber Elbaz was appointed Artistic Director for Lanvin womenswear. Elbaz's designs are infused with a raw and sensuous elegance, which has become his trademark. His debut Lanvin collection, shown for Autumn-Winter 2002, saw him inspired in part by founder Jeanne Lanvin, with spontaneous bursts of huge sequins, loosely sewn ribbons and chemise-like dresses nodding at the 1920s flapper. Reconciling the modern and the feminine, grown-up tailoring was loosened up with gently unfinished edges and simple leather thongs whipped around waists. One of the biggest hits of Paris Fashion Week, Alber Elbaz looks like he has finally found a place to let his remarkable talent shine.

Alber Elbaz kam als jüngster von zwei Brüdern und zwei Schwestern im marokkanischen Casablanca zur Welt. Seine Mutter, eine Künstlerin aus Spanien, zog ihn in der Vorstadt von Tel Aviv allein groß, nachdem sein Vater, ein israelischer Friseur, schon früh gestorben war. Elbaz studierte am Shenkar College of Textile Technology and Fashion, Tel Aviv. Nach dem Abschluss ging er nach New York, wo er sieben Jahre lang die rechte Hand des amerikanischen High-Society-Designers Geoffrey Beene war. Im September 1996 wurde Elbaz Chefdesigner der Prêt-à-Porter-Linien bei Guy Laroche, wo er erfolgreiche Kollektionen entwarf, in denen er vergangene Hits des Hauses mit einem kraftvollen neuen Beat unterlegte. Der nächste Karriereschritt war die Ernennung zum Artistic Director der Damenmode bei Yves Saint Laurent Rive Gauche im November 1998, was bedeutete, dass er die Designerpflichten von Monsieur Saint Laurent höchstpersönlich übernahm. Obwohl er eine neue, junge Klientel ansprach – so trug etwa Chloë Sevigny anlässlich einer Oscar-Verleihung eines seiner Kleider – verließ Elbaz das Unternehmen Anfang 2000, nachdem es vom Gucci-Konzern gekauft worden war. Nach einem kurzen, aber von der Kritik viel-beachteten Intermezzo beim Mailänder Modehaus Krizia im Oktober 2001 folgte die Ernennung zum Artistic Director für die Damenmode bei Lanvin. Elbaz' Kreationen sind von einer rauen, sinnlichen Eleganz, die inzwischen als sein Markenzeichen gilt. Für seine Debütkollektion bei Lanvin, Herbst/Winter 2002, ließ er sich zum Teil von der Firmengründerin Jeanne Lanvin inspirieren: riesige Pailletten, locker angenähte Bänder und Hemdblusenkleider erinnerten an die Mädchen der Golden Twenties. Er versöhnte das Moderne mit dem Femininen und lockerte die gestrenge Schneiderkunst mit unvollendeten Säumen oder lose um die Taille geschlungenen einfachen Lederbändern auf. Nachdem seine Schau einer der größten Erfolge bei der Pariser Modewoche war, scheint es, als hätte Elbaz endlich den Platz gefunden, an dem sein bemerkenswertes Talent perfekt zur Geltung kommt.

Petit dernier de deux frères et deux sœurs, Alber Elbaz est né à Casablanca au Maroc. Il grandit dans la banlieue de Tel Aviv auprès de sa mère, une artiste espagnole, car son père, un Israélien coiffeur pour hommes, meurt quand Alber est encore petit. Elbaz étudie le textile et la mode au Shenkar College of Textile Technology and Fashion de Tel Aviv. Une fois diplômé, il part pour New York où, pendant sept ans, il sera le bras droit de Geoffrey Beene, le styliste de la haute société américaine. En septembre 1996, Elbaz est nommé directeur de la création du prêt-à-porter chez Guy Laroche, pour qui il produit des collections réussies qui revisitent les plus grands succès passés de la maison à travers une approche inédite et pleine de vie. En novembre 1998, Elbaz devient directeur artistique de la ligne féminine Yves Saint Laurent Rive Gauche, succédant avec efficacité à M. Saint Laurent en personne. Bien qu'il parvienne à attirer une nouvelle clientèle plus jeune – Chloé Sevigny portait l'une de ses robes aux Oscars – Elbaz quitte la maison début 2000 après le rachat de l'entreprise par le Groupe Gucci. Ensuite, il travaille quelques mois pour la maison milanaise Krizia où ses collections sont saluées par une critique unanime. En octobre 2001, Alber Elbaz est nommé directeur artistique des collections pour femme de Lanvin. Ses créations se distinguent par l'élégance brute et sensuelle qui est aujourd'hui devenue sa signature. Pour sa première collection Lanvin Automne-Hiver 2002, il s'inspire en partie du style de la fondatrice Jeanne Lanvin, avec des explosions spontanées de grosses paillettes, de cascades de rubans et de robes-chemises en clin d'œil à la garçonne des années 1920. Réconciliant modernité et féminité, les coupes classiques sont actualisées à travers des ourlets sans finition et de simples lanières de cuir lacées autour de la taille. Chouchou de la Semaine de la Mode de Paris, Alber Elbaz semble avoir finalement trouvé un lieu où laisser éclater son remarquable talent.

"I want to re-introduce fragility and emotion to fashion, my way"

PORTRAIT BY ROBERTO FRANCKENBERG

ALBER ELBAZ

What are your signature designs? Clothes with emotions **What are your favourite pieces from any of your collections?** Always the first three or four pieces from each collection **How would you describe your work?** A continual process of making mistakes **What's your ultimate goal?** For all women of different backgrounds and age groups to wear my clothes in their own way **What inspires you?** People, places and friends **What do you have in mind when you design?** A blank sheet of paper in front of me **Is the idea of creative collaboration important to you?** Absolutely, very much **Who has been the greatest influence on your career?** Geoffrey Beene and the House of Saint Laurent **How have your own experiences affected your work as a designer?** They have made me more focused **Which is more important in your work: the process or the product?** The ultimate goal is the final product **Is designing difficult for you and, if so, what drives you to continue?** Yes, it is difficult. The imperfection of my last collection always makes me go on **What's your definition of beauty?** Beauty is constant but fashion is not **What's your philosophy?** I am not a philosopher **What is the most important lesson you've learned?** To doubt yourself

Could clothes be any more cheerful than those designed by Eley Kishimoto? This husband and wife team's signature is vivacious and artistic print-work, which has established their label as a model of happy, inspiring fashion. Born in Sapporo, Japan in 1965, Wakako Kishimoto graduated from Central Saint Martins in 1992 with a BA in fashion and print; Mark Eley was born in Bridgend, Wales in 1968, and graduated from Brighton Polytechnic in 1990 with a BA in fashion and weave. They founded Eley Kishimoto together in 1992, designing prints for Joe Casely-Hayford (1992–94), Hussein Chalayan (1995–96) and Alexander McQueen (1996–97), amongst others. In 1995, Eley Kishimoto produced their first collection, 'Rainwear' – printed PVC-coated fabrics turned into umbrellas, waterproof coats and gloves. Since then, Eley Kishimoto have not only gained a reputation for their print commissions (including Jil Sander, Versace, Yves Saint Laurent and Clements Ribeiro), but for their own quirky, colourful take on fashion. The duo presented their first on-schedule show during London Fashion Week for Autumn-Winter 2001: a series of afternoon tea parties, rather than a catwalk presentation. The label has also expanded to include crockery, furniture, wallpaper, luggage, sneakers, lingerie and sunglasses. Today Eley Kishimoto prints are commissioned by international designers including Marc Jacobs and Louis Vuitton, but despite the scale of their industry, the couple work quietly with a crew of dedicated craftspeople from a workshop in South London.

Kann Mode fröhlicher sein als die von Eley Kishimoto entworfenen Stücke? Das Markenzeichen dieses Designer-Ehepaars sind lebhafte, kunstvolle Muster, die ihr Label zu einem Paradebeispiel für lustige, inspirierende Mode gemacht haben. Die 1965 in Sapporo geborene Wakako Kishimoto schloss das Central Saint Martins 1992 mit einem Bachelor in Mode und Textildruck ab; Mark Eley, 1968 in Bridgend, Wales, geboren, verließ das Polytechnikum Brighton 1990 mit einem BA in Mode und Weben. Gemeinsam gründeten die beiden 1992 Eley Kishimoto und entwarfen Prints unter anderem für Joe Casely-Hayford (1992–94), Hussein Chalayan (1995–96) und Alexander McQueen (1996–97). 1995 produzierte man die erste eigene Kollektion namens 'Rainwear': Regenschirme, wasserdichte Mäntel und Handschuhe aus bedruckten, PVC-beschichteten Stoffen. Seit damals genießt das Label nicht nur Reputation für seine Printaufträge (u. a. von Jil Sander, Versace, Yves Saint Laurent und Clements Ribeiro), sondern eben auch für die eigenwillige, farbenfrohe Mode. Eine erste offizielle Show bei der Londoner Modewoche präsentierte das Designerduo für Herbst/Winter 2001. Allerdings handelte es sich dabei eher um eine Reihe von Afternoon-Tea-Parties als um eine klassische Catwalk-Show. Inzwischen produziert das Label auch Geschirr, Möbel, Tapeten, Reisegepäck, Turnschuhe, Dessous und Sonnenbrillen. Internationale Unternehmen wie Marc Jacobs und Louis Vuitton lassen nach wie vor Stoffmuster bei Eley Kishimoto entwerfen, doch trotz des Auftragsvolumens arbeitet das Designerehepaar zurückgezogen mit einem Team engagierter Handwerker in einer Werkstatt im Süden von London.

Existe-t-il des vêtements plus réjouissants que ceux d'Eley Kishimoto? Ce couple marié crée des pièces immédiatement reconnaissables à leurs imprimés amusants et artistiques qui ont établi cette griffe joyeuse et inspirée comme un modèle à suivre. Née en 1965 à Sapporo au Japon, Wakako Kishimoto sort diplômée de Central Saint Martins en 1992 avec un BA en mode et impression; Mark Eley est né en 1968 à Bridgend au Pays de Galles et étudie à l'école polytechnique de Brighton, où il obtient un BA en mode et tissage en 1990. Ensemble, ils fondent Eley Kishimoto en 1992 et commencent à dessiner des imprimés pour Joe Casely-Hayford (1992–94), Hussein Chalayan (1995–96) et Alexander McQueen (1996–97), entre autres. En 1995, la première collection d'Eley Kishimoto, «Rainwear», est coupée dans des tissus PVC imprimés et transformés en parapluies, manteaux et gants imperméables. Depuis, Eley Kishimoto doit sa réputation à ses nombreuses commandes d'imprimés (notamment pour Jil Sander, Versace, Yves Saint Laurent et Clements Ribeiro), mais également à sa vision étrange et colorée de la mode. Le duo présente son premier défilé officiel pendant la London Fashion Week Automne-Hiver 2001, une présentation qui ressemble plus à une «tea party» qu'à un véritable défilé. La griffe propose actuellement une ligne de vaisselle, des meubles, des papiers peints, des bagages, des baskets, de la lingerie et des lunettes de soleil. Aujourd'hui, les imprimés Eley Kishimoto sont commandés par des créateurs internationaux tels que Marc Jacobs et Louis Vuitton, mais en dépit d'une production à grande échelle, le couple continue de travailler tranquillement avec une petite équipe d'artisans dévoués dans son atelier de South London.

"We control colour better than other people. We're not afraid to put a print in your face"

PORTRAIT BY FLO KOLMER

MARK ELEY & WAKAKO KISHIMOTO

What are your signature designs? Uplifting bold printed separates **What's your favourite piece from any of your collections?** There is always a firm favourite from each collection that we like individually. I can't say that one item is the 'one', but the enjoyment has come along with the momentum of witnessing the favourite item still appearing in a different guise each season **How would you describe your work?** Enjoyable **What inspires you?** We are 'creatives' and therefore each and every experience is digested and can be called inspiration **Can fashion still have a political ambition?** Absolutely. The ability to have a voice, a platform and an audience is all you need to express any politics **Who do you have in mind when you design?** Girls that know a thing or two **Is the idea of creative collaboration important to you?** Very important. The foundation of our business is dependant on relationships with creative people **What has been the greatest influence on your career?** There are many people, places and experiences that have influenced and have been party to the development of our business. It's difficult to name one person or occasion as such a commitment to one thing would be detrimental to the many minor influences **How have your own experiences affected your work as designers?** All experiences are part of our make-up, and we make decisions on a daily basis that are answered from our instinct, so therefore our route has been guided with the help of past acknowledgements **Which is more important in your work: the process or the product?** There's no reason to separate these two aspects because the beauty of any work is the unity of both **Is designing difficult for you and, if so, what drives you to continue?** Designing is not difficult. It's the physical limitations of time which sometimes test **Have you ever been influenced or moved by the reaction to your designs?** Yes, it's quite overwhelming when a reaction to our product is expressed and is parallel to our own notions of what we are doing **What's your definition of beauty?** This is a little too personal and quite difficult to define. We both have very different ideas of what we think is held within beauty **What's your philosophy?** We have many, but here is one: 'We are surface decorators and everything has a surface' **What is the most important lesson you've learned?** To be honest

Timothy Everest is one of the most successful practitioners of contemporary bespoke tailoring. Born in Southampton in 1962, his career began with an apprenticeship to Tommy Nutter, maverick London tailor for the Rolling Stones and The Beatles. Like his mentor, Everest's own career has managed to side-step much of the stuffiness that can be associated with Savile Row, whilst still employing its high standards of craftsmanship. Everest's head office, workshop and fitting rooms are based in Spitalfields in London's East End and his tailoring operation takes all four floors of a Georgian townhouse. It is from this typically English location that Everest undertakes commissions, offering a surprisingly informal atmosphere and a decent cup of tea alongside his more traditional services. Everest has over 3,000 clients – recent commissions include a personal order from David Beckham and to dress actor Tom Cruise for the 'Mission: Impossible' films. In addition to a successful bespoke service (Everest took his first bespoke order in 1989) and producing ready-to-wear collections (since 1999), Everest is Group Creative Director of Daks. Everest has given some much-needed direction to the British house, overseeing the launch of a younger diffusion line for men and women called London E1, plus the more directional Daks Collection, also for men and women. Everest is also responsible for rejuvenating the existing Daks signature line whilst sensitively respecting its rich heritage.

Timothy Everest ist einer der erfolgreichsten Vertreter der modernen Maßschneiderei. Er wurde 1962 in Southampton geboren und begann seine Laufbahn mit einer Lehre bei Tommy Nutter, dem Außenseiter unter Londons Schneidern, der etwa für die Rolling Stones und die Beatles arbeitete. Wie seinem Mentor gelang es auch Everest, in seiner Karriere viel von der Spießigkeit zu vermeiden, die man gemeinhin mit der Savile Row assoziiert, und trotzdem deren hohem handwerklichem Anspruch zu genügen. Hauptbüro, Atelier und Anproberäume der Firma Everest befinden sich in Spitalfields im Londoner East End und nehmen dort alle vier Etagen eines Stadthauses im georgianischen Stil ein. An diesem typisch englischen Unternehmenssitz nimmt Everest ganz traditionelle Aufträge entgegen, und zwar in überraschend zwangloser Atmosphäre, bei einer stilechten Tasse Tee. Genäht wird für mehr als 3000 Kunden – dazu gehören Aufträge für den Privatmann David Beckham oder die Kostüme von Tom Cruise in den 'Mission Impossible'-Filmen. Neben der erfolgreichen Maßschneiderei (seinen ersten Auftrag nahm Everest 1989 entgegen) und eigenen Prêt-à-Porter-Kollektionen (seit 1999) ist Everest noch Group Creative Director bei Daks. Er gab dem britischen Modehaus eine dringend benötigte neue Richtung und überwachte die Einführung einer jüngeren Nebenlinie für Herren und Damen namens London E1. Zugleich ist er auch für die maßvolle Verjüngung der eher klassischen Damen- und Herrenkollektionen verantwortlich – immer mit Rücksicht auf die große Tradition des Hauses, versteht sich.

Timothy Everest est l'un des tailleurs contemporains qui rencontre le plus de succès. Né en 1962 à Southampton, il débute sa carrière comme apprenti de Tommy Nutter, le célèbre tailleur londonien des Rolling Stones et des Beatles. A l'instar de son mentor, Everest réussit à se départir du côté «vieux jeu» de Savile Row tout en conservant les standards élevés du savoir-faire à façon. Les bureaux, l'atelier et les salons d'essayage d'Everest se trouvent à Spitalfields dans l'East End de Londres et occupent les quatre étages d'un immeuble Georges V. C'est dans ce lieu typiquement anglais qu'Everest réalise ses commandes, au sein d'une atmosphère étonnamment informelle où le client se voit offrir une bonne tasse de thé aux côtés de services plus traditionnels. Everest compte plus de 3000 clients : récemment, il a reçu une commande personnelle de David Beckham et a créé les costumes de Tom Cruise pour les deux opus de «Mission : Impossible». Outre sa réussite en tant que tailleur sur mesure (Everest a reçu sa première commande en 1989) et la production de collections de prêt-à-porter (depuis 1999), Everest est aussi directeur de la création du groupe Daks. Il a insufflé la nouvelle orientation tant attendue par la maison anglaise, supervisant le lancement d'une ligne plus jeune pour homme et femme baptisée London E1, ainsi que Daks Collection, une gamme plus expérimentale, également pour homme et femme. Everest a également réussi à rajeunir la ligne principale de Daks tout en respectant la richesse de son héritage.

"I'd like to be remembered as someone who made people take British clothing seriously"

PORTRAIT COURTESY OF TIMOTHY EVEREST

TIMOTHY EVEREST

PHOTOGRAPHY BY DONALD CHRISTIE, STYLING BY JAMES SLEAFORD. JUNE 2000

What are your signature designs? For me, it's not a particular style. It's about making sure a garment has the best fit, the best fabric, the best things for the job **What's your favourite piece from any of your collections?** An old blazer, which I've had for about eight years. It's very low key **How would you describe your work?** Individual styles for individual people **What's your ultimate goal?** To be remembered as someone who made people take British clothing seriously, who made it internationally acceptable **What inspires you?** People, movies, travel, situations, challenges. I think visually so I get very inspired by aesthetics **Can fashion still have a political ambition?** Yes, I suppose so. To be yourself is the only way you can be modern. I just think people need depth and reason **Who do you have in mind when you design?** Somebody who is aware of their heritage, what the value of that is now and for the future, and who is sensitive to what's going on internationally on all levels **Is the idea of creative collaboration important to you?** Yes, it helps you grow and actually addresses reality. Smaller companies can bring a lot of nuances to bigger companies and bigger companies can help smaller companies. For us it's been very, very positive **Which is more important in your work: the process or the product?** All of it. It's no good having a concept without being able to make it work. The whole process, I love it. And the whole team makes it work, not just you **Who has been the greatest influence on your career?** Probably my uncle and his job in a dodgy old tailors. I got a job there when I was about 17. It was really old-fashioned, but the best grounding I could have had. It was about old-fashioned retail and service, and proper standards. Tommy Nutter is also one of my biggest influences. He was a very modest person and able to articulate to his generation what tailoring was about **Is designing difficult for you and, if so, what drives you to continue?** I don't find it difficult to design in the sense of putting together what I think, the concept, the range and how it goes together. But sometimes it's difficult because I don't have the time to do much of anything because I am constantly running around **Have you ever been influenced or moved by the reaction to your designs?** I like the compliments which are not necessarily to your face – you just hear things and that is really, really nice **What's your philosophy?** Hard work is important and you must learn your trade. Be yourself and believe in yourself. Then everything is possible **What is your definition of beauty?** Depth and subtlety. I like those things you have to study **What is the most important lesson that you've learned?** To be patient with my impatience, that was what my old boss told me. What goes around comes around. Be very careful what you say about people, because you can go down as well as up, and believe in what you can do

PHOTOGRAPHY BY THOMAS SCHENK, STYLING BY JOANNE BLADES. MARCH 2000

Fendi is a house of extremes: big furs and little handbags, a family business with worldwide recognition, a sincere chic past and an ironic cool future. The Fendi empire was founded in 1925 by Adele Fendi from a small leather goods shop and workroom in Rome, where she and her husband Eduardo worked with private clients. The family business expanded with the opening of a bigger shop in 1946, but it wasn't until the death of Eduardo eight years later that their five daughters started to carve the modern Fendi image, injecting the little company with their youthful glamour and spirit. Adele died in 1978 and each sister inherited a corner of the empire to look after: Paola (born 1931) did the furs, Anna (born 1933) the leather goods, Franca (born 1935) the customer relations, Carla (born 1937) the business coordination and Alda (born 1940) the sales. By the end of the 1980s, the label had become synonymous with jet-set elitist luxury thanks to its furs and double F logo. In the '90s climate of anti-bourgeois political correctness, Fendi returned to its heritage and the bags of Adele Fendi. The Baguette was re-born and Fendi's star was in the ascendant yet again, defining the craze for baroque excess. In 1999, LVMH and Prada bought a 51 percent stake in the label, LVMH eventually becoming the sole partner in 2001. But Fendi is still very much a family business: the future being Maria Silvia Venturini Fendi, daughter of Anna Fendi, who created the Fendissime line in 1987 and is now the Head of the Style Department. Karl Lagerfeld, as Chief Designer, continues to work with the sisters as he has since 1965, designing the double F logo and reworking the mould of Fendi's signature fabric, fur.

Fendi ist ein Modehaus der Extreme – mit opulenten Pelzen und winzigen Handtäschchen, ein Familienbetrieb von Weltrang mit einer distinguiert-eleganten Vergangenheit und einer witzig-coolen Zukunft. Gegründet wurde das Fendi-Imperium 1925 von Adele Fendi in einem kleinen römischen Lederwarengeschäft mit angeschlossener Werkstatt. Dort arbeiteten sie und ihr Mann Eduardo für einen kleinen Kreis von Privatkunden. 1946 expandierte man und eröffnete einen größeren Laden. Doch erst nach dem Tod Eduardos acht Jahre später begannen die fünf Töchter das moderne Image von Fendi zu prägen, indem sie ihren jugendlichen Eifer und Esprit in das kleine Unternehmen einbrachten. Adele starb 1978 und hinterließ jeder Tochter einen eigenen Bereich: der 1931 geborenen Paola die Pelzabteilung, der 1933 geborenen Anna die Lederwaren, die 1935 geborene Franca war für Werbung und PR zuständig, Carla, Jahrgang 1937, koordinierte die Finanzen und die 1940 geborene Alda den Verkauf. Ende der 1980er Jahre hatte die Marke sich zum Synonym für den elitären Luxus des Jet-Sets gemausert, vor allem dank ihrer Pelze und ihres Doppel-F-Logos. In den anti-bourgeoisen, von Political Correctness geprägten 1990er Jahren besann man sich auf seine Wurzeln und die Taschen von Adele Fendi. Die Baguette-Form wurde wieder entdeckt, und der Stern des Unternehmens war wieder im Steigen begriffen – nur stand er jetzt für die plötzlich wieder gefragte barocke Üppigkeit. 1999 kauften LVMH und Prada 51 Prozent der Anteile; zwei Jahre später wurde LVMH alleiniger Partner. Trotzdem hat Fendi nach wie vor viel von einem Familienbetrieb. Die Zukunft der Firma liegt heute in den Händen von Maria Silvia Venturini Fendi, der Tochter von Anna Fendi. Sie gründete 1987 die Linie Fendissime und ist jetzt Chefin des Modebereichs. Karl Lagerfeld prägt seit 1965 als Chefdesigner den Stil des Hauses. Er hat unter anderem das Doppel-F-Logo entworfen und Fendis klassischem Material zu neuem Ansehen verholfen: dem Pelz.

Fendi est la marque des extrêmes : grosses fourrures et petits sacs à main, entreprise familiale et reconnaissance internationale, passé vraiment chic et futur plutôt cool et ironique. L'empire Fendi a été fondé en 1925 par Adele Fendi à partir d'un petit atelier de maroquinerie de Rome où, avec son mari Eduardo, elle travaillait pour une clientèle privée. L'entreprise familiale se développe grâce à l'ouverture d'une plus grande boutique en 1946, mais ce n'est que huit ans plus tard, à la mort d'Eduardo, que leurs cinq filles commencent à sculpter l'image moderne de Fendi, insufflant à la petite entreprise tout leur glamour et leur jeunesse. Quand Adele meurt en 1978, chaque sœur hérite d'un morceau de l'empire : Paola (née en 1931) s'occupe des fourrures, Anna (née en 1933) de la maroquinerie, Franca (née en 1935) des relations avec les clients, Carla (née en 1937) de la coordination et Alda (née en 1940) des ventes. A la fin des années 1980, la griffe est devenue synonyme de luxe élitiste et jet-set grâce à ses fourrures et son logo en double F. Au sein du climat politiquement correct et anti-bourgeois des années 1990, Fendi replonge vers ses racines et ressort les sacs d'Adele Fendi. La Baguette est ressuscitée et l'étoile de Fendi remonte au firmament, incarnant la nouvelle folie pour les excès baroques. En 1999, LVMH et Prada rachètent 51% de la griffe, mais LVMH finit par devenir l'unique partenaire en 2001. Toutefois, Fendi reste encore une affaire très familiale : son avenir repose sur les épaules de Maria Silvia Venturini Fendi, fille d'Anna Fendi, qui a créé la ligne Fendissime en 1987 et occupe aujourd'hui le poste de directrice du département Style. Karl Lagerfeld, directeur de la création, continue à travailler pour les sœurs comme il l'a toujours fait depuis 1965. C'est lui qui a créé le célèbre logo en double F et retravaillé la fourrure, matière Fendi s'il en est.

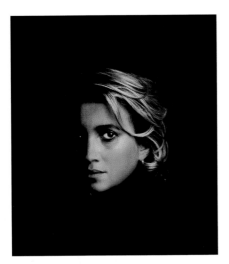

"Irony allows me to dampen the creative obsession"

PORTRAIT BY KARL LAGERFELD

SILVIA VENTURINI FENDI

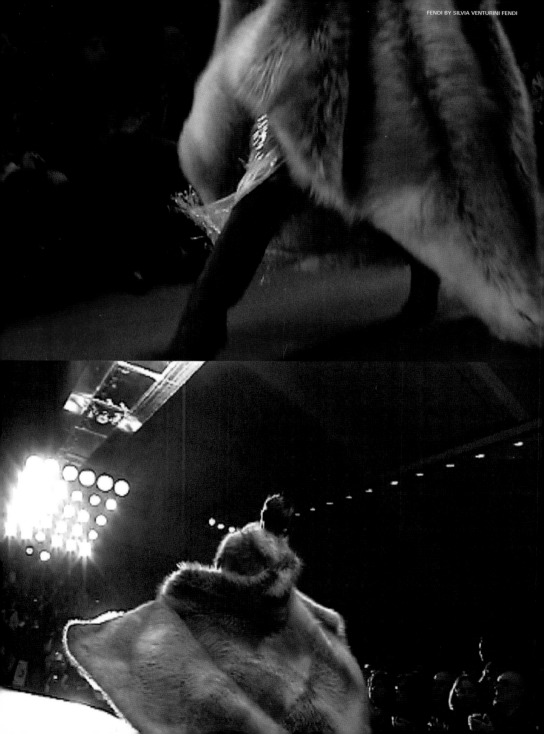

PHOTOGRAPHY BY GUSTAVO TEN HOEVER, STYLING BY GARETH GRIFFITHS. FEBRUARY 2002

What are your signature designs? Manual ability and technique **What's your favourite piece from any of your collections?** The Baguette **How would you describe your work?** Dreaming and realising **What's your ultimate goal?** The Ostrik bag **What inspires you?** Anything, but above all, the challenges **Can fashion still have a political ambition?** It should not – but it can because fashion has a great power when it influences costume and society **What do you have in mind when you design?** It depends. Sometimes I have in mind images, sometimes I have only sensations which I would call 'visionary' **Is the idea of creative collaboration important to you?** Creativity grows when it is shared **Who has been the greatest influence on your career?** My mother **How have your own experiences affected your work as a designer?** Irony, which I have acquired through my life experiences, allows me to have a sort of detachment and to dampen the creative obsession **Which is more important in your work: the process or the product?** It is impossible to separate one from the other. However, the process is the longer and more fascinating phase, which culminates in the realisation of the product **Is designing difficult for you and, if so, what drives you to continue?** It is not easy, but always challenging **Have you ever been influenced or moved by the reaction to your designs?** Yes, because creativity is neither blind nor deaf **What's your definition of beauty?** Energy **What's your philosophy?** To be afraid of convictions and to have the courage of changing ideas **What is the most important lesson you have learned?** To be ready to reverse the norms that up to that moment seemed to be absolute

Alberta Ferretti is one of the doyennes of Italian fashion. A Ferretti chiffon dress, beaded and embellished with ribbons or embroidery, is a recognisable designer signature and her line for younger women, Philosophy, one of the most successful diffusion collections. Ferretti is also a powerful businesswoman: her company, Aeffe, was founded in 1980 and is now a major luxury brand group. Ferretti was born in 1950 in Cattolica on the north Adriatic coast, the daughter of a dressmaker. She cites her mother's atelier as a major inspiration, but also credits the glamorous presence of the Fellini movie productions that were being made around her local area in the 1950s. Aged just 18, Ferretti opened a boutique in her home town, but in 1974 she exchanged selling for designing and launched her own label. Six years later she created Aeffe with her brother, Massimo. During the 1980s, Ferretti built up her brand of pretty, lyrical dressing, making her debut on the Milan runway in 1981 and launching Philosophy di Alberta Ferretti in 1984. In 1994, the small medieval village of Montegridolfo became the home of Aeffe; by this time the group was also producing collections for Moschino, Gaultier and Narciso Rodriguez. Today Aeffe is a major and acquisitive player in the luxury goods market, but Ferretti's aesthetic remains steadfast and she firmly believes in women designing for women. Her collections of filmy dresses, princess coats and neat, girlish knitwear have been augmented by new underwear and accessory lines, but ultimately she knows her clients: feminine, romantic women with a taste for delicate, antique decoration and simple lines.

Alberta Ferretti ist eine der dienstältesten Leitfiguren der italienischen Mode. Mit Perlen und Bändern oder Stickereien verzierte Chiffonkleider gelten als Markenzeichen der Designerin. Ihre Linie Philosophy für jüngere Frauen zählt zu den erfolgreichsten Zweitlinien überhaupt. Ferretti ist denn auch eine einflussreiche Geschäftsfrau: Ihre 1980 gegründete Firma Aeffe hat sich zu einem Großkonzern für Luxusmarken entwickelt. Die Tochter einer Schneiderin wurde 1950 in Cattolica an der nördlichen Adria geboren. Das Atelier ihrer Mutter war ein wichtiger Ansporn für sie, aber auch die glamourösen Filme Fellinis, die in den 1950er Jahren in dieser Gegend gedreht wurden, haben sie geprägt. Mit gerade 18 Jahren eröffnete Ferretti ein Modegeschäft in ihrer Heimatstadt. 1974 startete sie ihr eigenes Label, wandte sie sich vom Verkauf ab und dem Entwerfen zu. Sechs Jahre später gründete sie die Firma Aeffe zusammen mit ihrem Bruder Massimo. Im Verlauf der 1980er Jahre machte sich Ferretti einen Namen mit hübschen, romantischen Kreationen. Das Debüt auf dem Laufsteg in Mailand erfolgte 1981. Philosophy di Alberta Ferretti wurde erstmals 1984 präsentiert. Der kleine mittelalterliche Ort Montegridolfo ist seit 1994 Sitz von Aeffe. Zu dieser Zeit produzierte der Konzern auch Kollektionen für Moschino, Gaultier und Narciso Rodriguez. Heute mischt Aeffe als erfolgreicher Global Player auf dem Markt der Luxusgüter mit. Ferrettis Ästhetik ist davon jedoch weitgehend unberührt geblieben. Die Designerin steht fest zu ihrem Grundsatz: Mode von Frauen für Frauen. Ihre Kollektionen aus duftigen Kleidern, Prinzessmänteln und adretten, mädchenhaften Strickwaren wurden um neue Dessous- und Accessoire-Linien erweitert. Doch letztlich kennt Ferretti ihre Kundinnen ganz genau: Es sind feminine, romantische Frauen mit einem Faible für elegantes, traditionelles Dekor und klare Linien.

Alberta Ferretti est l'une des doyennes de la mode italienne. Impossible de ne pas reconnaître au premier coup d'œil sa célèbre robe en mousseline de soie perlée, ornée de rubans et de broderies. De plus, Philosophy, collection destinée aux clientes plus jeunes, est l'une des lignes de diffusion qui se vend le mieux actuellement. Alberta Ferretti est donc aussi une femme d'affaires influente : Aeffe, la société qu'elle a fondée en 1980, est aujourd'hui un important groupe de luxe. Fille de couturière, Alberta Ferretti est née en 1950 à Cattolica au nord de la côte Adriatique. Naturellement inspirée par l'atelier de sa mère, elle se dit aussi influencée par le glamour des films de Fellini tournés dans sa région dans les années 1950. A l'âge de 18 ans, Alberta Ferretti ouvre une boutique dans sa ville natale. En 1974, elle délaisse la vente au profit de la création et lance sa propre griffe. Six ans plus tard, elle fonde Aeffe avec son frère Massimo. Pendant les années 1980, Alberta Ferretti impose sa marque de vêtements ravissants et poétiques. Elle fait ses débuts aux défilés de Milan en 1981 avant de lancer la ligne Philosophy di Alberta Ferretti en 1984. En 1994, Aeffe s'installe dans le petit village médiéval de Montegridolfo ; à cette époque, le groupe produit également des collections pour Moschino, Gaultier et Narciso Rodriguez. Aujourd'hui, Aeffe est devenu un acteur incontournable et redouté sur le marché du luxe, mais l'esthétique Ferretti reste la même, la créatrice tenant toujours à ce que des femmes dessinent pour des femmes. A ses collections de robes vaporeuses, de manteaux de princesse et d'élégantes pièces en maille très jeune fille viennent s'ajouter de nouvelles lignes de lingerie et d'accessoires. En fait, Alberta Ferretti connaît parfaitement ses clientes : féminines et romantiques, ce sont des femmes qui aiment les décorations délicates anciennes et les lignes simples.

"I try to emphasise the personality and elegance of women"

ALBERTA FERRETTI

ALBERTA FERRETTI

PHOTOGRAPHY BY KAYT JONES, STYLING BY BELLAN CASADEVALL. APRIL 2001. MODEL: LIBERTY ROSS

PHOTOGRAPHY BY GLEN ERLER, STYLING BY RACHAEL ZILLI, SEPTEMBER 2004. MODEL: SADIE FROST

"Beauty is the harmony created by the dress and the woman who wears it"

What is the signature of your designs? Lightness **What's your favourite piece from any of your collections?** The one I'll make tomorrow **How would you describe your work?** Challenging, stimulating, satisfying **What inspires you?** From a single cloud to a woman's gesture **Can fashion still have a political ambition?** Particular styles in dressing can underline the belonging to a group with a specific and identifiable ideology. Only in that sense can we say that fashion has political ambition **What do you have in mind when you design?** A silhouette in motion… a story to be told **Is the idea of creative collaboration important to you?** Collaborating with others is essential, to go on and forward **Who has been the greatest influence on your career?** I, myself: from the endless challenges I face, to the effort I make to improve myself and to always reach new goals **Which is more important in your work: the process or the product?** There is no outcome with no process; elaborating without producing is sterile. The result really comes only from the union of these two phases **Is designing difficult for you?** No, designing is my passion **Have you ever been influenced or moved by the reaction to your designs?** I consider the opinion of others, but I have always tried to advance by maintaining my concept of elegance and femininity **What's your definition of beauty?** Beauty is the harmony created by the dress and the woman who wears it **What's your philosophy?** I try to emphasise the personality and elegance of women

It's often said creative minds, no matter where their itineraries take them, never really cut loose the threads of their roots. This theory applies perfectly to Sardinian Angelo Figus (born 1975). Growing up in a small agricultural village, he first moved to Milan to study architecture, then a year later, in 1996, took off to Antwerp, Belgium, to study fashion at the prestigious Royal Academy. Figus immediately made his mark: his June 1999 graduation collection, 'Quore di Cane', received so much attention from the international press present that it was staged again a month later during Paris Haute Couture week, despite it being menswear. In February 2000, Angelo Figus translated his uncompromising, often dramatic but poetic style to women's fashion with his first prêt-à-porter collection, presented in Paris and loosely based on the osmosis of clothes and interior design. This set the tone for his signature approach: deeply personal, dreamlike even, but combined with both the romance of Sardinian childhood memories and the turmoil of adult emotions. More alchemist than mathematician, Figus masterfully drapes, pleats and contorts fabric. His idiosyncratic tailoring and sensuous presentations got him noticed by international buyers and press alike, as well as the theatrical arts: in 2000, he designed the costumes for Ugo Rondinone's performance in Ghent, Belgium. Figus was also commissioned by the Dutch Opera to design costumes for Claude Vivier's opera 'Rêves d'un Marco Polo' in 2000 and Wagner's opera 'Lohengrin', staged by Pierre Audi, in February 2002.

Es heißt oft, dass kreative Menschen – egal wohin das Schicksal sie führt – ihre Wurzeln niemals ganz kappen. Auf den sardischen Designer Angelo Figus trifft das genau zu. 1975 geboren, wuchs er in einem kleinen Bauerndorf auf und ging 1995 zunächst nach Mailand, um dort Architektur zu studieren. Ein Jahr später zog er ins belgische Antwerpen, um an der angesehenen Königlichen Akademie ins Modefach zu wechseln. Und schon bald machte Figus von sich reden: Seine Abschlusskollektion 'Quore di Cane' erregte im Juni 1999 in der internationalen Presse solches Aufsehen, dass sie schon einen Monat später bei der Pariser Haute-Couture-Woche erneut gezeigt wurde – und das, obwohl es sich um Herrenmode handelte. Im Februar 2000 brachte der Italiener seinen kompromisslosen, oft dramatischen, aber immer poetischen Stil mit seiner ersten Prêt-à-Porter-Kollektion auch in der Damenmode zum Ausdruck. Die Kreationen waren zutiefst persönlich, geradezu verträumt und verbanden romantische Erinnerungen an eine Kindheit auf Sardinien mit dem Aufruhr der Gefühle eines jungen Erwachsenen. Mehr Alchemist als Techniker, versteht es der junge Designer meisterhaft, Stoffe zu drapieren, zu plissieren und zu raffen. Seine unverwechselbaren Entwürfe und deren sinnliche Präsentation weckten nicht nur Interesse bei Kunden und Journalisten in aller Welt, sondern auch in der Theaterszene. So entwarf er im Jahr 2000 die Kostüme für die Performance von Ugo Rondinone im belgischen Gent. Das Opernhaus Amsterdam beauftragte Figus 2000 mit dem Entwurf der Kostüme für Claude Viviers Oper 'Rêves d'un Marco Polo' sowie 2002 für Wagners 'Lohengrin' unter der Regie von Pierre Audi.

On dit souvent que les esprits créatifs ne coupent jamais vraiment le lien avec leurs racines, où que leur carrière les amène. Cette théorie s'applique parfaitement au Sarde Angelo Figus. Né en 1975 dans un petit village de paysans, il s'installe d'abord à Milan pour étudier l'architecture, puis un an plus tard, en 1996, il part pour la Belgique où il étudie la mode à la prestigieuse Académie Royale d'Anvers. Figus s'y fait immédiatement remarquer : en juin 1999, sa collection de fin d'études, «Quore di Cane», suscite un tel enthousiasme auprès de la presse internationale qu'il est invité un mois plus tard à présenter son travail à la Semaine de la Haute Couture de Paris, bien qu'il ne dessine que pour les hommes. En février 2000, Angelo Figus applique son style intransigeant, souvent théâtral mais toujours poétique, à la mode pour femme dans une première collection de prêt-à-porter présentée à Paris et caractérisée par une osmose entre vêtements et design d'intérieur, un événement annonciateur de son style : sa mode profondément personnelle, voire onirique, combine à la fois le romantisme de ses souvenirs d'enfance en Sardaigne et les émois de l'âge adulte. Plus alchimiste que mathématicien, Figus maîtrise les drapés, les plis et les contorsions de tissus à la perfection. Ses coupes typiques et ses présentations voluptueuses ont non seulement attiré l'attention des acheteurs internationaux et de la presse, mais également celle du théâtre : en l'an 2000, il conçoit les costumes du spectacle d'Ugo Rondinone à Gand en Belgique. La même année, le Dutch Opera fait appel à lui pour dessiner les costumes de «Rêves d'un Marco Polo», l'opéra de Claude Vivier. Il renouvelle l'expérience en février 2002 pour le «Lohengrin» de Wagner mis en scène par Pierre Audi.

"For me, fashion is sharing different thoughts with others"

PORTRAIT BY TERRY JONES

ANGELO FIGUS

What's your favourite piece from any of your collections? At this stage of my development I'm still completely involved with all the pieces. They all relate to a situation. Besides that, I don't want to be classified for some pieces, as their ensemble is straight **How would you describe your work?** Free association of elements and feelings in the most abstract and simple way **What's your ultimate goal?** To share with others my different thoughts **What inspires you?** Nature, tradition **Can fashion still have a political ambition?** Life is politics, politics is economy and economy is also fashion: fashion is politics (as everything) **Who do you have in mind when you design?** The same person as last time, like always **Is the idea of creative collaboration important to you?** Creation is individualism; it is like giving something that you both can share. Some have lots of people around but it is never equal. I believe in duos **Who has been the greatest influence on your career?** All the people I have loved, lost or discovered **How have your own experiences affected your work as a designer?** I'm fascinated by memories, but never autobiographic **Which is more important in your work: the process or the product?** The process is more exciting and very involving, playful; but the product gives sense to it **What's your definition of beauty?** Beauty is to feel confident and comfortable with yourself **What is the most important lesson you've learned?** Tomorrow's

PHOTOGRAPHY BY CRAIG MCDEAN, STYLING BY EDWARD ENNINFUL. JUNE/JULY 2002. MODEL: KATE MOSS

Tom Ford has redefined the role of fashion designer. No longer a troubled artist, the new paradigm is at ease with the commercial aims of large fashion companies, as brilliant at brand rejuvenation and marketing strategies as he is at design. Tom Ford was born in Austin, Texas, in 1961. He spent his teenage years in Santa Fe, New Mexico, before enrolling on an art history course at New York University. In Manhattan, Ford's extracurricular activities included acting in TV advertisements and hanging out at both Studio 54 and Warhol's Factory. He eventually transferred to Parsons School of Design in New York and Paris, studying architecture, but by the end of the course Ford had realised that he wanted to work in fashion. In 1986, back in New York, he joined the design studio of Cathy Hardwick, moving to Perry Ellis two years later as Design Director. In 1990, Ford became womenswear designer at Gucci, the Italian accessories company which had been ailing since its 1960s heyday. In 1994, Ford was made Creative Director at Gucci and the following March showed a landmark collection. His velvet hipster trousers and jewel-coloured satin shirts – unbuttoned to the navel and impossibly lean – were part of a slick, alluring package of unapologetic flash and sex appeal. The Mario Testino ad campaigns, the moodily-lit new boutiques – even the carrier bags – appeared to be made of the same sultry fabric. Almost overnight, Gucci became a byword for desirability, offering the most aspirational and hedonistic kind of fashion. Since January 2000, when the Gucci Group purchased Yves Saint Laurent, Ford has designed menswear and womenswear for Yves Saint Laurent Rive Gauche, using his expert ability to revolutionise the house with collections that have been an enormous critical and commercial triumph. Tom Ford has received dozens of industry awards, including three from the prestigious CFDA; in 2002, the Council named him Accessory Designer of the Year for his work at YSL. He is now Creative Director of the Gucci Group.

Tom Ford hat die Rolle des Modeschöpfers neu definiert. Im Gegensatz zum geplagten Künstler kommt der neue Typus des Designers mit den kommerziellen Zielvorgaben großer Modeunternehmen zurecht und bewährt sich bei der Verjüngung einer Marke und der Entwicklung von Marketingstrategien ebenso brillant wie beim Entwerfen. Tom Ford wurde 1961 in Austin, Texas, geboren. Seine Teenagerzeit verbrachte er in Santa Fe, New Mexico, bevor er sich zum Studium der Kunstgeschichte an der New York University einschrieb. In Manhattan gehörten zu seinen außeruniversitären Aktivitäten Auftritte in TV-Werbespots und das Herumhängen im Studio 54 und in Andy Warhols Factory. Schließlich wechselte er an die Parsons School of Design in New York und zeitweise nach Paris, um Architektur zu studieren, doch gegen Ende der Ausbildung erkannte Ford, dass er eigentlich in der Modebranche arbeiten wollte. 1986 schloss er sich, nach New York zurückgekehrt, dem Designatelier von Cathy Hardwick an. Zwei Jahre später ging er als Design Director zu Perry Ellis. 1990 wurde er Designer für Damenmode bei Gucci, dem italienischen Accessoire-Hersteller, der seit seiner besten Zeit in den 1960er Jahren vor sich hin kränkelte. Dort wurde Ford 1994 zum Creative Director befördert und zeigte im darauf folgenden März eine Kollektion, die den Wendepunkt darstellen sollte. Seine Hüfthosen aus Samt und Satinblusen in Edelsteintönen – bis zum Nabel aufgeknöpft und unglaublich schmal geschnitten – waren Teil eines raffinierten, verführerischen, keineswegs zurückhaltenden sexy Looks. Die Werbekampagnen von Mario Testino, die stimmungsvoll ausgeleuchteten neuen Boutiquen – ja selbst die Tragetaschen schienen aus ein und demselben erotisierenden Material gemacht zu sein. Fast über Nacht wurde Gucci zum Synonym für Begehrlichkeit, zu einem Label, das die ambitionierteste und hedonistischste Mode von allen bot. Seit Januar 2000, als die Gucci-Gruppe Yves Saint Laurent erwarb, designt Ford die Damen- und Herrenmode für Yves Saint Laurent Rive Gauche. Dabei hat er dieses Haus dank seiner langjährigen Erfahrung mit Kollektionen revolutioniert, die sowohl bei den Kritikern als auch bei den Käufern ein Riesenerfolg waren. Dafür gab es Dutzende Preise der Textilindustrie, darunter allein drei des angesehenen CFDA. 2002 verlieh ihm das Council für seine Arbeit bei YSL den Titel Accessory Designer of the Year. Heute ist Tom Ford Creative Director der gesamten Gucci-Konzerns.

Tom Ford a redéfini le rôle du créateur de mode. Au diable le mythe de l'artiste maudit, le nouveau styliste se réconcilie avec les objectifs commerciaux des grandes marques de mode, aussi doué pour créer que pour rajeunir les griffes et définir les stratégies marketing. Tom Ford est né en 1961 à Austin au Texas. Il passe son adolescence à Santa Fe au Nouveau-Mexique avant de suivre un cours d'histoire de l'art à l'Université de New York. A Manhattan, Ford utilise son temps libre pour tourner dans des spots de pub et on le retrouve régulièrement au Studio 54 et à la Factory de Andy Warhol. Il finit par s'inscrire à la Parsons School of Design de New York, puis part étudier l'architecture à Paris. Ce n'est qu'une fois ses études terminées que Ford prend enfin conscience de sa vocation. En 1986, de retour à New York, il rejoint le studio de création de Cathy Hardwick, avant de partir travailler deux ans plus tard chez Perry Ellis comme directeur de la création. En 1990, Ford devient styliste pour femme chez Gucci, fabricant d'accessoires italien qui périclite depuis son âge d'or dans les années 1960. En 1994, Ford est nommé directeur de la création de Gucci et présente au mois de mars une collection qui fait date : ses pantalons taille basse en velours et ses chemises en satin aux couleurs de pierres précieuses, déboutonnées jusqu'au nombril et très près du corps, font partie d'une collection séduisante et maligne au sex-appeal sans complexe. Qu'il s'agisse des campagnes publicitaires de Mario Testino, des nouvelles boutiques à l'éclairage sobre et étudié ou même des messenger bags, tout semble taillé dans la même étoffe sensuelle. Quasiment du jour au lendemain, Gucci devient une marque indispensable en proposant la mode la plus désirable et la plus hédoniste du moment. Depuis janvier 2000, date du rachat d'Yves Saint Laurent par le Groupe Gucci, Ford dessine les collections pour homme et pour femme d'Yves Saint Laurent Rive Gauche, utilisant sa grande expertise pour révolutionner la maison avec des collections qui remportent toutes un immense succès tant critique que commercial. Tom Ford a reçu des dizaines de prix, notamment trois du prestigieux CFDA qui le consacre également Accessory Designer of the Year pour son travail chez YSL en 2002. Tom Ford est aujourd'hui directeur de la création du Groupe Gucci.

"I like to think that I brought a certain hedonism back to fashion"

PORTRAIT BY TERRY RICHARDSON

TOM FORD

PHOTOGRAPHY BY PAOLO ROVERSI, STYLING BY EDWARD ENNINFUL. APRIL 2002

PHOTOGRAPHY BY MATT JONES. STYLING BY SARAH HACKETT. JANUARY 2001. MODEL: GISELE

PHOTOGRAPHY BY KAYT JONES, STYLING BY GERIADA KEFFORD. NOVEMBER 2002. MODEL: LIBERTY ROSS

PHOTOGRAPHY BY NATHANIEL GOLDBERG, STYLING BY SORAYA DAYANI. JULY 2001

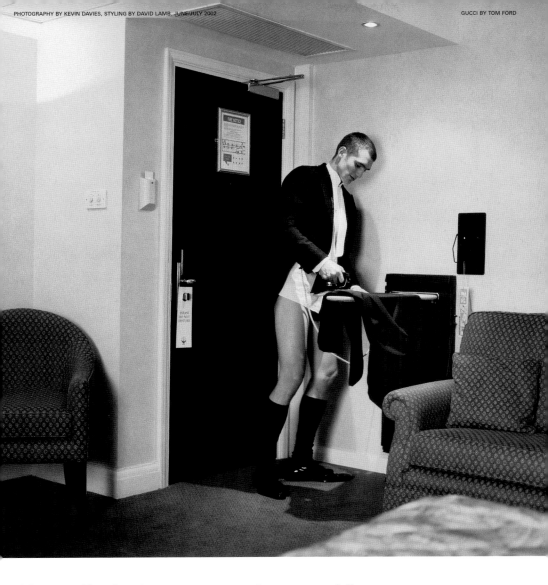

"Sensuality is always present in my work"

What are your signature designs? I like to think that in the mid '90s I brought a certain hedonism back to fashion. Sensuality is always present in my work **How would you describe your work?** Hard. I love what I do but it can be incredibly draining to constantly generate things that feel fresh and new **Who do you have in mind when you design?** A woman who's confident, intelligent and uses fashion to express different aspects of her personality. And who knows how to walk in heels **Can fashion still have a political ambition?** I don't think that clothes can start a revolution, but I do believe that fashion is often a manifestation of a sociological or political climate **What has been the greatest influence on your career?** My constant drive **How have your own experiences affected your work as a designer?** If you are a writer you write about what you know, if you are a designer you design for the world that you know. My experiences are my work **Is designing difficult for you and, if so, what drives you to continue?** No. I become bored very easily and I love change **What inspires you?** Chicks with Dicks

PHOTOGRAPHY BY STEVEN KLEIN, STYLING BY EDWARD ENNINFUL. MAY 2002. MODEL: NATALIA V

John Galliano is one of Britain's fashion heroes. Born in 1960, the son of working class émigrés, he was christened Juan Carlos Antonio. His mother is Spanish and his father from Gibraltar, the British colony where Galliano was born and grew up, leaving at the age of six for South London. But this background, with its religious ceremonies and colourful sun-drenched culture, has been a constant inspiration for Galliano; the Latin tradition of 'dressing-up' is now his signature, eclecticism is his handwriting. Having attended Wilson's Grammar School for boys, Galliano won a place at Central Saint Martins, graduating in 1984. It was that graduation collection – inspired by the French Revolution and called 'Les Incroyables' – that was bought by Joan Burstein of Browns and catapulted him into the spotlight. In 1990, after a past famous for its problems with backers and collections deemed uncommercial because they dared to dream beyond the conventional, Galliano started to show in Paris and finally moved there in 1992. Having championed the bias cut dress and the dramatic tailoring of 1950s couture whilst minimalism and grunge dominated fashion, it was announced in 1995 that Galliano would succeed Hubert de Givenchy at the fashion house that bore his name. It was the start of the English invasion of Paris and the revival of haute couture. Two seasons later and with an unprecedented four British Designer of the Year Awards under his belt, Galliano became Creative Director at Christian Dior, showing his first collection for Spring-Summer 1997 couture. Since then, Galliano has revitalised the house, both financially and creatively, and redefined the purpose of Paris couture as a theatrical bonanza. Galliano still designs and shows his own label collection in Paris, and with the mighty hand of LVMH behind him, has let loose his imagination, his creativity seemingly knowing no bounds.

Er ist eine der Ikonen des britischen Modebusiness. John Galliano wurde 1960 als Arbeiterkind geboren und auf den Namen Juan Carlos Antonio getauft. Die Mutter ist Spanierin, der Vater stammt aus Gibraltar, wo auch Galliano bis zu seinem sechsten Lebensjahr aufwuchs, bevor er mit seiner Familie ins südliche London zog. Diese Vergangenheit mit ihren religiösen Ritualen und der sonnendurchfluteten Umgebung inspirieren den Designer bis heute. Die südländisch-katholische Tradition des 'Sich-schön-Anziehens' ist nach wie vor sein Markenzeichen; seine modische Handschrift ist vom Eklektizismus geprägt. Nach dem Besuch von Wilson's Grammar School for Boys eroberte Galliano einen Studienplatz am Central Saint Martins, das er 1984 verließ. Seine Abschlusskollektion, die von der französischen Revolution inspiriert war und den Titel 'Les Incroyables' trug, katapultierte ihn ins Rampenlicht und wurde von Joan Burstein aus dem Hause Browns gekauft. Die nächsten Jahre waren überschattet von Problemen mit Geldgebern und Kollektionen, die als unkommerziell abgetan wurden, weil sie es wagten, mit Konventionen zu brechen. 1990 begann Galliano dann, seine Entwürfe in Paris zu präsentieren, wohin er 1992 auch seinen Wohnsitz verlegte. Nachdem er den Diagonalschnitt und die dramatische Couture der 1950er Jahre favorisiert hatte, während Minimalismus und Grunge den Ton in der Mode angaben, wurde Galliano 1995 Nachfolger von Hubert de Givenchy in dessen gleichnamigem Modehaus. Das war der Beginn der so genannten englischen Invasion in Paris und markierte das Revival der Haute Couture. Zwei Saisons später wurde Galliano als erster viermaliger Preisträger des British Designer of the Year Award Creative Director bei Christian Dior. Sein erste Kollektion dort war die Couture für Frühjahr/Sommer 1997. Seit damals hat der Designer das Modehaus revitalisiert – und zwar sowohl finanziell als auch in kreativer Hinsicht – und sogar der gesamten Pariser Couture ihren Sinn als Quelle des Theatralischen zurückgegeben. Galliano entwirft und präsentiert die Kollektionen seines eigenen Labels nach wie vor in Paris. Mit der Finanzkraft des Konzerns LVMH im Rücken scheint seine Kreativität keine Grenzen zu kennen.

John Galliano est un héros de la mode britannique. Né en 1960, ses parents, des ouvriers émigrés, le baptisent Juan Carlos Antonio. Sa mère est espagnole et son père vient de Gibraltar, colonie anglaise où Galliano naît et grandit avant de partir pour le sud de Londres à l'âge de six ans. Ces origines, avec leurs cérémonies religieuses et leur culture du soleil et de la couleur, représentent une source d'inspiration constante pour Galliano ; la tradition du « chic latin » est devenue sa signature et l'éclectisme son écriture. En sortant du lycée pour garçons Wilson's Grammar School, Galliano réussit à entrer à Central Saint Martins et en sort diplômé en 1984. Sa collection de fin d'études, inspirée de la Révolution Française et intitulée « Les Incroyables », est achetée par Joan Burstein de chez Browns, ce qui le catapulte directement sur le devant de la scène. En 1990, après de célèbres déboires avec ses financiers et des collections vouées à l'échec commercial parce qu'elles osaient défier les conventions, Galliano commence à présenter ses défilés à Paris et finit par s'y installer en 1992. Fervent défenseur des coupes asymétriques et de la haute couture théâtrale des années 1950 au sein d'une mode alors dominée par le minimalisme et le grunge, sa nomination à la succession d'Hubert de Givenchy dans la maison éponyme est annoncée en 1995. C'est le début de l'invasion anglaise à Paris et du renouveau de la haute couture. Deux saisons plus tard et fort de quatre British Designer of the Year Awards, un exploit sans précédent, Galliano devient directeur de la création chez Christian Dior et présente sa première collection aux défilés haute couture Printemps-Eté 1997. Depuis, Galliano a redonné vie à la maison Dior, tant au plan financier que créatif, tout en replaçant la haute couture parisienne à l'avant-garde de l'innovation. Galliano continue de dessiner et de présenter les collections de sa propre griffe à Paris, et grâce à la toute puissance du groupe LVMH qui le soutient, il peut enfin laisser libre cours à son imagination, avec une créativité qui ne semble pas connaître la moindre limite.

"My work is about pushing the boundaries of creation"

PORTRAIT BY SEAN ELLIS

JOHN GALLIANO

PHOTOGRAPHY BY ELLEN VON UNWERTH. STYLING BY PATTI WILSON. JUNE 2001. MODEL: LINA

HY BY ELLEN VON UNWERTH, STYLING BY CATHERINE AYME. MARCH 2002.

JOHN GALLIANO

nion has become too sophisticated, too serious.
:en up! You should enjoy it, like a good wine"

your signature designs? The bias cut **What's your favourite piece from any of your collections?** It would be like choosing which ldren you like best **How would you describe your work?** It is about femininity and romance, about pushing the boundaries of is a constant search for new creative solutions **What's your ultimate goal?** To live life to the fullest, to hold on to every minute as if last **Who do you have in mind when you design?** In the course of my career I have discovered that having a specific muse (either figure or a living person) can be inhibiting rather than inspiring. Now I would say that I think of a more abstract notion of a modern , someone who is assertive and controls her own destiny **Who or what has been the greatest influence on your career?** My mother ndmother and their love of life and their sense of occasion for dress have been the first and lasting influence on me. When I lived in go to school in Spain I had to go through Tangiers. The souks, the markets, the fabrics, the carpets, the smells, the herbs, the ean colour is where my love of textiles comes from. Later, when I started my studies at Saint Martins, I was greatly influenced by the achers I had and by the theatre **Is designing difficult for you and, if so, what drives you to continue?** I have always seen work as hallenge. I love what I am doing, I love the very act of creating. Even in my darkest moments I would continue working – I have no n and now, it was all I could and can do **Have you ever been influenced or moved by the reaction to your designs?** A few weeks showing of the Autumn-Winter 2002 collection, I received a letter with some drawings from a ten-year-old boy. It turns out that he e Dior show on TV. He did not want to go to sleep and stayed up until two in the morning drawing the clothes. His mother was first but then moved by his enthusiasm and she sent us the drawings. The drawings were so lovely I was very touched. I invited the boy show and met him afterwards. Something like this makes it all worthwhile **What's your definition of beauty?** A woman in charge destiny **What is the most important lesson you've learned?** Mr Arnault once told me: 'John, you have to learn to live with your t was a very good lesson

A certain schizophrenia seems ever present with Jean Paul Gaultier. From his tag as the 'enfant terrible' of French fashion, although he was born in 1952, to the balance of the radical and the traditional at the centre of his work – for instance his iconic corset, the most traditional of undergarments, was merely changed from innerwear to outerwear. Above all, to the seeming divide between 'Mr Gaultier' the couturier and 'Jean Paul' the media personality. In fact, it is these binary oppositions that have made Jean Paul Gaultier one of the most significant designers of the past 20 years. Despite his couture training with Pierre Cardin and Jean Patou in the early 1970s, from his first ready-to-wear collection in 1976 it was apparent that the punk-spirited Gaultier was not content to contain himself within a high fashion world. Later, his image and style spread far and wide – from being instrumental in the impact of diffusion lines with Junior Gaultier (launched 1988), to fragrances (1993), film work and the high profile collaborations with Madonna (including 1990s 'Blonde Ambition' tour), Gaultier truly brought high fashion to the masses, becoming one of the most successful independent designers. Conversely, Gaultier also brought the street onto the catwalk and combined it with an element of 'political shock', with the changing boundaries of gender, race and sexuality featuring as constant themes in his women's and menswear collections. Yet it wasn't until he embarked upon the ultra-elitist pursuit of haute couture in 1997 that Gaultier gained full recognition from the fashion establishment. It was a natural return to his roots – couture was his initial inspiration for becoming a designer. That, and his first taste of fashion notoriety, gained as a literal 'enfant terrible' aged seven, when the designer found himself in trouble for drawing a Folies-Bergère dancer in class. He liked the fishnet stockings.

Jean Paul Gaultier passt einfach in keine Schublade. So gilt er, obwohl er Jahrgang 1952 ist, nach wie vor als Enfant terrible der französischen Mode. Außerdem schafft er es, in seiner Arbeit radikal und zugleich traditionell zu sein – wie beispielsweise bei dem untrennbar mit seinem Namen verbundenen Korsett, dem traditionsreichsten Dessous überhaupt, das er einfach von einer Unter- zur Oberbekleidung machte. Und dann gibt es da natürlich noch die scheinbare Trennung zwischen Monsieur Gaultier, dem Couturier, und der Medienfigur Jean Paul. Wahrscheinlich sind es genau diese komplementären Gegensätze, die Jean Paul Gaultier zu einem der wichtigsten Designer der letzten zwanzig Jahre gemacht haben. Trotz seiner Ausbildung in der Haute Couture bei Pierre Cardin und Jean Patou in den frühen 1970er Jahren war schon an seiner ersten Prêt-à-Porter-Kollektion 1976 erkennbar, dass sich dieser von der Punkbewegung inspirierte Designer nicht auf die Welt der High Fashion beschränken würde. Etwas später sollte sich sein Image und sein Stil immens verbreiten. Sein Einfluss reichte von Nebenlinien wie Junior Gaultier (1988 eingeführt), über Düfte (ab 1993) und die Mitarbeit beim Film bis hin zur vielbeachteten Ausstattung von Madonna (unter anderem für die 'Blonde Ambition'-Tour in den Neunzigern). Auf all diesen Wegen brachte Gaultier die High Fashion einem breiten Publikum nahe und avancierte gleichzeitig zu einem der erfolgreichsten unabhängigen Designer. Umgekehrt brachte er aber auch die Straßenkultur auf den Catwalk und kombinierte sie mit gesellschaftlich schockierenden Elementen; die Infragestellung der Grenzen von Geschlecht, Rasse und Sexualität war ein immer wiederkehrendes Thema seiner Damen- und Herrenkollektionen. Dennoch wurde Gaultier vom Mode-Establishment erst mit seinem Einstieg in die ultra-elitäre Haute Couture 1997 wirklich anerkannt. Eigentlich war das die nur natürliche Rückkehr zu seinen Wurzeln – die Couture hatte ihn schließlich überhaupt erst auf den Gedanken gebracht, Designer zu werden. Das und ein erster Vorgeschmack auf die Verrufenheit der Mode, als er im Alter von sieben Jahren – damals im wahrsten Sinne des Wortes noch ein Enfant terrible – erwischt wurde, als er im Schulunterricht eine Tänzerin der Folies-Bergère zeichnete. Ihm gefielen einfach deren Netzstrümpfe.

Le travail de Jean Paul Gaultier semble toujours empreint d'une certaine schizophrénie. Surnommé «l'enfant terrible» de la mode française, bien qu'il soit né en 1952, Jean Paul Gaultier cherche à trouver un équilibre entre mode radicale et traditionnelle, par exemple avec son célèbre corset, le plus classique des sous-vêtements, qu'il a transformé en vêtement de dessus. Mais cette schizophrénie concerne avant tout la distinction évidente qui existe entre «M. Gaultier» le couturier et «Jean Paul» le chouchou des médias. En fait, ce sont ces ambivalences qui ont fait de lui l'un des créateurs les plus importants de ces 20 dernières années. Malgré une formation en haute couture chez Pierre Cardin et Jean Patou au début des années 1970, Gaultier le punk prouve dès sa première collection de prêt-à-porter en 1976 qu'il ne peut se plier aux contraintes de la mode de luxe. Plus tard, son image et son style se reconnaissent dans le monde entier : il joue un rôle essentiel dans le succès des lignes de diffusion avec Junior Gaultier (1988), il lance des parfums (1993), crée des costumes pour le cinéma et collabore même avec Madonna (notamment pour la tournée «Blonde Ambition» de 1990). En démocratisant réellement la haute couture, Gaultier est aujourd'hui l'un des créateurs indépendants les plus appréciés. Inversement, il fait monter la mode de la rue sur les podiums et l'associe à un élément de «choc politique» tandis qu'il estompe les frontières entre les sexes, les races et les sexualités, un thème fil rouge dans ses collections pour femme et pour homme. Néanmoins, ce n'est qu'en 1997, lorsqu'il se lance dans l'univers ultra-élitiste de la haute couture, que Gaultier gagne vraiment la reconnaissance de ses pairs. Cette démarche marque un retour à ses racines ; en effet, c'est pour travailler dans la haute couture qu'il a souhaité devenir créateur de mode. Cette première inspiration, associée à son goût précoce pour la notoriété, est née lorsqu'il avait sept ans, le jour où «l'enfant terrible» a dû s'expliquer pour avoir dessiné une danseuse des Folies-Bergère pendant la classe : il aimait beaucoup les bas résille.

"I didn't want to be famous"

PORTRAIT BY CHRISTIAN BADGER

JEAN PAUL GAULTIER

PHOTOGRAPHY BY DAVID LACHAPELLE, STYLING BY PATTI WILSON, SEPTEMBER 2002

PHOTOGRAPHY BY DONALD CHRISTIE, STYLING BY KARL PLEWKA. SEPTEMBER 2001

PHOTOGRAPHY BY KAYT JONES, STYLING BY GERIADA KEFFORD. DECEMBER 2002

of the provocative things I've done were not urposefully, but instead came quite naturally"

signature designs? The corset is probably the thing I am known for **What are your favourite pieces from any of your** ⟨pr⟩obably the ones that other people have liked most, because I do the collections for people to like. And through that, to like me. ⟨clo⟩thes which they love, because it makes me loved **What inspires you?** I think that to look is my biggest pleasure. I love to go out ⟨...⟩ Once I was in Ibiza, in a very, very bad club, and there was a live parrot in a cage. And I just looked at him for three hours. I ⟨abso⟩rb all the colours. And that inspired a dress in my first couture show. I had no photo, nothing but my memory. I truly love that ⟨...h⟩ave in mind when you design? Not one person, because I want to be open to difference. That would be too restrictive. I like ⟨ty⟩pes of people, different types of beauty, different types of living. I am influenced by many things at the same time **Is the idea of** ⟨collab⟩oration important to you?** I enjoy collaboration… Exactly what kind of collaboration do you mean? **What has been the greatest** ⟨...y⟩our career?** Seeing the scandal Yves Saint Laurent caused in the '70s was important, because he captured everything that I love – ⟨s⟩exual aggressiveness and even political shock. It was all the things that ever made me dream about being a part of the world of ⟨...⟩ne did definitely influenced me later and also made me realise the point in fashion: that if you are too much in advance, it appears ⟨...o⟩n **How have your own experiences affected your work as a designer?** I was quite rejected at school because, let's say, I was ⟨...⟩te. So I was always on my own, sketching. One time, when I was about seven, I saw the Folies-Bergère on TV – the feathers, the ⟨...⟩ I drew it at school the next day. The teacher, wanting to punish me, pinned it to my back and made me walk from class to class. ⟨...⟩vas smiling. So I thought, well, people like you when you do your sketches. It comforted me and gave me a lot of confidence. After ⟨...⟩t of fishnets and feathers **Is designing difficult for you and, if so, what drives you to continue?** I love fashion and I love making ⟨...to⟩ deal with problems of organisation is not exactly my cup of coffee **What's your definition of beauty?** I don't have one. You can ⟨...ev⟩erywhere **What's your philosophy?** In fashion you are supposed to hate what you have loved before. I cannot do that. And I do ⟨...⟩ that part of the industry. It's a kind of snobbery. You feel like you have to hate something to show that you are a part of the new ⟨...no⟩t embarrassed at all to welcome something that I like **What is the most important lesson you've learned?** To be yourself. I am ⟨...I⟩ suppose you'd say I have a complex that people only like me because of what I do

In 1997, aged 26 and a relative unknown, Nicolas Ghesquière was given the role of Head Designer at the Parisian house of Balenciaga. He was a year old in 1972 when Cristobal Balenciaga, the couturier described by Dior as 'the master of us all' died. It seemed the young designer had a lot to live up to. Yet, within the past five years, he has become one of the most fêted of contemporary talents. Although he had no formal training, Ghesquière actually became involved in the fashion industry at a precocious age, completing work placements at Agnès B. and Corinne Cobson while still at school in Loudon, central France. After leaving school aged 19, he became one of the assistant designers at Jean Paul Gaultier. Simultaneous to stints with Mugler, Kelian and the position of Head Designer at Trussardi, Ghesquière worked freelance for the Balenciaga licenses collections from 1995 onwards. It was there his talent was spotted for the main line. In his work, Nicolas Ghesquière frequently uses a dialogue of extremes. He displays the divide between a certain cerebral, architectural style and then expertly combines and contrasts it with an over-the-top form of ornamentation. But his collections could be seen to be playing out the perceived binary oppositions within the history of the house of Balenciaga: the differences between the past and the present, haute couture and ready-to-wear, austerity and excess. It points to his interest in absorbing the past without copying or dwelling nostalgically, and also to the idea of collective consciousness. Among other plaudits, Nicolas Ghesquière received the Vogue/VH1 Avant Garde Designer of the Year Award in 2000. In 2001, the Gucci Group purchased the house of Balenciaga; that same year Ghesquière launched bag and footwear lines. In 2002 menswear was incorporated into the label.

1997, im Alter von 26 Jahren, wurde der noch relativ unbekannte Nicolas Ghesquière zum Chefdesigner des Pariser Modehauses Balenciaga ernannt. Dabei war er erst ein Jahr alt gewesen, als der Couturier Cristobal Balenciaga, den Dior 'unser aller Meister' nannte, 1972 starb. Demnach hatte der junge Designer ziemlich großen Erwartungen gerecht zu werden. In den letzten fünf Jahren avancierte er jedoch zu einem der gefeiertsten Talente der aktuellen Modeszene. Auch wenn er keine herkömmliche Ausbildung vorzuweisen hat, kam Ghesquière zumindest schon früh mit der Modebranche in Kontakt. So jobbte er noch während seiner Schulzeit in Loudon bei Agnès B. und Corinne Cobson. Nachdem er die Schule mit 19 Jahren verlassen hatte, fing er als einer der Assistenzdesigner bei Jean Paul Gaultier an. Ab 1995 arbeitete Ghesquière an Aufträgen für Mugler, Kelian sowie in der Verantwortung eines Chefdesigners bei Trussardi als freischaffender Designer an den Lizenzkollektionen von Balenciaga mit. Hier entdeckte man sein Talent für die Hauptlinie. Nicolas Ghesquière führt oft einen Dialog der Extreme. Er zeigt bewusst die Grenzen zwischen einem gewissermaßen kopfgesteuerten architektonischen Stil und einer gekonnt damit kombinierten, kontrastierenden, übersteigerten Form von Ornamentierung. Seine Kollektionen spielen aber auch offensichtlich mit den unverkennbaren Gegensätzen in der Geschichte des Hauses Balenciaga: den Unterschieden zwischen Vergangenheit und Gegenwart, Haute Couture und Prêt-à-Porter, Nüchternheit und Überfluss. Seine Mode macht das Interesse des Designers an der Integration der Vergangenheit deutlich, allerdings ohne diese zu kopieren oder nur in Nostalgie zu schwelgen; außerdem wird seine Begeisterung für die Idee eines kollektiven Bewusstseins sichtbar. Neben anderen Auszeichnungen erhielt Ghesquière im Jahr 2000 den Vogue/VH1 Avant Garde Designer of the Year Award. 2001, als der Gucci-Konzern Balenciaga kaufte, stellte Ghesquière eine Taschen- und eine Schuhkollektion vor. Ein Jahr später wurde erstmals Herrenmode unter dem Label Balenciaga präsentiert.

En 1997, le jeune Nicolas Ghesquière de 26 ans est nommé styliste de la maison Balenciaga à Paris alors qu'il est encore relativement inconnu. Il n'a qu'un an lorsque meurt Cristobal Balenciaga en 1972, couturier décrit par Dior comme « notre maître à tous ». A l'époque, tout le monde s'accorde à dire que le jeune designer doit faire la preuve de ses compétences. En cinq ans, il s'est pourtant imposé comme l'un des talents contemporains les plus appréciés. Bien qu'il n'ait pas suivi de réelle formation, Ghesquière s'est intéressé à la mode à un âge précoce, notamment par le biais de stages chez Agnès B. et Corinne Cobson alors qu'il était encore lycéen à Loudon, dans le centre de la France. A 19 ans, une fois ses études terminées, il devient assistant-styliste chez Jean Paul Gaultier. Parallèlement à ses collaborations avec Mugler et Kelian et un poste de styliste chez Trussardi, Ghesquière travaille en free-lance pour les collections sous licence de Balenciaga dès 1995. C'est là que son talent est remarqué et pressenti pour la ligne principale. Dans son travail, Nicolas Ghesquière affectionne particulièrement le dialogue des extrêmes, combinant habilement un style cérébral et architectural à une forme d'ornementation plutôt surchargée. Néanmoins, ses collections jouent sur les contrastes qui ont forgé l'histoire de la maison Balenciaga : les différences entre passé et présent, haute couture et prêt-à-porter, austérité et excès. Elles témoignent de son goût pour le passé, qu'il intègre sans copier et sans insister sur la nostalgie, mais également d'une certaine conscience collective. Parmi d'autres distinctions, Nicolas Ghesquière a reçu en l'an 2000 le prix Avant Garde Designer of the Year décerné par Vogue et la chaîne VH1. En 2001, le groupe Gucci a racheté la maison Balenciaga ; la même année, Ghesquière a lancé des lignes de sacs et de chaussures. En 2002, il complète sa griffe d'une collection pour homme.

"I like to confuse people, throw them slightly off balance"

PORTRAIT BY DAVID SIMS

NICOLAS GHESQUIÈRE

PHOTOGRAPHY BY TERRY TSIOLIS, STYLING BY SAMIRA NASR. SEPTEMBER 2002

What are your signature designs? I can't define what I do and I don't really want to. If people interpret this or that in a certain way, it's fine. It's done for that reason – to be open **How would you describe your work?** What I do is always because of last season, not a reaction against it. I always want to find a surprising way to go, but beneath that I want to try and say the same things **What's your ultimate goal?** I've never really wanted to be famous. That, for me, is not the intention **What inspires you?** I'm an 1980s child, so it's completely natural for me to be inspired by that decade. I've always used those references. I think, in a way, you always have to use the same thing in fashion, but you must find a new way to tell it **Who do you have in mind when you design?** Any girl who puts on Balenciaga is a muse. I don't like to think of one in particular when I'm designing **How have your own experiences affected your work as a designer?** The history of the house is incredible, which means I can work with a lot of freedom. Cristobal Balenciaga discovered so many things, was so inventive, it's astonishing. I can work on something and then look back through the archives and find it already. I am very respectful of Balenciaga, but this is another time and it is my vision of what Balenciaga is now **What's your philosophy?** For me it's about evolution, not revolution **What is the most important lesson you've learned?** If you want to be happy, then keep yourself a little hidden

PHOTOGRAPHY BY MATT JONES, STYLING BY WILLIAM BAKER AND SIMONEZ. JANUARY/FEBRUARY 1998

With a creative partnership that has spanned more than 30 years, Marithé and François Girbaud's combined efforts to improve on the classic blue jean with experimental washes and softening techniques has revolutionised the denim industry. Consistently injecting innovative thinking into denim manufacture, the Girbaud brand is responsible for some of the most wildly popular jean styles in contemporary history. Marithé Bachellerie was born in Lyon in 1942 and François Girbaud in Mazamet, France in 1945. Meeting in 1960, they began to import American cowboy wear to Paris. Softening the harsh, raw denims with emery boards led them to the invention of 'stonewash' – now an industrial necessity. By 1968, they had worked together on their first collection, CA, and in 1972 opened their first retail store, Boutique, in the Les Halles area of Paris, known at that time only for its food market and honky-tonk women. Working under different licences and titles, including Compagnie des Montagnes et des Forêts and Closed, the duo continued to explore new techniques. It was not until 1986 that Marithé and François Girbaud began to design under their own name and show at Paris Fashion Week. During the 1990s the brand was as creatively adventurous as ever, slowly evolving as the Girbauds began to collaborate with large denim manufacturers and open flagship stores and franchises worldwide. Laser cut, torn and distressed, thermally fused, tattooed, branded, lycra-stretch, seamless structural overhauls: Marithé and François Girbaud continue to innovate, to design for the body, not current fashion trends. The Girbaud brand now includes denim and leather lines, shoes and accessories, sportswear and skiwear, eyewear and a US-based 'peace movement' education project to promote racial unity.

Im Laufe ihrer über dreißigjährigen Partnerschaft haben Marithé und François Girbaud mit ihren Weiterentwicklungen der klassischen Blue Jeans durch Waschexperimente und Weichmachertechniken die Jeansindustrie revolutioniert. Dank ihrer permanent innovativen Ideen zur Jeansherstellung zeichnet die Marke Girbaud für einige der wichtigsten Trends in der Geschichte der Jeansmode verantwortlich. Marithé Bachellerie wurde 1942 in Lyon geboren, François Girbaud 1945 in Mazamet. Nachdem sie sich 1960 kennen gelernt hatten, begannen die beiden, amerikanische Cowboy-Kleidung nach Paris zu importieren. Den steifen, rauen Denim schmirgelten sie zunächst mit Schleifpapier glatt, was letztlich zur Erfindung des heute in der Jeansindustrie unverzichtbaren Stonewash-Verfahrens führte. 1968 stellten sie ihre Kollektion namens CA zusammen. Vier Jahre später wurde ihr erster Laden mit dem Namen 'Boutique' in der Nähe von Les Halles in Paris eröffnet. Damals war dieses Viertel nur für seinen Markt und leichte Mädchen bekannt. Mit diversen Lizenzen und unter verschiedenen Markennamen wie Compagnie des Montagnes et des Forêts und Closed erforschte das Designerteam weitere neue Techniken. Erst 1986 begannen Marithé und François Girbaud unter eigenem Namen zu entwerfen und ihre Kreationen bei der Pariser Modewoche zu präsentieren. Während der 1990er Jahre war ihre Marke so kreativ und innovationsfreudig wie eh und je. Sie entwickelte sich kontinuierlich, während die Girbauds mit großen Jeansherstellern zu kooperieren begannen sowie weltweit Flagship Stores eröffneten sowie Franchise-Lizenzen vergaben. Mit Laser geschnitten, zerfetzt, angekokelt, tätowiert, gebrandmarkt, mit Lycra durchzogen, nahtlos – Marithé und François Girbaud forschen weiter, um körpergerecht und nicht nach gängigen Modetrends zu entwerfen. Zur Marke Girbaud gehören inzwischen Jeans- und Lederkollektionen, Schuhe und Accessoires, Sport- und Skimode, Brillen sowie 'Peace Movement', ein Jugendprojekt gegen Rassismus mit Sitz in den USA.

Partenaires dans la création depuis plus de 30 ans, Marithé et François Girbaud ont uni leurs efforts pour faire évoluer le blue-jean classique en expérimentant les délavages et les techniques d'assouplissement qui ont révolutionné cette industrie. Injectant régulièrement une bonne dose d'innovation dans la production du denim, la marque Girbaud est à l'origine de quelques styles de jeans parmi les plus vendus de l'histoire contemporaine. Marithé Bachellerie est née en 1942 à Lyon et François Girbaud en 1945 à Mazamet. Ils se rencontrent en 1960 et commencent à importer les uniformes des cow-boys américains à Paris. En assouplissant les denims rigides et bruts à l'aide de cartons d'émeri, ils inventent le « stonewash », procédé industriel aujourd'hui incontournable. Jusqu'en 1968, ils travaillent ensemble à leur première collection, CA, puis en 1972, ils ouvrent un premier point de vente baptisé Boutique dans le quartier des Halles à Paris, alors surtout réputé pour son marché et ses femmes de petite vertu. Travaillant sous différentes licences et divers noms, notamment « Compagnie des Montagnes et des Forêts » et « Closed », le duo continue d'explorer les nouvelles techniques. Il faut attendre 1986 pour que Marithé et François Girbaud commencent à dessiner sous leur propre nom et à présenter leur collection à la Semaine de la Mode de Paris. Pendant les années 1990, la marque est plus aventureuse et créative que jamais, évoluant tranquillement alors que les Girbaud se mettent à travailler avec de gros fabricants de denim et ouvrent boutiques et franchises à travers le monde entier. Le jean est déchiré et vieilli, coupé au laser, structuré sans couture par thermocollage, tatoué, griffé ou en Lycra stretch : Marithé et François Girbaud ne cessent d'innover en dessinant pour le corps, sans se soucier des tendances de la mode. La marque Girbaud inclut aujourd'hui des lignes de vêtements en jean et en cuir, des chaussures et des accessoires, du sportswear, des tenues de ski et une ligne de lunettes. Par ailleurs, les Girbaud ont lancé aux Etats-Unis un projet éducatif qui vise à promouvoir la paix et l'unité raciale.

"What we do is related to our lives – we are the John Lennon generation of rock 'n' roll"

PORTRAIT COURTESY OF MARITHÉ & FRANÇOIS GIRBAUD

MARITHÉ & FRANÇOIS GIRBAUD

What are your signature designs? In the past, it was a big revolution. I think it's very difficult now and I cannot pretend to summarise my work. For me it's reducing 40 years to one sentence. I'm not working in fashion, I'm working in garments. People will recognise that it is Girbaud **What's your favourite piece from any of your collections?** I don't have one. Because what people like, what people remember, was always something very painful for us **Can fashion still have a political ambition?** It's difficult today. Especially the people representing a revolution, what the people wear to create a movement today, we have to call them 'sir' **What do you have in mind when you design?** What we do is related to our lives – we are the John Lennon generation of rock 'n' roll **Is the idea of creative collaboration important to you?** Girbaud is a collaboration, a worldwide collection of people working from different companies, but we continue to exchange and share ideas **What has been the greatest influence on your career?** Comic books, Tintin, cartoons, cowboys. The America we imagine, not the real America. The one in the European mind **Which is more important in your work: the process or the product?** I don't define myself as a designer. I mean, I'm responsible for working with chemicals, fabrics, yarn, development, weaving… all these things, in association with the best fabric makers in the world. It's not just designing clothes. I have to work with them too **Is designing difficult for you and, if so, what drives you to continue?** Is designing painful? Yes, a bit, but I don't see designing as a job. I design to express, to make my ideas three-dimensional **Have you ever been influenced or moved by the reaction to your designs?** Yes, every time **What's your definition of beauty?** I think beauty is inside a person **What's your philosophy?** I love people. I love human beings **What is the most important lesson you've learned?** That to pretend to invent is ridiculous. We always reinvent something that's already there in nature

Best known for his interpretations of classic military designs for men and his innovative utilitarian twists on everyday garments (his self-explanatory sleeping bag jacket being a good example), Jeff Griffin's designs are as conceptual as they are functional. Born in 1967 in Petersfield, Portsmouth, he graduated from Central Saint Martins with an MA in Fashion Design in 1990. Subsequently moving to Italy to work for the Gian Marco Venturi design team, Griffin was headhunted by Little Italy Family design studio, working across an array of houses including Valentino, Ferré and Fiorucci. Eventually, in 1993, he set up his own label, Griffin Laundry (now known as Griffin). After four successful catwalk shows, Griffin decided to move away from the traditional show concept, choosing instead to produce a technological installation for the British Design Council. Later presentations have included launching his collection on the internet in 1998, followed by a joint cinematic venture with Channel Four for the showing of his collection in 1999. Collaboration is also important to Griffin: past projects include work with Sony, Mandarina Duck, Kenzo Ki and Hugo Boss, plus his long-time friend, photographer Donald Christie. February 2001 saw the opening of the Griffin concept store in West London, while in May of the same year he jointly established the Parka Rock surf and streetwear label. Jeff Griffin is now based in rural Wiltshire with his wife and children, where he has his design studio.

Am bekanntesten sind Jeff Griffins Interpretationen klassischer Militäruniformen für Männer und seine zweckmäßigen Neuerungen bei Alltagskleidung (bestes Beispiel: die für sich selbst sprechende Schlafsack-Jacke). Seine Entwürfe sind ebenso künstlerisch wie funktional. 1967 im englischen Petersfield (Portsmouth) geboren, verließ er 1990 das Central Saint Martins mit einem Abschluss in Modedesign. Danach zog er nach Italien, um für das Designteam von Gian Marco Venturi zu arbeiten. Nachdem das Designstudio Little Italy Family auf ihn aufmerksam geworden war, entwarf Griffin für eine Reihe großer Häuser wie Valentino, Ferré und Fiorucci. 1993 schließlich gründete er mit Griffin Laundry – das inzwischen nur noch Griffin heißt – sein eigenes Label. Nach vier erfolgreichen Präsentationen auf dem Catwalk entschloss sich der Designer, vom traditionellen Konzept der Modenschau abzuweichen, und produzierte stattdessen eine technisch ausgefeilte Installation für das British Design Council. 1998 zeigte er seine Kollektion im Internet und präsentierte die Modelle für das darauf folgende Jahr im Rahmen einer Koproduktion mit dem TV-Sender Channel Four. Grundsätzlich hält Griffin viel von Synergien: In der Vergangenheit arbeitete er unter anderem mit Sony, Mandarina Duck, Kenzo Ki, Hugo Boss und natürlich mit seinem langjährigen Freund, dem Fotografen Donald Christie, zusammen. Im Februar 2001 wurde Griffins Concept Store im Westen Londons eröffnet. Das Gemeinschaftslabel Parka Rock für Surf- und Streetwear entstand im Mai desselben Jahres. Heute lebt Jeff Griffin mit seiner Frau und seinen Kindern auf dem Land in Wiltshire, wo sich auch sein Atelier befindet.

Surtout connu pour son interprétation des uniformes militaires classiques pour homme et son détournement innovant et utilitaire des vêtements de tous les jours (dont la veste-sac de couchage offre un bon exemple), Jeff Griffin crée une mode tout aussi conceptuelle que fonctionnelle. Né en 1967 à Petersfield près de Portsmouth, il obtient un MA en Mode à Central Saint Martins en 1990. Il part ensuite pour l'Italie, où il travaille avec l'équipe de création de Gian Marco Venturi. Repéré par le studio de création Little Italy Family, il travaille ensuite pour de nombreuses maisons, notamment Valentino, Ferré et Fiorucci. Finalement, en 1993, il fonde sa propre griffe, Griffin Laundry (aujourd'hui rebaptisée Griffin). Après quatre présentations très remarquées, Griffin décide de s'éloigner du concept traditionnel des défilés, préférant produire une installation technologique pour le British Design Council. En 1998, il lance une collection sur Internet, suivie d'un partenariat cinéma avec Channel Four pour la présentation de sa collection en 1999. Griffin aime travailler avec les autres : parmi ses projets passés figurent des collaborations avec Sony, Mandarina Duck, Kenzo Ki et Hugo Boss, ainsi qu'avec son ami de longue date le photographe Donald Christie. En février 2001, il ouvre une boutique-concept dans le West London, tandis qu'en mai de la même année il participe à la création de la griffe surf et streetwear Parka Rock. Jeff Griffin vit actuellement avec sa femme et ses enfants à la campagne dans le Wiltshire, où il a également installé son studio de création.

"What comes through as a signature for me is this continuous fight: fashion versus anti-fashion"

PORTRAIT BY SOPHIE DELAPORTE

JEFF GRIFFIN

What are your signature designs? What comes through as a signature is this continuous fight: fashion versus anti-fashion **How would you describe your work?** We're a small company with a lot of ideas, still in love with what we do **What's your ultimate goal?** To actually design something men can wear which doesn't fall into a stereotype. Also, to continue doing our own thing **What inspires you?** Japan: they love and recognise what Griffin does there. It also inspires because it pays me well, which means that I can travel the world and do different things **Can fashion still have a political ambition?** No, everything has become so corporation-based. I think people are too scared to upset anybody else **Who do you have in mind when you design?** The only reason I started up Griffin, which seems like a very basic concept, was because it was so difficult to find interesting menswear. There's still not really that much and it's such a fine line with menswear, from being fashion victim to being boring **Is the idea of creative collaboration important to you?** The idea of having our own company is that we can work with as many other talented people as possible. It makes life more interesting rather than just 'I am, I am, I am'. I think fashion is full of enough twats and people up their own arse **What has been the greatest influence on your career?** Japan as a country. Every season I go there, it just inspires me to keep designing. They live fashion without looking like fashion victims. And John Galliano – he's so modern. Can you imagine him doing a casualwear collection? It would be fantastic. He can think on all those levels, he's not just a couturier **How have your experiences affected your work as a designer?** Everything I do with Griffin is relating to where I am at a certain point. You're addressing what is clothing and you're thinking into it quite a lot. Each piece is a piece of art; you're being quite deep and philosophical about everything. Take the millennium – at that time I suppose we were acting like scientists in the world of clothing **Which is more important in your work: the process or the product?** The whole design process is interesting because of using different people, collaborating with different people, to actually come up with a product which is something you all believe in **Is designing difficult for you and, if so, what drives you to continue?** It's very natural for me. I think the difficult thing is working in a market which is so money-based **Have you ever been influenced or moved by the reaction to your designs?** Yes, particularly with the Griffin shop, when you see someone prepared to pay for your stuff over everyone else's stuff **What's your definition of beauty?** I can get really excited about industrial or military things. Every military garment you see just looks so correct for some reason. And the other thing is Thailand. I think Asia is just beautiful **What's your philosophy?** If the people around you are nice, you know that the company's nice. That's what we try and give: a very honest approach to what we're doing. It should be fun. I think that's what has to come across in the clothes **What is the most important lesson you've learned?** You can only really do what you enjoy and what you love, because otherwise you just don't know from your heart if it's right or wrong

PHOTOGRAPHY BY ORION BEST, STYLING BY CLAIRE DURBRIDGE. MARCH 2000

In the early 1980s, when English creativity was at the forefront of design, Katharine Hamnett emerged as one of the country's dominant fashion forces. Born in 1948, much of her childhood was spent abroad – her father was in the Royal Air Force – and both the detail of military uniforms and cultural diversity have influenced her work. Graduating from Central Saint Martins in 1970, Hamnett worked as a freelance designer before setting up her own label in 1979, working with functional fabrics like parachute silks and cotton jersey. Her work was characterised by an uncompromising precision, which in the decade of designer denim earned her jeans a loyal following. Hamnett's shops in London's Sloane Street and Brompton Cross also became well-known during the 1980s for their idiosyncratic design. She is most famous, however, for inventing the 'slogan' T-shirt – an idea as simple as it was effective. The type was large and bold so it would stand out, particularly in photographs, and it was something she wanted to be ripped off – prompting pop acts like Frankie Goes To Hollywood and Wham! to create memorable variations of their own. The slogan T-shirt highlighted Hamnett's socio-political concerns – in 1984, she attended a Downing Street reception hosted by Prime Minister Margaret Thatcher wearing a T-shirt that read '58% DON'T WANT PERSHING'. She has since worked with organic cotton and highlighted the side effects of processes such as bleaching. Despite changes in trends and business practices, Hamnett still practises what she preaches; successfully selling around the world, particularly in Japan.

In den frühen 1980er Jahren galt englische Kreativität als Speerspitze der Designermode, und Katharine Hamnett erwies sich als eine der dominantesten Kräfte in der Mode- branche ihres Heimatlandes. Die 1948 geborene Designerin, deren Vater bei der Royal Air Force war, verbrachte aus eben diesem Grund einen Großteil ihrer Kindheit im Ausland. Sowohl die Details von Armeeuniformen als auch multikulturelle Impressionen haben ihre Arbeit geprägt. Das Central Saint Martins schloss sie 1970 ab. Danach arbeitete Ham- nett zunächst als freischaffende Designerin, bevor sie 1979 ihr eigenes Label gründete. Sie verwendete oft funktionale Materialien wie Fallschirmseide und Baumwolljersey. Ihre Kreationen zeichneten sich durch kompromisslose Präzision aus, was ihr im Jahrzehnt der Designerjeans eine treue Anhängerschaft bescherte. Die beiden Londoner Hamnett- Shops in der Sloane Street und am Brompton Cross waren in den 1980ern auch für ihre unverwechselbaren Entwürfe bekannt. Am berühmtesten ist die britische Designerin jedoch für ihre Erfindung des 'Slogan'-T-Shirts – eine ebenso simple wie geniale Idee. Die Schriftzüge waren groß und fett gedruckt, so dass sie deutlich ins Auge fielen, vor allem auf Fotos. Außerdem waren diese T-Shirts mit einer Message etwas, das die Modeschöpferin gern kopiert haben wollte – so brachte sie Popbands wie Frankie Goes To Hollywood und Wham! dazu, eigene, denkwürdige Variationen zu kreieren. Die T-Shirts unterstrichen Hamnetts gesellschaftspolitisches Engagement. So trug die Designerin etwa bei einem Empfang der damaligen Premierministerin Margaret Thatcher 1984 in der Downing Street ein T-Shirt mit dem Schriftzug '58% DON'T WANT PERSHING'. Hamnett verarbeitet auch schon seit langem Öko-Baumwolle und weist immer wieder auf die Umweltbelastung bei Verfahren wie dem Bleichen hin. Allen wechselnden Mode- trends und Geschäftspraktiken zum Trotz beherzigt Hamnett nach wie vor selbst, wovon sie überzeugt ist. Ihre Mode verkauft sich weltweit – besonders in Japan – mit großem Erfolg.

Au début des années 1980, alors que les Anglais occupent l'avant-garde de la création, Katharine Hamnett s'impose comme un acteur incontournable de la mode britannique. Née en 1948, elle passe la majeure partie de son enfance à l'étranger, suivant un père qui travaille dans la Royal Air Force. Les détails des uniformes militaires et la diversité des cultures de son enfance ont largement influencé son travail. Diplômée de Central Saint Martins en 1970, Katharine Hamnett travaille comme styliste free-lance avant de créer sa propre griffe en 1979, utilisant des tissus utilitaires tels que les soies de parachute et le jersey de coton. Son travail se distingue alors par une précision intransigeante qui, à l'époque des jeans de créateur, attire une clientèle fidèle vers ses pièces en denim. Dans les années 1980, ses boutiques de Sloane Street et Brompton Cross à Londres sont très courues pour leur design si particulier, mais Katharine Hamnett est surtout connue comme l'inventrice du T-shirt « slogan », une idée aussi simple qu'efficace. Elle utilise une typographie large et audacieuse qui ressort particulièrement bien sur les photos, une idée qu'elle espère se faire piquer : les plus grandes stars de la pop comme Frankie Goes To Hollywood et Wham! s'en inspirent et créent des variations mémorables de leur propre cru. Le T-shirt slogan lui permet d'exprimer ses opinions socio-politiques : en 1984, invitée à Downing Street pour une réception donnée par le Premier Ministre Margaret Thatcher, elle arbore un T-shirt qui proclame « 58% DON'T WANT PERSHING ». Depuis, elle a travaillé le coton biologique et mis en valeur les effets inattendus de divers procédés tels que le blanchiment. Malgré les changements de tendances et de méthodes commerciales, Katharine Hamnett met toujours en pratique ce qu'elle prêche, vendant avec succès dans le monde entier et plus particulièrement au Japon.

"You can make political statements about society by the clothes that you wear. It's something I've kept going on about for the last 20 years"

PORTRAIT BY HAMISH BROWN

KATHARINE HAMNETT

What are your signature designs? I really have no idea. You ask any creative about their past work and they're simply not interested. They're only concerned with what they're doing now. I just try and make clothes that I feel are right for the moment. When they work they become a signature, but I like to play with everything from the utterly simple to the incredibly complicated to the totally modern **What's your favourite piece from any of your collections?** I like some of the things that I was doing in the '80s. I love the slogan T-shirts, though they were getting attention that I just thought was excessive and obscene. But I thought it was wonderful that they were worn and copied **How would you describe your work?** It's just a service – I really hate that ego thing. You try to make something that will fit everybody and, if they feel good, then you give them a good time **What's your ultimate goal?** The hope of making clothing that is environmentally friendly. And using fair labour and making a success of it. It's something I've kept going on about for the last 20 years **What inspires you?** Living, I guess **Can fashion still have a political ambition?** Why not? You can make a political statement about your views on society by the clothes that you wear. I think trading is important too, because some countries increase their work by how well they trade and clothing is something that we all need **Who do you have in mind when you design?** Only myself, my friends and the people I love **Is the idea of creative collaboration important to you?** The experience of working in a good team is a bit like working in an orchestra: mind-blowing. I tend to be a bit of a loner, though **What has been the greatest influence on your career?** My father was in the air force and he got posted everywhere, so it's probably travel. Just being in different cultures. Being in some very formal situation where you didn't know what clothes you could wear for dinner and what was appropriate **Which is more important in the work: the process or the product?** The product, because that's what it is all about. The process is just a path that you take to get the end result. A really good garment is one that just comes alive, as if it's magical. It's really quite beautiful and it makes me feel humble **Is designing difficult for you and, if so, what drives you to continue?** No, it's really easy. It's like a unique entertainment; it gives me pleasure and I love it. It's a kind of escapism too **Have you ever been influenced or moved by the reaction to your designs?** I really loved it when people liked those T-shirts, as I didn't think I'd even sell one. I was totally thrilled by that reaction **What's your definition of beauty?** Beauty is everywhere, you just have to find it. It could be some manifestation of a crumpled piece of paper or the way the mud's dried on a landscape. It's quite universal and it's not just objects **What's your philosophy?** If you look back on this life, the only things that make you happy is when you've helped other people **What is the most important lesson you've learned?** You have to follow what's really close to your heart

Whether Bless counts as a fashion label at all is a moot point. Preferring to describe their venture as 'a project that presents ideal and artistic values to the public via products,' Desirée Heiss (born 1971) and Ines Kaag (born 1970) formed Bless in 1995, positioning themselves as a collaborative experiment in fashion. The business is split between two European capitals: Heiss, who graduated from the University of Applied Arts in Vienna in 1994, is based in Paris, while Kaag, who graduated from the University of Arts and Design in Hanover in 1995, is based in Berlin. The two met by chance when their work was shown adjacently at a Paris design competition. The Bless modus operandi is to re-invent existing objects to produce new garments and accessories, which are released quarterly in limited editions and available through subscription. Their work has included fur wigs for Martin Margiela's Autumn-Winter '97 collection, customisable trainers for Jean Colonna, and the creation of 'Human-Interior-Wear' for Levi's. While these all function as wearable garments, many of their products cross entirely into the realm of art. 'Embroidered Flowers', for instance, is a series of photographic prints, while their 'Hairbrush Beauty-Product' (a brush with human hair for bristles) is closer to the work of Joseph Beuys or Marcel Duchamp than any fashion designer. Consequently, when the 'Bless Shop' goes on tour, it visits Europe's alternative galleries, rather than department stores. Heiss and Kaag's success is in providing a unique comment on fashion that you can also (usually) wear.

Die Frage, ob Bless ein Modelabel im eigentlichen Sinne darstellt, ist rein akademischer Natur. Desirée Heiss, Jahrgang 1971, und Ines Kaag, Jahrgang 1970, nennen ihr Unternehmen lieber 'ein Projekt, das der Öffentlichkeit ideelle und künstlerische Werte mittels diverser Produkte präsentiert'. Gegründet wurde Bless 1995 als eine Art gemeinsames Modeexperiment mit Sitz in zwei europäischen Hauptstädten: Heiss, die bis 1994 an der Wiener Universität für angewandte Kunst studiert hat, arbeitet in Paris, Kaag, die bis 1995 die Fachhochschule für Kunst und Design Hannover besucht hat, ist von Berlin aus tätig. Kennen gelernt haben sich die beiden zufällig, als ihre Arbeiten bei einem Design-Wettbewerb in Paris nebeneinander ausgestellt wurden. Das Konzept von Bless besteht darin, bereits existierende Produkte – seien es Kleidungsstücke oder Accessoires – neu zu erfinden. Die Kreationen werden vierteljährlich in limitierten Auflagen vornehmlich an Abonnenten ausgeliefert. Zu den Arbeiten der beiden Designerinnen gehören unter anderem die Pelzperücken für Martin Margielas Herbst-/Winter-Kollektion 1997, 'Customisable Trainers' für Jean Colonna und eine Kreation namens 'Human-Interior-Wear' für Levi's. Die genannten Stücke lassen sich alle tragen, doch zahlreiche andere Bless-Produkte sind reine Kunstobjekte. So etwa die Fotoserie 'Embroidered Flowers'. Mit dem 'Hairbrush Beauty-Product' (einer Bürste mit Borsten aus Menschenhaar) nähern sich Heiss und Kaag zweifellos stärker als jeder andere Modedesigner an die Arbeiten von Joseph Beuys oder Marcel Duchamp an. Da erscheint es nur logisch, dass der 'Bless Shop' mit seinen Ausstellungen statt in großen Kaufhäusern in den alternativen Galerien Europas Station macht. Der Erfolg des Designerduos besteht wohl darin, einzigartige Kommentare zum Thema Mode abzugeben, die man – zumindest in den meisten Fällen – sogar anziehen kann.

Peut-on vraiment considérer Bless comme une marque de mode? Desirée Heiss (née en 1971) et Ines Kaag (née en 1970) décrivent plutôt leur association comme «un projet présentant au public des valeurs idéales et artistiques par le biais de produits». Elles créent Bless en 1995 dans l'optique d'une collaboration expérimentale autour de la mode. Leur activité se divise entre deux capitales européennes: Desirée Heiss, diplômée de l'Université des Arts Appliqués de Vienne en 1994, travaille à Paris, tandis qu'Ines Kaag, diplômée de l'Université des Arts et du Design de Hanovre en 1995, est installée à Berlin. Elles se sont rencontrées par hasard à Paris lors d'un concours de design où leurs travaux respectifs étaient présentés côte à côte. Le modus operandi de Bless consiste à ré-inventer les objets existants pour produire de nouveaux vêtements et accessoires, commercialisés chaque trimestre en édition limitée et uniquement par abonnement. Entre autres, elles ont créé des perruques en fourrure pour la collection Automne-Hiver 1997 de Martin Margiela, des survêtements personnalisables pour Jean Colonna et travaillé sur un concept de «Human-Interior-Wear» pour Levi's. Bien que toutes ces pièces soient portables, la plupart de leurs produits s'apparentent entièrement au domaine de l'art. Par exemple, «Embroidered Flowers» est une série d'impressions photographiques, tandis que leur «Hairbrush Beauty-Product» (une brosse en cheveux humains) relève davantage du travail de Joseph Beuys ou de Marcel Duchamp que de la pure création de mode. Quand le «Bless Shop» part en tournée, il préfère donc faire étape dans les galeries d'art alternatives d'Europe plutôt que dans les grands magasins. Le succès de Desirée Heiss et d'Ines Kaag repose avant tout sur leur approche unique d'une mode qu'on peut aussi porter, la plupart du temps.

"We need to design to fill existing gaps: who would do what we do, if we wouldn't do it?"

PORTRAIT BY DESIRÉE HEISS

DESIRÉE HEISS & INES KAAG

What are your signature designs? Always the newest. But the most famous are still: No 00 Furwig, No 06 Customisable Footwear, No 07 Living Room Conquerors, No 12 Bedsheets/Adidas Sneakers/Materialmix Jewellery **How would you describe your work?** Design (reflections) in a general sense. This can touch fashion, accessories, industrial fields, art, photography, food… anything **What's your ultimate goal?** To establish a company that gives us the freedom to evolve in whatever direction, without limits. A company that stands for a quality product or service, in whatever way they appear. To change prefixed definitions of all kind of things and to refresh ways of thinking in disturbing the usual way slightly **What inspires you?** We don't like the word inspired. We act upon needs, either personal ones that come along and need to be satisfied, or other people's and/or institutional ones that come to us and want to be served **Can fashion still have a political ambition?** Can anything ever have no political ambition? **Is the idea of creative collaboration important to you?** We love to mix our view with other ones. We don't like to see only us, our thoughts, designs **What has been the greatest influence on your career?** Many people on the way and lucky coincidences **How have your own experiences affected your work as designers?** Sport is important to calm the mind **Which is more important in your work: the process or the product?** If the product is able to transmit the message we want to give, the product. If not, the process **Is designing difficult for you and, if so, what drives you to continue?** Sometimes it is, sometimes not. We need to do it to fill existing gaps: who would do what we do, if we wouldn't do it? **Have you ever been influenced or moved by the reaction to your designs?** First of all, our products have to fulfil our vision/their mission, but then yes, very much so. We want to provide a good service. If people like it, there is no better reason to continue **What's your definition of beauty?** Everything that is very, very close or very, very far away is beautiful **What's your philosophy?** To be open for whatever might come along **What is the most important lesson you've learned?** To be patient

PHOTOGRAPHY BY MICHEL MOMY, STYLING BY KANAKO B KOGA. MAY 2000

Of Romanian and Polish origin, Alexandre Herchcovitch was born in São Paulo, Brazil in 1971. He attended the local Jewish Orthodox school and by the age of 10 had already decided he wanted to be a fashion designer, making his own clothes and often dressing up his mother when she went out. After graduating from the city's Santa Marcelina College for the Arts, he presented his first ready-to-wear collection in 1993. Herchcovitch is Brazil's most important and internationally recognised designer, celebrated for his distinctly original approach to fashion. He is politically as well as aesthetically inspired, and treats his work as wearable art, concentrating on creating unusual and experimental men's and women's wear. Shapes are directional and inventive – in autumn 1996, he produced a woollen pair of 'Skousers', a tailor-made skirt constructed with legs – but his references are often prompted by Brazilian history and religious folklore. Herchcovitch's complex collections display an appreciation of an elegant form infused with the narrative of his country. He first showed outside of Brazil in February 1999 at London Fashion Week and now exhibits in Paris. Herchcovitch has two gallery-style stores in São Paulo and, as well as selling his own label to shops around the world, works as the head fashion consultant for Zoomp, an enormous high street chain with hundreds of outlets across Brazil.

Der Designer rumänisch-polnischer Abstammung wurde 1971 in São Paulo geboren. Er besuchte die dortige jüdisch-orthodoxe Schule und fasste schon mit zehn Jahren den Entschluss, Modedesigner zu werden. Bereits damals entwarf er seine eigenen Kleider und beriet seine Mutter, wenn sie ausging. Nach Abschluss der örtlichen Kunsthochschule, Santa Marcelina College for the Arts, präsentierte Herchcovitch 1993 seine erste Prêt-à-Porter-Kollektion. Heute ist er Brasiliens wichtigster international bekannter Designer und berühmt für seinen absolut originellen Zugang zur Mode. Politisch und künstlerisch interessiert, betrachtet er seine Arbeit als tragbare Kunst und konzentriert sich vornehmlich auf außergewöhnliche und experimentelle Kreationen für Frauen wie für Männer. Seine Schnitte sind klar und erfindungsreich – so entwarf er etwa für Herbst 1996 einen wollenen Hosenrock, 'Skousers' –, ihre Wurzeln haben diese Kleidungsstücke aber oft in der brasilianischen Geschichte und der volkstümlichen Religiosität. Herchcovitchs komplexe Kollektionen zeigen seine Vorliebe für elegante Silhouetten und sind zugleich geprägt vom historischen Vermächtnis seines Heimatlandes. Seine erste Modenschau außerhalb Brasiliens fand im Februar 1999 im Rahmen der London Fashion Week statt; heute präsentiert er in Paris. Herchcovitch betreibt zwei galerieähnliche Läden in São Paulo, vertreibt seine Kreationen aber zusätzlich über Geschäfte in aller Welt. Außerdem ist er der wichtigste Consultant in Sachen Mode bei Zoomp, einer gehobenen brasilianischen Textilkette mit Hunderten von Outlets im ganzen Land.

D'origine roumaine et polonaise, Alexandre Herchcovitch est né en 1971 à São Paulo au Brésil. A l'âge de 10 ans, alors qu'il est inscrit à l'école juive orthodoxe de son quartier, il sait déjà qu'il deviendra créateur de mode. En effet, il crée ses propres vêtements et habille souvent sa mère pour ses soirées. Une fois diplômé du Santa Marcelina College for the Arts de la ville, il présente sa première collection de prêt-à-porter en 1993. Célébré pour son approche unique et originale de la mode, Herchcovitch est le designer brésilien le plus important et le plus reconnu sur la scène internationale. Inspiré tant par la politique que l'esthétique, il considère son travail comme de « l'art à porter » et se spécialise dans la création de vêtements inhabituels et expérimentaux pour homme et pour femme. Ses formes sont directionnelles et inventives : à l'automne 1996, il invente le « Skousers », sorte de jupe en laine avec des jambes coupée sur mesure ; toutefois, ses références sont plus souvent issues de l'histoire et du folklore religieux du Brésil. Les collections complexes d'Herchcovitch témoignent de sa prédilection pour une forme d'élégance marquée par l'art de la narration propre à son pays. Son premier défilé à l'extérieur du Brésil a lieu en février 1999 lors de la London Fashion Week ; depuis, il présente également ses collections à Paris. Herchcovitch possède deux boutiques-galeries à São Paulo et, outre la vente de sa propre griffe aux boutiques du monde entier, il travaille en tant que consultant principal pour Zoomp, énorme chaîne de magasins de vêtements qui compte des centaines de points de vente à travers le Brésil.

"Beauty is something that challenges the imagination"

PORTRAIT BY LUKE THOMAS

ALEXANDRE HERCHCOVITCH

What are your signature designs? The way I work with contrasts of shape, texture, fabric, weight and colour **What are your favourite pieces from any of your collections?** A dress with a tail that turns into a jumpsuit with an apron (Autumn-Winter 1998); patchwork dresses with aluminium chains inserted (Spring-Summer 2002); a T-shirt with a 'Pomba-Gira' (an Afro-Brazilian goddess from Umbanda, she's a bit of a devil-woman) print (Spring-Summer 1995); unisex skirt with the legs of trousers attached, later called 'skousers' (Autumn-Winter 1996) **How would you describe your work?** A formal research on clothes-making, and a way to express my emotions and thoughts and criticise society from a very personal point of view **What's your ultimate goal?** To achieve full creative freedom, with money enough and conditions to support it **What inspires you?** My own daily life, my own work and the people on the streets **Can fashion still have a political ambition?** It must, especially at times when it seems to move away from politics **Who do you have in mind when you design?** It's a bit of a mess. I'm too emotional sometimes, but I rationally think about shape and how to make what I'm designing **Who has been the greatest influence on your career?** When I was a teenager, Boy George was a great influence to me, and I think that his attitude towards fashion and sexuality drove me to the vision I have of fashion **How have your own experiences affected your work as a designer?** A lot, especially the ones of my adolescence: studying in a Jewish Orthodox school, being a fan of Boy George, the support my mother gave to me when I decided to be a designer etc **Is designing difficult for you and, if so, what drives you to continue?** No, designing is not difficult for me. But it is difficult to run my company and pay the bills. Sometimes that makes me want to quit **Have you ever been influenced or moved by the reaction to your designs?** When I run out of money, maybe. But usually not at all **What's your definition of beauty?** Something that challenges the imagination of the viewer **What's your philosophy?** Fashion is a language that people use to communicate with and hide from each other **What is the most important lesson you've learned?** That I must carry on with my own beliefs, always

PHOTOGRAPHY BY KENT BAKER, STYLING BY MARK ANTHONY. JANUARY/FEBRUARY 2000

With its striking red, white and blue logo – an encapsulation of the American spirit – the Tommy Hilfiger brand was pre-eminent in reviving, and sustaining, the perennial Ivy League look of chinos and Oxford shirts in the early 1990s: a style which crossed over from the Hampton set to the homeboys of Brooklyn. One of nine children, Hilfiger was born in 1951 in the backwaters of Elmira, near New York. His retail career began in 1969 with, the story goes, two friends, $150 and 20 pairs of bell-bottomed jeans. He quickly opened his first store, called People's Palace, in upstate New York, and unable to find the clothes his customers said they wanted, began to design them himself. Being self-taught did not prove a hindrance. Other Hilfiger labels came and went, among them Click Point, an architectural womenswear line in the Japanese tradition. A decade later, he moved to New York City to set up shop as a fashion designer under his own name, introducing his first collection in 1984. It was announced with a bold ad campaign that stated, bluntly, that here was a new leader in men's fashion. It proved right, not least because in 1995 Hilfiger was the CFDA's Menswear Designer of the Year. By 1992 Hilfiger (the name hails from Bavaria) and his partners had taken the company public; by 1998 it had reacquired the licences for its womenswear and jeanswear businesses, while in 2000 it opened its first flagship store. The company is now established as one of the leading, and most diverse, global American clothing brands, encompassing everything from jeans to shoes, sunglasses to handbags, scents to bath products, golf to swimwear, clothes for babies and home furnishings for their parents.

Mit ihrem auffallenden Logo in Rot, Weiß und Blau – der farblichen Quintessenz des American Spirit – war die Marke Tommy Hilfiger in den frühen 1990er Jahren führend an der Wiederbelebung und Pflege des zeitlosen Ivy-League-Looks mit seinen Chinos und Oxford-Hemden beteiligt. Dieser Stil verband die bessere Gesellschaft der Hamptons mit den Kids aus Brooklyn. Als eines von neun Geschwistern wurde Hilfiger 1951 in der tiefsten Provinz, genauer gesagt, in Elmira nahe New York, geboren. Seine Verkaufskarriere begann der Legende nach mit zwei Freunden, 150 Dollar und zwanzig Jeans mit Schlag. Bald eröffnete Hilfiger seinen ersten Laden namens People's Palace in der New Yorker Provinz. Weil es ihm nicht gelang, die Kleidungsstücke aufzutreiben, die seine Kunden wollten, begann er, selbst zu entwerfen. Dabei ließ er sich von der Tatsache, dass er in Sachen Mode Autodidakt war, nicht im geringsten beeindrucken. Weitere Hilfiger-Labels kamen und gingen, darunter Click Point, eine geometrische Damenmodelinie im japanischen Stil. Zehn Jahre später zog der ehrgeizige Geschäftsmann nach New York City, um dort unter seinem eigenen Namen zu eröffnen. 1984 stellte er schließlich seine erste Kollektion vor. Die wurde mit einer großangelegten Werbekampagne angekündigt, die unverblümt behauptete, hier käme eine neue führende Marke in der Herrenmode. Das stellte sich als richtig heraus, und zwar schon vor 1995, als Hilfiger vom CFDA zum Menswear Designer of the Year gekürt wurde. 1992 hatte Hilfiger (dessen Namen übrigens ursprünglich aus Bayern stammt) zusammen mit seinen Partnern das Unternehmen an die Börse gebracht. Die Lizenzen für Damenmode und Jeans kaufte man 1998 zurück und eröffnete im Jahr 2000 den ersten Flagship Store. Heute hat sich Hilfiger als einer der führenden und vielseitigsten global vertretenen Textilhersteller der USA etabliert. Man produziert fast alles, von Jeans über Schuhe, Sonnenbrillen, Handtaschen, Düfte und Badeartikel, Golf- und Bademode, Kinderkleidung bis hin zu Heimtextilien.

Avec son logo rouge, blanc et bleu très accrocheur qui capture tout l'esprit de l'Amérique, la marque Tommy Hilfiger joue un rôle prédominant au début des années 1990 en rajeunissant et pérennisant l'éternel style Ivy League des khakis et des chemises Oxford: un look qui a depuis traversé les frontières de Hampton pour devenir l'uniforme des homeboys de Brooklyn. Hilfiger est né en 1951 à Elmira, un trou perdu des environs de New York, dans une famille de neuf enfants. La petite histoire raconte qu'il a débuté sa carrière de vendeur en 1969 avec deux amis, 150 dollars en poche et 20 paires de jeans à pattes d'éléphant. Rapidement, il ouvre une première boutique, People's Palace, dans le nord de l'Etat de New York. Incapable de trouver les vêtements que ses clients lui réclament, il décide de les créer lui-même. Sa formation d'autodidacte s'est avérée un atout. D'autres griffes Hilfiger se succèdent, parmi lesquelles Click Point, ligne féminine de vêtements architecturaux au style japonais. Dix ans plus tard, Hilfiger s'installe à New York pour ouvrir une boutique de créateur à son propre nom et présente sa première collection en 1984. L'audacieuse campagne publicitaire qui l'accompagne le présente sans complexe comme un nouveau leader de la mode pour homme. Une annonce prémonitoire, car en 1995 Hilfiger reçoit le prix de Menswear Designer of the Year du CFDA. En 1992, Hilfiger (nom d'origine bavaroise) et ses partenaires ouvrent le capital de l'entreprise; en 1998, il rachète ses licences pour femme et pour homme et ouvre la première boutique Tommy Hilfiger en l'an 2000. L'entreprise est désormais considérée comme l'une des multinationales américaines du vêtement les plus importantes et les plus diversifiées, regroupant toutes sortes de produits: jeans, chaussures, lunettes de soleil, sacs à main, parfums, produits pour le bain, tenues de golf, maillots de bain, vêtements pour bébé et mobilier, entre autres.

"I grew up wearing button-down shirts and badly-cut chinos, knowing that one day I wanted to change the way that these classics were made"

PORTRAIT COURTESY OF TOMMY HILFIGER

TOMMY HILFIGER

PHOTOGRAPHY BY MATT JONES, STYLING BY CATHY DIXON. JANUARY/FEBRUARY 2000

What are your signature designs? All-American classics with a modern twist **What are your favourite pieces from any of your collections?** My favourite pieces are my white shirts with Ithaca stripe detailing on the collars and my beige trench with tartan lining and, of course, my jeans **How would you describe your work?** Fresh, understated, easy clothes for the young at heart **What's your ultimate goal?** To live long, be happy and healthy **What inspires you?** My children and America **Can fashion still have a political ambition?** I don't think fashion should have any political ambitions **Who do you have in mind when you design?** You, me – anyone with a young attitude, a dose of confidence and a good smile **Is the idea of creative collaboration important to you?** Yes. My team is the most important asset I have – I love to work with diverse creative minds and ideas. This is what keeps me excited and inspired **What has been the greatest influence on your career?** Americana and music **How have your own experiences affected your work as a designer?** Everything I design comes from my own experiences. I grew up wearing button-down shirts and badly-cut chinos, knowing that one day I wanted to change the way that these classics were cut. My first store was inspired by the music I was listening to at the time – The Stones, T Rex – and by the fact that no-one where I grew up could find cool clothes. I started by bringing a car-load of great pieces back from Manhattan and selling them straight from the trunk of my car **Which is more important in your work: the process or the product?** The product – the processes vary so much, but if at the end of the day the process doesn't inspire a great product, what's the point? **Is designing difficult for you?** No, because it's my passion. I love designing and when you love something it doesn't seem like work **Have you ever been influenced or moved by the reaction to your designs?** I love seeing people wear my clothes – I take great pleasure when I see people wearing my clothes in ways that I had never thought of or customising pieces to make them their own **What's your definition of beauty?** Honesty – it shows all over your face **What's your philosophy?** Trust in what you believe and know to be right **What is the most important lesson you've learned?** Be true to yourself

One and one equals two, but for Dutch duo Viktor & Rolf, working together means one vision and one goal. Inseparable since they met while studying at Arnhem's fashion academy, Viktor Horsting and Rolf Snoeren (both born 1969) decided to join forces after graduating in 1992. Their first feat was winning three awards at the 1993 Hyères Festival with a collection that already betrayed their preference for sculptural, experimental clothes. Soon afterwards, they joined the ranks of Le Cri Néerlandais, a loose collective of like-minded young designers from Holland who organised two shows in Paris. Once Le Cri disbanded, Viktor & Rolf continued to make collections, although the time didn't seem right for their headstrong, conceptual designs (a 1996 collection was called 'Viktor & Rolf On Strike', decrying the lack of interest from press and buyers). They decided to clarify their stance on the industry by creating a toy-like miniature fashion show, a fake perfume bottle and accompanying ad campaign: these artefacts, presented in Amsterdam art gallery Torch in 1996, established them as upcoming upstarts with an agenda. But what really launched their career was the introduction into Parisian haute couture: from Summer 1998 on, Viktor & Rolf stunned ever-growing audiences with their highly innovative creations based on exaggerated volumes and uncommon shapes, all peppered with a sly sense of humour and a true aspiration for glamour. To everyone's surprise/delight, the duo managed to translate their spectacular couture designs into wearable yet ground-breaking prêt-à-porter pieces, showing their first ready-to-wear collection for Autumn-Winter 2000. Clinging to a love of ruffles, ribbons and perfectly-cut smokings, Viktor & Rolf have since staged five ready-to-wear shows. They continue to work and live in Amsterdam.

Eins plus eins macht eigentlich zwei, doch für das niederländische Designerduo Viktor & Rolf bedeutet ihre Zusammenarbeit die Verwirklichung *einer* Vision und *eines* Zieles. Seit der gemeinsamen Studienzeit an der Modeakademie Arnhem sind Viktor Horsting und Rolf Snoeren, beide Jahrgang 1969, unzertrennlich. Daher war es nur konsequent, dass sie sich nach Abschluss ihrer Ausbildung 1992 zusammentaten. Ihr erster Streich waren drei Auszeichnungen auf dem Festival von Hyères 1993, und zwar mit einer Kollektion, die bereits ihr Faible für skulpturale, experimentelle Kleidung verriet. Bald danach schlossen sie sich Le Cri Néerlandais an, einem lockeren Kollektiv gleich gesinnter junger Designer aus Holland, die zwei Modenschauen in Paris organisierten. Nach der Auflösung von Cri erarbeiteten Viktor & Rolf neue Kollektionen, obwohl die Zeit für ihre kopflastigen, konzeptualen Entwürfe nicht gerade günstig war. So hieß dann auch eine Kollektion von 1996 'Viktor & Rolf On Strike' – quasi als Kritik am mangelnden Interesse von Presse und Publikum. Um ihren Standpunkt noch deutlicher zu machen, kreierten die beiden eine Miniatur-Modenschau im Spielzeugformat, eine Parfumflakon-Attrappe und eine begleitende Werbekampagne. All diese Artefakte wurden 1996 in der Kunstgalerie Torch in Amsterdam präsentiert und etablierten ihre Schöpfer als aufstrebende Newcomer mit einem eigenen Programm. Doch was ihrer Karriere wirklich Schub gab, war der Zutritt zur Welt der Pariser Haute Couture: ab Sommer 1998 erstaunten Viktor & Rolf ein immer größer werdendes Publikum mit ihren höchst innovativen Kreationen, die auf extrem voluminösen, ungewöhnlichen Silhouetten basierten und allesamt versteckten Humor sowie ein echtes Streben nach Glamour ausstrahlten. Zur allgemeinen Überraschung gelang es dem Designerduo, seine spektakulären Couture-Entwürfe in tragbare, aber immer noch bahnbrechende Prêt-à-Porter-Mode zu transponieren, wie ihre erste Kollektion für Herbst/Winter 2000 bewies. Die Liebe zu Rüschen, Bändern und perfekt geschnittenen Jacken ist in den bisher fünf Prêt-à-Porter-Schauen immer unverkennbar gewesen. Viktor & Rolf leben und arbeiten übrigens nach wie vor in Amsterdam.

Un et un font deux, mais pour le duo hollandais Viktor & Rolf, la collaboration doit reposer sur une seule vision et un même objectif. Inséparables depuis leur rencontre sur les bancs de l'académie de mode d'Arnhem, Viktor Horsting et Rolf Snoeren (tous deux nés en 1969) décident de travailler ensemble après l'obtention de leurs diplômes en 1992. Ils réalisent un premier exploit en remportant trois prix au Festival de Hyères en 1993 grâce à une collection qui trahit déjà leur prédilection pour une mode sculpturale et expérimentale. Peu de temps après, ils rejoignent les rangs du Cri Néerlandais, collectif libre de jeunes designers hollandais partageant tous le même état d'esprit et qui a présenté deux défilés à Paris. Après la dissolution du Cri, Viktor & Rolf continuent à travailler sur leurs collections, bien que leurs créations têtues et conceptuelles soient un peu en avance sur leur époque (en 1996, ils baptisent l'une de leurs collections « Viktor & Rolf On Strike » pour dénoncer le manque d'intérêt de la presse et des acheteurs à leur égard). Ils décident de clarifier leur position sur le marché en créant un mini-défilé jouet, un faux flacon de parfum et une campagne publicitaire pour l'accompagner : ces artefacts, présentés dans la galerie d'art Torch d'Amsterdam en 1996, les imposent comme de nouveaux rebelles à suivre de très près. Mais c'est lorsqu'ils débarquent dans la haute couture parisienne que leur carrière décolle enfin : dès l'été 1998, Viktor & Rolf éblouissent un public sans cesse croissant grâce à des créations très innovantes qui jouent sur l'exagération des volumes et sur des formes inhabituelles, le tout saupoudré d'un humour malicieux et d'une véritable aspiration au glamour. A la surprise générale et pour le plus grand bonheur de tous, le duo parvient à traduire ses créations haute couture spectaculaires sous forme de vêtements prêt-à-porter à la fois portables et novateurs, qu'ils présentent pour la première fois aux collections Automne-Hiver 2000. Revendiquant leur amour des volants, des rubans et des vestes aux coupes irréprochables, Viktor & Rolf ont depuis présenté cinq défilés de prêt-à-porter. Aujourd'hui, ils vivent et travaillent toujours à Amsterdam.

"More important than the designs themselves is their capacity to communicate"

PORTRAIT BY ANUSCHKA BLOMMERS AND NIELS SCHUMM

VIKTOR HORSTING & ROLF SNOEREN

PHOTOGRAPHY BY DAVID LACHAPELLE, STYLING BY PATTI WILSON. MARCH 2002

PHOTOGRAPHY BY RICHARD BURBRIDGE. STYLING BY EDWARD ENNINFUL. MARCH 2001. MODEL: STELLA TENNANT

"The illusion that next time it might be perfect keeps us going"

What are your signature designs? The ones that received the most attention. More important than the designs themselves is their capacity to communicate. Our signature designs are the designs that communicate best **What is your favourite piece from any of your collections?** The Babushka collection: the 'fashion dream' miniatures **How would you describe your work?** Difficult question **What's your ultimate goal?** 'Wanna be famous, wanna be rich, wanna be a star' **What inspires you?** Fashion itself **Can fashion still have a political ambition?** Yes, fashion is a reflection of all aspects of life **Who do you have in mind when you design?** We have never designed with a specific person in mind, but always regarded our collections as autonomous: once the designs are finished, they are for whoever appreciates them. Recently however we are becoming more and more aware of the reality of the product we are creating. It was an inspiration to see our clothes worn by Tilda Swinton, who really brought them to life in a way we had imagined, but not yet seen in real life **Is the idea of creative collaboration important to you?** Collaborating is the essence of Viktor & Rolf. Working in tandem gives us an opportunity to go deeper. We have known each other for a long time and formed a very strong bond that is the basis of everything we do. Sometimes this can make it difficult to let other people in, but when they do succeed it can feel like a breath of fresh air **Who has been the greatest influence on your career?** Inez van Lamsweerde and Vinoodh Matadin: they forced us to think in a more realistic way about fashion without being ashamed of it **How have your own experiences affected your work as designers?** Our work is always very personal. We try to translate our lives into our work. If we are down, we feel it is better to turn it into creative energy than to let it beat you. That is how the 'Black Hole' collection was born, for example **Which is more important in your work: the process or the product?** The result is the only thing that counts **Is designing difficult for you and, if so, what drives you to continue?** Being a fashion designer is a challenging profession because it requires a variety of skills that go far beyond designing. Designing itself is very difficult, but the illusion that next time it might be perfect keeps us going **Have you ever been influenced or moved by the reaction to your designs?** We never take candy from strangers, however if it's enough candy from an important stranger etc **What's your definition of beauty?** Originality **What's your philosophy?** Viktor and Rolf first **What's the most important lesson you've learned?** There are others too

PHOTOGRAPHY BY CRAIG MCDEAN. STYLING BY EDWARD ENNINFUL. OCTOBER 1999. MODEL: GUINEVERE

Marc Jacobs designs must-have fashion. Yet the roots of his most cultish garments are often in classic American clothing. Familiar items borrowed from preppy uniforms, sportswear or jeanswear are transformed into brilliantly cut, luxurious fashion. This straightforward approach, with its high regard for quality, has earned him fame and a loyal following worldwide. Marc Jacobs was born in New York in 1963, entering Parsons School of Design in 1981. Jacobs was a star pupil, winning numerous student awards and selling his early hand-knit designs to New York boutique Charivari. In 1984 Jacobs formed a business partnership with Robert Duffy; the two still work together today. In 1986, Jacobs designed his first collection bearing the Marc Jacobs label. The following year, he became the youngest-ever recipient of the CFDA's New Fashion Talent Award and has since won numerous industry awards, including the Council's Women's Designer of the Year twice. In 1989 Jacobs and Duffy joined Perry Ellis, overseeing the design of the sportswear label's womenswear collections. In 1992, Jacobs famously showed a collection for Perry Ellis inspired by the downbeat dress of grunge fans, raw-edged and layered haphazardly. In autumn 1993 Marc Jacobs International was founded and the following year saw a flurry of licensing deals for the brand. In 1997, Jacobs was appointed Artistic Director of Louis Vuitton, overseeing the design of womenswear, menswear and all accessories. Jacobs has revolutionised the company's image with collections that redefine luxury, subtlety and desirability, placing Louis Vuitton alongside major fashion labels where previously it was perceived solely as a luggage brand. Parent company LVMH's share in Jacobs' own label has since allowed considerable expansion, including several new boutiques and a fantastically successful accessories collection. A secondary fashion line, the best-selling Marc by Marc Jacobs, was launched in Spring 2001, followed by fragrances for both men and women.

Marc Jacobs entwirft Mode, die man einfach haben muss. Ihren eigentlichen Ursprung haben die meisten seiner Kleider mit Kultcharakter erstaunlicherweise jedoch in amerikanischen Klassikern. So nimmt der Designer Anleihen bei bekannten Bestandteilen von Preppie-Look, Sportswear oder Jeansmode und transformiert sie zu brillant geschnittenen Luxuskreationen. Dieser geradlinige Stil mit besonderem Augenmerk auf Qualität hat Jacobs berühmt gemacht und ihm eine treue Fangemeinde in der ganzen Welt eingebracht. Geboren wurde Marc Jacobs 1963 in New York. Nachdem er 1981 sein Studium an der Parsons School of Design aufgenommen hatte, avancierte er zum Star unter seinen Kommilitonen, der zahlreiche Studentenpreise gewann und seine frühen handgestrickten Entwürfe an die New Yorker Boutique Charivari verkaufte. 1984 ging Jacobs eine Geschäftsbeziehung zu Robert Duffy ein, mit dem er bis heute zusammenarbeitet. Zwei Jahre später entwarf er seine erste eigene Kollektion, mit der er zugleich das Label Marc Jacobs begründete. Schon im darauf folgenden Jahr hieß der jüngste Preisträger aller Zeiten, der den New Fashion Talent Award des Council of Fashion Designers of America erhielt, Marc Jacobs; seither wurden ihm viele Auszeichnungen der Textilindustrie verliehen, darunter auch zweimal der Titel Women's Designer of the Year des CFDA. 1989 gingen Jacobs und Duffy zu Perry Ellis, wo sie fortan für das Design der Damenkollektion des Sportswear-Labels verantwortlich waren. Jacobs' Schau einer Kollektion für Perry Ellis von 1992, inspiriert vom depressiven Grunge-Stil mit seinen Ecken und Kanten und scheinbar willkürlich übereinander angezogenen Schichten, gilt inzwischen als legendär. Im Herbst 1993 wurde Marc Jacobs International gegründet, im darauf folgenden Jahr schloss man zahlreiche Lizenzverträge für die Marke ab. Jacobs' Ernennung zum Artistic Director von Louis Vuitton erfolgte 1997. Fortan entwarf er Damen- und Herrenmode sowie Accessoires. Mit Kollektionen, die das Verständnis von Luxus, Raffinesse und Begehrlichkeit neu definierten, gelang es dem Designer, das Image des Unternehmens zu revolutionieren. Plötzlich war die Marke Louis Vuitton, die man bislang ausschließlich als Erzeuger von Reisegepäck wahrgenommen hatte, in die Riege der großen Modelabels aufgenommen. Die Beteiligung des Mutterkonzerns LVMH an Jacobs' eigenem Label ermöglichte seither ein beträchtliches Wachstum, unter anderem einige neue Läden und eine außerordentlich erfolgreiche Accessoire-Kollektion. Eine Zweitlinie für Mode, Marc by Marc Jacobs, die ebenfalls Bestsellerqualitäten hat, wurde im Frühjahr 2001 vorgestellt. Die jüngsten Kreationen des Designers sind Düfte für Herren und Damen.

Marc Jacobs dessine des vêtements absolument «indispensables». Pourtant, ses pièces les plus cultes sont souvent inspirées par la mode américaine la plus classique. Il emprunte des éléments familiers aux uniformes universitaires, au sportswear ou au jean pour créer une mode luxueuse aux coupes magistralement exécutées. Jacobs doit sa célébrité internationale et sa clientèle fidèle à son approche directe et son grand souci de la qualité. Né en 1963 à New York, Marc Jacobs entre à la Parsons School of Design de la ville en 1981. Etudiant surdoué, il remporte de nombreux prix et vend ses premières pièces tricotées main à la boutique Charivari de New York. En 1984, Jacobs signe un partenariat commercial avec Robert Duffy, avec qui il travaille encore aujourd'hui. En 1986, il dessine sa première collection sous la griffe Marc Jacobs. L'année suivante, il devient le plus jeune lauréat du New Fashion Talent Award décerné par le CFDA qui depuis l'a également couronné Women's Designer of the Year à deux reprises. En 1989, Jacobs et Duffy rejoignent Perry Ellis pour travailler à la création des collections pour femme de la griffe sportswear. En 1992, Jacobs présente une collection Perry Ellis désormais célèbre, inspirée par les tenues relax de la jeunesse grunge, coupée brute et superposée de façon aléatoire. A l'automne 1993, il crée Marc Jacobs International et l'année suivante, la marque conclut de nombreux accords de licence. En 1997, Jacobs est nommé directeur artistique de Louis Vuitton, chez qui il supervise la création des lignes pour femme, pour homme et de tous les accessoires. Grâce à des collections qui proposent une nouvelle définition du luxe, de la subtilité et de la séduction, Jacobs révolutionne l'image de la maison et hisse Louis Vuitton aux côtés des grands de la mode alors que la marque était depuis toujours considérée comme un simple fabricant de bagages. La participation de la société-mère LVMH dans la propre griffe de Jacobs a permis à l'entreprise de connaître une expansion considérable, notamment avec l'ouverture de plusieurs boutiques et le lancement d'une collection d'accessoires au succès phénoménal. Une ligne secondaire, Marc by Marc Jacobs, est commercialisée au printemps 2001, suivie de parfums pour homme et pour femme.

"I find it easy to make things seem naughty. I quite like the idea of doing something more intelligent"

PORTRAIT BY DUC LIAO

MARC JACOBS

PHOTOGRAPHY BY GREG LOTUS, STYLING BY PATTI WILSON. JULY 2001. MODEL: ANOUCK LEPERE

PHOTOGRAPHY BY TESH, STYLING BY EDWARD ENNINFUL, OCTOBER 2002. MODEL: ANGELA LINDVALL

PHOTOGRAPHY BY ELLEN STAGG. STYLING BY KAREN LEVITT. OCTOBER 2001. MODEL: SCARLETT JOHANSSON

PHOTOGRAPHY BY WILLY VANDERPERRE, STYLING BY OLIVER RIZZO. MARCH 2002

"I do love rock 'n' roll, I do love going out, I do love partying and having a good time. When it comes to fashion I'm inspired by those things, but I try not to hold a mirror up to them and present a sort of clichéd, surface poseur version"

What's your favourite piece from any of your collections? Although there are pieces that I love, it's not only about the piece, but the piece on the right girl. What I really, truly love is the whole image **How would you describe your work?** I find it easy, perhaps too easy, to make things seem naughty or too – I hate this word – edgy. I find that all too easy. I quite like the idea of doing something more intelligent **What's your ultimate goal?** People say, 'Well, what's left? What do you want to do?' All I want to do is what I'm doing today. And I would like to be able to do it tomorrow **What inspires you?** I do love rock 'n' roll music, I do love going out, I do love partying and having a good time. When it comes to fashion I'm inspired by those things, but I try not to hold a mirror up to them and present a sort of clichéd, surface poseur version **What do you have in mind when you design?** I like to think that the clothes could have a life after the show is over. And that's important, because everything we make is some kind of fantasy; even if it's quite practical, it's still a heightened reality. But I like the believability factor in clothes, so I like to think that a person I know, or some person I don't know who has an eclectic sense of style, could actually be walking down a street in one of those looks. It's important for me to think that it's not just an exercise in runway high jinx **Is the idea of creative collaboration important to you?** I love working with people. Everybody brings something to the party **Who has been the greatest influence on your career?** I've always been very influenced by Yves Saint Laurent and the mystique of the House of Saint Laurent. That's my fashion fantasy. But I guess I'm just influenced by people who are really, really passionate about their work. That could be musicians or artists or fashion designers, whoever, just somebody being so committed, and so truly connected, always inspires me **How have your own experiences affected your work as a designer?** I can imagine there were seasons when certain designers did such a good collection they must have felt like they were 'it' for the season. But I've never felt like 'it' and I don't think I ever will. I feel very outside. I'm comfortable acting within the fashion system. But I think I'm quite separate in a way **Which is more important in your work: the process or the product?** You can't have one without the other **Is designing difficult for you and, if so, what drives you to continue?** I define design as a series of creative choices. And there are so many choices that one can make. I don't know how it is with other people, but for me it is a very painful process because I feel like there has to be integrity and meaning in the choices. And I doubt myself a lot, I don't really have a lot of self-confidence. But I really, really enjoy being a part of this process and, even though it's painful for me sometimes, there's nothing else I'd rather be doing. I guess it's a gift to feel so passionate about something. What got us to this point is doing what we believe in our hearts is right **Have you ever been influenced or moved by the reaction to your designs?** Yeah, I have. I love it when I see strangers wearing my clothes, because there is such a vast amount of choice out there, and somebody choosing the work that we've done over somebody else's is a big thing. That's really the reward **What is the most important lesson you've learned?** It has very little to do with fashion. The most important lesson I've learned is to just be present. Enjoy life today

Shortly before his tragically early death at the age of 44 in 1994, Franco Moschino discussed the future of the label which bore his name with Rossella Jardini, his right-hand woman at the company since its inception in 1983. His message was simple: she was to keep the house going and to use her position to continue to raise money for charity. Few could have expected that a label so synonymous with the charismatic irreverence of Moschino himself would thrive under any other designer, but Jardini's low-key approach and rather austere appearance belied the fact that she had been integral in Moschino's tongue-in-cheek deconstruction of the ridiculousness of fashion; a parody of a parody, as they would have it. Born in Bergamo in 1952, Jardini opened a small boutique in the early 1970s, selling avant-garde designs by the likes of Issey Miyake, before moving to work at Cadette, a womenswear line designed by the young Moschino. Jardini briefly parted company with her new best friend to design accessories for Bottega Veneta, but she was tempted back when Moschino launched his own label in 1983. The Moschino mixture of parody, trompe l'oeil effects and classic cut proved the perfect blend in the fashion-obsessed 1980s. Their cheeky slogans are perhaps the best example of how Moschino pricked the self-obsessed couture bubble. Fashionistas lapped up the chance to laugh at themselves with a 'This Is A Very Expensive Shirt' shirt, while 'Ready To Where?' summed up the herd-like vacuity of the age. Following Moschino's death, the 'court jester of high fashion' tag that the label had shared with Jean Paul Gaultier began to grate with the conceptual seriousness of the 1990s, but Jardini has succeeded in turning the company's fortunes around, aided by a recent revival in vintage Moschino and a determination never to take fashion too seriously.

Kurz vor seinem tragischen frühen Tod mit nur 44 Jahren im Jahr 1994 diskutierte Franco Moschino mit Rossella Jardini über die Zukunft der Marke, die seinen Namen trug. Jardini war seit der Gründung der Firma 1983 seine rechte Hand. Die Marschrichtung war damals klar: Sie sollte das Unternehmen fortführen und ihre Position nutzen, um weiterhin Geld für wohltätige Zwecke zu sammeln. Doch kaum jemand hätte erwartet, dass sich eine Marke, die praktisch mit der charismatischen Respektlosigkeit von Moschino selbst identisch war, unter irgendeinem anderen Designer oder einer anderen Designerin florieren könnte. Doch Jardinis Zurückhaltung und ihre eher nüchterne Erscheinung täuschten über die Tatsache hinweg, dass sie entscheidend an Moschinos klammheimlicher Demontage der Mode in all ihrer Lächerlichkeit, dieser Parodie einer Parodie, beteiligt gewesen war. Geboren wurde Rossella Jardini 1952 in Bergamo. In den frühen 1970er Jahren eröffnete sie eine kleine Boutique, in der sie Avantgarde-Mode von Issey Miyake und anderen verkaufte. Als nächstes ging sie zu Cadette, einer Damenmode-Linie, die der junge Moschino entwarf. Danach trennte sich ihr Weg und der ihres neuen besten Freundes nur noch einmal kurz, während sie Accessoires für Bottega Veneta kreierte. Als er 1983 sein eigenes Label gründete, holte Moschino sie zurück. Der Moschino-Mix aus Parodie, Trompe-l'œil-Effekten und klassischen Schnitten erwies sich als perfekt für die modebesessenen 1980er Jahre. Die frechen Slogans sind der vielleicht beste Beleg dafür, wie Moschino die große Seifenblase der von sich selbst so faszinierten Couture-Szene anpiekte. Fashion-Freaks nutzten begierig die Gelegenheit, mit einem 'This Is A Very Expensive Shirt'-Hemd über sich selbst zu lachen. 'Ready To Where?' brachte die geistige Leere der Zeit, die nur vom Herdentrieb bestimmt schien, auf den Punkt. Nach Moschinos Tod passte das Etikett 'Hofnarr der Haute Couture', das man sich mit Jean Paul Gaultier geteilt hatte, nicht zuletzt wegen der konzeptionellen Ernsthaftigkeit der 1990er Jahre nicht mehr. Rossella Jardini gelang es jedoch, das Schicksal der Firma zu wenden. Dabei kam ihr nicht zuletzt das jüngste Revival der alten Moschino-Kreationen zu Hilfe und natürlich der Grundsatz, Mode niemals zu ernst zu nehmen.

Peu de temps avant sa mort tragique à l'âge de 44 ans (1994), Franco Moschino discutait de l'avenir de sa griffe éponyme avec Rossella Jardini, son bras droit à la direction de l'entreprise depuis sa création en 1983. Son message était clair: Rossella devait faire vivre la maison et utiliser sa position pour continuer à collecter des fonds au profit d'actions caritatives. Rares étaient ceux qui croire qu'une griffe aussi intimement liée à l'irrévérence charismatique du personnage de Moschino pourrait prospérer sous l'impulsion d'un autre créateur, mais l'approche discrète et l'apparence plutôt austère de Rossella Jardini ont confirmé son importance cruciale dans la déconstruction Moschino très second degré du ridicule de la mode, sorte de parodie de parodie. Née en 1952 à Bergame, Rossella ouvre une petite boutique au début des années 1970 pour vendre les pièces de couturiers avant-gardistes tels qu'Issey Miyake, puis part travailler chez Cadette, une ligne pour femme dessinée par le jeune Moschino. Elle fausse brièvement compagnie à son nouveau meilleur ami pour créer des accessoires chez Bottega Veneta, mais revient en 1983 quand Moschino décide de lancer sa propre griffe. Le mélange de parodie, d'effets trompe-l'œil et de coupe classique qui distingue Moschino s'avère un ticket gagnant pendant les années 1980, une décennie marquée par l'obsession de la mode. Les slogans impertinents de Moschino offrent peut-être le meilleur exemple de la façon dont il parvient à crever la bulle de cette haute couture égocentrique. Les fashion victims saisissent la chance de l'autodérision en arborant une chemise proclamant «Cette chemise coûte très cher», tandis que l'accroche «Ready To Where?» résume bien la vacuité de l'époque. A la mort de Moschino, l'appellation de «bouffon de la mode» que partageait la griffe avec Jean Paul Gaultier commence à faire grincer des dents au milieu du sérieux conceptuel des années 1990. C'était compter sans Rossella Jardini, qui a réussi à rétablir l'image de l'entreprise, notamment grâce au récent retour en grâce des anciennes pièces Moschino et de sa ferme détermination à ne jamais prendre la mode trop au sérieux.

"Try to work with honesty"

ROSSELLA JARDINI

PHOTOGRAPHY BY EDDIE MONSOON, STYLING BY JUDY BLAME. NOVEMBER 1999

PHOTOGRAPHY BY DONALD CHRISTIE, STYLING BY GIANNIE COUJI. OCTOBER 2002. MODEL: LISA RATLIFFE

What are your signature designs? Formal tailleurs **How would you describe your work?** Hard work **What's your ultimate goal?** My objective is to keep the name of Franco Moschino to his high level – a thing in which I hope we've succeeded **What inspires you?** Moschino's whole company **Can fashion still have a political ambition?** It should have a strong social context, but this is far away from politics **Who do you have in mind when you design?** Franco Moschino **Is the idea of creative collaboration important to you?** It is fundamental **Who has been the greatest influence on your career?** Coco Chanel, Yves Saint Laurent and Franco Moschino **How have your own experiences affected your work as a designer?** In my case, personal experience was decisive. I was a close friend of Franco Moschino, so I was strongly influenced by a deep love which led me to follow his work **Is designing difficult for you and, if so, what drives you to continue?** It's the only thing I've ever done in my life and it's the only job I'm able to do **Have you ever been influenced or moved by the reaction to your designs?** Many times I have been shocked by critics – however I was hopefully able to interpret them in a constructive way **What's your definition of beauty?** Elegance **What's your philosophy?** Try to work with honesty **What is the most important lesson you've learned?** Humbleness

PHOTOGRAPHY BY TESH, STYLING BY EDWARD ENNINFUL. MARCH 2001. MODEL: KATE MOSS

The term 'mad hatter' could have been most endearingly coined for Stephen Jones. Born in 1957, he graduated from Central Saint Martins in 1979 with a BA in Fashion Design and was immediately commissioned to create a hat collection for Fiorucci. A year later, he opened a hat salon in London's Covent Garden which became a magnet for New Romantic club kids and 1980s pop heroes such as Visage, Culture Club and Spandau Ballet. Stephen Jones has always understood fashion's popular climate and catered accordingly. In 1984 he was the first hat designer to be drafted into Paris, where he collaborated with Comme des Garçons, Jean Paul Gaultier and Thierry Mugler. Since then he has worked with numerous designers, producing hats every season to compliment their work. He is currently best known for flamboyantly groundbreaking collaborations with his friend John Galliano, for whom he designs both haute couture and prêt-à-porter ranges for Galliano's own line as well as for Christian Dior. In 1990, the Stephen Jones empire expanded to include two diffusion collections – Miss Jones and Jonesboy – plus there are also Jonesgirl hats, scarves, sunglasses and handbags produced under licence in Japan. In addition, Jones consults for Shiseido as a colour creator. Worn by celebrities including Björk, Barbra Streisand and the Rolling Stones, his designs are playful, artistic and, above all, original. Stephen Jones's work is on display in museums worldwide, including London's Victoria & Albert Museum, the Louvre in Paris and the Fashion Institute of Technology in New York.

Die Figur des verrückten Hutmachers aus 'Alice im Wunderland' könnte auch eine liebevolle Hommage an Stephen Jones sein. Der wurde 1957 geboren und schloss 1979 das Central Saint Martins mit einem Bachelor of Arts im Fach Modedesign ab. Gleich danach erhielt er den Auftrag, eine Hutkollektion für Fiorucci zu entwerfen. Ein Jahr später eröffnete der junge Designer einen Hutsalon in Covent Garden, der sich rasch zum Anziehungspunkt für Fans von New Romantic und für Popidole der 1980er Jahre wie Visage, Culture Club und Spandau Ballet entwickelte. Stephen Jones bewies immer ein gutes Gespür für populäre Modetrends und bediente diese entsprechend. 1984 war er der erste Hutdesigner, den man nach Paris berief, wo er mit Comme des Garçons, Jean Paul Gaultier und Thierry Mugler zusammenarbeitete. Seither hat er noch für viele andere Designer Hüte entworfen und deren Kreationen damit Saison für Saison optimal zur Geltung gebracht. Gegenwärtig macht Jones vor allem durch seine auffallenden und bahnbrechenden Entwürfe für seinen Freund John Galliano von sich reden. Er designt sowohl Haute Couture als auch Prêt-à-Porter für Gallianos eigene Linie und für das Haus Christian Dior. 1990 expandierte das Stephen-Jones-Imperium mit zwei Nebenkollektionen – Miss Jones und Jonesboy. Dazu kommen noch Hüte, Schals, Sonnenbrillen und Handtaschen des Labels Jonesgirl, die in Lizenz in Japan hergestellt werden. Jones selbst arbeitet gleichzeitig auch als Colour Creator für Shiseido. Prominente wie Björk, Barbra Streisand und die Rolling Stones tragen seine verspielten, kunstvollen und vor allem originellen Hutkreationen. Arbeiten von Stephen Jones findet man aber auch weltweit in Museen, etwa im Londoner Victoria & Albert Museum, im Pariser Louvre oder im Museum des Fashion Institute of Technology in New York.

Le mot « chapelier fou » aurait pu être inventé pour Stephen Jones. Né en 1957, il sort diplômé de Central Saint Martins en 1979 avec un BA en mode. Fiorucci l'engage immédiatement pour créer une collection de chapeaux. Un an plus tard, il ouvre à Covent Garden une boutique de mode qui attire comme un aimant nouveaux clubbers romantiques et héros pop des années 1980 tels que Visage, Culture Club et Spandau Ballet. Stephen Jones a toujours su saisir le climat populaire de la mode et l'alimenter en conséquence. En 1984, il est le premier modiste appelé par Paris, où il collabore avec Comme des Garçons, Jean Paul Gaultier et Thierry Mugler. Depuis, Jones a travaillé avec de nombreux couturiers, produisant chaque saison les chapeaux qui viendront compléter leurs collections. Actuellement, il est surtout connu pour ses collaborations révolutionnaires et flamboyantes avec son ami John Galliano, pour qui il dessine des chapeaux haute couture et prêt-à-porter, que ce soit pour la propre griffe de Galliano ou pour Christian Dior. En 1990, l'empire Stephen Jones s'enrichit de deux autres collections : Miss Jones et Jonesboy, sans mentionner les chapeaux, les écharpes, les lunettes de soleil et les sacs à main Jonesgirl produits sous licence au Japon. Par ailleurs, Jones conseille Shiseido pour ses gammes de maquillage. Portées par des célébrités comme Björk, Barbra Streisand et les Rolling Stones, ses créations sont artistiques et pleines d'humour mais toujours originales. Le travail de Stephen Jones est exposé dans plusieurs musées à travers le monde, notamment au Victoria & Albert Museum de Londres, au Louvre à Paris et au Fashion Institute of Technology de New York.

"It's never just a process, never just a product: it's my life"

PORTRAIT BY PETER ASHWORTH

STEPHEN JONES

What are your signature designs? Developments of the top hat, incorporating glamour and hauteur, wit and sex **How would you describe your work?** Beyond fabulous, of course! **What's your ultimate goal?** Higher, wider, bigger and more lights on! **What inspires you?** Everything from a piece of chewing gum to the universe **Can fashion still have a political ambition?** Yes, without it fashion has no real relevance – but it can be just eye-candy too **Who do you have in mind when you design?** I try to have no-one in mind; I am very good at adapting my designs to suit an individual, but they would suit only her and no-one else **Is the idea of creative collaboration important to you?** Yes, because it is a journey into the unknown and it re-focuses my idea of beauty versus ugliness **Who has been the greatest influence on your career?** Shirley Hex who taught me how to make hats, Michael Roberts and Robert Forrest who encouraged me, and the designers with whom I have collaborated: (in chronological order) Jean Paul Gaultier, Thierry Mugler, Comme des Garçons, Claude Montana and, latterly, John Galliano **How have your own experiences affected your work as a designer?** I was extremely driven until I was made aware of AIDS in about 1982, when I was 25. This stopped me in my tracks and I realised that there was more to life than mauve chenille spotted veiling **Which is more important in your work: the process or the product?** It's never just a process, never just a product: it's my life **Is designing difficult for you and, if so, what drives you to continue?** It's the best fun in the world **Have you ever been influenced or moved by the reaction to your designs?** I remember making a hat for a fabulous client of a certain age, who wanted one of my most extravagant creations for Dior. After the final fitting, she modelled it for her husband and, wet-eyed, he applauded, repeating, 'My darling, you are so very beautiful, so beautiful, exquisite…' **What's your definition of beauty?** Purity and honesty, complexity and lies; take your pick! **What's your philosophy?** Don't look before you leap **What is the most important lesson you've learned?** I've learned nothing (fortunately!)

PHOTOGRAPHY BY BARNABY ROPER, STYLING BY DAVID LAMB. OCTOBER 2002

With her mother a showroom model, her father a tailor and even her stepfather in the business, it was almost inevitable Donna Karan would go on to study fashion at her hometown New York's Parsons School of Design. She didn't finish her course though. Offered a job while on work placement at Anne Klein, her apprenticeship as designer and businesswomen began in earnest. Indeed, in 1969 Karan was named as the successor to Klein and by 1974, following Klein's death, she was made head of the company. Her time at Anne Klein proved the foundry for Karan's signature sassy practicality: easy luxury sportswear separates, typically in navy and black shades of draped or stretch fabrics. Karan left in 1984 to launch her own label with her late husband, Stephan Weiss. Although she was just as likely to throw in a hand-painted devoré dress, the popular utility of her designs was clear from her first key 'New York' collection in 1985, focusing on her concept of 'seven easy pieces', including the wraparound skirt and – the quintessential Karan item – the black bodysuit. Certainly, while the designer has won big industry gongs (she has been named CFDA Best Womenswear Designer four times) she has rarely offered the radical. But she has pioneered a new attitude towards dressing. The Karan look is also (along with that of Michael Kors and, latterly, Marc Jacobs) the bedrock of chic celebrity-supported New York style. 'New York' even features on her labelling. The business now encompasses menswear (launched 1992), childrenswear, perfume, 'New York Home', her fast-fashion diffusion line DKNY (launched in 1989) and all the other departments of a global lifestyle brand. Donna Karan's business was publicly traded in 1996 and sold for $643m to LVMH in 2001.

Bei einer Mutter, die als Modell, und einem Vater, der als Schneider arbeitete, sowie einem Stiefvater in der Textilbranche war es fast unvermeidlich, dass Donna Karan an der Parsons School of Design in ihrer Heimatstadt New York Mode studierte. Sie beendete ihre Ausbildung dort allerdings nicht, denn während eines Aushilfsjobs bei Anne Klein bot man ihr eine Stelle an, mit der ihre Lehrzeit als Designerin und Geschäftsfrau beginnen sollte. 1969 wurde sie bereits zu Kleins Nachfolgerin ernannt, und nach dem Tod der Chefin im Jahr 1974 übernahm sie die Firmenleitung. Ihre Zeit bei Anne Klein sollte das Fundament für Karans Markenzeichen – schicke und zugleich praktische Mode – legen: leichte, luxuriöse Sportswear-Separates, typischerweise in Marinetönen oder Schwarz aus schön fallenden oder elastischen Stoffen. Karan verließ die Firma 1984, um mit ihrem inzwischen verstorbenen Ehemann Stephan Weiss ein eigenes Label zu gründen. Auch wenn die Designerin gelegentlich mit einem handbemalten Devoré-Kleid überraschte, stand die populäre Vielseitigkeit ihrer Entwürfe schon mit der ersten richtungsweisenden 'New-York'-Kollektion von 1985 fest. Sie konzentrierte sich darin auf ihr Konzept von 'sieben einfachen Stücken', zu denen unter anderem ein Wickelrock und – als wesentlicher Karan-Artikel – ein schwarzer Body gehörten. Auch wenn die Designerin eine Menge bedeutender Preise der Industrie gewonnen hat (allein viermal wurde sie vom Council of Fashion Designers of America, CFDA, als Best Womenswear Designer ausgezeichnet), mutete sie ihren Fans selten Radikales zu. Der Karan-Look ist (wie der von Michael Kors und später von Marc Jacobs propagierte) die Basis des schicken, auch von Stars gepflegten typischen New Yorker Stils. New York taucht sogar auf ihren Labels auf. Das Unternehmen produziert inzwischen Herrenmode (seit 1992), Kinderkleidung, Parfums, 'New York Home', die schnelllebige Nebenlinie DKNY (seit 1989) und ist außerdem in all den anderen Bereichen vertreten, die man heute von einer Weltmarke in Sachen Lifestyle erwartet. 1996 ging Donna Karan an die Börse und wurde 2001 für 643 Millionen Dollar an den Konzern LVHM verkauft.

Entre une mère mannequin-cabine, un père tailleur et un beau-père travaillant dans le milieu de la mode, il n'est pas surprenant que Donna Karan décide d'étudier la mode à la Parsons School of Design de New York. Elle ne terminera pas son cursus: alors qu'elle est en stage chez Anne Klein, l'entreprise lui propose un poste qui lui permet d'entamer très sérieusement sa formation de styliste et de femme d'affaires. En 1969, Donna Karan est nommée à la succession d'Anne Klein puis, à la mort de cette dernière en 1974, elle reprend la direction de l'entreprise. C'est au cours de son expérience chez Anne Klein qu'elle a développé ce sens pratique si caractéristique de son travail: séparés sportswear luxueux et faciles à porter, généralement taillés dans des tissus drapés ou stretch aux nuances bleu marine et noires. Donna Karan quitte l'entreprise en 1984 pour lancer sa propre griffe avec Stephan Weiss, son mari aujourd'hui décédé. Bien qu'elle soit capable d'agrémenter ses collections de pièces très complexes, l'aspect utilitaire de ses créations transparaît de façon évidente dès son premier défilé de 1985, « New York », qui présente son concept des « seven easy pieces », avec la jupe portefeuille et, modèle Karan par excellence, le bodysuit noir. Elle a déjà remporté les plus hautes distinctions de l'industrie de la mode (elle a été consacrée quatre fois Best Womenswear Designer par la CFDA), bien qu'elle ait rarement flirté avec le radical. Pourtant, Donna Karan a proposé une nouvelle approche de l'habillement. Le look Karan est devenu le style new-yorkais de base que soutiennent les stars (comme c'est le cas de Michael Kors et plus récemment de Marc Jacobs). D'ailleurs, le mot « New York » apparaît sur toutes ses étiquettes. L'activité regroupe aujourd'hui une ligne pour homme (lancée en 1992), une ligne pour enfant, un parfum, « New York Home », sa ligne de grande consommation DKNY (lancée en 1989) et tous les autres départements dignes d'une vraie marque mondiale de lifestyle. L'entreprise Donna Karan a été introduite en bourse en 1996 et vendue pour 643 millions de dollars à LVMH en 2001.

"I never see one woman when I design, it's a universe of women. Clothes are a canvas to their individuality"

PORTRAIT COURTESY OF DONNA KARAN

DONNA KARAN

PHOTOGRAPHY BY FRANCESCA SORRENTI. JULY 2002

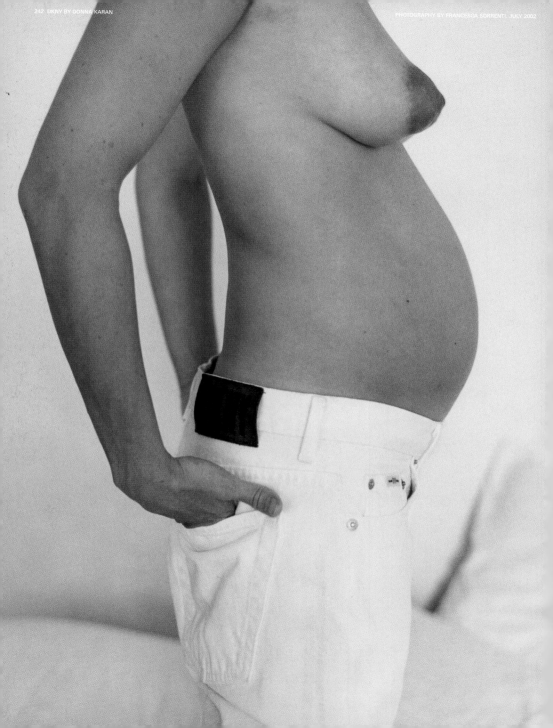

What are your signature pieces? My seven easy pieces wardrobe. It's a simple, sophisticated system of dressing that takes a woman from day into evening, weekday to weekend **How would you describe your work?** Sensual, urban and body conscious **What's your ultimate goal?** Professionally, it's always what I haven't done that excites me. But my ultimate goal in life is to find peace and happiness **What inspires you?** Any and everything. Passion. Sensuality. Nature – the textures of the beach, the melding colours of water, the electricity of the night. I really try to stay open and take in the beauty that's all around me **Can fashion still have a political ambition?** Absolutely. When you're creating something, you must be sensitive to what people want and the times they live in. However innovative it is, what you create must be relevant and reflect the here and now **Who do you have in mind when you design?** I never see one woman when I design, it's always a universe of women. Strong passionate women, women who are true to themselves and their visions. I see clothes as a canvas to their individuality. The woman is the first thing you see, not the clothes **Is the idea of creative collaboration important to you?** You are only as good as the people behind you. It can't be done alone. It takes team effort **Who has been the greatest influence on your career?** Anne Klein – her passing pushed me into becoming a designer. It wasn't something I was sure I wanted to do **How have your own experiences affected your work as a designer?** My own personal needs – what works and doesn't work – affect my work. The fact that I'm a woman and, like all women, want to be taller, thinner and look sophisticated without a lot of effort. Everything I create works to that end **Which is more important in your work: the process or the product?** When all becomes one. When the product fulfils the dream of inspiration **Is designing difficult for you and, if so, what drives you to continue?** The challenge of creation. I try to stay open to new things. To live is to move forward, to discover new means of expression **Have you ever been influenced or moved by the reaction to your designs?** Yes – I have to think twice about the way people react. People's reactions can motivate me to another level. That's how you evolve **What's your definition of beauty?** Beauty is about individuality. There is nothing more attractive than a woman who values her uniqueness. She has the confidence to express herself, to say something new, to create from within **What's your philosophy?** Never stop exploring or challenging yourself. When I design, I'm always looking for a balance between purpose and expression **What is the most important lesson you've learned?** No matter how bad or good it is, it will always change. Everything is in constant motion

Rei Kawakubo is a visionary. As the driving force behind Comme des Garçons, she is one of the most important fashion designers working today. Since her arrival from Japan 20 years ago, Kawakubo has challenged Western ideals of body shape and garment construction, of society's sexism and use of colour. She has misplaced and exaggerated the female form with big blobs of padded fabric; created finished garments from tailor's calico or turned clothes inside-out so that the innards of their construction become decoration; perfected androgyny with her flat shoes (she hates high heels), baggy men's trousers and sloping shouldered jackets. Kawakubo has, in short, revolutionised fashion. Born in Tokyo in 1942, she started school in US-occupied Japan, studying literature at Keio University before going to work as a stylist in the advertising department of a chemicals manufacturer. The Comme des Garçons label was born in 1969 after Kawakubo learned how to make clothes and sell them to supplement her income, but it wasn't until that shocking Paris show in 1981 that she became so influential, directly challenging the status quo of the era's heady glamour. Her creations are often tagged with the word 'art' because of their conceptual and intellectual rigour, but this hasn't stopped her from building one of the biggest independent fashion empires, with over 80 stores in Japan alone. Her domain includes one of the most idiosyncratic fragrance collections (launched in 1994), revolutionary stores that challenge both architectural design and the shopping experience (including her most recent project in 2002 with 10 Corso Como's Carla Sozzani for a shop in Tokyo that pioneers the concept of fashion designer collaborated collections) and her protégé, Junya Watanabe, who designs his own collection for the Comme stable. Her work has featured in numerous books and exhibitions, including the '2 Women: Gabrielle Chanel and Rei Kawakubo' in Antwerp as part of the 'Fashion 2001 Landed/Geland' project.

Rei Kawakubo ist eine Visionärin. Als treibende Kraft hinter Comme des Garçons zählt sie zu den wichtigsten Modedesignerinnen und -designern unserer Zeit. Seit sie Japan vor zwanzig Jahren verlassen hat, stellt Kawakubo die westlichen Ideale von Statur und Schnitt, aber auch den Sexismus der hiesigen Gesellschaft und die Verwendung von Farbe in Frage. Sie hat die weibliche Gestalt mit großen Mengen aufgebauschten Stoffes überzeichnet, aufwändige Kleider aus ungebleichtem Baumwollstoff kreiert oder Kleidungsstücke auf links gedreht und so die Nähte zur Dekoration umfunktioniert. Den androgynen Look perfektionierte sie mit flachen Schuhen (High Heels sind der Designerin ein Graus), weiten Männerhosen und Jacken mit abfallenden Schultern. Kawakubo hat, kurz gesagt, die Mode revolutioniert. Geboren wurde die Designerin 1942 in Tokio. Als sie in die Schule kam, stand Japan noch unter amerikanischer Militärherrschaft. Kawakubo studierte an der Keio-Universität Literatur, bevor sie als Stylistin in der Werbeabteilung eines Chemiekonzerns begann. Ihr Label Comme des Garçons gründete sie 1969, nachdem sie gelernt hatte, Kleider zu nähen und mit deren Verkauf ihr Einkommen aufzubessern. Doch erst nach der die Branche schockierenden Schau in Paris 1981 erlangte sie solchen Einfluss, dass sie sich erlauben konnte, den Status Quo des gedankenlosen Glamours jener Zeit in Frage zu stellen. Ihre Kreationen werden wegen ihrer konzeptionellen und intellektuellen Schärfe oft mit dem Etikett 'Kunst' versehen, doch hat das deren Schöpferin nicht davon abgehalten, eines der größten unabhängigen Modeimperien aufzubauen. Heute gehören dazu allein in Japan über achtzig eigene Läden. Zu deren Sortiment zählt unter anderem seit 1994 eine der eigenwilligsten Duftkollektionen überhaupt. Und auch die Geschäfte selbst sind revolutionär, sowohl was die Architektur als auch was das Einkaufserlebnis betrifft. Kawakubos jüngstes Projekt war 2002 zusammen mit Carla Sozzani von 10 Corso Como ein Shop in Tokio, in dem erstmals das Konzept der Fashion Designer Collaborated Collections angewandt wird. Fester Bestandteil des Konzerns ist auch Kawakubos Protegé Junya Watanabe, der eigene Kollektionen bei Comme des Garçons entwirft. Kawakubos Werk ist in zahlreichen Büchern und Ausstellungen dokumentiert, darunter '2 Women: Gabrielle Chanel und Rei Kawakubo', die in Antwerpen als Teil des Projekts 'Mode 2001 Landed/Geland' gezeigt wurde.

Rei Kawakubo est une visionnaire. Cerveau de la griffe Comme des Garçons, elle compte parmi les créateurs de mode les plus importants actuellement en exercice. Depuis qu'elle a débarqué de son Japon natal il y a 20 ans, Rei Kawakubo remet systématiquement en question les idéaux occidentaux sur la forme du corps et la construction du vêtement, sur le sexisme de la société et l'utilisation de la couleur. Elle a déplacé et exagéré la forme du corps féminin à travers de gros morceaux de tissu rembourrés, créé des vêtements finis à partir de calicot de tailleur ou retourné les vêtements à l'envers pour transformer les entrailles de leur construction en éléments décoratifs. Elle a perfectionné l'androgynie avec ses chaussures plates (elle déteste les talons hauts), ses pantalons baggy masculins et ses vestes aux épaules tombantes. En d'autres termes, Rei Kawakubo a révolutionné la mode. Née en 1942 à Tokyo, elle commence à étudier la littérature à l'Université Keio dans un Japon sous occupation américaine, avant de travailler comme styliste pour le département Publicité d'un fabricant de produits chimiques. Rei Kawakubo, qui a appris entre temps à confectionner des vêtements et à les vendre pour arrondir ses fins de mois, lance la griffe Comme des Garçons en 1969. Mais c'est depuis son scandaleux défilé parisien de 1981 qu'elle est devenue si influente, s'attaquant directement au status quo du glamour entêté de l'époque. Ses créations sont souvent étiquetées comme « artistiques » en raison de leur rigueur conceptuelle et intellectuelle, mais cela ne l'a pas empêchée de bâtir l'un des plus grands empires indépendants de la mode, avec plus de 80 boutiques sur le seul territoire du Japon. Son champ d'action inclut l'une des collections de parfums les plus particulières qui soient (lancée en 1994). Ses boutiques révolutionnaires remettent en question l'architecture d'intérieur et l'expérience d'achat, comme c'est le cas de son projet le plus récent (2002) réalisé avec Carla Sozzani, la boutique-concept 10 Corso Como de Tokyo où sont présentés les résultats de collaborations entre designers. Son protégé, Junya Watanabe, dessine sa propre collection pour l'écurie Comme des Garçons. Le travail de Rei Kawakubo a fait l'objet de nombreux ouvrages et de plusieurs expositions, notamment « 2 Women: Gabrielle Chanel and Rei Kawakubo » dans le cadre du projet anversois « Mode 2001 Landed/Geland ».

"It is clear to me that designing creatively becomes harder. But I have to continue, I don't believe I have achieved all I can yet"

PORTRAIT BY TIMOTHY GREENFIELD

REI KAWAKUBO

PHOTOGRAPHY BY PAOLO ROVERSI, STYLING BY EDWARD ENNINFUL. SEPTEMBER 2000

VIDEO STILLS BY TERRY JONES. AUTUMN-WINTER 2002

PHOTOGRAPHY BY RICHARD BURBRIDGE, STYLING BY EDWARD ENNINFUL. MARCH 2001

What's your favourite piece from any of your collections? I haven't yet made clothes that I have been totally satisfied with and maybe I never will **How would you describe your work?** Comme des Garçons is not just about making clothes. Where the clothes are sold is just as important as the clothes. Even the name-card of the staff is important. I design the company, in fact. I am not only the designer of the company **What's your ultimate goal?** A good analogy is to talk about climbing a mountain. When you are going up, you don't look behind you all the time to see how far you have come – you are focused on where you are going next. And I still haven't reached the top yet **What do you have in mind when you design?** Every time is different **How have your own experiences affected your work as a designer?** The problem is that you can't do away with your own experience **Which is more important in your work: the process or the product?** What's almost as difficult as the idea is how to turn it into a business. The business part doesn't start after the show, it's always a parallel process going on at the same time. The question is always, how is this going to be sold in stores? **Is designing difficult for you and, if so, what drives you to continue?** The situation is more tough now. The more experienced you are, the more difficult it is to do something different each time. One can look at it as one collection adding something to the last – but to do something from zero, that gets more and more difficult as the weight of experience gets heavier **Have you ever been influenced or moved by the reaction to your designs?** I have never changed what I wanted to do whatever people's reaction has been. I think it is totally normal and right that there are reactions both ways. Right from the start, I wanted to challenge people and move them to have a reaction. Whether it is a good reaction or a bad one is unimportant **What's your philosophy?** Freedom

PHOTOGRAPHY BY RICHARD BURBRIDGE, STYLING BY EDWARD ENNINFUL. OCTOBER 2001. MODEL: SVETA

Calvin Klein's pitch may be one of simplicity – minimalistic sportswear in the American luxury tradition: unisex loose trousers, shirt-jackets, blazers and pea-coats in a neutral palette – but it is revolutionary, award-winning simplicity (in 1993, Klein picked up both CFDA Best Womenswear and Best Menswear designer awards, the first time a designer had won the double). And his global reputation may be founded on those undergarments (launched 1982) which financially bolstered business and gave men a new sex appeal, but Klein's design pedigree is solid. Born in 1942 in the Bronx, Klein taught himself to cut and sew before studying at New York's School of Art and Design, and the Fashion Institute of Technology, graduating in 1962. From there he worked as an assistant to designer Dan Millstein, before working with a number of the city's leading dressmakers. By 1968, Klein had launched his own women's coat business. Encouraged by fashion store executives, a full sportswear line followed in the mid 1970s, together with the invention of 'designer denim', tightly moulded round a teen Brooke Shields claiming 'nothing comes between me and my Calvins.' Certainly Calvin's advertising has always pushed the envelope to give sometimes mainstream fare a raw quality – from the buffed body of Mark Wahlberg straining from his Y-fronts (Klein began a trend for using performers rather than models in ads) to the extensive employment of then-waifish Kate Moss. But controversy has been founded on wily business: Klein's cK brand may be among the most high-profile of diffusion lines, but his knack for creating best-selling fragrances (among them Obsession, Eternity and cKOne, the first unisex fragrance) is matched only by Armani.

Calvin Kleins Geheimnis mag denkbar einfach sein – minimalistisch sportliche Mode in bester gehobener amerikanischer Tradition: locker geschnittene Unisex-Hosen, Hemd-blusen, Jacken und Caban-Jacken in neutralen Farben – doch diese Schlichtheit war revolutionär und brachte dem Designer diverse Auszeichnungen ein. So wurde Klein 1993 als erstem Designer sowohl der Preis für Best Womenswear als auch der für Best Menswear vom Council of Fashion Designers of America verliehen. Und auch wenn sein welt-weiter Ruf sich auf die 1982 herausgebrachte Unterwäsche gründete, die dem Unternehmen finanziellen Erfolg brachte und Männern neuen Sexappeal verlieh, ist der Werde-gang des Designers grundsolide. Der 1942 in der Bronx geborene Klein brachte sich selbst das Nähen bei, bevor er ein Studium an der New Yorker School of Art and Design und am Fashion Institute of Technology begann, das er 1962 abschloss. Danach arbeitete er zunächst als Assistent für den Designer Dan Millstein und mit einigen der wichtigsten Schneider der Stadt. 1968 führte er bereits eine eigene Konfektionsfirma für Damenmäntel. Nachdem Einkäufer großer Kaufhäuser ihn dazu ermutigt hatten, erweiterte Klein Mitte der 1970er Jahre sein Angebot zu einer kompletten Sportswear-Kollektion. Gleichzeitig erfand er die sogenannte Designerjeans. Diese saß wie angegossen an dem Teenager-Model Brooke Shields, die behauptete, sie lasse nichts zwischen sich und ihre Calvins. Zweifellos hat die Werbung für Calvin Klein immer dazu beigetragen, eigentlich alltäglichen Produkten den Reiz des Besonderen zu verleihen – angefangen beim wohlgeformten Body eines Mark Wahlberg, den ein Y-Front-Slip umspannt (Klein begann als erster, in seinen Kampagnen mit Schauspielern anstelle von Models zu arbeiten), bis hin zum damals geradezu verwahrlost aussehenden Lieblingsmodel Kate Moss. Diese Widersprüche funktionierten jedoch nur auf der Basis klugen Geschäftsgebarens. So zählt Kleins Marke cK wohl zu den profiliertesten Nebenlinien, und sein Gespür für Düfte mit Bestsellerpotential (wie Obsession, Eternity und das erste Unisexparfum cKOne) wird nur noch von Armani übertroffen.

Le style de Calvin Klein se définit sans doute comme un sportswear à la simplicité minimaliste, dans la pure tradition du luxe américain : pantalons larges unisexe, vestes-chemises, blazers et cabans aux couleurs neutres ; mais cette simplicité-là est vraiment révolutionnaire, comme le prouvent les nombreux prix décernés à Calvin Klein (en 1993, il a raflé à la fois le Best Womenswear Designer Award et le Best Menswear Designer Award de la CFDA, un fait sans précédent). Klein doit probablement sa réputation mon-diale aux sous-vêtements (lancés en 1982) qui ont soutenu l'entreprise financièrement et donné aux hommes un nouveau sex-appeal, mais le style de Klein n'en reste pas moins solide. Né en 1942 dans le Bronx, Klein apprend lui-même à tailler le tissu et à coudre avant d'étudier à la School of Art and Design de New York puis au Fashion Institute of Technology, dont il sort diplômé en 1962. Ensuite, il devient assistant du designer Dan Millstein avant de travailler pour de nombreux grands couturiers de la ville. En 1968, Klein a déjà lancé sa propre société de fabrication de manteaux pour femme. Encouragé par les responsables des boutiques de mode, une ligne complète de sportswear suit au milieu des années 1970. Il invente le « jean de créateur », étroitement moulé sur une Brooke Shields alors adolescente qui proclame « il n'y a rien entre moi et mon Calvin ». Sans aucun doute, les campagnes publicitaires de Calvin ont toujours un peu poussé le bouchon pour donner à cette mode mainstream une qualité brute : du corps huilé de Mark Wahlberg archi-moulé dans son slip (Klein a lancé la tendance qui consiste à faire appel à des artistes plutôt qu'à des mannequins pour les pubs) jusqu'aux apparitions récurrentes de la frêle Kate Moss. Les controverses ainsi déclenchées ont porté leurs fruits : certes, la marque cK de Klein figure parmi les lignes de « diffusion » les plus prestigieuses, mais son talent pour créer des parfums à succès (notamment Obsession, Eternity et cKOne, le premier parfum unisexe) n'est égalé que par Armani.

"I am inspired by the pursuit of a kind of purity"

PORTRAIT COURTESY OF CALVIN KLEIN

CALVIN KLEIN

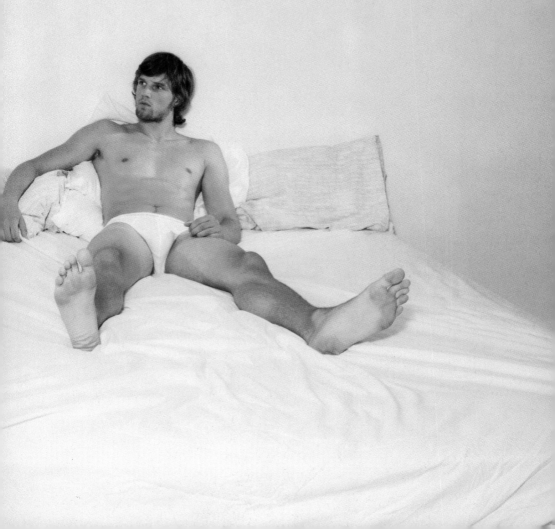

"The challenge is to introduce ease into a complex way of life"

What are your signature designs? Modern interpretations of the elements of American style: pants cut like a jean, the slip dress, the T-shirt, the pea-coat **How would you describe your work?** Clothing that is pared down to the modern essentials – pure, clean and simple **What's your ultimate goal?** The challenge of modern design is to introduce ease, simplicity and clarity into a complex way of life **What inspires you?** The pursuit of a certain perfection, a kind of purity. The modern woman who leads an active busy life **Can fashion still have a political ambition?** Ambition yes, politics no; politics is for politicians, fashion is for designers **Who do you have in mind when you design?** The modern woman, a woman with confidence who leads many lives in one **Is the idea of creative collaboration important to you?** Absolutely, it enhances and stimulates creativity because the design process relies on surprise, the unexpected; the more talented minds you have working together, the better. Collaboration among a group of people on the same wavelength is what makes design move forward: it provokes change, leads to better solutions and new ideas **Who or what has been the greatest influence on your career?** There are so many influences, conscious and unconscious, that filter through daily life to contribute to your aesthetic. For me, they include people (Coco Chanel, Baron Nicolas de Gunzburg), places (New York City), artists (Donald Judd, Mark Rothko) and, as always, the modern woman **Which is more important in your work: the process or the product?** The process is what leads to the product – and trusting the process is what creating is about. Design, more than anything, is a process and, like any creative process, it involves editing, paring down to the essential, which is what we're about – so process becomes the product **Is designing difficult for you and, if so, what drives you to continue?** I thrive on challenge – that's what drives me. If anything, the challenge is to take design to the next level, to keep the process stimulating, to discover new solutions. If design ever becomes easy or boring, I would have to do something else **Have you ever been influenced or moved by the reaction to your designs?** Hard as it is not to be, you can't let yourself be overly influenced by reactions **What is the most important lesson you've learned?** You have to be passionate about your work, believe in yourself, trust your instincts – and with luck, everything else will follow

The Greek-born, London-based designer Sophia Kokosalaki returns to her homeland again and again in her collections. Born in Athens in 1972, she was brought up on a rich diet of history and mythology, which she continues to feed on voraciously. After studying Greek Literature at the University of Athens, she attended Central Saint Martins; since leaving in 1998, she has pick'n'mixed her way through everything from the Minoan culture to those wafty silk chiffon dresses worn by Barbra Streisand on holiday in Mykonos in the 1970s. A master at playing with fabric, Kokosalaki's genuine feel for craft is evident in her work. Her grandmother, a dab hand at macramé, lit the first spark. Now Kokosalaki works through a back catalogue of ancient skills using appliqué, pintucking, cording, plaiting, ruching and patchwork to embellish a range of fabrics including her signature leather and silk jersey. And yet, for all her research and technique, she manages to keep a supreme simplicity to her work by leaving her design to intuition. Her dresses seem so light and pretty they are almost deviant – but Kokosalaki just wants her clothes to look assertive. Balancing light and dark sentiment, the feminine and masculine, she has worked as a designer for Ruffo Research (Spring-Summer and Autumn-Winter 2001) and a consultant for Fendi. In 2002 she produced a range for TopShop in London. A front-runner in British fashion, she was the first designer to be awarded a £10,000 fellowship by Britain's Arts Foundation.

Die aus Griechenland stammende und heute in London lebende Designerin Sophia Kokosalaki kehrt in ihren Kollektionen immer wieder zu ihren mediterranen Wurzeln zurück. Sie wurde 1972 in Athen geboren und wuchs mit reichlich Geschichte und Mythologie auf, wovon sie bis heute nicht genug bekommen kann. Nach dem Studium Griechischer Literatur an der Universität von Athen besuchte sie das Central Saint Martins in London. Seit ihrem Abschluss dort im Jahr 1998 hat sie von der minoischen Kultur bis zu den wehenden Kleidern aus Seidenchiffon, die Barbra Streisand in den 1970ern im Urlaub auf Mykonos trug, kaum eine Inspirationsquelle ausgelassen. Kokosalakis echte Begeisterung für alles Handwerkliche und ihre Meisterschaft im Spiel mit Stoffen sind unübersehbar. Ihre Großmutter, eine wahre Makramé-Künstlerin, brachte Sophia auf den Geschmack. Inzwischen schöpft Kokosalaki aus einem wahren Fundus althergebrachter Techniken wie Applizieren, mit Biesen oder Kordeln Versehen, Flechten oder Steppen, um die verschiedensten Stoffe zu verzieren, darunter ihre Lieblingsmaterialien Leder und Seidenjersey. Allen neuesten Entwicklungen und technischen Errungenschaften zum Trotz gelingt es der Designerin, ihren Entwürfen letztlich eine erhabene Schlichtheit zu bewahren, indem sie nach wie vor intuitiv arbeitet. Ihre Kleider fallen durch Schönheit und Leichtigkeit auf. Kokosalaki legt besonderen Wert auf positive Ausstrahlung. Als Designerin, die es versteht, lichte und düstere Gefühle sowie das feminine und das maskuline Element ins Gleichgewicht zu bringen, hat sie für Ruffo Research (Frühjahr/Sommer und Herbst/Winter 2001) und als Beraterin bei Fendi gearbeitet. Im Jahr 2002 entwarf sie eine Kollektion für TopShop in London. Als eine der Galionsfiguren der britischen Mode wurde Kokosalaki von der Britain's Arts Foundation als erste Designerin mit einem Stipendium in Höhe von 10 000 Pfund gefördert.

Dans ses collections, la créatrice londonienne Sophia Kokosalaki fait sans cesse référence à ses origines. Née à Athènes en 1972, elle grandit dans un univers riche d'histoire et de mythologie qu'elle continue d'alimenter avec voracité. Après avoir étudié la littérature grecque à l'Université d'Athènes, elle suit des cours à Central Saint Martins, dont elle sort en 1998. Depuis, elle puise son inspiration dans toutes sortes de choses, de la culture de la Crète antique aux robes vaporeuses en mousseline de soie que portait Barbra Streisand pendant ses vacances à Mykonos dans les années 1970. Maîtrisant parfaitement les tissus, Sophia Kokosalaki démontre un talent artisanal authentique qui apparaît de façon évidente dans son travail, une passion qui lui vient de sa grand-mère, surdouée du macramé. Aujourd'hui, Sophia Kokosalaki utilise un large éventail de techniques anciennes telles que les appliqués, les nervures, les ganses, les tresses, les ruchés et les patchworks pour embellir toutes sortes de tissus, notamment son cuir et son jersey de soie si caractéristiques. En dépit de ses nombreuses recherches et de son grand savoir-faire, elle réussit tout de même à conférer une extrême simplicité à ses créations en travaillant par intuition. Ses robes sont si belles et si légères qu'elles en paraîtraient presque perverses : mais Sophia Kokosalaki cherche simplement à créer des vêtements expressifs. Jouant sur les contrastes entre ombre et lumière, féminin et masculin, elle a travaillé comme styliste pour Ruffo Research (collections Printemps-Eté et Automne-Hiver 2001) et en tant que consultante pour Fendi. En 2002, elle a dessiné une ligne pour TopShop à Londres. A l'avant-garde de la mode britannique, elle a été la première créatrice à bénéficier d'une bourse de 10 000 livres de la Britain's Arts Foundation.

"My aim is always to hit a chord"

PORTRAIT BY ELLEN NOLAN

SOPHIA KOKOSALAKI

What are your signature designs? A signature design would happen to involve elaborate hand-work, traditional or military elements and an alternative or Teutonic silhouette **What's your favourite piece from any of your collections?** A draped patchwork leather and jersey dress from my Spring-Summer 2000 collection as it was one of my first experiments **How would you describe your work?** Complex and labour intensive, but also light and contemporary **What's your ultimate goal?** Achieving perfect balance between life and work **What inspires you?** It is usually a combination of elements and situations **Can fashion still have a political ambition?** No, but it can have an emotional feel **Who do you have in mind when you design?** Nobody specific **Is the idea of creative collaboration important to you?** Yes, dialogue with people that share a similar aesthetic can be unexpectedly conclusive and productive **What has been the greatest influence on your career?** The need to be independent was the one thing that controlled my career **How have your own experiences affected your work as a designer?** In a decisive way because experiences define your personality and my personality interferes with my work a lot **Which is more important in your work: the process or the product?** Both **Is designing difficult for you and, if so, what drives you to continue?** Designing is never difficult but the technical complexities can be a challenge **Have you ever been influenced or moved by the reaction to your designs?** Of course, because with my work my aim is always to hit a chord **What's your definition of beauty?** It changes constantly but a slight imperfection always adds more allure **What's your philosophy?** It's never as hard as it seems **What is the most important lesson you've learned?** You can never start working early enough

Michael Kors designs pure American opulence: luxurious, perfectly tailored sportswear in contrasting textures of leather and cashmere with a cheeky flash of pelt. Growing up in deepest suburbia, Kors (born Long Island) always had a healthy focus on fashion and the city of New York. After studying design at the Fashion Institute of Technology, New York, by the age of 19 he was designing and merchandising for Lothar's boutique. The attention this received by the fashion press led him to launch the Michael Kors label in 1981. The Kors Michael Kors bridge line followed in 1995. After launching a capsule menswear collection in 1997, Kors was named the first women's ready-to-wear designer for the house of Céline. By February 1999 he had become Creative Director for the luxury label, overseeing all women's products. 1999 was a remarkable year for Kors: he was awarded the CFDA Award for Womenswear Designer of the Year, The New York Times Award, and announced plans for the first Michael Kors flagship store on Madison Avenue, NYC – a homecoming of sorts. A signature scent was launched in 2000, with a cologne Michael for Men appearing in 2001. A Kors Michael Kors store opened in SoHo, New York, in 2002. As Michael Kors' vision unfolds further to shoes and eyewear, he continues to design to a sophisticated ethic, a sexy American Dream.

Michael Kors entwirft amerikanische Opulenz in Reinkultur: luxuriöse, perfekt geschnittene Freizeitmode aus Leder und Kaschmir als Materialien mit kontrastierender Textur, dazu frech aufblitzender Pelz. Aufgewachsen ist der auf Long Island geborene Kors in der Vorstadt, doch hatte er bereits dort die Mode und New York City genau im Blick. Nach dem Studium am New Yorker Fashion Institute of Technology entwarf er schon mit 19 erfolgreich für Lothar's Boutique. Nachdem er damit die Aufmerksamkeit der Modepresse auf sich gezogen hatte, wagte er sich 1981 an die Gründung eines eigenen Labels mit seinem Namen. Die profitable preiswertere Nebenlinie Kors Michael Kors folgte 1995. Nach der Präsentation einer kleinen Herrenkollektion im Jahr 1997 wurde Kors erster Designer für die Prêt-à-Porter-Damenmode im Hause Céline. Bis Februar 1999 war er zum Creative Director des Luxuslabels aufgestiegen und fortan für alle Damenprodukte zuständig. 1999 war aber auch in anderer Hinsicht ein bemerkenswertes Jahr für Kors: Das CFDA ernannte ihn zum Womenswear Designer of the Year, er erhielt den New York Times Award und gab außerdem seine Pläne für den ersten Michael Kors Flagship Store auf der New Yorker Madison Avenue bekannt – eine Art Nachhausekommen. 2000 stellte der Designer einen Duft mit seinem Namen vor, im darauf folgenden Jahr das Eau de Parfum 'Michael for Men'. Ein 'Kors-Michael-Kors'-Laden im New Yorker Stadtviertel SoHo kam 2002 dazu. Während Michael Kors seine Kreativität jetzt auch in den Bereichen Schuh- und Brillenmode spielen lässt, setzt er die Arbeit am Design eines sexy American Dream fort.

Michael Kors crée dans la plus pure tradition de l'opulence américaine : sportswear luxueux aux coupes impeccables, taillé dans des matières constrastées de cuir et de cachemire, avec quelques touches audacieuses de peau ça et là. Né à Long Island et élevé en banlieue, Kors a toujours eu une vision plutôt saine de la mode et de la ville de New York. Après des études de design au Fashion Institute of Technology, dès l'âge de 19 ans il commence à dessiner pour la boutique Lothar's. Encouragé par l'intérêt de la presse spécialisée, il crée la griffe Michael Kors en 1981, suivie en 1995 par la ligne de vêtements de voyage Kors Michael Kors. Après le lancement d'une mini-collection pour homme en 1997, Kors est nommé styliste principal du prêt-à-porter féminin de la maison Céline. En février 1999, il devient directeur de la création de la griffe de luxe et supervise tous les produits pour femme. 1999 est une année en or pour Kors : il reçoit le Womenswear Designer of the Year Award du CFDA, le New York Times Award et annonce l'ouverture de la première boutique Michael Kors sur Madison Avenue à New York, retour au foyer s'il en est. Il lance un parfum éponyme en l'an 2000, suivi d'une eau de Cologne Michael for Men en 2001. Il ouvre une boutique Kors Michael Kors dans SoHo à New York en 2002. Tandis qu'il continue sur sa lancée avec une ligne de chaussures et de lunettes, Kors conserve toutefois une éthique sophistiquée, dessinant un rêve américain plus sexy.

"There's no point in design for design's sake. Everything I believe in is about getting women dressed"

MICHAEL KORS

What are your signature designs? The mix of something glamorous with something casual **What are your favourite pieces from any of your collections?** I always have a great white shirt, camel coat, trench, grey flannel trousers, the perfect cashmere pullover, brown croc slingbacks and a black sheath as part of my collections in one way or another… it's not necessarily about 'favourite', just pieces that should be part of every woman's wardrobe **How would you describe your work?** Chic, sexy, luxurious American sportswear **What's your ultimate goal?** To have more free time **What inspires you?** Women and their ever-changing moods and needs **Can fashion still have a political ambition?** I think fashion has a sociological impact rather than political **Who do you have in mind when you design?** I don't necessarily have a 'muse' or one woman in mind, rather it's about a group of women who constantly inspire me. Everyone from clients, to celebrities, to the women who work with me, to my mom **Is the idea of creative collaboration important to you?** I surround myself with people who have a strong opinion and I love the collaborative dialogue that takes place in my office on a daily basis, even if it is exhausting at times. Also, working with people in related fields is always inspiring, like Fabien Baron who works with me on all of our creative materials, and Daniel Rowen our architect **Who or what has been the greatest influence on your career?** Pop culture – everything from film and theatre to television and music – and my mother and grandmother **How have your own experiences affected your work as a designer?** I think that who I am and everything that I do comes out in my work. Whether it be a destination I'm dreaming of going to that inspires a collection, or the colour of water at my beach house that might inspire a palette for the season… it's all intertwined in my mind **Which is more important in your work: the process or the product?** Definitely the product…there's no point in design for design's sake. Everything I believe in is about getting women dressed. It has to be somewhat practical: I might love something throughout the process, but if a woman can't get into it because it has no zipper, or can't walk because it has no slit, then what's the point? **Is designing difficult for you?** If it was, I wouldn't still be doing this after 20-plus years **What's your definition of beauty?** Confidence and a great sense of humour **What's your philosophy?** Glamour combined with comfort is the only modern answer **What is the most important lesson you've learned?** Listen to your gut instinct and always remain open and curious

Christian Lacroix's wit, his Provençal taste for hot pinks and reds, his kaleidoscopic vision of lavish embroidery, sequins and beads, and his brave new silhouettes all mark him out as a true original. Born in Arles, France in 1951, Lacroix grew up immersed in the Southern culture: bullfighting costumes and gypsy traditions have consistently inspired his highly decorative style. In 1973 Lacroix moved to Paris, studying at the Sorbonne and the Ecole du Louvre, planning a career as a museum curator. The same year he met his future wife, Françoise, who persuaded him to abandon musty exhibits in favour of fashion drawing. Hermès was his first employer, in 1978, then Guy Paulin, in 1980. A year later, Lacroix had his first taste of haute couture, designing for Jean Patou. Lacroix revived the waning art, producing season after season of fantastical, opulent fashion. In the mid 1980s, he suddenly found success. His 1986 collection of 'puffball' cocktail dresses propelled him into international celebrity and the prestigious haute couture prize, the Golden Thimble. In 1987, Bernard Arnault founded the house of Christian Lacroix, the first new haute couture house to open since Saint Laurent in 1962. Lacroix became one of the most sought-after labels of the day, and his shadow still looms large over 1980s fashion history; to many, his clothes conveyed decadence, and as such, they symbolise that decade not just in terms of fashion, but also as social history. Prêt-à-porter followed in 1987, the Bazar line in 1994. In Spring 2002, Christian Lacroix was appointed designer for the house of Pucci.

Sein Esprit, seine provençalische Vorliebe für kräftige Pink- und Rottöne, seine kaleidoskopartige Vision von üppigen Stickereien, Ziermünzen und Perlen sowie gewagte neue Silhouetten – all das verleiht Christian Lacroix' Entwürfen solche Originalität. Der 1951 im französischen Arles geborene Designer wuchs mit der Lebensart des Südens auf: Die Kostüme der Stierkämpfer und Zigeunertradition haben seinen überaus dekorativen Stil nachhaltig geprägt. Nachdem er 1973 nach Paris gezogen war, studierte er zunächst Kunstgeschichte an der Sorbonne und der Ecole du Louvre, um Museumkurator zu werden. Im selben Jahr lernte er jedoch seine spätere Frau Françoise kennen, die ihn überredete, die musealen Ambitionen zugunsten einer Laufbahn als Modezeichner aufzugeben. Sein erster Arbeitgeber war 1978 Hermès, ab 1980 Guy Paulin. Ein Jahr später machte Lacroix mit Entwürfen für Jean Patou seine ersten Schritte auf dem Parkett der Haute Couture. Durch ihn erfuhr diese schon im Schwinden begriffene Kunst neuen Auftrieb, denn er entwarf Saison für Saison phantastisch opulente Modelle. Mitte der 1980er Jahre stellte sich dann plötzlich der große Erfolg ein. Seine 1986er Kollektion von Cocktailkleidern mit 'Pouf', einem kurzen Ballonrock, brachte ihm internationale Anerkennung und den renommierten Goldenen Fingerhut der Haute Couture ein. 1987 gründete Bernard Arnault mit dem Label Christian Lacroix das erste neue Couture-Haus seit Saint Laurent (1962). Damit avancierte Lacroix zu einem der gefragtesten Designer jener Zeit, der die Modegeschichte entscheidend geprägt hat. Viele kritisierten seine Kleider als dekadent, doch gerade das prädestiniert sie zu Symbolen dieses Jahrzehnts – nicht nur in modischer, sondern auch in sozialer Hinsicht. 1987 präsentierte Lacroix seine erste Prêt-à-Porter-Kollektion, seit 1994 Sportswear unter dem Label Bazar. Im Frühjahr 2002 wurde Christian Lacroix Designer im Hause Pucci.

L'intelligence de Christian Lacroix, son goût typiquement provençal pour les roses et rouges vifs, sa vision kaléidoscopique des broderies luxueuses, des sequins et des perles, ainsi que ses silhouettes inédites et audacieuses le distinguent comme un original à part entière. Né en 1951 à Arles, Lacroix grandit immergé dans la culture du Sud de la France : les costumes des corridas et les traditions gitanes ont toujours inspiré son style hautement décoratif. En 1973, Lacroix s'installe à Paris pour étudier à la Sorbonne et à l'Ecole du Louvre afin de devenir conservateur de musée. La même année, il rencontre sa future femme, Françoise, qui le persuade de délaisser les musées poussiéreux au profit de la création de mode. Hermès est la première maison à l'embaucher en 1978, puis en 1980 il part travailler chez Guy Paulin. Un an plus tard, Lacroix touche pour la première fois à la haute couture en dessinant pour Jean Patou. Il redonne vie à cet art qu'on disait moribond en produisant, saison après saison, une mode fantastique et opulente. Au milieu des années 1980, il rencontre soudainement le succès. En 1986, sa collection de robes de cocktail « boule » le propulse au rang de célébrité internationale et lui vaut le prestigieux Dé d'Or de la haute couture. En 1987, Bernard Arnault fonde la maison de haute couture Christian Lacroix, la première à ouvrir ses portes depuis celle de Saint Laurent en 1962. Lacroix devient l'une des griffes les plus recherchées de l'époque, exerçant une énorme influence sur la mode des années 1980 ; nombreux sont ceux qui pensent que ses vêtements véhiculent une certaine décadence, symbolisant ainsi la décennie, non seulement en termes de mode, mais également d'histoire de la société. Il lance une ligne de prêt-à-porter en 1987, suivie en 1994 par la ligne Bazar. Au Printemps 2002, Christian Lacroix est nommé directeur artistique de la maison Pucci.

"I would like to express much more violence in my work"

PORTRAIT BY KEVIN DAVIES

CHRISTIAN LACROIX

PHOTOGRAPHY BY KATE JONES, STYLING BY GERIADA KEFFORD. NOVEMBER 2002. MODEL: LIBERTY ROSS

"Beauty is not a very well-balanced thing; it has to be disturbing and uncomfortable"

What are your signature designs? Let's say – red. Something crazy! **How would you describe your work?** It's based on individuality and self-expression. It's not exactly anti-fashion, but it's contrary to the way that fashion is. My fashion is much more a way of living life with your roots, and finding your own true self, than having a logo put on your back **Can fashion still have a political ambition?** I would like to express much more violence in my work. I'm very, very angry when I see all this globalisation. If we want the most sensual things in life, we have to fight for them. My house is based on an ethnic art and on gypsies, and I hope that through it I will succeed in expressing their heritage, something that is stronger than the poor everyday life that globalisation would like us to have **Who do you have in mind when you design?** A kind of gypsy. Everybody who is free enough to express this way of life **Who has been the greatest influence on your career?** My wife: if I had not met her, I would be in the South of France, eating goat's cheese. I was lazy, I was shy and she gave me a spine **What's your definition of beauty?** Beauty is not a very well-balanced thing; it has to be disturbing and uncomfortable. It's about the period and art rather than anything physical **What's your philosophy?** I'm totally despairing and totally joyful at the same time

'Fashion is not something that exists only in clothes. Fashion is in the air. It has something to do with ideas, with the way in which we live, with what happens around us.' Coco Chanel made this often-quoted remark in the first half of the 20th century. She was perhaps the first designer to anticipate the all-encompassing 'lifestyle brand' that would dominate the century's end. And, in many ways, it would be her current heir at the house, Karl Lagerfeld (born Hamburg, 1938), who would bring it about. Early in his career, Lagerfeld caught on to the direction that fashion was moving in. In the 1960s, he realised the future was no longer in couture but ready-to-wear. After work as an assistant to Pierre Balmain aged just 17, then the role of Artistic Director at Jean Patou three years later, he eschewed the establishment of his own couture house, instead taking on the role of freelance designer. With bases in France, Italy, England and Germany, he designed everything related to fashion: clothing, fabric and accessories. Although unconsciously, to a great extent he defined himself in opposition to Yves Saint Laurent, with whom he had won the International Wool Secretariat competition in 1955. Both would go on to determine the face of fashion during the next 50 years. Karl Lagerfeld is a designer in the truly modern sense: his genius is in adapting to and articulating each of his given roles supremely well. Whether it be his work at Fendi (beginning with the fur collection in 1965 and now all of their lines), his two periods at Chloé (1963–83 and 1992–97), his artistic direction at Chanel (from 1983), his own Karl Lagerfeld label (begun 1984) and now Lagerfeld Gallery (1998), which combines his passions for fashion, books and photography, each project has been imbued with its own distinct style and character. Then there's his interest in perfume (as important for Lagerfeld as clothing), the opera, ballet and illustration work, the photography of his own advertising campaigns, the magazine shoots, the series of art titles… It's with good reason that Karl Lagerfeld is known as the hardest working man in fashion.

'Mode ist nicht etwas, das nur in Form von Kleidung existiert. Mode liegt in der Luft. Sie hat mit Ideen zu tun, mit der Art, wie wir leben, mit dem, was um uns herum geschieht.' Coco Chanel tat diesen vielzitierten Ausspruch in der ersten Hälfte des 20. Jahrhunderts. Und vielleicht war sie damit die erste Designerin, die jene alles umfassenden 'Lifestyle-Marken', die am Ende des Jahrhunderts dominieren würden, vorausahnte. Und in vielerlei Hinsicht sollte ihr Nachfolger im Hause Chanel, der 1938 in Hamburg geborene Karl Lagerfeld, daran mitwirken. Schon früh in seiner Karriere erfasste Lagerfeld, in welche Richtung die Mode sich entwickelte. In den 1960er Jahren war ihm bereits klar, dass die Zukunft weniger in der Haute Couture, sondern eher im Bereich Prêt-à-Porter lag. Nach seiner Arbeit als Assistent von Pierre Balmain mit erst 17 Jahren und als Artistic Director bei Jean Patou nur drei Jahre später, entschied er sich gegen die Eröffnung eines eigenen Couture-Ateliers und für die Laufbahn eines freischaffenden Designers. An seinen Stützpunkten in Frankreich, Italien, England und Deutschland kreierte er praktisch alles, was mit Mode zu tun hat: Kleidung, Stoffe und Accessoires. Obwohl er sich dessen wohl nicht bewusst war, behauptete er sich in weiten Teilen als Gegenspieler von Yves Saint Laurent, seitdem beide gleichzeitig 1955 den Wettbewerb des International Wool Secretariat gewonnen hatten. Beide sollten in den kommenden fünfzig Jahren das Antlitz der Mode bestimmen. Karl Lagerfeld ist ein Designer nach modernem Verständnis: Auf geradezu geniale Weise passt er sich an jede vorgegebene Rolle an und füllt sie auf das Beste aus. Ob es seine Tätigkeit für Fendi ist (die mit der Pelzkollektion von 1965 begann und jetzt alle Linien des Hauses umfasst), seine zwei Schaffensperioden bei Chloé (1963–83 und 1992–97), die künstlerische Leitung des Hauses Chanel (seit 1983), das eigene Label Karl Lagerfeld (1984 gegründet) oder nun die Lagerfeld Gallery (seit 1998), wo der Allrounder seine Leidenschaften für Mode, Bücher und Fotografie auslebt – jedes dieser Projekte war oder ist durchdrungen von einem ganz eigenen Stil und Charakter. Dann wäre da noch Lagerfelds Faible für Düfte, die ihm ebenso wichtig sind wie seine Mode, außerdem seine Liebe zur Oper, zum Ballett und zu Illustrationen, nicht zu vergessen die Fotos für seine eigenen Werbekampagnen, für Zeitschriften, eine Reihe von Kunstbüchern … Aus gutem Grund gilt Lagerfeld als der vielbeschäftigtste Mann der Modebranche.

« La mode, ce n'est pas que des vêtements. La mode est dans l'air. Elle a quelque chose à voir avec les idées, avec nos modes de vie, avec ce qui se passe autour de nous. » Souvent cité, ce commentaire de Coco Chanel date de la première moitié du XXe siècle. Elle était peut-être la première couturière à anticiper le concept global de « lifestyle » qui allait dominer la fin du siècle. Et à de nombreux égards, c'est son héritier actuel à la tête de la maison, Karl Lagerfeld (né en 1938 à Hambourg), qui lui donnera forme. Dès le début de sa carrière, Lagerfeld sait quelle direction la mode va prendre. Dans les années 1960, il prend conscience que l'avenir n'appartient plus à la haute couture mais au prêt-à-porter. Après avoir travaillé comme assistant de Pierre Balmain dès l'âge de 17 ans, puis trois ans plus tard comme directeur artistique de Jean Patou, Lagerfeld décide de ne pas créer sa propre maison de haute couture, préférant travailler en free-lance. Depuis différentes bases en France, en Italie, en Angleterre et en Allemagne, il dessine tout ce qui touche de près ou de loin à la mode : vêtements, tissus et accessoires. Bien que ce soit de façon inconsciente, Lagerfeld s'est défini dans une large mesure par opposition à Yves Saint Laurent, aux côtés duquel il a remporté le concours International Wool Secretariat en 1955. Ces deux couturiers devaient en effet dessiner le visage de la mode pendant les cinquante années suivantes. Karl Lagerfeld est un créateur au sens le plus actuel du terme : son génie réside dans sa capacité d'adaptation et la facilité suprême avec laquelle il concilie chacun de ses différents rôles. Que ce soit son travail chez Fendi (débuté par une collection de fourrures en 1965, aujourd'hui pour toutes les lignes de la maison italienne), ses deux périodes d'activité chez Chloé (1963–83 et 1992–97), la direction artistique de Chanel (depuis 1983), sa propre griffe Karl Lagerfeld (lancée en 1984) et aujourd'hui Lagerfeld Gallery (1998) qui lui permet de combiner ses passions pour la mode, les livres et la photographie, chacun de ses projets est imprégné de son style si particulier et de son caractère bien trempé. Outre son intérêt pour le parfum (aussi important à ses yeux que les vêtements), Lagerfeld nourrit une passion pour l'opéra, le ballet et l'illustration. Il photographie ses propres campagnes publicitaires, réalise des shootings pour les magazines, a créé une série de livres d'art… Ce n'est pas pour rien que Karl Lagerfeld est considéré comme le travailleur plus acharné de la mode.

"I've survived quite a few generations. That's because I never lost my enthusiasm. I wake up every morning like on Christmas Day, waiting for the gifts"

PORTRAIT BY GAUTHIER GALLET

KARL LAGERFELD

PHOTOGRAPHY BY GAUTHIER GALLET. JULY 2001

PHOTOGRAPHY BY TERRY RICHARDSON, STYLING BY PATTI WILSON. NOVEMBER 2002

PHOTOGRAPHY BY ROBERT WYATT, STYLING BY LUCY EWING, MARCH 2001. MODEL: BRIDGET HALL

CHANEL BY KARL LAGERFELD

PHOTOGRAPHY BY SOPHIE DELAPORTE. STYLING BY KARL PLEWKA. MAY 2001

"I don't want to be my own souvenir, or a typical symbol of the '60s. I'm from no generation, I'm part of no group. I'm totally floating and this is the whole story, and why I can survive"

What's your philosophy? Never compare, never compete **What's the most important lesson you've learned?** What not to do. That's what I've learned in life. I vaguely know what not to do, but I don't know yet what I should do. And I have to work to find out. I always think the next step will be better, I will improve. That's why I don't do retrospectives, that's why I never looked at old things I did, that's why I never keep clothes or documents. I have nothing, nothing, nothing. It's only now and tomorrow

Helmut Lang is simultaneously one of the most influential and one of the most copied designers of the last decade. Starting his label in Vienna in 1977, without any formal training, the Austrian designer (born 1956) showed his first fully formed ready-to-wear collection in Paris in 1986. He was already displaying the shape of things to come: his austere, utilitarian and sportswear-inspired design would go on to dominate the 1990s. Lang formulated the prevailing, stripped-down silhouette of that decade and applied it to both sexes – he was one of the first to show men's and womenswear together. He experimented and introduced techno fabrics to a catwalk style, playing with technology further by showing one collection solely on the Internet, the first designer to do so. While Giorgio Armani is sometimes credited as the father of it and Jil Sander was another early pursuer, it is Lang who fully articulated what has become known as 'minimalism' – a term that he personally doesn't like. Maybe that dislike stems from Lang's almost autobiographical approach to his design: the combination of the formal and the casual at the heart of his aesthetic comes from the strict business suits he was made to wear as a teenager by his stepmother. Rather than 'trends', there is the sense of experimentation within a single identity in his collections. In 1998, Helmut Lang relocated his fashion house to New York. A year later he sold 51 percent of his company to the Prada Group. This has proved the start of a new phase for the designer, with a move into a more 'luxe' aesthetic, together with the launch of a perfume and accessories range.

Helmut Lang zählt zu den einflussreichsten und meistkopierten Designern des vergangenen Jahrzehnts. Der 1956 geborene Österreicher gründete 1977 in Wien als völliger Autodidakt in Sachen Mode sein eigenes Label. Die erste formvollendete Prêt-à-Porter-Kollektion präsentierte er 1986 in Paris. Dort bekam man bereits einen Vorgeschmack auf die Zukunft, denn sein nüchternes, funktionales und von der klassischen Sportbekleidung inspiriertes Design sollte die 1990er Jahre dominieren. Lang prägte die vorherrschende reduzierte Silhouette jener Dekade und verordnete sie Männern wie Frauen – er war auch einer der ersten, die Herren- und Damenmode zusammen präsentierten. Der experimentierfreudige Österreicher brachte synthetische Fasern auf den Laufsteg. Seine Vorliebe für moderne Technologie ging sogar so weit, dass er als erster Designer eine neue Kollektion ausschließlich im Internet zeigte. Auch wenn manchmal Giorgio Armani als Vater des Minimalismus bezeichnet wird und Jil Sander als eine seiner frühen Vertreterinnen gilt, so war es doch Lang, der diesen Stil als erster regelrecht ausarbeitete – und das, obwohl er persönlich den Begriff Minimalismus keineswegs schätzt. Vielleicht entspringt diese Abneigung dem fast autobiografischen Verhältnis des Designers zu seinen Entwürfen. Die Kombination von Strenge und Lässigkeit als Basis seiner Ästhetik mag ihren Ursprung in den formellen Anzügen haben, die er als Teenager auf Geheiß seiner Stiefmutter tragen musste. Statt neue Trends vorzugeben, experimentiert Lang in seinen Kollektionen eher mit den Möglichkeiten einer einzigen Persönlichkeit. 1998 verlegte der Designer sein Modehaus nach New York. Im folgenden Jahr verkaufte er 51 Prozent seines Unternehmens an den Prada-Konzern. Damit begann für Lang eine neue Schaffensphase, in der er sich einer etwas luxuriöseren Ästhetik verschrieben und neben einem Parfum auch eine Reihe von Accessoires kreiert hat.

Helmut Lang (né en 1956) est l'un des créateurs de mode les plus influents et les plus copiés de ces dix dernières années. Sans formation préalable, il lance sa propre griffe à Vienne en 1977. En 1986, le créateur autrichien présente à Paris une première collection complète de prêt-à-porter qui préfigure déjà la tendance à venir : ses créations austères, utilitaires et d'inspiration sportswear devaient en effet dominer la mode des années 1990. Lang définit la silhouette épurée qui symbolise cette décennie et l'applique aux deux sexes : il est d'ailleurs l'un des premiers à présenter vêtements pour homme et pour femme au cours d'un même défilé. Il expérimente les nouveaux tissus techno et les adapte au style « podium ». Jouant avec la technologie, il fait figure de pionnier en présentant une collection uniquement sur Internet. Bien que Giorgio Armani en soit parfois considéré comme le père et Jil Sander comme l'une des premières disciples, c'est pourtant Lang qui a entièrement articulé ce qu'il convient d'appeler aujourd'hui le « minimalisme », un terme qu'il n'aime pas. Ce rejet découle peut-être de la vision presque autobiographique que porte Lang sur ses créations : la combinaison du formel et du décontracté qui se trouve au cœur de son esthétique lui vient des costumes stricts que sa belle-mère l'obligeait à porter quand il était adolescent. Plutôt que des « tendances », ses collections présentent avant tout un sens de l'expérimentation vraiment unique. En 1998, la maison Helmut Lang s'installe à New York. Un an plus tard, il cède 51% de son entreprise au Groupe Prada. Ce tournant marque le début d'une nouvelle phase pour le créateur, qui se dirige désormais vers une esthétique plus « luxe », accompagnée par le lancement d'un parfum et d'une ligne d'accessoires.

"I think I always had a good sense of seeing things that were coming and was never afraid to explore them"

PORTRAIT BY ANTHONY WARD

HELMUT LANG

PHOTOGRAPHY BY RICHARD BURBRIDGE, STYLING BY EDWARD ENNINFUL. APRIL 2001. MODEL: SVETA

PHOTOGRAPHY BY MATT JONES, STYLING BY KATE YOUNG. DECEMBER/JANUARY 2002. MODEL: RYAN GOSLING

PHOTOGRAPHY BY ELFIE SEMOTAN, STYLING BY SABINA SCHREDER. MARCH 1999

"Always be open-minded, curious, forward-thinking and then suspicious"

What are your signature designs? Everything What's your favourite piece from any of your collections? Everything How would you describe your work? Nobody does it better What's your ultimate goal? The right balance What inspires you? Contradictions Can fashion still have a political ambition? Not now. It might happen again though Who do you have in mind when you design? Nobody in particular but everybody special Is the idea of creative collaboration important to you? Yes, very much so. I have worked with Melanie Ward for a long time What has been the greatest influence on your career? People and time How have your own experiences affected your work as a designer? Without experience you cannot develop in life and you cannot progress in your work Which is more important in your work: the process or the product? Both Is designing difficult for you and, if so, what drives you to continue? I don't know Have you ever been influenced or moved by the reaction to your designs? Yes, all the time What's your definition of beauty? Everything goes What's your philosophy? Always be open-minded, curious, forward-thinking, and then suspicious What's the most important lesson you've learned? Never give up

PHOTOGRAPHY BY WILLY VANDERPERRE, STYLING BY OLIVIER RIZZO. AUGUST 2002

Ralph Lauren is one of the dominant lifestyle brands of the late 20th Century, with that small polo pony the fashion world's most recognised logo. Its appeal? An 'elitist' design sensibility aiming to capture the gentrified Ivy League manner, reworking the preppy tradition and aspirational lifestyle of the classic East Coast collegiate scene: button-down shirts and twin-sets, blazers and Bermuda shorts, ruffled blouses and full skirts. Once appropriated and reworked by urban black youth, Ralph Lauren became the American uniform, from Wall Street to Harlem. It has been a remarkable 35 years of empire building for the New York born (in 1939) and based designer: as a teen, he would spend the money earned from an after-school job on pricey suits. After two years in the army, he sold gloves at Brooks Brothers while, tellingly, studying business at Manhattan's City College night school. He joined A Rivetz & Co Neckwear in 1967 where, against trend, he designed wider ties and created the Polo brand. In 1968, a $50,000 loan led to the creation of his own company, Polo Designs, including men's and womenswear by 1971 and an eponymous collection of essentially updated classics in 1972. But fashion design was always just one element of what is now a $900m company. Lauren sells not just clothes, bed linen, paint or perfume, but class. And like others of his brand status, his marketing skills were canny from the outset: he was the first designer to open his own store (1971) and the first US designer to open in Europe (1981). Ralph Lauren remains the only designer to receive all five of the CFDA's awards, including that for humanitarian leadership (in 1989 he founded a centre for breast cancer research at Georgetown University; in 1994 initiated the Fashion Targets Breast Cancer fundraising campaign; and in 2000 established the Ralph Lauren Center for cancer care in Harlem). He most recently launched a new womenswear range, Blue Label (2002), which updates his heritage classics.

Ralph Lauren war eine der dominierenden Lifestylemarken des späten 20. Jahrhunderts und das kleine Polopferd das bekannteste Logo der Modewelt. Was den Appeal dieses Labels ausmachte? Sein Gespür für 'elitäres' Design, das dem Ivy-League-Stil nachempfunden war und eine Wiederbelebung der Preppy-Tradition und des ambitionierten Lebensstils der klassischen Ostküsten-Colleges bedeutete: Button-down-Hemden und Twinsets, Blazer und Bermudashorts, Rüschenblusen und weite Röcke. Nachdem die schwarze Jugend der Städte sich die Marke angeeignet und auf ihre Bedürfnisse zugeschnitten hatte, wurde Ralph Lauren von der Wall Street bis nach Harlem zu einer Art amerikanischer Uniform. Der 1939 in New York geborene und bis heute dort lebende Designer hat beachtliche 35 Jahre an seinem Imperium gearbeitet. Als Teenager gab Ralph Lauren das Geld, das er sich mit einem Job nach der Schule verdiente, für preiswerte Anzüge aus. Nach zwei Jahren in der Armee verkaufte er bei Brooks Brothers Handschuhe und studierte gleichzeitig in Abendkursen am Manhattan City College bezeichnenderweise Wirtschaft. 1967 trat er in die Firma A Rivetz & Co Neckwear ein, wo er entgegen dem damaligen Trend breitere Krawatten entwarf und das Polo-Logo erfand. Mit Hilfe eines Kredits von 50 000 Dollar gründete Lauren 1968 seine eigene Firma Polo Designs. 1971 produzierte er bereits Herren- und Damenmode, ab 1972 auch eine Kollektion gründlich modernisierter Klassiker unter seinem eigenen Namen. Doch Mode war immer nur ein Bereich des heute 900 Millionen Dollar schweren Unternehmens. Lauren verkaufte nicht nur Kleidung, Bettwäsche, Farbe oder Parfum, sondern Klasse. Und wie Kollegen von Marken mit ähnlichem Status erwies auch er sich von Anfang an als Marketinggenie: So war Ralph Lauren 1971 der erste Designer, der einen eigenen Laden eröffnete, und 1981 der erste US-Designer, der eben dies in Europa tat. Lauren ist auch bis heute der einzige Designer, dem alle fünf Auszeichnungen des Council of Fashion Designers of America verliehen wurden – einschließlich des Preises für vorbildliches humanitäres Verhalten (1989 gründete er an der Georgetown University ein Zentrum zur Erforschung von Brustkrebs; 1994 rief er die Kampagne Fashion Targets Breast Cancer ins Leben, um Geld für die Forschung zu sammeln; 2000 wurde in Harlem das Ralph Lauren Center für Krebskranke gegründet). Zuletzt hat der Designer im Jahr 2002 Blue Label auf den Markt gebracht, eine neue Nebenlinie für Damen mit seinen eigenen aktualisierten Klassikern.

Ralph Lauren compte parmi les plus importantes marques de «lifestyle» de la fin du XXᵉ siècle et le petit poney de ses polos est aujourd'hui le logo de mode le plus connu au monde. Le secret de Ralph Lauren? Une approche «élitiste» de la création qui vise à capter le style Ivy League aristocrate en revisitant l'héritage BCBG et le mode de vie plein d'ambition des universités de la Côte Est: chemises avec col à pointes boutonnées et twin-sets, blazers et bermudas, chemises à volants et jupes amples. La jeunesse black urbaine s'approprie et revisite le style Ralph Lauren, qui depuis s'est imposé comme l'uniforme américain de Wall Street à Harlem. Né en 1939 à New York, Ralph Lauren travaille sans relâche pendant 35 ans pour bâtir son empire: adolescent, il dépense l'argent qu'il gagne avec ses petits jobs pour acheter des costumes hors de prix. Après deux ans passés dans l'armée, il vend des gants chez Brooks Brothers tandis que, fait révélateur s'il en est, il étudie la gestion d'entreprise aux cours du soir du City College de Manhattan. En 1967, il rejoint A Rivetz & Co Neckwear où, à contre-courant des tendances, il dessine des cravates plus larges et crée la marque Polo. En 1968, un prêt de 50 000 dollars lui permet de fonder sa propre entreprise, Polo Designs, qui lance des lignes pour homme et pour femme en 1971 ainsi qu'une collection éponyme de classiques remis au goût du jour en 1972. Mais la mode n'est qu'un élément de ce groupe qui pèse actuellement 900 millions de dollars. Lauren ne vend pas que des vêtements, de la literie ou des parfums, il vend aussi de la classe. Et comme d'autres créateurs de sa stature, ses compétences en marketing étaient aiguisées dès le départ: il est le premier couturier à ouvrir sa propre boutique (1971) et le premier styliste américain à ouvrir une boutique en Europe (1981). Ralph Lauren est aujourd'hui le seul créateur à avoir reçu les cinq prix du CFDA, notamment celui qui récompense les initiatives à vocation humanitaire (en 1989, Ralph Lauren a créé un centre de recherche sur le cancer du sein à l'Université de Georgetown; en 1994, il a lancé la campagne de collecte de fonds Fashion Targets Breast Cancer; en l'an 2000, il a ouvert le Centre de traitement du cancer Ralph Lauren à Harlem). Récemment, Ralph Lauren a lancé Blue Label (2002), une nouvelle collection pour femme qui revisite les classiques de la marque.

"I've never been about fashion and trends. I believe in design that has a lasting integrity"

PORTRAIT COURTESY OF RALPH LAUREN

RALPH LAUREN

PHOTOGRAPHY COURTESY OF RALPH LAUREN. SPRING-SUMMER 2002.

RALPH LAUREN

PHOTOGRAPHY BY TAKAY, STYLING BY MARK ANTHONY. OCTOBER 200

What are your signature designs? Several of my collections have been referred to as signature – Sante Fe, Safari, some of the nautical or western collections **What is your favourite piece from any of your collections?** I don't really think in terms of pieces, although elements of certain collections were definitely standouts. The coats inspired by native American blankets, leather fringed jackets with whipstitching, menswear for women **What inspires you?** Each season I'm inspired by something different. Sometimes it's a film or even a photograph. It's not a literal thing – I just sense a mood, and that leads me in a new direction **Who has been the greatest influence on your career?** My family – my wife, Ricky, and my children, Andrew, David and Dylan. So much of what I've accomplished in my career has been inspired by different experiences we've had as a family. I got into womenswear because I wanted to put together a collection that would be right for Ricky. It was the same for the children's and even the home collection **How have your own experiences affected your work as a designer?** Some of my collections were inspired by travel and vacations I've taken with my family – an African safari, time we've spent in Colorado or Jamaica. As a New Yorker, I also respond to the energy of the city – an urban sensibility **Is designing difficult for you and, if so, what drives you to continue?** The design process can be challenging, but I'm always excited at the start of a new season. With so many collections, and such a diverse company, there is always something happening… it's that momentum that keeps things new **Have you ever been influenced or moved by the reaction to your designs?** I'm most concerned with how my customers respond to a collection. Can they see themselves wearing my clothes? Do they fit in with their lifestyle? **What's your definition of beauty?** Beauty is an attitude – it's an expression of elegance and confidence **What's your philosophy?** I've never been about fashion and trends. I believe in design that has a lasting integrity. Whatever it is – a jacket, a gown, furnishings for the home – it must be part of a lifestyle and become more personal with time **What is the most important lesson you've learned?** To maintain a consistent point of view and a clarity of vision

Christophe Lemaire's work is articulated around the concept of elegant functionality: an effortless blend of the luxurious with the practical. His signature designs are zipped jackets and printed shirts, always very wearable, but with enough panache to mark them out as directional pieces. Lemaire, born in Besançon, France in 1965, first studied literature before turning his hand to fashion. Lemaire has a wealth of design experience, having worked first with Thierry Mugler, then Jean Patou and Christian Lacroix, also assisting at the Yves Saint Laurent design studio. He established his eponymous womenswear label in 1990; menswear followed in 1994. Since Spring-Summer 2002, Lemaire has also held the position of Creative Director for the world-famous Lacoste sportswear brand. His skill with colour, cut and innovation – combined with a respectful reverence for the heritage of his employer – have helped to re-establish Lacoste as a leading directional sportswear company. Lemaire designs both the men's and womenswear collections, and oversaw the label's first-ever catwalk presentation in June 2001. Following a two-season break from his own line, enabling the designer to concentrate solely on Lacoste, Lemaire is once again working on his own collections for men and women, which will be presented in Paris for Spring-Summer 2003.

Christophe Lemaires Arbeit basiert auf dem Konzept eleganter Funktionalität, auf der mühelosen Verbindung des Luxuriösen mit dem Praktischen. Markenzeichen dieses Designers sind Reißverschlussjacken und bedruckte Shirts – alles sehr gut tragbar, aber aufwändig genug, um als Statement zu taugen. Der 1965 in Besançon geborene Lemaire studierte Literatur, bevor er sich der Mode zuwandte. Entsprechende Erfahrungen hat der Franzose reichlich gesammelt: zunächst bei Thierry Mugler, dann bei Jean Patou und Christian Lacroix sowie als Assistent im Atelier von Yves Saint Laurent. Das nach ihm selbst benannte Damenmodelabel gründete Lemaire 1990; in der Herrenmode ist er seit 1994 vertreten. Seit Frühjahr/Sommer 2002 wirkt der Designer zusätzlich als Creative Director der weltberühmten Sportmodemarke Lacoste. Sein Talent im Umgang mit Farben, Schnitten und Innovationen – sowie der angemessene Respekt vor der Tradition dieses Hauses – hat ihm geholfen, Lacoste wieder als führenden, richtungsweisenden Sportswear-Hersteller zu etablieren. Lemaire entwirft sowohl die Herren- als auch die Damenkollektion und verantwortete im Juni 2001 die allererste Catwalk-Präsentation des Labels. Nach zwei Saisons Pause mit seiner eigenen Linie, um sich ganz auf Lacoste konzentrieren zu können, entwirft der Designer für Frühjahr/Sommer 2003 auch wieder eigene Kollektionen für Damen und Herren, die er in Paris vorstellen wird.

Le travail de Christophe Lemaire s'articule autour du concept de l'élégance fonctionnelle, mêlant luxe et sens pratique avec une déconcertante facilité. Parmi ses modèles les plus caractéristiques, ses vestes zippées et ses chemises imprimées, très faciles à porter, n'en sont pas moins très innovantes et pleines de panache. Né en 1965 à Besançon, Lemaire commence par étudier la littérature avant de s'orienter vers la mode. Il possède un CV bien rempli, avec une première expérience chez Thierry Mugler, puis chez Jean Patou et Christian Lacroix, sans parler de son poste d'assistant au studio de création Yves Saint Laurent. Lemaire lance sa griffe éponyme pour femme en 1990, suivie d'une ligne masculine en 1994. Depuis le Printemps-Eté 2002, Lemaire est également directeur de la création de Lacoste, marque de sportswear célèbre dans le monde entier. Son talent en matière de couleurs, de coupe et d'innovation, combiné à son immense respect pour la riche tradition de son employeur, l'ont aidé à faire revenir Lacoste sur le devant de la scène sportswear. Lemaire dessine à la fois les collections pour femme et pour homme. Il a supervisé le tout premier défilé de la marque en juin 2001. Pendant deux saisons, Lemaire laisse donc de côté sa propre griffe pour se consacrer entièrement à Lacoste. Aujourd'hui, il travaille à nouveau sur ses collections masculine et féminine, qu'il présentera à Paris au Printemps-Eté 2003.

"Look for quality in everything"

PORTRAIT BY TERRY JONES

CHRISTOPHE LEMAIRE

PHOTOGRAPHY BY TAKAY, STYLING BY MARK ANTHONY. NOVEMBER 2001

What are your signature designs? Printed shirts, zipped jackets, pants… **How would you describe your work?** I want to create clothes, accessories and objects that are essential and charming, functional with taste, precise and funky, simple and special **Can fashion still have a political ambition?** Fashion really is about aesthetics… Of course, if we think of fashion as an expression of individuality, as style, as attitude towards others, then yes, style can have a political meaning. I would rather say that fashion must have a cultural meaning **Who do you have in mind when you design?** I am generally inspired by people from the music scene, like Nick Cave, Serge Gainsbourg, PJ Harvey, Deborah Harry… I always found people connected to music are more stylish, free-minded and expressive than the majority of the fashion crowd **Is the idea of creative collaboration important to you?** Fundamental. That's what everyday life should be about – sharing ideas. My work as a designer would mean nothing without the team around me **What has been the greatest influence on your career?** Japanese culture, rock 'n' roll (Stooges, Ramones) and Yves Saint Laurent **How have your own experiences affected your work as a designer?** Too complex, unconscious, to answer precisely! **Which is more important in your work: the process or the product?** As a designer, what really matters at the end of the day is the product: is it good or is it bad? But through the years, I also learned how essential the process was. A better process – creative, focused, positive – makes a better product **Is designing difficult for you and, if so, what drives you to continue?** I find designing actually quite natural and exciting. What's more difficult for me and demands more discipline and concentration (I am rather impulsive and impatient) is all the process to make the design happen, become real and faithful to my first intuition. That's why the process is as important as the product **Have you ever been influenced or moved by the reaction to your designs?** I am probably too sensitive to the opinions of others and I try to free myself from that dependence. I can easily lose my confidence if I don't feel good reactions to my work **What's your philosophy?** Listen to my heart as much as my brain, fight against laziness, conformism, mediocrity (starting with my own) and look for quality in everything. Show respect to others **What is the most important lesson you've learned?** Patience

Véronique Leroy's clothes are sexy: pure and simple. Born in Liège, Belgium, in 1965, Leroy arrived in Paris in 1984 where she began her design career at Studio Berçot, leaving after three years to assist Didier Renard, then Azzedine Alaïa and Martine Sitbon. Leroy established her own label in 1991 and, from the start, her emphasis was on accentuating the female form. Her clothes consistently toy with the proportions of a woman's body – Leroy is a designer unafraid to juxtapose sharply tailored and voluminous garments, something which she does with great panache. She cuts to flatter, but not necessarily in a figure-hugging manner like one might expect of someone who trained with Alaïa. Leroy's idea of what constitutes sexy operates on an intellectually mature, more conceptual level, always with an independent and rebellious streak. She is well known for her graphic swimwear designs, which are extremely popular. After many years, Leroy continues to collaborate with photographic team Inez van Lamsweerde and Vinoodh Matadin, whose style has helped to shape the image of her label. Leroy has been awarded many accolades during her career, including the Canette d'Or, the Courtelle award and the Vénus de la Mode prize for 'Le Futur Grand Créateur' three times. Although technically a Belgian designer, Leroy has spent her working life in Paris and prefers to work independently of any movement – indicative of her strong spirit and undiminished individuality.

Die Mode von Véronique Leroy ist sexy, makellos und schlicht. Die 1965 in Liège geborene Belgierin ging 1984 nach Paris, wo sie ihre Designerkarriere im Studio Berçot begann. Nach drei Jahren wechselte sie als Assistentin zunächst zu Didier Renard, anschließend zu Azzedine Alaïa und dann zu Martine Sitbon. Ihr eigenes Label gründete Leroy 1991. Dabei legte sie von Anfang an besonderes Augenmerk auf die Akzentuierung der weiblichen Formen. Ihre Kreationen spielen permanent mit den Proportionen des Frauenkörpers. Die Designerin schreckt jedoch nicht davor zurück, figurnah geschnittene und voluminöse Stücke miteinander zu konfrontieren, was sie sogar mit großem Aufwand tut. Ihre Schnitte schmeicheln, allerdings nicht unbedingt auf figurbetonte Weise, wie man das von einer Alaïa-Schülerin vielleicht erwarten würde. Leroys Vorstellung davon, was sexy ist, bewegt sich auf einem intellektuell gereiften, eher konzeptionellen Niveau, und immer ist eine Spur Unabhängigkeit und Rebellion mit im Spiel. Die Designerin ist besonders für ihre außerordentlich beliebten grafisch gestalteten Bademoden bekannt. Seit vielen Jahren arbeitet sie mit dem Fotografenteam Inez van Lamsweerde und Vinoodh Matadin zusammen, deren Stil das Image ihres Labels mitgeprägt hat. Im Laufe ihrer Karriere hat Leroy schon viele Auszeichnungen erhalten, darunter die Canette d'Or, den Courtelle-Preis und dreimal die Vénus de la Mode für ›Le Futur Grand Créateur‹. Genau genommen ist sie zwar Belgierin, doch hat die Designerin ihr gesamtes bisheriges Berufsleben in Paris verbracht. Außerdem schätzt sie es, unabhängig von jeglicher Gruppe oder Strömung zu arbeiten – ein Beleg ihrer ausgeprägten Persönlichkeit und ihres ungebrochenen Individualismus.

Les créations de Véronique Leroy sont purement et simplement sexy. Née en 1965 à Liège en Belgique, Véronique Leroy débarque à Paris en 1984. Elle passe trois ans au Studio Berçot puis devient assistante styliste de Didier Renard, d'Azzedine Alaïa puis de Martine Sitbon. Elle lance sa propre griffe en 1991 et, dès le départ, cherche à accentuer les formes féminines. Ses créations jouent souvent sur les proportions du corps de la femme : Véronique Leroy n'a pas peur de juxtaposer vêtements aux coupes sévères et pièces plus volumineuses, un mélange dans lequel elle excelle avec un certain panache. Ses coupes flattent le corps, mais pas nécessairement en soulignant ses formes comme on pourrait s'y attendre de la part d'une créatrice formée chez Alaïa. Sa vision du sexy opère à un niveau plus conceptuel et plus abouti intellectuellement, mais toujours avec une touche d'indépendance rebelle. Véronique Leroy est surtout connue pour ses maillots de bain graphiques, qui remportent un énorme succès. Depuis de nombreuses années, elle collabore avec l'équipe de photographes formée par Inez van Lamsweerde et Vinoodh Matadin, dont le style a contribué à former l'image de sa griffe. Véronique Leroy a reçu de nombreuses distinctions tout au long de sa carrière, notamment la Canette d'Or, le prix Courtelle et trois fois le prix de « Futur Grand Créateur » décerné par les Vénus de la Mode. Bien qu'elle soit techniquement une créatrice belge, Véronique Leroy a toujours travaillé à Paris, préférant évoluer indépendamment de tout mouvement : la preuve que cette forte tête a su garder intact son individualisme si particulier.

"Making clothes isn't exciting –
what is exciting is being able
to give them a soul"

PORTRAIT BY KARL LAGERFELD

VÉRONIQUE LEROY

What are your signature designs? They have more to do with cut, shape and attitude than decoration **How would you describe your work?** Designing for me is to succeed in translating my ideas and envies; it's being able to give them a shape, an attitude. Because making clothes isn't exciting – what is exciting is being able to give them a soul **What's your ultimate goal** To still like this job and to carry on being passionate about what I am doing **What inspires you?** I have been trying to understand this, but still don't know. I can say that everything is inspiring, it just depends how you look at things **Who do you have in mind when you design?** When I draw a collection I have no-one in particular in mind – I'm looking more into making clothes that I like. A person or a personality appears when the collection is almost finished **Is the idea of creative collaboration important to you?** I always collaborate with my team, but from time to time with people from the 'outside' also; my collaboration with Inez van Lamsweerde, for example, is very important because it allows me to go further **What has been the greatest influence on your career?** Everything: my life, my friends, other relationships, politics, trading and, above all, my own choices **How have your own experiences affected your work as a designer?** There is no gap between V Leroy and V Leroy the designer, so any experiences have affected my work **Which is more important in your work: the process or the product?** The process as it leads to the product **Is designing difficult for you and, if so, what drives you to continue?** Designing isn't difficult. The thing that is most difficult is to get into it, when you're looking for the rhythm. But when you feel that you have caught it then you get moments of grace, moments 'hanging in time'. I think it's the pleasure you feel in those moments which makes it vital to continue **Have you ever been influenced or moved by the reaction to your work?** I don't think so. Maybe indirectly **What's your definition of beauty?** Beauty is the combination of a moment and a sight. It's very abstract; you can find beautiful one day something you didn't like weeks ago. Beauty has more to do with feeling **What is the most important lesson you've learned?** Nothing is ever granted

PHOTOGRAPHY BY STEEN SUNDLAND, STYLING BY JAMES SLEAFORD. NOVEMBER 2000

From Giorgio Armani to Marc Jacobs, designers almost universally have one wish: to have invented jeans. In fact, they were created by a San Francisco trader called Levi Strauss and a Reno tailor called Jacob Davis, who bought denim from Strauss. Davis began riveting trousers for a client who complained that his tore too easily. When other customers asked for the same service, he decided to patent the idea, but couldn't afford to alone. So he asked Strauss to help him and in 1873 they produced the first 'patented riveted overall'. The double arc they stitched onto the pockets is now the oldest continuously used clothing trademark in the US. A century later, Levi's were still being produced but the denim market was struggling and had no obvious leader. In 1985, everything changed when Levi's began one of the most memorable ad campaigns in history: Nick Kamen stripping off his jeans to the sound of Marvin Gaye, increasing sales of 501s by an incredible 820 percent. The 1990s was a terrible time for denim companies, as military and thrift clothing was universally adopted. In the late 1990s fortunes turned again, denim re-emerging with a more fervoured interest than ever seen before. Levi's have been both quick and clever in capitalising on this, setting up two new lines: Levi's RED (1999) and Levi's Vintage Clothing. The first, designed by Rikke Korff, utilises Levi's history and iconography to respond to current trends, bursting onto the market with their 'twisted' designs. LVC, meanwhile, has concentrated on carefully replicating pieces from the company archives. The discovery of a pair of jeans in an attic in summer 2001 caused excitement around the world after they were put on eBay because they pre-dated the oldest known pair. The rivets proved they were Levi's, who bought them at auction for $46,532. This is testimony to the enduring appeal of a true original, a symbol of the 20th century that was born before, and will doubtless long outlive it.

Von Giorgio Armani bis Marc Jacobs wünschen sich eigentlich alle Designer dasselbe: die Jeans erfunden zu haben. Tatsächlich sind sie die Idee eines Kaufmanns namens Levi Strauss aus San Francisco und des Schneiders Jacob Davis aus Reno, der von Strauss Denim kaufte. Davis begann, die Hosen für einen Kunden zusammenzunieten, nachdem dieser sich darüber beschwert hatte, dass sie zu leicht zerreißen würden. Als andere Kunden den gleichen Service verlangten, entschloss sich der Schneider, seine Idee patentieren zu lassen, wofür er allein jedoch nicht genug Geld hatte. Also bat er Strauss, ihm auszuhelfen, und so produzierten die beiden 1873 den ersten 'patentierten genieteten Overall'. Der doppelte Bogen, den sie auf die Taschen stickten, ist heute das am längsten verwendete Markenzeichen für Textilien in den USA. Hundert Jahre nach ihrer Erfindung produzierte Levi's immer noch Jeans, doch der Markt für Textilien aus Denim war hart umkämpft, und es gab keine Marke, die ihn klar dominierte. Das sollte sich 1985 ändern, als Levi's eine der denkwürdigsten Werbekampagnen aller Zeiten startete: Nick Kamen zog sich zum Sound von Marvin Gaye seine Jeans aus und steigerte damit den Absatz der Levi's 501 um unglaubliche 820 Prozent. Die 1990er waren wieder eine schwere Zeit für die Jeanshersteller, da Militär- und Second-Hand-Kleidung allgemein im Trend lagen. Gegen Ende des Jahrzehnts wendete sich das Blatt erneut und Denim war angesagter denn je. Levi's hatte rasch und umsichtig reagiert – mit zwei neuen Linien: Levi's RED (1999) und Levi's Vintage Clothing (LVC). Erstere wurde von Rikke Korff designt und bediente sich der Geschichte und Ikonographie des Hauses, um auf aktuelle Trends zu reagieren; so stürmte man etwa den Markt mit 'twisted' Jeans. Bei LVC konzentrierte man sich derweil auf detailgetreue Repliken von Stücken aus dem Firmenarchiv. Im Sommer 2001 versetzte die Entdeckung einer uralten Jeans auf einem Dachboden die ganze Welt in Aufregung, weil sie älter war als die bislang älteste noch erhaltene Jeans. Die Nieten waren der Beweis für die Herkunft aus dem Hause Levi's, das dann die Hose schließlich auch für 46 532 Dollar beim Internet-Auktionshaus eBay ersteigerte. Das kann man wohl als Beweis für den ungebrochenen Reiz eines wahren Originals nehmen. Die Jeans ist ein Symbol des 20. Jahrhunderts, obwohl sie deutlich vor dessen Beginn erfunden wurde und es zweifellos lange überleben wird.

De Giorgio Armani à Marc Jacobs, les créateurs de mode sont nombreux à partager le même rêve : avoir inventé le jean. En fait, son invention revient à Levi Strauss, négociant de San Francisco, et Jacob Davis, un tailleur de Reno qui achetait du denim à Strauss. Au départ, Davis a l'idée de poser des rivets sur les pantalons pour satisfaire un client qui se plaignait de voir les siens se déchirer trop facilement. D'autres clients commencent à exiger le même service et Davis décide de breveter son idée. Comme il n'a pas les moyens de le faire seul, il fait appel à Strauss et en 1873, ils produisent le premier «jean à rivets breveté ». L'arc doublé qu'ils surpiquent sur les poches est aujourd'hui le motif le plus ancien et le plus utilisé dans la production de vêtements aux Etats-Unis. Un siècle plus tard, la marque Levi's est toujours produite mais le marché du jean est submergé par une telle offre qu'aucun leader ne s'y distingue vraiment. En 1985, tout bascule lorsque Levi's lance l'une des campagnes publicitaires les plus mémorables de l'histoire : Nick Kamen retire son jean sur une chanson de Marvin Gaye et les ventes de 501 enregistrent une incroyable augmentation de 820%. Les années 1990 marquent une décennie désastreuse pour les fabricants de jeans car à cette époque, le monde entier ne jure plus que par les tenues militaires recyclées et les vêtements d'occasion. A la fin des années 1990, la chance tourne à nouveau et le denim revient en force dans les garde-robes. Levi's mise rapidement et à bon escient sur cette tendance en lançant deux nouvelles lignes : Levi's RED (1999) et Levi's Vintage Clothing. La première, conçue par Rikke Korff, reprend l'histoire et l'iconographie de Levi's pour satisfaire les attentes du moment, explosant des records de vente avec son modèle «Twisted », tandis que LVC réplique des pièces issues des archives de la compagnie. A l'été 2001, la découverte d'un jean dans un grenier fait sensation dans le monde entier : antérieur à la plus vieille paire de Levi's connue, il est mis aux enchères sur le site d'eBay. Les rivets prouvant son authenticité, Levi's le rachète pour 46 532 dollars. Cette anecdote démontre l'attrait éternel qu'exerce un véritable original, symbole du XXe siècle bien qu'il lui soit antérieur et qu'il semble bien parti pour lui survivre encore longtemps.

"The goal is to inspire youth to re-appropriate denim in new ways"

PORTRAIT COURTESY OF GARY HARVEY, CREATIVE DIRECTOR LEVI'S EUROPE, MIDDLE EAST & AFRICA

LEVI'S

PHOTOGRAPHY BY TAKAY, STYLING BY MARK ANTHONY. OCTOBER 2002. MODEL: NOLAN HEMMINGS

What are your signature designs? Levi's 501, the original jeans; Levi's Engineered jeans; the new Levi's Type 1 jeans collection **What's your favourite piece from any of your collections?** The 1947 501 – it's the ultimate combination of silhouette, shrink to fit fabrication and denim styling **How would you describe your work?** The best job in the world! Taking inspiration from products in our archives and combining that with the future aspirations of the consumer, creating a complete jeanswear image for young people, from basic denim jeans to pioneering new forms of jeanswear **What's your ultimate goal?** To inspire youth to re-appropriate denim and jeanswear in new ways that suit their own lifestyle and image **What inspires you?** People and their potential for change **Can fashion still have a political ambition?** If personal identity is a statement of an individual's current beliefs then politics and fashion are inextricably linked, although apathy appears to dominate politics and fashion at times **Who do you have in mind when you design?** I do not have a person in mind, I have an attitude or feeling: rebellious, fuck-you and sexy. I try to think of the values the guys and girls who buy the jeans associate with the Levi's brand **Is the idea of creative collaboration important to you?** Yes, the best ideas come from using the best resources available. I work with some of the most talented designers and stylists in the business **Who has been the greatest influence on your career?** No single person or event has specifically influenced my career, although every person I have met to date has had some influence on my life **How have your own experiences affected your work as a designer?** Positively – a straightforward common sense approach **Which is more important in your work: the process or the product?** The product is the ultimate goal and a good process is designed with that in mind **Is designing difficult for you and, if so, what drives you to continue?** Any design involves a challenge and this is what stimulates me. So long as people continue to exert choice in their identity and our culture continues to evolve then designing will always be interesting **Have you ever been influenced or moved by the reaction to your designs?** I get energised and excited by the reactions whenever we launch a new range – the response to Levi's Type 1 jeans has been fantastic and our new Levi's girls fits are doing really well – but the real measure of success is seeing the stuff worn on the street. That gives me the biggest buzz **What's your definition of beauty?** If it excites you, it's beautiful **What's your philosophy?** Relax and enjoy it, you'll be dead soon enough **What is the most important lesson you've learned?** You have a choice in everything you do

Renowned for his intricate work in leather and experimental use of colour in the form of geometric patterns, Markus Lupfer's designs have an intangible sense of belonging to, and being of, London, where he is now permanently based. Born in Kißlegg, South Germany, in 1968, Lupfer studied fashion design in his home country before transferring to London's University of Westminster, graduating in 1997 with first class honours. His final year collection was sold to London boutique Koh Samui, instantly marking him out as a serious talent with a strong commercial edge. Following his graduation, Lupfer went to work with Clements Ribeiro, a training that is still evident today in his skill with knitwear, and established his own label a year later in 1998. Lupfer's designs are youthful and playful, whilst being simultaneously sophisticated and carefully crafted. Lupfer has been an 'on-schedule' London Fashion Week presence since 1999 and is currently one of the event's biggest attractions for international buyers and press. The Spring-Summer 2002 season saw the launch of Lupfer's accessory range, reiterating his reputation for desirable and expertly finished pieces in worked and woven leather. Lupfer's talent and pragmatic approach to fashion has resulted in a collaboration with influential high street retailer TopShop since 1999, for whom he produces a capsule collection.

Mit seinen raffinierten Lederkreationen und seiner experimentellen Verwendung von Farbe in geometrischen Mustern gibt Markus Lupfer dem Betrachter die unbestimmte Gewissheit, dass diese Mode aus seiner Wahlheimat London kommt und auch dorthin gehört. Dabei stammt der 1968 geborene Designer eigentlich aus dem süddeutschen Kißlegg. Lupfer studierte zunächst auch in Deutschland Mode, bevor er auf die University of Westminster in London wechselte, die er 1997 mit Auszeichnung verließ. Die Kollektion seines Abschlussjahres verkaufte Lupfer an die Londoner Boutique Koh Samui. Damit war unmissverständlich klar, dass es sich bei ihm um ein ernsthaftes Talent mit starken kommerziellen Qualitäten handelte. Gleich nach dem Studium arbeitete der Jungdesigner für Clements Ribeiro, und diese Erfahrung ist bis heute an seinen Fähigkeiten im Bereich Strickwaren ablesbar. Die Gründung des eigenen Labels erfolgte ein Jahr später, 1998. Lupfers Kreationen sind jung und verspielt, gleichzeitig aber auch elegant und handwerklich perfekt. Seit 1999 ist Lupfer fester Programmpunkt der Londoner Modewoche. Gegenwärtig gilt er dort in den Augen internationaler Einkäufer und Journalisten sogar als eine der größten Attraktionen. In der Saison Frühjahr/Sommer 2002 brachte Lupfer auch eine Accessoire-Kollektion heraus, die seinen Ruf als Designer begehrter und kunstvoller Kreationen aus bearbeitetem oder gewebtem Leder weiter festigte. Sein Talent und seine pragmatische Einstellung zur Mode veranlassten Lupfer 1999 zu einer Kooperation mit der einflussreichen Einzelhandelskette TopShop, für die er eine eigene Nebenkollektion entwirft.

Réputé pour son travail complexe du cuir et son utilisation expérimentale de la couleur sous forme de motifs géométriques, Markus Lupfer crée des vêtements marqués par le style de Londres, où il est désormais installé. Né en 1968 à Kißlegg dans le sud de l'Allemagne, Lupfer étudie la mode dans son pays natal avant d'obtenir un transfert à la Westminster University de Londres, dont il sort diplômé en 1997 avec les félicitations du jury. La boutique londonienne Koh Samui achète sa collection de fin d'études, ce qui le distingue immédiatement comme un créateur de talent doublé d'un véritable homme d'affaires. Après l'université, Lupfer travaille pour Clements Ribeiro, une formation qui transparaît encore aujourd'hui de façon évidente dans ses pièces en maille. Un an plus tard, en 1998, il lance sa propre griffe. Les créations de Lupfer sont jeunes et pleines d'humour mais restent néanmoins sophistiquées et exécutées avec le plus grand soin. Depuis 1999, Lupfer est un rendez-vous officiel de la London Fashion Week, les acheteurs internationaux et la presse ne ratant pas un seul de ses défilés. Au Printemps-Eté 2002, Lupfer lance une gamme d'accessoires qui confirme sa réputation grâce à des pièces hautement désirables aux finitions expertes, en cuir ouvragé ou tissé. Depuis 1999, Lupfer produit également une mini-collection pour la célèbre chaîne TopShop qui a su apprécier son talent et son approche pragmatique de la mode.

"I've always liked the idea of being very open. Clothes should be for everyone"

PORTRAIT BY DENNIS SCHOENBERG

MARKUS LUPFER

What are your signature designs? Leather and print **What's your favourite piece from any of your collections?** One of the very first prints I developed, which had faces all over it **How would you describe your work?** Simple, sexy, comfortable, good quality and easy to wear – but special. Always special elements, special details **What's your ultimate goal?** To set up my own production company. The strongest designers have all done that **What inspires you?** Different things: music, books, street, country, just things I see. Day-to-day things, even. Sometimes very trivial **Can fashion still have a political ambition?** Yes, it can. But I don't think people want to know. Nobody takes fashion that seriously. At the end of the day, design is more for feeling good than making statements **Who do you have in mind when you design?** I've always liked the idea of being very open. Clothes should be for everyone **Is the idea of creative collaboration important to you?** It's nice to have different angles **What has been the biggest influence on your career?** Growing up in Southern Germany, I felt like I was very far away from fashion. That made me very determined, because I really wanted to design and the only way was to go somewhere else **Which is more important in your work: the process or the product?** Sometimes I think that is the difference between design and art. With art, it matters more how you get there, rather than the end product. With design, it's about what you produce **Is designing difficult for you and, if so, what drives you to continue?** The possibilities are what I find exciting **Have you ever been influenced or moved by the reaction to your designs?** When I started designing accessories, suddenly there was a demand for them and that was brilliant. It's what keeps you going **What's your definition of beauty?** At the end of the day it's the inside, not the outside. How people are rather than how they look **What's your philosophy?** Good quality is very important **What is the most important lesson you've learned?** Always do what you believe in. Be true to yourself and know yourself. If you don't do that, it doesn't work

PHOTOGRAPHY BY TESH, STYLING BY EDWARD ENNINFUL. AUGUST 2001. MODEL: ANOUCK LEPERE

Before anyone knew he was actually a fashion designer, German-born Lutz became a familiar face (and body) after appearing in Wolfgang Tillmans' now infamous fashion story 'Like Sister Like Brother', published in i-D's Sexuality Issue of November 1992. He kept popping up in his friend's pictures, but in retrospect it's now clear that Lutz was not gearing up to be a model. After making the move from his native village near Cologne to London, he studied fashion at Central Saint Martins. Graduating in 1995, he got an internship at Martin Margiela's Paris atelier, becoming Margiela's assistant and focusing on knitwear and the production of the Belgian designer's 'artisanale' line (garments based on vintage and found pieces). With three years of professional training under his belt, he returned to London to accept a teaching job at his former school, a position he holds to this day. In 2000, he set up his own company, presenting his first women's collection in Paris for Autumn-Winter 2000. Taking the garment and its emotional versatility as a starting point, Lutz makes the unconventional wearable and beautiful by cutting up and subsequently assembling different pieces, as well as giving them a new identity through transformation. Sweaters become sleek dresses with the aid of smartly placed zips, bomber jackets are decorated with smoking lapels: in order to make sense (and innovative fashion), Lutz above all throws the unexpected and the fragmented into the equation. He now lives and works in Paris.

Bevor irgendjemand wusste, dass er eigentlich Designer ist, machte sich der in Deutschland geborene Lutz einen Namen als Fotomodell: Sein Gesicht und sein Körper waren in Wolfgang Tillmans' inzwischen legendärer Modegeschichte 'Like Sister Like Brother' in der Sex-Nummer von i-D im November 1992 zu sehen. Danach tauchte er immer mal wieder in den Bildern seines Freundes auf, aus heutiger Sicht ist jedoch klar, dass er es nicht auf eine Karriere als Model abgesehen hatte. Nach dem Umzug aus seinem Heimatdorf bei Köln nach London studierte er Mode am Central Saint Martins. Nachdem er 1995 seinen Abschluss gemacht hatte, bekam Lutz einen Praktikumsplatz im Pariser Atelier von Martin Margiela, wurde anschließend Assistent des belgischen Designers und konzentrierte sich auf Strickwaren sowie die Produktion der Linie 'artisanale' (auf der Basis von Vintage-Mode und Fundstücken). Nach diesen drei Jahren zusätzlicher Berufsausbildung kehrte Lutz nach London zurück und begann an seinem ehemaligen College zu unterrichten, was er bis heute tut. Im Jahr 2000 gründete er eine eigene Firma und präsentierte in Paris seine erste Herbst/Winter-Kollektion für Damen. Ausgehend von der emotionalen Vielseitigkeit jedes Kleidungsstücks, macht der junge Designer das Unkonventionelle tragbar. Die Schönheit seiner Mode entsteht, indem er verschiedene Stücke auftrennt, anders zusammenfügt und ihnen durch diese Verwandlung eine neue Identität verleiht. So verwandeln sich Pullover mit Hilfe von klug platzierten Reißverschlüssen in schmal geschnittene Kleider, Bomberjacken werden mit Smokingrevers aufgeputzt. Um innovative Mode mit Verstand zu kreieren, bringt Lutz vor allem Unerwartetes und Fragmente ins Spiel. Heute lebt und arbeitet der Designer in Paris.

Avant d'être connu comme créateur de mode, l'Allemand Lutz s'est fait surtout remarquer pour son visage (et son corps), apparu dans le célèbre article de Wolfgang Tillmans « Like Sister Like Brother » publié dans le numéro Sexualité du magazine i-D en novembre 1992. Il continue pendant quelque temps à poser pour ses amis photographes, mais avec le recul, il semble aujourd'hui évident que Lutz n'était pas destiné à une carrière de mannequin. Après avoir quitté son village natal près de Cologne pour venir à Londres, il étudie la mode à Central Saint Martins. Une fois diplômé en 1995, il fait un stage dans l'atelier parisien de Martin Margiela et devient son assistant. Il travaille principalement sur la maille, ainsi qu'à la production de la ligne artisanale du créateur belge (composée de pièces « vintage » et de vêtements dénichés à droite à gauche). Fort de trois années d'expérience professionnelle, il revient à Londres pour accepter un poste d'enseignant dans son ancienne école, une position qu'il occupe encore aujourd'hui. En l'an 2000, il monte sa propre entreprise et présente sa première collection pour femme à Paris aux défilés Automne-Hiver 2000. Avec le vêtement et sa flexibilité émotionnelle comme points de départ, Lutz rend la mode non-conformiste à la fois belle et portable, découpant et assemblant différentes pièces pour qu'elles trouvent une nouvelle identité à travers la transformation. Les pulls se métamorphosent en de sublimes robes grâce à des zips astucieusement placés et les blousons d'aviateur se parent de revers de veston d'intérieur : pour que tout cela ait un sens (et pour innover dans la mode), Lutz s'attache avant tout à réunir l'inattendu et le fragmenté. Aujourd'hui, il vit et travaille à Paris.

"I've never been interested in fashion as a product, but as something which defines identity"

PORTRAIT BY KAYT JONES

LUTZ

What are your signature designs? Really sporty and masculine clothes, with bits of eveningwear hanging on long strings **What's your favourite piece from any of your collections?** My favourite at the moment is a parka skirt **How would you describe your work?** It's important that it means something. I don't want to do work that's here today and then gone tomorrow. There are certain things I love that I always wear because I feel comfortable in them. Ideally, it would be nice to make clothes which do the same thing for other people **What's your ultimate goal?** For the time being, it's just to be able to continue with what I'm doing. I'm happy doing that **What inspires you?** I always look at how people wear their clothes. And then I wonder what it says about them. I've never been interested in fashion as a product, but as something which defines identity **Can fashion still have a political ambition?** I think it should have. If it doesn't have a political or a human dimension that goes further than just product, it doesn't mean anything **Who do you have in mind when you design?** Not one person **What has been the greatest influence on your career?** Studying at Central Saint Martins was the best thing that happened to me. When you come from Germany, there is no chaos. Everything is very much thought through and planned. To come to a college that is completely based on chaos, to just do whatever you like… it was a complete culture shock. It really changed my life **How have your own experiences affected your work as a designer?** Working with Martin Margiela was important because at that time he was the only designer who was not working with fashion as a status symbol. And that's the thing that touched me most. Fashion as a money-spinning operation just doesn't interest me. So that was an inspiration. He was saying that it was possible to see clothes in a different way **Have you ever been influenced or moved by the reaction to your designs?** The thing that touches me most right now is when I see people wearing my clothes. That's incredible. It's one thing to sit and design, but in the end it doesn't matter if it doesn't touch anybody outside, somebody who is willing to pay for something I've thought of **What is the most important lesson you've learned?** If you think you have something to say, then you should try and say it

'I don't want to be avant-garde,' says Julien Macdonald of his in-yer-face showgirl brand of glamour. 'I like beautiful clothes. I don't care what people think about me.' Born in Merthyr Tydfil, Wales, in 1974, Macdonald studied fashion at Brighton University then went on to London's Royal College of Art, graduating in 1996 with a stellar collection styled by Isabella Blow. As 'Brother Julien' he had already designed for Koji Tatsuno, Alexander McQueen and Karl Lagerfeld, for whom he worked as Head Knitwear Designer for Chanel Haute Couture, Chanel Prêt-à-Porter and the Karl Lagerfeld collections in 1997. Since then, Macdonald has gone on to make his name as the Prince Charming of London glamour, dressing his poptastic princesses in barely-there crochet slips of cobwebs and crystals. Macdonald is the guy who furnishes the unspoken agreement between paparazzi and personality, the man who can guarantee a front-page picture and headline for his clothes that are more about undressing than dressing. His catwalk antics, including appearances from Scary Spice, and an Autumn-Winter 2001 presentation held at the Millennium Dome and directed by hip hop video supremo Hype Williams, have earned him a reputation as a showmaster. It was with little surprise that Macdonald won the British Glamour Designer of the Year Award in 2001 and then was appointed successor to Alexander McQueen as the Creative Director of Givenchy later that same year. Under his direction, sales for the luxury label are steadily increasing. Macdonald continues to show his own collections in London.

'Ich möchte nicht avantgardistisch sein', sagt Julien Macdonald über seine knallige, glamouröse Revuegirl-Mode. 'Ich mag hübsche Klamotten. Was die Leute von mir denken, ist mir egal.' Er wurde 1974 im walisischen Merthyr Tydfil geboren, studierte Mode an der Brighton University und ging dann auf das Londoner Royal College of Art, das er 1996 mit einer von Isabella Blow gestylten Star-Kollektion abschloss. Als 'Brother Julien' hatte er damals bereits Entwürfe für Koji Tatsuno, Alexander McQueen und Karl Lagerfeld gemacht. Für letzteren arbeitete er im darauf folgenden Jahr als Head Knitwear Designer der Chanel Haute Couture, der Prêt-à-Porter-Kollektion von Chanel sowie der Karl-Lagerfeld-Kollektionen. Seit damals genießt Macdonald den Ruf eines Märchenprinzen des Londoner Glamours und kleidet seine poptastischen Prinzessinnen in hauchfeine Häkelslips, die aussehen wie Spinnweben mit Kristallen darin. Macdonald ist der Typ, dem der Spagat zwischen Paparazzo und eigenständiger Persönlichkeit gelingt; er sorgt mit seinen Kleidern für Titelseiten und Headlines, in denen es eher ums Aus- als ums Anziehen geht. Seine schrillen Schauen mit Auftritten von Scary Spice oder die Präsentation der Herbst/Winter-Kollektion im Millenium Dome unter der Regie der Hiphop-Video-Ikone Hype Williams haben dem Designer den Ruf eines Showmasters eingebracht. So überraschte es auch niemanden, dass er 2001 den British Glamour Designer of the Year Award einheimste und noch im selben Jahr als Nachfolger von Alexander McQueen Creative Director bei Givenchy wurde. Unter seiner Ägide steigen die Umsätze des Luxuslabels kontinuierlich. Nach wie vor präsentiert Macdonald aber auch eigene Kollektionen in London.

« Je ne cherche pas à être avant-garde », dit Julien Macdonald de son glamour tout sauf subtil et digne des showgirls de Las Vegas. « J'aime les beaux vêtements. Je me fiche pas mal de ce que les gens pensent de moi. » Né en 1974 à Merthyr Tydfil au Pays de Galles, Macdonald étudie la mode à l'Université de Brighton puis au Royal College of Art de Londres, dont il sort diplômé en 1996 avec une collection exceptionnelle mise en style par Isabella Blow. Sous le nom de « Brother Julien », il avait déjà collaboré avec Koji Tatsuno, Alexander McQueen et Karl Lagerfeld, pour lequel il a travaillé en tant que responsable de la maille pour Chanel Haute Couture, Chanel Prêt-à-Porter et les collections Karl Lagerfeld en 1997. Aujourd'hui, Macdonald fait figure de Prince Charmant du glamour londonien, habillant ses princesses pop de combinaisons très osées, réalisées au crochet en toile d'araignée et ornées de cristaux. Macdonald est celui qui arrive à passer des accords tacites entre stars et paparazzi, celui qui peut assurer une couverture et les gros titres à ses vêtements qui déshabillent plus qu'ils n'habillent. Ses défilés extravagants, avec des apparitions de Scary Spice, et la présentation de sa collection Automne-Hiver 2001 au Millennium Dome sous la direction du parrain de la vidéo hip hop Hype Williams, lui ont valu une réputation de maître du spectacle. Il n'est donc pas surprenant que Macdonald ait reçu le British Glamour Designer of the Year Award en 2001, avant de prendre plus tard dans l'année la succession d'Alexander McQueen à la direction de la création de la maison Givenchy. Sous son impulsion, les ventes de la griffe de luxe ne cessent d'augmenter. Aujourd'hui, Macdonald continue de présenter ses propres collections à Londres.

"I don't want to be avant-garde. I like beautiful clothes. I don't care what people think about me"

PORTRAIT BY CORINNE DAY

JULIEN MACDONALD

PHOTOGRAPHY BY TAKAY, STYLING BY JO BARKER NOVEMBER 2002

PHOTOGRAPHY BY ANUSCHKA BLOMMERS AND NIELS SCHUMM, STYLING BY KARL PLEWKA. NOVEMBER 1999

What are your signature designs? Ultra-sexy, ultra-glamorous, sparkly and short: that sums up what I do **What's your favourite piece from any of your collections?** The hand crocheted or cobweb knits are my favourites. There's nothing of them, so they look best on people with gorgeous bodies who just want to squeeze into something small **How would you describe your work?** It's dangerous, exciting, high-octane glamour but, most of all, it's fun. I create clothes people would notice when you walk into a room **What's your ultimate goal?** To build up both my brand name and my label – I've got a goal in both fashion and power **What inspires you?** Life itself **Can fashion still have a political ambition?** I think fashion is basically a service provider, it's as simple as that **Who do you have in mind when you design?** I suppose I design for a kind of Amazonian woman; someone who's not afraid of her body and wants to go out and show it **Is the idea of creative collaboration important to you?** As a designer you basically work on your own. You have an idea for a collection and then you just bring in different people to help you achieve it. The designer is the person it stems from – without them, there's nothing **Who has been the greatest influence on your career?** I spent two years working with Karl Lagerfeld at Chanel and he educated me in the way a woman with culture and status dresses **How have your own experiences affected your work as a designer?** I think that the older you get, the more interesting you become as a person and the more interesting you become as a designer. If you'd asked me these questions five years ago, the answers would have been very different **Which is more important in your work: the process or the product?** People don't pay attention to the process – they just want the product **Is designing difficult for you and, if so, what drives you to continue?** I don't think designing is difficult. What is difficult is managing and running a business **Have you ever been influenced or moved by the reaction to your designs?** There's nothing more satisfying than seeing a woman looking fantastic in one of your outfits. My aim is to make women feel comfortable, happy and glamorous **What's your definition of beauty?** Beauty is in the eye of the beholder, as they say. Beauty can be very cruel or very pretty. It's a difficult one **What's your philosophy?** I don't really have one. I just want to design clothes and be happy and enjoy what I do – if you don't enjoy it, give up **What is the most important lesson you've learned?** Always be nice

PHOTOGRAPHY BY TERRY RICHARDSON, STYLING BY SABINA SCHREDER. JULY 2000

Martin Margiela is the fashion designer's fashion designer. Normally this comment could be read as casual cliché, but in the case of Margiela it is justified. For unlike any other designer, he produces work which could be seen as a distinct form of 'metafashion': his clothes are essentially about clothes. With his own peculiar yet precise vision, he is one of the most influential and iconoclastic designers to have emerged over the past 15 years. Born in 1959 in Limbourg, Belgium, he studied at the Royal Academy Antwerp and was part of the first wave of talent which would emerge from the city. Between 1984 and 1987 he assisted Jean Paul Gaultier; in 1988, Maison Martin Margiela was founded in Paris and his first womenswear collection for Spring-Summer 1989 was shown that same year. Struggling to come to terms with a definition of Margiela's fashion, with its exposure of and mania for the process and craft of making clothes, the press would label this new mood 'deconstruction'. Eschewing the cult of personality that attends many designers, Martin Margiela has instead fostered a cult of impersonality, further deconstructing the conventions of the fashion industry. Never interviewed in person or as an individual ('Maison Margiela' answers faxed questions), even the label in his clothing remains blank (as in the main womenswear line) or simply has a number circled ('6' for women's basics and '10' for menswear). Martin Margiela is truly a designer whose clothes speak for themselves, which made his appointment as head designer of Hermès womenswear in 1997 – when 'personality' appointments were in abundance – seem inspired and more successful. In 2000, the first Margiela shop opened in Tokyo, followed in 2002 by Brussels and Paris; each carry the full range of Margiela products including footwear ('22'), publications and objects ('13'). Margiela has also participated in numerous exhibitions, including 'Radical Fashion' at London's Victoria & Albert Museum in 2001.

Martin Margiela ist der Modedesigner der Modedesigner. Diese Aussage könnte wie ein unbedachtes Klischee klingen, doch im Fall von Margiela hat sie tatsächlich ihre Berechtigung. Im Unterschied zu allen anderen Modeschöpfern erschafft er etwas, das man als besondere Form von 'Meta-Mode' bezeichnen könnte: Seine Kleider sind die Quintessenz ihrer selbst. Dank seiner eigenwilligen, aber präzisen Vorstellungen ist er einer der einflussreichsten und umstürzlerischsten Designer, der in den vergangenen 15 Jahren von sich reden gemacht hat. Geboren wurde Margiela 1959 im belgischen Limbourg. Nach seinem Studium an der Königlichen Akademie in Antwerpen gehörte er zur ersten Welle neuer Talente aus dieser Stadt. Von 1984 bis 1987 arbeitete Margiela als Assistent für Jean Paul Gaultier, 1988 gründete er dann in Paris sein Label Maison Martin Margiela und präsentierte noch im selben Jahr seine erste Damenkollektion für Frühjahr/Sommer 1989. Die Presse taufte diese neue Strömung Dekonstruktivismus, weil es ihr so schwer fiel, den Stil des Designers mit seiner Ablehnung und seiner gleichzeitigen Leidenschaft für den Entstehungsprozess von Mode exakt zu definieren. Margiela lehnt den Personenkult ab, den so viele Designer pflegen, und förderte stattdessen eher die Unpersönlichkeit als Kult, was einen weiteren Bruch mit den Konventionen der Modeindustrie darstellt. Der Designer lässt sich weder fotografieren noch als Person oder Individuum interviewen – Maison Margiela beantwortet lediglich gefaxte Anfragen. Und selbst die Etiketten in seinen Kleidern bleiben leer (wie in der Hauptkollektion für Damen) oder tragen nur einen Kreis mit einer Nummer darin (eine 6 für Damen-Basics, eine 10 für Herrenmode). So gesehen ist Martin Margiela ein Designer, der wirklich und ausschließlich seine Kreationen für sich sprechen lässt. Das war vielleicht auch das Erfolgsgeheimnis seiner Ernennung zum Chefdesigner der Damenmode bei Hermès im Jahr 1997, zu einer Zeit also, als die Ernennung von 'Persönlichkeiten' gerade besonders en vogue war. Der erste Margiela-Laden wurde 2000 in Tokio eröffnet, 2002 folgten Filialen in Brüssel und Paris. Jedes dieser Geschäfte führt die gesamte Palette der Margiela-Kreationen, darunter auch Schuhe (die die Nummer 22 tragen) sowie Publikationen und Objekte (mit der Nummer 13 versehen). Margiela hat bereits an zahlreichen Ausstellungen teilgenommen, darunter auch 'Radical Fashion', die 2001 im Londoner Victoria & Albert Museum gezeigt wurde.

Martin Margiela est le créateur de mode par excellence et, en l'occurrence, ce banal cliché est tout à fait justifié. Contrairement à tout autre créateur, il produit un travail qui s'apparente à une forme distincte de « métamode » : en effet, ses vêtements parlent avant tout de vêtements. Sa vision particulière et bien définie l'a imposé comme l'un des stylistes les plus influents et les plus iconoclastes qui ont émergé ces 15 dernières années. Né en 1959 à Limbourg en Belgique, Margiela étudie à l'Académie Royale d'Anvers et fait partie de la première vague de nouveaux talents de la ville. Entre 1984 et 1987, il est assistant de Jean Paul Gaultier ; en 1988, il fonde Maison Martin Margiela à Paris et présente sa première collection pour femme Printemps-Eté 1989 la même année. Cherchant désespérément à définir le mode de Margiela, avec sa franchise et sa manie du procédé artisanal, la presse baptise ce nouveau style « déconstruction ». Evitant le culte de la personnalité qui attend de nombreux designers, Martin Margiela cherche au contraire à développer un culte de l'impersonnalité en s'affranchissant des conventions de l'industrie de la mode. Jamais pris en photo, jamais interviewé en personne (c'est Maison Margiela qui répond aux questions envoyées par fax), même la griffe de ses vêtements reste vierge (comme c'est le cas de la ligne principale pour femme) ou comporte simplement un numéro dans un cercle (« 6 » pour les basiques féminins et « 10 » pour les hommes). Martin Margiela crée vraiment des vêtements qui parlent d'eux-mêmes et Hermès l'a bien compris : à l'époque où il est de bon ton d'engager des « personnalités » à la direction de la création, la maison Hermès l'engage en 1997 comme styliste principal de sa ligne pour femme, un choix qui s'est avéré depuis très inspiré. En l'an 2000, la première boutique Margiela ouvre ses portes à Tokyo, suivie en 2002 par Bruxelles et Paris ; chacune d'elles présente la gamme complète des produits Margiela, y compris des chaussures (« 22 »), des livres et des objets (« 13 »). Margiela a participé à de nombreuses expositions, notamment « Radical Fashion » au Victoria & Albert Museum de Londres en 2001.

"There should be as little philosophising as possible. The head, when used in support of the heart and an informed sense of good, will rarely lead astray"

PHOTOGRAPHY BY MICHEL MOMY

MARTIN MARGIELA

PHOTOGRAPHY BY TESH, STYLING BY EDWARD ENNINFUL. MARCH 2001. MODEL: KIM PEERS

PHOTOGRAPHY BY MICHEL MOMY, STYLING BY FIONA DALLANEGRA. MARCH 1999

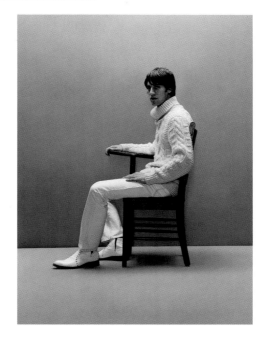

What are your signature designs? Though clearly others will have a totally different view on our work, we will venture to suggest some individual garments, as well as a few overriding themes of our collections, that might be worthy of being remembered after we are long gone! Among these might be: Our work for every collection since our first on what we refer to as our 'Artisanal Production' – the reworking of men's and women's vintage garments, fabrics and accessories. The silhouette that dominated our first ten collections – the 'cigarette' shoulder for which a roll of fabric was placed above the shoulder leaving the wearer's natural shoulder line to define the garment. These were usually worn with long apron skirts in washed man's suiting fabric or men's jeans and suit trousers that were opened and reworked as skirts. The Martin Margiela 'Tabi' boot 6, Spring-Summer 1989 to the present day – based on a Japanese 'Tabi' sock, these have been present in all of our collections and first commercialised in 1995. They were made up in leather, suede and canvas and mounted on a wooden heel of the diameter of the average human heel. Since 1990, vintage jeans and jeans jackets painted by hand. Winter 1991/92 – a sweater made entirely from opened and assembled military socks. The heels of the original socks helped form the shoulders, elbows and bust of the sweater. Autumn-Winter 1994/95 – elements of a doll's wardrobe were enlarged 5.2 times to a human scale. The disproportions and structures of the doll's pieces were maintained in the upscaled reproductions, often rendering oversized knit, collars, buttons and zips etc. Summer 1996 – a wardrobe for summer of photographed elements of a man's and women's winter wardrobe. The photographs were printed on light fluid summer fabrics. Summer 1997 and Winter 1997/98 – garments evoke the trial and development of prototype garments as worked on with a 'Tailor's Dummy'. A jacket of each of these seasons was in the shape of a 'Tailor's Dummy'. Spring-Summer 2000 to Spring-Summer 2002 – a work on scale. The creation of a fictive Italian size 78. Elements of a man's and woman's wardrobe – dress jackets, suit jackets, bombers, pants and jeans – are proposed in this one size and over the seasons the ways of treating these up-scaled garments varied. Trousers are fit to size by folding them over and stitching them. The final version was for Spring–Summer 2002 when these garments were raw cut to the waistline of the wearer **What's your favourite piece from any of your collections?** Impossible to say – so many have their own place, importance and significance for us in our memory of our work and development **How would you describe your work?** A continuation and the deepening of our technical experience, collaboration and craft **What's your ultimate goal?** Keep going while seeking out those new challenges that continue to stimulate us **What inspires you?** Integrity, conviction and courage **Who do you have in mind when you design?** Not one person, male or female, in particular – more an overall, and sometimes specific, attitude **Is the idea of creative collaboration important to you?** Yes, though this is not often easy! A creative point of view often has little to do with democracy in its expression – it is for this reason that individual conviction within a team often demands the respect of which it is so worthy **Who has been the greatest influence on your career?** Those who support us and, above all, those who encourage us by assimilating that which we produce into their own wardrobes and style **How have your own experiences affected your work as a designer?** We will all have another approach to this – yet, in the main, a constant questioning of purpose and point of view **Which is more important in your work: the process or the product?** The process and the result – as it hangs on the hanger and more so… on the body! **Is designing difficult for you and, if so, what drives you to continue?** Yes! Designing and those designs touching the wearer **Have you ever been influenced or moved by the reaction to your designs?** Constantly, thankfully **What's your definition of beauty?** What is 'within' being given the chance to blossom and surface **What's your philosophy?** That there should be as little 'philosophising' as possible! The head when used in support of the heart and an informed sense of 'Good' will rarely lead astray **What's the most important lesson you've learned?** That to be 'right' is subjective and only ever half the battle

PHOTOGRAPHY BY STEFANO MORO, STYLING BY CHRISTINE FORTUNE. AUGUST 2002

Born in Alghero in Sardinia in 1962, Antonio Marras had no formal schooling in fashion but, via his father's fabric store, developed enough of a passion for textiles to convince an entrepreneur from Rome to back him to create his first ready-to-wear collection. The resulting label, launched in 1988, was named Piano Piano Dolce Carlotta – after the Robert Aldrich horror movie of the 1960s: Marras' tribute to his inspiration, the film's lead star Bette Davis. He continued to work freelance for the next four years, winning the Contemporary Linen prize for a wedding dress that revealed the Sardinian influence which is his trademark. In 1992 he decided to concentrate on one collection, finally making his haute couture debut under his own name in Paris in 1996. A meditation on the theme of collective memory, the collection was a triumph of exquisite detailing: burn marks on precious fabrics, frayed gauze, visible hems and brocades. His first own label ready-to-wear collection followed in Milan in 1999, with the shapes and colours of Sardinian costume again a major influence, together with Byzantine symbolism. His use of masculine tailoring and fabrics is often interlaced with the most delicate detailing in silk tulle and chiffon. Marras' 'Laboratorio' enables him to explore an area between couture and ready-to-wear; each garment is unique, born as it is from the remnants of fabrics combined in ways that cannot be duplicated. Aware of the influence his roots have on his work, Marras continues to make Sardinia his home, living and working with his extended family in a home-workshop overlooking the sea.

Der 1962 in Alghero auf Sardinien geborene Antonio Marras absolvierte zwar keine spezielle Ausbildung in Sachen Mode, doch durch das Stoffgeschäft seines Vaters hatte er eine Leidenschaft für Textilien entwickelt, die genügte, um einen Unternehmer aus Rom zur Finanzierung seiner ersten Prêt-à-Porter-Kollektion zu bewegen. Das dafür gegründete und 1988 präsentierte Label trug nach Robert Aldrichs Horrorfilm aus den 1960er Jahren den Namen Piano Piano Dolce Carlotta. Das war Marras' Tribut an seine Inspiration – die weibliche Hauptfigur des Films, gespielt von Bette Davis. Danach arbeitete der Designer vier Jahre lang selbstständig und gewann in dieser Zeit den Contemporary-Linen-Preis für ein Brautkleid, bei dem der Einfluss seiner sardischen Heimat – inzwischen sein Markenzeichen – unverkennbar war. 1992 beschloss er, sich ganz auf eine Kollektion zu konzentrieren und gab schließlich 1996 in Paris sein Haute-Couture-Debüt unter eigenem Namen. Es war eine Meditation zum Thema kollektives Gedächtnis, die vor allem durch ungewöhnliche Details bestach: Brandlöcher in kostbaren Stoffen, ausgefranste Gaze, sichtbare Säume und Brokat. Die erste Prêt-à-Porter-Kollektion seines eigenen Labels folgte 1999 in Mailand. Auch hier war der Einfluss der Schnitte und Farben sardischer Trachten deutlich, dazu kamen noch Symbole aus der byzantinischen Kunst. Marras' maskuline Schnitte und typische Herrenstoffe sind oft verwoben mit zartesten Details aus Seidentüll und Chiffon. In seinem 'Laboratorio' erkundet der Designer das nicht genau definierte Terrain zwischen Haute Couture und Prêt-à-Porter: Jede seine Kreationen ist ein Einzelstück aus verschiedenen Stoffresten, die sich genau so kein zweites Mal zusammenfügen lassen. Weil er sich seiner stark ausgeprägten Wurzeln und deren Wirkung auf seine Arbeit bewusst ist, lebt und entwirft Marras auf Sardinien, wo er mit seiner Großfamilie ein Haus samt Atelier mit Blick aufs Meer bewohnt.

Né en 1962 à Alghero en Sardaigne, Antonio Marras ne suit pas de formation formelle en mode mais, dans le magasin de tissus de son père, il développe une telle passion pour les textiles qu'il réussit à convaincre un entrepreneur romain de financer sa première collection de prêt-à-porter. Il lance sa griffe en 1988, qu'il baptise Piano Piano Dolce Carlotta, en référence au thriller tourné par Robert Aldrich dans les années 1960 : Marras rend ainsi hommage à sa plus grande source d'inspiration, la star du film Bette Davis. Il continue à travailler en free-lance pendant quatre ans et remporte le prix Contemporary Linen pour une robe de mariée qui révélait déjà l'influence sarde qui définit son style. En 1992, il décide de se concentrer sur une seule collection et finit par faire ses premiers pas dans la haute couture à Paris en 1996. Méditation sur le thème de la mémoire collective, la collection voit triompher les détails les plus exquis : marques de brûlure sur des tissus précieux, gaze effilochée, ourlets apparents et brocarts. En 1999, il présente sa première collection de prêt-à-porter à Milan, où les formes et les couleurs du costume traditionnel sarde constituent encore une influence majeure, aux côtés du symbolisme byzantin. Son utilisation des coupes et des tissus de la mode pour homme se marie souvent aux détails les plus délicats en tulle et en mousseline de soie. Le «Laboratorio» de Marras lui permet d'explorer la frontière qui sépare la haute couture du prêt-à-porter ; chaque vêtement est unique, engendré tel quel à partir de coupons de tissu qu'il combine de façon inimitable. Conscient de l'impact de ses racines sur son travail, Marras vit toujours en Sardaigne, où il habite et travaille avec sa grande famille dans une maison-atelier avec vue sur la mer.

"I don't work for a purpose. What interests me is the trip and not the destination"

PORTRAIT BY CRICCHI AND FERRANTE

ANTONIO MARRAS

What are your signature designs? I don't know, really I don't know. I hate definitions and labels. I consider my collections an expression of what I like and enjoy **What are your favourite pieces from any of your collections?** All of them! As they say in Naples, 'They are the pieces of my heart' **How would you describe your work?** It isn't a job but a way of life. A world without boundaries between hobbies, passions, interests and duties, between family and collaborators **What's your ultimate goal?** I don't work for a purpose. What interests me is the trip and not the destination **What inspires you?** I feel like a sponge which absorbs everything, almost without filters, without consciousness, letting the things that strike me most leave a mark **Can fashion still have a political ambition?** Usually fashion tends to follow, record and eventually underline certain changes. I don't believe that designers nowadays can instill any kind of political influence by means of their work. Indeed, I feel that certain initiatives and stances that exploit wars, injustices, current issues for imprudent promotional purposes are opportunist rather than absurd. Instead, I appreciate moral choices such as not using furs, as well as not taking advantage of underpaid manufacturing work in less developed countries **Who do you have in mind when you design?** I don't think – my mind is empty, or better, too full and dedicated to what I'm doing, as if I were in a trance **Who has been the greatest influence on your career?** I consider my encounter with Maria Lai crucial. She's an 80-year-old Sardinian artist who works with fabrics and sewing machines as if she were an alchemist, who opened a universe I didn't even know I was a part of **How have your own experiences affected your work as a designer?** I was brought up in the family boutique so I am aware of a woman's needs in choosing a dress, I know how to interpret her look in the mirror coming out of the dressing room. It is important to be familiar with the codes in order to override them **Is designing difficult for you and, if so, what drives you to continue?** The most difficult thing is the relationship with the productive system. We are fond of the most difficult pieces; the company is fond of the one that sells best. It's a matter of finding a common language, which isn't always easy **Have you ever been influenced or moved by the reaction to your designs?** I listen to everybody and don't pay attention to anyone **What's your definition of beauty?** When my son Effi was four years old, he surprised us all with the following statement: 'What is beautiful, IS BEAUTIFUL!' Unquestionable, right? **What's your philosophy?** 'Woe betide those who don't pursue their own pureness with rage' (Mario Trejo, Argentina, 1926) **What is the most important lesson you've learned?** Never take anything for granted

PHOTOGRAPHY BY ALASDAIR MCLELLAN, STYLING BY SORAYA DAYANI. OCTOBER 2002. MODEL: JAYNE WINDSOR

The writing was on the wall for Stella McCartney (born London, 1971) the day she first stumbled into her mother's wardrobe, brimming with Chloé. In 1997, at the age of just 25, she won top spot at the Parisian house after showing only two of her own collections since graduating from Central Saint Martins. And despite relentless and unwarranted criticism of her connections, McCartney has shown a remarkable resilience throughout her short career in fashion. She not only turned Chloé around financially, but gave it the kind of cool that comes from being a Portobello party girl with a string of friends that include Kate Moss, Gwyneth Paltrow and Madonna. McCartney knew what made chicks tick and proved it by being queen of the pop pickers when it came to the must-have airbrushed T-shirt and diamanté-studded aviator sunglasses. She knew women wanted to wear sharp trouser suits and vintage-style dresses. And, importantly, she stayed true to her brash sense of humour and ballsy femininity by making Chloé fun and saucy, with the sort of pineapple-emblazoned bikinis that would provoke an 'ooo-er missus' in a 'Carry On' film. McCartney's Chloé shows mirrored her jet-setting life but the clothes also paid homage to her homebody nature and commitment to animal rights – she refuses to use leather or fur in her designs. Gucci's Tom Ford knew McCartney had everything it took to be successful: the drive, the will, the intelligence and taste that could turn a dusty brand into a money-spinner. Thanks to his support she once again designs under her own name, having held her first Gucci-backed show for Spring-Summer 2002 in Paris. Stella McCartney launches her first perfume in 2003.

Ihre Karriere war eigentlich vorgezeichnet, seit die 1971 in London geborene Stella das erste Mal ins Ankleidezimmer ihrer Mutter spazierte, das voll mit Chloé-Kreationen war. 1997 übernahm sie mit erst 25 Jahren die Spitzenposition in dem Pariser Modehaus, und das nur zwei Kollektionen nach ihrem Abschluss am Central Saint Martins. Auch wenn man ihr ungerechterweise immer wieder ihren Namen und ihre guten Verbindungen vorwarf, hat McCartney in ihrer bisherigen kurzen Karriere erstaunliches Stehvermögen bewiesen. Chloé profitierte nicht nur in finanzieller Hinsicht von ihr, sondern auch von ihrer Coolness, ein Portobello-Party-Girl zu sein und beispielsweise Kate Moss, Gwyneth Paltrow oder Madonna zur Freundin zu haben. McCartney weiß genau, was die Mädels mögen, und trat den Beweis dafür als Pop-Picker-Queen an, als ihre Airbrush-T-Shirts und mit Diamanten besetzte Pilotensonnenbrillen der letzte Schrei waren. Sie spürte einfach, dass Frauen scharfe Hosenanzüge und Kleider im Vintage-Look anziehen wollten. Und was mindestens genauso wichtig war: Sie behielt ihren frechen Humor und ihre forsche Weiblichkeit, während sie Chloé witziger und kesser machte, etwa mit gewagten Ananasbikinis, die in jeder Familienserie Entsetzen ausgelöst hätten. McCartneys Chloé-Schauen spiegelten ihr Jet-Set-Leben, wurden aber zugleich auch ihrem bodenständigen Charakter und ihrem Engagement als Tierschützerin gerecht. So weigert sich die Designerin bis heute, in ihren Kreationen Leder oder Pelz zu verarbeiten. Tom Ford von Gucci wusste, dass McCartney das Zeug zum Erfolg hatte: den Drive, den Willen, die Intelligenz und den Geschmack, um aus einer leicht angestaubten Traditionsmarke wieder eine Goldgrube zu machen. Dank seiner Unterstützung entwirft sie inzwischen wieder unter eigenem Namen. Ihre erste von Gucci finanzierte Schau für Frühjahr/Sommer 2002 fand in Paris statt. 2003 wird das erste Parfum der Designerin auf den Markt kommen.

Le chemin de Stella McCartney (née en 1971 à Londres) semble tout tracé depuis le jour où elle a ouvert la garde-robe de sa mère, remplie de vêtements Chloé. En 1997, à peine âgée de 25 ans, elle décroche un poste important dans la maison parisienne alors qu'elle n'a présenté que deux collections depuis l'obtention de son diplôme à Central Saint Martins. Malgré une critique incessante et injustifiée qui l'accuse d'être une « pistonnée », Stella McCartney a fait preuve d'une remarquable flexibilité tout au long de sa courte carrière dans la mode. Non seulement elle a remis la maison Chloé à flots sur le plan financier, mais elle lui a également apporté toute la « cool attitude » d'une fêtarde de Portobello grâce à sa bande de copines, parmi lesquelles Kate Moss, Gwyneth Paltrow et Madonna. Stella McCartney sait ce qu'aiment les filles et l'a prouvé en devenant la reine des fashion victims quand a déferlé la mode des indispensables T-shirts aérographiés et des lunettes de soleil cloutées de strass. Elle savait que les femmes voulaient porter des tailleurs-pantalon aux lignes sévères et des robes d'inspiration « vintage ». Mais surtout, elle est restée fidèle à son ironie effrontée et sa féminité sans complexe, transformant Chloé en une marque drôle et impertinente, notamment grâce à ses graphiques sexuellement provocants mais toujours empreints d'une bonne dose d'humour très british. Les défilés de Stella McCartney pour Chloé reflétaient sa vie de jet-setteuse, mais les vêtements rendaient également hommage à son goût du cocooning et son engagement dans la protection des animaux : en effet, elle se refuse à utiliser du cuir ou de la fourrure. Chez Gucci, Tom Ford pressent que Stella McCartney a tout ce qu'il faut pour réussir : l'énergie, la volonté, l'intelligence et le goût qui peuvent transformer une marque poussiéreuse en véritable poule aux œufs d'or. Grâce à son soutien, elle peut à nouveau dessiner sous son propre nom. Elle a présenté sa première collection financée par Gucci aux défilés parisiens Printemps-Eté 2002. De plus, Stella McCartney compte lancer son premier parfum en 2003.

"I think I have a place in the industry. I have a role; I represent something for women. I've built up trust with them and that's important"

PORTRAIT BY KAYT JONES

STELLA MCCARTNEY

PHOTOGRAPHY BY DONALD CHRISTIE, STYLING BY GIANNIE COUJI. OCTOBER 2002. MODEL: CHRISTINA KRUSE

"I keep doing this because I'm a fucking glutton for punishment and am trying to prove myself"

What are your signature designs? Sexy trousers! **What's your favourite piece from any of your collections?** I don't have one. I love them all. Is that allowed? **How would you describe your work?** It hopefully covers all facets of a woman: sexy, feminine, humorous, confident and fucking cool **What's your ultimate goal?** I'm in the process, hopefully, of achieving it. My ultimate goal is to be happy. If my company succeeds and that means I'm happy, or if it doesn't but I'm still happy, it's all for the good **What inspires you?** My mum **Who do you have in mind when you design?** Me and my friends **Can fashion still have a political ambition?** Sure it can. You can take it as seriously as you want, but fashion on a daily basis is always political because it's people expressing themselves **Is the idea of creative collaboration important to you?** I just did a T-shirt with Gary Hume and I think that collaborating with people, doing limited editions and one-off pieces, is really exciting. I'm increasingly interested in trying to make individual, special pieces rather than mass producing things **Who has been the greatest influence on your career?** Just the customer. The girls that I know that wear my clothes. Only the cool ones, of course **Which is more important in your work: the process or the product?** The product. Because if the process is brilliant but the product's shit... who cares? **Is designing difficult for you and, if so, what drives you to continue?** If I'd settled for being a cliché of myself and just making tons of money, it'd be fine. I've taken an option that's a bit more difficult and I'm pushing myself. But I love it. And I do it for the genuine reason that I think I have a place in the industry. I have a role; I represent something for women. I've built up trust with them and I think that's important. And I keep doing it because I'm totally a fucking glutton for punishment and am trying to prove myself, though to God knows who **Have you ever been influenced or moved by the reaction to your designs?** I had an event at a store a few months ago to meet my clients. This woman came in who was about 75 years old and she was so stylish. And she said to me, 'Your clothes make me so happy'. And she really meant it. She wasn't a fashion person. She was a client. And I just thought, that's what it's all about, that is really what it's all about for me. I never would have thought a 75-year-old woman would wear my clothes. And she was fucking cool. And that definitely moved me **What's your definition of beauty?** Inner peace **What's your philosophy?** Be true to yourself, believe in yourself and shine on **What is the most important lesson you've learned?** Do unto others as you would have them do unto you

Karl Lagerfeld once suggested that Lee Alexander McQueen was closer in spirit to shock artist Damien Hirst than Hubert de Givenchy, whose couture house McQueen inherited in 1996. This observation goes to the heart of McQueen's appeal: as a designer of skill and substance who understood he was, in the first instance, in the business of theatre and generating a reaction rather than polite applause. But after almost 15 years in the industry, now with a partner in the Gucci Group who understands the potential of the total McQueen proposition, he is finally delivering on his promise and developing a global luxury brand bearing his name. Born to an East End taxi driver in 1969, at 16 Alexander McQueen began an apprenticeship at Anderson & Sheppard on Savile Row, eventually becoming a pattern cutter at Romeo Gigli after stints with theatrical costumier Angel & Bermans and the Milan-based designer Koji Tatsuno. Returning to London, McQueen graduated from Central Saint Martins in 1992 and was immediately dubbed 'enfant terrible' by the press, becoming known for his brutally sharp tailoring and extravagant presentations. Four years later, aged 26, he won the British Designer Of The Year Award, the first of three such prizes and, more importantly, was appointed head designer at Givenchy, replacing John Galliano. In December 2000 the Gucci Group bought a controlling stake in McQueen's own line and he left Givenchy three months later. McQueen's Autumn-Winter 2002 collection, presented during Paris Fashion Week with few theatrical diversions, was his strongest to date: tailored tweed with leather strapping, naughty schoolgirls and the sexiest sixth formers, the glimpse of lace, thigh-high boots, bodices and corsets. Fetishism made empowerment, at once romantic and perverse, it was a clear statement of intent: McQueen was ready to do business. In July 2002, McQueen launched a bespoke menswear collection made by Huntsman of Savile Row. An Alexander McQueen flagship store opened in New York in 2002, with London, Milan and Los Angeles stores following in 2003.

Karl Lagerfeld meinte einmal, Lee Alexander McQueen sei eher ein Seelenverwandter des Schock-Künstlers Damien Hirst als von Hubert de Givenchy, für dessen Couture-Haus er ab 1996 entwarf. Diese Einschätzung trifft exakt McQueens besonderen Reiz: Er ist ein selbstbewusster talentierter Designer, der erkannt hat, dass es im Modezirkus nicht an erster Stelle auf höflichen Beifall, sondern auf das Provozieren von Reaktionen ankommt. Nach rund 15 Jahren in der Branche und mittlerweile als Partner des Gucci-Konzerns, der das Potenzial der McQueen-Philosophie erkannt hat, löst er jetzt sein Versprechen ein: Er ist dabei, eine internationale Luxusmarke zu entwickeln, die seinen Namen trägt. Geboren wurde McQueen 1969 als Sohn eines Taxifahrers im Londoner East End. Mit 16 Jahren begann er eine Schneiderlehre bei Anderson & Sheppard in der Savile Row. Nachdem er außerdem Erfahrungen bei der Kostümschneiderei Angel & Bermans und dem Designer Koji Tatsuno in Mailand gesammelt hatte, wurde er zunächst Zuschneider bei Romeo Gigli. Wieder in London, absolvierte er 1992 das Central Saint Martins und wurde danach wegen seiner messerscharfen Schnitte und extravaganten Präsentationen von der Presse praktisch sofort mit dem Etikett Enfant terrible versehen. Vier Jahre später, mit nur 26, gewann er den British Designer of the Year Award – seinen ersten von bisher dreien dieser Preise. Fast zeitgleich wurde er, was noch wichtiger war, als Nachfolger von John Galliano Chefdesigner bei Givenchy. Im Dezember 2000 erwarb die Gucci-Gruppe die Kontrollmehrheit von McQueens eigenem Label. Drei Monate später verließ der Designer das Haus Givenchy. Seine im Rahmen der Pariser Modewoche mit erstaunlich wenig Pomp präsentierte Kollektion für Herbst/Winter 2002 gilt als bislang stärkste Arbeit McQueens: tadellos sitzender Tweed mit Lederriemen, kesse Schulmädchen und die verführerischsten Schulabgängerinnen, eine Ahnung von Spitze, schenkellange Stiefel, Mieder und Korsetts. Fetischismus als Symbol von Macht, romantisch und verrucht zugleich – die Botschaft war eindeutig: McQueen ist endlich bereit, auch die Verkäuflichkeit seiner Kreationen zu berücksichtigen. Im Juli 2002 präsentierte der Designer eine bei Huntsman in der Savile Row gearbeitete Maßkollektion für Herren. Im selben Jahr wurde auch ein Alexander McQueen Flagship Store in New York eröffnet. Weitere Läden in London, Mailand und Los Angeles folgen 2003.

Karl Lagerfeld a un jour laissé entendre que Lee Alexander McQueen serait plus proche du parfum de scandale qui entoure Damien Hirst que de l'esprit Hubert de Givenchy, maison de haute couture dont McQueen reprend la direction en 1996. Un commentaire qui résume parfaitement l'essence du style McQueen : ce styliste aux talents évidents comprend dès le départ que la mode est un grand théâtre dans lequel il vaut mieux provoquer une réaction plutôt que des applaudissements polis. Pourtant, avec aujourd'hui près de 15 ans de métier derrière lui et le soutien du Groupe Gucci, un partenaire qui a su saisir le potentiel de son radicalisme, McQueen tient finalement ses promesses et développe une marque de luxe mondiale à son propre nom. Né en 1969 d'un père chauffeur de taxi dans l'East End, Alexander McQueen commence son apprentissage à 16 ans chez Anderson & Sheppard de Savile Row. Il travaille ensuite comme traceur de patrons chez Romeo Gigli après une expérience chez le costumier de théâtre Angel & Bermans et le styliste Koji Tatsuno basé à Milan. De retour à Londres, McQueen sort diplômé de Central Saint Martins en 1992. Immédiatement qualifié d'enfant terrible par la presse, il se fait remarquer par ses coupes brutales et sévères et ses défilés extravagants. Quatre ans plus tard, à l'âge de 26 ans, il remporte le prix de British Designer of the Year, le premier d'une série de trois, mais surtout il est nommé directeur de la création chez Givenchy, où il succède à John Galliano. En décembre 2000, le Groupe Gucci acquiert une part majoritaire dans la griffe de McQueen, qui quitte Givenchy trois mois plus tard. La collection Automne-Hiver 2002 de McQueen, présentée à la Semaine de la Mode de Paris avec quelques diversions cinématographiques, est à ce jour la plus aboutie : tweed de tailleur avec lanières de cuir, écolières malicieuses et lycéennes ultra-sexy, une touche de dentelle, bottes montantes et moulantes, corsages et corsets. Un fétichisme à la fois romantique et pervers donne le ton de cette collection qui, pour McQueen, est une déclaration d'intention sans détour : il est enfin prêt à vendre. En juillet 2002, il lance une collection pour homme « à façon » créée par Huntsman de Savile Row. La même année, il ouvre une boutique éponyme à New York, qui sera suivie par Londres, Milan et Los Angeles en 2003.

"I use things that people want to hide in their heads. War, religion, sex: things we all think about but don't bring to the forefront. But I do and I force them to watch it"

PORTRAIT BY CORINNE DAY

ALEXANDER MCQUEEN

PHOTOGRAPHY BY DAVID LACHAPELLE, STYLING BY PATTI WILSON. SEPTEMBER 2002. MODEL: JAMIE BOCHERT

PHOTOGRAPHY BY ANETTE AURELL, STYLING BY ANNETT MONHEIM, OCTOBER 2000

PHOTOGRAPHY BY ELLEN VON UNWERTH, STYLING BY PATTI WILSON. JUNE 2001. MODEL: TAMMI

"I used to be conflicted about the whole industry. Now I'm happy and balanced. Well, still a little off balance, I suppose"

What are your signature designs? Signature pieces include the bumster, the frock coat, anything trompe-l'oeil **What are your favourite pieces from any of your collections?** The wooden fan kilts from Spring-Summer 1999, the red slide dress from Spring-Summer 2001, the jellyfish dress from Autumn-Winter 2002 **How would you describe your work?** Electric, eccentric **What is your ultimate goal?** To offer haute couture pieces as an integral part of the ready-to-wear collection **What inspires you?** I find a multitude of influences inspiring – homeless to the rich, vulgar to the common **Can fashion still have a political ambition?** Because fashion is so indicative of the political and social climate in which we live, what we wear will always be a symptom of our environment. But I do believe that often the results are the opposite of what we expect – when the economic climate is hard, escapism is essential **Who do you have in mind when you design?** A strong independent woman who loves and lives fearlessly in equal measures **Is the idea of creative collaboration important to you?** Collaborations give me the opportunity to work with peers who I admire as well as pushing myself creatively. What's the point otherwise? **Who has been the greatest influence on your career?** Anyone I come into contact with and find a connection with **How have your own experiences affected your work as a designer?** Working with the atelier at Givenchy showed me the possibilities that only haute couture can give a designer, where craftsmanship suddenly becomes state of the art **Which is more important in your work: the process or the product?** Design development allows you to make mistakes; without screwing up once in a while you can't ever move forward **Is designing difficult for you and, if so, what drives you to continue?** I enjoy putting the whole picture together – from the initial design phase to the shows and the stores. It's rewarding to see the entire concept work in unison. There is still a lot I want to achieve, my mind works very quickly and there isn't any room for complacency in this head! **Have you ever been influenced or moved by the reaction to your designs?** When I watched Shalom Harlow being spray painted as the finale of my Spring-Summer 2000 show I was very moved. She was so poetic and elegant that I could hear the audience gasp – it really moved me to hear such an immediate reaction to my work **What's your definition of beauty?** An image that combines opposing or unusual aesthetics **What's your philosophy?** To make a piece that can transcend any trend and will still hold as much presence in 100 years time when you find it in an antique store as when you bought it in my store yesterday **What is the most important lesson you've learned?** How trust really works

PHOTOGRAPHY BY JAMES COCHRANE AND KIM WESTON ARNOLD. OCTOBER 2000

Born in Normandy, Yvan Mispelaere abandoned his multimedia installation course at the Villa Arçon in Nice to pursue his first love, fashion – relocating to Paris to study at Studio Berçot. In 1989 he went on to cut his fashion teeth with Claude Montana, who then was head of haute couture at Lanvin. Five years later, Mispelaere left Paris for Rome to work with Valentino, eventually defecting to Prada in 1998, where you will remember his work in leather leaves that tumbled down duffel coats and that famous red mouth print pouting from pleated skirts. But it was on his return to Paris for the revival of the dusty old Parisian house of Louis Féraud that Mispelaere's vision was given free reign and his talent made obvious. That first collection, shown at the Autumn-Winter 2000 couture collections, was a highlight of the week, propelling the craft into new realms of enchantment. Using the lack of a Féraud identity to forge a fresh image for a new generation of customer, Mispelaere sliced the most delicate shapes from a monochromatic palette, decorating them with sequins, beads, lace medallions and abstract-shaped appliqués, all formed into graphic Art Déco-esque patterns. Never had so many ideas and so much attention to detail looked so effortless. A few seasons later and the Féraud/Mispelaere union looks to have ended. The fashion world eagerly awaits the fruit of Mispelaere's own label, rumoured to be debuting in early 2003.

Der in der Normandie geborene Yvan Mispelaere brach seine Ausbildung zum Multimedia-Experten in der Villa Arçon in Nizza ab, um sich dem Studium seiner ersten Liebe – der Mode – zu widmen. Dazu ging er nach Paris, um im Studio Berçot zu lernen. Erste Berufserfahrung in Sachen Mode sammelte er dann 1989 bei Claude Montana, dem damaligen Chef der Haute Couture bei Lanvin. Fünf Jahre später wechselte Mispelaere vom Paris nach Rom, um zunächst bei Valentino zu arbeiten und ab 1998 bei Prada. Aus jener Zeit hat man noch seine Blätter aus Leder in Erinnerung, die an Dufflecoats herabfallen, und den berühmten roten Schmollmund, der auf Faltenröcke gedruckt war. Doch erst nach seiner Rückkehr nach Paris mit dem Auftrag, das leicht angestaubte alte Modehaus Louis Féraud neu zu beleben, hatte Mispelaere freie Bahn für seine Visionen und konnte sein Talent richtig entfalten. Jene erste Haute-Couture-Kollektion für Herbst/Winter 2000 war ein Höhepunkt der damaligen Modewoche und trieb die Zunft in neue Sphären des Entzückens. Mispelaere nutzte das Fehlen einer eigenen Identität bei Féraud, um ein frisches Image für eine neue Kundengeneration zu erschaffen. Aus einer mono-chromen Farbpalette schnitt er raffinierteste Silhouetten, die er mit Pailletten, Perlen, Spitzen, Medaillons und abstrakten Applikationen – allesamt im grafischen Stil des Art Déco angeordnet – verzierte. Nie zuvor hatten so viele Ideen und eine solche Liebe zum Detail derart mühelos ausgesehen. Nach ein paar Saisons scheint es mit dem Féraud/Mispelaere-Look zu Ende zu gehen. Die Modewelt wartet gespannt auf die Kreationen von Mispelaeres eigenem Label, das angeblich Anfang 2003 vorgestellt werden soll.

Né en Normandie, Yvan Mispelaere abandonne son cours d'installation multimédia à la Villa Arçon de Nice pour étudier la mode, sa première passion, au Studio Berçot de Paris. En 1989, il affine ses talents auprès de Claude Montana, alors en charge de la collection haute couture de Lanvin. Cinq ans plus tard, Mispelaere quitte Paris pour Rome et travaille avec Valentino. En 1998, il part chez Prada où son travail ne passera pas inaperçu, notamment grâce à ses duffle-coats surchargés de cascades de feuilles en cuir et ses célèbres lèvres rouges imprimées qui font la moue sur les jupes plissées. De retour à Paris, Mispelaere est engagé par Louis Féraud pour dépoussiérer l'ancienne maison et il peut enfin laisser libre cours à sa vision et faire reconnaître ses talents. Sa première collection, présentée aux défilés haute couture Automne-Hiver 2000, est le clou de la semaine de la mode, hissant cet art vers de nouvelles sphères enchanteresses. Tirant parti du manque d'identité de Féraud pour forger une image originale à l'attention d'une nouvelle génération de clients, Mispelaere coupe ses formes délicates dans une palette monochrome et les décore de paillettes, de perles, de médaillons en dentelle et d'applications abstraites, le tout avec un graphisme très Art Déco. Il n'a jamais paru aussi facile d'avoir des idées et de porter une telle attention au détail. Quelques saisons plus tard, il semble que le divorce Féraud/Mispeleare soit prononcé. Le monde de la mode attend impatiemment de découvrir la griffe de Mispelaere qui, selon la rumeur, devrait présenter le résultat de son travail début 2003.

"In my work I am always looking for something that will make me feel bizarre, almost uncomfortable"

PORTRAIT BY DUC LIAO

YVAN MISPELAERE

What are your signature designs? A balance between a surgical construction and free sensuality, a contrast between stiff geometrical logic and light femininity are always recurrent in a way in my designs. There's a 'techno-romantic' something in those obsessive origami foldings, in those stratified volumes and naive graphics. I always try to re-build a personal poetry using an accumulation of things, working on clashes or combinations, looking for something that will make me feel bizarre, almost uncomfortable. I like to think about my work as an intricate collage that would not show obviously what it is made of. When the object doesn't reveal all, keeping some mystery, some foggy secret **How would you describe your work?** An absolute work in progress. Being able to perceive and take care of every single thing, event and person that happens during the whole process of a collection. Not pretending to stay completely fixed to your first idea, but letting it move outside your mind, get richer and alive. That makes the work totally exciting. It's all about excitement, isn't it? **What's your ultimate goal?** Making sure that I will go on enjoying what excites me in my work and what makes it so special, by creating a special situation for it. Making collections under my name – that's a privilege! **What inspires you?** People's lives, all of ours. Past, present, future **Who do you have in mind when you design?** Characters of all my stories, 'personal movies' and fantasies, hoping they might exist somehow… **Is the idea of creative collaboration important to you?** It's the essence of any creative issue – I don't believe in creative loneliness, but rather in creative motion, exchanges **What has been the greatest influence on your career?** A personal accident gave me the energy to dare to 'talk' – like a spark. And I am becoming talkative more and more… **How have your own experiences affected your work as a designer?** As atomic dynamics: producing energy by hitting one thing on the other **Which is more important in your work: the process or the product?** The product as the living evidence of the whole process and as the opening of other coming processes **Is designing difficult for you and, if so, what drives you to continue?** A lot! It's never achieved or satisfying. Time makes the pressure and gives the beat. But I am ingenuously stubborn **Have you ever been influenced or moved by the reaction to your designs?** All the time! It doesn't mean you change yourself because of that, but you go on building, breaking and restarting your own thing in an everlasting lively dialogue, a permanent exchange **What's your definition of beauty?** Poetry, emotion **What's your philosophy?** Enjoying… by living emotions and making poetry… and vice versa! **What is the most important lesson you've learned?** Carpe diem and just do it!

PHOTOGRAPHY BY PETE DRINKELL, STYLING BY RACHAEL ZILLI. APRIL 2002

Angela Missoni has carried her family name forward into the 21st century with assurance and individuality, and in doing so has maintained the cachet of one the biggest brands in Italian fashion. The Italian preference for keeping it in the family has, on this occasion, paid dividends: Angela Missoni has won new converts for the label with her sexy, sporty take on the house's colourful knits and prints. The Missoni company was founded as a knitwear producer in 1953 by her parents, Ottavio and Rosita; over 40 years of technical innovation and experimentation with abstract pattern and beguiling colour combinations have made the Missoni brand world-famous. Angela and her two brothers, Luca and Vittorio, all work for the family company but it was Angela, born in Milan in 1958, who had the natural inclination towards fashion design. She worked in the Missoni company for 20 years, experiencing all aspects of the business, designing alongside her mother while also raising three children. In the spring of 1993, she launched her own label, Angela Missoni, produced by the family company; when Rosita and Ottavio retired from designing the main line in 1997, their daughter was ready to take over. Angela Missoni has managed to achieve what many established fashion brands hope for when they hire a new creative director. She has updated the house signatures for a younger customer who probably doesn't recall the 1970s heyday of Missoni; the instantly recognisable zig-zags, Greek key patterns, stripes and patchworks are seen afresh, cut into hip-hugging trousers or floating chiffon tunics. Angela Missoni's look is still 'put-together' – a phrase coined in 1975 by the American press to describe the Missoni taste for layered, mis-matching patterns – but the attitude is of a new generation.

Angela Missoni hat ihren Familiennamen mit Selbstsicherheit und Eigenständigkeit ins 21. Jahrhundert gebracht, ohne dabei den Charakter einer der bedeutendsten Marken in der Modeszene Italiens zu gefährden. Die italienische Vorliebe für Familienbetriebe hat sich in diesem Fall mehr als bezahlt gemacht: Angela Missoni hat mit den verführerischen und sportlichen Kreationen aus den farbenfrohen Strickstoffen ihres Hauses neue Kunden für die Marke gewonnen. Das Unternehmen Missoni war 1953 als reine Strickwarenproduktion von ihren Eltern Ottavio und Rosita gegründet worden. Mehr als vierzig Jahre technischer Innovationen und Experimente mit den abstrakten Mustern und faszinierenden Farbkombinationen haben Missoni seither weltberühmt gemacht. Angela und ihre beiden Brüder Luca und Vittorio arbeiten allesamt im Familienunternehmen, aber es war die 1958 in Mailand geborene Tochter des Hauses, die sich von jeher zum Modedesign hingezogen fühlte. Zwanzig Jahre lang war sie in allen Bereichen für die Firma tätig, neben ihrer Mutter auch in der Designabteilung, und zog außerdem noch drei Kinder auf. Im Frühjahr 1993 präsentierte sie ihr eigenes Label – Angela Missoni – das ebenfalls im eigenen Haus produziert wurde. Als die Eltern 1997 mit dem Design der Hauptkollektion aufhörten, war ihre Tochter bereit, diese Aufgabe zu übernehmen. Angela Missoni ist gelungen, was viele etablierte Modeunternehmen sich erhoffen, wenn sie einen neuen Kreativdirektor einstellen. Sie hat die Markenzeichen ihres Hauses für eine jüngere Kundschaft, die sich vermutlich nicht an den Missoni-Boom der 70er erinnern kann, aktualisiert. Die unverkennbaren Zickzack- und Mäandermuster, Streifen und Patchworks präsentieren sich mit neuen Schnitten auf Hüfthosen oder fließenden Chiffontuniken. Der Look, den Angela Missoni kreiert, entspricht zwar dem Geschmack einer neuen Generation, er ist jedoch nach wie vor 'put-together' – ein Ausdruck, den die amerikanische Presse 1975 prägte, um die für Missoni so typischen Lagen verschiedener, eigentlich nicht zusammenpassender Muster zu charakterisieren.

Angela Missoni a réussi à faire entrer le nom de sa famille dans le XXIe siècle avec assurance et individualité tout en préservant le cachet de l'une des plus grandes marques de mode italiennes. Dans ce cas précis, la tradition typiquement italienne de l'entreprise familiale a porté ses fruits : Angela Missoni a gagné de nouveaux clients pour la griffe grâce à son interprétation sexy et sport de la maille et des imprimés multicolores caractéristiques de la maison. Ses parents, Ottavio et Rosita, ont fondé l'entreprise Missoni en 1953 en commençant par produire des vêtements en maille ; plus de 40 ans d'innovation technique et d'expérimentation sur des motifs abstraits et des combinaisons de couleurs étonnantes ont valu à la marque Missoni sa reconnaissance internationale. Angela et ses deux frères, Luca et Vittorio, travaillent tous pour l'entreprise familiale, mais c'est Angela, née en 1958 à Milan, qui présente un don naturel pour la création de mode. Pendant 20 ans, elle travaille pour la maison Missoni et touche à tous les aspects du business, dessinant avec sa mère tout en élevant ses trois enfants. Au printemps 1993, elle lance sa propre griffe, Angela Missoni, produite par l'entreprise familiale ; lorsque Rosita et Ottavio arrêtent de dessiner pour la ligne principale en 1997, leur fille est prête à reprendre le flambeau. Angela Missoni a relevé le défi que de nombreuses marques de mode bien établies espèrent surmonter lorsqu'elles engagent un nouveau créateur. Elle a remis au goût du jour les modèles signature de la maison en les adaptant à une cible plus jeune qui n'a probablement pas connu l'âge d'or de Missoni dans les années 1970 ; elle a revisité les zigzags, les motifs grecs, les rayures et les patchworks immédiatement identifiables de la marque en les taillant sous forme de pantalons étroits aux hanches ou de tuniques vaporeuses en mousseline de soie. Le style Angela Missoni se caractérise toujours par son côté « put-together », expression lancée en 1975 par la presse américaine pour décrire son goût pour les assemblages de motifs superposés et non assortis. Toutefois, le look Angela Missoni n'en est pas moins celui d'une nouvelle génération.

"A certain harmony of colours instantly reflects my work"

PORTRAIT COURTESY OF ANGELA MISSONI

ANGELA MISSONI

PHOTOGRAPHY BY PAUL WETHERELL, STYLING BY SORAYA DAYANI. MARCH 2002

"I try to put comfort into the clothes: a kind of freedom"

What are your signature designs? A certain harmony of colours instantly reflects Missoni **What's your ultimate goal?** To maintain the 50-year tradition that my parents invented but keep moving forward **What inspires you?** I am inspired of course by the work of my parents. But it's more a continual, on-going thing. And I am inspired by life itself **Who do you have in mind when you design?** I live in the country and I'm always thinking about the women who are trying to live in the city. So I try to put this kind of comfort into the clothes: a kind of freedom **Who has been the greatest influence on your career?** Number one would have to be my mother, because I learned a lot from her. But I still have my way of doing things **How have your own experiences affected your work as a designer?** Everything is related for me: my passion, my love, my life, my children, my job **Which is more important in your work: the process or the product?** The process is what keeps you going on. The results stay there for such a small amount of time **Have you ever been influenced or moved by the reaction to your designs?** Of course, you are happy if people like what you are doing. But if people don't like what you do then the factory closes tomorrow. That is a big responsibility **What's your definition of beauty?** Uniqueness is more beautiful than 'perfect' beauty **What's your philosophy?** I need to work in harmony: in my love life and with my friends **What is the most important lesson you've learned?** My father says, 'Why gain more money if you don't have time to spend it?'

Issey Miyake (born Hiroshima, 1938) was one of the first Japanese designers to show on the European catwalks in 1973, almost a full decade before Yohji Yamamoto and Comme des Garçons. After studying graphic design at Tama Art University, Miyake moved to Paris in 1964, working for Guy Laroche and Hubert de Givenchy. Before returning to Tokyo to set up his own company, Miyake Design Studio, he also worked for Geoffrey Beene in New York. Each affected Miyake's work as a designer: Beene with his subtlety of form, Laroche and Givenchy with their distinctly Parisian sense of cut and structure. However, Miyake's own collections were something entirely new. He was the first to marry Japanese design with that of the West: aside from looking at the textures and dyeing of traditional Japanese fabrics (such as farmers' smocks), he also utilised some of the notions of Japanese dress, such as universal sizing. This fitted well with his desire to create practical and democratic clothing; a universality later expressed through his choice of models – a show in 1976 used all black girls, another cast women in their 80s. Issey Miyake's designs immediately received acclaim beyond the fashion world and in 1986 he started collaborating with the photographer Irving Penn, who has created an impressive body of work that clearly visualises Miyake's ideas. Besides his own-name label (designed by Naoki Takizawa since 1999), Issey Miyake also produces a line of entirely pleated clothing, Pleats Please, and the collection (designed with his assistant, Dai Fujiwara) he now dedicates his time to, A-POC (A Piece Of Cloth). A genuinely new way of constructing clothes, thread is fed into a knitting machine, creating a 3-D tube of fabric with demarcation lines that, when cut, form a complete wardrobe from large dresses to a simple pair of socks. A-POC was first seen at the Paris collections in October 1998, when 23 models appeared on the catwalk all connected by a piece of cloth. The technique is a closely guarded secret at the Miyake Design Studio, with a patent pending.

Issey Miyake, 1938 in Hiroshima geboren, war 1973 einer der ersten japanischen Designer, die ihre Kreationen auf den Laufstegen Europas präsentierten, fast zehn Jahre vor Yohji Yamamoto und Comme des Garçons. Nach einem Grafikdesign-Studium an der Tokioter Tama Art University ging Miyake 1964 nach Paris, wo er für Guy Laroche und Hubert de Givenchy arbeitete. Bevor er nach Tokio zurückkehrte, um dort mit dem Miyake Design Studio sein eigenes Unternehmen zu gründen, sammelte er noch Erfahrungen bei Geoffrey Beene in New York. Jeder dieser Modeschöpfer hat Miyakes Stil als Designer geprägt: Beene mit seinen raffinierten Silhouetten, Laroche und Givenchy mit ihrem Pariser Gespür für Schnitte und Strukturen. Trotzdem waren Miyakes eigene Kollektionen etwas völlig Neues. Er vereinte als Erster japanisches und westliches Design: Abgesehen von den Texturen und Färbetechniken traditioneller japanischer Gewänder (wie etwa dem Bauernkittel) übernahm er auch einige Eigentümlichkeiten japanischer Kleidung, etwa die universelle Größe. Das passte auch gut zum Vorsatz des Designers, praktische, demokratische Mode zu kreieren. Diese Universalität kam später auch durch die Wahl der Models zum Ausdruck – so liefen bei einer Schau 1976 nur farbige Frauen, bei einer anderen nur Frauen über achtzig. Issey Miyakes Kleider riefen sofort auch außerhalb der Modewelt Begeisterung hervor. 1986 begann die Zusammenarbeit mit dem Fotografen Irving Penn, der eine beeindruckende Werkgruppe schuf, die Miyakes Vorstellungen visuell umsetzte. Neben dem Label, das seinen Namen trägt (und für das seit 1999 Naoki Takizawa entwirft), produziert Issey Miyake noch eine Linie mit ausschließlich plissierten Stücken – Pleats Please. Heute widmet Miyake (gemeinsam mit seinem Assistenten Dai Fujiwara) seine Zeit hauptsächlich A-POC (A Piece Of Cloth). Dabei handelt es sich um eine völlig neue Produktionstechnik: Ein Faden wird in eine Strickmaschine eingeführt, die daraus eine dreidimensionale Stoffröhre mit Trennungslinien macht; wenn man an diesen Linien entlang schneidet, entsteht eine vollständige Garderobe, von langen Kleidern bis zu einem schlichten Paar Socken. A-POC wurde erstmals mit den Pariser Kollektionen im Oktober 1998 gezeigt, als 23 mit einem einzigen Stück Stoff verbundene Models auf den Laufsteg traten. Die Technologie, die hinter dieser Methode steckt, ist ein wohl gehütetes Geheimnis des Miyake Design Studios; die Erteilung des entsprechenden Patents steht noch aus.

En 1973, Issey Miyake est l'un des premiers créateurs japonais à présenter ses collections sur les podiums européens, presque dix ans avant Yohji Yamamoto et Comme des Garçons. Né en 1938 à Hiroshima, Issey Miyake fait des études de graphisme à la Tama Art University, puis s'installe à Paris en 1964 où il travaille pour Guy Laroche et Hubert de Givenchy. Avant de revenir à Tokyo pour créer sa propre entreprise, Miyake Design Studio, il fait un détour par New York et travaille pour Geoffrey Beene. Chacune de ces expériences a influencé son travail en tant que créateur de mode : Beene par ses formes subtiles, Laroche et Givenchy par leur sens typiquement parisien de la coupe et de la structure. Pourtant, les collections de Miyake proposent quelque chose d'entièrement nouveau. Il est le premier à marier le style japonais à celui de l'Occident : outre son intérêt pour les textures et la teinture des tissus japonais traditionnels (tels que les blouses de fermiers), il reprend également à son compte certaines notions de l'habillement japonais, notamment la taille universelle. Ces idées cadrent bien avec son désir de créer une mode pratique et démocratique, une universalité qui s'exprimera par la suite à travers son choix de mannequins : dans un défilé de 1976, il fait uniquement appel à des filles noires, puis à des octogénaires pour une autre présentation. Les créations d'Issey Miyake sont immédiatement applaudies bien au-delà des cercles de la mode et, en 1986, il entame une collaboration avec le photographe Irving Penn, dont le travail impressionnant traduit parfaitement les idées de Miyake. Outre sa griffe éponyme (conçue par Naoki Takizawa depuis 1999), Issey Miyake produit également une ligne de vêtements entièrement plissés, Pleats Please, ainsi qu'une collection (conçue avec son assistant Dai Fujiwara) à laquelle il consacre tout son temps, A-POC (A Piece Of Cloth). Dans cette nouvelle technique originale de construction des vêtements, le fil est inséré dans une machine à tricoter qui débite un tube de tissu en 3D doté de lignes de démarcation qui, une fois coupées, permettent de créer une garde-robe complète, des vêtements les plus amples aux simples paires de chaussettes. La première présentation d'A-POC a lieu en octobre 1998 sur les podiums parisiens, qui voient défiler 23 mannequins reliés par une même pièce de tissu. Le secret de cette technique, dont le brevet est en cours, est étroitement gardé au studio de création Miyake.

"I am a part of my past, but I look to the future"

PORTRAIT COURTESY OF ISSEY MIYAKE

ISSEY MIYAKE

PHOTOGRAPHY BY MARK LEBON, STYLING BY MIRANDA WARBURTON. DECEMBER 2001/JANUARY 2002

"The goal is that our work will be of use"

What's your favourite piece from any of your collections? Always whatever piece I am working upon. At this stage of the year 2002, I work on A-POC with Dai Fujiwara **How would you describe your work?** A-POC is the innovative process of making reality **What's your ultimate goal?** It is that our work will be a part of our daily lives and be of use. To realise it, we are just trying to establish the method and system **What inspires you?** Life **Who do you have in mind when you design?** People **Is the idea of creative collaboration important to you?** Sometimes important. Sometimes dangerous **What has been the greatest influence on your career?** People, nature and technologies **How have your own experiences affected your work as a designer?** I am a part of my past but I look to the future **Which is more important in your work: the process or the product?** Both **Is designing difficult for you?** Making things is a natural extension of myself **Have you ever been influenced or moved by the reaction to your designs?** I always learn from other people **What's your definition of beauty?** Joy **What's your philosophy?** Advancing **What is the most important lesson you've learned?** Honesty

Anna Molinari's Blumarine label is the first stop for any aspiring coquette: her signature mink-collared cardigans are the most famous example of her taste for girlish, lavishly trimmed fashion. Blumarine is always utterly feminine, using beading, embroidery, leopardskin patterns and floral prints – particularly of roses – to decorate delicate chiffon dresses and lightweight knits. Born in 1949 in Carpi, Italy, where she still lives and works, Molinari was introduced to fashion by her parents, who owned a large knitwear factory. On leaving school, she joined the family company. By 1977 Molinari had learned enough from her parents' business to found a new company, Blumarine, with her husband Gianpaolo Tarabini. In 1981 Blumarine made its catwalk debut at Milan Fashion Week. Molinari and her husband incorporated their company in 1988 as Blufin SpA, based in her hometown. Blumarine now has over 700 stockists and 20 own-label boutiques worldwide, selling Blugirl, Blumarine Uomo and Anna Molinari alongside the Blumarine collections. Molinari has made her company a family affair: her husband is managing director while both her daughter Rossella and her son Gianguido have major design roles. Blumarine achieved must-have status in the mid 1990s when delicate slip dresses became fashion editors' favourites: Molinari's little cardigans were the perfect accompaniment to these lingerie-inspired looks. Blumarine continues to have a committed following among women who favour clothes with a vivacious, romantic allure.

Anna Molinaris Label Blumarine ist die erste Wahl für jede Frau, die als kokettes Mädchen in Erscheinung treten will: Die Strickjacken mit Nerzkragen sind das berühmteste Markenzeichen der Designerin für mädchenhafte, üppig aufgeputzte Mode. Blumarine wirkt stets überaus feminin; typisch sind Perlen, Stickereien, Leoparden- und Blumenmuster – insbesondere Rosen – auf zarten Chiffonkleidern und federleichten Stricksachen. Molinari wurde 1949 im italienischen Carpi geboren, wo sie bis heute lebt und arbeitet. Über ihre Eltern, Besitzer einer großen Strickwarenfabrik, kam sie erstmals mit der Modebranche in Berührung. Nachdem sie die Schule beendet hatte, trat Anna ins Familienunternehmen ein. 1977 hatte sie genug gelernt, um gemeinsam mit ihrem Mann Gianpaolo Tarabini die eigene Firma Blumarine zu gründen. 1981 erfolgte das Debüt auf dem Laufsteg bei der Mailänder Modewoche. Seit 1988 firmiert das Unternehmen als Blufin SpA mit Sitz in Molinaris Heimatstadt. Inzwischen gibt es weltweit über 700 Fachhändler und zwanzig eigene Läden, die außer den Blumarine-Kollektionen auch die Nebenlinien Blugirl, Blumarine Uomo und Anna Molinari verkaufen. Dennoch ist Blufin ein Familienbetrieb geblieben: Annas Mann fungiert als Geschäftsführer, während sowohl Tochter Rossella als auch Sohn Gianguido bereits Schlüsselfunktionen im Bereich Design übernommen haben. Mitte der 1990er Jahre, als zarte Kleidchen im Dessous-Stil zum Lieblingslook der Moderedakteurinnen avancierten, war Blumarine unverzichtbar. Molinaris kleine Strickjacken passten perfekt zu diesen an Unterröcke erinnernden Kreationen. Doch auch heute hat Blumarine noch zahlreiche treue Kundinnen unter den Frauen, die romantisch verspielte Mode bevorzugen.

Toute coquette qui se respecte considère la griffe Blumarine d'Anna Molinari comme indispensable à sa garde-robe : ses cardigans à col en vison si caractéristiques offrent le meilleur exemple de son goût pour une mode très jeune fille et richement ornée. Blumarine est avant tout une marque extrêmement féminine, avec des robes délicates en mousseline de soie et des pièces en maille légère souvent décorées de perles, de broderies, de motifs léopard et d'impressions florales, de roses en particulier. Née en 1949 à Carpi en Italie, où elle vit et travaille toujours, Anna Molinari découvre la mode à travers ses parents, propriétaires d'une grande usine de vêtements en maille. Une fois ses études terminées, elle rejoint l'entreprise familiale. Dès 1977, elle en a suffisamment appris auprès de ses parents pour fonder une nouvelle entreprise, Blumarine, avec son mari Gianpaolo Tarabini. En 1981, Blumarine présente son premier défilé à l'occasion de la Milan Fashion Week. En 1988, Anna Molinari et son mari fondent la société Blufin SpA, installée dans leur ville natale. Blumarine possède aujourd'hui plus de 700 stockistes et 20 boutiques indépendantes à travers le monde, qui commercialisent les lignes Blugirl, Blumarine Uomo et Anna Molinari aux côtés des collections Blumarine. Anna Molinari a transformé son entreprise en une véritable affaire familiale : son mari en est le directeur général tandis que sa fille Rossella et son fils Gianguido jouent un rôle majeur dans la création. Blumarine s'est imposée comme une marque indispensable à toute garde-robe au milieu des années 1990, lorsque les rédactrices de mode ne juraient plus que par les délicates robes-combinaisons : en effet, les petits cardigans d'Anna Molinari accompagnaient à merveille ces robes inspirées de la lingerie. Blumarine compte toujours de nombreuses fidèles, autant de femmes qui aiment les vêtements au style espiègle et romantique.

"Fashion is art and it must remain a dream that materialises in beautiful clothes, free of any scheme"

PORTRAIT BY STEFANO GUINDANI

ANNA MOLINARI

What are your favourite pieces from any of your collections? I really like my embroidered dresses, my knitwear with little rose prints and big cardigans worn with light dresses **How would you describe your work?** A choice of life, something that gives me great satisfaction as well as problems! Anyhow, my work represents everything for me, after my family **What's your ultimate goal?** I always want to improve myself as a woman, a mother and as a fashion designer **What inspires you?** Anything: a picture, a film, a beautiful garden in flower, the colours of nature, people walking in the streets, a song **Can fashion still have a political ambition?** I don't think so. Fashion is art and it must remain a dream that materialises in beautiful clothes, free of any scheme **Who do you have in mind when you design?** I often think about my mother, a wonderful woman who used to work with the greatest fashion designers in the '60s. She taught me everything I know and transmitted to me a love for beauty and generosity towards people who are not as lucky as I am. I think about my daughter Rossella, whom I love more than myself and who is like my mother. They are both in my heart and I usually get the energy to start my work by thinking of my mother's attitude and my daughter's creative talent **Is the idea of creative collaboration important to you?** I usually listen to my assistants' opinions, but when I make a decision I always try to persuade them to follow my ideas **Who has been the greatest influence on your career?** My mother's elegance, love for beauty and lifestyle have made me become as I am. My husband Gianpaolo, who is the sole manager of the company, has always been my greatest supporter **How have your own experiences affected your work as a designer?** I consider myself a very strong and lucky woman because I have a great family and I had a wonderful childhood. The infinite love and protection that my husband and our sons give me every day have made me a happy woman. This feeling always influences me and my work; my light but strong dresses are the most natural way I have to express this feeling **Is designing difficult for you and, if so, what drives you to continue?** It is always very difficult. Sometimes I think I could go on holiday, but then… I would be so sad if women couldn't wear my clothes **Have you ever been influenced or moved by the reaction to your designs?** I always listen to the critics and, when they are true, I usually try to adjust my mistakes in order to improve myself **What's your definition of beauty?** Goodness, forgiveness and generosity towards other people, this is the real beauty! **What is your philosophy?** Freedom for all human beings, not meant as anarchy but as having the possibility to live a happy life **What is the most important lesson you've learned?** To be a good person. To be somebody who is able to love and to protect people who ask for my help

Born in South Africa in 1968, Hamish Morrow moved to London in 1989 to study fashion at Central Saint Martins – but promptly left with financial difficulties and a change of heart. It was only after pursuing a career as a freelance designer and pattern cutter that he went to the Royal College of Art in 1996, graduating with an MA in Menswear. Since then, Morrow has worked the ateliers and studios of New York, Milan and Paris. This international training lent his work an air of authority that brought him to the attention of the American press. Morrow's second show, 'The Life Cycle Of An Idea' for Autumn-Winter 2001, proved that off-schedule (as he was then) didn't mean off the boil. The show, which used flowers from bud to full bloom to wilting death, marked Morrow out as one to watch at a time when London was suffering the loss of McQueen and Chalayan to Paris. His use of the finest fabrics (the same Chantilly lace that was used by Monsieur Yves Saint Laurent and tweeds from Chanel's mill) and attention to detail were worthy of a Parisian atelier. But for all the comparisons to couture, Morrow's particular brand of elegance has that unconventional London edge within his conceptual approach to design. Morrow's collections are finally available to buy; he is also one of the young London designers collaborating with TopShop.

Der 1968 in Südafrika geborene Hamish Morrow zog 1989 nach London, um am Central Saint Martins Mode zu studieren. Bald besann er sich jedoch eines anderen und brach, nicht zuletzt wegen finanzieller Probleme, die Ausbildung ab. Erst nachdem er als freier Designer und Zuschneider Karriere gemacht hatte, ging Morrow 1996 noch aufs Londoner Royal College of Art, das er mit einem Magister in Herrenmode abschloss. Danach arbeitete er in diversen Ateliers in New York, Mailand und Paris. Erst diese internationale Erfahrung verlieh seiner Arbeit genügend Autorität, um auch die amerikanische Presse für ihn zu interessieren. Morrows zweite Modenschau unter dem Titel 'The Life Cycle of an Idea' für Herbst/Winter 2001 bewies, dass das, was außerhalb des offiziellen Terminkalenders stattfindet, nicht automatisch unbeachtet bleibt. Das Dekor zur Show bestand aus Blumen in allen Entwicklungsstadien, von der Knospe über die volle Blüte bis zum Verwelken. Morrow erreichte damit große Aufmerksamkeit, als London gerade unter McQueens und Chalayans Weggang nach Paris litt. Seine Verwendung edelster Stoffe (etwa Chantilly-Spitze, wie auch Monsieur Yves Saint Laurent sie benutzte, oder Tweed aus der gleichen Produktion wie Chanel) und die Liebe zum Detail hätten einem Pariser Atelier alle Ehre gemacht. Aber trotz aller Parallelen zur Couture hat die für Morrow so typische Eleganz einen gewissen unkonventionellen Londoner Touch. Inzwischen kann man die Stücke aus seinen Kollektionen endlich auch kaufen, denn er ist einer der jungen Designer, die mit TopShop zusammenarbeiten.

Né en 1968 en Afrique du Sud, Hamish Morrow s'installe à Londres en 1989 pour étudier la mode à Central Saint Martins, mais il change d'avis et abandonne les cours à la suite de problèmes d'argent. Ce n'est qu'en 1996, après avoir travaillé en free-lance dans la création et la coupe de patrons, qu'il entre au Royal College of Art où il obtient un MA en mode pour homme. Depuis, Morrow a travaillé dans plusieurs ateliers de New York, Milan et Paris ; cette formation internationale lui confère une certaine autorité qui attire l'attention de la presse américaine. Le deuxième défilé Automne-Hiver 2001 de Morrow, « The Life Cycle of an Idea », prouve que défiler « off » (comme c'était son cas à l'époque) ne veut pas nécessairement dire qu'on ne bouillonne pas d'idées. Ce défilé, avec ses fleurs bourgeonnantes, écloses et fanées, impose Morrow comme quelqu'un qu'il faudra suivre de près à une époque où Londres souffre du départ de McQueen et de Chalayan pour Paris. Son utilisation des plus beaux tissus (la même dentelle Chantilly que celle de Monsieur Yves Saint Laurent et les tweeds de l'usine Chanel) et son grand souci du détail sont dignes d'un atelier parisien. Malgré les comparaisons à la haute couture, son approche conceptuelle de la création de mode se distingue par une élégance particulière et non-conformiste dans le plus pur esprit londonien. Les collections de Morrow sont finalement disponibles à la vente ; il fait également partie des jeunes créateurs londoniens qui ont collaboré avec TopShop.

"It is my dissatisfaction with everything I do that drives me"

PORTRAIT BY DENNIS SCHOENBERG

HAMISH MORROW

What are your signature designs? The blend of glamour with industrial, technical with luxury and sport with architectural **What is your favourite piece from any of your collections?** The gathered Prince of Wales wool dresses and skirts with incorporated industrial draped web tape and the Swarovski crystal harnesses **How would you describe your work?** Very controlled, technical and analytical **What's your ultimate goal?** To lose control **What inspires you?** Ideas and their evolution **Can fashion still have a political ambition?** Yes, but it would be unwise **Who do you have in mind when you design?** I never design with anyone in mind, muse or customer. My work is entirely ideas-based, and through their evolution, I eventually relate those ideas to the human body, anybody not somebody **What has been the greatest influence on your career?** Music and art **How have your own experiences affected your work as a designer?** They have taught me what I don't want to achieve. This doesn't solve the problem of what I do want, but it helps to narrow it down a little **Which is more important in your work: the process or the product?** I prefer the evolution of process; however the success of the product is the final affirmation of the process and is ultimately more important **Is designing difficult for you and, if so, what drives you to continue?** Designing is not difficult, however evolution of concept can sometimes be demanding and slow. It is my dissatisfaction with everything I do that drives me **Have you ever been influenced or moved by the reaction to your designs?** Once your work goes out before an audience, it no longer belongs to you – the reaction can either be distressing or elating **What's your definition of beauty?** Beauty is not pretty **What's your philosophy?** Life is short **What is the most important lesson you've learned?** You reap what you sew

Roland Mouret has become London's hot ticket without actually having to play the predictable game of showmanship. Touted as a new designer, in fact he has been involved in the fashion industry for a good 15 of his 41 years. And whilst Mouret is labelled the Next Big Thing, his aesthetic and design philosophies are quietly intimate. Born in 1961 in Lourdes, France, he moved to Paris where he started modelling for Jean Paul Gaultier at the age of 22, before going on to become a stylist, working on fashion shoots and in the music business, then as an art director for shoemaker Robert Clergerie. Mouret moved to London in the late 1980s, establishing the Freedom Café in Soho, along with the fashion label People Corporation, a street style-inspired collection. But he first began to make his mark in fashion as part of a new school of designer – the demi-couturier – whose work revives old school craftsmanship and ideas of individuality. Since establishing the Roland Mouret label in 1998, his signature draped pieces of fabric – which he works on each client's body – have become an alternative to the It Dress, his tailoring evoking the glamour of film noir. However Mouret's collections are not exclusive to atelier work, having included prêt-à-porter pieces and a jewellery range, RM Rough, which was the first to use raw diamonds. He continues to show in London.

Roland Mouret gilt als Londoner Geheimtipp, ohne dass er die dafür eigentlich notwendige Show hätte abziehen müssen. Hinter vorgehaltener Hand empfiehlt man ihn als neuen Designer, obwohl er doch schon gut 15 seiner bisher 41 Lebensjahre in der Modebranche zugebracht hat. Und selbst wenn man ihn als einen der kommenden ganz Großen apostrophiert, sind die ästhetischen und designerischen Grundsätze von Mouret unaufregend vertraut. Geboren wurde er 1961 im französischen Wallfahrtsort Lourdes. Mit 22 Jahren ging er nach Paris, um für Jean Paul Gaultier zu modeln, bevor er Stylist wurde, bei Modeaufnahmen und in der Musikbranche jobbte und schließlich als Art Director für den Schuhhersteller Robert Clergerie tätig war. Ende der 1980er Jahre zog es Mouret nach London, wo er neben dem Freedom Café in Soho mit einer vom Street-Style inspirierten Kollektion das Modelabel People Corporation gründete. In der Modebranche machte er jedoch erst als Mitglied einer neuen Designergruppe – der Demi-Couturiers – von sich reden. Diese beleben in ihren Arbeiten die alte hohe Schule der Schneiderkunst und die Grundsätze der Individualität aufs Neue. Seit der Gründung des nach ihm benannten Labels 1998 sind die typischen drapierten Stoffbahnen, die Roland Mouret jeder Kundin auf den Körper schneidert, die Alternative zum It Dress. Diese Form der Schneiderei evoziert den Glamour des Film noir. Dennoch bestehen die Kollektion von Mouret nicht nur aus exklusiven Atelierstücken. Es gibt auch Prêt-à-Porter sowie eine Schmucklinie unter dem Label RM Rough, die als erste Rohdiamanten als solche beließ. Seine Mode präsentiert Roland Mouret nach wie vor in London.

Roland Mouret est devenu un acteur clé de la scène londonienne sans avoir eu à en faire des tonnes. Vendu à 41 ans comme un « nouveau créateur », il est pourtant impliqué dans l'industrie de la mode depuis une bonne quinzaine d'années. Et bien que Mouret soit considéré comme la prochaine sensation, son esthétique et sa philosophie de la création restent plutôt tranquilles et intimistes. Né en 1961 à Lourdes, il s'installe à Paris où il débute comme mannequin pour Jean Paul Gaultier à l'âge de 22 ans. Ensuite, il devient styliste et travaille sur des plateaux photo et dans l'industrie de la musique avant de décrocher un poste de directeur artistique chez le créateur de chaussures Robert Clergerie. Mouret part pour Londres à la fin des années 1980. Il ouvre le Freedom Café à Soho et crée la griffe People Corporation, une collection inspirée du streetwear. En fait, Mouret commence vraiment à attirer l'attention en tant que membre d'une nouvelle école de créateurs, le « demi-couturier », dont le travail remet au goût du jour le savoir-faire à l'ancienne et les concepts d'individualité. Depuis la création de sa griffe éponyme en 1998, ses pièces drapées si caractéristiques, qu'il travaille sur le corps de chaque client, ont offert une alternative aux « effets podium » des défilés grâce à des coupes qui évoquent tout le glamour du film noir. Néanmoins, les collections de Mouret ne sont pas toutes réalisées sur mesure en atelier, puisqu'il a aussi lancé une collection de prêt-à-porter et une ligne de bijoux baptisée RM Rough, la première à utiliser des diamants bruts. Aujourd'hui, Roland Mouret continue de présenter ses collections à Londres.

"I'm not interested in fantasies but a fresh reality. What can we offer women today?"

PORTRAIT BY KEVIN DAVIES

ROLAND MOURET

What are your signature designs? I aim to make clothes that look effortless – that's my signature **What's your favourite piece from any of your collections?** I don't have a favourite piece; I have favourite moments of seeing women wearing my clothes **How would you describe your work?** It's the central thing in my life and it allows me to have a straight life ten hours a day! **What's you ultimate goal?** A house in Camargue, South of France **What inspires you?** A remembered emotion, movement or philosophy **Can fashion still have a political ambition?** Does it need to? **Who do you have in mind when you design?** Sharai, Laura, Fanny, Kate, Sharon, Jo, Kim, Sera, Alex, Georgie, Annabel, Michelle, Lorraine, Becky, Anna and Madame Ma **Is the idea of creative collaboration important to you?** Without it I would just be a dressmaker – it's vital **What has been the greatest influence on your career?** Women – a lot of women! The first one was my grandmother and the latest is my business partner **How have your own experiences affected your work as a designer?** It was the first question I asked myself when I decided to put my name on a piece of fabric. My clothes are the answer to my past and allow me to translate and close doors on my life **Which is more important in your work: the process or the product?** How do you define pleasure without understanding pain, black without white? **Is designing difficult for you and, if so, what drives you to continue?** The unknown is always scary, but I couldn't imagine my life any other way **Have you ever been influenced or moved by the reaction to your designs?** Yes, it would be inhuman not to be! **What's your definition of beauty?** Non-perfection **What's your philosophy?** I'm a fashion designer. It's impossible to answer that question without sounding like I'm totally up my own arse **What is the most important lesson you've learned?** How to be an adult – a child who can take responsibility

Born in Dresden, East Germany in 1959, Kostas Murkudis had a quiet, television-free childhood in West Berlin. Of Greek origin, he was destined to study chemistry and live out a staid existence. It was a shock then (not least to him) that Murkudis strayed so far from the path laid out by his parents: abandoning his science degree to study fashion in Berlin. Murkudis left the Berlin Lette-Verein fashion school in 1983, briefly assisted Wolfgang Joop and soon met Helmut Lang, who was about to show for the first time. Murkudis became Lang's assistant, a position he held for almost seven years, leaving in 1994 to launch his own label in Paris, finally previewing his own collection in 1997 to international acclaim. For a designer who has always valued the themes of utility and masculinity, Murkudis' garments are sensitive, feminine and bravely colourful. He approaches the sharpness and strength of essentially male tailoring with sensitivity, slowing the beat to explore a softer, more luxurious edge. These hidden layers fascinate Murkudis: secrets that remain glimpsed or unseen, a complex relationship with the masculine. To translate these themes, Murkudis' garments can be reversed, opaquely layered and see-through laced, but are always forward-thinking and unique. Murkudis gave up his own signature collection in 2000 to become Head Designer and Creative Director of Diesel's New York Industrie line, showing his first collection that Autumn-Winter. He continues to design for strong, decadent women with delicious, dark secrets.

Der 1959 in Dresden geborene Kostas Murkudis verlebte eine stille, fernsehfreie Kindheit in West-Berlin. Eigentlich schien der Designer griechischer Herkunft dazu bestimmt, Chemie zu studieren und insgesamt ein gesetztes Leben zu führen. Deshalb war es vermutlich zunächst auch ein ziemlicher Schock – nicht zuletzt für ihn selbst –, dass er so weit von dem Weg, den seine Eltern ihm vorgezeichnet hatten, abwich: Er entschied sich gegen die Naturwissenschaften, um in Berlin Mode zu studieren. Die Berufsfachschule für Modedesign des Berliner Lette-Vereins verließ Murkudis 1983 für ein kurzes Engagement bei Wolfgang Joop. Bald lernte er jedoch Helmut Lang kennen, der damals gerade seine erste Modenschau vorbereitete. Murkudis wurde in den nächsten sieben Jahren dessen erster Assistent. 1994 stellte er in Paris ein eigenes Label vor und erntete schließlich 1997 für die Preview seiner ersten eigenen Kollektion internationalen Beifall. Für einen Designer, der immer Wert auf Zweckmäßigkeit und männliche Erscheinung gelegt hat, sind Murkudis' Kreationen ausgesprochen sinnlich, feminin und geradezu gewagt bunt. Er begegnet der Schärfe und Strenge des im Grunde genommen männerdominierten Schneiderhandwerks mit Sensibilität und einer Langsamkeit, die weichere, luxuriösere Entwürfe hervorbringt. Diese verborgenen Schichten faszinieren Murkudis: Geheimnisse, die man nur erahnt oder die völlig im Dunkeln bleiben, ein komplexes Verhältnis zum Maskulinen. Um diese Themen in Mode zu transponieren, wendet der Designer manchmal althergebrachte Techniken an – blickdicht unterlegte oder durchsichtige Spitze – dennoch ist sein Denken zukunftsorientiert und unverwechselbar. Die Kollektion unter seinem eigenen Namen gab Murkudis im Jahr 2000 auf, um Chefdesigner und Creative Director der Linie New York Industrie bei Diesel zu werden. Im selben Jahr präsentierte er dort seine erste Kollektion für Herbst/Winter. Nach wie vor sind seine Entwürfe wie geschaffen für starke Frauen mit pikanten, dunklen Geheimnissen.

Né en 1959 à Dresde en Allemagne de l'Est, Kostas Murkudis passe une enfance tranquille et sans télévision à Berlin Ouest. D'origine grecque, il semble bien parti pour faire des études de chimie et vivre une existence paisible. C'est donc un sacré choc pour ses parents lorsque Murkudis décide de s'éloigner du chemin qu'ils lui avaient tracé : il abandonne son cursus scientifique pour étudier la mode à Berlin. En fait, Murkudis quitte l'école de mode du Lette-Verein de Berlin en 1983, assiste Wolfgang Joop pendant quelque temps puis rencontre rapidement Helmut Lang, qui s'apprête alors à présenter son tout premier défilé. Murkudis devient son assistant, un poste qu'il occupe pendant près de sept ans. Il part en 1994 pour lancer sa propre griffe à Paris, avant de présenter en 1997 une collection éponyme qui rencontrera un succès international. Malgré la grande valeur qu'il a toujours accordée aux thèmes de l'utilité et de la masculinité, Murkudis dessine des vêtements sensibles et féminins dans des couleurs audacieuses. Il aborde la sévérité et la force des coupes classiques pour homme avec une grande sensibilité, en quête d'un style plus doux et plus luxueux. Tout ce qui est caché fascine Murkudis : secrets encore inconnus ou à peine dévoilés, il entretient une relation complexe avec le masculin. Pour traduire ces thèmes, Murkudis peut retourner ses vêtements à l'envers, les recouvrir de superpositions opaques ou de dentelle transparente, ses créations restent toujours visionnaires et uniques en leur genre. En l'an 2000, Murkudis abandonne sa propre collection pour devenir styliste principal et directeur artistique de la ligne New York Industrie de Diesel, présentant la même année un premier défilé aux collections Automne-Hiver. Aujourd'hui, il continue à dessiner pour les femmes sûres d'elles et décadentes qui cachent des secrets sombres et délicieux.

"These clothes are made for using with a smile on your lips"

PORTRAIT COURTESY OF KOSTAS MURKUDIS

KOSTAS MURKUDIS

What are your signature designs? These clothes are made for using with a smile on your lips (24 hour soul moisturiser) **What's your favourite piece from any of your collections?** Always the next **How would you describe your work?** A fusion of contrasts **What's your ultimate goal?** Still having ideas to work out **What inspires you?** The unknown and unexpected **Can fashion still have a political ambition?** It's the wrong platform **Who do you have in mind when you design?** People with their own dreams **Is the idea of creative collaboration important to you?** Collaboration is very inspiring **What has been the greatest influence on your career?** I was shocked and motivated at the same time when I saw my first shows in Paris in 1984 **Which is more important in your work: the process or the product?** An idea needs to be transformed into a product. That's a beautiful moment **Is designing difficult for you and, if so, what drives you to continue?** I love to get through difficult procedures, to find new answers. The chance to evolve is very inspiring **Have you ever been influenced or moved by the reaction to your designs?** No **What's your definition of beauty?** When an idea becomes its own life **What's your philosophy?** Listen to your own voice **What is the most important lesson you've learned?** Respect

The Moscow-based design duo of Nina Neretina (born 1968) and Donis Poupis (born 1969) have been collaborating on ready-to-wear collections under the Nina Donis label since 1992. Having met at the Moscow Textile Academy, where they both studied from 1987-92, their progress has been bound up with one of the most turbulent periods of political history. Not surprisingly, like other designers who have emerged from the former Soviet Union in recent years, their clothing often appears as a reaction to, and an interaction with, the political climate. Nina Donis' designs are a million miles away from the 'boy meets tractor' aesthetic of the Socialist Realism of old; instead there is a debt to the British pop eccentricity found in early Westwood, Galliano and McQueen. Yet, at the same time, their work is tinged with a certain kind of Russian romantic nostalgia which, according to the designers, relates to the optimistic period of Perestroika (the beginnings of reform in the economic and political system of the former USSR). It was at this time, in 1989, that Donis Poupis decided to make Moscow his permanent home (he grew up in Cyprus, with a Cypriot father and Russian mother). He had already started collaborating at art college with Nina Neretina, who comes from just outside Voronezh, a city in central Russia. Since then, Nina Donis have shown at home and abroad, gaining sales in both places, and have exhibited at the designers exhibition during London Fashion Week.

Das in Moskau lebende und arbeitende Designerduo Nina Neretina, Jahrgang 1968, und Donis Poupis, Jahrgang 1969, entwirft seit 1992 gemeinsam Prêt-à-Porter-Kollektionen unter dem Markennamen Nina Donis. Kennen gelernt haben sie sich an der Moskauer Textilakademie, an der beide von 1987 bis 1992 studierten. Ihre Erfolgsstory ist eng mit einer der politisch turbulentesten Phasen in der Geschichte ihres Landes verbunden. Daher überrascht es auch nicht, dass ihre Mode, ähnlich der anderer Kollegen aus der ehemaligen Sowjetunion, wie eine Reaktion auf das politische Klima und eine Interaktion mit diesem wirkt. Von der alten Ästhetik des sozialistischen Realismus à la 'Junge mit Traktor' sind die Kreationen von Nina Donis Lichtjahre entfernt. Eher noch entdeckt man Bezüge zur britischen Popexzentrik der frühen Arbeiten von Westwood, Galliano und McQueen. Zugleich haben die Entwürfe von Nina Donis einen Hauch dieser gewissen romantischen russischen Nostalgie, die nach Aussage der beiden Designer mit dem Optimismus der Perestroika zu tun hat. Genau zu jener Zeit, nämlich 1989, entschloss sich Donis Poupis, der als Kind eines zypriotischen Vaters und einer russischen Mutter auf Zypern aufgewachsen war, auf Dauer in Moskau zu bleiben. Er hatte damals schon begonnen, mit seiner Studienkollegin Nina Neretina, die aus einem kleinen Ort nahe Woronesch in Zentralrussland stammt, zusammenzuarbeiten. Seither präsentiert das Label Nina Donis seine Kollektionen zu Hause und im Ausland und steigert hier wie dort seine Umsätze. Auch bei der Designer-Ausstellung im Rahmen der Londoner Modewoche war man schon vertreten.

Le duo moscovite formé par Nina Neretina (née en 1968) et Donis Poupis (né en 1969) présente des collections de prêt-à-porter sous la griffe Nina Donis depuis 1992. Ils se sont rencontrés sur les bancs de l'Académie Textile de Moscou, où ils ont été étudiants de 1987 à 1992. Leur progression est intimement liée à l'une des périodes les plus turbulentes de l'histoire politique. A l'instar d'autres créateurs de l'ex-Union soviétique qui ont émergé ces dernières années, il n'est pas étonnant que leurs créations soient souvent considérées comme une réaction au climat politique ambiant et comme une interaction avec celui-ci. Les vêtements de Nina Donis se trouvent à des années-lumière de l'esthétique de «glorification du travail» propre au Réalisme Socialiste d'antan; en fait, ils s'inspirent plutôt de l'excentricité pop britannique des premières pièces de Vivienne Westwood, Galliano et McQueen. Pourtant, leur travail témoigne parallèlement d'une certaine nostalgie du romantisme russe qui, selon les créateurs, est à mettre en relation avec la période d'optimisme de la Perestroïka (les premières réformes du système économique et politique de l'ex-URSS). C'est à cette époque, en 1989, que Donis Poupis décide de s'installer de façon permanente à Moscou (il est né à Chypre d'un père chypriote et d'une mère russe). Etudiant en arts, il commence à travailler avec Nina Neretina, originaire des environs de Voronezh, une ville du centre de la Russie. Depuis, Nina Donis a présenté et réussi à vendre ses collections en Russie comme à l'étranger. La griffe a également été présentée à l'exposition des créateurs de la London Fashion Week.

"We try to focus on the positive aspects of living in Russia now and hope this sensibility comes through in the clothes that we design: quite hard-edged but maybe with a touch of romanticism"

PORTRAIT BY GLEB KOSORUKOV

NINA NERETINA & DONIS POUPIS

What are your signature designs? It's difficult for us to say. We'd have to be able to look at our work objectively, through the eyes of someone else, which is not easy **What's your favourite piece from any of your collections?** In each collection we have favourites. But once we've started work on the next collection we become too involved to think about work we liked in the past **How would you describe your work?** We'd like someone else to do that. Someone of our choice! **What's your ultimate goal?** Just to carry on having the drive, the means and the ability to do what we're doing for as long as possible **What inspires you?** Our friends, music, nature, our memories, new people we meet, new ideas **Can fashion still have a political ambition?** Definitely. A political idea or slogan can provide the inspiration that drives a collection. Less directly, everything about us, including how we think, influences what we do **Who do you have in mind when you design?** The people who best fit the image and the mood which we're trying to give in any collection **Is the idea of creative collaboration important to you?** Well, of course! **Who has been the greatest influence on your career?** We've been each other's greatest influence **How have your own experiences affected your work as designers?** In every way! Even in many ways that we're not conscious of **Which is more important in your work: the process or the product?** The process. The more interesting and inspired the process, the better the work **Is designing difficult for you and, if so, what drives you to continue?** Sometimes. But the feeling we get when we think we've achieved something helps us to carry on. Anyway, it's what we like doing best. It's actually the only thing we like doing! **Have you ever been influenced or moved by the reaction to your designs?** If it's the reaction of someone whose opinion we respect and value **What's your definition of beauty?** Do we have to define beauty? **What's your philosophy?** To try and appreciate what one has now, today **What is the most important lesson you've learned?** That we should trust our feelings and our reason and listen to our conscience

A Bathing Ape, or BAPE as it is sometimes known, is the brainchild of a Japanese designer known as Nigo. An elusive personality, Nigo keeps his real name, age and just about everything else a closely guarded secret. A huge fan of the 1970s cult film 'Planet Of The Apes', Nigo started his label in 1993 with a run of limited edition T-shirts featuring simian imagery. A close friend of Undercover's Jun Takahashi, whom he met while studying fashion at the Bunka Fashion College in 1988, they collaborated together before setting up their respective companies. While still a student, Nigo worked as a stylist and writer for hip street magazines such as 'Popeye' and 'Last Orgy 2'. A Bathing Ape perfectly reflects the new market featured in those titles: a generation that has emerged in the last 15 years and been influenced not by designer fashion, but instead the dress codes of their heroes, such as hip hop stars and sportsmen. Nigo's designs offer comfort and quality to a burgeoning group of young men who believe style should be relaxed, subtle and reflect their lifestyle and interests. Today, A Bathing Ape is much more than a clothes line, incorporating all manner of accessories such as furniture and action toys. Given that Nigo's interest in fashion lies as much in its social context as in design itself, it is hardly surprising that in 2000 he released an album on his friend James Lavelle's Mo'Wax label. Today A Bathing Ape is one of the most sought-after street labels by cognoscenti from Tokyo to New York.

A Bathing Ape oder BAPE, wie das Label manchmal auch genannt wird, ist die Erfindung eines japanischen Designers namens Nigo. Dieser Nigo hält seinen richtigen Namen, sein Alter und alle anderen persönlichen Informationen streng geheim. Als glühender Verehrer des Siebziger-Jahre-Kultfilms 'Planet Of The Apes' (Planet der Affen) startete Nigo sein Unternehmen 1993 mit einer limitierten Auflage von T-Shirts mit Affenmotiven. Zuvor hatte er mit Jun Takahashi von Undercover, einem engen Freund seit der gemeinsamen Studienzeit am Tokioter Bunka Fashion College 1988, zusammengearbeitet, bis beide ihre eigenen Firmen gründeten. Schon während des Studiums war Nigo als Stylist und Autor für verschiedene angesagte Straßenmagazine wie 'Popeye' und 'Last Orgy 2' tätig. A Bathing Ape entspricht exakt dem neuen Publikum, das auch diese Zeitschriften anvisieren: eine Generation, die in den letzten 15 Jahren herangewachsen ist und sich nicht von Designermode, sondern von den Dresscodes ihrer Idole, Hiphop-Musikern oder Sportlern, beeinflussen lässt. Nigos Kreationen bieten Bequemlichkeit und Qualität für die ständig wachsende Gruppe junger Männer, die eine ihrem Lebensstil und ihren Interessen entsprechende lockere, raffinierte Mode erwarten. Inzwischen steht A Bathing Ape für viel mehr als nur Kleidung – alle Arten von Accesoires, Möbel und Action-Toys gehören zum Sortiment der Marke. Wenn man bedenkt, dass Nigos Interesse an Mode ebensoviel mit deren soziokulturellem Kontext wie mit ihrem Design an sich zu tun hat, überrascht es nicht, dass der Designer im Jahr 2000 ein Album beim Label Mo'Wax seines Freundes James Lavelle veröffentlicht hat. Heute zählt A Bathing Ape bei Kennern in Tokio wie in New York zu den begehrtesten Streetlabels.

A Bathing Ape, ou BAPE comme on l'appelle parfois, est l'invention d'un créateur japonais connu sous le nom de Nigo. Personnalité insaisissable, Nigo cache son vrai nom, son âge et presque tout le reste comme un précieux secret. Fan numéro 1 du film culte des années 1970 « La Planète des Singes », Nigo lance sa propre griffe en 1993 avec une série de T-shirts à l'imagerie simienne en édition limitée. En 1988, il rencontre son grand ami Jun Takahashi d'Undercover sur les bancs du Bunka Fashion College et entame une collaboration avec lui avant que les deux stylistes se consacrent à leurs entreprises respectives. Pendant ses études, Nigo travaille comme styliste et rédacteur pour des revues underground telles que « Popeye » et « Last Orgy 2 ». A Bathing Ape reflète parfaitement le nouveau marché ciblé par cette presse : la nouvelle génération qui a émergé ces 15 dernières années, influencée non pas par la mode des créateurs mais plutôt par les codes vestimentaires de ses héros, sportifs et stars du hip hop. Les créations de Nigo apportent confort et qualité à ce groupe émergent de jeunes hommes qui recherchent un style décontracté et subtil reflétant leur style de vie et leurs centres d'intérêt. Aujourd'hui, A Bathing Ape est bien plus qu'une simple ligne de vêtements et propose toutes sortes d'accessoires, des meubles et des jouets. Aussi intéressé par le contexte social de la mode que par la création en soi, Nigo sort un album sur le label Mo'Wax de son ami James Lavelle en l'an 2000. De Tokyo à New York, A Bathing Ape est actuellement l'une des griffes branchées les plus recherchées par les aficionados.

"I'm an editor really"

PORTRAIT COURTESY OF NIGO

NIGO

What are your signature designs? A Bathing Ape **What's your favourite piece from any of your collections?** Ape camo **How would you describe your work?** Simple **What's your ultimate goal?** I don't know. If it is here, I've already reached the goal **What inspires you?** Everything around my life. Everything that I would see **Can fashion still have a political ambition?** No **What do you have in mind when you design?** Nothing on my mind **Is the idea of creative collaboration important to you?** Yes **Who has been the greatest influence on your career?** Nobody **How have your own experiences affected your work as a designer?** My experiences haven't affected my work **Which is more important in your work: the process or the product?** Product is more important, but process is enjoyable **Is designing difficult for you?** Easy! **Have you ever been influenced or moved by the reaction to your designs?** No **What's your definition of beauty?** Perfect thing-making **What's your philosophy?** Ape shall never kill Ape **What is the most important lesson you've learned?** I have never had it. I'm not good at learning from someone

Although customisation's major player Jessica Ogden has been ripped off more times than she cares to remember, nothing will stop her staying true to her unique way with vintage fabrics and clothes. Completely self-taught, a free-spirited element skips through Ogden's work. The daughter of a commercials director and Bounty model, she was born in Jamaica in 1970 and brought up by her parents' extended family. She studied sculpture at London's Byam Shaw School of Art, then after turning a heap of old clothes into some exciting new ideas for Oxfam's NoLoGo label in the early 1990s, set up her own label in 1993. Enhancing the personality of old fabrics with hand applications of darning or delicate lines of running stitches is a labour of love for this true bohemian. Ogden is obsessed with craft – but that's not to say her work is solely about surface decoration. Nothing clings in her collections, she makes her samples in a size 12 and uses real people in all shapes, sizes, colours and ages as models. Creating clothes that empower the wearer the way they empower her is her therapy. No wonder hippy chick popsters like Neneh Cherry and Tori Amos are fans. And little surprise that she is seen as one of fashion's true artists by the Arts Council, Crafts Council, Design Museum and Design Council, London, all of whom have invited her to exhibit. Her talent also struck designer Jean Touitou, who continues to send samples from old APC collections for her to breathe new life into each season.

Auch wenn sie als eine der wichtigsten Vertreterinnen der Customization von der Kritik schon öfter regelrecht zerfetzt wurde, lässt sich Jessica Ogden nicht von ihrem unverwechselbaren Stil abbringen, in dem sie Vintage-Stoffe und -Modelle verarbeitet. Den Arbeiten dieser völligen Autodidaktin haftet etwas Freigeistiges an. Als Tochter eines Regisseurs für Werbefilme und eines Bounty-Models wurde die 1970 auf Jamaika geborene Ogden von der Großfamilie ihrer Eltern aufgezogen. An der Londoner Byam Shaw School of Art studierte sie Bildhauerei, verwandelte dann in den frühen 1990er Jahren einen Haufen alter Klamotten in ein paar aufregende neue Kleidungsstücke für das Oxfam-Label NoLoGo und gründete schließlich 1993 ihr eigenes Label. Für die echte Bohemienne Ogden ist es eine Art Liebesdienst, die Persönlichkeit alter Stoffe durch handgenähte Applikationen oder zarte Stickmuster zu unterstreichen. Sie ist von allem Kunsthandwerklichen fasziniert – was nicht heißen soll, ihre Arbeit wäre allein vom oberflächlichen schönen Schein bestimmt. In ihren Kollektionen gibt es nichts Hautenges; sie entwirft in Größe 38, und ihre Models sind normale Menschen von jeglicher Statur, Größe, Hautfarbe sowie unterschiedlichen Alters. Ogdens Geheimnis sind Kleider, die dem Menschen, der sie trägt, genau so viel Kraft geben, wie sie ihr beim Designen geschenkt haben. Kein Wunder also, das Stars wie Neneh Cherry und Tori Amos, die sich dem Hippie-Chic verschrieben haben, zu ihren Fans zählen. Und es ist auch nicht erstaunlich, dass die Designerin beim Arts Council, dem Crafts Council, dem Design Museum und dem Design Council in London als eine der echten Künstlerinnen der Modeszene gilt – all diese Institutionen haben sie nämlich zu Ausstellungen eingeladen. Ein weiterer Bewunderer von Ogdens Talent ist ihr Kollege Jean Touitou, der ihr regelmäßig Stücke aus alten APC-Kollektionen schickt, damit sie ihnen neues Leben einhaucht.

Bien que la « reine du custom » Jessica Ogden se soit fait copier un nombre incalculable de fois, rien ne pourra jamais l'empêcher de rester fidèle à sa façon si unique de travailler les vieux tissus et les vêtements d'occasion. Complètement autodidacte, Jessica Ogden présente des créations parcourues d'un élément de libre pensée. Fille d'un père réalisateur de spots publicitaires et d'une mère mannequin pour les barres Bounty, elle est née en 1970 en Jamaïque, élevée par la famille de ses parents. Elle étudie la sculpture à la Byam Shaw School of Art de Londres, puis, au début des années 1990, elle transforme tout un tas de vieux vêtements en nouveaux modèles pour la griffe NoLoGo d'Oxfam avant de lancer sa propre griffe en 1993. Pour cette véritable bohémienne, rien n'est plus beau que les vieux tissus, dont elle fait ressortir la personnalité avec des applications reprisées à la main ou des lignes délicates de coutures apparentes. Jessica Ogden est obsédée par l'artisanat, mais son travail ne tourne pas uniquement autour des décorations de surface. Rien n'est moulant dans ses collections, elle conçoit ses prototypes en taille 40 et choisit ses mannequins parmi de « vrais gens » aux formes, tailles, races et âges variés. Sa thérapie consiste à créer des vêtements qui rendront heureux ceux qui les portent, comme c'est le cas pour elle. Il n'est donc pas étonnant qu'elle compte quelques stars hippie pop comme Neneh Cherry et Tori Amos parmi ses fans. Ni qu'elle soit considérée comme l'une des vraies artistes de la mode par l'Arts Council, le Crafts Council, le Design Museum et le Design Council, Londres, autant d'institutions qui l'ont invitée à exposer ses créations. Son talent a également séduit le designer Jean Touitou, qui lui envoie régulièrement les prototypes de ses anciennes collections APC pour renouveler son inspiration chaque saison.

"Clothes are about much more than just cloth. It's giving the wearer something more than a garment. It's transferring emotion"

PORTRAIT BY JOHN SPINKS

JESSICA OGDEN

What are your signature designs? I'm known for pieces with patchwork, random stitch or appliqué. Also, for using antique fabrics What's your favourite piece from any of your collections? A very tattered patchwork dress from Spring-Summer 1999, which I daren't wear because it will probably fall apart How would you describe your work? Quite gentle and subtle. It's a body of work that changes over time, rather than each season What's your ultimate goal? Just to continue – if the label grows or if it stays or if it just comes back to working alone, that's all fine What inspires you? Being able to make my own clothes. I'm still thrilled by that idea Can fashion still have a political ambition? Of course it can, if that's your motivation. Whether it's actually transferred into the outer world is a different question Who do you have in mind when you design? I'm still making clothes for myself Is the idea of creative collaboration important to you? Working with people you're close to is very important. All through my career there have been people who have had a positive influence over me – who have come into my life and opened up new worlds and encouraged me to dream How have your own experiences affected your work? I always think that garments are about much more than just cloth – there's a huge amount of emotion there too. And that comes from still having clothes that my mum sewed for me as a child, from seeing her work and remembering how that made me feel. It's giving the wearer something more then a garment. It's transferring emotion Which is more important in your work: the process or the product? It's very much the whole process of work. I guess that through being self-taught, I don't have an end vision all the time. This is the reason why I can't draw a dress I want – I have to go through a process to get it. But when it comes out, you can see that process, you can see there has been time spent. To sew is a beautiful thing Is designing difficult for you and, if so, what drives you to continue? It is difficult in some ways because I can't give a team of people a drawing and say 'this is what I want'. Rather, it's working with people, which is not about an instant result. It's not difficult in the way that it's really hard work – it's good work Have you ever been influenced or moved by the reaction to your designs? Yes, it's really nice when someone enjoys what a piece gives them What's your definition of beauty? It definitely comes from within What's your philosophy? Expression is important What is the most important lesson you've learned? Listening to yourself – and allowing yourself time to do that

José Enrique Oña Selfa has an aesthetic fetish for sado-masochistic strictness. His muse is the nun, the Latin widow, the horse rider, the Latino dancer. Discipline lubricated by delicious torture is what floats Oña Selfa's fashion boat. Born in 1975, his parents are from Andalusia, Southern Spain, and moved to Brussels in the 1960s, where Oña Selfa was raised. He studied fashion at the Ecole Nationale Supérieure des Arts Visuels de la Cambre, graduating in 1999 with a Masters of the highest distinction. By that point he had already been working with fellow student Olivier Theyskens for two years, assisting him as a pattern cutter and knitwear designer when Theyskens dropped out to launch his own label. Oña Selfa started his own company in 2000, presenting a debut show for Autumn-Winter to international acclaim. The collection featured directional and revolutionary knitwear that was very much a product of Oña Selfa's mixed heritage, the fusion of passionate Latin energy and brooding Belgian romance. Sex sells and Oña Selfa's aesthetic had the cut and thrust that Loewe, a relatively unknown label compared to LVMH's other brands, was looking for. (Other womenswear designers for Loewe have included Karl Lagerfeld, Giorgio Armani and Narciso Rodriguez.) Despite his relatively short career history, he was hired as the company's new designer. Like Helmut Newton bullfighting infantas, girls stormed in at Oña Selfa's first Loewe collection for Autumn-Winter 2002 in his mix of bourgeoise luxury and high voltage sexual energy crafted in the house fabric: Nappa leather. Sex has seldom looked so expensive. Oña Selfa also continues to show his own collection in Paris.

José Enrique Oña Selfa ist in ästhetischer Hinsicht von sadomasochistischer Strenge besessen. Seine Musen sind Klischees: die Nonne, die südländische Witwe, die Reiterin und die Latino-Tänzerin. Oña Selfas Mode schwimmt auf einer Welle von Disziplin und lustvoller Qual. Seine Eltern stammen aus Andalusien, zogen jedoch in den 1960er Jahren nach Brüssel, wo auch ihr 1975 geborener Sohn aufwuchs. Oña Selfa studierte an der Ecole Nationale Supérieure des Arts Visuels de la Cambre, die er 1999 mit Auszeichnung und einem Magistertitel verließ. Zu jenem Zeitpunkt hatte er bereits zwei Jahre lang mit seinem Kommilitonen Olivier Theyskens zusammengearbeitet und ihm als Zuschneider und Strickmode-Designer assistiert, nachdem Theyskens das Modestudium abgebrochen und sein eigenes Label gegründet hatte. Oña Selfa startete im Jahr 2000 seine eigenes Unternehmen mit der Präsentation einer international mit Beifall aufgenommenen Debütkollektion für Herbst und Winter. Diese Kollektion enthielt revolutionäre Strickmode, die ganz deutlich ein Produkt der multikulturellen Herkunft ihres Designers war: Er verschmolz leidenschaftliche südländische Kraft mit elegischer Romantik, die als typisch belgisch gilt. Sex verkauft sich immer, und Oña Selfas Ästhetik besaß die innere Dynamik, nach der Loewe, ein relativ unbekanntes Label unter dem Dach des Konzerns LVMH, damals gerade suchte. Trotz seiner relativ geringen Berufserfahrung wurde Oña Selfa als neuer Designer des Hauses eingestellt. (Zu seinen namhaften Vorgängern, die bereits Damenmode für Loewe entworfen hatten, zählten Karl Lagerfeld, Giorgio Armani und Narciso Rodriguez.) Wie Helmut Newtons Stierkämpferinnen stürmten die Mädchen bei seiner ersten Loewe-Schau für Herbst/Winter 2002 auf den Laufsteg. Diese Mischung aus bourgeoisem Luxus und sexueller Hochspannung war im Lieblingsmaterial des Hauses verarbeitet: Nappaleder. Selten hat Sex so kostbar ausgesehen. Oña Selfa präsentiert seine eigene Kollektion weiterhin in Paris.

José Enrique Oña Selfa est obsédé par l'esthétique sévère du fétichisme et du sado-masochisme. Les muses qui l'inspirent sont la nonne, la veuve italienne, l'écuyère ou encore la danseuse Latino, dans une mode alimentée par la discipline et les délices de la torture. Dans les années 1960, ses parents originaires d'Andalousie s'installent à Bruxelles où grandit Oña Selfa (né en 1975). Il étudie la mode à l'Ecole Nationale Supérieure des Arts Visuels de la Cambre, puis décroche un Masters avec les félicitations du jury en 1999. A cette époque, il travaille déjà depuis deux ans avec son ami Olivier Theyskens qui a quitté l'école pour lancer sa propre griffe. Il l'assiste dans la coupe des patrons et dessine des pièces en maille. Oña Selfa crée sa propre entreprise en l'an 2000 et présente un premier défilé Automne-Hiver qui remporte un succès mondial. Les pièces en maille révolutionnaires de cette collection établissent une nouvelle référence, résultat évident de l'héritage mixte de Oña Selfa : fusion entre passion des pays latins et romantisme désabusé de la Belgique. Le sexe fait vendre et l'esthétique de Oña Selfa présente le style et l'énergie que Loewe, griffe relativement inconnue par rapport aux autres marques du groupe LVMH, recherche alors (parmi les précédents stylistes pour femme de Loewe figurent Karl Lagerfeld, Giorgio Armani et Narciso Rodriguez). Malgré sa brève expérience du métier, il devient le nouveau styliste de la maison. Telles les infantes des corridas de Helmut Newton, les filles se précipitent sur la première collection Automne-Hiver 2002 de Oña Selfa pour Loewe, séduites par ce mélange de luxe bourgeois et d'énergie sexuelle explosive taillé dans le tissu de la maison : le cuir Nappa. Le sexe a rarement paru si cher. Par ailleurs, Oña Selfa continue à présenter sa propre collection à Paris.

"I love the essence of women"

PORTRAIT BY DUC LIAO

JOSÉ ENRIQUE OÑA SELFA

PHOTOGRAPHY BY DONALD CHRISTIE, STYLING BY KARL PLEWKA. SEPTEMBER 2002. MODEL: SARAH MURRAY

"Women's fashion shouldn't be to pleasure a gay man, because after he has no use for her"

What are your signature designs? Those made from leather. Quality **What's your favourite piece from any of your collections?** To mention one, a tweed outfit (the inside made from pink leather) **How would you describe your work?** Sensual, elegant **What's your ultimate goal?** Constant evolution **What inspires you?** The atmosphere created by reading, writing and structuring all these into a 'woman' **Can fashion still have a political ambition?** In certain ways, yes **What do you have in mind when you design?** The 'envy' of fashion **Is the idea of creative collaboration important to you?** Yes, it is **What has been the greatest influence on your career?** The will of fashion **Which is more important in your work: the process or the product?** Everything is linked. One after another **Is designing difficult for you and, if so, what drives you to continue?** Over again, the pleasure and the will of fashion **Have you ever been influenced or moved by the reaction to your designs?** Not really **What's your definition of beauty?** Allure **What's your philosophy?** Work **What is the most important lesson you've learned?** To trust myself

PHOTOGRAPHY BY ALEX HOERNER. MAY 2002. MODEL: MICHELE LAMY

Away from the glittering turquoise pools of David Hockney and an unrelenting 'Hooray for Hollywood', there is another Los Angeles. Louche, lean, decadent and more than a bit malign, it's the LA that designer Rick Owens seems to evoke in his clothing. Owens has been producing collections in his adopted hometown since 1994. Despite garnering a fashion audience from Barneys to Browns, he only started showing formally in New York in February 2002. He has no plans to move east. Born in 1961 and brought up in Porterville (a small town in Southern California), in between pot, beer and Lynnard Skynnard there was French Vogue, Mugler and Mahler – Owens was always attracted by the idea of wicked city sophistication. He initially made the move to LA in 1979, studying painting at Otis Parsons. Becoming disillusioned with the art world, Owens specialised in pattern cutting at a technical college and later worked in the knock-off garment district. Although unconventional, this training has given a strict technical underpinning to what Owens does. He also cites historical influences including Vionnet, Fortuny and Grès, all famed for their sculptural approach to design for the body. It adds up to a subtlety and quietness in the clothing: elegant elongated forms, a subdued palette and the concentration on luxurious yet experimental fabrication. Mixed together with the down-at-heel atmosphere of Hollywood Boulevard, his work feels like all of the above run over by a stolen car.

Abseits der türkis glitzernden Pools von David Hockney und der unreflektierten Begeisterung für Hollywood gibt es noch ein anderes Los Angeles. Anrüchig, mager, dekadent und mehr als ein bisschen boshaft – ein solches LA scheint der Designer Rick Owens mit seiner Mode heraufzubeschwören. Owens produziert schon seit 1994 eigene Kollektionen in seiner Wahlheimat. Trotz namhafter Kunden von Barneys bis Browns begann er mit offiziellen Schauen in New York erst im Februar 2002. Allerdings plant er nach wie vor nicht, an die Ostküste zu ziehen. Geboren und aufgewachsen ist Owens in der südkalifornischen Kleinstadt Porterville, wo es neben Hasch, Bier und Lynnard Skynnard auch die französische Vogue, Mugler und Mahler gab. Die Vorstellung von der verruchten, blasierten Großstadt faszinierte ihn schon immer, und so zog er 1979 erstmals nach LA, um bei Otis Parsons Malerei zu studieren. Nachdem er seine Illusionen über den Kunstbetrieb verloren hatte, spezialisierte sich Owens an einem Technischen College aufs Zuschneiden und arbeitete anschließend im heruntergekommenen Garment District. Diese unkonventionelle Ausbildung verleiht Owens' Arbeit bis heute eine solide technische Basis. Der Designer bekennt sich aber auch zu historischen Einflüssen, etwa von Vionnet, Fortuny und Grès, die für den skulpturalen Ansatz ihrer Mode berühmt sind. All das resultiert in Finesse und Ruhe: elegante, gestreckte Silhouetten, gedämpfte Farben und Konzentration auf luxuriöse, aber dennoch experimentelle Herstellungsverfahren. Versetzt mit der leicht heruntergekommenen Atmosphäre des Hollywood Boulevard, wirkten seine Arbeiten wie von einem gestohlenen Auto überfahren.

Loin des piscines turquoise scintillantes de David Hockney et de l'attitude agressive pro-Hollywood, il existe un autre Los Angeles. Louche, pauvre, décadent et plus qu'un peu malfaisant, c'est le L.A. que semble évoquer le designer Rick Owens dans ses vêtements. Owens produit des collections dans sa ville d'adoption depuis 1994. Bien qu'il ait séduit un public d'avertis de Barneys à Browns, il n'a commencé à présenter ses collections de façon formelle qu'en février 2002 à New York. Il n'a pas l'intention de s'installer sur la Côte Est. Né en 1961 et élevé à Porterville (petite ville de Californie du Sud), Owens fume de l'herbe, boit de la bière et écoute Lynnard Skynnard, mais il lit aussi le Vogue français, découvre Mugler et apprécie la musique de Mahler: il était déjà attiré par l'idée d'une sophistication urbaine déjantée. En 1979, il s'installe d'abord à L.A. pour étudier la peinture à Otis Parsons. Déçu par le monde de l'art, Owens entre alors dans un collège technique et se spécialise dans la coupe de patrons avant de travailler pour des fabricants de vêtements bas de gamme. Bien que non conventionnelle, sa formation procure à Owens de solides bases techniques. Il cite également des influences historiques telles que Madeleine Vionnet, Fortuny et Grès, autant de couturiers réputés pour leur approche sculpturale du corps. Cette inspiration ajoute subtilité et douceur à ses vêtements: formes allongées et élégantes, palette discrète, fabrication luxueuse mais expérimentale. Avec leur touche « miséreuse » à la Hollywood Boulevard, ses vêtements donnent l'impression d'avoir été écrasés par une voiture volée.

"Dirty habits – that's what my clothing is all about"

PORTRAIT BY TERRY JONES

RICK OWENS

"My references all share an elegance tinged with a bit of the barbaric"

What are your signature designs? The silhouette I return to regularly is a small, controlled, sharp shoulder, draping down to a trail of smoke. I like the sloppiness of something dragging; there's probably a mythological reference there too. Colours are usually kind of sombre, muted non-colours – pearls, greys, nudes, shadows. I love flowers but I don't need to compete with them **How would you describe your work?** I try to give everything I make a worn, softened feeling. I admit there's the attraction of melancholy damage, but there's also an earthy comfort. And of course the implication of a little perspiration and musk **Who do you have in mind when you design?** I try to make clothes the way Lou Reed does music. Minimal chord changes and direct. Sweet, but kinda creepy. There's so much stimulation in the world that I'd like to offer the alternative of quiet and familiarity. Not the beige reserve of someone who wants to play it safe, but the place you find when you've explored and experimented. A contentment from satisfying a healthy appetite. The luxury of not caring **What inspires you?** The bleak, romantic social conscience of artist Joseph Beuys. The minimal but grand precision of interior designer Jean Michel Frank. The languid modernism of Vionnet. These are some of my favourite references and I think they all share an elegance tinged with a bit of the barbaric **What's your definition of beauty?** If there's a theme, it's probably something about the cycle of youthful utopian idealism softening into sadder but wiser tranquility. The memory of the glory of bloody mosh-pit noses. Strauss's Salome's lust reduced to a head on a plate. That kind of stuff **What's your philosophy?** It's not art. At least not in my case. But it gets kinda close. It's sort of telling a story bit by bit, season after season. You build up a history of ideas, little connotations, observations, and try and turn it into a whole. Something of beauty, a mood. You're culling subtle references whose combination strikes a chord with your generation. I'm by myself a lot and this is the best way I've found to comfortably engage with the world

Marjan Pejoski is a designer as colourful, eccentric and energetic off the catwalk as his creations are on it. Resolutely flamboyant, Pejoski's work is noted for its exceptional finishing touches and a trademark use of crochet, beadwork and sequins. His designs are labour-intensive and blur the boundaries between ready-to-wear and couture, whilst always mixing in a generous helping of humour. Born in Skopje, Macedonia (then part of Yugoslavia) in 1968, the son of a politician, Pejoski studied economics and business before deciding to move to London, where he took courses in jewellery design at Westminster, shoe design at Cordwainers College and fashion illustration at Chelsea College of Art and Design. Pejoski then went on to complete a BA in womenswear at Central Saint Martins in 1999. His graduation collection caused a sensation with its transparent showpiece dress, filled with water and tropical fish. The same year, Pejoski was propelled into the spotlight when he dressed Björk for the Cannes film festival. Pejoski and Björk's shared sense of the unconventional led to an inevitable friendship and she regularly wears his clothes; most famously, his egg-laying swan dress to the 2001 Oscars ceremony. Pejoski co-founded the London and Paris Kokon Tozai boutiques, for which he buys the work of other young and radical designers. He now shows his collections during Paris Fashion Week.

Marjan Pejoski ist als Designer ebenso vielseitig, exzentrisch und energiegeladen, wie die Kreationen, die er auf den Laufsteg bringt. Seine bewusst extravaganten Arbeiten sind bekannt für ihren außergewöhnlichen letzten Schliff; Häkelspitzen, Perlen und Pailletten dienen als Markenzeichen. Die arbeitsintensiven Stücke liegen irgendwo zwischen Prêt-à-Porter und Haute Couture, sind jedoch stets mit einer großzügigen Portion Humor versehen. Pejoski wurde 1968 in Skopje, damals noch Jugoslawien, heute Mazedonien, als Sohn eines Politikers geboren. Nach einem Betriebswirtschaftsstudium beschloss er, nach London zu gehen, wo er an der University of Westminster Kurse für Schmuck-design belegte, am Cordwainers College Schuhdesign und am Chelsea College of Art and Design Modeillustration studierte. 1999 machte Pejoski schließlich noch einen Bache-lor of Arts in Damenmode am Central Saint Martins. Seine Abschlusskollektion, u. a. ein transparentes Kleid, das mit Wasser und tropischen Fischen gefüllt war, erregte unglaub-liches Aufsehen. Im selben Jahr stand Pejoski noch einmal im Rampenlicht, und zwar mit dem Kleid, das er für Björks Auftritt bei den Filmfestspielen von Cannes entworfen hatte. Der Designer und die Sängerin teilen den gleichen Hang zum Unkonventionellen und wurden deshalb fast zwangsläufig zu Freunden. Seither trägt Björk regelmäßig Pejoski-Kreationen, darunter auch das berühmte Schwanenkleid anlässlich der Oscar-Verleihung 2001. Pejoski ist Mitbegründer der Kokon-Tozai-Läden in London und Paris, für die er Arbeiten anderer junger, radikaler Designer ankauft. Die eigenen Kollektionen präsentiert er inzwischen bei der Pariser Modewoche.

Dans la vie, Marjan Pejoski est un designer aussi haut en couleurs, excentrique et énergique que le sont ses créations sur le podium. Résolument flamboyant, le travail de Pejoski se distingue par des touches de finition exceptionnelles et une utilisation originale du crochet, des perles et des sequins. Ses créations nécessitent de nombreuses heures de travail et estompent la frontière entre prêt-à-porter et haute couture, le tout saupoudré d'une bonne dose d'humour. Né en 1968 à Skopje en Macédoine (territoire de l'ex-Yougoslavie) d'un père homme politique, Pejoski étudie l'économie et la gestion d'entreprise avant de partir pour Londres, où il suit des cours de création de bijoux à la University of Westminster, de création de chaussures au Cordwainers College et d'illustration de mode au Chelsea College of Art and Design. En 1999, Pejoski obtient un BA en mode féminine à Central Saint Martins. Sa collection de fin d'études fait sensation grâce à « l'effet podium » d'une robe transparente remplie d'eau et de poissons tropicaux. La même année, Pejoski se voit propulsé sous les feux de la rampe en habillant Björk pour le festival de Cannes. Le goût commun de Pejoski et de Björk pour le non-conformisme marque la naissance d'une belle amitié. Elle porte régulièrement ses vêtements et s'est fait particulièrement remarquer avec sa robe « cygne » qui pondait des œufs à la céré-monie des Oscars 2001. Pejoski est le co-fondateur des boutiques Kokon Tozai de Londres et de Paris, pour lesquelles il achète les œuvres d'autres jeunes créateurs radicaux. Il présente désormais ses collections à la Semaine de la Mode de Paris.

"My philosophy is obviously freedom of expression"

PORTRAIT COURTESY OF MARJAN PEJOSKI

MARJAN PEJOSKI

What are your signature designs? It's the texture and the embroideries that I use. And the 3-D, almost sculptural pieces that I do sometimes **How would you describe your work?** I play with visuals, colours and textures. It's my way of talking instead of using words **What's your ultimate goal?** Freedom of expression **What inspires you?** Films, places, people, music, theatre, books… anything **Can fashion still have a political ambition?** Of course fashion is a statement. You can have a slogan on yourself, whatever. But that's not my fashion **Who do you have in mind when you design?** It can be quite a fragile character, but it is somebody who believes in themselves and who knows what they want, in a sense of having their own taste. And somebody who is quite interested in experimenting with colours and shapes. Wearing clothes in their own way and maybe re-organising those clothes in the sense of customising or mixing them in any possible way **How have your own experiences affected your work as a designer?** It's such a cliché, but I have loved fashion ever since I was very young. I never knew it was going to be my final profession, that I would make a career out of it. It was just something I knew I loved. So when I came to London first, I tried out all these different things – photography, sculpture, painting, shoe design, jewellery – to try and know myself. It was my tutors who knew and who pushed me always towards fashion **What's your definition of beauty?** I love eccentric people. Someone who believes in originality, who doesn't follow any given ways of doing things **What's your philosophy?** It is obviously freedom of expression **What is the most important lesson you've learned?** Don't compromise

Jurgi Persoons deforms classics, ripping out necklines and splitting linings, twisting and stitching them all together again. Born near Brussels in 1969, Persoons studied at the Royal Academy Antwerp then briefly assisted Walter Van Beirendonck in 1994 before designing his first womenswear collection in 1996. From the beginning, Persoons has worked with a fashion aesthetic that explores all the natural imperfections of the creative process. Just as muted and faded vintage garments are perceived to have character and value, Persoons also allows his pieces to evolve naturally. Tiny flaws are noted and tentatively nurtured; original classics are thrown off balance. Early collections have titles like: 'Resurrection Of Eighties Ungaro Tramps Out Of Their Graves'. The result is obsessively hand-worked: intricate pieces with rough textures and ragged crinkle-cut edges, signature white-on-black stitching and a classic, near masculine cut. Building a reputation for dramatic static exhibitions, the preview of Persoons' Autumn-Winter 1999 collection (his first proper 'show') involved models imprisoned in glass cages along the banks of the Seine, which the audience had to travel to by taxi and 'discover'. In one installation, models were stuck like butterflies on huge perspex blocks; others turned blue in the winter cold as they climbed scaffolding outside the Musée d'Art Moderne. Perhaps mellowing slightly, Persoons' Autumn-Winter 2002 show came in the form of a sedately posed school photograph on the steps of the Palais Galliera.

Jurgi Persoons entstellt Klassiker, indem er ihre Kragen abtrennt, ihr Futter aufschlitzt, alles dreht, wendet und wieder neu zusammennäht. Der 1969 in der Nähe von Brüssel geborene Belgier studierte an der Königlichen Akademie in Antwerpen und war 1994 kurze Zeit Assistent von Walter Van Beirendonck. Zwei Jahre später entwarf er seine erste eigene Damenkollektion. Von Beginn an vertrat der Designer eine Ästhetik, die alle natürlichen Unzulänglichkeiten des kreativen Prozesses mit einschließt. So wie die zerstückelten, verblichenen Vintage-Stücke Wert und Charakter ausstrahlen, erlaubt Persoons auch seinen neuen Kreationen, sich quasi natürlich zu entwickeln. Kleine Fehler werden registriert und sogar sorgsam gehegt. Ursprüngliche Klassiker stößt er dagegen bewusst von ihren Sockeln. Frühe Kollektionen von Persoons tragen so bezeichnende Namen wie: 'Resurrection Of Eighties Ungaro Tramps Out Of Their Graves'. Das Ergebnis ist leidenschaftlich handgearbeitet: komplizierte Stücke mit rauen Texturen und ausgefransten, krumm geschnittenen Kanten, weiße Stiche auf schwarzem Grund als Markenzeichen und ein klassischer, beinahe maskuliner Schnitt. Seinen Ruf als Meister dramatischer, statischer Präsentationen erwarb sich Persoons schon mit der Preview seiner Kollektion für Herbst/Winter 1999 – seiner ersten eigenen Show: Hierfür waren Models in Glaskäfige entlang des Seineufers gesperrt; das Publikum musste im Taxi an ihnen vorbeifahren und sie 'entdecken'. Bei einer anderen Installation hatte er die Models wie Schmetterlinge auf riesigen Blöcken aus Plexiglas fixiert. Bei einer weiteren Präsentation waren die Models von der winterlichen Kälte regelrecht blaugefroren, während sie auf einem Gerüst an der Fassade des Musée d'Art Moderne herumkletterten. Vielleicht ist der Designer inzwischen doch etwas milder geworden, denn seine Kollektion für Herbst/ Winter 2002 präsentierte er in Form eines unbewegt aufgenommenen Klassenfotos auf den Stufen des Palais Galliera.

Jurgi Persoons se plaît à déformer les classiques : il arrache les décolletés et déchire les doublures avant de tordre et de recoudre l'ensemble. Né en 1969 près de Bruxelles, Persoons étudie à l'Académie Royale d'Anvers. En 1994, il travaille brièvement comme assistant de Walter Van Beirendonck avant de lancer sa première collection pour femme en 1996. Dès ses débuts, Persoons adopte une esthétique de la mode qui vise à explorer toutes les imperfections naturelles du processus de création. Il donne du caractère et de la valeur à ses pièces « vintage » aux couleurs sourdes et vieillies et laisse ses vêtements évoluer naturellement. Dans sa quête expérimentale, il traque les plus petits défauts pour les mettre en valeur, déséquilibrant les grands classiques délibérément et avec originalité. Ses premières collections portent des titres aussi saugrenus que « Salopes Ungaro eighties ressuscitées de leurs tombes ». Persoons nourrit une véritable obsession pour le fait main : pièces complexes taillées dans des textures grossières aux bords crantés et effilochés, coutures blanc sur noir caractéristiques et coupe classique presque masculine. Persoons bâtit sa réputation autour de ses présentations statiques très théâtrales. Pour l'avant-première de sa collection Automne-Hiver 1999 (son premier vrai « défilé »), il présente des mannequins emprisonnés dans des cages de verre le long des quais de la Seine que le public doit parcourir en taxi s'il tient à « découvrir » les créations. Dans une autre installation, les mannequins sont collés comme des papillons sur de grands blocs de plexiglas ; d'autres bleuissent dans le froid hivernal alors qu'elles escaladent les échafaudages du Musée d'Art Moderne. Pour son défilé Automne-Hiver 2002, peut-être un peu plus soft, Persoons opte pour une photo de classe où les mannequins posent sagement sur les marches du Palais Galliera.

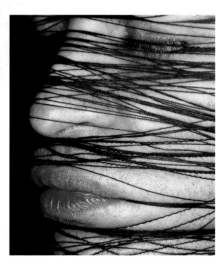

"I just prefer to make beautiful clothes"

PORTRAIT BY RONALD STOOPS

JURGI PERSOONS

What are your signature designs? Clothes with artisanal or sophisticated finishings **What's your favourite piece from any of your collections?** My favourite piece is a patchwork tartan skirt with more than two kilometres of hand stitching **How would you describe your work?** Very classic **What's your ultimate goal?** To be able to do what I want to do **What inspires you?** Watching other people **Can fashion still have a political ambition?** No idea. I just prefer to make beautiful clothes **Who do you have in mind when you design?** I don't have any special muse **Is the idea of creative collaboration important to you?** Yes, it is very motivating and opens other points of view **Who has been the greatest influence on your career?** Actually, I don't know yet **How have your own experiences affected your work as a designer?** No idea **Which is more important in your work: the process or the product?** The product. The process you forget quickly **Is designing difficult for you and, if so, what drives you to continue?** It needs a lot of concentration. That's why sometimes it is so difficult **Have you ever been influenced or moved by the reaction to your designs?** Yes, of course **What's your definition of beauty?** Something intriguing **What's your philosophy?** To follow my feelings **What is the most important lesson you've learned?** To think before I follow my feelings

Phoebe Philo, Creative Director at Chloé, is the talented understudy who wound up headlining the show. Until early 2001, Philo was known as Stella McCartney's Design Assistant and best buddy, an inspiring deputy who helped McCartney make her mark at the Parisian house. Philo has a particular talent for translating her own idiosyncratic personal style into instantly desirable – and therefore sell-out – fashion, moving with ease between street culture and high glamour. Born in Paris in 1973, Philo grew up in London and studied fashion at Central Saint Martins. McCartney was in the year above her at college and the two became friends. In 1996, Philo graduated with a Latino-inspired collection and, after working briefly for London designer Pamela Blundell, began assisting McCartney with her fledgling label. When McCartney was headhunted for Chloé by the Richemont Group in 1997, she asked her new bosses to allow Philo to join her in Paris. Under McCartney and Philo, the romanticism of previous Chloé collections was replaced by a sexy, youthful image that often featured low-slung trousers, witty prints and pretty camisole tops. So successful were the duo that when McCartney departed Chloé in April 2001, her assistant was named as successor. In October 2001, Philo made her debut as Chief Designer, her first solo show since her graduation presentation. The transition was judged a runaway success, with the now-hallmark narrow trousers and playfully detailed blouses drawing Chloé's young customers into 270 outlets worldwide.

Phoebe Philo, Creative Director bei Chloé, ist die talentierte Zweitbesetzung, die am Ende unerwartet Schlagzeilen machte. Bis Anfang 2001 kannte man Philo nur als Stella McCartneys Designassistentin und beste Freundin – eine Art kreative Stellvertreterin, die der bekannten Designerin half, dem Pariser Modehaus Chloé ihren Stempel aufzu-drücken. Philo hat ein besonderes Talent dafür, ihren eigenen charakteristischen Stil in heiß begehrte und deshalb absolut verkäufliche Mode umzusetzen. Dabei wechselt sie mit Leichtigkeit zwischen Streetwear und edelstem Glamour. Geboren wurde Phoebe Philo 1973 in Paris. Sie wuchs in London auf und studierte dort auch Mode am Central Saint Martins. Stella McCartney war einen Jahrgang über ihr, und die beiden freundeten sich an. 1996 schloss Philo ihr Studium mit einer lateinamerikanisch angehauchten Kol-lektion ab. Nach kurzer Tätigkeit für die Londoner Designerin Pamela Blundell wurde sie Assistentin von McCartney, deren eigenes Label damals gerade erste Erfolge verzeichne-te. Als McCartney 1997 von der Richemont Group für Chloé angeworben wurde, bat sie ihre neuen Chefs, Philo zu sich nach Paris holen zu dürfen. Unter der Ägide der beiden wurde die Romantik früherer Chloé-Kollektionen durch ein verführerisches, jugendliches Image ersetzt, bei dem tief sitzende Hosen, witzige Muster und hübsche Mieder-Tops eine wichtige Rolle spielten. Das Designerinnenteam war so erfolgreich, dass man, als McCartney Chloé im April 2001 verließ, die bisherige Assistentin zu ihrer Nachfolgerin be-stimmte. Im Oktober desselben Jahres gab Philo ihr Debüt als Chefdesignerin mit ihrer ersten Solo-Schau seit der Abschlusspräsentation am College. Der Neuanfang für Chloé wurde allgemein als durchschlagender Erfolg gewertet. Und die inzwischen typischen schmalen Hosen und verspielten Blusen locken Chloés junge Kundschaft nach wie vor in die 270 Outlets überall auf der Welt.

L'histoire de Phoebe Philo, directrice de la création chez Chloé, est celle de la doublure aux talents cachés qui finit par prendre le haut de l'affiche. Jusqu'au début 2001, Phoebe Philo était surtout connue en tant qu'assistante inspirée et meilleure amie de Stella McCartney, qu'elle a aidée à imprimer sa marque sur la maison parisienne. Aussi à l'aise avec la culture de la rue que le grand glamour, Phoebe Philo possède un talent particulier pour traduire son style personnel si caractéristique en une mode immédiatement désirable et rapidement en rupture de stock dans les boutiques. Née à Paris en 1973, Phoebe Philo grandit à Londres et étudie la mode à Central Saint Martins. C'est là qu'elle devient l'amie de Stella McCartney, alors une classe au-dessus d'elle. En 1996, Phoebe Philo obtient son diplôme avec une collection d'inspiration Latino puis, après avoir brièvement travaillé pour la styliste londonienne Pamela Blundell, elle commence à aider Stella McCartney sur sa nouvelle griffe. En 1997, lorsque Stella est repérée par le Groupe Richemont pour travailler chez Chloé, elle demande à ses nouveaux patrons de faire venir Phoebe à Paris. Sous l'impulsion des deux Anglaises, le romantisme des précédentes collections de Chloé fait place à une image plus jeune et plus sexy, avec des pantalons à taille très basse, des imprimés pleins d'esprit et d'adorables tops caraco. Le duo remporte un tel succès que lorsque Stella McCartney quitte Chloé en avril 2001, son assistante est nommée à sa succession. En octobre 2001, Phoebe Philo fait ses débuts en tant que directrice de la création et présente son premier défilé en solo depuis sa collection de fin d'études. La transition est réussie et la collection remporte un succès foudroyant, avec des pantalons étroits aujourd'hui devenus absolument indispensables et des chemisiers aux détails ingénieux qui continuent d'attirer les jeunes clientes de Chloé dans ses 270 points de vente à travers le monde.

"My trousers do give a lovely bottom"

PORTRAIT COURTESY OF PHOEBE PHILO

PHOEBE PHILO

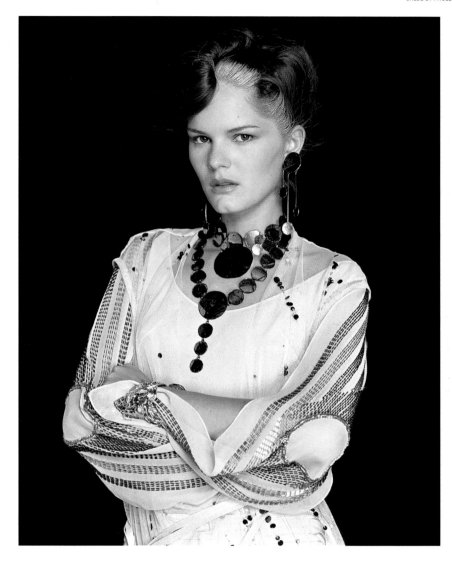

What are your signature designs? There's not one thing that sums it up. A bit of everything. Although the trousers do give a lovely bottom **What's your favourite piece from any of your collections?** Often the least commercial **How would you describe your work?** Work in progress **What's your ultimate goal?** To enjoy **What inspires you?** Sunsets, sunrises, being with horses and a lot of love **Can fashion still have a political ambition?** Tricky… **Who do you have in mind when you design?** People that inspire me **Is the idea of creative collaboration important to you?** I like the idea, although I haven't done much yet **What has been the greatest influence on your career?** Relationships probably with family, friends, people I have met in the street, life in Cuba and learning to bogle **How have your own experiences affected your work as a designer?** I try not to assess it too much. Things are just the way they are. My reactions to experiences in my life can't be divided between me and me as a designer **Is designing difficult for you and, if so, what drives you to continue?** Sometimes it is relentless but when it is good, it is great **Have you ever been influenced or moved by the reaction to your designs?** Seeing someone you really love or respect wearing something you created can drive and move you **What's your definition of beauty?** My friend Mel **What's your philosophy?** A bit of everything is good **What is the most important lesson you've learned?** Don't fuck with people

Carol Christian Poell is one of the only avant-garde designers living and working in Milan. In a city that prides itself on the successful marriage of commerce and creativity, Poell (born in Linz, Austria in 1966) is something of an anomaly. 'Curious' is perhaps the most appropriate adjective for this designer, whose presentations (he never offers conventional catwalk shows) ask as many questions as they offer solutions. Poell became interested in fashion at an early age, helping out in his stepfather's clothes factory from the tender age of eight. After graduating from Milan's Domus Academy, Poell showed his first menswear collection for Autumn-Winter 1996, immediately provoking enthusiastic reactions with his unique vision. His particular talent is an ability to challenge established ideas – for example, his use of human hair as an alternative to wool – combined with unrivalled tailoring skills. Since 1999, he has put these to good use by also presenting a womenswear collection; his women's trousers, in particular, are much sought-after. Poell's designs can often be perceived as quite simple – many of them long, lean examples of precision tailoring – but that would be to ignore his immense craftsmanship. Poell doesn't design collections in the usual sense, preferring to work on individual garments, working and reworking them with such attention to detail that they become faultless and timeless.

Carol Christian Poell ist einer der wenigen Avantgarde-Designer, die in Mailand leben und arbeiten. Er gilt als Ausnahmeerscheinung in dieser Stadt, die doch so stolz auf ihre erfolgreiche Verbindung von Kommerz und Kreativität ist. Der Begriff 'neugierig' umschreibt den 1966 in Linz geborenen Designer vielleicht am besten. So veranstaltet er niemals herkömmliche Catwalk-Shows und wirft bei seinen Präsentationen mindestens so viele Fragen auf wie er Antworten bietet. Poell begann schon sehr früh, sich für Mode zu interessieren; bereits mit acht Jahren machte er sich in der Textilfabrik seines Stiefvaters nützlich. Nach dem Studium an der Mailänder Domus Academy präsentierte der Designer seine erste Herrenkollektion für Herbst/Winter 1996 und sorgte mit unverwechselbaren visionären Entwürfen sofort für Begeisterung. Sein besonderes Talent besteht darin, etablierte Vorstellungen in Frage zu stellen – beispielsweise benutzt er Menschenhaar als Ersatz für Wolle. Dazu kommt noch seine überragende fachliche Qualifikation. Diese nutzt er seit 1999 auch erfolgreich für eine Damenkollektion. Daraus sind insbesondere die Hosen heiß begehrt. Poells Entwürfe wirken oft ganz schlicht – viele lange, schmale, präzise gearbeitete Stücke, denen man das unglaubliche handwerkliche Können ihres Schöpfers erst auf den zweiten Blick ansieht. Der Designer liefert keine Kollektionen im herkömmlichen Sinne ab, sondern bevorzugt die Arbeit an Einzelstücken, die er mit solcher Liebe zum Detail herstellt und so lange verändert, bis sie schließlich vollkommen und zeitlos sind.

Carol Christian Poell est l'un des rares créateurs d'avant-garde qui vit et travaille à Milan. Dans cette ville qui se flatte d'incarner la réussite du mariage entre commerce et créativité, Poell (né en 1966 à Linz en Autriche) fait vraiment figure d'anomalie. « Curieux » est sans doute l'adjectif qui décrit le mieux ce designer dont les présentations posent autant de questions qu'elles apportent de réponses (il n'a jamais présenté de défilé traditionnel). Très tôt, Poell commence à s'intéresser à la mode en aidant son beau-père dans son usine de vêtements. Une fois diplômé de la Domus Academy de Milan, Poell présente une première collection pour homme Automne-Hiver 1996 qui, grâce à son approche unique, suscite immédiatement beaucoup d'enthousiasme. Son talent particulier réside dans sa capacité à remettre en question les idées reçues – par exemple en utilisant des cheveux humains en alternative à la laine – ainsi que dans ses compétences inégalées en matière de coupe. Depuis 1999, il applique ce potentiel à la mode féminine et ses pantalons pour femme sont aujourd'hui très recherchés. Le style de Poell est souvent considéré comme assez simple, avec ses vêtements longs et près du corps pourtant parfaitement coupés, mais cette simplicité-là doit beaucoup à son immense savoir-faire. Poell ne dessine pas de « collections » à proprement parler ; il préfère travailler et retravailler chaque vêtement en portant une grande attention aux détails afin d'aboutir à des pièces parfaites et intemporelles.

"Clothes should speak to you, communicate a sensibility"

PORTRAIT BY ARMIN LINKE

CAROL CHRISTIAN POELL

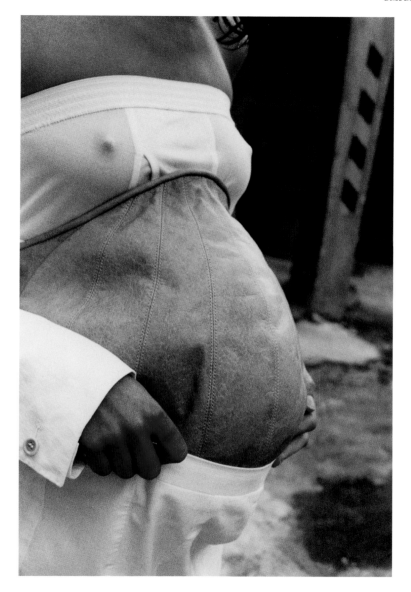

What are your signature designs? I don't have any **How would you describe your work?** Undecided **What's your ultimate goal?** To continue **What inspires you?** Problems **Can fashion still have a political ambition?** If political means power and money, yes **What do you have in mind when you design?** A jacket, a shirt… **Is the idea of creative collaboration important to you?** Yes, when necessary **What has been the greatest influence on your career?** Coincidence **How have your own experiences affected your work as a designer?** Questioning myself in my work **Which is more important in your work: the process or the product?** The process of producing the product **Is designing difficult for you and, if so, what drives you to continue?** Yes – I don't know **Have you ever been influenced or moved by the reaction to your designs?** Impossible not to be **What's your definition of beauty?** Beauty cannot be defined **What's your philosophy?** To doubt **What is the most important lesson you've learned?** Not everything sells

Zac Posen's extreme youth belies his talent for cutting lascivious, glamorous dresses that seduce both starlets and stylists alike. Born in New York in 1980, the son of a painter, he grew up on Spring Street, SoHo. As a child, Posen constantly made fashion sketches, and on leaving St Ann's School for the Arts in Brooklyn, set his sights on Central Saint Martins in London. He started a BA in womenswear there in 1999, while also cultivating a private client list; the success of his own designs led him to abandon study in 2001 to focus on his own label, based at his parent's house in New York. Even before Posen's catwalk debut he was attracting excited headlines: in February 2001, The New York Times ran a feature on him entitled 'A Star Is Born'. His much-anticipated first collection, shown for Spring-Summer 2002, drew further acclaim, and each month since has brought more enthusiastic buyers, more award nominations and more celebrity admirers. The Victoria & Albert Museum in London recently acquired a leather dress by Posen for its permanent costume exhibition. Museums have played a key role in the development of this young designer's career: he spent two years as an intern at the Metropolitan Museum's famed Costume Institute. His time among the Vionnet and Dior originals has left Posen with a keen sense of fashion history, which informs many of his techniques: ruffled satin, fishtail hemlines, swooping necklines and bias-cut silhouettes dominated his second collection for Autumn-Winter 2002.

Zac Posens Talent beim Entwerfen lasziver, glamouröser Roben, die Starlets wie Stylisten gleichermaßen begeistern, ist umso erstaunlicher, wenn man das Alter des Designers bedenkt. Er wurde 1980 als Sohn eines Malers in New York geboren und wuchs in der Spring Street in SoHo auf. Schon als Kind machte Posen ständig Modezeichnungen, und nach dem Abschluss der St. Ann's School for the Arts in Brooklyn kam für ihn nur das Londoner Central Saint Martins in Frage. 1999 begann er dort mit dem Bachelor-Studium im Fach Damenmode. Schon damals arbeitete er für eine Reihe von Privatkunden. Angesichts des Erfolgs seiner eigenen Kreationen brach er die Hochschule 2001 ab, um sich auf sein eigenes Label zu konzentrieren, das er in seinem Elternhaus in New York gründete. Noch vor seinem Debüt auf dem Catwalk machte Posen Schlagzeilen. Im Februar 2001 erschien in der New York Times ein Feature unter der Überschrift 'A Star Is Born'. Die von großen Erwartungen begleitete erste Kollektion für Frühjahr/Sommer 2002 erntete noch mehr Lob, und Monat für Monat wächst die Zahl der begeisterten Käufer, der Nominierungen für diverse Preise und der prominenten Bewunderer. Kürzlich erwarb das Londoner Victoria & Albert Museum ein Lederkleid von Posen für seine Dauerausstellung zum Thema Kostüm und Mode. Überhaupt haben Museen in der bisherigen Karriere dieses jungen Designers eine Schlüsselrolle gespielt: Zwei Jahre lang war er Praktikant am berühmten Costume Institute des New Yorker Metropolitan Museum. Diese Zeit zwischen den Originalen von Vionnet und Dior hat Posens Sinn für historische Vorbilder geschärft und ihn in vielerlei Hinsicht geprägt. So dominierten Satinrüschen, Fischschwanz-Säume, tiefe Dekolletés und diagonal geschnittene Silhouetten seine zweite Kollektion für Herbst/Winter 2002.

Le jeune âge de Zac Posen surprend quand on constate avec quel talent il coupe ses robes glamour et provocantes qui plaisent autant aux starlettes qu'aux stylistes. Né en 1980 à New York d'un père peintre, il grandit à SoHo dans Spring Street. Enfant, Posen passe son temps à dessiner des croquis de mode, et lorsqu'il quitte la St Ann's School pour l'école d'art de Brooklyn, il a déjà des vues sur Londres et Central Saint Martins. En 1999, il y entame un BA en mode féminine tout en travaillant pour des clients privés; en 2001, le succès de ses créations l'incite à abandonner les études pour se consacrer à plein temps à sa propre griffe, dont il installe l'atelier chez ses parents à New York. Zac Posen attire rapidement l'attention de la presse alors qu'il n'a même pas encore présenté son premier défilé : en février 2001, le New York Times lui consacre un article intitulé « Une Etoile Est Née ». Très attendue, sa première collection Printemps-Eté 2002 suscite encore plus d'enthousiasme et depuis, il attire chaque mois de nouveaux acheteurs, des clients célèbres et se voit nominé pour de nombreux prix. Le Victoria & Albert Museum de Londres a récemment acquis l'une de ses robes en cuir pour l'intégrer à son exposition permanente de costumes. Les musées ont joué un rôle décisif dans la carrière de ce jeune créateur : il a fait un stage de deux ans au célèbre Costume Institute du Metropolitan Museum. Le temps qu'il a passé au milieu des pièces originales de Madeleine Vionnet et de Dior a permis à Posen de se forger un sens aigu de l'histoire de la mode, qui se traduit dans nombre de ses techniques : en effet, sa deuxième collection pour l'Automne-Hiver 2002 est dominée par les volants de satin, les ourlets en queue de poisson, les décolletés plongeants et les coupes en biais.

"I design thinking about the kind of woman that I would be: intelligent, powerful and eccentric"

PORTRAIT BY VANINA SORRENTI

ZAC POSEN

What are your signature designs? At the moment, my trumpet dresses are my signature item. But I think that the suits will become signature **How would you describe your work?** I do very technical clothing. It's a strong feminine silhouette, fierce, flirtatious and intelligent. My mother is a feminist and I love women. There are designers who love women and some that hate women. I want to try and challenge some of the barriers that are still placed upon them. My idea of fashion is that it should be worn by many different kinds of women, all ages and sizes. The Autumn-Winter 2002 collection was about combining feminism, sex and beauty **What's your ultimate goal?** I'd love to design for couture. At some point I want to have a very large fashion house, but right now I'm exploring **What inspires you?** The great artists of the past – Francis Bacon and Hieronymus Bosch and Velazquez **Can fashion still have a political ambition?** I think it's beyond political. Politics is very small compared to ideas of the role between man and woman and sex **Who do you have in mind when you design?** I think the kind of clothing and the kind of woman that I would be: intelligent, powerful and eccentric. And open to experiences **Who has been the greatest influence on your career?** My father. He was a painter. And my sister, who is a mask-maker and a mime and a visual artist and is the creative director of my company. In terms of fashion designers? First, there's the great Balenciaga. And Chanel, I think she was a political designer. And Azzedine Alaïa. And Galliano **How have your own experiences affected your work as a designer?** I keep my eyes open. At all times. And I've learned to surround myself with people who are looking to the future **Which is more important in your work: the process or the product?** They're equal. One's personal and the other, the product, is a gift to society **Is designing difficult for you?** No, I love it. I love what I do and it's not difficult at all **What's your definition of beauty?** I think beauty is very diverse. And I like finding it in the most awkward places **What's the most important lesson you've learned?** In fashion, it's perfection. And in life, it's generosity. And willpower. You have to have willpower. Otherwise you're fucked

In 1971 Miuccia Prada entered the family business. Twenty years later, the highly traditional leather goods company had changed beyond all recognition. The innovation of something as simple as a nylon bag meant there was no looking back: Prada was on the way to redefining luxury, subtlety and desirability in fashion. Prada the company – led by the designer and her husband, Patrizio Bertelli, who started work with Prada in 1977 and is now CEO of the Prada Group – seem to have an uncanny ability to capture the cultural climate in fashion. This second sense has been unashamedly teamed with commercial savvy, which has made the brand's influence over the past decade vast and its growth enormous. From bags and shoes to the first womenswear collection (1988), the Miu Miu line for the younger customer (1993), menswear (1994), Prada Sport (1997) and Prada Beauty (2000), all are directly overseen by Miuccia Prada herself. Yet, unlike many other Leviathan brands, there is something both unconventional and idiosyncratic in Miuccia Prada's aesthetic. Much of this may be down to her contradictory character. Born in Milan in 1950, Miuccia Prada studied political science at the city's university and was a member of Italy's Communist Party, yet is said to have worn Yves Saint Laurent on the barricades. The designer, who has made the Wall Street Journal's '30 Most Powerful Women In Europe' list, also spent a period studying to be a mime artist. These dualities have led to her expert ability in balancing the contrary forces of art and commerce within the superbrand: Prada has its own art foundation and the company's most recent large-scale project was a collaboration with the architect Rem Koolhaas for a New York store which opened in 2001. From the late 1990s, the Prada Group has embarked upon a policy of rapid expansion, confirming its position as a leading player in the global luxury goods market. Amongst others it owns, or has a large stake, in Helmut Lang, Jil Sander, Church & Co, Azzedine Alaïa and Genny. It also owns and races a very big yacht.

1971 trat Miuccia Prada in das Familienunternehmen ein. Zwanzig Jahre danach hat sich die bis dahin eher traditionelle Lederwarenfabrik bis zur Unkenntlichkeit verändert. Etwas so Simples wie eine Nylonhandtasche markierte den Neuanfang. Prada sorgte für die Neudefinition von Begriffen wie Luxus, Raffinesse und Begehrlichkeit in Sachen Mode. Unter der Leitung der Designerin und ihres Mannes Patrizio Bertelli, der 1977 in das Unternehmen eintrat und heute CEO des Konzerns ist, beweist Prada einen untrüglichen Instinkt, wenn es darum geht, aktuelle Modeströmungen aufzunehmen. Dieses Gespür, gepaart mit dem nötigen Geschäftssinn, sorgte in den letzten zehn Jahren für das ungeheure Wachstum und den enormen Einfluss der Marke. Von den Taschen und Schuhen, der ersten Damenkollektion (1988), dem Label Miu Miu für jüngere Kundinnen (1993) über Männermode (1994) und die Linie Prada Sport (1997) bis hin zu Prada Beauty (2000) unterstehen alle Bereiche nach wie vor Miuccia Prada. Doch im Unterschied zu anderen großen Marken ist Miuccias Ästhetik höchst unkonventionell und individuell. Vieles davon mag auf den ungewöhnlichen Werdegang der Designerin selbst zurückzuführen sein. 1950 in Mailand geboren, studierte Miuccia Prada in ihrer Heimatstadt Politikwissenschaft und war Mitglied der Kommunistischen Partei Italiens. Doch angeblich trug sie selbst auf den Barrikaden Yves Saint Laurent. Die vom Wall Street Journal zu den '30 mächtigsten Frauen Europas' gekürte Geschäftsfrau absolvierte auch eine Schauspielausbildung. Diese Vielseitigkeit mag dazu beitragen, dass es ihr immer wieder hervorragend gelingt, Kunst und Kommerz unter dem Dach der Supermarke miteinander auszusöhnen. Und das ist gelegentlich durchaus wörtlich zu nehmen: So betreibt Prada eine eigene Kunststiftung, und das jüngste Großprojekt war die 2001 eröffnete New Yorker Filiale, die der Architekt Rem Koolhaas gestaltet hat. Seit Ende der 1990er Jahre setzt der Prada-Konzern auf rasche Expansion, um seine Position als Global Player auf dem Markt für Luxusgüter zu behaupten. Zu dieser Geschäftspolitik passen auch Beteiligungen an Labels wie Helmut Lang, Jil Sander, Church & Co, Azzedine Alaïa und Genny. Eine große Rennyacht gehört ebenfalls zum Firmenbesitz.

Miuccia Prada rejoint l'entreprise familiale en 1971. Vingt ans plus tard, ce maroquinier ultra-classique a subi une transformation si radicale qu'il en est devenu méconnaissable. Une innovation telle que le sac en nylon prouvait bien que la maison ne regardait plus en arrière : Prada était sur le point de redéfinir le luxe, la subtilité et les avantages de la mode. Patrizio Bertelli, mari de Miuccia mais également directeur de l'entreprise, designer et actuel PDG du Groupe Prada, avait commencé à travailler pour l'entreprise en 1977. La société semble jouir d'une étrange facilité à capter le climat culturel de la mode. Cette intuition se mêle sans complexe à un esprit de conquête commerciale qui n'a fait qu'augmenter l'influence de la marque ces dix dernières années et lui a permis de connaître une croissance vertigineuse. Des chaussures aux sacs en passant par la première collection de vêtements pour femme (1988), la ligne Miu Miu pour les jeunes (1993), la mode masculine (1994), Prada Sport (1997) et Prada Beauty (2000), tout est directement supervisé par Miuccia Prada en personne. Contrairement à la plupart des grandes marques, l'esthétique de Miuccia Prada se distingue par son non-conformisme très caractéristique. Cette ambivalence repose en grande partie sur l'esprit de contradiction de Miuccia. Née à Milan en 1950, elle étudie les sciences politiques à l'université de la ville et s'inscrit au Parti Communiste Italien, n'hésitant pas à monter sur les barricades habillée en Yves Saint Laurent. La créatrice, incluse dans la liste des « 30 femmes les plus puissantes d'Europe » du Wall Street Journal, a également suivi une formation pour devenir comédienne. Ces dualités lui ont permis de réconcilier les forces contradictoires de l'art et du commerce au sein de la « super-marque », parfois même au pied de la lettre : Prada possède sa propre fondation artistique et pour son grand projet le plus récent, l'entreprise a collaboré avec l'architecte Rem Koolhaas, qui a conçu la boutique de New York ouverte en 2001. Dès la fin des années 90, le groupe Prada a adopté une politique d'expansion rapide, confirmant sa position de leader sur le marché mondial du luxe. L'entreprise possède, en totalité ou en majorité, les griffes Helmut Lang, Jil Sander, Church & Co, Azzedine Alaïa et Genny. Elle dispose également d'un très grand yacht qui participe à diverses courses en mer.

"I don't believe in people who think that clothes are not important"

PORTRAIT BY MARC QUINN

MIUCCIA PRADA

PHOTOGRAPHY BY VANINA SORRENTI, STYLING BY FIONA DALLANEGRA. DECEMBER 2001/JANUARY 2002

PHOTOGRAPHY BY TAKAY, STYLING BY MARK ANTHONY. APRIL 2001

PHOTOGRAPHY BY MATT JONES, STYLING BY KATE YOUNG. DECEMBER 2001/JANUARY 2002. MODEL: LIV TYLER

PHOTOGRAPHY BY MARIO SORRENTI, STYLING BY JANE HOW. SEPTEMBER 2000

"I hate it when people call me a minimalist. That black nylon period only lasted two years"

What are your signature designs? I hope I design clothes that have harmony – and make sense **How would you describe your work?** I hate it when people call me a minimalist. That black nylon period lasted only about two years, but it is all that some people remember. The way I want to deal with fashion is a very personal, feminine, and not an intellectual way of doing things **What's your ultimate goal?** Everyone imagines we have this detailed strategy, but we don't. We just do what feels right and what interests us. We don't have military planning, we have disorganisations – but maybe now that has to change. There are a lot of negative feelings towards global businesses now. It is time to do something more individual and personal **Can fashion still have a political ambition?** I don't want to sound stupid or too clever, but anything you do is political. The way you treat women, you have respect for them or not – this is a political choice. I think I've always done clothes for people who respect themselves and express themselves through clothing. I don't think that if you are interested in politics, you have to have bad clothing **What do you have in mind when you design?** For some designers fashion is everyday theatre. I'm not interested in that. I decided early on that I wanted to be creative but in a way that is real: fashion for real people **Who has been the greatest influence on your career?** If it weren't for my husband I would still just be doing bags. I was pushed to do shoes. I was pushed to do ready-to-wear. I was pushed to do menswear. I was always resisting. Then I realised that every time I was asked to do something new, I got excited and interested **How have your own experiences affected your work as a designer?** When I realise I'm becoming too arty or intellectual, I stop and think: 'Would I like to wear this? Will it make me beautiful?' People don't believe me, they think I'm serious, but I can get crazy about a pair of pink shoes! **Is designing difficult for you and, if so, what drives you to continue?** In the beginning it was a nightmare. I used to go mad with Patrizio because he always drove me so hard, but now I see that it is the best thing for me. On my own I could be a bit lazy. I don't like being stressed and frightened, but I think probably it is useful. Doing new things is a way of keeping your mind open **Have you ever been influenced or moved by the reaction to your designs?** There is pleasure in a job done well **What's your definition of beauty?** When the clothes do not reveal, it gives you the freedom to reveal your mind **What's your philosophy?** I am more interested in what I don't want to do than what I do want **What is the most important lesson you've learned?** Life did not change for me from being successful. I can buy more jewels or paintings, but that does not change the inner self

Whether it's George Michael wearing his ubiquitous Destroy jacket in the video to the song 'Faith' or Bryan Adams photographing his new collection, John Richmond's career has often been surrounded by the rock and pop aristocracy. Born in 1961 in Manchester, Richmond graduated from Kingston Polytechnic in 1982 and immediately began working under his own name as well as designing freelance for Emporio Armani, Joseph Tricot and Fiorucci. In 1984 he formed the Richmond-Cornejo label with Ravensbourne graduate Maria Cornejo. The pair's avant-garde, street- and clubwear-inspired collections earned them a cult following, appropriating a distressed punk aesthetic with anarchy logos and slogans of alienation, ripped-off sleeves and skintight trousers. Since 1987, Richmond has worked under his own name producing a mainline collection and two diffusion ranges: his leather jackets, printed either with slogans or tattoo designs, being perhaps his most enduring, definitive pieces. His passion for music and its iconography, plus a unique balance between precise tailoring and irreverent styling, informs Richmond's designs. Street culture is still a significant influence in his work, with recent seasons mixing the smartness of the mod aesthetic with heavy metal detailing. In 1995, Richmond avoided the fate of many of his British contemporaries by looking to Europe for support, achieving significant global growth thanks to Italy's Falber SRL (production) and Moschillo (sales and distribution). He now shows both men's and womenswear at Milan Fashion Week. As well as his men's and women's mainline collections, he also runs the diffusion lines John Richmond X and Richmond Denim, and produces bag and shoe collections.

George Michael trägt seine allgegenwärtige Destroy-Jacke in dem Video zu dem Song 'Faith', und Bryan Adams hat seine neue Kollektion fotografiert – in John Richmonds Karriere spielen oft Rock- und Popgrößen eine Rolle. Der 1961 in Manchester geborene Richmond absolvierte sein Studium am Kingston Polytechnic und begann 1982 unter seinem eigenen Namen sowie als freier Mitarbeiter für Emporio Armani, Joseph Tricot und Fiorucci zu entwerfen. 1984 gründete er zusammen mit dem Ravensbourne-Absolventin Maria Cornejo das Label Richmond-Cornejo. Die avantgardistischen, von der Street- und Clubwear inspirierten Kollektionen des Designerduos hatten bald eine treue Fangemeinde. Diese statteten sie mit Punk-Ästhetik, anarchistischen Logos, verfremdeten Slogans, abgeschnittenen Ärmeln und hautengen Hosen aus. Seit 1987 arbeitet Richmond auch unter eigenem Namen und bringt eine Haupt- sowie zwei Nebenkollektionen heraus. Die maßgeblichen und zeitlosesten Stücke darin sind seine mit Slogans oder Tattoos versehenen Lederjacken. Die Leidenschaft des Designers für Musik und deren Ikonografie sowie eine einzigartige Harmonie zwischen exaktem Schneiderhandwerk und respektlosem Styling – all das prägt Richmonds Kreationen. Die Straßenkultur übt nach wie vor beträchtlichen Einfluss auf seine Arbeit aus; in den jüngsten Kollektionen vermengt er auch den Chic moderner Ästhetik mit Elementen des Heavy Metal. 1995 entging Richmond dem Schicksal vieler anderer britischer Designer und suchte sich Unterstützung auf dem Kontinent. Mit Hilfe der italienischen Firmen Falber SRL (im Bereich Produktion) und Moschillo (bei Verkauf und Vertrieb) konnte er bald beträchtliche Zuwächse auf dem internationalen Markt verzeichnen. Inzwischen präsentiert Richmond seine Herren- wie seine Damenmode auf der Mailänder Modewoche. Außer den Hauptkollektionen betreibt er die Nebenlinien John Richmond X und Richmond Denim und produziert zusätzlich Taschen- und Schuhkollektionen.

Entre George Michael qui ne quitte pas un seul instant sa veste Destroy dans le clip de « Faith » et Bryan Adams qui photographie sa nouvelle collection, la carrière de John Richmond a souvent été entourée par la crème du rock et de la pop. Né en 1961 à Manchester, Richmond sort diplômé de l'école polytechnique de Kingston en 1982 et commence immédiatement à travailler sous son propre nom, tout en dessinant en free-lance pour Emporio Armani, Joseph Tricot et Fiorucci. En 1984, il crée la griffe Richmond-Cornejo avec Maria Cornejo, diplômée de Ravensbourne. Leurs collections avant-gardistes, inspirées par la mode de la rue et le clubwear, sont considérées comme « culte » et suivies par de nombreux fidèles qui adoptent cette esthétique punk chaotique aux logos anarchiques et slogans d'aliénation, manches déchirées et pantalons ultra-moulants. Depuis 1987, Richmond travaille sous son propre nom et produit une collection principale et deux lignes secondaires : ses vestes en cuir, imprimées de slogans ou de tatouages, sont sans doute ses pièces les plus abouties. Les créations de Richmond témoignent de sa passion pour la musique et son iconographie, ainsi que d'un équilibre unique entre précision de coupe et style irrévérencieux. La culture de la rue joue encore un rôle significatif sur son travail ; il a récemment présenté une collection mêlant le raffinement de l'esthétique Mod à des détails Heavy Metal. En 1995, Richmond échappe au sort de ses nombreux contemporains britanniques en se tournant vers l'Europe, enregistrant une importante croissance à l'échelle mondiale grâce au soutien des Italiens Falber SRL (pour la production) et Moschillo (ventes et distribution). Aujourd'hui, il présente des collections pour homme et pour femme à la Semaine de la Mode de Milan. En parallèle, il produit également les lignes John Richmond X et Richmond Denim, ainsi que des collections de sacs et de chaussures.

"People always say, 'Oh, you're the guy who did the leather jackets'"

PORTRAIT COURTESY OF JOHN RICHMOND

JOHN RICHMOND

PHOTOGRAPHY BY ORION BEST, STYLING BY JAMES SLEAFORD. MARCH 1999

What are your signature designs? People always say, 'Oh, you're the guy who did the leather jackets', so I think the public have probably decided for me. But I get more enjoyment out of creating the next design **How would you describe your work?** Masculine and feminine at the same time. Quite contradictory, like me. Considered but not throwaway; not ephemeral **What inspires you?** Everything. You have to be like a sponge, constantly soaking up information **Can fashion still have a political ambition?** It's very difficult in our society to exert any honesty in being political when you don't really suffer. I'm sure it's different for someone in Afghanistan, but I think it's a bit hypocritical for us to pretend we can be honest in the same way **Who do you have in mind when you design?** When I'm doing menswear it's for myself. For womenswear it's a certain look, the John Richmond woman: androgynous but feminine **Is the idea of creative collaboration important to you?** It's hard to collaborate in fashion on a pure design level; it's a very singular image that you have to create. But you still need a fantastic team around you to achieve that **Which is more important in your work: the process or the product?** The process is much more enjoyable because you are never happy with the end result. You're always looking to improve on the last design **Is designing difficult for you?** No. The people who work for me hate me, because I design too much **Have you ever been influenced or moved by the reaction to your designs?** Sometimes. It's obviously easier when people like what you do. But also you've just got to have the guts to stick to your guns **What's your definition of beauty?** Proportion is one of the most important aspects of every form of design. That's proportion of body and mind. It's about the way you carry yourself. **What's your philosophy?** Destroy. Disorientate. Disorder **What is the most important lesson you've learned?** That you never stop learning

C. P. Company started life as Chester Perry in 1974, set up by Massimo Osti. A graphic artist from Bologna, he switched full-time to fashion after designing a successful run of T-shirts. From the outset, Osti attempted to sidestep the ephemeral quality of fashion, instead seeking lasting practical solutions to everyday needs. Many ideas were derived from military clothing, an approach to design which was completely new at that time. An emphasis on production and construction highlighted the label's ethos of quality and function, striking a chord with young Italian men who shied away from overtly 'designed' clothes; later it became an essential for young English lads, who copied the styles of their Italian counterparts. In 1982, to meet the demands of an ever-growing audience, a diffusion line, Stone Island, was created, which specialised in surface treatment of fabrics and dyeing techniques. Through the GFT Group, Carlo Rivetti became a major shareholder in the company in 1983, when they created a partnership. Since his arrival, Rivetti has been the driving force in the company's continued development, keeping Osti's original ideas alive in both labels. In 1993 Rivetti bought the company outright, bringing in Moreno Ferrari to design the C. P. Company line. Ferrari intrinsically understands the objectives of Osti, in particular recognising that many people today live an almost 'nomadic' existence, moving frequently. With this in mind, and again influenced by the military, he has created some of C. P. Company's most iconic designs, such as the coat-cum-tent and the jacket-cum-chair. The company's ever-growing fanbase is proof of its unrivalled ability to create clothes that are fashionable, practical and curious simultaneously.

Die C. P. Company wurde 1974 unter dem Namen Chester Perry von Massimo Osti gegründet. Der Grafiker aus Bologna wandte sich ganz der Mode zu, nachdem er eine erfolg-reiche T-Shirt-Kollektion entworfen hatte. Von Anfang an versuchte Osti, nichts Kurzlebiges zu kreieren, sondern dauerhafte praktikable Lösungen für alltägliche Bedürfnisse zu finden. Viele Ideen waren von Uniformen abgeleitet, was damals einen völlig neuen Ansatz darstellte. Die Bedeutung, die dem Material und seiner Verarbeitung beigemessen wurde, unterstrich den Anspruch der Marke hinsichtlich Qualität und Funktionalität. Das kam besonders bei den jungen männlichen Kunden in Italien gut an, die zu offensicht-lich designte Kleidung ablehnten. Dieser Trend wurde später auch von modebewussten jungen Briten übernommen. 1982 gründete man, um die stetig steigende Nachfrage zu befriedigen, das Nebenlabel Stone Island; hier wurde noch größerer Wert auf die Oberflächenbehandlung der Stoffe und auf Färbetechniken gelegt. Durch die Fusion mit der GFT-Gruppe wurde Carlo Rivetti 1983 einer der wichtigsten Aktionäre des Unternehmens. Seither fungiert er als treibende Kraft bei der Weiterentwicklung der Firma und sorgt dafür, dass bei beiden Labels die ursprünglichen Vorstellungen des Firmengründers Osti weiterhin berücksichtigt werden. 1993 kaufte Rivetti schließlich das gesamte Unternehmen und beauftragte Moreno Ferrari mit dem Design der Linie C. P. Company. Ferrari hat Ostis Ziele genau verstanden, insbesondere die Rücksicht auf die geradezu nomadische Lebensweise vieler Menschen heutzutage. Mit diesen Vorgaben und ebenfalls unter dem Einfluss soldatischer Kleidung hat der Designer einige der bekanntesten Stücke von C. P. Company entworfen: den Regenmantel, der zugleich auch ein Zelt ist, oder den Parka, der sich zu einem Sessel aufblasen lässt. Die permanent wachsende Fangemeinde der Firma ist der beste Beweis für deren konkurrenzlose Fähigkeit, Kleider zu entwerfen, die modisch, praktisch und originell zugleich sind.

Massimo Osti crée la griffe C. P. Company en 1974 sous le nom de Chester Perry. Après avoir dessiné une série de T-shirts à succès, ce graphiste de Bologne se lance à plein temps dans la mode. Dès le départ, il tente d'échapper au côté éphémère de la mode, préférant trouver des solutions pratiques et durables aux besoins de tous les jours. De nombreuses idées lui sont inspirées par les vêtements militaires, une approche de la création complètement inédite à cette époque. L'accent porté sur la production et la construction met en valeur le génie de la griffe en termes de qualité et d'aspect fonctionnel, touchant les jeunes Italiens qui ne se reconnaissent pas dans les vêtements ouvertement « stylés »; plus tard, les jeunes Anglais adopteront le même uniforme que leurs homologues italiens. En 1982, Osti lance Stone Island, ligne secondaire qui vient répondre à la demande d'une clientèle en pleine croissance et est spécialisée dans le traitement de surface des tissus et dans les techniques de teinture. Grâce à un partenariat avec le Groupe GFT, Carlo Rivetti devient l'un des actionnaires majoritaires de l'entreprise en 1983. Depuis son arrivée, Rivetti est le véritable moteur du développement de l'entreprise, donnant vie aux idées originales d'Osti pour les deux griffes. En 1993, Rivetti rachète l'intégralité de la société et y fait entrer Moreno Ferrari pour dessiner la ligne C. P. Company. Ferrari comprend de façon instinctive les objectifs d'Osti, notamment en reconnaissant qu'aujourd'hui, de nombreuses personnes mènent une existence presque nomade et se déplacent souvent. Dans cette optique et toujours influencé par les tenues militaires, il a créé certaines des pièces les plus représentatives de C. P. Company, telles que le manteau-tente et la veste-chaise. Les clients de l'entreprise, toujours plus nombreux, prouvent le talent inégalé de C. P. Company quand il s'agit de créer des vêtements à la fois mode, utiles et insolites.

"Fashion must be ethical"

PORTRAIT BY TERRY JONES

CARLO RIVETTI

390

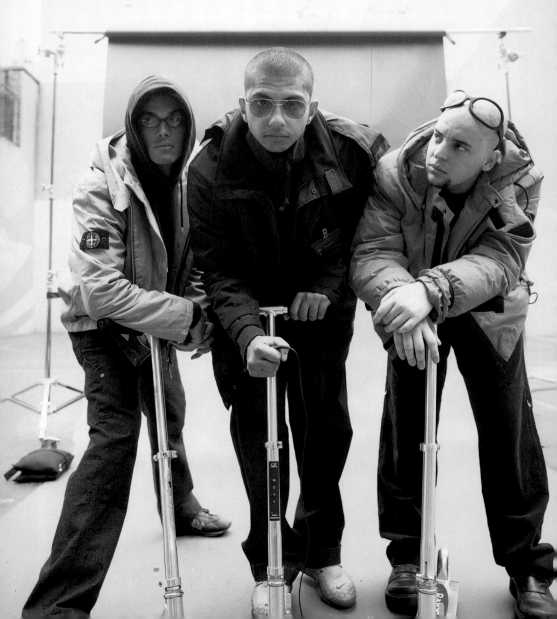

What are your signature designs? A refined elegance in an informal context **How would you describe your work?** The real fascination of this job is the fabrics. Textiles are a living, fascinating material. They change constantly. And this means you can carry on experimenting. Starting from the same canvas, every six months you can interpret and reinterpret, evolve, refine and blend forms, materials and colours, keeping an eye on the street and on society. This is a job that continues 24 hours a day because everything can be used to stimulate research. My company is a machine dedicated to translating all this into something that can be manufactured on an industrial scale **What's your ultimate goal?** To see a C. P. Company or Stone Island garment displayed alongside the Olivetti Lettera 22 at MoMA in New York **Can fashion still have a political ambition?** Undoubtedly. Today, like everything else, fashion must be ethical. It must be ethical at every step of the supply chain **What do you have in mind when you design?** I don't entirely agree that the consumer is central to the whole process. The consumer himself often doesn't know what he wants. Or what he wants is already 'old'. Ideas and innovations must always be in line with the brand philosophy and its historic heritage. So that we can offer innovative solutions that are also reassuring, showing complete respect for the expectations and taste of consumers who identify with the brands **Is designing difficult for you and, if so, what drives you to continue?** Today's market is driven by increasingly tight schedules that are counterproductive for pure creativity. We are one of the few companies that can afford to finish projects without being slaves to collections or seasons. When we feel that an innovative product for C. P. Company or Stone Island is ready – and it can take years – we include it in the collection. We do not follow the logic of what the market wants, but strangely in the long term, it is just what the market 'wanted' **What's your definition of beauty?** A harmonious balance in everything **What's your philosophy?** I am a very strong believer in ethics **What is the most important lesson you've learned?** That everything can be lost in a trice. Therefore, you shouldn't get too attached to things. Never look back and never have any regrets. Seize the moment and, with conscience, enjoy what you have

For Narciso Rodriguez, it's all a matter of getting the balance right. His is a minimalist take on luxury, opting for subtle and sexy over wham-bam glam. He claims to take inspiration from New York streetwear, yet he is most famous for designing the dress for the American society wedding of the 1990s: Carolyn Bessette's marriage to John F. Kennedy Jr. Born in Newark, New Jersey in 1961 to Cuban-American parents, Rodriguez studied at Parsons School of Design in New York, graduating in 1982. Following freelance work in the city's garment industry, he joined Anne Klein under Donna Karan in 1985, moving to Calvin Klein six years later to design womenswear. In 1995, Rodriguez became Design Director of TSE, simultaneously designing luxe tailoring for Cerruti. Two years later, he launched his own label: the first Narciso Rodriguez womenswear collection was shown in Milan for Spring-Summer '98. His move to Europe was significant, following the route of fellow Parsons graduates Tom Ford (at Gucci) and Marc Jacobs (at Louis Vuitton). In the same year, Rodriguez was appointed Womenswear Designer at Loewe, a position he held until 2001. Combining the European tradition of fine tailoring with his unique mixture of sleek New York glamour and Latino roots, Rodriguez returned to New York to show his Autumn-Winter 2001 signature collection. Beauty is, as ever, in the detail: his accessories reveal an understated mastery over form and material — not least his shoes, from cashmere-covered Birkenstocks to his penchant for stilettos — which, he insists, provide the wearer with 'instant plastic surgery'.

Für Narciso Rodriguez ist alles eine Frage des Gleichgewichts. Er bevorzugt Luxus der minimalistischen Art, subtile Verführung statt schrillem Glamour. Angeblich holt er sich seine Inspirationen bei der New Yorker Streetwear, doch sein bisher berühmtestes Stück war das Brautkleid zu *dem* gesellschaftlichen Ereignis Amerikas in den 1990er Jahren: die Hochzeit von Carolyn Bessette und John F. Kennedy Jr. Der 1961 in Newark, New Jersey, geborene Sohn kubanisch-amerikanischer Eltern absolvierte sein Studium an der Parsons School of Design in New York. Nach dem Abschluss 1982 arbeitete er zunächst als Freelancer in der New Yorker Textilbranche, bevor er 1985 unter Donna Karan bei Anne Klein anfing. Sechs Jahre später wechselte er zu Calvin Klein, um dort Damenmode zu entwerfen. 1995 wurde Rodriguez Design Director bei TSE, kreierte gleichzeitig aber auch Luxus-Couture für Cerruti. Die Gründung des eigenen Labels erfolgte zwei Jahre später, und die erste Narciso-Rodriguez-Damenkollektion für Frühjahr/Sommer 1998 präsentierte der Designer in Mailand. Der Wechsel nach Europa war bezeichnend. Er folgte damit dem Beispiel anderer Parsons-Absolventen wie Tom Ford, der zu Gucci ging, und Marc Jacobs, der bei Louis Vuitton arbeitete. Rodriguez wurde Designer für Damenmode bei Loewe — eine Position, die er bis 2001 innehatte. Er kombinierte die europäische Tradition der hohen Schneiderkunst mit seiner einzigartigen Mischung aus dezentem New Yorker Chic sowie seinen Latino-Wurzeln und kehrte mit einer Kollektion seines Namens für Herbst/Winter 2001 nach New York zurück. Deren Schönheit liegt wie immer im Detail: Seine Accessoires weisen ihn als zurückhaltenden Meister der Form und des Materials aus. Dies gilt nicht zuletzt für seine Schuhe, angefangen bei Birkenstock-Sandalen mit Kaschmirüberzug bis zu seinem Lieblingsschuhwerk: Stilettos. Letztere, so beharrt er, wirken wie bei der Frau, die sie trägt, wie eine 'sofortige Schönheitsoperation'.

Pour Narciso Rodriguez, tout n'est qu'une question d'équilibre. Son approche de la mode privilégie un luxe minimaliste, optant pour le subtil et le sexy plutôt que pour un glamour tapageur. Bien qu'il se dise inspiré par la mode des rues de New York, Narciso Rodriguez s'est surtout fait connaître en dessinant la robe du mariage le plus jet-set de l'Amérique des années 1990 : celui de Carolyn Bessette et de John F. Kennedy Jr. Né en 1961 à Newark dans le New Jersey de parents d'origine cubaine, Rodriguez fait ses études à la Parsons School of Design de New York, dont il sort diplômé en 1982. Après une période en free-lance dans l'industrie vestimentaire de la ville, il rejoint Anne Klein chez Donna Karan en 1985, avant de partir chez Calvin Klein six ans plus tard, pour qui il dessinera des vêtements pour femme. En 1995, Rodriguez devient directeur de la création chez TSE, travaillant en parallèle pour la ligne de luxe de Cerruti. Deux ans plus tard, il lance sa propre griffe : sa première collection pour femme est présentée à Milan aux défilés Printemps-Eté 1998. Son départ pour l'Europe revêt une signification particulière dans la mesure où il marche sur les traces d'autres diplômés de Parsons tels que Tom Ford (chez Gucci) et Marc Jacobs (chez Louis Vuitton). La même année, Rodriguez est nommé directeur de la création pour la ligne féminine de Loewe, un poste qu'il occupe jusqu'en 2001. Combinant la tradition du luxe européen à son cocktail unique entre pur glamour new-yorkais et racines Latino, Rodriguez revient à New York à l'Automne-Hiver 2001 pour présenter sa collection éponyme. Comme toujours, sa beauté réside dans le détail : ses accessoires révèlent une maîtrise subtile des formes et des matières. C'est notamment le cas de ses chaussures, des Birkenstock recouvertes de cachemire aux nombreux modèles à talons aiguille, dont il aime affirmer qu'ils ont sur celles qui les portent un effet « chirurgie esthétique » instantané.

"As hard and painful as designing can be, it is the thing I have always been most passionate about"

PORTRAIT BY TONY TORRES

NARCISO RODRIGUEZ

What are your signature designs? A dress What's your favourite piece from any of your collections? Fall-Winter 2000 black look on Carmen Kass opening the show How would you describe your work? Clean, tailored, feminine What inspires you? Life on the streets Can fashion still have a political ambition? Anything is possible Who do you have in mind when you design? A modern woman Who has been the greatest influence on your career? Cristobal Balenciaga Which is more important in your work: the process or the product? Both Is designing difficult for you and, if so, what drives you to continue? As hard and painful as it can be, it is the thing I have always been most passionate about Have you ever been influenced or moved by a reaction to your designs? Whether you're slammed or applauded, you're always moved What's your definition of beauty? Grace What's your philosophy? Keep it simple! What is the most important lesson you've learned? To appreciate every day what life has to offer

Throughout his career as a designer, Gilles Rosier has sought to define an 'Other Couture' by creating unadorned, made-to-measure garments for the modern age. His keen interest in colour and in natural form stems, no doubt, from a childhood spent on the move in sun-drenched locations. Born in Paris in 1961, his father's job as an engineer took him to Algiers, Port-Gentil and Kinshasa, before Rosier undertook studies at the Ecole de la Chambre Syndicale de la Couture , graduating in 1982. After an initial apprenticeship at Pierre Balmain and another with Christian Dior, followed by a stint with Guy Paulin, he became Jean Paul Gaultier's assistant in 1987. Five years later, Rosier created the first men's prêt-à-porter collection for Léonard, taking on the role of Artistic Director. His unbridled work ethic was further illustrated by not only creating another label, GR816, in the same year, but also establishing his eponymous label. Rosier's couture training lends his designs a fluidity, yet they are also characterised by a precise sense of proportion and non-threatening innovation. His mastery of cutting led him to become responsible for the main Kenzo Paris collection in 1998. Since 1999, Rosier has been Artistic Director for all of Kenzo women's lines – Paris, Jungle, Jeans and accessories – while simultaneously developing his own collections. Astonishingly, he even finds time to act in theatrical productions of Shakespeare and Chekhov when not designing. Considering that Kenzo means 'travel through time and space', it all makes perfect sense.

Während seiner gesamten Designerlaufbahn hat sich Gilles Rosier darum bemüht, eine 'andere' Couture zu kreieren – schlichte, maßgeschneiderte und vor allem zeitgemäße Mode. Sein großes Interesse an Farbe und natürlicher Form hat seinen Ursprung zweifellos in einer Kindheit, die er an mehreren von der Sonne verwöhnten Orten verbrachte. Nachdem er 1961 in Paris zur Welt gekommen war, kam er durch den Ingenieurberuf des Vaters nach Algier, von dort nach Port-Gentil und schließlich nach Kinshasa. Sein Studium an der Ecole de la Chambre Syndicale de la Couture in Paris schloss er 1982 ab. Nach ersten Lehrjahren bei Pierre Balmain und weiteren bei Christian Dior folgten Erfahrungen bei Guy Paulin und schließlich 1987 die Assistenz bei Jean Paul Gaultier. Weitere fünf Jahre später entwarf Rosier die erste Prêt-à-Porter-Herrenkollektion für Léonard und wurde dort Artistic Director. Seine unbändige Lust an der Arbeit belegt nicht nur die Gründung eines weiteren Labels, nämlich GR816, noch im selben Jahr, sondern auch die Etablierung einer Marke mit seinem Namen. Rosiers Erfahrungen in der Haute Couture verleihen seinen Kreationen ein fließendes Erscheinungsbild; charakteristisch für ihn sind aber auch das präzise Gespür für Proportionen und nicht zu gewagte Innovationen. Seine meisterhafte Schnittkunst bescherte ihm 1998 die Verantwortung für die Hauptkollektion von Kenzo Paris. Seit 1999 ist Rosier Artistic Director aller Kenzo-Linien für Damen – Paris, Jungle, Jeans und Accessoires – während er gleichzeitig auch noch seine eigenen Kollektionen entwirft. Erstaunlicherweise findet Rosier darüber hinaus noch Zeit, als Schauspieler an Theaterproduktionen von Shakespeare- und Tschechow-Stücken mitzuwirken. Wenn man bedenkt, dass Kenzo auf Deutsch 'Reise durch Raum und Zeit' bedeutet, erscheint dies alles sehr einleuchtend.

Tout au long de sa carrière de designer, Gilles Rosier a cherché à définir une «autre couture» en créant des vêtements sur mesure épurés de toute décoration et destinés à la nouvelle ère. Son grand intérêt pour la couleur et les formes naturelles provient sans aucun doute d'une enfance passée entre diverses destinations ensoleillées. Né à Paris en 1961, il suit un père ingénieur qui part travailler à Alger, Port-Gentil et Kinshasa. Rosier entame des études à l'Ecole de la Chambre Syndicale de la Couture, dont il sort diplômé en 1982. Après un premier apprentissage chez Pierre Balmain et Christian Dior, suivi d'une collaboration avec Guy Paulin, il devient assistant de Jean Paul Gaultier en 1987. Cinq ans plus tard, Rosier crée la première collection de prêt-à-porter pour homme de Léonard en tant que directeur artistique. Son éthique professionnelle débridée continue à s'illustrer, non seulement à travers la création d'une autre marque, GR816, mais également par le lancement de sa griffe éponyme la même année. La formation haute couture de Rosier confère à ses créations une grande fluidité, mais elles se distinguent également par un sens précis des proportions et une innovation tranquille. Sa parfaite maîtrise de la coupe le conduit à devenir responsable de la collection principale Kenzo Paris en 1998. Depuis 1999, Rosier est directeur artistique de toutes les lignes féminines de Kenzo (Paris, Jungle, Jeans et accessoires) et continue à développer ses propres collections en parallèle. Curieusement, il réussit à trouver le temps de jouer dans des pièces de théâtre de Shakespeare et de Tchekhov. Si l'on considère que Kenzo signifie «voyager à travers le temps et l'espace», tout s'explique.

"My designs are always romantic"

PORTRAIT BY DUC LIAO

GILLES ROSIER

KENZO BY GILLES ROSIER

What are your signature designs? A look with a refined patchwork of influences from elsewhere, oppositions between masculine and feminine, asymmetric draped pieces, but always romantic **What are your favourite pieces from any of your collections?** The ones I create for shows, especially the leather pieces which are really worked on with cut-out laser perforations, hand-painted, vintage or tattooed **How would you describe your work?** Modern and architectural with reference to historical details. It's very thought-out **What's your ultimate goal?** To be acknowledged for my work and eventually get the opportunity to do an haute couture collection **What inspires you?** I get inspiration from all my travels, hence the ethnic influences; dance, theatre, exhibitions, films, books, anything British, my childhood spent in Africa... Also the street influences **Can fashion still have a political ambition?** If you want to, and believe strongly in something, I think you can get a point of view across on anti-racism, anti-fur... **Who do you have in mind when you design?** All types of women, the beautiful and not so beautiful, the famous and not so famous **Is the idea of creative collaboration important to you?** It's really important for my two collections to have teams behind me, especially as there is so much work involved and the deadlines are so short. I really need professional people who love what they do around me – it's impossible at this level to do everything myself **Who has been the greatest influence on your career?** I had the good fortune to work for houses such as Christian Dior, Guy Paulin and Jean Paul Gaultier; these were very important experiences for me. Also with Claude Sabah when I did my first company, GR 816 **Which is more important in your work: the process or the product?** You need the product to sell and be worn, otherwise there's not much point in doing it. However, to get to that point you need to go through the whole procedure, and then one can't really exist without the other **Is designing difficult for you?** On the contrary, it's a pleasure because I'm passionate about it. It's something I've loved from a really early age **Have you ever been influenced or moved by the reaction to your designs?** I'm only human, so any compliments I get for my work are a real pleasure to hear. It makes all the tough moments worthwhile when someone appreciates what you do **What's your definition of beauty?** Something or someone surprising. Rarity **What's your philosophy?** Trust and be trusted. Live and love. Treat people as you wish to be treated **What is the most important lesson you've learned?** Through my professional experiences, I've learned to give back to the public images, feelings, impressions and inspirations I have felt

Diesel has come to be recognised as much for its image and advertising – by turns controversial, confrontational, ironic and iconic – as its collections of bright, innovative casualwear and denim. The man behind the Italian company is Renzo Rosso. Born in Padua in 1955, he studied industrial textile manufacturing before co-founding the influential Genius Group to develop new fashion brands, among them Replay and, in 1978, Diesel. From the start Diesel broke away from the restrictions of dominant trends, creating lines based instead on the design team's often eccentric instincts. It has worked: successfully pulling off the balancing act of rebellion and individuality whilst embracing mass consumerism. Indeed, its now-famed and multi-award winning advertising catchline – 'Diesel: For Successful Living' – parodies advertising's traditional message that 'things will make you happy'. In 1985 Rosso, something of an entrepreneurial master, acquired the company. By 1991 it had unified its first global marketing strategy and by 1996 it opened a flagship store in New York, a fully licensed, truly international brand name. In 2000 it acquired Staff International, manufacturer of licensed products for Martin Margiela and Vivienne Westwood among others. It now has a turnover in excess of 550m euros. New brands – autonomous spin-offs – have also been launched, among them Diesel Kids, 55DSL and the experimental Diesel Style Lab. In 2002, Diesel collaborated with Karl Lagerfeld on jeans for his Autumn-Winter Lagerfeld Gallery collection. Diesel also has its own hotel, the Art Déco Pelican on South Beach, Miami. It is an architectural expression of the quirky Diesel philosophy: each of the 30 rooms are themed, among them 'Me Tarzan, You Vain'.

Die Marke Diesel ist inzwischen für ihr Image und ihre abwechselnd kontroverse, provozierende, ironische und ikonenhafte Werbung ebenso berühmt wie für ihre Kollektionen fröhlicher, innovativer Freizeit- und Jeansmode. Der Mann, der hinter dem italienischen Unternehmen steht, heißt Renzo Rosso. Er wurde 1955 in Padua geboren und studierte Textilingenieurwesen, bevor er sich an der Gründung der einflussreichen Genius Group beteiligte, die diverse neue Modemarken, darunter auch Replay und 1978 Diesel, kreierte. Von Anfang an emanzipierte sich Diesel von den Einschränkungen herrschender Trends und setzte bei seinen Produktlinien eher auf die oft exzentrischen Instinkte des Designteams. Und siehe da, es funktionierte: Mit Erfolg schaffte man den Balanceakt zwischen Rebellion und Individualismus und war noch dazu massenkonsumtauglich. Genau besehen ist der heute berühmte und vielfach ausgezeichnete Werbeslogan – 'Diesel: For Successful Living' – eine Parodie auf die traditionelle Werbebotschaft, wonach bestimmte Dinge die Menschen glücklich machen. 1985 kaufte Rosso das Unternehmen, und das war sozusagen sein unternehmerisches Meisterstück. Die erste globale Marketingstrategie hatte man bis 1991 erarbeitet; 1996 wurde ein Flagship Store in New York eröffnet. Damit war Diesel zur voll lizenzfähigen, wirklich internationalen Marke avanciert. Im Jahr 2000 kaufte der Dieselkonzern mit Staff International einen Hersteller von Lizenzprodukten für Martin Margiela, Vivienne Westwood und andere namhafte Designer. Der Umsatz liegt zur Zeit bei über 550 Millionen Euro. Inzwischen sind neue Marken – unabhängige Spin-offs – dazugekommen, etwa Diesel Kids, 55DSL und das experimentierfreudige Diesel Style Lab. 2002 arbeitete Diesel mit Karl Lagerfeld an Jeans für dessen Herbst/Winter-Kollektion seiner Lagerfeld Gallery zusammen. Dem Unternehmen gehört inzwischen mit dem Pelican in South Beach, Miami, sogar ein eigenes Hotel. Es ist der architektonische Ausdruck der eigenwilligen Diesel-Philosophie. Jedem der dreißig Zimmer des Art-Déco-Hotels ist ein eigenes Motto zugeordnet, darunter beispielsweise 'Me Tarzan, You Vain'.

Aujourd'hui, la marque Diesel est aussi célèbre pour son image et ses campagnes publicitaires, tour à tour ironiques, iconiques, sujettes à la controverse et aux polémiques, que pour ses collections brillantes et innovantes de casualwear et de jeans. L'homme à l'origine de ce succès s'appelle Renzo Rosso. Né en 1955 à Padoue, il étudie la fabrication textile industrielle avant de co-fonder l'influent Groupe Genius pour développer de nouvelles griffes de mode, parmi lesquelles Replay et, en 1978, Diesel. Dès le départ, Diesel ignore les tendances qui dominent la mode, préférant laisser libre cours aux instincts souvent excentriques de l'équipe de création. Et ça marche : rébellion et individualisme trouvent leur place dans le consumérisme de masse. En effet, le slogan publicitaire désormais célèbre et maintes fois primé « Diesel : For Successful Living » parodie le message traditionnel de la publicité qui cherche à faire croire aux gens que les « choses » peuvent les rendre heureux. En 1985, Rosso rachète l'entreprise en homme d'affaires avisé. En 1991, Diesel unifie sa première stratégie marketing mondiale et en 1996, la griffe ouvre une boutique à New York et s'impose comme une marque vraiment globale. En l'an 2000, Diesel acquiert Staff International, fabricant de produits sous licence pour Martin Margiela et Vivienne Westwood, entre autres. La marque enregistre aujourd'hui un chiffre d'affaires de plus de 550 millions d'euros. Diesel se diversifie à travers de nouvelles marques secondaires autonomes, telles que Diesel Kids, 55DSL et l'expérimental Diesel Style Lab. En 2002, la marque collabore avec Karl Lagerfeld pour créer les jeans de la collection Automne-Hiver de Lagerfeld Gallery. Diesel possède également son propre hôtel à South Beach Miami, l'Art Deco Pelican, où chacune des 30 chambres de l'hôtel tourne autour d'une thématique différente, par exemple « Moi Tarzan, Toi Vaine ».

"The product comes first"

PORTRAIT COURTESY OF RENZO ROSSO

RENZO ROSSO

DIESEL BY RENZO ROSSO

PHOTOGRAPHY BY TAKAY, STYLING BY RACHAEL ZILLI. JANUARY 2001

"Beauty is everything that gives you a vibration"

What are your signature designs? I would definitely say Diesel's innovative and sometimes extreme treatments on denim **What's your favourite piece from any of your collections?** Truly, I love them all. They are all like pieces of a special puzzle **How would you describe your work?** An immeasurable passion for detail and the urge to always do something better and before anybody else **What's your ultimate goal?** Quality is differentiation **What inspires you?** Everything can inspire me: a venue, a sound, a face, a book, an image **Can fashion still have a political ambition?** What is politics today anyway? **Who do you have in mind when you design?** An independent mind and spirit. Someone who enjoys creating his or her own style, and refuses any uninformed approach to fashion **Is the idea of creative collaboration important to you?** Essential. I believe in team work and in a constant flow of inspiration. I love to learn from anybody **What has been the greatest influence on your career?** At the beginning of my career, my inspiration was USA in the '50s **How have your own experiences affected your work as a designer?** Every single work and life experience, positive or negative, wises you up and improves your skills **Which is more important in your work: the process or the product?** Diesel is a unique company because the product comes first. The process is directly influenced by and follows the product **Is designing difficult for you and, if so, what drives you to continue?** I'm not a designer. I spend much of my time travelling around the world. I read about 150 international magazines a month, I meet people from various cultures and I enjoy surfing the net… all of these experiences excite me, provide me with impulses and supply me with stirring ideas for my design team. It keeps me alive, because each single day of my life I can achieve something new and exciting **Have you ever been influenced or moved by the reaction to your designs?** I am always proud when people appreciate what we do. At the same time, when asked what I think is our best collection or product to date, I always answer 'the next one!' **What's your definition of beauty?** Beauty is everything that gives you a vibration **What's your philosophy?** Work with satisfaction and enjoy your life **What is the most important lesson you've learned?** The education my parents gave me

Sonia Rykiel is a bastion of French chic. Famous for her knitwear and shock of red hair, Rykiel has come to embody the elegance and sophistication of the established Paris fashion scene. A pregnant Rykiel created her first designs in 1962, making her own sweaters and maternity dresses for the boutique Laura. Four years later, she established the Sonia Rykiel company and opened her first boutique on the Left Bank in Paris, championing the 'démodé' aesthetic with her inside-out seams and elimination of hems and linings, whilst developing a look that included signature stripes, Rhinestones and words written across sweaters. Since then, the Rykiel brand has gone on to develop a childrenswear range, designed by her daughter Nathalie Rykiel, plus menswear, perfumes, cosmetics and accessories. In 2001 she launched Modern/Vintage Sonia Rykiel, a range of 'greatest hits'. But Rykiel is more than a fashion designer. She has had considerable success as a writer, having written books on fashion, children's fairy tales and a novel, 'Les Lèvres Rouges', as well as having countless books written about her. More homage to Rykiel has been paid in exhibitions and special anniversary fashion shows around the world, in her commissions to redecorate some of Paris' finest hotels and, with the help of Jean-Pierre Guillot Rosaries, a Sonia Rykiel rose. Rykiel also starred in Robert Altman's film 'Prêt à Porter' in 1994 and performed a duet with Malcolm McLaren on his 'Paris' album the same year. Three National Orders later, Rykiel still rocks the fashion world.

Sonia Rykiel ist eine Bastion der französischen Eleganz. Die für ihre Strickmode und ihren roten Schopf berühmte Designerin verkörpert inzwischen den Chic und den Anspruch der etablierten Pariser Modeszene. Während ihrer Schwangerschaft 1962 machte Rykiel die ersten eigenen Entwürfe: Pullover und Umstandskleider für die Boutique Laura. Vier Jahre später gründete sie die Firma Sonia Rykiel und eröffnete ihre erste Boutique am linken Seineufer in Paris. Ihr Markenzeichen war eine Anti-Mode, die sie selbst als 'démodé' bezeichnet: außen getragene Nähte, keine Säume, kein Futter, dafür Streifen, Rheinkiesel und Schriftzüge quer über Pullover. Inzwischen gehören zur Marke Rykiel auch eine Kinderkollektion, entworfen von Tochter Nathalie Rykiel, sowie Herrenmode, Parfums, Kosmetika und Accessoires. 2001 wurde Modern/Vintage Sonia Rykiel präsentiert, quasi eine Kollektion der 'Greatest Hits'. Doch Rykiel ist mehr als eine Modedesignerin. Sie hatte beachtlichen Erfolg als Autorin von Modebüchern, Kindergeschichten und dem Roman 'Les Lèvres Rouges'. Und natürlich ist sie auch selbst Thema zahlreicher Bücher. Außerdem ehrte man sie in Ausstellungen und besonderen Jubiläums-Modenschauen in aller Welt und über das Rosarium von Jean-Pierre Guillot mit einer Rose, die ihren Namen trägt. Die Designerin gestaltete auch die Inneneinrichtung einiger Pariser Spitzenhotels. 1994 spielte sie sich in Robert Altmans Film 'Prêt à Porter' selbst und nahm ein Duett mit Malcolm McLaren für dessen Album 'Paris' auf. Nach der Auszeichnung mit drei wichtigen Orden ihres Heimatlandes ist Rykiel nach wie vor im Stande, die Modewelt in Aufregung zu versetzen.

Sonia Rykiel est un bastion du chic français. Célèbre pour ses pièces en maille et sa flamboyante chevelure rousse, Sonia Rykiel incarne aujourd'hui l'élégance et la sophistication de la mode parisienne. Enceinte, Sonia Rykiel crée ses premiers vêtements en 1962 en confectionnant ses propres pulls et robes de futures mamans pour la boutique Laura. Quatre ans plus tard, elle fonde la société Sonia Rykiel et ouvre sa première boutique rive gauche à Paris. Défendant l'esthétique du « démodé », avec des coutures apparentes et l'élimination des ourlets et des doublures, elle définit un look inimitable, caractérisé par des rayures, des strass et des inscriptions en travers des pulls. Depuis, la marque Rykiel a sorti une ligne pour enfants dessinée par la fille de Sonia, Nathalie Rykiel, ainsi qu'une collection pour homme, des parfums, une ligne de produits cosmétiques et des accessoires. En 2001, elle lance Modern/Vintage Sonia Rykiel, une ligne de « best of ». Mais Sonia Rykiel a d'autres cordes à son arc. Elle a remporté un succès considérable en tant qu'écrivain pour ses livres sur la mode, ses contes de fées pour enfants et son roman « Les Lèvres Rouges », sans parler des innombrables ouvrages qui lui ont été consacrés. D'autres hommages lui ont été rendus dans le monde entier à l'occasion d'expositions et de défilés anniversaires, notamment pour son implication dans la redécoration de certains des plus beaux hôtels parisiens et pour la création de la rose Sonia Rykiel, avec l'aide des Roseraies Jean-Pierre Guillot. En 1994, elle a fait une apparition dans le film « Prêt à Porter » de Robert Altman et chanté un duo avec Malcolm McLaren sur son album « Paris ». Après avoir reçu trois décorations nationales, Sonia Rykiel n'a pourtant pas fini de secouer le monde de la mode.

"I think I am in love with what I am doing"

PORTRAIT BY SARAH MOON

SONIA RYKIEL

PHOTOGRAPHY BY PETE DRINKELL, STYLING BY RACHAEL ZILLI. SEPTEMBER 2002

"Getting old is terrible but if you keep your childish soul, everything inspires you"

What are your signature designs? It used to be knitwear. But now I think it's not just that **How would you describe your work?** Fashion is liberty. Complete liberty. But you have to know what you do. If you just make liberty it means nothing, you have to mix together liberty and 'know-how'. I make fashion, but also I make so many things around that. I have to, because if I don't make so many things around my fashion, my fashion will become completely dumb **What inspires you?** I think I am in love with what I am doing. Every day is a discovery of something new. Getting old is terrible; it is impossible. But if you keep the fresh air and your childish soul, everything inspires you, every moment **Can fashion still have a political ambition?** Absolutely. I care about politics, completely. And I know that politics is a part of my fashion. Also, I think that everything is political **Who do you have in mind when you design?** For me, the Rykiel woman is an intelligent woman. She is impulsive, frivolous and likes to be artificial. Because artificial is also art. She knows the way to walk, the way to play with words and with herself. She's a liar. She's evil. She is a terrible woman… She has two different sides to her character. She's perverse, sweet. She is very sophisticated and she is also very simple. Simplicity means to know what you are **How have your own experiences affected your work as a designer?** Creative people are not like other people: they can't just hear something, they can't see something, they can't learn something, read something – there has to be a reason for everything. Creative people are slaves! **Which is more important in your work: the process or the product?** Both **What's your definition of beauty?** I don't like perfection. At all. Perfection for me is finish. And I like when it's not finished. For me, the real beauty is something just on the good side **What's your philosophy?** Luxury is to know what you want **What is the most important lesson you've learned?** I still keep learning every day

Ghost is the brainchild of ex-model Tanya Sarne, who set up the label with just £11,000 in 1984. Now the West London-based company has a multi-million pound turnover, hundreds of stockists, four of its own boutiques scattered on either side of the Atlantic and several fragrances. Sarne has received much recognition from the British fashion establishment for her company, which has been nominated for, and won, numerous industry awards. Ghost has also designed successful capsule collections for the British retail giant Marks & Spencer. The key to Ghost's success is practicality. The label specialises in clothing made from a textile that, despite having the appearance of vintage crepe, can be flung into a washing machine and worn unironed. At Ghost's inception, sole owner and creative director Sarne adopted an ingenious new fashion fabric: initially stiff and grey, a viscose that, when dyed, shrinks and takes on a delicate antique appearance. To allow for the huge shrinkage, garments have to be cut to outsized patterns. The process is time-consuming and not always predictable. Finished Ghost pieces are unstructured, soft, feminine and gently bohemian; perennial Ghost looks such as bias-cut dresses, narrow or floppy trousers and embroidered vests or tunics are cut to flatter curvaceous or boyish bodies alike. After a brief decampment to New York, Tanya Sarne continues to show the Ghost collections during London Fashion Week.

Ghost ist die Erfindung des Ex-Models Tanya Sarne, die das Label 1984 mit nur 11 000 Pfund Startkapital gründete. Heute macht das Unternehmen mit Sitz im Westen Londons pro Jahr mehrere Millionen Pfund Umsatz, beliefert Hunderte von Einzelhändlern, darunter vier eigene Läden dies- und jenseits des Atlantik, und hat auch mehrere Parfums im Angebot. Sarne genießt die Anerkennung des britischen Mode-Establishments und hat mit ihrem Unternehmen diverse Preise der Textilindustrie gewonnen. Von Ghost stammen auch gefragte Minikollektionen für die englische Kaufhauskette Marks & Spencer. Das Erfolgsrezept des Labels sind praktische Kreationen, vor allem aus einem Stoff, der aussieht wie klassischer Crêpe, sich aber in die Waschmaschine stecken lässt und nicht gebügelt werden muss. In der Anfangsphase entdeckte Sarne – Alleineigentümerin und Creative Director von Ghost in einer Person – einen geniales neues Material: Die zunächst graue, steife Viskose zieht sich nach dem Färben zusammen und erhält ein leicht antikes Aussehen. Um das starke Schrumpfen zu berücksichtigen, müssen die Zuschnitte extrem großzügig ausfallen. Dieser Herstellungsprozess ist sehr zeitaufwändig und nicht immer vorhersehbar. Fertige Ghost-Kreationen sind fließend, weich, feminin und ein bisschen bohemehaft. Über Jahre tragbare Looks wie Kleider im Diagonalschnitt, schmale oder weite Hosen, bestickte Westen und Tuniken sind so geschnitten, dass sie kurvenreichen wie knabenhaften Figuren gleichermaßen schmeicheln. Nach einem kurzen Intermezzo in New York präsentiert Tanya Sarne die Kollektionen von Ghost jetzt wieder im Rahmen der Londoner Modewoche.

En 1984, l'ex-mannequin Tanya Sarne crée la griffe Ghost avec seulement 11 000 livres en poche. Aujourd'hui, l'entreprise du West London enregistre un chiffre d'affaires de plusieurs millions de livres, compte des centaines de stockistes, quatre boutiques réparties des deux côtés de l'Atlantique et plusieurs parfums. Tanya Sarne a été largement adoptée par l'establishment de la mode britannique qui a nominé et récompensé sa marque à de nombreuses reprises. Ghost a également conçu plusieurs mini-collections à succès pour le géant britannique de la distribution Marks & Spencer. La clé de la réussite de Ghost réside dans son sens pratique. La griffe se spécialise dans les vêtements taillés à partir d'un textile qui, bien qu'il ressemble à du crêpe ancien, peut être lavé en machine et porté sans repassage. A la création de Ghost, l'unique propriétaire et directrice de la création Tanya Sarne utilisait un nouveau tissu très mode et ingénieux : une viscose initialement rigide et grise qui, une fois teinte, rétrécit et prend un aspect ancien raffiné. Pour prévoir leur rétrécissement, les vêtements doivent être coupés sur des patrons surdimensionnés, un procédé qui prend beaucoup de temps et ne donne pas toujours les résultats escomptés. Les pièces finies de Ghost sont déstructurées, douces, féminines et légèrement bohème ; ses indémodables tels que les robes asymétriques, les pantalons étroits ou souples et les gilets et tuniques brodés sont coupés de façon à flatter les corps voluptueux comme les physiques androgynes. Après un bref passage à New York, Tanya Sarne continue de présenter les collections de Ghost à la London Fashion Week.

"My career was influenced by men refusing to take me seriously"

PORTRAIT COURTESY OF TANYA SARNE

TANYA SARNE

What are your signature designs? The real signature of Ghost lies in the unique group of viscose fabrics that it has developed. Stylewise, it would have to be the bias-cut spaghetti-strap slip dress **What are your favourite pieces from any of your collections?** The pieces I always come back to are the really easy classic basics, like the bias sheath dresses, vests and T-shirts **How would you describe your work?** Challenging and exciting, but pressurised. I have to make it all work, which is a far larger brief than just designing **What's your ultimate goal?** To live to an old age and enjoy it **What inspires you?** Nature **Can fashion still have a political ambition?** Fashion reflects the spirit of an era. It belongs to social history, not politics **Who do you have in mind when you design?** I design with women in mind, and how best to make them feel good **Is the idea of creative collaboration important to you?** There are so many sides to design – fabric, colour, cut, make, style, etc – that creative collaboration is a necessity **What has been the greatest influence on your career?** Initially my career was influenced by men refusing to take me seriously **How have your own experiences affected your work as a designer?** Originally I was motivated by my need to make a living and the fact that I could not find beautiful, functional, affordable fashion. I had two small children and no money, and there was not much available between high street and expensive designerwear. I set out to fill that gap **Is designing difficult for you and, if so, what drives you to continue?** I love fashion and I love women. It is a constant challenge to design clothes that enhance a women's life on every level. It's not easy – but then nothing worthwhile ever is **Have you ever been influenced or moved by the reaction to your designs?** I am extremely moved when women tell me I have changed their lives by giving them feminine, functional, comfortable fashion as opposed to structured, uncomfortable clothing requiring dry cleaning **What's your definition of beauty?** I do not believe beauty can be defined. The supermodel of today would have been considered ugly 200 years ago. Beauty is subjective **What's your philosophy?** Every woman is beautiful in some respect. For this beauty to manifest itself, a women must be confident. Confidence comes from being confident inside and out. I believe that clothes designed to bring out the femininity in women and mould to a women's body, rather than the body having to fit the clothes, makes a woman comfortable and therefore confident **What is the most important lesson you've learned?** There are a few. A: Timing is all important. Being too avant-garde or late with a trend is to miss out on sales. B: Sales and press are worlds apart and it is extremely difficult to reconcile the two. C: Never panic. Things always work out in the end and panicking can only make things worse

The subtle work of Stephan Schneider reflects this reserved designer's opinion on the beauty of what he warmly refers to as 'boring dailyness.' Schneider, the son of a chemist and hairdresser, was born in Duisburg, Germany, in 1969. Educated at Antwerp's Royal Academy (the city where he is still based), Schneider graduated top of his class in 1994; on the strength of this final collection, he was awarded an exhibition stand during Paris Fashion Week. Schneider's work in both men's and womenswear is based on the everyday, the normality of life. This is not to say that it can be dismissed simply as 'normal': on the contrary, he subverts familiar garments, using the commonplace as his inspiration. His signature pieces boast fine print-work, elasticated waistbands on formal trousers, and wide-hemmed and sometimes belted shirts. Schneider's work has an almost tangible mood of calmness and control; he uses the same fabrics for men as he does for women, lending a greater sense of austerity to his womenswear and a gentler character to his menswear, achieving an 'unbalanced balance'. Schneider has shown his menswear collections in Paris since July 2000 and is known for his unusual presentations: these have included a school gym party scenario, a live karaoke performance and for Spring-Summer 2003 his models paced not to the tune of music, but to the gentle rhythm of moving water sprinklers. Schneider currently has over 70 stockists worldwide, a flagship store in Antwerp (opened in 1996) and another in Tokyo (Japan being his biggest market), which opened in 2001.

Die feinsinnigen Kreationen von Stephan Schneider reflektieren die Haltung dieses zurückhaltenden Designers gegenüber der Schönheit des vermeintlich langweiligen Alltäg-lichen. Der Sohn eines Chemikers und einer Friseurin wurde 1969 in Duisburg geboren. Seine Ausbildung erhielt er an der Königlichen Akademie in Antwerpen, wo er bis heute lebt und arbeitet. Er beendete sein Studium 1994 als Klassenbester, und weil seine Abschlusskollektion dermaßen überzeugte, wurde er dafür mit einem Ausstellungsstand auf der Pariser Modewoche belohnt. Schneiders Kreationen – sowohl für Frauen wie für Männer – basieren auf dem Alltäglichen, der Normalität. Das soll natürlich nicht heißen, seine Mode sei schlichtweg 'normal'. Ganz im Gegenteil stellt Schneider vertraute Kleidungsstücke in Frage und nutzt modische Gemeinplätze als Inspiration. Seine Marken-zeichen sind feine Muster, elastische Bündchen an streng geschnittenen Hosen sowie Hemden mit weitem Saum, manche davon gegürtet. Schneiders Arbeiten strahlen eine fast fühlbare Ruhe und Kontrolliertheit aus. Er verwendet übrigens für Frauen wie für Männer die gleichen Stoffe, nur sind die Damenkollektionen eine Spur strenger, die Herren-sachen etwas sanfter, was zu einem 'ungleichen Gleichgewicht' führt. Seit Juli 2000 präsentiert Schneider seine Herrenkollektionen in Paris und ist dort für unkonventionelle Schauen bekannt: Einmal war das Szenario einer Schulparty nachempfunden, ein andermal gab es eine Karaoke-Performance, und bei der Kollektion Frühjahr/Sommer 2003 bewegten sich seine Models nicht zum Takt von Musik, sondern im Rhythmus von kleinen Wasserfontänen. Weltweit ist der Designer momentan bei über siebzig Fachhändlern vertreten. Außerdem gibt es je einen Flagship-Store in Antwerpen (seit 1996) und in Tokio (seit 2001), da Japan für Schneider den größten Markt darstellt.

Le travail subtil de Stephan Schneider reflète l'opinion de ce designer réservé sur la beauté de ce qu'il aime appeler « l'ennui du quotidien ». Schneider est né en 1969 à Duisburg en Allemagne d'un père chimiste et d'une mère coiffeuse. Formé à l'Académie Royale d'Anvers, ville où il vit toujours, Schneider sort premier de sa promotion en 1994 ; grâce à la force de sa collection de fin d'études, on lui accorde un stand d'exposition à la Semaine de la Mode de Paris. Qu'il dessine pour les femmes ou pour les hommes, le travail de Schneider repose toujours sur le quotidien, sur la normalité de la vie. Cela ne veut pas dire pour autant que l'étiquette de « normal » lui convienne : bien au contraire, il détourne les vêtements familiers en s'inspirant de l'ordinaire. Ses pièces les plus caractéristiques présentent de magnifiques imprimés, des ceintures élastiques sur des pantalons clas-siques et des chemises à large ourlet, parfois ceinturées. Le travail de Schneider est empreint d'un calme et d'un contrôle presque tangibles ; il utilise les mêmes tissus pour les hommes et les femmes et confère ainsi plus d'austérité à ses collections pour femme et plus de douceur à sa mode masculine, en quête d'un « équilibre déséquilibré ». Schneider présente ses collections pour homme à Paris depuis juillet 2000, remarqué pour ses défilés très originaux : soirée dans un gymnase de lycée, performances karaoké en live et pour le Printemps-Eté 2003, ses mannequins ne défilaient pas en phase avec la musique mais sur le rythme tranquille d'arroseurs mobiles. Schneider possède actuellement plus de 70 stockistes à travers le monde, ainsi qu'une boutique à Anvers (ouverte en 1996) et une autre à Tokio (le Japon étant son plus gros marché), ouverte en 2001.

"Fashion is a lot about dreaming. But I am not a dreamer. My philosophy is to bring a daily averageness back to fashion"

PORTRAIT COURTESY OF STEPHAN SCHNEIDER

STEPHAN SCHNEIDER

What are your signature designs? When you see my real signature, I have big problems at the bank because I change it quite often. I think for some people my design is just as difficult to follow. I jump from one theme to the other **What's your favourite piece from any of your collections?** Once you start designing, other things come with it. Nasty things like having to build up a company, deliveries, schedules… So I think about the thing I am most emotional about: my first collection. You are so innocent, so fresh then. Two years after it, I thought 'Oh my God, this is terrible.' Now, five years later, I just think 'Wow!' **How would you describe your work?** Perhaps because of my German background, I am very realistic. Fashion is a lot about dreaming, about escape from reality, escape to other centuries, escape to the future. I am busy with the low key boring dailyness **What's your ultimate goal?** Sometimes I wish I had one **What inspires you?** I am most inspired when I am really bored. When I am happy and enjoying life, I hate my work and want to do anything but work **Can fashion still have a political ambition?** When I think about the '80s, I still think about the Katharine Hamnett T-shirt which had such a strong political statement, and I look with a lot of nostalgia to this ambition for engagement. Today we are not interested in anything **What do you have in mind when you design?** I don't have this dream person in my mind. I start always from a hunger **Is the idea of creative collaboration important to you?** Designers are quite… egoistic is the wrong word, but let's say egocentric. And I think that makes fashion strong, because it's so personal **What has been the greatest influence on your career?** First of all, I don't really like the word career. I am just continuing day by day. I am not really conscious about influences **How have your own experiences affected your work as a designer?** My experiences in my life are always like pain – I forget quickly. I want to change and I want to learn from experiences, but I never do. I am like a virgin waking up each morning and starting all over again **Which is more important in your work: the process or the product?** I'd love to say the process. But that would be a very pretentious answer because the customer can never see the process, they can't participate. So I have to answer that the product is the more important. Unfortunately. Because the process is so much more fun **Have you ever been influenced or moved by the reaction to your designs?** Actually yes, very much so. Designing is asking for a dialogue, asking for a reaction. I don't design for myself. I live for those reactions, and I am moved and influenced by them **What's your definition of beauty?** If I knew this definition I could design from a sort of pragmatic structure, but beauty has no structure, no rule. Like love, it is difficult to define. I wish I could – I'd have less pain in my life **What's your philosophy?** I am not a dreamer. My philosophy is to bring a daily averageness back to fashion **What is the most important lesson you have learned?** I live from day to day. I really appreciate basic dull values like politeness. I appreciate honesty. I see a quality in those values, rather than a quality in dreams

Jeremy Scott's story is the stuff of fairy tales and syndicated gameshows. Born in 1974 and raised in Kansas City, Missouri, Scott was the boy who read Italian 'Vogue' between classes and wrote about fashion in French essays. After graduating from New York's Pratt Institute, the 21-year-old Scott made a pilgrimage to Paris where his collection, made out of paper hospital gowns and inspired by the body-modifying artist Orlan, would go down in fashion folklore. And his first formal runway presentation in October 1997, 'Rich White Women', presenting asymmetrically cut trousers and multifunctional T-shirts, would establish Scott as a considerable Paris presence. But controversy clings to the designer like a Pierre Cardin teddy bear brooch – later collections, such as March 1998's infamous 'Contrapied' show, have met with a mixture of incredulity, derision and bemusement, all the while establishing key details of the Scott aesthetic: attention to volume, an obsession with logos (including the best-selling back-to-front Paris print), a hard-edged Mugler-esque glamour and a wicked way with fur. In Autumn 2001, Scott relocated to Los Angeles, a city that has welcomed his über-trash, parodic style with wide-open arms. So much so that in January 2002, Scott achieved one of his longterm ambitions when he appeared as a celebrity contestant on 'Wheel Of Fortune' and dressed hostess Vanna White for a five night showcase of his glamour gowns and denim wear. He is currently recording a single with DJ friend Michel Gauberg. As Scott himself might say, *vive l'avant-garde!*

Jeremy Scotts Biografie klingt wie ein Märchen oder wie Stoff für eine typische Fernsehshow. Der 1974 geborene und in Kansas City, Missouri, aufgewachsene Scott las tat-sächlich schon als Schüler in der Pause die italienische Vogue und schrieb in Französisch Aufsätze über Mode. Nach einem Abschluss am New Yorker Pratt Institute pilgerte der damals 21-jährige nach Paris, wo seine Kollektion aus papierenen Krankenhaushemden in die Modegeschichte einging. Dazu inspiriert hatte ihn die Künstlerin Orlan, die ihren Körper u. a. durch Schönheitsoperationen zum Kunstobjekt machte. Scotts erste offizielle Laufsteg-Show präsentierte im Oktober 1997 unter dem Titel 'Rich White Women' asymmetrisch geschnittene Hosen und multifunktionale T-Shirts, mit denen der Designer sich in der Pariser Szene etablierte. Doch haftet ihm Widersprüchlichkeit wie eine Teddy-bär-Brosche von Pierrre Cardin an. So wurden spätere Kollektionen, wie etwa die berüchtigte Show 'Contrapied' vom März 1998, zwar mit einer Mischung aus Skepsis, Spott und Verwirrung aufgenommen, setzten aber dennoch Maßstäbe für die Markenzeichen von Scotts Ästhetik: Volumen, eine Leidenschaft für Logos (inklusive des Bestsellers in Gestalt eines umlaufenden Parisdrucks), ein kantiger, an Mugler erinnernder Glamour und ein verrücktes Faible für Pelz. Im Herbst 2001 verlegte Scott seinen Wohnsitz nach Los Angeles – in die Stadt, die seinen extrem kitschigen, ironischen Stil begeistert aufgenommen hatte. Die Resonanz war sogar so groß, dass im Januar 2002 ein lange gehegter Wunsch Scotts in Erfüllung ging: Er war Stargast in der TV-Show 'Wheel of Fortune' und stattete Vanna White, die Buchstabenfee der Sendung, fünf Abende lang mit seinen glamourösen Roben und Jeans-Kreationen aus. Das jüngste Projekt des Designers war die Aufnahme einer Single mit dem befreundeten DJ Michel Gauberg – getreu dem Motto: *Vive l'avant-garde!*

L'histoire de Jeremy Scott est une affaire de contes de fées et de jeux télévisés. Né en 1974, il grandit à Kansas City dans le Missouri, où il est bien le seul à lire le « Vogue » italien entre les cours et à disserter sur la mode dans ses rédactions de français. Une fois diplômé du Pratt Institute de New York à 21 ans, Scott part en pèlerinage à Paris. La collection qu'il y présente marque un véritable tournant dans l'histoire de la mode, avec ses robes d'hôpitaux en papier inspirées par l'œuvre de l'artiste plasticien Orlan. En octobre 1997, lors de son premier défilé officiel intitulé « Rich White Women », il présente des pantalons asymétriques et des T-shirts multifonctions qui assoient sa présence sur la scène parisienne. Mais la controverse s'accroche au créateur comme une broche-nounours de Pierre Cardin : les collections suivantes, notamment le terrible défilé « Contre-pied » de mars 1998, sont accueillies dans un mélange d'incrédulité, de dérision et de stupéfaction, bien que certains détails clés parviennent à imposer l'esthétique de Scott : l'attention portée au volume, l'obsession des logos (notamment l'imprimé « Paris » qui s'est très bien vendu), un glamour « Mugleresque » aux lignes acérées et une utilisation scandaleuse de la fourrure. A l'automne 2001, Scott s'installe à Los Angeles où son style parodique et ultra-trash est accueilli à bras ouverts. A tel point qu'en janvier 2002, Scott réalise l'un de ses plus vieux rêves : il participe à la « Roue de la Fortune » en tant que célébrité-candidat et habille l'animatrice Vanna White de ses robes glamour et de ses pièces en denim pour un show-case de cinq soirées. Il enregistre actuellement un single avec son ami DJ Michel Gauberg. Comme le dirait Scott lui-même, *vive l'avant-garde !*

"I'm just interested in trying to provoke people"

PORTRAIT BY ALEX HOERNER

JEREMY SCOTT

What are your signature designs? Just something unexpected. Something that is always out there **What's your favourite piece from any of your collections?** I don't think I have a favourite. There's different moods to my designs, different personalities – I go through phases. They all have an importance **How would you describe your work?** I don't know if it's a challenge – I'm just interested in trying to provoke people. For each collection, there's something that I want to really convey: a message, an idea or a thought. That's for other people to think about **What's your ultimate goal?** To rule the world! To leave behind a legacy of design, a visual archive so that in 100 years some fashion fanatic opens up a book and says 'What the fuck was that?' Totally flipping out because it's still exciting and challenging, something that makes a statement even in the future **What inspires you?** Los Angeles is a major eye candy **Can fashion still have a political ambition?** Oh yes **Who do you have in mind when you design?** There are different people around me that I consider. Obviously a part of it is purely just fantasy gone wild **Is the idea of creative collaboration important to you?** It's like a puzzle. I do share with people, talk about what I'm doing. I don't think it's bad to collaborate, but I think in the end I'm pretty single-minded **What has been the greatest influence on your career?** My own goals **Which is more important in your work: the process or the product?** I think the process dictates the work, not the product. Everything along the way actually defines the product **Is designing difficult for you?** No, it's not hard. Designing is pretty serious, though **Have you ever been influenced or moved by the reaction to your designs?** I have had major, heavy, strong criticism and I continue to have it. There's no way you can somehow manage not to react to that. But I still believe in trying to push new ideas **What's your definition of beauty?** Unusual **What's your philosophy?** Get up, do it again, do it better. Do it better all the time. I don't know if that's my philosophy, but fashion is kind of like that **What is the most important lesson you've learned?** Believe in yourself

Although he is now one of the indisputable kings of menswear, Raf Simons (born 1968) never took a single fashion course. Instead, he studied industrial design in Genk, Belgium, close to his hometown Neerpelt. Nevertheless he took an internship at the Walter Van Beirendonck Antwerp office while still at school, citing fashion as a major point of interest. Afterwards Simons started working as a furniture designer, but gradually grew unhappy with this direction. In 1995, after moving to Antwerp and meeting up with Linda Loppa, head of the fashion department at the city's Royal Academy, he decided to switch career. Obsessed both by traditional, formal menswear and the rebellious dress codes of present and past youth cultures, Simons distilled a groundbreaking new style from these inspirations. From his first collection for Autumn-Winter 1995 on, he drew a tight, linear silhouette executed in classical materials that encapsulated references like English schoolboys, gothic music, punk, Kraftwerk and Bauhaus architecture. Despite international acclaim, Raf Simons surprisingly shut down his company after presenting his Autumn-Winter 1999 collection, in order to take a sabbatical and re-arrange the internal structure of his business. After sealing a close co-operation with Belgian manufacturer CIG, Simons returned for Autumn-Winter 2000 with a new, multi-layered and radical look, worn as ever by non-professional models scouted on the streets of Antwerp. These teenage boys were the subject of a collaboration with David Sims, resulting in photographs compiled in a book ('Isolated Heroes', 1999) and presented on the art gallery circuit. Raf Simons designed the Ruffo Research men's collections for Spring-Summer and Autumn-Winter 1999. Since October 2000, he has taught fashion at the University of Applied Arts in Vienna. Raf Simons also guest edited the February 2001 issue of i-D.

Obwohl er heute unbestreitbar zu den Königen der Herrenmode zählt, hat der 1968 geborene Raf Simons nie auch nur ein einziges Seminar zum Thema Mode besucht. Stattdessen studierte er im belgischen Genk, nahe seiner Heimatstadt Neerpelt, Industriedesign. Vorher absolvierte er noch zu Schulzeiten ein Praktikum im Antwerpener Büro von Walter Van Beirendonck. Schon damals war Mode einer der Bereiche, die ihn am meisten interessierten. Seine berufliche Karriere begann Simons als Möbeldesigner, was ihn jedoch nicht besonders lange glücklich machte. Nachdem er 1995 nach Antwerpen gezogen war und dort Linda Loppa, die Leiterin des Fachgebiets Mode an der Königlichen Akademie, kennen gelernt hatte, entschloss er sich zu einer anderen Karriere. Weil er von der traditionellen, formellen Herrenmode ebenso begeistert war wie von den rebellischen Dresscodes der Jugendkultur von heute und gestern, entwickelte Simons aus diesen Inspirationen einen bahnbrechenden neuen Stil. Schon in seiner ersten Kollektion für Herbst/Winter 1995 entschied er sich für eine schmale, lineare Silhouette und klassische Materialien. Außerdem zitierte er in seinen Entwürfen englische Schuluniformen, Gothic Music, Punk, Kraftwerk und Bauhaus-Architektur. Trotz internationaler Anerkennung schloss Simons seine Firma überraschenderweise nach der Präsentation seiner Kollektion für Herbst/Winter 1999, um sich ein Jahr Auszeit zu nehmen, in der er sein Geschäft neu strukturierte. Nach der Vereinbarung einer engen Kooperation mit dem belgischen Hersteller CIG kehrte er mit einer Kollektion für Herbst/Winter 2000 auf den Laufsteg zurück. Dieser neue, radikale Look aus vielen Lagen wurde wie immer von nicht-professionellen Models vorgeführt, die man auf den Straßen Antwerpens rekrutiert hatte. Diese Teenager-Jungs wirkten auch an einem Projekt mit David Sims mit, das in dem Fotoband 'Isolated Heroes' (1999) dokumentiert ist und in diversen Kunstgalerien präsentiert wurde. Für Ruffo Research entwarf Raf Simons die Herrenkollektionen für Frühjahr/Sommer und Herbst/Winter 1999. Seit Oktober 2000 lehrt der Designer Mode an der Universität für Angewandte Kunst in Wien. An der Februarausgabe 2001 von i-D wirkte er als Gastredakteur mit.

Bien qu'il soit sans conteste devenu l'un des rois de la mode pour homme, Raf Simons (né en 1968) n'a jamais suivi la moindre formation en mode. En fait, il a étudié le design industriel à Genk, près de sa ville natale de Neerpelt en Belgique. Pendant ses études, il fait toutefois un stage au bureau anversois de Walter Van Beirendonck car la mode figure parmi ses principaux centres d'intérêt. Ensuite, Simons commence à travailler comme designer de meubles, mais s'avère progressivement insatisfait par cette orientation. En 1995, après avoir emménagé à Anvers et rencontré Linda Loppa, directrice du département mode de l'Académie Royale de la ville, il décide de changer de carrière. Obsédé à la fois par la mode masculine classique et les codes vestimentaires de la jeunesse rebelle d'hier et d'aujourd'hui, Simons puise dans ces inspirations et invente un nouveau style révolutionnaire. Dès sa première collection pour l'Automne-Hiver 1995, il définit une silhouette étroite et linéaire, façonnée dans des matières classiques pleines de références aux collégiens anglais, à la musique gothique, au punk, à Kraftwerk ou encore à l'architecture Bauhaus. Malgré un succès international, contre toute attente, Raf Simons ferme sa maison après avoir présenté sa collection Automne-Hiver 1999, décidant de prendre un congé sabbatique et de revoir la structure interne de son entreprise. Il signe ensuite un accord d'étroite coopération avec le fabricant belge CIG, puis revient à l'Automne-Hiver 2000 avec un nouveau look radical aux multiples facettes, présenté comme toujours sur des mannequins non professionnels recrutés dans les rues d'Anvers. Ces adolescents font d'ailleurs l'objet d'une collaboration avec David Sims, qui sort un livre de photographies («Isolated Heroes», 1999) également présentées dans les galeries d'art. Par ailleurs, Raf Simons a conçu la collection masculine Ruffo Research Printemps-Eté et Automne-Hiver 1999. Depuis octobre 2000, il enseigne la mode à l'Université des Arts Appliqués de Vienne. Raf Simons a également été invité au comité de rédaction du numéro de février 2001 du magazine i-D.

"I can't see myself as being only a fashion designer. The clothes themselves are just a medium to make clear a certain aesthetic"

PORTRAIT BY DAVID SIMS

RAF SIMONS

PHOTOGRAPHY BY WILLY VANDERPERRE, STYLING BY OLIVIER RIZZO. FEBRUARY 2001. MODELS: ROBBIE & CHLOE

SOUND

"My goal is true independence, both in my work and my mind"

What are your signature designs? Tailoring meets youth culture **What's your favourite piece from any of your collections?** White all-over printed bomber made in collaboration with Peter De Potter, inspired by an i-D photo from Nigel Shafran and Melanie Ward, and by Ashley Bickerton's self-portrait **How would you describe your work?** Individualism for individuals **What's your ultimate goal?** True independence, both in my work and my mind **What inspires you?** People, friends, personal memories, street culture, art… **Can fashion still have a political ambition?** Yes **Who do you have in mind when you design?** Not a person, an attitude **Is the idea of creative collaboration important to you?** Yes, I am extremely attracted to other individuals' creativity and worlds, and vice versa. Often the collaborations result in the most memorable moments and creations for me (ie – David Sims, Simon Periton, Peter De Potter, Willy Vanderperre) **What has been the greatest influence on your career?** Too long a list, don't know where to start **How have your own experiences affected your work as a designer?** I took a break once because I felt uncomfortable with the business of fashion. Creative freedom may never be compromised, otherwise I stop **Which is more important in your work: the process or the product?** The process, although I hate ordering buttons and zippers. I like the social interaction involved in the process. I also like the fact that I can transfer the process to other fields, areas with the same philosophy but another product **Is designing difficult for you?** No, it is not difficult **Have you ever been influenced or moved by the reaction to your designs?** Of course, it is my drive. For example, I only work with non-professional models; people that I cast myself, usually not related to the fashion world, because their reactions are different, fresh. They make me think more; they inspire me more **What's your definition of beauty?** Purity that transcends the common taste. For me that kind of purity is usually isolated **What's your philosophy?** Order through disorder **What is the most important lesson you've learned?** It is love and life that matters

You could say the exotic comes naturally to Martine Sitbon. Born in 1951 in Casablanca to a French father and Italian mother, Sitbon moved to Paris at the age of ten, witnessing at firsthand the social upheaval of the late 1960s, before enrolling at the famed Studio Berçot. Her early interest in fashion was fired by visiting the flea markets of Paris and London and, after graduating in 1974, she continued her practical education by travelling extensively. From Hong Kong and India to Mexico, via Milan and New York, she gained inspiration from the local fabrics and textiles she sourced on her journeys. Her own designs eventually premiered in 1985: a debut that saw her unique but sober cultural melange – from bloomers to monks' habits – launched to the strains of the Velvet Underground. Sitbon thrives on paradox, playing with masculine and feminine conventions and producing seemingly traditional designs in unexpected fabrics. From 1988 until 1992, Sitbon designed Chloé's ready-to-wear collection, toning down the brash 1980s silhouettes in favour of a simpler look inspired by 1960s geometric prints. In the same year that she joined Chloé, Sitbon also launched her Martine Sitbon Fantasy range. In the 1990s Sitbon found herself associated with the 'grunge' movement in fashion. Given her androgynous approach and delicate, flea market-inspired chic, this was an obvious, but overly simplistic, appraisal of her work. Her 1999 menswear collection perfectly complemented her continual use of men's garments in womenswear. In 2001 she joined Byblos as womenswear designer, bringing the attentive choice of material and heterogeneous approach synonymous with her work. In April 2002 she left to fully concentrate on her eponymous men's and womenswear label, where she continues to inspire with her beautifully constructed designs.

Man könnte sagen, dass Exotik für Martine Sitbon das Natürlichste der Welt ist. Sie wurde 1951 in Casablanca als Kind eines französischen Vaters und einer italienischen Mutter geboren, zog im Alter von zehn Jahren nach Paris, wo sie die Studentenunruhen der späten 1960er Jahre hautnah miterlebte, und schrieb sich schließlich als Studentin im berühmten Studio Berçot ein. Ihr frühes Interesse an Mode wurde durch den regelmäßigen Besuch der Flohmärkte von Paris und London geweckt. Nach Beendigung ihres Studiums 1974 sammelte sie auf ausgedehnten Reise weiter praktische Erfahrungen. In Indien und Mexiko, aber auch in Städten wie Hongkong, Mailand und New York ließ sie sich von einheimischen Stoffen und Kleiderstilen inspirieren. Die Premiere ihrer eigenen Entwürfe fand schließlich 1985 statt: Es war eine einzigartige, aber unsentimentale Melange verschiedenster Kulturen – von altmodischen Pumphosen bis hin zu Mönchskutten –, die sie zu Klängen von Velvet Underground präsentierte. Sitbon liebt das Paradoxe, spielt mit männlichen und weiblichen Konventionen und produziert scheinbar traditionelle Entwürfe aus ganz unerwarteten Materialien. Von 1988 bis 1992 kreierte sie die Prêt-à-Porter-Kollektion bei Chloé, wo sie die protzigen Silhouetten der 1980er Jahre durch einen schlichteren Look ersetzte, der an die geometrischen Drucke der Sixties angelehnt war. In dem Jahr, als sie anfing, für Chloé zu arbeiten, präsentierte sie auch die Kollektion Martine Sitbon Fantasy. In den 1990er Jahren wurde die Designerin als Teil der sogenannten Grunge-Bewegung wahrgenommen. Angesichts ihres androgynen, von Flohmarktfunden inspirierten zarten Chics ist das eine zwar nahe liegende, aber wohl doch zu stark vereinfachende Einschätzung ihrer Arbeit. Die Herrenkollektion von 1999 jedenfalls ergänzte die kontinuierliche Verwendung von Männerkleidung in ihrer Damenmode auf das Beste. 2001 übernahm Sitbon das Design der Damenkollektion bei Byblos, wo sie ihre besondere Aufmerksamkeit für die Materialwahl und den heterogenen Stil einbrachte. Seit April 2002 konzentriert sich die Designerin ausschließlich auf ihre eigenen Labels für Herren- und Damenmode und begeistert weiterhin mit wunderschönen Entwürfen.

Chez Martine Sitbon, l'exotisme est quelque chose de naturel. Née en 1951 à Casablanca d'un père français et d'une mère italienne, Martine Sitbon arrive à Paris à l'âge de dix ans et assiste aux premiers mouvements sociaux de la fin des années 1960 avant d'étudier au célèbre Studio Berçot. Son intérêt précoce pour la mode naît en visitant les marchés aux puces de Paris et de Londres puis, une fois diplômée en 1974, elle continue sa formation pratique en parcourant le monde, Hong Kong, l'Inde et le Mexique en passant par Milan et New York, elle trouve son inspiration dans les tissus et textiles locaux qu'elle rapporte de ses voyages. Elle finit par présenter ses propres créations en 1985 : au son du Velvet Underground, son premier défilé témoigne d'un mélange culturel unique mais sobre, avec ses salopettes et ses tenues monastiques. Martine Sitbon excelle dans le paradoxe, elle joue avec les conventions masculines et féminines et produit des pièces apparemment traditionnelles dans des tissus inattendus. De 1988 à 1992, elle dessine la collection prêt-à-porter de Chloé, atténuant les silhouettes effrontées des années 1980 au profit d'un look plus simple inspiré par les imprimés géométriques des sixties. L'année où elle rejoint Chloé, Martine Sitbon lance également sa ligne Martine Sitbon Fantasy. De par son approche androgyne et son chic délicat très « marché aux puces », elle se retrouve malgré elle associée au mouvement grunge qui déferle sur la mode dans les années 1990, une évaluation par trop simpliste de son travail. En 1999, sa collection pour homme vient couronner l'utilisation constante des vêtements masculins dans sa mode pour femme. En 2001, elle devient styliste des collections pour femme de Byblos, portant une grande attention au choix des matières et insufflant à la marque l'approche hétérogène qui caractérise son travail. En avril 2002, elle quitte Byblos pour se consacrer exclusivement à sa griffe éponyme qui continue de séduire hommes et femmes grâce à des pièces magnifiquement construites.

"I mix ordinary clothes with extraordinary pieces, respecting reality"

PORTRAIT COURTESY OF MARTINE SITBON

MARTINE SITBON

What are your signature designs? The mix of opposites – femininity and androgyny, fragility and rock, reality and dream – defines my style. I work contrasts; I try in each collection to distance myself from obvious references. Mix up. Confuse **What's your favourite piece from any of your collections?** This season I really liked the look that Anne Catherine wore, a grey dress, almost classic, with an almost futuristic silver waistcoat. Last winter I loved the big military coat with the very fragile Edwardian drapery. As for my past collections, the velour burn-out dresses **How would you describe your work?** Always a dichotomy between old clothes from the military and tailoring to flowing bias and draping. A mix of ordinary clothes with extraordinary pieces, respecting reality **What inspires you?** I accumulate extremely diverse emotions that may come from films, rock concerts, ballet, exhibitions… then somehow they all smoothly come out together to form a soft mixture **Can fashion have a political ambition?** I hope so, everything shouldn't come down solely to commercialism **Who do you have in mind when you design?** A girl who is lively, off-beat, original… **Is the idea of creative collaboration important to you?** Definitely. I love to work as a team; there is a synergetic effect, stimulation and an exchange of ideas invaluable in creative work **Who has been the greatest influence on your career?** When I was young, David Bowie, the Rolling Stones and Syd Barrett gave me the desire to do fashion **How have your own experiences affected your work as a designer?** Music has brought a lot to me and going to secondhand markets has been a fundamental start-point of my research in making looks. Later, contemporary dance and art have left an impression on me. I have the impression that everything I have experienced has affected my work **Which is more important in your work: the process or the product?** With the product, history becomes real but the most interesting part is the process **Is designing difficult for you and, if so, what drives you to continue?** The perpetual restart of fashion is very interesting and this permanent evolution is what pushes me to stay in this profession. We can never sleep, we cannot count on anything and there is a real idea of a game **Have you ever been influenced or moved by the reaction to your designs?** Success, like failure, pushes you to do your work better **What's your philosophy?** Keep your feet on the ground and your head in the clouds

Luxuriously tailored designs with a subtle, subversive twist; a coherent blending of couture tradition and unflinching modernism; a lean, sexy, often androgynous silhouette: these are the signatures of designer Hedi Slimane. Born in Paris in 1968, Slimane began making clothes as a teenager. Perhaps surprising given his focus on precision cut and tailoring, Slimane received no formal training, instead choosing to study History of Art at Ecole du Louvre. He joined French designer José Lévy in 1992, becoming assistant to Jean-Jacques Picart, and working in various behind-the-scene roles for the next five years. In July 1997, the relatively unknown Slimane was appointed Artistic Director of Yves Saint Laurent Rive Gauche Homme. Over the next three years at YSL, he would reinvigorate their ready-to-wear menswear line, combining a respectful appreciation of Yves Saint Laurent history with a sharp, often erotic take on modern glamour. Following the Gucci Group's purchase of Yves Saint Laurent, Slimane left Rive Gauche Homme in March 2000; his swan song, the 'Black Tie' collection for Autumn-Winter 2000, would stand as a touchstone for his uncompromising vision of male elegance. After a two season hiatus, Slimane was appointed Creative Director for Menswear at Christian Dior. His first collection for the French house, reworking his razor slim silhouette with brutally perforated leather tuxedos, met with universal acclaim. In February 2002, the first Dior Homme boutique opened in Milan and in April, he was named Designer of the Year by the CFDA. Concurrent with his design work, Slimane has also presented an installation at the 62nd Pitti Immagine Uomo Fair in Florence, accompanied by a book of his photography, 'Transmission'. He continues to play a central role in redefining the shape – and significance – of menswear within contemporary fashion. 'I'd like men to think about evolving into something more sophisticated, more seductive,' he has declared. 'To explore the possibility of an entirely new kind of masculinity.'

Luxuriöse, perfekt sitzende Kreationen mit leicht subversivem Touch, eine harmonische Melange aus traditionsbewusster Couture und unerschrockenem Modernismus, dazu eine schmale, erotische und doch oft androgyne Silhouette: All das kennzeichnet die Handschrift des Designers Hedi Slimane. 1968 in Paris geboren, begann Slimane schon als Teenager, Kleider zu nähen. Angesichts des Augenmerks, das der Designer auf Schnitt und Verarbeitung legt, erstaunt es vielleicht, dass er keinerlei entsprechende Ausbildung besitzt. Stattdessen studierte er Kunstgeschichte an der Ecole du Louvre. Ab 1992 war er tätig für den französischen Designer José Lévy, wurde danach Assistent von Jean-Jacques Picart und arbeitete in den darauf folgenden Jahren in diversen Funktionen hinter den Kulissen. Im Juli 1997 wurde Slimane als noch ziemlich unbeschriebenes Blatt zum Artistic Director von Yves Saint Laurent Rive Gauche Homme ernannt. Innerhalb der nächsten drei Jahre gelang es ihm, die Prêt-à-Porter-Linie für Herren neu zu beleben, indem er mit dem gebührenden Respekt das Vermächtnis von Yves Saint Laurent und ein klares, oft erotisches Verständnis von modernem Glamour kombinierte. Nach dem Verkauf des Hauses YSL an den Gucci-Konzern verließ Slimane das Unternehmen im März 2000. Rückblickend war seine Abschiedskollektion namens 'Black Tie' für Herbst/Winter 2000 der Prüfstein seiner kompromisslosen Vorstellung von männlicher Eleganz. Nach einer zwei Saisons dauernden Auszeit meldete sich Slimane zurück, und zwar als Creative Director for Menswear bei Christian Dior. Seine erste Kollektion für dieses Haus, eine Überarbeitung seiner rasiermesserscharfen Silhouetten, etwa mit gnadenlos durchlöcherten Smokings, rief allgemeine Begeisterung hervor. Im Februar 2002 wurde die erste Boutique von Dior Homme in Mailand eröffnet, und im April desselben Jahres kürte das Council of Fashion Designers of America (CFDA) Slimane zum Designer of the Year. Neben seiner üblichen Arbeit als Designer präsentierte der vielseitige Franzose auch eine Installation auf der 62. Pitti Immagine Uomo Fair in Florenz. Aus diesem Anlass erschien unter dem Titel 'Transmission' auch ein Buch mit seinen Fotos. Slimane spielt weiterhin eine zentrale Rolle bei der Neudefinition von Erscheinung und Bedeutung der Herrenbekleidung in der zeitgenössischen Mode. 'Ich wünsche mir, dass Männer mehr Eleganz, mehr Verführerisches entwickeln', hat er erklärt. 'Es geht darum, die Möglichkeiten einer ganz neuen Form des Maskulinen auszuloten.'

Coupes luxueuses aux formes subtiles et subversives, mélange cohérent entre tradition haute couture et modernité assurée, silhouette longiligne, sexy et souvent androgyne : telle est la signature du créateur Hedi Slimane. Né en 1968 à Paris, Slimane commence à faire des vêtements alors qu'il est encore adolescent. Fait surprenant étant donné la précision de sa coupe et de son style, Slimane n'a suivi aucune formation particulière, préférant étudier l'histoire de l'art à l'Ecole du Louvre. Il rejoint le styliste français José Lévy en 1992 et devient l'assistant de Jean-Jacques Picart, occupant divers postes en coulisses pendant cinq ans. En juillet 1997, le quasi-inconnu Slimane est nommé directeur artistique d'Yves Saint Laurent Rive Gauche Homme. Pendant les trois années qu'il passe chez YSL, il revitalise la ligne de prêt-à-porter masculin : dans le plus grand respect de l'histoire de la maison, il insuffle à la collection son sens aiguisé d'un glamour moderne et souvent érotique. Slimane quitte Rive Gauche Homme en mars 2000 après le rachat d'Yves Saint Laurent par le Groupe Gucci ; son chant du cygne, la collection « Black Tie » pour l'Automne-Hiver 2000, impose sa vision intransigeante de l'élégance masculine. Après une interruption de deux saisons, Slimane est nommé directeur de la création pour homme chez Christian Dior. Sa première collection Dior, pour laquelle il retravaille ses silhouettes « au rasoir » avec des smokings en cuir brutalement perforés, reçoit un accueil sans réserve. En février 2002, la première boutique Dior Homme ouvre à Milan et en avril, le CFDA le consacre « Designer of the Year ». Parallèlement à son activité de créateur, Slimane a également présenté une installation à la 62ᵉ Pitti Immagine Uomo Fair de Florence, accompagnée d'un livre de photographies, « Transmission ». Aujourd'hui, Slimane continue de jouer un rôle central au sein de la mode contemporaine en redéfinissant la forme et l'importance de la mode pour homme. « J'aimerais que les hommes évoluent vers quelque chose de plus sophistiqué, de plus séduisant, pour explorer un type de masculinité entièrement nouveau », explique Slimane.

"I'd like men to think about evolving into something more sophisticated, more seductive. To explore the possibility of an entirely new kind of masculinity"

PORTRAIT BY WOLFGANG TILLMANS

HEDI SLIMANE

PHOTOGRAPHY BY KAYT JONES. STYLING BY GIANNIE COUJI. OCTOBER 2001.

"I'm not interested in the cosmetic effect of fashion"

What are your signature designs? I was always interested by this archaic dichotomy between daywear and eveningwear. It translates into a codified and ritualistic wardrobe **What's your favourite piece from any of your collections?** Not any particular clothes. I usually remember a character and a moment **How would you describe your work?** Arhythmic **What's your ultimate goal?** Enjoy **What inspires you?** Watching people interacting. Interfering as little as possible **Can fashion still have a political ambition?** I don't think it ever had. It has always been more of a social catalyser. Isn't political a little presumptuous for fashion? You can be subversive but political is a little bit of a joke, maybe **Who do you have in mind when you design?** No one. I think about movement. Just like when they test resistance on new aircraft **Is the idea of creative collaboration important to you?** Not really. I like to work mostly in isolation. I collaborate on satellite projects **What has been the greatest influence on your career?** Doing my degree at Saint Laurent, when Saint Laurent was still Saint Laurent **How have your own experiences affected your work as a designer?** It is still a little early to know. I think for many years you just do things, you produce; eventually it makes sense with the distance. I think we tend to be too impatient and fast with appreciation and judgement **Which is more important in your work: the process or the product?** The process I suppose, but it only makes sense if it translates into a product. In the early '20s, modernity was built on repetition, and access. Already the process before, or for the product **Is designing difficult for you and, if so, what drives you to continue?** Don't need any driver. I feel very fortunate to design. There are more painful things, I think **Have you ever been influenced or moved by the reaction to your designs?** You just pursue an idea, and if it is clear enough and you are focused, you tend to forget any reaction **What's your definition of beauty?** I don't have one. It has to evolve anyway **What's your philosophy?** Move on, don't look back **What is the most important lesson you've learned?** It is not that simple, things are never the way they appear

Paul Smith's rise to the position of Britain's most financially successful fashion designer began as a gofer in a clothing warehouse. But he didn't stay there long. In 1970, Smith (born 1946) opened a store in his native Nottingham, selling designer wear and his own early, unbranded designs – all the stuff he wanted for himself but was unable to find. It soon became a serious proposition: Smith studied fashion at evening classes in Nottingham Polytechnic and extended his range with the assistance of his wife, Pauline Denyer, a Royal College of Art fashion graduate. By 1974 the shop became a full-time business. And Smith had stepped on the escalator to the top: just two years later, he showed his first full menswear collection in Paris. Smith may be noted for his revival of boxer shorts and the Filofax in the early 1980s, but it is the very accessibility of his essentially traditional clothes that are their appeal – English eccentricity made in the best, if sometimes unexpected, fabrics. He has also been instrumental in introducing menswear to bold, often irreverent prints. Indeed, London-based Smith is as much witty retailer as designer. His first London shop, an updated gentleman's club, opened in 1979; his first international outposts following in New York in 1987 and Paris in 1993. He now has over 200 shops in Japan. It's hardly surprising that this selffinanced business – covering everything from womenswear (1994) to childrenswear and most recently furniture, and for which the luxury goods conglomerates have made tempting offers – now turns over some £233m. Paul Smith has been given innumerable awards: in 1991 he scooped the prestigious Royal British Designer for Industry award, was made a CBE in 1994 and then knighted in 2001.

Paul Smiths Aufstieg zu einem der kommerziell erfolgreichsten Modedesigner Großbritanniens begann mit einem Job als Laufbursche in einem Lagerhaus für Textilien. Dort blieb Smith, Jahrgang 1946, jedoch nicht lange. 1970 eröffnete er einen eigenen Laden in seiner Heimatstadt Nottingham. Er verkaufte zunächst Designermode und erste eigene, noch namenlose Entwürfe – lauter Kleidungsstücke, die er selbst suchte, aber nirgends bekommen konnte. Daraus entwickelte sich bald ein ernsthaftes Projekt: Smith studierte am Polytechnikum von Nottingham in Abendkursen Mode und erweiterte sein Sortiment mit Hilfe seiner Frau Pauline Denyer, einer Absolventin des Royal College of Art im Fach Mode. 1974 war der Laden ein Fulltimejob, und Smith hatte sozusagen die Rolltreppe nach ganz oben betreten. Nur zwei Jahre später präsentierte er seine erste komplette Herrenkollektion in Paris. Smith mag für das Revival von Boxershorts und Filofax in den frühen 1980er Jahren bekannt sein, doch ist es eher die bloße Verfügbarkeit seiner im Grunde genommen traditionellen Mode, die ihren Reiz ausmacht – englische Exzentrik aus besten, manchmal ungewöhnlichen Stoffen. Er war auch Vorreiter, was kräftige, oft respektlose Muster in der Herrenmode betraf. Genau genommen ist der heute in London lebende Smith als Verkäufer ebenso genial wie als Designer. Seinen ersten Londoner Laden eröffnete er 1979 in einem ehemaligen Herrenclub; die ersten internationalen Standorte folgten 1987 in New York und 1993 in Paris. Inzwischen betreibt Smith unter anderem über 200 Läden in Japan. Wenn man bedenkt, dass mit dem inzwischen kompletten Angebot von Damenmode (seit 1994) über Kinderkleidung bis hin zu Möbeln pro Jahr etwa 233 Millionen Pfund umgesetzt werden, überrascht es kaum, dass dieses Unternehmen immer wieder verlockende Angebote von den Luxusgüter-Konzernen bekommt. Paul Smith selbst hat im Laufe der Zeit unzählige Auszeichnungen erhalten, beispielsweise 1991 den angesehenen Royal British Designer for Industry Award. 1994 wurde er Commander of the Order of the British Empire und 2001 sogar geadelt.

Avant d'incarner le plus grande réussite financière de Grande-Bretagne dans le domaine de la mode, Paul Smith a démarré son ascension dans un entrepôt de vêtements pour lequel il travaillait comme coursier, un poste qu'il n'a pas occupé bien longtemps. En 1970, Paul Smith (né en 1946) ouvre une boutique dans sa ville natale de Nottingham, vendant des pièces de créateurs aux côtés de ses premiers modèles sans marque, tous ceux qu'il avait envie de porter mais ne trouvait nulle part. Son intérêt pour le vêtement se développe petit à petit: Smith étudie la mode aux cours du soir de l'école polytechnique de Nottingham et élargit la palette de ses talents, secondé par sa femme Pauline Denyer, diplômée en mode du Royal College of Art. En 1974, la boutique l'occupe à temps plein et Smith semble avoir posé un pied sur l'escalator du succès: à peine deux ans plus tard, il présente sa première collection complète pour homme à Paris. Au début des années 1980, Smith se fait remarquer pour les boxer shorts et le Filofax qu'il remet au goût du jour, mais c'est surtout la grande accessibilité de ses vêtements, traditionnels pour l'essentiel, qui fait leur attrait: l'excentricité anglaise taillée dans les plus beaux tissus, parfois inattendus. Il a également joué un rôle décisif en introduisant des imprimés audacieux et souvent irrévérencieux dans la mode pour homme. Une fois installé à Londres, le créateur s'avère également un homme d'affaires avisé. Sa première boutique londonienne, dans le style «club pour gentlemen», ouvre ses portes en 1979, suivie par des avant-postes internationaux à New York en 1987 et Paris en 1993. Il possède aujourd'hui plus de 200 boutiques au Japon. Il n'est donc pas surprenant que cette affaire autofinancée, convoitée par les grands groupes de luxe comme le prouvent de nombreuses offres de rachat très tentantes, qui s'étend de la mode féminine (1994) aux vêtements pour enfants en passant par une récente ligne de mobilier, enregistre aujourd'hui un chiffre d'affaires de près de 233 millions de livres sterling. Par ailleurs, Paul Smith a reçu un nombre incalculable de prix: en 1991, on lui remet la prestigieuse distinction de Royal British Designer pour services rendus à l'industrie de la mode. En1994, il est fait Commandeur de l'Empire Britannique, puis Chevalier en 2001.

"The thing I'm most interested in is continuity. I've always worked hard at not being today's flavour"

PORTRAIT BY IDESU OHAYO

PAUL SMITH

PHOTOGRAPHY BY ... STYLING BY ... SLEAFORD. JANUARY/FEBRUARY 2000

PHOTOGRAPHY AND STYLING BY REBECCA LEWIS, MARCH 2001

"I never think about design.
Ideas seem to come naturally"

What are your signature designs? Tradition mixed with the unexpected **What's your favourite piece from any of your collections?** I have no favourite piece, but the simplicity of my suits mixed with the eccentricity of special linings I like very much **How would you describe your work?** Curious **What's your ultimate goal?** Keeping things simple and having a business with a heart **What inspires you?** Observation and thinking **Can fashion still have a political ambition?** In my case, no **Who do you have in mind when you design?** People who want to show their own character **Is the idea of creative collaboration important to you?** A creative collaboration should be inspiring – if it is, then it is important **Who has been the greatest influence on your career?** My father and my wife **How have your own experiences affected your work as a designer?** They go hand in hand **Which is more important in your work: the process or the product?** Personally the process, but the product pays my wages **Is designing difficult for you and, if so, what drives you to continue?** I never think about design, the ideas seem to come naturally **Have you ever been influenced or moved by the reaction to your designs?** As my designs are not radical, this has never come to mind **What's your definition of beauty?** Something that is natural and not forced **What's your philosophy?** Making clothes for people from everyday walks of life **What is the most important lesson you've learned?** Always give yourself time to answer important requests

San Francisco-based designer Wynn Smith (born 1967) constantly betrays his fondness for the well-bred American brat gone decidedly wrong: a Wasp with a sting in the tail is the very model of the Wink girl. Launched in the spring of 1997 and shown in New York ever since, a complicated cross-section of American youth culture is frequently cited in his Wink label – the Manson family, student uprisings, hippies, preppies, grunge, even the Amish get the occasional nod. But it is the society gal gone bad who is ever-present; from Sunny von Bülow to Patty Hearst, at least one is chosen as a 'heroine' for each collection. But it wasn't always this way. Before Wink, Smith actually dressed the well-heeled in his couture-like Wynn line (started in 1995 but discontinued with the advent of Wink) and while catering for private clients in San Francisco. He had previously learned his trade working with Geoffrey Beene in New York in 1987, later studying privately with a tailor in Paris from 1989-90. Furthermore, he was brought up in Arkansas by his ultra lady-like grandmother, Evelyn Smith, who thought it improper for women to wear trousers. In fact, with rigorous attention to cut and detail and homages to designers such as Courrèges, Kawakubo and Armani, there is a wit and elegance to the Wink collections which owe as much of a debt to the history of fashion as they do to the history of social unrest.

Der in San Francisco lebende, 1967 geborene Designer Wynn Smith hat keine Vorliebe für wohlerzogene amerikanische Mädchen aus gutem Hause: Das eigentliche Vorbild des Wink-Girls ist eine widerspenstige Wasp (White Anglosaxon Protestant). Mit seinem 1997 gegründeten und seither in New York präsentierten Label zeigt der Designer immer wieder amerikanische Jugendkultur im Querschnitt – die Manson-Family, Studentenunruhen, Hippies, Preppies, Grunge, selbst die Amish People kommen hin und wieder vor. Omnipräsent sind jedoch die bösen Mädchen der besseren Gesellschaft, von Sunny von Bülow bis Patty Hearst. Mindestens eine von ihnen ist 'Heldin' jeder Kollektion. Doch das war nicht immer so. Vor Wink belieferte Smith von 1995 bis 1997 tatsächlich die Gutbetuchten mit seiner Couture-Linie Wynn und arbeitete außerdem für Privatkunden in San Francisco. Sein Handwerk hat der Designer 1987 bei Geoffrey Beene in New York und danach in den Jahren 1989 und 1990 im Rahmen einer Privatausbildung bei einem Pariser Schneider gelernt. Nicht zuletzt wurde Smith von seiner extrem damenhaften Großmutter, Evelyn Smith, geprägt, die ihn als Jungen in Arkansas aufzog und es beispielsweise unpassend fand, dass Frauen Hosen trugen. Die Kollektionen von Wink zeichnen sich durch große Sorgfalt hinsichtlich des Schnittes und der Details aus, zugleich kann man sie als Hommage an Designer wie Courrèges, Kawakubo und Armani interpretieren. Mit ihrem Esprit und ihrer Eleganz spiegeln sie Modegeschichte wie auch die gesellschaftliche Unruhe früherer und heutiger Zeiten wider.

Né en 1967, le designer Wynn Smith de San Francisco trahit constamment sa prédilection pour la pétasse américaine de bonne famille qui a mal tourné : la wasp déchue est le modèle même de la fille Wink. Depuis son lancement au printemps 1997, sa griffe Wink est présentée chaque année à New York, incarnant un échantillon complexe de la culture des jeunes Américains : clins d'œil occasionnels à la famille Manson, aux révoltes étudiantes, aux hippies, aux preppies, au grunge, et même à la communauté Amish. Mais c'est toujours la fille jet-set un peu trash qui fait office de fil conducteur ; de Sunny von Bülow à Patty Hearst, il choisit au moins une « héroïne » pour chacune de ses collections. Pourtant, ça n'a pas toujours été le cas. En fait, avant Wink, Smith habillait les riches avec les vêtements couture de sa ligne Wynn (lancée en 1995 mais interrompue lors de la création de Wink), tout en dessinant pour ses clients privés de San Francisco. Wynn Smith apprend le métier dès 1987 en travaillant avec Geoffrey Beene à New York, avant de devenir l'élève d'un tailleur parisien entre 1989 et 1990. Par ailleurs, il a grandi en Arkansas, élevé par une grand-mère très « lady » dans l'âme, Evelyn Smith, qui s'offusquait de voir des femmes porter le pantalon. En fait, grâce à l'attention rigoureuse qu'il porte à la coupe et aux détails, à des hommages aux couturiers tels que Courrèges, Rei Kawakubo et Armani, les collections Wink révèlent beaucoup d'esprit et d'intelligence, qui doivent tant à l'histoire de la mode qu'à celle du désordre social.

"The reaction to my work has left me insulted and elated"

PORTRAIT BY JAN-WILLEM DIKKERS

WYNN SMITH

What are your signature designs? Classics: the tailored coat and blazer, the T-shirt, the nightgown, jeans and trousers How would you describe your work? Contrasts: the sissy and the tomboy, the rare with the humble, the cool and the uncool What's your ultimate goal? To buy a '64 Mustang What inspires you? Humour, elitism, perversion Can fashion still have a political ambition? Not to me Who do you have in mind when you design? A detached blonde Is the idea of creative collaboration important to you? Extremely What has been the greatest influence on your career? Halloween and my great-grandmother, Gertrude Pilkington How have your own experiences affected your work as a designer? Growing up in Oklahoma. Going to military school. Training in Paris. Working for Geoffrey Beene. Living in San Francisco… Do the math Which is more important in your work: the process or the product? The product Is designing difficult for you and, if so, what drives you to continue? Yes. Simple, I love to make clothes Have you ever been influenced or moved by the reaction to your designs? Yes, both insulted and elated What's your definition of beauty? Brooke Shields at age 14 What's your philosophy? Sex is gross What is the most important lesson you've learned? The past does not equal the future

PHOTOGRAPHY BY RAINER HOSCH, STYLING BY KARL PLEWKA. JANUARY/FEBRUARY 1998

Stephen Sprouse, often referred to as one of the few designers with true rock spirit, does indeed walk it like he talks it. With money earned from selling the first two dresses from his debut collection, he bought an electric guitar. Although his music teacher soon gave up hope of ever teaching Sprouse to play, the anecdote speaks volumes about the freewheeling way he likes to operate. Born in Columbus, Indiana in 1953, Sprouse spent his high school years mimicking his art heroes Frank Stella and Andy Warhol. At the age of 17, he moved to New York and worked as Halston's assistant for two years, befriending Steven Meisel and Debbie Harry (for whom he would go on to design outfits when she became the lead singer of pop group Blondie). In 1984, he showed his first collection at the New York Ritz. Fusing the best elements of punk, Pop Art and 1960s fashion, his day-glo and sequinned dresses and graffiti-sprayed T-shirts went down a storm, but his business folded due to financial problems. In 1987 he returned, opening a three-storey NYC shop selling clothes, jewellery and his own line in make-up. From this period stems his seminal 'Hardcore' 1988 collection, which scrambled American flags, hardcore logos and mod-style tailoring. Following another financial setback, Sprouse ventured into the art world with the paintings he had been doing all along, some of them featuring icons like Jim Morrison or Iggy Pop. In 1995, he served as the fashion curator of the Rock 'n' Roll Hall of Fame and Museum in Cleveland, Ohio. In 1996, the Andy Warhol Foundation gave Sprouse exclusive rights to the entire catalogue of Warhol's images for use in his men's and womenswear. Invited by his friend and admirer Marc Jacobs, Sprouse customised the Spring-Summer 2001 Louis Vuitton handbag range with his typical graffiti-style handwriting.

Stephen Sprouse, der oft zu den wenigen Designern mit echtem Rockerethos gezählt wird, lebt tatsächlich so, wie er sich gibt. Mit dem Geld aus dem Verkauf der ersten zwei Kleider seiner Debütkollektion erstand er eine E-Gitarre. Und auch wenn sein Musiklehrer bald die Hoffnung aufgab, Sprouse jemals das Spielen darauf beibringen zu können, spricht diese Anekdote Bände über das sorglose Wesen dieses Designers. Der 1953 in Columbus, Indiana, geborene Sprouse verbrachte seine Highschool-Zeit damit, seine Künstleridole Frank Stella und Andy Warhol zu imitieren. Im Alter von 17 Jahren ging er nach New York und arbeitete zwei Jahre lang als Assistent bei Halston, wo er sich mit Steven Meisel und Debbie Harry anfreundete. (Für Letztere sollte er später Bühnenoutfits designen, nachdem sie Leadsängerin der Popband Blondie geworden war.) 1984 präsentierte Sprouse seine erste Kollektion im New Yorker Ritz. Die Verschmelzung der besten Elemente von Punk, Pop und 60er-Jahre-Mode, die Kleider in fluoreszierenden Neontönen und mit Paillettenbesatz sowie die T-Shirts mit aufgesprayten Graffiti schlugen zwar wie eine Bombe ein, doch aufgrund finanzieller Probleme machte die Firma trotzdem Pleite. 1987 meldete Sprouse sich zurück und eröffnete in New York einen Laden über drei Etagen, in dem er Kleidung, Schmuck und seine eigene Make-up-Linie verkaufte. Aus dieser Phase stammt auch seine folgenreiche Kollektion 'Hardcore' von 1988, in der er amerikanische Flaggen, Hardcore-Logos und Mode im Mod-Style wild durcheinander mixte. Nach einem weiteren finanziellen Rückschlag machte Sprouse, der nebenher immer auch gemalt hatte, mit Bildern von Ikonen wie Jim Morrison und Iggy Pop einen Abstecher in die Kunst. 1995 wirkte er als Mode-Kurator für die Rock 'n' Roll Hall of Fame and Museum in Cleveland, Ohio. Im folgenden Jahr überließ ihm die Andy Warhol Foundation exklusiv die Rechte an allen Bildern des Künstlers zu deren Verwendung in seiner Herren- und Damenmode. Auf Einladung seines Freundes und Bewunderers Marc Jacobs versah Sprouse die Handtaschenkollektion von Louis Vuitton für Frühjahr/Sommer 2001 mit seiner typischen Handschrift im Graffiti-Stil.

Souvent considéré comme l'un des rares créateurs à l'esprit rock, Stephen Sprouse fait toujours ce qu'il dit. Avec l'argent que lui rapporte la vente des deux premières robes de la collection de ses débuts, il achète une guitare électrique. Bien que son professeur de musique abandonne rapidement tout espoir de lui apprendre un jour à jouer, l'anecdote en dit beaucoup sur l'indépendance avec laquelle opère Sprouse. Né en 1953 à Columbus dans l'Indiana, il passe ses années de lycée à imiter ses héros Frank Stella et Andy Warhol. A 17 ans, il s'installe à New York et travaille comme assistant de Halston pendant deux ans avant de devenir l'ami de Steven Meisel et Debbie Harry (qu'il continuera à habiller quand elle deviendra chanteuse du groupe Blondie). En 1984, il présente sa première collection au Ritz de New York. Mêlant les meilleurs éléments du punk, du Pop Art et de la mode des années 1960, ses robes fluo et pailletées et ses T-shirts tagués remportent un succès incroyable, mais à la suite de difficultés financières, il est contraint au dépôt de bilan. En 1987, Sprouse fait son grand retour en ouvrant à New York une boutique de trois étages dans laquelle il vend des vêtements, des bijoux et sa propre ligne de maquillage. Cette période lui inspire sa collection « Hardcore » de 1988, qui fait date avec son mélange de drapeaux américains, de logos hardcore et de coupes Mod. Après un autre revers de fortune, Sprouse se lance dans le monde de l'art avec des toiles de son cru, certaines à l'effigie de Jim Morrison ou d'Iggy Pop. En 1995, le Rock 'n' Roll Hall Of Fame and Museum de Cleveland dans l'Ohio le nomme conservateur de l'exposition de vêtements. En 1996, la Fondation Andy Warhol lui cède les droits exclusifs de toutes les images de Warhol pour qu'il puisse les utiliser sur ses vêtements masculins et féminins. Sur l'invitation de son ami et admirateur Marc Jacobs, Sprouse a customisé la gamme Printemps-Eté 2001 de sacs à main Louis Vuitton avec son écriture graffiti si typique.

"My ultimate goal is to design clothes for the first Mars settlers"

PORTRAIT BY RAINER HOSCH

STEPHEN SPROUSE

What are your signature designs? Day glo and graffiti in the '80s, techno and velcro in the '90s, space and 3D in the '00s **What's your favourite piece from any of your collections?** The Satellite dress with metal rings from the '90s **How would you describe your work?** Colourful or black **What's your ultimate goal?** To design clothes and rooms for the first Mars settlers **What inspires you?** Music, technology and space **Can fashion still have a political ambition?** Not unless people start making free clothes **Who do you have in mind when you design?** Human collaboration as much as creative collaboration **Who or what has been the greatest influence on your career?** Andy Warhol, Eero Saarinen, Bernini, Italian sculpture **Which is more important in your work: the process or the product?** Both **What's your definition of beauty?** Outward and inward – and if you've got both, that's pretty good **What is the most important lesson you've learned?** To never give up?

Lawrence Steele was born in Hampton, Virginia. After graduating with first class honours in fine art from the School of the Art Institute in Chicago, Steele spent several months in Tokyo as a design assistant. His big break came in the mid-1980s when he moved to Milan, working with Franco Moschino for the next five years. In 1990 Steele joined Prada, assisting with womenswear design at a pivotal time when the family leatherwear business was becoming one of the world's most influential fashion houses. Steele left in 1994 to launch his own label in Milan, armed with years of invaluable experience. His signature style, a commercial fusion of American attitude and European chic, quickly won the designer a loyal following. Steele is known for simple, sensuous, feminine clothing in luxurious and technically advanced materials, designed with a vision that is both sexy and elegant. Steele has numerous celebrity clients; in 2000 he designed the dress actress Jennifer Aniston wore for her wedding to Brad Pitt. In 2001, Steele collaborated with artist Vanessa Beecroft in Genoa for her performance 'VB48'. As well as the women's main line, Lawrence Steele now also incorporates a knitwear collection and Lawrence Steele Design. Launched in 1999, Design is based around the idea of sportswear but remains every bit as luxurious and precise as everything else that Steele touches.

Lawrence Steele stammt aus Hampton, Virginia. Nachdem er das School of the Art Institute in Chicago mit Auszeichnung absolviert hatte, ging er für einige Monate als Design-Assistent nach Tokio. Den großen Durchbruch erlebte Steele Mitte der 1980er Jahre, als er nach Mailand kam, um fünf Jahre lang mit Franco Moschino zu arbeiten. 1990 wechselte er zu Prada, wo er als Assistent im Bereich Damenmode ausgerechnet in der Zeit wirkte, als das Unternehmen den entscheidenden Schritt vom Familienbetrieb für Lederwaren zu einem der einflussreichsten Modehäuser der Welt machte. Ausgerüstet mit der unschätzbaren Berufserfahrung vieler Jahre verließ der Designer 1994 Prada, um in Mailand sein eigenes Label zu gründen. Der für ihn typische Stil – eine gut verkäufliche Mischung aus amerikanischem Way-of-Life und europäischem Chic – sorgte rasch für eine treue Gefolgschaft. Steele ist bekannt für seine schlichten, sinnlichen, femininen Kreationen aus luxuriösen und technisch ausgefeilten Materialien. Die Vision des Designers ist sexy und elegant zugleich. Wohl auch deshalb beliefert Steele zahlreiche prominente Kunden. So entwarf er etwa 2000 Jennifer Anistons Brautkleid für ihre Hochzeit mit Brad Pitt. 2001 arbeitete er zusammen mit der Künstlerin Vanessa Beecroft in Genua an deren Performance ›VB48‹. Neben der zentralen Damenkollektion gibt es inzwischen auch eine Strickwarenkollektion sowie die Nebenlinie Lawrence Steele Design. Beim seit 1999 bestehende Design-Label handelt es sich zwar grundsätzlich um Sportswear, doch diese ist genauso luxuriös und perfekt wie alles, was Steele anfasst.

Lawrence Steele est né à Hampton en Virginie. Diplômé en beaux-arts du School of the Art Institute de Chicago avec les félicitations du jury, Steele travaille d'abord plusieurs mois à Tokyo comme assistant styliste. En fait, sa carrière décolle au milieu des années 1980 lorsqu'il s'installe à Milan pour y travailler avec Franco Moschino pendant cinq ans. En 1990, Steele rejoint Prada en tant qu'assistant styliste de la ligne féminine, au moment où l'affaire familiale de maroquinerie devient l'une des maisons de mode les plus influentes du monde. Armé d'une solide d'expérience de plusieurs années, Steele quitte Prada en 1994 pour lancer sa propre griffe à Milan. Fusion commerciale de l'attitude américaine et du chic européen, son style signature permet au créateur de gagner rapidement une clientèle fidèle. Steele est connu pour ses vêtements simples, sensuels et féminins qu'il coupe dans des matières haute technologie toujours luxueuses et conçoit à partir d'une vision à la fois sexy et élégante. Steele compte de nombreuses célébrités parmi ses clients ; en l'an 2000, il dessine la robe de mariée de l'actrice Jennifer Aniston pour son mariage avec Brad Pitt. En 2001, Steele collabore avec l'artiste Vanessa Beecroft sur sa performance génoise « VB48 ». Outre sa ligne principale pour femme, Lawrence Steele propose également une collection de pièces en maille et la ligne Lawrence Steele Design. Lancée en 1999, Design s'apparente plus au sportswear mais reste en tout point aussi luxueuse et précise que tout ce que touche Steele.

"Growing up as a Black American on military bases throughout Europe, I've always been a person that's out of context with my environment and I like to create thinking about that kind of individual, an outsider"

PORTRAIT BY HELMUT NEWTON

LAWRENCE STEELE

What are your signature designs? What I am known for is languid, curvy, very feminine clothes **What's your favourite piece from any of your collections?** Usually there's a piece from each collection that's my favourite, but something I've gone back to a lot is the glove jacket from 1996. It was a jacket that was basically made in glove leather and skin tight, so it formed to your body as you wore it **How would you describe your work?** Timeless objects of desire **What's your ultimate goal?** To continue to make beautiful clothes. Just that **What inspires you?** Body gestures. The way that women tend to be women through their movements and their gestures. How they cross their legs, how they are different from men, how they're unique creatures **Can fashion still have a political ambition?** Clothes don't really have a soul, but when they are put together in a human context they become political statements in one way or another. Then it depends on a particular time and culture for it to be a strong statement, or not **Who do you have in mind when you design?** Probably me. It's an abstract idea of woman that's in my mind **Is the idea of creative collaboration important to you?** I collaborate on every level. When I start designing, I work with pattern makers and fabric companies, and the ultimate product comes through many kinds of collaborations **How have your own experiences affected your work as a designer?** Growing up as a Black American on military bases throughout Europe, I've always been a person that's out of context with my environment and I like to create thinking about that kind of individual. Someone who is not necessarily part of a whole thing, but an outsider inside a particular context **Which is more important in your work: the process or the product?** The product. The process is whatever it takes to get a good result at the end. Obviously it needs to be fun to do; if the process was not enjoyable it would get in the way. At the end of the day, the thing that I really care about is whatever object is going to remain after the creative process, that it is outstanding or particularly right **Is designing difficult for you and, if so, what drives you to continue?** It can be. There are times when things just pop into your head and it's very easy. The thing that is difficult is creating a certain number of pieces within a certain amount of time – I tend to be very slow in my creative process. I continue to do it because it's what I love **Have you been influenced or moved by the reaction to your designs?** I can't exactly say how I am influenced. If there is a bad reaction to what I do, it hurts; if there is a good reaction to what I do, it inspires me to do more, better **What's your definition of beauty?** Good God… **What's your philosophy?** No philosophy **What is the most important lesson that you've learned?** It has something to do with being self-sufficient. Whatever my work is about, it's about me at the end of the day. I guess it's trusting your instincts

Few brands have revolutionised the clothing business like Stüssy. Redefining casualwear to create a style that encompassed high fashion, sports and workwear, Stüssy has continued to invigorate the industry while remaining close to its sandy-cheeked beach bum roots. Shawn Stüssy was a surfer who shaped his own boards for friends and locals in Laguna Beach, California. Along with the surfboards, Stüssy began to screen his graffiti tag signature logo onto tees and shorts in 1980, casualwear that soon caught on in boutiques and speciality markets. In 1986, the first Stüssy showrooms opened in New York and Los Angeles, selling pieces based around the original printed tees with smoky Rasta imagery, 1950s Americana and the odd runaway dinosaur. Stüssy slowly unfolded a style based on hip hop, skate and surf subcultures; a market previously ignored and unexplored. Building an international network of like-minded individuals who lived the lifestyle and wore the clothes, Stüssy never lost its underground appeal. It was from this bank of originals that Stüssy appointed Art Director Paul Mittleman in 1996, who now heads the brand's small design teams. Stüssy's freshness, simplicity and sense of humour has always been at odds with more traditional fashion giants, but answers a genuine need for something different. Under Mittleman's direction, Stüssy has become truly international, encompassing menswear, womenswear, footwear, eyewear, accessories and smaller indulgent projects (like toy airplanes). As the label continues to grow organically, its lasting influence has been not only to help shape the streetwear market, but to create it.

Nur wenige Marken haben bisher das Modebusiness so revolutioniert wie Stüssy. Mit der Neudefinition von Freizeitkleidung durch einen Stil, der Haute Couture, Sport- und Arbeitskleidung vereint, hat Stüssy der Textilindustrie neue Impulse gegeben und ist trotzdem den eigenen Wurzeln, d. h. den braungebrannten Strandjungs, treu geblieben. Shawn Stüssy war ein Surfer, der Boards für Freunde und Nachbarn im kalifornischen Laguna Beach baute. Außer auf die Surfboards begann Stüssy 1980 seinen Namen als Graffiti-Logo auch auf T-Shirts und Shorts zu sprayen. Schon bald war diese Casualwear in ausgewählten Geschäften zu haben. 1986 wurden die ersten Stüssy-Showrooms in New York und Los Angeles eröffnet. Dort verkaufte man Kollektionen rund um die originell bedruckten T-Shirts mit verschwommenen Rastabildern, 50er-Jahre-Americana und dem komischen flüchtenden Dinosaurier. Langsam entwickelte Stüssy einen Stil, der auf den Subkulturen von Hiphop-, Skater- und Surferszene basierte. Dieser Markt war bis dahin ignoriert worden und noch gänzlich unerschlossen. Auch wenn sich ein internationales Netzwerks aus gleichgesinnten Individualisten bildete, die den gleichen Lebensstil pflegten und die gleichen Kleider trugen, verlor Stüssy doch nie seinen Underground-Appeal. In dieser günstigen Ausgangslage ernannte Stüssy 1996 Paul Mittleman, der bis heute das kleine Designteam der Marke führt, zum Art Director. Man unterschied sich schon immer durch Unverbrauchtheit, Schlichtheit und Sinn für Humor von den traditionelleren Modegiganten und befriedigte gerade dadurch das tatsächlich vorhandene Bedürfnis nach dem etwas Anderen. Unter Mittlemans Leitung ist die Marke wirklich international geworden und stellt heute Herren- und Damenmode, Schuhe, Brillen und Accessoires her. Dazu kommen Liebhaberprojekte wie etwa Spielzeugflieger. Das organisch gewachsene Unternehmen hat den Markt für Streetwear nicht nur dauerhaft geprägt, sondern ihn bis zu einem gewissen Grad überhaupt erst erschaffen.

Peu de marques ont révolutionné le marché du vêtement comme Stüssy. En redéfinissant le casualwear pour donner vie à un style inspiré par la mode d'avant-garde, le sport et les uniformes de travail, Stüssy continue de vivifier l'industrie tout en restant fidèle à ses racines de squatteur de plages. Au début, le surfeur Shawn Stüssy commence par fabriquer des planches pour ses amis et les habitants de Laguna Beach en Californie. Outre les surfboards, Stüssy appose dès 1980 son logo signature en forme de tag sur des T-shirts et des shorts, vêtements relax qui se vendent très bien dans les boutiques et les magasins spécialisés. En 1986, les premiers showrooms Stüssy ouvrent à New York et Los Angeles et vendent des pièces qui reprennent les imprimés originaux des T-shirts : images de Rastas fumeurs, symboles américains très fifties et parfois, un dinosaure qui passe. Progressivement, Stüssy donne vie à un look inspiré par les sous-cultures du hip hop, du skate et du surf, un marché jusqu'alors ignoré et inexploré. Grâce à un réseau international d'individus qui partagent tous le même état d'esprit, le même mode de vie et portent les mêmes vêtements, Stüssy n'a jamais perdu son attrait underground. En 1996, Paul Mittleman devient directeur artistique de Stüssy et dirige désormais les petites équipes de création de la marque. La fraîcheur, la simplicité et le sens de l'humour de Stüssy ont toujours été à l'encontre des géants de la mode, mais répondent à un besoin réel de nouveauté. Sous la direction de Mittleman, Stüssy est devenue une vraie marque internationale regroupant des lignes pour homme et pour femme, des chaussures, des lunettes et des projets moins ambitieux (comme des avions-jouets). Alors que la griffe continue à évoluer de façon naturelle, son influence durable n'a pas seulement favorisé la formation du marché streetwear, elle l'a tout simplement créé.

"We have in mind the street-savvy consumer who wants more than less but not so much that it becomes too fashionable"

PORTRAIT COURTESY OF PAUL MITTLEMAN

STÜSSY

PHOTOGRAPHY BY KIRBY KOH, STYLING BY NADINE SHAW, JANUARY 2091

What are your signature designs? The reinvention of the baseball cap, the personalised and branded baseball jacket and the new and traditional use of camo **What are your favourite pieces from any of your collections?** The beach pant (circa 1983), original skull hat (1984), Ralph Cramden jacket (1987), hood coach snap shell with crown print (1989), all-over rasta print (1989), reggae dot letterman jacket (1990), gramps collection (1994) and the leather track jacket (2000) **How would you describe your work?** A simple pursuit of traditional Stüssy products that represents the Stüssy history with a view to reinventing **What inspires you?** The desire to get it right for the times **Can fashion still have a political ambition?** Fashion has no ambition but to be fashionable **Who do you have in mind when you design?** We have in mind the street-savvy consumer who wants more than less but not so much that it becomes too fashionable. We want style **Is the idea of creative collaboration important to you?** No. Unbiased ideas, yes **Who or what has been the greatest influence on your career?** There have been many who's. The what is punk from London and hip hop from New York **How have your own experiences affected your work as a designer?** Saint Martins taught me to always want to be better. Italy and Japan taught me to recognise quality. Reality taught me not to take myself too seriously. It is style that counts **What's more important in your work: the process or the product?** The product. It justifies the process **Is designing difficult for you and, if so, what drives you to continue?** Designing is not difficult. Successful designing is **Have you ever been influenced or moved by the reaction to your designs?** We've stayed limited in volume and directional because people have reacted passionately to good design **What's your definition of beauty?** Youth and confidence is beauty in fashion **What's your philosophy?** Increase the peace **What is the most important lesson you've learned?** Forget fashion. Stay real

PHOTOGRAPHY BY SERGE LEBLON, STYLING BY TAMARA CINCIK. APRIL 2001

Having Chloë Sevigny as your creative director and the Son of God as your namesake is no guarantee of success, but in the fabulous world of fashion it probably helps. Staging your debut New York show in an East Village funeral parlour is quite a canny move too. And so it goes with Imitation Of Christ, aka Tara Subkoff (born 1974) and Matt Damhave (born 1979), respectively a sometime actress and a Maryland Institute College of Art drop-out, who in the space of a few short seasons have created the kind of fashion stir many would indeed die for. Meeting outside a Champs gig in San Francisco two years ago, the pair embarked on an anti-corporate, anti-fashion, anti-cheap crusade: resurrecting old thrift store designs (through restructuring, slashing and embellishing with graffiti) to near-instantaneous acclaim ('Is this the death of fashion?' screamed an hysterical 'Fashion Wire Daily', after witnessing their morbidly-inclined NY outing). Possibly not, but still the duo have made a little reworking and a lot of philosophising ('sincerity is the new vulgarity') go incredibly far; the saintly set-up have even spawned their own copycat collective, Imitation of Imitation of Christ. Later seasons have seen them screen a short film on the perils of fame, starring Selma Blair, Reese Witherspoon and Lisa Marie, and persuade models and fashion editors to switch roles for Spring-Summer 2002. Although the pair have gone their separate ways, Subkoff will be continuing the name whilst also concentrating on her acting career; she has recently completed a TV movie with Larry Clark.

Chloë Sevigny als Creative Director und Gottes Sohn als Namenspatron sind zwar keine Garantie für Erfolg, dürften in der exzentrischen Modewelt aber wohl ein wenig helfen. Sein New Yorker Debüt in den Geschäftsräumen einer Bestattungsfirma im East Village zu geben, kann man ebenfalls gewagt nennen. Aber das alles ist typisch für Imitation of Christ, d. h. für die 1974 geborene Tara Subkoff und ihren Partner Matt Damhave, Jahrgang 1979. Die Gelegenheitsschauspielerin und der Abbrecher des Maryland Institute College of Art haben tatsächlich mit wenigen Kollektionen einen Modestil kreiert, den viele zum Sterben schön finden. Vor zwei Jahren lernten sich die beiden bei einem Gig von Champs in San Francisco kennen und begannen ihren Kreuzzug gegen Marken, etablierte Mode und Billigprodukte. Sie hauchten Second-Hand-Stücken neues Leben (durch Umnähen, Aufschlitzen und Graffiti-Dekor) ein, was sofortige Begeisterung beim Publikum hervorrief. 'Ist das der Tod der Mode?', titelte der 'Fashion Wire Daily' nach dem morbiden New Yorker Auftritt hysterisch. Wohl kaum, aber zweifellos hat das Designerduo mit wenig Umarbeiten und einer Menge eigener Philosophie ('Offenheit ist die neue Vulgarität') unheimlich viel bewegt. Das so heilig klingende Label hat sogar sein eigenes Nachahmer-Kollektiv hervorgebracht: Imitation Of Imitation Of Christ. Nach ein paar Kollektionen folgte ein Kurzfilm über die Gefahren des Ruhms mit Selma Blair, Reese Witherspoon und Lisa Marie als Akteurinnen. Für die Kollektion Frühjahr/Sommer 2002 gelang es Subkoff und Damhave, Models und Moderedakteurinnen dazu zu bringen, kurzfristig die Rollen zu tauschen. Auch wenn das Designerpaar inzwischen getrennte Wege eingeschlagen hat, wird Subkoff den Namen des Labels weiterführen. Außerdem kümmert sie sich verstärkt um ihre Karriere als Schauspielerin und drehte zuletzt einen Fernsehfilm mit Larry Clark.

Le fait d'avoir Chloë Sevigny à la direction de la création et le Fils de Dieu comme homonyme ne garantit pas nécessairement le succès, mais dans le monde merveilleux de la mode, ça aide certainement. L'idée de présenter un premier défilé new-yorkais dans un salon funéraire de l'East Village était également une bonne trouvaille. Telle est l'histoire de Imitation of Christ, c'est-à-dire Tara Subkoff (née en 1974), ancienne actrice, et de Matt Damhave (né en 1979), diplômé du Maryland Institute College of Art. En l'espace de quelques saisons, ils ont suscité le genre d'enthousiasme pour lequel de nombreux créateurs de mode seraient prêts à donner leur vie. Après une première rencontre il y a deux ans à la sortie d'un concert de Champs à San Francisco, le duo se lance dans une croisade anti-entreprise, anti-mode et anti-cheap : ils redonnent une nouvelle vie aux vieux vêtements des « thrift stores » (en les restructurant, les tailladant et les ornant de graffitis) et rencontrent un succès presque instantané (« Est-ce la mort de la mode ? », hurlait un journaliste du « Fashion Wire Daily » après avoir assisté à leurs morbides débuts new-yorkais). Sans doute pas, mais toujours est-il que ces deux-là ont chamboulé pas mal de choses avec une philosophie qui voit loin (« la sincérité est la vulgarité d'aujourd'hui ») ; le duo sacré a même inspiré ses propres imitateurs, Imitation Of Imitation Of Christ. Par la suite, ils ont tourné un court métrage sur les dangers de la notoriété avec Selma Blair, Reese Witherspoon et Lisa Marie. Ils ont même réussi à persuader mannequins et rédacteurs de mode d'échanger les rôles pour la saison Printemps-Eté 2002. Bien que les membres du duo aient emprunté des voies différentes, Tara Subkoff perpétuera le nom tout en se concentrant sur sa carrière d'actrice ; elle a terminé le tournage d'un téléfilm avec Larry Clark.

"I am not a designer"

PORTRAIT BY MATT JONES

TARA SUBKOFF

What are your signature designs? I'm not a designer **What's your favourite piece from any of your collections?** I don't have one **How would you describe your work?** Indescribable **What's your ultimate goal?** Top secret **What inspires you?** Can't tell, it's a secret **Can fashion still have a political ambition?** I feel the only political ambition fashion can have is within fashion. By paying attention to where and how garments are made, and if they are exploiting workers or destroying the environment by using chemicals or dyeing processes that are unnecessary. The fashion community should take responsibility for what they are doing. I don't want to hear about another designer who 'didn't know' that the factory licensed out to make their underwear is one of the worst sweatshops with 14 or 15-year-old girls making $.03 an hour, working off a $10,000 recruiting fee they owe in order to get their 'fantastic job' in 'America'. Meanwhile that same 'designer' is raising money to cure the rainforest or paediatric AIDS. Not that these charities aren't important, but clean up your own backyard first **Is the idea of creative collaboration important to you?** Yes. Very **Who has been the greatest influence on your career?** Stephen Baldwin **Which is more important in your work: the process or the product?** They should be equally important **What's your definition of beauty?** Probably what other people find unattractive **What's your philosophy?** It's been talked about to death but always changing **What is the most important lesson you've learned?** It's a tie: 'Don't do it for money'. Or: 'Shut up and make nice. No-one really cares what you think'

Anna Sui was born in a small suburb of Detroit Rock City in 1955. As other children played with their dolls, Sui would wryly style hers, clipping outfits from fashion magazines while listening endlessly to rock music. A celebration of popular culture, love of music and an ability to connect creatively with the past is the key characteristic of her work today. Re-animating a more decadently remembered Woodstock, her exploration of romanticism, femininity and nostalgia is peppered with the shameless spirit of rock 'n' roll. Winning a scholarship to the Parsons School of Design, Sui moved to New York City at the age of 17 where she met photographer Steven Meisel, who would go on to become a close friend and collaborator. After graduating, Sui worked her way through a steady stream of sportswear design positions. A small signature line was introduced at the Boutique Show in 1980, immediately bought by Macy's and produced from Sui's apartment for the next ten years. After an acclaimed runway show in 1991, she opened her first boutique in New York, winning the CFDA Perry Ellis award for New Fashion Talent in 1993. Designing for both men and women, further boutiques opened in Tokyo, Osaka and Los Angeles, while Sui also launched a shoe collection plus ranges of cosmetics, eyewear, bags, jewellery, jeans and two best-selling fragrances. With a sly eye for vintage perfection, Sui remains serious about fashion, yet not overly serious about herself. A mature and respected designer, her work is infused with energy, bringing together a playful innocence with its defiant, incongruous opposite.

Anna Sui wurde 1955 in einem kleinen Vorort von Detroit geboren. Während andere Mädchen mit ihren Puppen einfach spielten, stylte Anna ihre auf eigenwillige Weise mit Outfits, die sie aus Modemagazinen ausschnitt; dazu hörte sie permanent Rockmusik. Ihre Begeisterung für die Popkultur, die Liebe zur Musik und die Fähigkeit, Vergangenes kreativ zu nutzen, prägen heute die Arbeit der Designerin. Neu belebte dekadente Erinnerungen an Woodstock, Versatzstücke aus Romantik, Weiblichkeit und Nostalgie kombiniert sie gnadenlos mit dem Geist des Rock 'n' Roll. Als Stipendiatin der Parsons School of Design zog Sui im Alter von 17 Jahren nach New York, wo sie den Fotografen Steven Meisel kennen lernte, der ihr ein enger Freund und kreativer Partner werden sollte. Nach Beendigung des Studiums arbeitete Sui nacheinander in mehreren Jobs im Bereich Sportswear-Design. 1980 stellte sie bei der Boutique Show eine kleine Kollektion unter ihrem eigenen Namen vor, die sofort von Macy's gekauft und in den nächsten zehn Jahren in Suis Apartment produziert wurde. Nach einer bejubelten Runway Show 1991 eröffnete die Designerin ihren ersten Laden in New York. 1993 erhielt sie von der CFDA den Perry Ellis Award for New Fashion Talent. Während sie inzwischen Damen- und Herrenmode entwarf, kamen weitere Läden in Tokio, Osaka und Los Angeles hinzu. Bis heute hat Sui außerdem eine Schuhkollektion, mehrere Kosmetiklinien, Brillen, Taschen, Schmuck, Jeans und zwei überaus erfolgreiche Parfums kreiert. Immer auf der Suche nach dem perfekten Vintage-Style, ist es der Designerin mit der Mode nach wie vor ernst. Nicht allzu ernst nimmt sie dagegen sich selbst. Auch als arrivierte und respektierte Modeschöpferin ist sie mit großem Elan bei der Sache und kombiniert verspielte Unschuld mit ihrem trotzigen, ungehörigen Gegenteil.

Anna Sui est née en 1955 dans une petite banlieue de Detroit, la « ville du rock ». Alors que les autres petites filles jouent à la poupée, Anna Sui habille la sienne avec une ironie désabusée et découpe les photos des magazines de mode en écoutant sans relâche ses disques de rock. Aujourd'hui, son travail célèbre la culture populaire et l'amour de la musique tout en faisant revivre le passé de façon créative. Ressuscitant un Woodstock plus décadent que ce qu'en ont gardé les mémoires, son exploration du romantisme, de la féminité et de la nostalgie est épicée d'une touche rock 'n' roll éhontée. Lauréate d'une bourse à la Parsons School of Design, Anna Sui s'installe à New York à l'âge de 17 ans. Elle y rencontre le photographe Steven Meisel, qui deviendra son ami et collaborateur. Une fois diplômée, Anna Sui poursuit son chemin, occupant divers postes de styliste dans le sportswear. En 1980, elle présente au Boutique Show une petite ligne originale immédiatement achetée par Macy's et qu'elle produira dans son appartement pendant dix ans. Après un défilé très remarqué en 1991, elle ouvre sa première boutique à New York. En 1993, elle remporte le prix Perry Ellis décerné aux nouveaux talents par le CFDA. Dessinant pour les hommes et les femmes, elle ouvre d'autres boutiques à Tokio, Osaka et Los Angeles. Elle lance une collection de chaussures, des produits cosmétiques, des lunettes, des sacs, des bijoux, des jeans ainsi que deux parfums à succès. Avec son sens aiguisé de la perfection « vintage », Anna Sui envisage la mode sérieusement sans jamais se prendre elle-même au sérieux. Créatrice mature et respectée, son travail plein d'énergie se distingue par son innocence ludique et son sens incongru de la provocation.

"I'm past the stage of being rebellious"

PORTRAIT BY GREG KADEL

ANNA SUI

What are your signature designs? When people think of my clothes they think romantic and feminine with a lot of embellishment. I love folkloric and vintage so there's all those elements thrown in. Then there's always rock 'n' roll… **How would you describe your work?** My favourite thing is discovering something, absorbing it and then putting it into my collection and showing it off to everybody. People who come to my fashion shows kinda go to a rock concert as I like to take them on a journey, an escapist journey. It's a fantasy, something that they are going to have fun with **What's your ultimate goal?** This is it! I like making beautiful clothes. I'm the ultimate consumer so there's nothing better than to be able to do products I love, plus cosmetics and perfumes **What inspires you?** I'm fortunate that everything I'm interested in I can use in my work. I'm just happy that there's some new rock bands around. Rock was at an all-time low a couple of years ago and suddenly there's a resurgence of rock-type bands. I've been listening to The Hives and I like that kind of music when people are playing instruments **Can fashion still have a political ambition?** I imagine it could – but that's not my intention. Perhaps I'm past the stage of being rebellious. It is possible to be really rebellious with fashion but usually it's a younger person who feels they need to make their statement that way. It's not an issue that I aspire to **Who do you have in mind when you design?** Again, there's always the selfish me… **Who has been the greatest influence on your career?** My parents. I think I got my creative and artistic side from my mother, and the practical and logical side from my father. If I didn't have that combination I wouldn't be able to do what I'm doing **How have your own experiences affected your work as a designer?** I can use all the things that I experience in my work. Particular things like the Tibet Freedom concert that inspired my 'Tibet Surfer' collection. Also, my travel has certainly been reflected in all of my work. I think the great thing about what I do is that whatever I've experienced somehow comes out in the work **Which is more important in your work: the process or the product?** I learned a long time ago that designing is a process which doesn't come overnight – you have to develop it to get the end result that you want. The more you develop your craft, the more the product becomes the ideal product and the thing that you were aiming for **Is designing difficult for you and, if so, what drives you to continue?** It's difficult and you are never happy. But that's part of the creative process **Have you ever been influenced or moved by the reaction to your designs?** The biggest compliment I've ever had is when a man who didn't really even know that much about fashion came up to me and said, 'You know, my wife looks her most beautiful when she wears a dress she bought from you eight years ago.' That really means something because it's heartfelt. An old dress that makes her feel happy every time she wears it… I mean, what more could you ask for? **What's your definition of beauty?** There are so many levels of beauty. There's the ideal beauty, but that's not always the most attractive thing. I think there's beauty in almost everything, if you look at it in a certain way **What's your philosophy?** Live your dream **What is the most important lesson you've learned?** That the world is a much bigger place than just fashion

Jun Takahashi, the creative force behind cult label Undercover, was born in Kiryu, Japan, in 1969. His first foray into fashion came in 1988 while he was still studying at Bunka Fashion College: Takahashi and his friend Nigo, now producer of the A Bathing Ape label, started a T-shirt label called Nowhere, an important stepping stone for both designers. After graduating in 1991, Takahashi went on to establish Undercover in 1994; the label now incorporates womenswear, for which it is best known, a concise menswear collection and some items of childrenswear. Undercover is a household name in Japan, with 17 stores throughout the country. Takahashi's is an elaborate look that whisks up a frenetic energy: his heavily layered, wearable silhouettes have an eclectic mix and match feel due to the free use of graphic print-work, pattern, colour and his excellent eye for proportion. Takahashi was personally invited by Rei Kawakubo to not only collaborate with her on a joint capsule collection, but to open a new Under Cover store as part of the 10 Corso Como Comme des Garçons shopping destination in Tokyo. Confirming Takahashi's credentials as a master of his particular craft, it has also attracted the eyes of the Western world to the talents of this young designer.

Jun Takahashi ist die kreative Kraft des Kultlabels Undercover. 1969 im japanischen Kiryu geboren, unternahm er 1988 noch während seines Studiums am Bunka Fashion College den ersten Ausflug ins Modegeschäft: Zusammen mit seinem Freund Nigo, der heute das Label A Bathing Ape betreibt, begann er eine T-Shirt-Produktion unter dem Namen Nowhere. Rückblickend erwies sich diese Unternehmung für beide Designer als Meilenstein. 1991 beendete Takahashi sein Studium, 1994 gründete er Undercover. Das Label umfasst heute Damenmode – für die es am bekanntesten ist – sowie eine kleine Herrenkollektion und einige Kindersachen. In Japan, wo es im ganzen Land 17 gleichnamige Läden gibt, ist Undercover allgemein bekannt. Der typische Takahashi-Look ist kunstvoll und strahlt eine ungeheure Energie aus. Seine tragbaren Silhouetten aus mehreren Lagen Stoff sind eine eklektische Mischung, aber dennoch vielseitig kombinierbar. Das verdanken sie der uneingeschränkten Verwendung von grafischen Drucken, Mustern, Farben und dem exzellenten Blick ihres Schöpfers für Proportionen. Takahashi wurde von Rei Kawakubo nicht nur persönlich eingeladen, mit ihr eine gemeinsame Kollektion zu entwerfen, sondern auch aufgefordert, einen neuen Undercover-Laden im Megastore 10 Corso Como von Comme des Garçons in Tokio zu eröffnen. Dieser weitere Beweis für Takahashis berechtigten Ruf als Meister seines Faches hat auch die Aufmerksamkeit der westlichen Welt auf diesen jungen japanischen Designer gelenkt.

Jun Takahashi, force créative de la griffe culte Undercover, est né en 1969 à Kiryu au Japon. En 1988, il fait une première incursion dans le monde de la mode alors qu'il est encore étudiant au Bunka Fashion College : Takahashi et son ami Nigo, aujourd'hui producteur de la griffe A Bathing Ape, lancent une marque de T-shirts baptisée Nowhere, pierre d'angle de la carrière des deux designers. Une fois diplômé en 1991, Takahashi poursuit son chemin et crée Undercover en 1994 ; la griffe propose aujourd'hui une collection pour femme qui lui a valu sa notoriété, ainsi qu'une courte collection pour homme et quelques vêtements pour enfant. Undercover est un nom que tout le monde connaît au Japon, avec ses 17 boutiques disséminées à travers tout le pays. Le look élaboré de Takahashi est secoué d'une énergie frénétique : ses silhouettes très portables et chargées de superpositions présentent un style éclectique qui repose sur la libre utilisation des imprimés graphiques, des motifs et de la couleur, ainsi que sur un œil aigu en terme de proportions. Takahashi a été convié par Rei Kawakubo en personne à collaborer avec elle sur une mini-collection, mais également à ouvrir un nouveau point de vente Undercover dans le cadre du magasin 10 Corso Como de Comme des Garçons à Tokyo. Ce geste de reconnaissance a confirmé la réputation de Takahashi et son art particulier, tout comme il a attiré l'attention de l'Occident sur les talents du jeune créateur.

"My philosophy is anarchy and peace"

PORTRAIT COURTESY OF JUN TAKAHASHI

JUN TAKAHASHI

What are your signature designs? Between 'mode' and street. Destructive What is your favourite piece from any of your collections? Spring-Summer 1999, 'Relief' What's your ultimate goal? Death What inspires you? Broken things Can fashion still have a political ambition? Yes Who do you have in mind when you design? Nobody in particular Is the idea of creative collaboration important to you? Sometimes important Who or what has been the greatest influence on your career? Rei Kawakubo. Punk rock Which is more important in your work: the process or the product? The product Is designing difficult for you? For the present, no Have you ever been influenced or moved by the reaction to your designs? No What's your definition of beauty? The opposite to beauty What's your philosophy? Anarchy and peace What is the most important lesson you've learned? Punk spirit

Naoki Takizawa (born Tokyo, 1960) is not an instantly recognisable name in the world of fashion. This is not because he is on the fringes or his designs unfamiliar. In fact, quite the opposite is true. Designer of both Issey Miyake menswear (since 1993) and womenswear (since 1999), Takizawa is one of the most important Japanese designers working today. Graduating from Kuwasawa Design Institute in 1982, he immediately joined the Miyake Design Studio. Initially he worked as designer of the newly formed Plantation line, a range that used natural fibres, focusing particularly on loose comfort and affordability. The Miyake Design Studio is renowned as a workplace for developing talent, but it also serves as a research base and, over the last ten years, Takizawa has been instrumental in the development of fabric and manufacturing techniques through new technologies. It is this, combined with the social function of clothing present in Miyake's early work, which currently defines his collections. His catwalk shows, both menswear and womenswear, are often theatrical affairs that attempt to explore the relationship between civilisation and clothes. Like many of his Japanese counterparts, Takizawa shies away from rigid tailoring and brings a gentle fluidity to both his men's and womenswear, conscious of the space between garment and wearer, something Miyake himself explored extensively. Aside from mixing colour and tone in his work, Takizawa has previously presented pieces influenced by sportswear and workwear. Through the appointment of Takizawa, Issey Miyake (who now devotes his time to the A-POC collection) has reinforced the Japanese desire for evolution and ensured that an inquisitive mind is still in charge of his eponymous label.

Der Name des 1960 in Tokio geborenen Designers Naoki Takizawa ist in der Modewelt nicht sonderlich geläufig. Das liegt jedoch keineswegs daran, dass er sich fernab vom Zentrum des Geschehens befände oder seine Kreationen zu unbekannt wären. Tatsächlich ist genau das Gegenteil der Fall. Als Designer der Herrenmode (seit 1993) und der Damenmode (seit 1999) bei Issey Miyake kann man Takizawa sicher mit Fug und Recht einen der bedeutendsten derzeit aktiven Designer Japans nennen. Nach seinem Abschluss am Kuwasawa Design Institute 1982 arbeitete er sofort für das Miyake Design Studio. Anfangs entwarf er für die neu gegründete Linie Plantation; bei dieser Kollektion aus Naturfasern legt man besonderen Wert auf Bequemlichkeit und verhältnismäßig moderate Preise. Das Miyake Design Studio ist als Talentschmiede bekannt, fungiert aber auch als Forschungszentrum. Und so war Takizawa in den letzten zehn Jahren entscheidend an der Entwicklung von Stoffen und neuen Verarbeitungsmethoden durch moderne Technologien beteiligt. Dies, aber auch die soziale Funktion von Kleidung, die in Miyakes Frühwerk besonders deutlich wird, bestimmen derzeit Takizawas Kollektionen. Seine Modenschauen sowohl für die Herren- wie für die Damenmode sind oft aufwändige Inszenierungen, mit denen der Designer das Verhältnis von Zivilisation und Kleidung genauer beleuchten will. Wie so viele seiner japanischen Kollegen schreckt auch Takizawa vor strengen Schnitten zurück und lässt seine Entwürfe für beide Geschlechter lieber weich fließen. Dabei scheint er sich der Distanz zwischen Kleidung und ihrem Träger, mit der sich ja auch Miyake intensiv auseinander setzte, sehr bewusst zu sein. Abgesehen von den Farben und Tönen, die er in seinen Kreationen mischt, hat Takizawa auch schon Stücke präsentiert, die sichtlich von Sport- und Arbeitskleidung inspiriert waren. Durch die Wahl Takizawas zu seinem Nachfolger hat Issey Miyake, der sich inzwischen ausschließlich der A-POC-Kollektion widmet, einerseits den japanischen Wunsch nach Weiterentwicklung erfüllt und andererseits sichergestellt, dass sich weiterhin ein aufgeschlossener Geist um das Label mit seinem Namen kümmert.

Naoki Takizawa (né en 1960 à Tokyo) n'est pas un nom qui fait tout de suite « tilt » dans le petit monde de la mode. Pourtant, ce couturier n'est pas en marge et ses créations ne sont pas inconnues. En fait, c'est exactement le contraire. Styliste pour la ligne homme (depuis 1993) et femme (depuis 1999) d'Issey Miyake, Takizawa est l'un des créateurs japonais les plus importants actuellement en exercice. Diplômé du Kuwasawa Design Institute en 1982, il commence immédiatement à travailler pour le Miyake Design Studio. Au départ, il dessine pour la nouvelle ligne Plantation, qui utilise des fibres naturelles et se concentre sur le confort et l'accessibilité. Connu comme lieu de formation des nouveaux talents, le Miyake Design Studio sert également de base de recherche et, ces dix dernières années, Takizawa a joué un rôle essentiel dans le développement de tissus et de techniques de production en tirant parti des nouvelles technologies. Cette curiosité, combinée à la fonction sociale du vêtement, un thème récurrent dans les premières pièces de Miyake, définit actuellement ses collections. Ses défilés pour homme et pour femme sont souvent mis en scène de façon théâtrale pour tenter d'explorer la relation entre mode et civilisation. Comme beaucoup de ses homologues japonais, Takizawa se départit d'une mode trop rigide et apporte douceur et fluidité à ses créations pour homme et pour femme, conscient de l'espace existant entre le vêtement et celui qui le porte, une idée que Miyake a lui-même largement explorée. Outre le mélange de couleurs et de tons qui caractérise son travail, Takizawa a également présenté des pièces inspirées du sportswear et des uniformes de travail. En engageant Takizawa, Issey Miyake (qui consacre désormais tout son temps à sa collection A-POC) a prouvé le désir d'évolution des Japonais et placé un esprit très curieux à la tête de sa griffe éponyme.

"I want to reach and touch people through my own expression"

PORTRAIT COURTESY OF NAOKI TAKIZAWA

NAOKI TAKIZAWA

VIDEO STILLS BY TERRY JONES. AUTUMN-WINTER 2001

What are your signature designs? The innovation in the process of making clothes **What's your favourite piece from any of your collections?** An unfinished piece which has so much possibility **How would you describe your work?** A new world of imagination **What's your ultimate goal?** To reach and touch people through my own expression **What inspires you?** Reality **Who do you have in mind when you design?** Imagined beauty **Is the idea of creative collaboration important to you?** Yes **Who has been the greatest influence on your career?** Issey Miyake **How have your own experiences affected your work as a designer?** Having a sense of value which is continually nurtured **Which is more important in your work: the process or the product?** The innovative process keeps me going **Is designing difficult for you and, if so, what drives you to continue?** Overflowing imagination **Have you ever been influenced or moved by the reaction to your designs?** Always **What's your definition of beauty?** Fear **What's your philosophy?** To always try and touch the five senses **What is the most important lesson you've learned?** To evolve

Rossella Tarabini's career is an object lesson in how the Italian tradition of family business can be highly creative as well as financially successful. Tarabini is Blumarine designer Anna Molinari's eldest daughter and Chief Designer of the collection named after her mother. A resolutely directional line, Anna Molinari is often inspired by vintage clothes and eccentric personalities. Tarabini succeeds in making reference to the Blumarine tradition of romantic decoration while also achieving a subtle 'destroyed' effect in her fabrics, which are often hand-dyed, bleached or deliberately weathered. Tarabini was born in Carpi, Italy, in 1968. When she was nine years old, her mother and her father, Gianpaolo Tarabini, founded the Blumarine label; there were early signs that the young Rossella had inherited her parents' talent when she chose to study arts at Modena's Liceo Linguistico, followed by Bologna University. After a stay in London, Tarabini returned to Italy in 1994, joining the family company as an assistant to the Blumarine art director. The following year, aged just 26, she finally achieved independent status, designing a new collection, Anna Molinari. Far from being a second or diffusion line, Anna Molinari has developed an eclectic, experimental character distinct from her mother's Blumarine label. Tarabini cites the personal stories that she invents for each collection as the thread that runs through her work. A glamorous heroine or an exotic location could inspire tomboy blazers or extravagant chiffon dresses, but whatever the season's story, Tarabini always has an acute sense of what pretty young things will want to wear.

Rossella Tarabinis Karriere ist ein Paradebeispiel dafür, dass das Festhalten an der italienischen Tradition des Familienbetriebs sich sowohl in kreativer als auch in finanzieller Hinsicht lohnen kann. Tarabini ist die älteste Tochter der Blumarine-Designerin Anna Molinari und Chefdesignerin der Kollektion, die den Namen ihrer Mutter trägt. Für deren klar ausgerichtete Linie ließ sich Anna Molinari oft von Vintage-Kleidern und exzentrischen Persönlichkeiten inspirieren. Als ihre Nachfolgerin besinnt sich Tarabini auf das traditionell romantische Dekor von Blumarine und erzielt gleichzeitig einen subtil gebrochenen Effekt mit Stoffen, die oft handgefärbt, gebleicht oder absichtlich 'verwittert' sind. Als die 1968 in Carpi geborene Rossella neun Jahre alt war, gründeten ihre Mutter und ihr Vater, Gianpaolo Tarabini, das Label Blumarine. Erste Anzeichen dafür, dass sie das Talent ihrer Eltern geerbt hatte, war ihre Entscheidung, an der Universität von Bologna Kunst zu studieren. Nach einem Studienaufenthalt in London kehrte sie 1994 nach Italien zurück und trat als Assistentin der Art Direction von Blumarine in das Familienunternehmen ein. Nur ein Jahr später, mit gerade 26 Jahren, genoss sie bereits totale Unabhängigkeit und entwarf die neue Kollektion mit dem Label Anna Molinari. Und dieses Label mit ganz eigenem eklektisch-experimentellem Charakter ist alles andere als nur eine Nebenlinie von Blumarine. Da sind diese ganz persönlichen Geschichten, die Tarabini quasi als roten Faden, der sich durch ihre Arbeit zieht, für jede Kollektion erfindet. Eine glamouröse Heldin oder eine exotische Location inspirieren sie zu Blazern für wilde Mädchen oder extravaganten Chiffonkleidchen. Aber wie die Geschichte auch ausgehen mag, Tarabini hat immer ein feines Gespür dafür, was hübsche junge Frauen in der nächsten Saison wohl anziehen wollen.

La carrière de Rossella Tarabini prouve que la tradition italienne des entreprises familiales permet d'atteindre des sommets de créativité tout en étant très rentable. Fille aînée d'Anna Molinari, la styliste de Blumarine, Rossella est directrice de la création pour la collection qui porte le nom de sa mère. La griffe Anna Molinari s'inspire souvent des vêtements «vintage» et des personnalités excentriques, thèmes récurrents dans les collections. Rossella réussit à intégrer les décorations romantiques de la tradition Blumarine tout en donnant un effet subtilement «destroy» à ses tissus, souvent teints à la main, blanchis ou délibérément vieillis. Rossella Tarabini est née en 1968 à Carpi en Italie. Elle a neuf ans lorsque sa mère et son père, Gianpaolo Tarabini, fondent la griffe Blumarine ; très vite, la jeune Rossella s'avère la digne héritière de ses parents et décide d'étudier l'art à l'Université de Bologne. Après avoir séjourné quelque temps à Londres, elle revient en Italie en 1994 pour rejoindre l'entreprise familiale en tant qu'assistante du directeur artistique de Blumarine. L'année suivante, à peine âgée de 26 ans, elle prend plus d'indépendance en dessinant la nouvelle collection baptisée Anna Molinari. Loin d'être une ligne secondaire ou de «diffusion», Anna Molinari se démarque de la griffe Blumarine par son style éclectique et expérimental. Pour chaque collection, Rossella dit s'inventer des histoires qui lui servent de fil conducteur dans son travail. Une héroïne glamour ou un lieu exotique peuvent inspirer des blazers très garçon manqué ou des robes extravagantes en mousseline de soie, mais quelle que soit l'histoire de la saison, Rossella Tarabini a toujours un sens très aigu de ce que les jeunes filles auront envie de porter.

"I don't like 'precise' and 'polished' – I find confusion much more interesting"

PORTRAIT COURTESY OF ROSSELLA TARABINI

ROSSELLA TARABINI

What are your signature designs? I really like dresses and shirts, so I would say those **What are your favourite pieces from any of your collections?** Some of the shirts I did in the last two collections, and from Autumn-Winter 2002, the super-long bias dress **How would you describe your work?** I believe in the power of contradiction: I think that from unfinished thinking, new energy can spark off. I don't like 'precise' and 'polished' – I find confusion much more interesting **What's your ultimate goal?** Try to dress all the people I like and admire **What inspires you?** Beautiful details **Who do you have in mind when you design?** Usually I start to build my fairytales, then I think what the character of the story would wear. It is not somebody real, it is somebody totally invented **Who has been the greatest influence on your career?** All the people who taught me something in an emotional way **How have your own experiences affected your work as a designer?** I think that all my personal experiences affect my work and am now convinced that people can see how I feel from the catwalk collection. Catwalk never lies **Which is more important in your work: the process or the product?** For me, the process is very difficult and important. I always need to find a story, a detail that links everything in my mind. If I don't find it, I honestly do not have a good product! **What's your definition of beauty?** Imperfections and contradictions can be so beautiful and charming **What is the most important lesson you've learned?** I have learned always to be honest with myself, to trust all the people I admire and never to think that the world is against me, it is just presumptuous

Certain designers, such as Atsuro Tayama (born in Kumamoto in 1955), shun the glare of fashion celebrity, instead forging fresh ideas away from the spotlight. Throughout the past three decades he has made his creative presence felt, quietly and persistently. Having graduated from the Bunka Fashion College, Tokyo, in 1975, shortly after winning the Pierre Cardin Fashion Prize, Tayama has designed for labels as diverse as Yohji Yamamoto (where he was Director of European Operations from 1978–82), for French house Cacharel in the early 1990s, and for his eponymous and AT Collection lines. In addition, he is director of brands such as INDIVI, OZOC and the Japanese menswear label Boycott. Tayama's finely-tuned sense of elegance – always underscored by comfort – has ensured his clothes are coveted by modern women. A deft way with fabric is one of his signatures: rayon and polyester that look like soft silk, or domestic blankets reworked into luxurious frocks. Paris-based Tayama is also noted for his skill at cutting seemingly complex, wrapped-and-ruched dresses, prompting one journalist to brand him 'fashion's Mr Twister'.

Manche Designer, wie auch der 1955 in Kumamoto geborene Atsuro Tayama, halten sich vom Rummel um die Fashion-Prominenz bewusst fern. Sie entwickeln neue Ideen lieber abseits vom Rampenlicht. Tayama hat in den vergangenen drei Jahrzehnten ruhig, aber beharrlich seine kreative Präsenz spüren lassen. 1975 absolvierte er das Bunka Fashion College in Tokio, gewann den Prix Pierre Cardin und entwarf anschließend für so unterschiedliche Label wie Yohji Yamamoto (wo er 1978–82 außerdem Director of European Operations war), in den frühen 1990er Jahren für das Haus Cacharel sowie für die nach ihm benannte Linie und die AT Collection. Inzwischen ist der Designer außerdem Chef der Marken INDIVI, OZOC und des japanischen Herrenmode-Labels Boycott. Tayamas hoch entwickeltes Gespür für Eleganz – ohne jegliche Einschränkung in punkto Bequemlichkeit – hat dafür gesorgt, dass moderne Frauen seine Entwürfe lieben. Der geschickte Einsatz unterschiedlichster Stoffe ist eines seiner Markenzeichen: Rayon und Polyester, die wie schmeichelnde Seide aussehen, oder luxuriöse Jacken aus umgearbeiteten schlichten Wolldecken. Geschätzt wird der in Paris lebende Tayama auch für seine meisterhaft geschnittenen, scheinbar komplizierten Wickel-und-Rüschen-Kleider, für die ihm eine Modejournalistin den Spitznamen 'Fashion's Mister Twister' verlieh.

Comme Atsuro Tayama (né en 1955 à Kumamoto), certains créateurs fuient les feux de la rampe, préférant travailler dans l'ombre pour trouver de nouvelles idées. Depuis trente ans, Atsuro Tayama fait sentir sa présence créative, tranquillement mais avec obstination. Diplômé du Bunka Fashion College de Tokyo en 1975, peu de temps après avoir remporté le Prix Pierre Cardin, Tayama commence à dessiner pour des griffes aussi variées que Yohji Yamamoto (où il est directeur des opérations européennes de 1978 à 1982), la maison Cacharel au début des années 1990, ainsi que pour ses propres lignes Atsuro Tayama et AT Collection. Par ailleurs, il dirige des marques telles qu'INDIVI, OZOC et la griffe japonaise pour homme Boycott. Le sens aiguisé de l'élégance qui distingue Tayama, toujours allié à un grand confort, garantit le succès de ses collections auprès des femmes d'aujourd'hui. Son habileté dans le maniement des tissus est également l'une de ses signatures : entre ses mains, la rayonne et le polyester prennent l'apparence de la soie et les couvertures de lit sont retravaillées pour se transformer en robes luxueuses. Aujourd'hui installé à Paris, Tayama est également réputé pour son talent dans la coupe de robes aux superpositions et ruchés apparemment complexes, ce qui a d'ailleurs amené un journaliste à le qualifier de « Fashion's Mr Twister ».

"I'm a clergyman who creates fashion"

PORTRAIT BY DUC LIAO

ATSURO TAYAMA

What are your signature designs? It's about mixing or combining. Combining feminine and masculine, East with West (that's because I'm Japanese), natural and artificial, beauty and destruction **What are your favourite pieces from any of your collections?** Incomplete jackets and dresses, which I continue making or completing **How would you describe your work?** A clergyman who creates fashion **What is your ultimate goal?** I don't have goals. It's all a process. For me, a finished line is yet another beginning **What inspires you?** A mixture of all feelings, such as confidence and anxiety **Can fashion still have a political ambition?** It depends on each designer. I do not place political ambition on my design **Who do you have in mind when you design?** I only think about clothing **Is the idea of creative collaboration important to you?** Yes. Collaboration is important and necessary. I collaborate with my staff **What has been the greatest influence on your career?** My first collection in Paris **How have your own experiences affected your work as a designer?** All my experiences affect my work. Connecting with people as well as solitude, sad as well as happy experiences **Is designing difficult for you and, if so, what drives you to continue?** Designing brings me joy. Nevertheless, it is difficult to maintain the environment where I can continue to design **Have you ever been influenced or moved by the reaction to your designs?** I have been influenced by the reactions to each of my collections **What's your definition of beauty?** Les belles choses ont une âme **What's your philosophy?** Continuation is everything **What is the most important lesson you've learned?** I've learned that I can destroy a dress beautifully

He lives in a 19th century brothel in Brussels, owns the head of a stuffed giraffe and makes macabre clothes riddled with sexual and religious connotations – but designer Olivier Theyskens is not as dark as he seems. He cries at 'ET', is David Attenborough's number one fan and would rather stay at home cooking than go out to some celeb-packed party. Theyskens fans include Smashing Pumpkins' Melissa Auf der Maur, who has catwalked for him, but the Belgian first made headline news when Madonna sent a personally faxed request on his 21st birthday. Born in Brussels in 1977, Theyskens dropped out of the city's Ecole Nationale Supérieure des Arts Visuels de la Cambre in January 1997 but presented his debut collection, 'Gloomy Trips', that August. Six months later, Madonna wore one of the dresses to the Oscars and a star was born. Theyskens' Gothic image was engendered on the catwalk: clothes were embroidered with real hair or decorated with dead skulls and stuffed birds, while his signature voluminous dresses, scarred with hook fasteners, made models look like beautiful Victorian governesses. And yet, for all his dramatic show-pieces, he knows he needs to sell. For Spring-Summer 2002 Theyskens followed with more romantic feats of construction, while for Autumn-Winter 2002 he spurned Paris Fashion Week in order to restructure his studio. Constantly discussed as a candidate for a big house, this is one designer who is not for turning, having famously declined Givenchy in order to concentrate on his own company. He continues to sell to 59 shops around the world.

Er lebt in einem ehemaligen Bordell aus dem 19. Jahrhundert in Brüssel, besitzt den ausgestopften Kopf einer Giraffe und macht makabre Mode voller sexueller und religiöser Anspielungen. Trotzdem ist der Designer Olivier Theyskens gar kein so düsterer Mensch, wie es vielleicht auf den ersten Blick scheint. Er weint bei 'E.T.', ist der größte Bewunderer von David Attenborough und bleibt lieber zu Hause, um zu kochen, als auf irgendeine Promi-Party zu gehen. Zu Theyskens' Fans gehört unter anderem Melissa Auf der Maur. Die ehemalige Bassistin der Smashing Pumpkins hat für den Designer auch schon bei Schauen gemodelt. In die Schlagzeilen kam der Belgier jedoch erstmals, als Madonna ihm an seinem 21. Geburtstag höchstpersönlich eine Bestellung faxte. Der 1977 in Brüssel geborene Theyskens brach zwar im Januar 1997 sein Studium an der Ecole Nationale Supérieure des Arts Visuels de la Cambre in seiner Heimatstadt ab, präsentierte jedoch schon im August desselben Jahres seine Debütkollektion 'Gloomy Trips'. Sechs Monate später trug Madonna eines dieser Kleider zur Oscar-Verleihung und machte dessen Designer damit über Nacht zum Star. Theyskens' Image als Gothic-Fan entstand auf dem Catwalk: durch Stoffe, die mit echten Haaren bestickt waren, Totenköpfe und ausgestopfte Vögel als Dekoration. Gleichzeitig ließen seine typisch voluminösen, mit zahllosen Häkchen versehenen Kleider die Models wie wunderschöne viktorianische Gouvernanten aussehen. Doch trotz all dieser theatralischen Schaustücke weiß der Jungdesigner, dass er auch etwas verkaufen muss. Deshalb legte er für Frühjahr/Sommer 2002 eher romantische Schnitte vor. Die Pariser Modewoche für Herbst/Winter 2002 ließ er jedoch aus, um sein Atelier neu zu strukturieren. Theyskens wird zwar permanent als ein Kandidat großer Modehäuser gehandelt, ist aber einfach nicht der Typ, der von seinem selbst vorgezeichneten Weg abweicht. So erregte es großes Aufsehen, als er ein Angebot von Givenchy ausschlug, um sich auf seine eigene Firma zu konzentrieren. Zur Zeit verkauft er seine Kreationen an 59 Läden in aller Welt.

Certes, Olivier Theyskens vit dans un bordel bruxellois du XIXᵉ siècle, possède une tête de girafe empaillée et crée des vêtements macabres aux connotations sexuelles et religieuses évidentes; et pourtant, ce créateur n'est pas aussi sombre qu'il y paraît. En larmes devant « E. T. » et fan numéro un de David Attenborough, il préfère rester chez lui et faire la cuisine plutôt que de courir les soirées people. Theyskens compte des fans célèbres, tels que Melissa Auf der Maur du groupe Smashing Pumpkins qui a défilé pour lui. Le Belge a même fait la une des journaux lorsque Madonna lui a faxé une commande le jour de son 21ᵉ anniversaire. Né à Bruxelles en 1977, Theyskens sort diplômé de l'Ecole Nationale Supérieure des Arts Visuels de la Cambre en janvier 1997 et présente sa première collection, « Gloomy Trips », dès le mois d'août suivant. Six mois plus tard, Madonna porte l'une de ses robes à la cérémonie des Oscars : une étoile est née. L'image gothique de Theyskens trouve son origine sur les podiums de ses défilés : il présente des vêtements brodés de vrais poils ou décorés de crânes et d'oiseaux empaillés, tandis que ses robes volumineuses si caractéristiques, déformées par des crochets, donnent aux mannequins un air de gouvernantes de l'ère victorienne. Pourtant, outre les tenues très théâtrales de ses défilés, Olivier Theyskens sait qu'il a besoin de vendre. Pour le Printemps-Eté 2002, il produit avec succès des constructions plus romantiques, tandis qu'à la saison Automne-Hiver 2002, il dédaigne la Semaine de la Mode de Paris pour se consacrer à la restructuration de son atelier. Souvent considéré comme un candidat idéal par les grandes maisons, ce créateur-là n'est pas du genre à s'écarter de son chemin, comme l'a prouvé son célèbre refus de travailler pour Givenchy, déclarant qu'il préférait se consacrer entièrement à sa propre entreprise. Aujourd'hui, ses collections sont vendues dans 59 boutiques à travers le monde.

"I like to imagine being in the skin of women"

PORTRAIT BY WILLY VANDERPERRE

OLIVIER THEYSKENS

PHOTOGRAPHY BY ANETTE AURELL, STYLING BY TAL BRENER. DECEMBER/JANUARY 2002

What are your signature designs? I'm looking towards a sort of balance. My character is quite logical and mathematical, and in the construction of my collections sometimes I find a logic – of balance, of creativity and a love for fashion. I don't actually know what my signature piece would be. I think rather it's a whole, a spirit **What are your favourite pieces from any of your collections?** The ones that make the girls more beautiful. My favourite one season can be a pair of trousers; the next time it can be a skirt or a dress. I never like the same things. The important thing is the impact at that precise moment **How would you describe your work?** I have to be disciplined but I also have to consider letting myself go, allowing myself to take risks in innovation or creativity. My role is not totally artistic. You have to be really practical and you also have to be a little bit anarchic **What's your ultimate goal?** I want to grow. Sometimes I think I also want to prove myself. But I love what I do, it gives me happiness, so my goal really is emotional **What inspires you?** I like to imagine being in the skin of women. In fact, the clothing sometimes doesn't express the real subject of the collection. Sometimes it's more a feeling – one of desperation or, at other times one of happiness. Behind the look and attitude, it's like something cinematic **Who do you have in mind when you design?** I give a lot of my time to rethinking the woman and her body, because I love the body. Sometimes it's more skinny, sometimes it's more soft, sometimes it's a more muscular body. That's always the first step **What has been the greatest influence on your career?** My childhood. Everything I saw in my childhood I think, unconsciously, I have inside me. I'm stimulated by TV, by media, by the women around me, by me. But I think childhood is very, very important **Is designing difficult for you and, if so, what drives you to continue?** What is difficult, in my case, is to put myself in the mood to design. Because when I'm good at designing, I draw very quickly, very precisely. The collections are done in just a few days. It's a situation where you are totally confident with yourself and totally okay to go in one direction and not another. That situation is difficult. Sometimes little things can break it completely: a fight with somebody, a stupid programme on TV can damage your mood. Sometimes I feel like an opera singer – very complicated! **Have you ever been influenced or moved by the reaction to your designs?** I have been disturbed sometimes **What's your definition of beauty?** It has to move me. When I see something beautiful, it brings me so much happiness that I may cry. It doesn't happen often – I'm very critical and cynical about what I see **What's your philosophy?** My philosophy is to learn and to leave bad things behind; you don't have to keep them in mind. You can learn and forget. What's interesting is to have lots of experiences, things that press you on to a higher level in your own humanity and in your own thinking. But things have to be good, not bad. And people also **What is the most important lesson you've learned?** Not to trust good-looking people! I've been innocent and naïve about the purpose of some people. I've been very naïve. I'm still naïve…

APC is a to-the-point fashion label. Not quite utility, but definitely user-friendly, it's a range that favours classic French simplicity and long-time desirability over seasonal ins and outs. Jean Touitou was born in Tunisia in 1951 and launched his 'Atelier de Production et de Création' (APC) line 36 years later in 1987. A graduate of history and linguistics from the Sorbonne in Paris, he never intended to work as a designer, becoming involved with Kenzo purely by chance in the late 1970s, later spending three years at Agnes B. But today Jean Touitou has found a recipe for fashion success and it involves olive oil. And a record label, and film and whatever else he feels like picking and choosing and working with that seems right at the time. Touitou is particularly skilled at collaboration and APC has been associated with many unexpected creative projects: in 1995 he launched a record label which has seen the likes of Sofia Coppola and Marc Jacobs make their musical debuts; in 2001, Touitou sponsored Zoe Cassavetes in a DVD-released film. Martin Margiela, Anna Sui and Martine Sitbon have all featured in the APC mail order catalogue (set up in 1993) as guest designers, while prints from Eley Kishimoto and Jessica Ogden's customisation skills have been used to give new life to old stock. APC's clothing for men and women is sold alongside music, aftershave, scented candles (and APC branded olive oil) at Touitou's three shops in Paris, four in Japan and one in London.

APC ist ein vollkommen unprätentiöses Modelabel. Die Kleidungsstücke sind nicht ausschließlich zweckmäßig, aber eindeutig sehr benutzerfreundlich. In der Kollektion dominieren klassische französische Schlichtheit und lange Tragbarkeit über saisonale In- und Out-Trends. Jean Touitou wurde 1951 in Tunesien geboren und gründete sein Label Atelier de Production et de Création, kurz: APC, im Jahr 1987. Nach einem Geschichts- und Linguistikstudium an der Pariser Sorbonne hatte er eigentlich niemals im Sinn, als Designer zu arbeiten, doch lernte er in den späten 1970er Jahren zufällig Kenzo kennen und arbeitete später drei Jahre bei Agnes B. Inzwischen hat Touitou ein Rezept für modischen Erfolg entwickelt, zu dem auch der Verkauf von Olivenöl gehört. Und ein Plattenlabel, das Filmgeschäft und womit sich zu beschäftigen und zu arbeiten er zum jeweiligen Zeitpunkt gerade Lust hat. Der Allrounder ist ein Kooperationsgenie, und so hat sich APC bislang an den ausgefallensten kreativen Projekten beteiligt: 1995 gründete Touitou ein Plattenlabel, beim dem Leute wie Sofia Coppola und Marc Jacobs ihr musikalisches Debüt gaben; 2001 sponserte der Designer einen bisher nur auf DVD erschienenen Film von Zoe Cassavetes. Modegrößen wie Martin Margiela, Anna Sui und Martine Sitbon haben bereits als Gastdesigner am Versandkatalog von APC (den es seit 1993 gibt) mitgewirkt. Mit Druckmustern von Eley Kishimoto und Jessica Ogdens Customization-Künsten wurden alte Lagerbestände aufgefrischt. Die Kollektionen von APC für Damen und Herren werden neben Musik, Aftershaves, Duftkerzen und dem hauseigenen Olivenöl in drei Touitou-Läden in Paris, vier in Japan und einem in London angeboten.

APC propose une mode qui va droit au but. Pas vraiment utilitaire mais résolument faite pour faciliter la vie de celui qui la porte, la collection APC préfère la simplicité française classique et les basiques indémodables aux va-et-vient saisonniers de la mode. Jean Touitou est né en 1951 en Tunisie. 36 ans plus tard, en 1987, il lance sa ligne Atelier de Production et de Création (APC). Diplômé de la Sorbonne en histoire et en linguistique, il n'a jamais cherché à devenir styliste. C'est donc par pur hasard qu'il se retrouve chez Kenzo à la fin des années 1970, avant de partir travailler pendant trois ans pour Agnès B. Aujourd'hui, Jean Touitou semble avoir trouvé la recette du succès : un soupçon d'huile d'olive, un label de musique, un film et tout ce qui colle à l'air du temps. Touitou excelle particulièrement dans les collaborations et APC a été associé à de nombreux projets créatifs inattendus : en 1995, il lance un label de musique et produit, entre autres, les premiers disques de Sofia Coppola et de Marc Jacobs ; en 2001, Touitou sponsorise Zoe Cassavetes dans un film sorti en DVD. Les stylistes Martin Margiela, Anna Sui et Martine Sitbon ont tous été invités à présenter leurs créations dans le catalogue de vente par correspondance d'APC (créé en 1993), tandis que les imprimés d'Eley Kishimoto et le talent de la « reine du custom » Jessica Ogden ont été utilisés pour ressusciter les pièces des collections passées. Les vêtements pour homme et pour femme d'APC sont vendus aux côtés de disques, de lotions après-rasage, de bougies parfumées (et de la fameuse huile d'olive APC) dans les trois boutiques parisiennes de Touitou, dans ses quatre boutiques au Japon, ainsi que dans sa boutique londonienne.

"What we do is not philosophy. We are only making clothes"

PORTRAIT BY TERRY JONES

JEAN TOUITOU

PHOTOGRAPHY COURTESY OF APC. AUTUMN-WINTER 2002

What are your signature designs? I am at a crossroads right now in terms of signature. Before, I thought the only dignifying signature was to be anonymous in such a way that it would make me hugely visible. Now, I am willing to let it go and show very different and mixed obsessions, but very few of them. In other words: minimalism used to be for me a lot of anonymous things. Now it's a very few maximised design items **What are your favourite pieces from any of your collections?** There have been a few mistakes over the years, but all the pieces are my favourites **How would you describe your work?** Waking up with a reason **What's your ultimate goal?** Read, build houses, build family, sail **What inspires you?** My past work and archives, some girls, some men too **Can fashion still have a political ambition?** I can't believe you're writing 'still'. Fashion has no clue of politics. It's all hype, poses, coteries, but not politics **What do you have in mind when you design?** Reaching the right proportion **Is the idea of creative collaboration important to you?** It's fundamental. I could do no work without it. It's challenging and dangerous **Who has been the greatest influence on your career?** Maybe Cristobal Balenciaga, because of the way he decided to stop. And Chuck Berry, because he refuses compromises and is still alive **Which is more important in your work: the process or the product?** Same thing to me. A wrong process can't lead to a right product. It would only be a gimmick **Is designing difficult for you and, if so, what drives you to continue?** Designing is not exactly difficult. What is difficult is to be alive. To make the house work. That is what hard work is. Because it's boring. Once this is out of the way, you kind of enjoy the difficulty of designing **Have you ever been influenced or moved by the reaction to your designs?** I've been influenced by my own reaction to my own designs. Two years ago I found out that what I was proposing was so boring, I knew I had to restart almost from scratch **What's your definition of beauty?** Sorry, I can't answer. It might be a philosopher's job. I'm into 'percepts' not concepts. It's too much for me **What's your philosophy?** I'm not a philosopher. I have no philosophy. Maybe in 25 years I will find out that I'm just cynical **What is the most important lesson you have learned?** There's no lesson I've learned that I did not know before being in fashion

Philip Treacy has caused a seismic shift in the perception of headwear as fashion wear. Along with fellow milliner Stephen Jones, he has ensured that hats are no longer eccentric ornament but a chic addition to a contemporary outfit. Born in Ahascragh, a country village in Western Ireland, in 1967, Treacy moved to Dublin to study fashion at the National College of Art and Design in 1985. There he made hats to go with the clothes he created, but millinery soon became the focal point of his concern. While on an MA course at London's Royal College of Art in 1988, he went to visit the style editor of 'Tatler', Isabella Blow, who has been his mentor ever since. At the age of 23 Philip Treacy started designing hats for Chanel. In 1993, after winning British Accessory Designer of the year twice in a row, he staged a debut catwalk show. It was a triumph and led him to open a shop in Belgravia the following year. In 1997, Treacy launched an accessories collection that was included in the V&A's 'Cutting Edge' exhibition; alongside bags, luggage and small leather goods, he now designs three own-name hat labels – Silver, Purple and Men's. Treacy collaborates with the world's finest artists and designers: he made hats for Givenchy in 1999 and collaborated with Vanessa Beecroft on an installation at the Venice Biennale in 2001. In 2000, he was invited to present the first-ever haute couture hat show in Paris. In 2002, Treacy won the Moët & Chandon fashion award and staged 'When Philip Met Isabella', a London Design Museum exhibition featuring the remarkable hats he has produced for Isabella Blow since they first met.

Philip Treacy hat für eine radikal veränderte Wahrnehmung von Kopfbedeckungen als Bestandteil der Mode gesorgt. Gemeinsam mit seinem Modistenkollegen Stephen Jones hat er bewirkt, dass Hüte nicht mehr als exzentrisches Dekor, sondern als schicke Ergänzung eines modernen Outfits gelten. Der 1967 in dem westirischen Dorf Ahascragh geborene Treacy ging 1985 nach Dublin, um am National College of Art and Design Mode zu studieren. Dort fertigte er zunächst Hüte, die zu den von ihm entworfenen Kleidern passten, doch bald rückte die Hutmacherei ganz in den Mittelpunkt seines Interesses. Während seines Magisterstudiums am Londoner Royal College of Art besuchte Treacy 1988 Isabella Blow, die Modechefin der Zeitschrift 'Tatler', die seitdem seine Mentorin ist. Mit 23 Jahren begann Treacy, Hüte für Chanel zu kreieren. Und nachdem er zweimal hintereinander British Accessory Designer of the Year geworden war, gab er 1993 sein Debüt mit einer eigenen Show auf dem Catwalk. Es war ein Triumph und ermunterte den Designer, im folgenden Jahr einen Laden in Belgravia zu eröffnen. 1997 stellte Treacy eine Accessoire-Kollektion vor, die auch in die Ausstellung 'Cutting Edge' im Londoner Victoria & Albert Museum aufgenommen wurde. Neben Taschen, Reisegepäck und kleinen Lederwaren designt er inzwischen Hüte für seine drei Labels – Silver, Purple und Men's. Dazu kommt noch die Zusammenarbeit mit den angesehensten Künstlern und Designern der Welt: 1999 entwarf er Hüte für Givenchy, 2001 schuf er zusammen mit Vanessa Beecroft eine Installation für die Biennale in Venedig. Im Jahr 2000 lud man Treacy zur ersten Haute-Couture-Schau aller Zeiten für Hüte nach Paris ein. 2002 brachte ihm den Modepreis von Moët & Chandon. Im selben Jahr inszenierte der Hutmacher auch 'When Philip Met Isabella' – eine Ausstellung im London Design Museum, die die bemerkenswerten Hüte zeigt, die er seit ihrer ersten Begegnung für Isabella Blow kreiert hat.

Philip Treacy a déclenché un véritable séisme en redonnant aux chapeaux une nouvelle place dans la mode. Aux côtés de son confrère modiste Stephen Jones, il a prouvé que le chapeau n'était plus un accessoire excentrique mais un « plus » très chic pour les tenues d'aujourd'hui. Né en 1967 à Ahascragh, petit village de l'ouest de l'Irlande, Treacy s'installe à Dublin en 1985 pour étudier la mode au National College of Art and Design. Pour accompagner les vêtements qu'il dessine, il commence à confectionner des chapeaux et cette activité devient rapidement son principal centre d'intérêt. En 1988, alors qu'il est encore étudiant au Royal College of Art de Londres, il rend visite à Isabella Blow, la styliste du magazine « Tatler », qui depuis est devenue son mentor. A 23 ans, Philip Treacy commence à dessiner des chapeaux pour Chanel. En 1993, après avoir remporté le British Accessory Designer of the Year Award deux années de suite, il présente son premier défilé : un véritable triomphe qui le conduit à ouvrir une boutique à Belgravia l'année suivante. En 1997, Treacy lance une collection d'accessoires présentée dans le cadre de l'exposition « Cutting Edge » du Victoria & Albert Museum ; outre les sacs, les bagages et les petits articles de maroquinerie, il dessine désormais des chapeaux pour trois griffes à son propre nom : Silver, Purple et Men's. Treacy travaille avec les plus grands artistes et couturiers du monde : il a créé des chapeaux pour Givenchy en 1999 et collaboré avec Vanessa Beecroft sur une installation à la Biennale de Venise en 2001. En l'an 2000, il a été convié à présenter le tout premier défilé de chapeaux haute couture à Paris. En 2002, Philip a reçu le Moët & Chandon Fashion Award et monté l'exposition « When Philip Met Isabella » au Design Museum de Londres pour présenter les magnifiques chapeaux qu'il a produits pour Isabella Blow depuis leur première rencontre.

"Making a hat is like throwing a party!"

PORTRAIT BY KEVIN DAVIES

PHILIP TREACY

What are your signature designs? Sculptural shape **What's your favourite piece from any of your collections?** My Ship hat **How would you describe your work?** An illusion **What's your ultimate goal?** To challenge people's perception of hats in the 21st century **Who inspires you?** Isabella Blow **Can fashion still have a political ambition?** Politics and fashion are a ridiculous mix **Who do you have in mind when you design?** Everybody **Is the idea of creative collaboration important to you?** Yes – when it's truly a collaboration **Who has been the greatest influence on your career?** My sister **How have your own experiences affected your work as a designer?** This is what creativity is all about **Which is more important in your work: the process or the product?** Both **Is designing difficult for you?** No **Have you ever been influenced or moved by the reaction to your designs?** Every day **What's your definition of beauty?** A hat **What's your philosophy?** The pursuit of perfection **What is the most important lesson you've learned?** Craftsmanship

Giambattista Valli is responsible for injecting a dose of cool kudos into what was one of the more conservative Parisian couture houses: Emanuel Ungaro. Established in 1965, Ungaro has had a kick up the derrière from Valli, who has catapulted it straight into the 21st century. Born in Rome in 1966, Valli attended the city's School of Art in 1980, where Cocteau's drawings, Gruau's illustrations for Dior, and Yves Saint Laurent's watercolours inspired him. After studying fashion at the European Design Institute in 1986, Valli achieved a degree in illustration at Central Saint Martins before going on to work with Capucci, Fendi (as Senior Designer for the Fendissime line) and Krizia (as Senior Designer for women's prêt-à-porter). Then, in 1996, Valli met Ungaro through a mutual friend and was appointed Head Designer for the label's prêt-à-porter and haute couture collections for two years, before becoming Artistic Director and finally Creative Director for prêt-à-porter. Valli has successfully managed to focus on the main philosophy of Ungaro – that particular French brand of femininity – and fuse it with the energy, edge and direction of a younger generation. Valli mixes Ungaro's trademark ruffles, clashing prints, chiffon dresses and slick tailoring with a post-modern ironic glamour inspired by his idols: Nan Goldin, Andy Warhol and Kurt Cobain.

Giambattista Valli bescherte Emanuel Ungaro, einem der eher konservativen Pariser Couture-Häuser, eine Menge Ansehen und sogar eine gewisse Coolness. Das 1965 gegründete Unternehmen bekam durch Valli solchen Schwung, dass es problemlos ins 21. Jahrhundert katapultiert wurde. Der 1966 in Rom geborene Valli besuchte 1980 die Kunstakademie seiner Heimatstadt, wo er sich von Cocteaus Zeichnungen, Gruaus Illustrationen für Dior und den Aquarellen Yves Saint Laurents inspirieren ließ. Nach dem Modestudium am European Design Institute 1986 machte Valli einen Abschluss in Illustration am Central Saint Martins in London, bevor er bei Capucci, Fendi (als Senior Designer für Fendissime) und Krizia (als Senior Designer für die Prêt-à-Porter-Damenkollektion) Erfahrungen sammelte. 1996 lernte er schließlich durch einen gemeinsamen Freund Ungaro kennen, der ihn für zwei Jahre zum Chefdesigner der Prêt-à-Porter-Kollektion sowie der Haute Couture machte. Danach wurde Valli zunächst Artistic Director und schließlich Creative Director des Prêt-à-Porter-Bereichs. Dabei gelang es ihm, sich erfolgreich auf die eigentliche Philosophie Ungaros zu konzentrieren – diese typisch französische Variation des Femininen – und sie mit der Energie, der Kantigkeit und anderen Strömungen einer jüngeren Generation zu vereinen. Valli mixt die für Ungaro so typischen Rüschen, kräftigen Muster, Chiffonkleider und raffinierten Schnitte mit einem postmodern-ironischen Glamour, zu dem seine eigenen Idole wie Nan Goldin, Andy Warhol und Kurt Cobain ihn inspirieren.

Giambattista Valli est l'homme qui a réussi à injecter une dose de jeunesse cool dans ce qui comptait parmi les maisons de haute couture parisiennes les plus conservatrices: Emanuel Ungaro. Fondée en 1965, la maison Ungaro a été littéralement révolutionnée par Valli, qui l'a directement catapultée dans le XXIᵉ siècle. Né à Rome en 1966, Valli entre à l'Ecole d'Art de la ville en 1980, où il est grandement inspiré par les dessins de Cocteau, les illustrations de Gruau pour Dior et les aquarelles d'Yves Saint Laurent. Après avoir étudié la mode à l'European Design Institute en 1986, Valli obtient un diplôme d'illustration de Central Saint Martins puis commence à travailler pour Capucci, Fendi (en tant que styliste senior de la ligne Fendissime) et Krizia (en tant que styliste senior du prêt-à-porter pour femme). En 1996, Valli rencontre Ungaro par le biais d'un ami commun: styliste pour les collections prêt-à-porter et haute couture pendant deux ans, il devient ensuite directeur artistique puis finalement directeur de la création pour le prêt-à-porter. Valli a réussi à préserver la philosophie d'Ungaro, c'est-à-dire cette touche de féminité à la française, tout en lui insufflant l'énergie, l'avant-gardisme et les aspirations de la nouvelle génération. Valli combine les volants, les imprimés surprenants, les robes en mousseline de soie et les coupes élégantes qui ont défini le style Ungaro à un glamour ironique et post-moderne inspiré par ses idoles: Nan Goldin, Andy Warhol et Kurt Cobain.

"It's about a woman that dedicates her beauty and femininity to her lover. In a way, it's quite voyeuristic"

PORTRAIT BY KEVIN DAVIES

GIAMBATTISTA VALLI

What are your signature designs? More than signature designs, I think I have signature fabrics, signature looks. I love to mix the old and the new. Even when something is completely new, I like it to look slightly 'distressed'. I am a perfectionist, but my idea of perfection is when something looks slightly out of place, although in fact I've done it on purpose. I am trying to break away from bourgeoisie and conquer a younger, cooler world and customer What's your favourite piece from any of your collections? The red cropped satin pants from Autumn-Winter 2001 **How would you describe your work?** Passionate. Enthusiastic. Endlessly curious. Constantly researching. Perfectionist **What's your ultimate goal?** To mark my era. That sounds pretentious, but I would love to be able to change my time **What inspires you?** Everything! I'm inspired every second of every day. I'm constantly researching and hungry for new ideas. I get my ideas from all over: The street - from Avenue Montaigne to the Marais to Moet and Sando to Portobello Road to Soho! Music - from Mary J Blige to Kylie Minogue to Kurt Cobain! Art - from Cocteau's drawings to Yves Saint Laurent's watercolours to Andy Warhol. Movies – 'Guépard' by Visconti, 'Diamonds Are A Girl's Best Friend', 'Blood & Sand', anything by Fellini. Photography - Nan Goldin's emotion. Travel – India, Japan, Marrakech **Can fashion still have a political ambition?** No. Politics is political whereas fashion should be free. As soon as politics becomes involved, fashion is polluted **Who do you have in mind when you design?** I don't have anyone in particular in mind. I am always thinking and researching. I do know that I am trying to get away from 'bourgeoisie'. I evolve with my time and adore the icons of my time. I love Jane Birkin, Gina Lollobrigida, Mary J Blige, Destiny's Child, Claudia Cardinale, Liberty Ross. **Is the idea of creative collaboration important to you?** Yes – I collaborate with Mr Ungaro and the rest of my design team. Together we make the dream become reality – it's a team effort **Who has been the greatest influence on your career?** Mr Ungaro. For his generosity, his friendship, his trust Which is more important in your work: the process or the product? The woman wearing the dress in the end! **Is designing difficult for you?** No. I can design all the time, every minute of the day, I adore it! I have so many ideas… just give me a pencil and paper! Have you ever been influenced or moved by the reaction to your designs? I guess I am moved when I see women wearing my designs, when my clothes become objects of envy and 'must haves' for women, it is always amazing. Suzy Menkes' opinion is very important to me and I am often moved when I read her reviews; she has such an understanding of fashion and respect for the designers. Even when she does not like a collection, she has a bonafide and legitimate opinion, this I respect immensely **What's your definition of beauty?** Something hidden, waiting to be discovered **What's your philosophy?** Freedom for everybody **What is the most important lesson you've learned?** To never judge people superficially. You can never change people's true natures

Belgian designer Walter Van Beirendonck (born 1955) has been photographed in a dragon suit with a frog sitting on his shaved head. He has sported the kind of mohican haircuts, big beards, tribal jewellery and extravagant goggles no other man of his impressive posture could get away with. But the most important thing is that over the last 19 years he has been designing clothes that easily eclipse these dare-all shenanigans. Incorporating strong graphics, bold messages and eye-popping colours into his often challenging designs, Van Beirendonck made it clear from the start that he was equally interested in the aesthetic, practical, sexual and sociological aspects of fashion. As part of the 'Antwerp Six', he got his breakthrough at the British Designer Show in 1987 with his own label. Between 1993 and 1999, he masterminded the W&LT (Wild & Lethal Trash) collections, culminating in theatrical multimedia fashion shows in Paris. Following this project, he re-launched his eponymous Walter Van Beirendonck collections; to this day he only sells these at his own Antwerp shop, Walter. A second line, Aestheticterrorists, founded in 1999, sells worldwide. Van Beirendonck is above all a communicator, at ease in music, art and publishing as well as fashion: 1989 saw his own comic book, 'King Kong Kooks', and in 1997 he dressed U2 for their 'Popmart' tour. 'Mutilate' (1998), a retrospective book of his career, came complete with stickers and cut-outs. In 2001, Van Beirendonck curated 'Mode 2001 Landed/Geland', the internationally acclaimed fashion project in Antwerp. Van Beirendonck also teaches fashion at the Royal Academy of Antwerp.

Es gibt ein Foto des belgischen Designers, auf dem er einen Drachenanzug trägt und ein Frosch auf seinem rasierten Kopf sitzt. Ansonsten trägt der 1955 geborene Walter Van Beirendonck Irokesenschnitt, Vollbart, Ethnoschmuck und extravagante Brillen – ein Outfit, das sich normalerweise kaum ein Mann von seiner Statur zulegen würde. Interessanter ist jedoch, dass der Exzentriker in den letzten 19 Jahren Mode kreiert hat, die diese gewagten Scherze leicht in den Schatten stellt. Indem er kräftige Muster, plakative Messages und grellste Farben in seine oft provozierenden Entwürfe integrierte, machte Van Beirendonck von Beginn an klar, dass ihn der ästhetischen, praktischen, sexuellen und soziokulturellen Aspekte von Mode gleichermaßen faszinieren. Als einer der 'Antwerp Six' erzielte er seinen Durchbruch mit dem eigenen Label 1987 auf der British Designer Show. Von 1993 bis 1999 war der Belgier der kreative Kopf hinter den Kollektionen von W&LT (Wild & Lethal Trash), die im Rahmen von theatralischen Multimedia-Modenschauen in Paris präsentiert wurden. Diesem Projekt folgte der Relaunch der Walter-Van-Beirendonck-Kollektionen. Übrigens verkauft der Designer diese bis heute exklusiv in seinem eigenen Antwerpener Laden namens Walter. Die 1999 gegründete Zweitlinie Aestheticterrorists wird hingegen weltweit vertrieben. Van Beirendonck ist ein Meister der Kommunikation und in der Musik-, Kunst- und Buchbranche ebenso zu Hause wie in der Mode: 1989 erschien sein Comic-Band 'King Kong Kooks', 1997 kleidete er U2 für die Popmart-Tour ein. Dem Buch 'Mutilate' (1998) über seine bisherige Karriere waren Aufkleber und Ausschneidebögen beigelegt. Im Jahr 2001 kümmerte sich Van Beirendonck als Kurator um das international gefeierte Antwerpener Modeprojekt 'Mode 2001 Landed/Geland'. Außerdem lehrt er Mode an der Königlichen Akademie in Antwerpen.

Le créateur belge Walter Van Beirendonck (né en 1955) a été photographié vêtu d'un costume orné d'un dragon et avec une grenouille perchée sur son crâne rasé. Il a arboré les coupes de cheveux à la Mohican, les longues barbes, les bijoux tribaux et les lunettes extravagantes qu'aucun autre homme de son impressionnante stature n'aurait jamais osé porter. Mais depuis 19 ans, il conçoit surtout des vêtements qui éclipsent aisément toutes ces supercheries. Intégrant des graphiques accrocheurs, des messages audacieux et des couleurs éclatantes à ses vêtements souvent provocateurs, Van Beirendonck fait clairement comprendre dès le départ qu'il s'intéresse autant à l'aspect esthétique, qu'à l'aspect pratique, sexuel et sociologique de la mode. En tant que membre du « Antwerp Six », il se fait connaître lors du British Designer Show de 1987 en présentant sa propre griffe. De 1993 à 1999, il supervise les collections de W&LT (Wild & Lethal Trash), collaboration qui culmine à travers des défilés multimédia spectaculaires présentés à Paris. A la suite de ce projet, il relance ses collections éponymes Walter Van Beirendonck ; à ce jour, il les vend uniquement dans sa propre boutique d'Anvers, Walter, tandis qu'Aestheticterrorists, autre ligne créée en 1999, est vendue dans le monde entier. Van Beirendonck est avant tout un homme de communication, aussi à l'aise dans la musique, l'art et l'édition que dans la mode : en 1989, il sort une bande dessinée « King Kong Kooks », et en 1997, il dessine les costumes de scène de U2 pour leur tournée « Popmart ». Le livre « Mutilate » (1998), rétrospective de sa carrière, est vendu avec des autocollants et des découpages. En 2001, Beirendonck a organisé « Mode 2001 Landed/Geland », projet de mode anversois salué dans le monde entier. Van Beirendonck enseigne également la mode à l'Académie Royale d'Anvers.

"My goal is to change the boundaries of fashion"

PORTRAIT BY TERRY JONES

WALTER VAN BEIRENDONCK

What are your signature designs? Experiments I did in every collection, designs to underline the silhouettes or statements of that particular collection **How would you describe your work?** A continuing challenge to create collections and clothes to reflect my personal vision and style independent from fashion trends and movements **What's your ultimate goal?** To change the boundaries of fashion and to achieve a personal satisfaction **What inspires you?** The world, my world, love… **Can fashion still have a political ambition?** Yes – fashion statements are still important, despite the fact that not many designers are thinking in that direction **Who do you have in mind when you design?** Nobody in particular. Gender, physique and age aren't important for my customers. It is more about being sensitive to my style, colours and forms **Is the idea of creative collaboration important to you?** Yes, very important. Most fascinating co-operations were with Stephen Jones, Bono, Mr Pearl, Mondino, Juergen Teller, Marc Newson, Paul Boudens **Who has been the greatest influence on your career?** My friend and colleague Dirk Van Saene **How have your own experiences affected your work as a designer?** I am still learning every day, but feel more mature than 20 years ago **Which is more important in your work: the process or the product?** Process and result are important. I do enjoy the process a lot **Is designing difficult for you and, if so, what drives you to continue?** I love it and despite the fact that it is a permanent (financial) struggle, I have never thought of giving it up **Have you ever been influenced or moved by the reaction to your designs?** Every reaction, good or bad, lets you think about what you are doing **What's your definition of beauty?** Rethink beauty! **What is your philosophy?** Think and dream **What is the most important lesson you've learned?** To stick to my own personality, style and ideas. A necessity in this fashion world

Dries Van Noten's culturally diverse style has made him one of the most successful of the 'Antwerp Six' designers who arrived at the London collections back in 1986. His signature scarves and saris are embroidered or beaded using the traditional folkloric techniques of India, Morocco or Eastern Europe – whichever far-flung culture has caught his attention that season. It's not only bohemian-minded women who adore Dries; the loosely layered, unstructured pieces of his menswear collections also have a loyal following. Born in Antwerp, Belgium in 1958 to a family of tailors, Van Noten enrolled at the city's Royal Academy of Fine Arts in 1977; his debut collection of men's shirts was bought by Barneys in New York and Whistles in London. He opened his own small shop in Antwerp in 1985, the larger Het Modepaleis replacing it in 1989. In 1992, he showed his menswear collection in Paris; his womenswear line followed a year later. Van Noten is perhaps the most accessible Belgian designer, but his theory of fashion is far from conventional. He prefers to design collections 'item by item', offering his clients a sense of individuality, rather than slavishly creating a collection around one silhouette. This pragmatic approach is contrasted by his constant experimentation with textiles and decorative techniques; a Dries Van Noten skirt might be dyed, embroidered, re-dyed and tailored in as many different countries. Despite his success – he now has three stores and around 500 outlets worldwide – Van Noten continues to live and work in his hometown.

Dries Van Notens von vielen Kulturen inspirierter Stil hat ihn zu einem der erfolgreichsten Designer der 'Antwerp Six' gemacht, die mit ihren Kollektionen erstmals 1986 in London für Aufsehen sorgten. Sein Markenzeichen sind mit Spitzen versehene oder perlenbestickte Schals und Saris in den traditionellen Techniken Indiens, Marokkos oder Osteuropas – je nachdem welches Land in der jeweiligen Saison seine Aufmerksamkeit besonders gefesselt hat. Und es sind nicht nur Damen mit einem Faible für die Boheme, die Dries lieben; auch die lose übereinander zu tragenden weiten Teile seiner Herrenkollektionen haben eine treue Fangemeinde. Van Noten kam 1958 als Sohn einer Schneiderfamilie in Antwerpen zur Welt, wo er 1977 sein Studium an der angesehenen Königlichen Akademie der Schönen Künste aufnahm. Die Herrenhemden seiner Debütkollektion kauften Barneys aus New York und Whistles aus London. 1985 eröffnete der Designer seinen ersten eigenen kleinen Laden in Antwerpen, 1989 zog er in das größere Het Mode-palais. Bei seiner ersten Show in Paris 1992 präsentierte er eine Herrenkollektion; sein Label für Damen folgte ein Jahr später. Obwohl Modeverständnis alles andere als konventionell ist, gelten Van Notens Modelle als die tragbarsten unter denen aller belgischen Designer. Statt sklavisch einen ganzen Look rund um eine Silhouette zu entwerfen, kreiert er seine Kollektionen lieber Stück für Stück und lässt seinen Kunden so mehr Raum für Individualität. Im Gegensatz zu dieser pragmatischen Einstellung steht seine anhaltende Lust am Experimentieren mit Materialien und dekorativen Techniken. So kann etwa ein Rock Dries Van Notens in einem Land gefärbt, in einem anderen bestickt, im dritten überfärbt und in einem weiteren schließlich genäht werden. Trotz seines Erfolgs – drei eigene Läden und rund 500 Outlets in aller Welt – lebt und arbeitet Van Noten immer noch in seiner belgischen Heimatstadt.

Parmi les jeunes créateurs du « Antwerp Six » qui ont débarqué à Londres pour les collections de 1986, Dries Van Noten, grâce à son style culturellement éclectique, est l'un de ceux qui ont rencontré le plus de succès. Selon la culture lointaine qui l'inspire pour la saison, il brode et perle ses écharpes et ses saris inimitables à l'aide de techniques traditionnelles folkloriques d'Inde, du Maroc ou d'Europe de l'Est. Les femmes à l'esprit bohème ne sont pas les seules à craquer pour Dries : les pièces non structurées aux superpositions floues de ses collections masculines ont aussi leurs fidèles. Né en 1958 à Anvers dans une famille de tailleurs, Van Noten entre à la prestigieuse Académie Royale des Beaux-Arts de la ville en 1977 ; sa première collection de chemises pour homme est achetée par Barneys à New York et Whistles à Londres. En 1985, il ouvre une petite boutique à Anvers, remplacée en 1989 par le plus imposant Het Modepaleis. En 1992, il présente sa collection pour homme à Paris, suivie d'une ligne féminine un an plus tard. Van Noten est sans doute le plus accessible des créateurs belges, mais sa théorie de la mode n'a pourtant rien de conventionnel. Pour offrir à ses clients un certain sens de l'individualité, il préfère dessiner les collections « pièce par pièce » plutôt que de concevoir servilement ses lignes autour d'une seule silhouette. Son expérimentation constante des textiles et des techniques décoratives vient contrebalancer cette approche pragmatique : une jupe Dries Van Noten peut être teinte, reteinte, brodée et coupée dans de nombreux pays différents. Malgré sa réussite – il a ouvert trois boutiques et compte près de 500 points de vente à travers le monde – Van Noten vit et travaille toujours dans sa ville natale.

"My work aims to give people the means to remain themselves, as close to their tastes as possible"

PORTRAIT BY PAUL WETHERELL

DRIES VAN NOTEN

PHOTOGRAPHY BY ELLEN NOLAN, STYLING BY THOM MURPHY. AUGUST 2002

PHOTOGRAPHY BY GUSTAVO TEN HOEVER, STYLING BY GARETH GRIFFITHS. FEBRUARY 2002

"Make the act of choosing what you wear a mark of self esteem"

What are your signature designs? A taste and a dialogue with the beautiful things of this world **What are your favourite pieces from any of your collections?** My favourites are always those that I am designing at the moment **How would you describe your work?** My work aims to give people the means to remain themselves, as close to their tastes as possible **What's your ultimate goal?** To make the act of choosing what you wear a mark of self esteem **What inspires you?** Everything that surrounds me surprises and captivates me every day **Can fashion still have a political ambition?** Fashion does not deliver any such message, even if it is inspired from time to time by current events **What do you have in mind when you design?** My dreams, wishes and tastes of the moment **What has been the greatest influence on your career?** Not really an influence, but an admiration for the Japanese designers when they first appeared in Europe **How have your own experiences affected your work as a designer?** It is difficult to make a distinction between my private and personal lives. The two are linked. My work is obviously influenced by this constant interplay **Which is more important in your work: the process or the product?** The success of the product, of course. This depends on a happy process **Is designing difficult for you and, if so, what drives you to continue?** My work thrills me. Working out difficult problems adds a little spice and avoids routine **Have you ever been influenced or moved by the reaction to your designs?** I have been stimulated by negative reactions, especially when said with frankness. These have proved that I was going in the wrong direction **What's your definition of beauty?** Beauty can only be perceived by the beholder **What's your philosophy?** Live each day as if it were your last **What is the most important lesson you've learned?** To trust yourself and not to stick needlessly to an idea in a moment of weakness

As part of the original 'Antwerp Six', Dirk Van Saene (born 1959) always set out to do his own thing, even if that meant both ignoring prevailing trends and refusing to play it safe by sticking to a signature style. This chameleon-like designer hates to be labelled – and his trajectory through fashion more than proves this headstrong attitude. After graduating from Antwerp's Royal Academy in 1981, Van Saene went against the grain by opening a small shop, Beauties And Heroes, selling his own home-made clothes. Two years later he won the gold award at Belgium's prestigious Golden Spindle contest. In 1987 he took part in the now-legendary 'Antwerp Six' presentation at the British Designer Show; three years later, he staged his first catwalk show in Paris. Ever since, Van Saene has used clever concepts to spice up his runway presentations: staging the backstage area, including the hairdresser's chairs and make-up tables, in front of the seated audience (Spring-Summer 1998), or handing out transistor radios to his models with each blaring out a different song (Spring-Summer 2000). Likewise, his designs hint at a kaleidoscopic approach: switching from deconstruction to couture-like refinement and back again, combining traditional fabrics with unusual materials like transparent latex or kitchen towels, assembling parts of different garments into a matching outfit, integrating trompe l'oeil lapels and pockets into pieces of clothing to create a 'flat' tailoring, and so on. Over the years he has also drawn inspiration from the fine arts, citing the work of Louise Bourgeois, Ellsworth Kelly and Diane Arbus as starting points for various collections. Always a great admirer of classic couture, Van Saene accepted the invitation to curate a Coco Chanel exhibition in Antwerp in 2001, part of the acclaimed fashion project 'Mode 2001 Landed/Geland'.

Als einer der echten 'Antwerp Six' war der 1959 geborene Dirk Van Saene schon immer darauf bedacht, seinem eigenen Instinkt zu folgen – selbst wenn er damit im Widerspruch zu herrschenden Trends steht und wegen fehlender Wiedererkennbarkeit seines Stils ein größeres Risiko eingeht. Dieser chamäleonhafte Designer hasst es einfach, in eine Schublade gesteckt zu werden – und seine bisherige Karriere im Modebusiness ist ein überdeutlicher Beweis für seine unverrückbare Haltung. Nach dem Abschluss seines Modestudiums an der Königlichen Akademie in Antwerpen 1981 tat Van Saene etwas völlig Unübliches und eröffnete einen kleinen Laden namens Beauties and Heroes, in dem er seine selbst genähten Sachen verkaufte. Zwei Jahre später holte er beim angesehenen belgischen Wettbewerb um die Golden Spindle Gold. 1987 war er an der inzwischen legendären Präsentation der 'Antwerp Six' im Rahmen der British Designer Show beteiligt. Drei Jahre danach fand seine erste Laufstegschau in Paris statt. Von jeher nutzt Van Saene clevere Ideen, um seine Catwalk-Präsentationen spannender zu gestalten: So holte er für die Kollektion Frühjahr/Sommer 1998 den Backstage-Bereich samt Frisierstühlen und Make-up-Tischen vor das im Saal sitzende Publikum auf die Bühne; für die Präsentation der Mode für Frühjahr/Sommer 2000 gab er jedem Model ein Transistorradio in die Hand, wobei jeder Apparat einen anderen Song spielte. Genauso kaleidoskopisch sind die Entwürfe des Designers: Er springt vom Dekonstruktivismus zu Couture-artiger Raffinesse und zurück, kombiniert traditionelle Stoffe mit ungewöhnlichen Materialien wie transparentem Latex oder Küchenhandtüchern, fügt verschiedenartigste Kleidungsstücke zu harmonischen Outfits zusammen, integriert Aufschläge und Taschen im Trompe-l'œil-Stil, um 'flache' Silhouetten zu erzielen, und so weiter. Im Laufe der Jahre hat er sich von verschiedenen bildenden Künstlern inspirieren lassen und Arbeiten von Louise Bourgeois, Ellsworth Kelly und Diane Arbus als Ausgangspunkte für verschiedene Kollektionen genutzt. Und weil er schon immer ein großer Bewunderer der klassischen Couture war, nahm Van Saene auch das Angebot an, 2001 in Antwerpen als Kurator eine Coco-Chanel-Ausstellung im Rahmen des angesehenen Projekts 'Mode 2001 Landed/Geland' zu inszenieren.

Membre original des «Antwerp Six», Dirk Van Saene (né en 1959) a toujours voulu faire cavalier seul, quitte à ignorer les tendances dominantes et à refuser de jouer la sécurité en collant à un style particulier. Véritable caméléon, ce créateur déteste les étiquettes et sa carrière dans la mode prouve bien son attitude entêtée. Diplômé de l'Académie Royale d'Anvers en 1981, Van Saene va à contre-courant en ouvrant une petite boutique, Beauties And Heroes, dans laquelle il vend des vêtements qu'il confectionne chez lui. Deux ans plus tard, il décroche l'or au prestigieux concours belge du Golden Spindle. En 1987, il participe à la présentation désormais légendaire des «Antwerp Six» au British Designer Show; trois ans plus tard, il présente son premier défilé à Paris. Depuis, Van Saene épice tous ses défilés d'idées astucieuses: par exemple, il présente les coulisses du podium, y compris les chaises de coiffeurs et les tables de maquillage, devant un public assis (Printemps-Eté 1998) ou distribue des postes de radio à ses mannequins, chacun diffusant une chanson différente (Printemps-Eté 2000). Dans le même esprit, ses créations adoptent une approche kaléidoscopique de la mode: allers-retours incessants entre déconstruction et raffinement haute couture, combinaison de tissus traditionnels et de matières inattendues telles que le latex transparent ou les torchons de cuisine, assemblages de pièces de différents vêtements qu'il transforme en tenue coordonnée, revers et poches en trompe-l'œil intégrés aux vêtements pour créer une coupe «plate», etc. Au fil des années, Van Saene s'inspirera également des beaux-arts, citant notamment les œuvres de Louise Bourgeois, d'Ellsworth Kelly et de Diane Arbus comme les points de départ de différentes collections. Admirateur fidèle de la haute couture classique, Van Saene a été invité à organiser une exposition Coco Chanel à Anvers en 2001 dans le cadre du célèbre projet «Mode 2001 Landed/Geland».

"Once in my life, I would like to be hyped!"

PORTRAIT BY ANDREW HOBBS

DIRK VAN SAENE

What are your signature designs? Spring-Summer 1998 'Transformations' collection: trenchcoats moulded and folded on corsets, transformed into dresses. Autumn-Winter 1998–99 'Fake Tailoring': all elements of tailoring (collars, pockets, belts, buttons) are trompe-l'oeil and integrated into the garments. Spring-Summer 2000: military overalls with velcro pads on which half a cocktail-dress, half a skirt, half a T-shirt can be added **How would you describe your work?** Inventive **What is your ultimate goal?** Once in my life, I would like to be hyped! **Can fashion still have a political ambition?** I am always sceptical about designers (ab)using political statements in order to promote their product **Is the idea of creative collaboration important to you?** Every collaboration is important, as long as it's creative **What has been the greatest influence on your career?** I have the feeling my career has not started yet! **How have your own experiences affected your work as a designer?** All experiences, good and bad, influence my way of thinking. It's obvious this reflects also in my work **Is designing difficult for you and, if so, what drives you to continue?** The designing part is the easiest. Everything else is difficult **Have you ever been influenced or moved by the reaction to your designs?** I am always moved by reactions, positive or negative, to my designs **What's your definition of beauty?** Beauty equals originality, honesty, intelligence **What's your philosophy?** Beautify life! **What is the most important lesson you've learned?** We're all equal

AF Vandevorst is the Belgian fashion label started by An Vandevorst (born 1968) and Filip Arickx (born 1971). A married couple, they first met at Antwerp's Royal Academy in 1987. Before setting up together in 1997, An worked as first assistant to Dries Van Noten and Filip worked as a freelance designer and stylist, after a three-year spell working with Dirk Bikkembergs. A design duo driven by a certain yin and yang, their work is the result of her intellectual musings and his more carefree, bohemian upbringing. Since their first Paris show in March 1998, AF Vandevorst have produced collections that succeed in capturing the zeitgeist while remaining unique. They often approach traditional clothing as a starting point for their work, turning it into something new and contemporary: previous collections have been based on horse riding equipment, an interpretation of the kimono and, most recently, their take on the bomber jacket. They create a curious femininity, both beautiful and modern, perhaps in part due to their masculine/ feminine duality. After only their second collection, AF Vandevorst were awarded the Vénus de la Mode award for 'Le Futur Grand Créateur', a prestigious prize given to young designers at Paris Fashion Week; a year later, they were invited to design the Ruffo Research collection for Spring-Summer and Autumn-Winter 2000, an accolade bestowed on young designers by the luxury Italian leather company Ruffo. In 2002, the AF Vandevorst collection included shoes, accessories and a lingerie range called 'Nightfall'.

Das belgische Label AF Vandevorst ist die Marke von An Vandevorst, Jahrgang 1968, und Filip Arickx, Jahrgang 1971. Das inzwischen verheiratete Paar lernte sich 1987 auf der Königlichen Akademie in Antwerpen kennen. Bevor sie 1997 ihre gemeinsame Firma gründeten, arbeitete An als erste Assistentin von Dries Van Noten. Filip war nach drei aufregenden Jahren bei Dirk Bikkembergs als freischaffender Designer und Stylist tätig. Zusammen sind die beiden ein Designerduo aus Yin- und Yang-Elementen. Von ihrer Seite fließen eher intellektuelle Überlegungen in die gemeinsame Arbeit ein, ihn prägt eher seine sorglos bohemehafte Jugend. Seit der ersten Schau in Paris im März 1998 hat AF Vandevorst Kollektionen herausgebracht, die einerseits den Zeitgeist widerspiegeln, andererseits trotzdem einzigartig sind. Die beiden Designer benutzen traditionelle Kleidung oft als Ausgangspunkt ihrer Arbeit und machen etwas Neues, Zeitgemäßes daraus. So beschäftigten sie sich in den bisherigen Kollektionen mit Reitkleidung, einer Interpretation des Kimonos und als letztes mit der Bomberjacke. Sie erzeugen eine merkwürdige Form des Femininen, die so schön wie modern ist, was vielleicht auch mit ihrer eigenen Männlichkeit bzw. Weiblichkeit zusammenhängt. Bereits nach Vorliegen der zweiten Kollektion wurde AF Vandevorst auf der Pariser Modewoche mit der begehrten Vénus de la Mode für 'Le Futur Grand Créateur' ausgezeichnet. Und nur ein weiteres Jahr danach lud man das Designerteam ein, die Frühjahr/Sommer- sowie die Herbst/Winter-Kollektion 2000 für Ruffo Research zu entwerfen. Diese prestigeträchtige Auszeichnung gewährt Ruffo, der italienische Hersteller von Luxuslederwaren, immer wieder vielversprechenden jungen Designern. 2002 umfasste die Kollektion von AF Vandevorst auch schon Schuhe, Accessoires und eine Dessouslinie namens 'Nightfall'.

AF Vandevorst est la griffe belge créée par An Vandevorst (née en 1968) et Filip Arickx (né en 1971). Aujourd'hui mariés, ils se sont rencontré pour la première fois en 1987 à l'Académie Royale d'Anvers. Avant de s'installer ensemble en 1997, An travaille comme première assistante de Dries Van Noten et Filip en tant que designer et styliste free-lance après trois ans passés au service de Dirk Bikkembergs. Sous-tendu par une notion de yin et de yang, le travail de ce duo est le fruit des rêveries intellectuelles d'An et de l'éducation plus laxiste et un peu bohème de Filip. Depuis son premier défilé parisien en mars 1998, AF Vandevorst produit des collections qui parviennent à capter l'air du temps tout en proposant quelque chose de vraiment unique. Dans leur travail, An et Filip adoptent souvent une approche traditionnelle du vêtement comme point de départ pour aboutir à une mode originale et contemporaine : leurs précédentes collections s'inspiraient des tenues d'équitation, du kimono et, plus récemment, du blouson d'aviateur. Le duo propose une étrange féminité à la fois belle et moderne qui découle peut-être en partie de leur dualité de masculin/féminin. A l'issue de sa deuxième collection, AF Vandevorst reçoit le prix de « Futur Grand Créateur» des Vénus de la Mode, récompense prestigieuse décernée aux jeunes créateurs pendant la Semaine de la Mode de Paris ; un an plus tard, ils sont invités par le maroquinier de luxe italien Ruffo à dessiner les collections Printemps-Eté et Automne-Hiver 2000 de Ruffo Research, une vraie marque de reconnaissance. En 2002, la collection AF Vandevorst s'est enrichie d'une ligne de chaussures, d'accessoires et d'une gamme de lingerie baptisée « Nightfall ».

"You can feel the combination of a man and a woman in our work. There's a balance in it"

PORTRAIT COURTESY OF AN VANDEVORST AND FILIP ARICKX

AN VANDEVORST & FILIP ARICKX

PHOTOGRAPHY BY PETE DRINKELL, STYLING BY RACHAEL ZILLI. JULY 2000

"Negative reactions to work can be the most constructive"

What are your signature designs? It's always difficult to say with your own work because you are in the middle of it **How would you describe your work?** It's a result of the two of us. We have lived together for 13 years. We do everything together. You can feel the combination of a man and a woman; there's a balance in it **What's your ultimate goal?** Together in the sun! Seriously, we hope to continue making everything in Belgium because we have a very personal contact with the manufacturers. And we'd like to expand and experiment with different things, making the AF Vandevorst universe as big as possible. It's always nice to challenge yourself. Right now it's not in our minds to design a sofa. But the best thing about being independent is that if you want to do something, you have the freedom to do it **What inspires you?** In one word, emotions **Can fashion still have a political ambition?** It's a tricky one. In the end, it's a product that you make and you can see there is a statement, but it ends up in a shop. And people buy it and it's only in the way you present it that you could possibly make a statement **Is the idea of creative collaboration important to you?** We are both into working together. Not only the two of us, but also with a lot of other people. We try to involve as many friends as we can **Which is more important in your work: the process or the product?** The process. In that process you try to build up a story; in our situation, tell something together. The first thing for both us is that we need to enjoy it **Is designing difficult for you and, if so, what drives you to continue?** If something is not working, our whole world doesn't fall apart. Earlier in our career we would be crying for a week, but you soon learn that it's just one problem after the other. In the beginning we would get mad. Now we laugh. Skip it and move onto the next thing. You can get a lot of energy from problem solving **Have you ever been influenced or moved by the reaction to your designs?** It always moves you a bit, whether it's positive or negative. But often negative reactions can be the most constructive. For example, our first collection was a chaos of ideas. We wanted to do this idea and this idea, and we presented it and nobody understood because there was no real point. Thus we learned that if it's too chaotic, nobody gets the message **What's your definition of beauty?** Happiness **What's your philosophy?** It's very important to have freedom. To do what you want to do. Always. That's why we want to be independent **What is the most important lesson you've learned?** Enjoy everything – it can soon all be over

Donatella Versace inherited one of the most august positions in the fashion industry – Artistic Director of the house of Versace – after the tragic death of her brother, Gianni, in 1997. Gianni Versace, who was born in 1946, had founded his own label in 1978 after working for Callaghan, Genny and Complice, going on to build one of the biggest fashion houses of the late 20th century. Gianni's brand of über-expensive, über-luxurious and über-glamorous fashion made him a key protagonist of popular culture, from the conspicuous spending and power dressing 1980s to the ghetto fabulous excess of the late 1990s. His signature use of prints, sex bomb silhouette and references to ancient Roman and Greek culture won him an A-list celeb clientele – in fact, it was his relationship with the rich and famous, especially rock stars and pop princesses, that made him an international superstar and made his clothes their uniform. Donatella, born in the 1960s in Reggio Calabria, was not only Gianni's sister but also his muse and right-hand woman. They first started working together while she was studying languages at Florence University. After graduating, Donatella's initial input was into the advertising campaigns, her domain eventually including the design of the accessories collections and licences, including Young Versace. From 1993, Donatella designed the Versus diffusion collection. Since taking over as Chief Designer (she is also Vice-President and Chief Executive Officer, along with her brother Santo), Donatella has successfully brought Versace into the 21st century, fusing her brother's hallmark high-octane baroque excess with her own sensuality. The Versace empire includes womenswear, menswear, sportswear, underwear, eyewear, jeans collections, fragrance and homewear, with recent additions of a make-up range and Palazzo Versace, the first six-star Versace hotel, which opened on the Gold Coast of Australia in 2000.

Donatella Versace übernahm nach dem tragischen Tod ihres Bruders Gianni im Jahr 1997 eine der angesehensten Positionen der Modebranche: Artistic Director des Hauses Versace. Der 1946 geborene Gianni Versace hatte nach Erfahrungen bei Callaghan, Genny und Complice 1978 sein eigenes Label gegründet und es zu einer der größten Mode-marken des ausgehenden 20. Jahrhunderts ausgebaut. Seine extrem teuren, extrem luxuriösen und extrem glamourösen Kreationen machten den Designer selbst zu einem der bedeutendsten Protagonisten der Popkultur, angefangen beim Prestigekonsum und dem Power-Dressing der Achtziger bis zu den unvorstellbaren Exzessen im Ghetto der Eliten in den späten Neunzigern. Seine Markenzeichen – üppige Muster, sexy Silhouetten und Anleihen bei der römischen und griechischen Antike – bescherten ihm eine Klientel aus den angesagtesten Prominenten. Genau genommen war es sein gutes Verhältnis zu den Reichen und Berühmten, insbesondere zu Rockstars und Pop-Prinzessinnen, das aus Versace selbst einen internationalen Superstar machte und dazu führte, dass seine Kleider zu ihrer Uniform werden ließ. Die in den 1960er Jahren in Reggio Calabria geborene Donatella war nicht bloß Giannis Schwester, sondern auch seine Muse und seine rechte Hand. Ihre Zusammenarbeit begann noch während ihres Sprachenstudiums an der Universität von Florenz. Nach ihrem Abschluss beteiligte sich Donatella zunächst an Werbekampagnen, später entwarf sie auch selbst Accessoire-Kollektionen und Nebenlinien wie Young Versace. Von 1993 an kreierte Donatella die Kollektionen von Versus. Seit sie (neben der Verantwortung als Vizepräsidentin und CEO, zusammen mit ihrem Bruder Santo) den Job der Chef-designerin übernommen hat, ist es ihr gelungen, Versace erfolgreich ins 21. Jahrhundert zu führen und dabei das Markenzeichen ihres Bruders, die barocke Üppigkeit, mit ihrer eigenen Sinnlichkeit zu vereinen. Das Imperium Versace umfasst Damen- und Herrenmode, Sportswear, Dessous, Brillen, Jeans, Düfte und Homewear. Die jüngsten Geschäfts-bereiche sind eine eigene Make-up-Linie sowie der Palazzo Versace, das 2000 eröffnete erste Sechs-Sterne-Versace-Hotel an der australischen Gold Coast.

A la mort tragique de son frère Gianni en 1997, Donatella Versace hérite d'une position parmi les plus enviées de l'univers de la mode : directrice de la création de la maison Versace. Gianni Versace, né en 1946, avait lancé sa propre griffe en 1978 après avoir travaillé pour Callaghan, Genny et Complice, développant sans relâche l'une des griffes de mode les plus importantes de la fin du XXᵉ siècle. Le goût de Gianni pour une mode très chère, très luxueuse et très glamour l'a imposé comme un acteur incontournable de la culture pop, tout au long des années 1980, du «power dressing» à prix prohibitif jusqu'aux excès tendance «ghetto de luxe» de la fin des années 1990. Son utilisation caractéristique des imprimés et des silhouettes de bombe sexuelle, ainsi que ses références constantes à la culture gréco-romaine de l'Antiquité lui ont valu une clientèle composée de la crème des célébrités : en fait, ce sont ses relations avec les grands de ce monde, notamment les stars du rock et les princesses pop, qui l'ont hissé au rang de star internationale et transformé ses vêtements en uniforme de la jet-set. Donatella, née dans les années 1960 à Reggio Calabria, est non seulement la sœur de Gianni mais également sa muse et son bras droit. Ils débutent leur collaboration alors qu'elle est encore étudiante en langues à l'université de Florence. Une fois diplômée, Donatella commence par s'impliquer dans les campagnes publicitaires de la marque avant de dessiner pour les collections d'accessoires et les licences, notamment Young Versace. Dès 1993, Donatella dessine pour la ligne Versus. Depuis sa nomination au poste de directrice de la création (elle est également vice-présidente et PDG aux côtés de son frère Santo), Donatella a réussi à faire entrer Versace dans le XXIᵉ siècle, fusionnant sa propre sensualité aux excès baroques et explosifs si typiques de son frère. L'empire Versace comprend des collections pour femme, des collections pour homme, du sportswear, des sous-vêtements, des lunettes, des collections de jeans, des parfums et une ligne de «homewear», sans parler du récent lancement d'une ligne de maquillage et de Palazzo Versace, premier hôtel Versace six étoiles ouvert sur la Gold Coast australienne en l'an 2000.

"I am always driven to push forward, searching for what is modern. That's what motivates me"

PORTRAIT COURTESY OF DONATELLA VERSACE

DONATELLA VERSACE

PHOTOGRAPHY COURTESY OF VERSACE, AUTUMN-WINTER 2002

PHOTOGRAPHY BY DAVID ARMSTRONG. NOVEMBER 2002

"I don't like to surround myself with 'yes' people. I am a great believer in the fact that creativity comes from a conflict of ideas"

What are your signature designs? The jungle print, the evening dress that Catherine Zeta Jones wore to the Oscars in 2001, the silk fringe dress that Sharon Stone wore to the Oscars in 2002, the leather pant suit with lace-up details and fringes **How would you describe your work?** The style and ideas behind the collection always come from the same thought channel: Versace, myself and my team. Everything that goes on the runway and every Versace item is something that I 'feel for' **What inspires you?** I am a very curious person and therefore get my inspiration from music, photographs, films, from meeting people, discovering new places, attitudes and new trends around the world **Who do you have in mind when you design?** Someone who has individuality, intelligence, with an inner confidence which reflects on the outside **Is the idea of creative collaboration important to you?** My design team is composed of 30 people from all over the world who are like family to me. I believe fashion derives from group work and I have a very open-minded team. Not everyone agrees with me, which is the way I prefer it – I don't like to surround myself with 'yes' people. I am a great believer in the fact that creativity comes from a conflict of ideas **Who has been the greatest influence on your career?** My brother has been the best maestro I could ever have. Everything I know I have learned from him, and everything that I do, and will do, will always have a touch of Gianni **How have your own experiences affected your work as a designer?** New ideas come from having an open mind. I live intensely all the moments of my life and, in each one of those moments, I try to find an interesting and stimulating aspect **Is designing difficult for you?** I adore the world of fashion. It's a passion for me, so I don't think I will ever get tired of it **What's your definition of beauty?** I am convinced that looking good can only come from the inside. It is how you feel about yourself **What's your philosophy?** I am always driven to push forward, searching for what is modern. That is what motivates me **What is the most important lesson you've learned?** To live every day to the full, as if it were the last

PHOTOGRAPHY BY RICHARD BURBRIDGE, STYLING BY EDWARD ENNINFUL. MARCH 2001. MODEL: STELLA TENNANT

Milan Vukmirovic has perhaps one of the toughest jobs in fashion. As a designer appointed by the Prada Group to succeed Jil Sander at the house she founded, Vukmirovic follows where many in the industry said it was not possible to follow. It's unquestionably a mark of his talent that the precision and pin-point temper – seductive but utterly restrained – of Sander's approach has not been lost. It has been a rapid climb up the fashion power escalator for Vukmirovic. Born in Chantilly, France in 1970 to a Yugoslavian family, Vukmirovic abandoned his formal fashion education after just eighteen months. Instead, he worked as an intern at 'Jardin des Modes' magazine in Paris for two years, going on to model for Matsuda in Japan, assisting on a Christian Lacroix show and finally working with Eric Bergère in Milan and Paris. After that he became designer for the Emmanuelle Fouks label, where he met mother and daughter team Colette and Sarah. In 1997 the trio founded the Parisian boutique Colette, pioneering a new kind of style fusion – mineral water meets art meets fashion objets, all carefully selected by Vukmirovic, the store's Creative Director and Head Buyer. In March 2000, Vukmirovic was appointed Design Director for the Gucci Group by Tom Ford, before swiftly moving to a high profile role as Creative Director for both men's and womenswear at Jil Sander. The politics of the situation made his position hard, but Vukmirovic has risen to the challenge, striking a difficult line of stamping his own ideas on the brand without making radical changes. It remains within the realm of what Sander's customers – many loyal since her first collection in 1973 – would expect: slim tapered lines, a clear sense of shape and proportion, a little colour to break up the monochrome and a graphic edge in the most refined fabrics. What Vukmirovic has brought to the label is a new and welcome emotion, infusing its cool simplicity with an obsessive attention to detail, an embodiment of the essence of discreet luxury. Jil Sander opened a flagship store in London in 2002, to be followed in 2003 by New York.

Milan Vukmirovic hat den vielleicht härtesten Job in der Modebranche. Der Designer wurde vom Prada-Konzern als Nachfolger von Jil Sander für das von ihr gegründete Modehaus verpflichtet. Viele Leute sagten dem Designer damals sein Scheitern voraus, weil eine Nachfolge in dieser Position schlichtweg unmöglich sei. Deshalb muss man es wohl als unzweifelhaften Beweis seines Talents werten, dass die Präzision und der Charakter des Jil-Sander-Stils – verführerisch, aber extrem reduziert – nicht verloren gegangen sind. Für Vukmirovic war es ein rascher Aufstieg in die mächtige Modeelite. Der 1970 in Chantilly geborene Sohn jugoslawischer Eltern brach die traditionelle Ausbildung zum Modemacher schon nach 18 Monaten ab. Stattdessen arbeitete er zwei Jahre lang als Praktikant bei der Zeitschrift 'Jardin des Modes' in Paris, modelte für Matsuda in Japan, assistierte bei einer Schau von Christian Lacroix und fand schließlich einen Job bei Eric Bergère in Mailand und Paris. Anschließend wurde er Designer für das Label Emmanuelle Fouks, wo er auch das Mutter-Tochter-Team Colette und Sarah kennen lernte. 1997 gründete das Trio die Pariser Boutique Colette, die den Weg für eine neue Art von Stilmix bereiten sollte: Mineralwasser trifft auf Kunst trifft auf Modekreationen. Die sorgsame Auswahl des Angebots verantwortete Vukmirovic als Creative Director und Chefeinkäufer in Personalunion. Im März 2000 wurde Vukmirovic von Tom Ford zum Design Director der Gucci-Gruppe berufen. Das war kurz vor seinem plötzlichen Wechsel in die hoch angesehene Position des Creative Director für die Herren- und Damenmode bei Jil Sander. Die Hintergründe der Situation machten ihm diese Arbeit nicht gerade leicht, doch Vukmirovic ist zweifellos an dieser Herausforderung gewachsen. Er wählte den schwierigen Weg, die Marke mit seinen eigenen Ideen zu prägen, ohne radikale Veränderungen einzuläuten. Die Marke blieb im Rahmen dessen, was Sanders Kundinnen – von denen viele der Designerin schon seit ihrer ersten Kollektion von 1973 die Treue halten – erwarteten: schmale, sich verjüngende Konturen, ein klares Gespür für Formen und Proportionen, ein wenig Farbe, um das Monochrome aufzubrechen, sowie ein grafisches Element bei den edelsten Materialien. Vukmirovic hat dem Label eine neue, willkommene Note verliehen, kühle Schlichtheit und eine geradezu obsessive Liebe zum Detail, die Verkörperung des diskreten Luxus. 2002 eröffnete das Haus Jil Sander einen Flagship Store in London, 2003 folgt ein weiterer in New York.

Milan Vukmirovic occupe sans doute l'un des postes les plus difficiles du monde de la mode. Nommé par le groupe Prada à la succession directe de Jil Sander, Vukmirovic a réussi là où de nombreux acteurs du marché le voyaient échouer. Preuve incontestable de son talent, il n'a rien perdu de la précision et de l'aspect méticuleux qui caractérisent le travail séduisant mais extrêmement sobre de Jil Sander. Cet exploit a permis à Vukmirovic de gravir rapidement les marches du succès. Né en 1970 à Chantilly dans une famille d'origine yougoslave, Vukmirovic abandonne sa formation en mode au bout de dix-huit mois. A la place, il opte pour un stage au magazine « Jardin des Modes » et y passe deux ans avant de travailler comme mannequin pour Matsuda au Japon, comme assistant sur les défilés Christian Lacroix puis finalement avec Eric Bergère à Milan et à Paris. Ensuite, il devient styliste de la griffe Emmanuelle Fouks, chez qui il rencontre la mère et la fille, Colette et Sarah. En 1997, le trio ouvre la boutique Colette à Paris et présente un nouveau concept dans la fusion des styles, où les eaux minérales côtoient les œuvres d'art et les vêtements, tous soigneusement sélectionnés par Vukmirovic, directeur artistique et acheteur principal de la boutique. En mars 2000, Vukmirovic est nommé directeur de la création du groupe Gucci par Tom Ford, puis décroche rapidement le poste plus convoité de styliste principal des lignes pour homme et pour femme de Jil Sander. L'aspect politique de la situation rend son travail difficile, mais Vukmirovic relève le défi en insufflant ses propres idées à la marque sans lui faire subir pour autant de changement radical. Les collections prennent l'orientation attendue par les clients Sander, très fidèles depuis sa première collection de 1973 : lignes élancées et fuselées, sens appuyé de la forme et des proportions, une touche de couleur pour briser le monochrome et un style graphique coupé dans les tissus les plus raffinés. Vukmirovic a apporté à la griffe une émotion nouvelle et bienvenue grâce à son goût de la simplicité et son obsession du détail qui incarnent l'essence de son luxe discret. En 2002, une boutique Jil Sander a ouvert à Londres; New York suivra en 2003.

"Reality for me doesn't mean boring"

PORTRAIT BY DAVID SIMS

MILAN VUKMIROVIC

PHOTOGRAPHY BY MATT JONES, STYLING BY KATE YOUNG. APRIL 2002

PHOTOGRAPHY BY TESH, STYLING BY EDWARD ENNINFUL. AUGUST 2001. MODEL: ELEANORA

"Designing is not difficult. That's when I enjoy myself most"

What are your signature designs? I think that's something you know when you stop doing fashion because then you look back. It's too early in my career to say **How would you describe your work?** I am responsible for all creative aspects of the Jil Sander company: men's and women's collections, advertising, image of stores, fragrances etc **What inspires you?** Mostly music and the young culture in the streets, which is quite far away from the fashion of the moment **Can fashion still have a political ambition?** I think it's always very dangerous to mix fashion and politics, because to many people fashion seems very futile. Fashion is not considered to be political, but when you are a fashion designer, I think you have a certain responsibility through your creations to leave a message. It happened to me when I designed the last men's collection – people asked why I used 'Clockwork Orange' as my theme, many people thought the movie was very violent. Actually, for me our times are very violent. What's violent to me is the growing manipulation by the media and the constant pressure of a consumerism that tends to unify everything, and that's why I want to fight for diversity and help people to cultivate their differences **Who do you have in mind when you design?** I watch a lot of movies. But the reality is that I am more and more influenced by real people, actually my friends, my very close friends. I have some women around me from different ages that I really look at. They are very different. I like to look at them because each one has a different elegance, a different sense of style and way to seduce **Is the idea of creative collaboration important to you?** Very, because I think nobody is doing anything alone. In the fashion system, it's very easy to become a megalomaniac and think that you are the only one to be right. It's dangerous and you have to share opinions. Creative collaboration makes you richer **Who has been the greatest influence on your career?** Yves Saint Laurent, because I feel very close to the sense of elegance he always had in his collections. Whatever was the trend, he almost suffered physically to fight for his own idea of femininity, elegance and beauty, and he stuck to this all his life **Which is more important in your work: the process or the product?** I have to say both, because I really enjoy the process. I like working with people and having creative collaborations. The beginning of a collection is usually one of my favourite moments. But in the end, what you create has to be worn. So I think it's both **Is designing difficult for you?** I think designing is not difficult at all. That is the moment when I enjoy myself the most **Have you ever been influenced or moved by the reaction to your designs?** Honestly, you have to read every critic; I'm always moved by them. You have to accept a different point of view and maybe sometimes it can help you to do better. A positive critic can be a great support. But I totally disagree when a negative review becomes too personal **What's your definition of beauty?** Beauty is like an emotion for me. I think emotion in life is very important. Life can be so difficult – it's beauty that makes it. Beauty also gives you a feeling of a certain eternity **What's your philosophy?** One of my biggest philosophies is that you have to fight for what you believe in. You have to believe in yourself; you have to stay true to yourself **What is the most important lesson you've learned?** You have to allow yourself and others to make mistakes, because you learn a lot from that

Junya Watanabe (born Tokyo, 1961) is the much-fêted protégé of Rei Kawakubo. Graduating from Bunka Fashion College in 1984, he immediately joined Comme des Garçons as a pattern-cutter. By 1987 he was designing their Tricot line. He presented his first solo collection in 1992 at the Tokyo collections; a year later, he showed at Paris Fashion Week. (Although designing under his own name, he is still employed by Comme des Garçons, who fund and produce the collections.) Despite an obvious debt to Rei Kawakubo in his work, Watanabe still stands apart from his mentor and friend with a vision that is indisputably his own. He has often used technical or functional fabrics, creating clothes that still retain a sense of calm and femininity. This was displayed most explicitly at his Autumn-Winter 1999 show, where the catwalk was under a constant shower of water: rain seemed to splash off the outfits, which were created in fabric by the Japanese company Toray, who develop materials for extreme conditions. Despite the wealth of creativity on display, Watanabe's clothes were a response to more fundamental issues: a practical answer to conditions and lifestyles. In contrast to this, Watanabe's designs are also an exercise in sensitivity and, through his remarkably complex pattern-cutting, his sculptural clothing presents a virtually unrivalled delicacy. In 2001, Watanabe presented his first menswear collection in Paris. Eschewing the intense craftsmanship of his womenswear, Watanabe prefers to twist simple men's garments. With an eye on Americana, his debut show – a collaboration with Levi's – was full of jeans and jeans jackets. His second lifted collegiate iconography, deftly creating visual effects through fabrics and colour. Part of the new generation of Japanese designers, Watanabe looks set to be as influential as his celebrated predecessors.

Der 1961 in Tokio geborene Junya Watanabe gilt als bereits viel gefeierter Protégé von Rei Kawakubo. Unmittelbar nach seinem Abschluss am Bunka Fashion College 1984 fing er als Zuschneider bei Comme des Garçons an. 1987 entwarf er bereits die Nebenlinie Tricot des japanischen Modehauses. Die erste Solokollektion präsentierte Watanabe dann 1992 in Tokio, ein Jahr später war er schon auf der Pariser Modewoche vertreten. (Selbst wenn er inzwischen unter eigenem Namen entwirft, ist der Japaner noch Angestellter des Unternehmens Comme des Garçons, das seine Kollektionen auch finanziert und produziert.) Obwohl er von Rei Kawakubo in seiner Arbeit entscheidend beeinflusst wurde, unterscheidet sich Watanabe doch mit einer zweifellos eigenständigen Vision von seiner Mentorin und Freundin. Oft benutzt er Mikrofasern und andere funktionale Stoffe für seine Kleider, die dennoch eine Aura von Gelassenheit und Weiblichkeit besitzen. Am deutlichsten wurde dies bisher bei seiner Schau für Herbst/Winter 1999, als er den Catwalk ununterbrochen beregnen ließ. Das Wasser schien von den Outfits abzuperlen, die aus einem Material der japanischen Firma Toray gefertigt waren. Dieses Unternehmen ist auf die Herstellung von Geweben für extreme Bedingungen spezialisiert. Doch trotz dieser originellen Präsentation waren die Kreationen von Watanabe die Reaktion auf fundamentalere Herausforderungen, nämlich eine praktische Antwort auf verschiedene Lebensumstände und -stile. Zugleich ist die Mode des Japaners aber auch eine Art Sensitivitätstraining, und dank der bemerkenswert komplexen Schnitte sind seine skulpturalen Entwürfe auch von einer noch nie da gewesenen Zartheit. 2001 präsentierte Watanabe seine erste Herrenkollektion in Paris. Hier verzichtete der Designer auf den großen handwerklichen Aufwand, den er in seiner Damenmode betreibt, und verfremdete eher schlichte Männerkleidung. Bei seiner Debütshow – einer Kooperation mit Levi's – schien er typisch Amerikanisches im Hinterkopf zu haben: So waren viele Jeans und Jeansjacken zu sehen. Bei der zweiten Schau kümmerte er sich dagegen nicht um eine akademische Ikonographie und setzte vor allem optische Effekte von Materialien und Farben gekonnt ein. Wie es aussieht, wird Watanabe so einflussreich sein wie seine berühmten japanischen Vorgänger.

Junya Watanabe (né en 1961 à Tokyo) est le célèbre protégé de Rei Kawakubo. Une fois diplômé du Bunka Fashion College en 1984, il commence immédiatement à travailler chez Comme des Garçons comme traceur de patrons. En 1987, il dessine déjà pour la ligne Tricot. En 1992, il présente sa première collection « en solo » aux défilés de Tokyo ; un an plus tard, il est invité à la Semaine de la Mode de Paris (bien qu'il dessine sous son propre nom, Watanabe est toujours employé par Comme des Garçons, qui finance et produit ses collections). Très marqué par l'influence de Rei Kawakubo, le travail de Watanabe se distingue toutefois de celui de son amie et mentor grâce à une approche indiscutablement personnelle. Les vêtements qu'il taille souvent dans des tissus techno et fonctionnels n'en sont pas moins empreints de calme et de féminité. Son talent apparaît de façon explicite à l'occasion de son défilé Automne-Hiver 1999, où les mannequins défilent sur un podium constamment aspergé d'eau : les gouttes de pluie rebondissent sur les vêtements coupés dans un tissu produit par Toray, une entreprise japonaise qui développe des matériaux résistant aux conditions extrêmes. Bien qu'ils démontrent l'immense créativité de Watanabe, ses vêtements apportent avant tout une réponse à des problèmes plus fondamentaux, une solution pratique aux divers climats et modes de vie. Ils témoignent également de la grande sensibilité de Watanabe qui, grâce à des coupes d'une complexité remarquable, confère à ses pièces sculpturales une délicatesse presque incomparable. En 2001, Watanabe présente sa première collection pour homme à Paris. Renonçant au savoir-faire artisanal qui caractérise sa ligne pour femme, Watanabe préfère proposer sa vision décalée des basiques masculins. Inspiré en partie par un style américain des plus « country », son premier défilé, en collaboration avec Levi's, fait la part belle aux jeans et aux vestes en denim. Son second défilé met en avant l'iconographie des uniformes universitaires, où tissus et couleurs se fondent pour créer des effets visuels étonnants. Issu de la nouvelle génération de créateurs japonais, Watanabe semble aujourd'hui bien parti pour devenir aussi influent que ses prédécesseurs.

"I'm surrounded by critical women. If I stopped challenging myself, they'd refuse to work with me. I like that"

PORTRAIT BY TERRY JONES

JUNYA WATANABE

PHOTOGRAPHY BY CHRISTOPHE RIHET, STYLING BY HAVANA LAFFITTE. MAY 2002

What are your signature designs? Strength and tenderness in clothes in a straightforward way **How would you describe your work?** I have the same attitude towards work and creativity that Rei Kawakubo has **Can fashion still have a political ambition?** While I respect the viewpoint that fashion reflects social and political issues, that is not where my interests lie **Who do you have in mind when you design?** I think the relationship between designer and customer is simple. That is, we do what we do and those who sympathise with our work will wear it **Is the idea of creative collaboration important to you?** In our work with Levi's, it is an inestimable experience and enrichment to profit from the weight of history **What has been the greatest influence on your career?** All I learned at fashion school was how to use a needle and thread and a sewing machine. Everything else I learned at Comme des Garçons **Which is more important to you in your work: the process or the product?** In women's fashion, each time I put all my energy into new challenges, the perfecting of new patterns and the search for unusual textures. But I'm also conscious that this experimentation is not an end in itself in garment design **Have you ever been influenced or moved by the reaction to your designs?** I have never thought about whether or not I am successful. Our aim is only to create a good collection

Vivienne Westwood, born in Derbyshire in 1941, is a true icon. Britain's greatest living designer, she is as much a symbol of England as the Queen or the black cab. Let It Rock, SEX, Seditionaries, urban Pirates and Buffalo girls: Westwood's collaborations with Malcolm McLaren, most famously the creation of punk's uniform, completely overturned perceptions of what fashion is. Since creating the final guise for the most famous address on London's King's Road – World's End – and severing business ties with McLaren, Westwood has gone on to become one of the fashion industry's most revered figures. In the 1980s she was famously hailed by WWD as one of its six most influential designers of all time – and all without a scrap of formal training. Through her tireless research of European costume, and her maniacal attention to detail, Westwood has invented clothing that has quoted historical precedent, upset conventional wisdom and has consistently been proved ahead of its time. Her designs are recognisable for their voluminous use of fabric, and she often creates shape and dimensions through elaborate folding, as well as unconventional pattern-cutting techniques. Awarded the OBE 15 years after being arrested on the night of the Queen's Silver Jubilee, she has now become as much part of the establishment as she is anti-establishment, reflecting the paradoxical nature of her clothing. Today she commands respect without culling any of her outspoken behaviour. In 2002 Westwood was guest professor of Fashion at the Berliner Universität der Künste, and her many awards include British Designer of the Year twice. She shows her ready-to-wear women's collection in Paris each season, and her menswear collection, MAN, in Milan, as well as producing a couture line, Gold. Her diffusion line, Anglomania, regularly references pieces from her earlier collections. Vivienne Westwood also has two best-selling women's fragrances, Libertine and Boudoir.

Die 1941 in Derbyshire geborene Vivienne Westwood ist eine echte Ikone der Modewelt. Als bedeutendste lebende Designerin Großbritanniens ist sie wie die Queen oder die schwarzen Londoner Taxis ein Symbol Englands. Let It Rock, SEX, Seditionaries, Urban Pirates oder die 'Buffalo-Girls'-Kollektion: Westwoods Zusammenarbeit mit Malcolm McLaren, insbesondere die berühmte Erfindung des Punker-Looks, hat die allgemein gültige Vorstellung, was Mode ist, völlig verändert. Seitdem sie selbst das Erscheinen von World's End, der berühmtesten Adresse in der Londoner King's Road, prägt und ihre Geschäftsbeziehungen zu McLaren abgebrochen hat, ist sie eine der meist verehrten Gestalten der Modeindustrie. In den 1980er Jahren wurde sie unter großem Jubel vom WWD zu einer der sechs einflussreichsten Designerinnen und Designer aller Zeiten gewählt – und das ohne die geringste professionelle Ausbildung. Dank ihrer unermüdlichen Beschäftigung mit europäischer Kostüm- und Modegeschichte und ihrer geradezu manischen Aufmerksamkeit für jedes Detail hat Vivienne Westwood Kleider kreiert, die historische Vorbilder zitierten, Konventionen außer Acht ließen und ihrer Zeit immer voraus waren. Ein Markenzeichen ihrer Entwürfe ist der verschwenderische Stoffkonsum. Oft erzielt sie Form und Volumen durch kunstvolles Falten oder ungewöhnliche Schnittmustertechniken. Mit dem Order of the British Empire wurde die Designerin genau 15 Jahre nach ihrer Verhaftung während des Silbernen Thronjubiläums der Queen ausgezeichnet. Heute gehört sie zum Establishment genau so wie zum Anti-Establishment, was auch dem paradoxen Charakter ihrer Mode entspricht. Und inzwischen flößt sie ihrer Umgebung Respekt ein, ohne ihre freimütige Art in irgendeiner Weise zügeln zu müssen. 2002 war sie Gastprofessorin für Mode an der Berliner Universität der Künste, und zu ihren vielen Auszeichnungen zählt der ihr bereits zweimal verliehene Titel British Designer of the Year. Ihre Prêt-à-Porter-Kollektion für Damen zeigt Vivienne Westwood jede Saison in Paris, die Herrenkollektion MAN in Mailand. Außerdem entwirft sie noch eine Couture-Linie namens Gold. Ihre Nebenlinie Anglomania bezieht sich regelmäßig auf Kreationen ihrer früheren Kollektionen. Vivienne Westwood hat mit Libertine und Boudoir auch zwei überaus erfolgreiche Damenparfums auf den Markt gebracht.

Vivienne Westwood, née en 1941 dans le Derbyshire, est une véritable icône. La plus grande créatrice britannique vivante symbolise l'Angleterre au même titre que la Reine ou les black cabs. Let It Rock, SEX, Seditionaries, Urban Pirates and Buffalo Girls : les nombreuses collaborations de Westwood avec Malcolm McLaren, notamment la création de l'uniforme punk, ont complètement révolutionné la perception des gens sur la mode. Depuis qu'elle a apporté la touche finale à sa boutique World's End, la plus célèbre adresse de King's Road, et mis un terme à ses relations d'affaires avec McLaren, Vivienne Westwood est devenue l'un des personnages les plus révérés par le monde de la mode. Dans les années 1980, WWD la classe parmi les six créateurs les plus influents de l'époque – le tout sans la moindre formation. A travers ses inlassables recherches sur le costume européen et son attention maniaque aux détails, elle a inventé des vêtements pleins de références historiques, renversé les idées reçues et régulièrement prouvé qu'elle était en avance sur son temps. On reconnaît ses vêtements à leur volume de tissu car la créatrice obtient souvent ses formes et ses dimensions grâce à un système de pliage très élaboré et des techniques de coupe de patrons inhabituelles. Décorée Officier de l'Empire Britannique 15 ans après son arrestation la nuit du jubilée d'argent de la Reine, elle est intégrée à l'establishment tout en restant anti-establishment, reflet des paradoxes de sa mode. Aujourd'hui, elle force le respect sans se départir le moins du monde de sa franchise. En 2002, Vivienne Westwood enseigne la mode à la Universität der Künste de Berlin, et parmi les nombreuses récompenses qu'elle a reçues, on compte deux fois le prix de British Designer of the Year. Chaque saison, elle présente sa collection de prêt-à-porter pour femme à Paris et sa collection pour homme, MAN, à Milan, tout en continuant à produire Gold, sa collection haute couture. Sa ligne secondaire, Anglomania, fait régulièrement référence aux pièces de ses anciennes collections. Elle a également lancé deux parfums féminins à succès, Libertine et Boudoir.

"It's difficult to be avant-garde today. People have got used to everything"

PORTRAIT BY KAYT JONES

VIVIENNE WESTWOOD

PHOTOGRAPHY BY ANETTE AURELL, STYLING BY ANNETT MONHEIM. OCTOBER 2000

"Power is sexy. I like the people that I dress to look important"

What are your signature designs? I think they're so well-known that you can fill this in yourself. One thing that people do forget is that I reintroduced the idea of fine knitwear into fashion. There's nothing more sexy than a twin set… more sexy still is the cardigan of the twin set, worn by itself with the buttons undone. You did not have this fine knitwear until I persevered getting it from English companies when the machinery to make it didn't even exist in fashion knitwear companies. I'm just making the point that the things I do are very, very fundamental sometimes to what filters into the fashion world **What's your favourite piece from any of your collections?** My favourite garment of all time is my knitted dress, which I've been wearing for at least the last five years. You just look so stunning wearing this dress with very high heels. It uses the technique of hand-knitting to perfection. I will mention also that in my career I've done three special trousers, which I think are just the greatest: bondage trousers, pirate trousers, alien trousers. Of course, I always like my latest collections the best of all, especially the dresses we have been doing for the last two or three seasons. They have only two or three seams, yet these seams meander in such way that we can get volume wherever we want. And they are just so dynamic **How would you describe your work?** Very simply, avant-garde **What's your ultimate goal?** It's a question of organisation, to make the clothes more easily available in order to satisfy the demand. I just want people, once they've got their money together, to go and buy something, to be able to see my things straight away in order to choose them **What inspires you?** I get my ideas from the work itself. When you start to do something, then you find another way to do it. It's only by doing something one way that you have an idea of how it could be done another way. Of course, I also get inspired by things I see, but I do not get inspired by the street these days **Can fashion still have a political ambition?** I look upon government as a one-way corridor, to facilitate the interests of business. At the same time, the government tries to convince everybody else that this is good for them. And so people are being trained by the media to be perfect consumers of mass manufactured rubbish. The people who wear this stuff have bought the system, and their appearance demonstrates the fact that their brains have been removed. I think it's important to make great clothes so that people can look individual and not a product of mass advertising **Who do you have in mind when you design?** The answer is nobody and everybody **What has been the greatest influence on your career?** I would say my World's End shop, which I've had since 1970. And that's because I was making clothes and selling them direct through the shop, so I always had access to the public and I always had customers. So I developed all my strengths without being frustrated in any way and I was always able to be the judge of my own work **How have your own experiences affected your work as a designer?** I had a cardinal change in my attitude after punk rock. I realised that my idea of attacking the establishment was naïve – if you try to attack the establishment, you actually feed the establishment. You give it all these ideas, it goes into mass manufacture and it has a big effect on the fashion world. So what I decided to do was go very fast and not care about attacking anything. Just to come up with the ideas and not be held back in any way. And since then, I've been miles down the road in front of anything **Is designing difficult for you and, if so, what drives you to continue?** When I view my catwalk show, my thought each season is the same: 'Six months ago that didn't exist; now it does exist. Nobody ever walked the planet wearing this before'. And that's what drives me on **What's your definition of beauty?** Everybody knows if a woman is beautiful or not. It's something that you can't deny. But I'm not terribly interested in beauty. What touches me is someone who understands herself **What's your philosophy?** Power is sexy. I like the men and women that I dress to look important. When I see that, I'm happy **What is the most important lesson you've learned?** Keep a smile on your face

PHOTOGRAPHY BY TESH, STYLING BY EDWARD ENNINFUL. DECEMBER/JANUARY 2002

While still studying at Antwerp's Royal Academy, Bernhard Willhelm (born 1972) already knew how to get to grips with his vocation. Trading in holidays for apprenticeships, he spent his summers working for Vivienne Westwood, Walter Van Beirendonck, Alexander McQueen and Dirk Bikkembergs. After graduating in 1998, Willhelm set up office in Antwerp, presenting his first womenswear collection in Paris a mere eight months later. This Autumn-Winter 1999 debut featured elements from Willhelm's childhood spent in the German Black Forest, as well as his already trademark humorous take on fashion. Mixing references from pop and street culture with handicraft and folklore, Bernhard Willhelm took on embroidering, pleating, folding and printing with enthusiasm. What really set him apart was his 'anything goes as long as it's beautiful' approach: subsequent collections have seen him working collage-style with checks, polka-dots, tapestry, handmade knits, lace, dinosaur and cookbook prints, ruffled tutus, kimono dresses and much, much more. Bored with the rigidity of the catwalk system, he presented his Autumn-Winter 2000 collection using a video projected on a silver screen. For Spring-Summer 2001, he introduced a series of menswear items, completing the existing range of womenswear and accessories. Proving such joyful eclecticism also works outside his atelier, Willhelm guest-curated Antwerp fashion magazine N°B (issue 2, February 2002), commissioning work by artists like Wolfgang Tillmans, Luc Tuymans and Attila Richard Lukacs, as well as poetry by Elfriede Jelinek and excerpts from texts written by the Dalai Lama, his personal hero. Willhelm has also posed naked for Butt magazine.

Schon während seines Studiums an der Königlichen Akademie von Antwerpen verstand es der 1972 geborene Bernhard Willhelm, sein Talent praktisch umzusetzen. Er nutzte die Semesterferien für Praktika und arbeitete jeweils einen Sommer lang für Vivienne Westwood, Walter Van Beirendonck, Alexander McQueen und Dirk Bikkembergs. Nach Abschluss seines Studiums 1998 machte sich der Deutsche in Antwerpen selbstständig und präsentierte nach nur acht Monaten seine erste Damenkollektion in Paris. Bei seinem Debüt für Herbst/Winter 1999 spielte er mit Elementen aus dem Schwarzwald, wo er seine Kindheit verbracht hatte. Schon damals war die humorvolle Einstellung zur Modebranche sein Markenzeichen. Willhelm mixte Zitate aus Pop- und Straßenkultur mit Kunsthandwerk und Folklore. Begeistert machte er sich ans Besticken, Plissieren, Falten und Bedrucken. Was ihn deutlich von der Konkurrenz abhob, war sein Grundsatz: Nichts ist unmöglich – solange es schön ist. So bekam man in seinen folgenden Kollektionen unter anderem Karomuster, Tupfen, Gobelins, Handgestricktes, Spitze, Dinosaurier- und Kochbuchdrucke, gerüschte Tutus und Kimonokleider zu sehen. Weil ihn die Strenge der traditionellen Laufstegpräsentation langweilte, zeigte der Jungdesigner seine Kollektion für Herbst und Winter 2000 als Video, das auf eine Leinwand projiziert wurde. Für Frühling/Sommer 2001 brachte er eine Reihe von Herrenkleidungsstücken heraus, die sein bisheriges Spektrum aus Damenmode und Accessoires komplettierten. Wie zum Beweis dafür, dass sein lustvoller Eklektizismus auch außerhalb seines Ateliers funktioniert, gestaltete der Designer als Gast eine Nummer des Antwerpener Modemagazins N°B (Nr. 2, Februar 2002) und verwendete dafür Arbeiten von Künstlern wie Wolfgang Tillmans, Luc Tuymans und Attila Richard Lukacs, aber auch Lyrik von Elfriede Jelinek und Auszüge aus Schriften des Dalai Lama – seines persönlichen Vorbilds. Willhelm hat übrigens auch schon nackt für die Zeitschrift Butt posiert.

Alors qu'il est encore étudiant à l'Académie Royale d'Anvers, Bernhard Willhelm (né en 1972) sait déjà comment mettre en pratique sa vocation. Préférant profiter de ses vacances pour faire des stages, il passe ses étés à travailler pour Vivienne Westwood, Walter Van Beirendonck, Alexander McQueen et Dirk Bikkembergs. Une fois diplômé en 1998, Willhelm s'établit à Anvers et présente sa première collection pour femme à Paris seulement huit mois plus tard. Ses débuts pour la saison Automne-Hiver 1999 sont marqués par les souvenirs d'une enfance passée dans la Forêt Noire allemande et témoignent de sa vision humoristique de la mode, déjà caractéristique de son style. Mélangeant des références à la culture pop et de la rue à une approche artisanale et folklorique, Bernhard Willhelm adopte les broderies, les plis et les imprimés avec enthousiasme. Il se démarque réellement grâce à son côté « tout est permis tant que c'est beau » : les collections suivantes verront défiler des carreaux, des pois, de la tapisserie, du tricoté main, de la dentelle, des imprimés de dinosaures et de livres de cuisine, des tutus à volants, des robes kimono et bien d'autres choses encore. Lassé par la rigidité des défilés, il présente sa collection Automne-Hiver 2000 par le biais d'une projection vidéo sur grand écran. Pour le Printemps-Eté 2001, il introduit une série de pièces masculines en complément de sa gamme de vêtements pour femme et d'accessoires. Cet éclectisme jubilatoire fait également des merveilles en dehors de son atelier, comme le prouve son invitation au comité de rédaction du numéro 2 de N°B (février 2002), magazine de mode anversois qui présentait les œuvres d'artistes tels que Wolfgang Tillmans, Luc Tuymans et Attila Richard Lukacs, ainsi que des poèmes d'Elfriede Jelinek et des extraits de textes du Dalaï Lama, son héros fétiche. Par ailleurs, Willhelm a posé nu pour le magazine Butt.

"Chaos is beautiful"

PORTRAIT BY WILLY VANDERPERRE

BERNHARD WILLHELM

What are your signature designs? I really don't know. It's up to other people to judge each of my designs. I totally leave it up to other people **What's your favourite piece from any of your collections?** Actually, all of them. But if there's anything I like to wear, it's an old dinosaur sweatshirt **How would you describe your work?** Chaotic, humorous and naïve **What's your ultimate goal?** To grow up **What inspires you?** At the moment, reading and love **Is the idea of creative collaboration important to you?** Collaboration, for me, is teamwork. If you call that collaboration, then yes. But I don't need to collaborate with magazines or whatever to express my ideas. It's a bit of an over-used word at the moment **Is designing difficult for you?** No **Which is more important in your work: the process or the product?** Both have the same value. Because if you have a very interesting, fantastic process and rubbish comes out of it, then it's worth nothing **What's your definition of beauty?** It's something that makes your heart beat. Beauty for me is something that you didn't expect... the unexpected. And the chaos, it has a lot to do with beauty for me **What's your philosophy?** Don't be lazy, but don't drive yourself crazy **What is the most important lesson you've learned?** You have to be kind and nice. The Dalai Lama helped me a lot with that

Matthew Williamson has a conviction in the use of colour very few designers are brave enough to match. He routinely splashes ultra pinks, fluorescent yellows and acid greens onto women's day and evening wear with an energising flourish. It's become a signature style since the debut of his first collection, 'Electric Angels', in 1997 – a combination of kaleidoscopic bias-cut dresses and separates, sometimes embroidered and fused with a bohemian edge. Modelled by friends Jade Jagger, Kate Moss and Helena Christensen, it was a presentation that affirmed the London-based designer's influences: fame, glamour and India. Celebrity was the all-important catalyst which made the fashion world sit up and pay attention to his work, but since that first collection it's been the intricate detail, contemporary styling and sexy silhouette clothes that have kept the applause coming. Born in Chorlton, Manchester, in 1971, Matthew Williamson graduated from Central Saint Martins in 1994 and set up his own label in 1996 after spending two years as consultant at UK high street chain Monsoon. 2002 has been an important year for Williamson: it saw the launch of his homewear range as well as a small collection of menswear, while his Autumn-Winter 2002 womenswear collection was presented for the first time at New York Fashion Week. He has also created a perfume, Incense, in conjunction with Lyn Harris, and is now working on developing his menswear collection more fully for Spring 2003. Matthew Williamson now sells to over 80 stores worldwide.

Matthew Williamson ist ein so überzeugter Benutzer von Farben wie kaum ein anderer Designer. Routinemäßig verteilt er mit schwungvoller Gebärde knallige Pink-, fluoreszierende Gelb- und Neongrüntöne in seiner Damenmode sowohl für den Tag wie für den Abend. Das ist sein Markenzeichen seit dem Debüt mit der Kollektion 'Electric Angels' 1997 – einer Mischung aus kaleidoskopischen Kleidern und Separates im Diagonalschnitt, teilweise bestickt und mit einem Hauch von Boheme. Die Schau, bei der Williamsons Freundinnen Jade Jagger, Kate Moss und Helena Christensen modelten, ließ unmissverständlich erkennen, was den Designer bei seinen Entwürfen beeinflusst hatte: Ruhm, Glamour und Indien. Zunächst war Prominenz der entscheidende Faktor, der seiner Arbeit die Aufmerksamkeit der Modewelt sicherte, doch nach dieser ersten Kollektion sorgten raffinierte Details, zeitgemäßes Styling und verführerische Silhouetten für den nötigen Applaus. Der 1971 in Chorlton, Manchester, geborene Matthew Williamson schloss sein Studium am Central Saint Martins 1994 ab und gründete 1996, nach zwei Jahren Beratertätigkeit für die britische Modekette Monsoon, sein eigenes Label. 2002 war ein wichtiges Jahr für den jungen Designer: Er brachte seine erste Homewear- sowie eine kleine Herrenkollektion heraus; die Damenkollektion für Herbst/Winter 2002 wurde erstmals bei der New Yorker Modewoche gezeigt. In Zusammenarbeit mit Lyn Harris kam mit Incense auch Williamsons erstes Parfum auf den Markt. Für Frühjahr 2003 ist eine erweiterte Herrenkollektion in Arbeit. Inzwischen werden die Kreationen von Matthew Williamson in mehr als achtzig exklusiven Läden weltweit verkauft.

Matthew Williamson utilise la couleur comme peu d'autres créateurs oseraient le faire. Régulièrement, il éclabousse avec panache ses tenues féminines de jour et du soir de roses flashy, de jaunes fluorescents et de verts acidulés. Depuis sa première collection «Electric Angels» en 1997, ce style s'est imposé comme sa signature : une combinaison de robes et de séparés kaléidoscopiques coupés en biais, parfois brodés et au look un peu bohème. Grâce à ses amies mannequins Jade Jagger, Kate Moss et Helena Christensen, ce défilé confirme les influences du créateur londonien : la gloire, le glamour et l'Inde. Ce sont d'abord les célébrités qui ont attiré l'attention du monde de la mode sur son travail, mais depuis cette première collection, il remporte un succès croissant grâce aux détails complexes, au style contemporain et à la silhouette sexy de ses vêtements. Né en 1971 dans le quartier Chorlton de Manchester, Matthew Williamson sort diplômé de Central Saint Martins en 1994. En 1996, après avoir travaillé deux ans comme consultant pour la chaîne de distribution britannique Monsoon, il crée sa propre griffe. 2002 est une année importante pour Williamson : il lance sa première gamme de vêtements pour la maison ainsi qu'une petite ligne pour homme et présente pour la première fois sa collection pour femme Automne-Hiver 2002 à la New York Fashion Week. Il a également créé un parfum, Incense, en collaboration avec Lyn Harris et travaille actuellement au développement de sa collection pour homme pour le Printemps 2003. A ce jour, les créations de Matthew Williamson sont vendues dans plus de 80 boutiques à travers le monde.

"Colour is the thing I'm best known for. If people pigeonhole me, so what? Long live the pink dress!"

PORTRAIT COURTESY OF MATTHEW WILLIAMSON

MATTHEW WILLIAMSON

What are your signature designs? My style is all about creating very feminine, sexy clothes that women really desire **What's your favourite piece from any of your collections?** I love the first dress that I ever did. It's pink with a turquoise cowl at the neck, so simple. But I love it most because of what it did for my career **What's your ultimate goal?** To be bought by an Italian or French house very quickly. You start out in London and it's great in the beginning because everyone is so hungry for new designers. But when you get to my stage, you're not new anymore. It's very difficult in this country because we don't take fashion seriously as a business **What inspires you?** Ultimately I'm most inspired by travel; by the places that I visit. I try to fuse Western style with a very Eastern, exotic feel. I pick up all of the colour and texture when I'm abroad, particularly in India, Thailand and Bali **Who do you have in mind when you design?** It's a combination of women **Is designing difficult for you and, if so, what drives you to continue?** If it was easy, it wouldn't be interesting **What's your definition of beauty?** I think people are most attractive when they appear confident and happy in themselves **What's your philosophy?** Everything in moderation **What is the most important lesson you've learned?** How to work for myself and be responsible. If shit goes wrong, I'm much more comfortable blaming myself

Yohji Yamamoto is one of the most important and influential fashion designers working today. As one of the industry's most mentally rigorous designers, the clothes he creates can be intellectual, sometimes difficult, but always beautiful. At once avant-garde and classic, transcending both time and culture, they sidestep gender altogether with their androgynous asexual aesthetic. His womenswear defies convention and body shape, wrapping the female form in exaggerated proportions. Born in Japan in 1943, Yamamoto's father died during the Second World War and he grew up with his seamstress mother. It was in an attempt to please her that Yamamoto enrolled at Keio University to study law, but later dropped out for a fashion degree at the Bunka Fashion College in Tokyo. After a trip to Paris, Yamamoto returned to Japan and started work fitting the customers at his mother's dressmaking shop. Having cut his fashion teeth, Yamamoto established his own label in 1971, holding his first fashion show in Tokyo in 1977. Already a financial success in Japan, Yamamoto held his debut Paris show in 1981, along with his girlfriend at the time, Rei Kawakubo, and her Comme des Garçons label. Yamamoto sent out grim-looking models, their faces painted white and wearing strange asymmetric black shapes, to the thud of an amplified electronic heartbeat. Whilst the fashion establishment cried 'Hiroshima Chic', a young generation of creative types embraced Yamamoto, who soon became a byword for the designer aspiration of the 1980s. This karate black belt and chief organiser of the Worldwide Karate Association still has a stronghold over the fashion industry, now with over 158 retail outlets across the globe, a successful partnership with Adidas, a fragrance (launched 1996), his diffusion collections Y's For Women (established in 1972) and Y's For Men (1979), and the unwavering admiration of a new generation of disciples. Yohji Yamamoto has also been represented in numerous books and exhibitions.

Yohji Yamamoto ist einer der bedeutendsten und einflussreichsten Modedesigner unserer Zeit. Er gilt als einer der Kompromisslosesten seiner Zunft, und die Mode, die er kreiert, kann manchmal intellektuell, gelegentlich sogar schwierig sein, besticht jedoch immer durch ihre Schönheit. Seine ebenso avantgardistischen wie klassischen Kreationen überwinden mühelos Epochen und Kulturen und lassen mit ihrer androgynen asexuellen Ästhetik den Geschlechterunterschied völlig außer Acht. Yamamotos Damenmode trotzt Konventionen und Körperformen, indem sie die Frauen in überdimensionierten Proportionen verhüllt. Geboren wurde der Designer 1943 in Japan. Sein Vater fiel im Zweiten Weltkrieg, so dass er allein mit seiner Mutter, die als Näherin arbeitete, aufwuchs. Um ihr eine Freude zu machen, schrieb sich Yamamoto zunächst auf der Keio-Universität für ein Jurastudium ein. Danach absolvierte er das Bunka Fashion College in Tokio. Nach einem Parisaufenthalt kehrte der junge Designer nach Japan zurück, wo er im Schneiderladen seiner Mutter zu arbeiten begann. Insbesondere war er für das Maßnehmen der Kundschaft zuständig. Sein eigenes Label gründete Yamamoto 1971; die erste Modenschau fand 1977 in Tokio statt. Nachdem er sich in Japan bereits wirtschaftlich etabliert hatte, gab Yamamoto 1981 sein Debüt in Paris, und zwar bei einer gemeinsamen Schau mit seiner damaligen Freundin Rei Kawakubo und ihrem Label Comme des Garçons. Er schickte finster dreinblickende Models mit weiß geschminkten Gesichtern und in befremdlichen asymmetrischen schwarzen Gewändern auf den Laufsteg. Dazu war das dumpfe Geräusch eines elektronisch verstärkten Herzschlags zu hören. Und während das Mode-Establishment 'Hiroshima Chic' heulte, nahm die junge Generation der Kreativen Yamamoto mit offenen Armen auf. In kürzester Zeit war sein Name der Inbegriff des Designer-Hypes der 1980er Jahre. Yamamoto, der unter anderem Träger des schwarzen Karategürtels und Funktionär der Worldwide Karate Association ist, übt immer noch beträchtlichen Einfluss auf die Modebranche aus: mit mehr als 158 Einzelhandels-Outlets in aller Welt, einer erfolgreichen Kooperation mit Adidas, einem Parfum (Markteinführung 1996), mit den Nebenkollektionen Y's For Women (seit 1972) und Y's For Men (seit 1979) und der ungebrochenen Bewunderung einer neuen Generation von Anhängern. Yohji Yamamotos Werk wurde in zahlreichen Büchern und Ausstellungen vorgestellt.

Yohji Yamamoto est l'un des créateurs de mode les plus importants et les plus influents actuellement en exercice. Comptant parmi les designers les plus rigoureux du monde de la mode, les vêtements qu'il crée peuvent être considérés comme intellectuels, parfois difficiles, mais ils sont toujours beaux. A la fois avant-gardistes et classiques, transcendant le temps et les cultures, ils estompent les différences entre homme et femme à travers une esthétique androgyne asexuée. Ses vêtements pour femme défient les conventions et la forme du corps, enveloppant les courbes féminines dans des proportions exagérées. Né en 1943 au Japon, Yamamoto devient orphelin de père pendant la Seconde Guerre Mondiale et grandit auprès d'une mère couturière. C'est en cherchant à lui faire plaisir qu'il entre à l'Université Keio pour étudier le droit, qu'il abandonnera plus tard au profit d'un cours de mode au Bunka Fashion College de Tokyo. Après un premier séjour à Paris, Yamamoto revient au Japon et commence à travailler en habillant les clients de l'atelier de sa mère. Ayant aiguisé son sens de la mode, Yamamoto crée sa propre griffe en 1971 et présente son premier défilé à Tokyo en 1977. Fort de ses premiers succès commerciaux au Japon, Yamamoto débute à Paris en 1981 aux côtés de sa petite amie de l'époque, Rei Kawakubo et de sa griffe Comme des Garçons. Ses mannequins à l'air sinistre ont le visage peint en blanc et portent d'étranges formes noires asymétriques, défilant sur le rythme sourd d'un battement de cœur électronique amplifié. Tandis que l'establishment de la mode crie au scandale, la nouvelle génération de créateurs des années 1980 adopte avec enthousiasme le « Chic Hiroshima » de Yamamoto qui incarne l'idéal auquel ils aspirent. Organisateur de l'Association Mondiale de Karaté et lui-même ceinture noire, Yamamoto exerce encore une grande influence sur le monde de la mode, avec aujourd'hui plus de 158 points de vente à travers le monde, un partenariat réussi avec Adidas, un parfum (lancé en 1996) et les lignes secondaires Y's For Women (1972) et Y's For Men (1979). Il bénéficie de l'admiration sans bornes d'une toute nouvelle génération de disciples. Le travail de Yohji Yamamoto a été présenté dans de nombreux ouvrages et plusieurs expositions.

"I want to achieve anti-fashion through fashion. That's why I'm always heading in my own direction. Because if you're not waking up what is asleep, you might as well just stay on the beaten path"

PORTRAIT BY CLAUDIO DELL'OLIO

YOHJI YAMAMOTO

THOMAS SCHENK, STYLING BY JOANNA BLADES. OCTOBER 2001. MODEL: STELLA TENNANT

PHOTOGRAPHY BY KAYT JONES. SEPTEMBER 2002. MODEL: CAMILLA RUTHERFORD

PHOTOGRAPHY BY MARTHA CAMARILLO, STYLING BY AVENA GALLAGHER, OCTOBER 2002

"I've already reached a goal. I'm enjoying the rest of my life"

What are your signature designs? Over-sized coats, over-sized shirts, over-sized jackets... Anyway, anything over-sized **What's your favourite piece from any of your collections?** In terms of 'piece', I don't have the feeling of a favourite. Psychologically, to be human is to forget about sadness or bitterness, so I have few memories of those emotions. I've always thought that I want to forget about the things which have already passed. I always think that it might have been done in a better way. In terms of the show collections, some of them are still quite impressive in my opinion, I guess **How would you describe your work?** I've played all of my cards **What's your ultimate goal?** I've already reached a goal. I'm enjoying the rest of my life. Now it's time to enjoy time, time to spend time **What inspires you?** Inspire... the word which has been thrown at me a thousand times, and to which every time I've replied in a different way. I guess it's every phenomenon that inspires us every moment. **Can fashion still have a political ambition?** If fashion has a role, it's to be immoral. A role to transfer the weak, humiliating and deplorable aspects of human nature into something charming. Art is always used or consumed by the authority of the time. Art co-operates by resistance. In this sense, fashion could have something to do with social ambition. But political ambition? I don't see it in fashion. But, if fashion does have such ambition, I would describe it as 'freedom'! **Who do you have in mind when you design?** The Sozzani sisters, Madonna, Jodie Foster. And Pina Bausch **Is the idea of creative collaboration important to you?** Important is not the right word. Creative collaboration can be used in a technological way; that is to combine technology with craftsmanship. But when we talk about creativity there must be ego, and when there are two egos we cannot help but compromise. So I don't find collaboration important in terms of creativity. I could find one collaboration in ten in which both sides influence each other in a good way. Conflict is expected from the beginning, so in a way you should go into collaboration with reason and intelligence **Who has been the greatest influence on your career?** Sigh-sigh-sigh. Mother... oh... Mother... again and forever. **How have your own experiences affected your work as a designer?** This is a matter which people should never speak about and which people never do speak about; this question is getting too close to it. It is trying to reach it. You could write a novel about it, I guess. Everyone has his own private stories, which he never speaks about, which he could never speak about and it's a bit impertinent to ask. It's difficult, isn't it? **Which is more important in your work: the process or the product?** This is the best of all questions! I cannot be happier than being in the process. Then the product is a reality – and reality hits. In a season which has done well, I feel 'Ah, I've compromised...,' and in a season which did not work as much, I think 'It was the wrong time, I have not done enough.' I feel the responsibility as a result. My heart is beating whilst in the process... but daybreak always comes **Is designing difficult for you and, if so, what drives you to continue?** It should be said in this way: I can keep on designing just because of its difficulty. You can say that designing is quite easy; the difficulty lies in finding a new way to explore beauty **Have you ever been influenced or moved by the reaction to your designs?** I have opposite feelings: one is feeling a bit embarrassed and saying 'It's not such good work.' The other is such a strong feeling that it can't be expressed with the words 'influenced' or 'moved' but the words 'I'll kill everyone!' would fit better. Sometimes, I find a smart critic who analyses the unconscious phase which lies in my work. It gives me a lesson **What's your definition of beauty?** Condition; coincidence and by chance. A beautiful flower does not exist. There's only a moment when a flower looks beautiful **What's your philosophy?** Oh, come on **What is the most important lesson you've learned?** I am what I am due to four or five women. Please give me compensation!

Gaspard Yurkievich is part of a new generation of designers emerging from Paris who combine the creative flair of London with the historic grandeure of France. Born in 1972 in Paris, of French and Argentine origin, Yurkievich studied at the Studio Berçot from 1991 to 1993. Whilst still at college, he undertook an internship with Thierry Mugler in 1992, moving to Jean Paul Gaultier a year later. In 1994 he went to assist Jean Colonna. This experience at an independent label was invaluable, allowing Yurkievich to absorb every facet of fashion design and production. In 1997 he started his own womenswear label; that same year he was awarded the prestigious womenswear prize at the Hyères Festival. In 1998 he received funding from ANDAM, an organisation set up by the French Ministry of Culture to support young designers, and showed his first collection in Paris. Yurkievich's work explores female sexuality and modern elegance alongside historic references, explicitly presented in shows such as his Spring-Summer 2002 collection, which was modelled by professional dancers and shown in the legendary Crazy Horse revue bar. His interest in shape – often long, lean and sharp – is reminiscent of Mugler, while his ability to inject something of the mood of his urban sprawl owes a little to Gaultier and Colonna. Yet Yurkievich adds his own unique and energetic spin with the use of sumptuous fabrics and witty interpretations of classic garments. Today Yurkievich is a leading representative of a new generation of young French designers, who effortlessly combine glamour with a youthful edge.

Gaspard Yurkievich gehört zu einer neuen Generation von Pariser Designern, die das kreative Flair Londons problemlos mit der historischen Grandeur Frankreichs vereinbaren. Der 1972 in Paris geborene Designer französisch-argentinischer Abstammung studierte von 1991 bis 1993 am Studio Berçot. Noch während dieser Ausbildung absolvierte er 1992 ein Praktikum bei Thierry Mugler und ein Jahr später eines bei Jean Paul Gaultier. 1994 wurde er Assistent bei Jean Colonna. Diese Erfahrung bei einem unabhängigen Label war für den jungen Designer unschätzbar wertvoll, weil er alle Bereiche von Modedesign und -herstellung kennen lernte. 1997 gründete Yurkievich sein eigenes Label für Damenmode und wurde noch im selben Jahr beim Festival von Hyères mit dem angesehenen Womenswear-Preis ausgezeichnet. Dank der Förderung durch ANDAM, eine vom französischen Kultusministerium gegründete Organisation zur Unterstützung junger Designer, konnte er 1998 seine erste Kollektion in Paris präsentieren. Yurkievichs Arbeiten ergründen die weibliche Sexualität, sind aber auch von moderner Eleganz und historischen Bezügen geprägt. Das kam beispielsweise in der Schau für die Kollektion Frühjahr/Sommer 2002 perfekt zum Ausdruck: Professionelle Tänzerinnen modelten im legendären Revuelokal Crazy Horse. Das besondere Augenmerk des Designers auf die Silhouette – meist lang, schmal und scharf geschnitten – erinnert an Mugler, während seine Fähigkeit, etwas von der urbanen Atmosphäre zu vermitteln, wohl eher auf die Einflüsse von Gaultier und Colonna zurückgeht. Doch Yurkievich verleiht seinen Kleidern durch die Verwendung kostbarer Stoffe und durch witzige Neuinterpretationen von Klassikern eine unübersehbar eigene Note. Inzwischen gilt er als Repräsentant einer neuen Generation französischer Designer, die es verstehen, Glamour ganz zwanglos mit jugendlichem Schwung zu verbinden.

Gaspard Yurkievich fait partie de cette nouvelle génération de créateurs parisiens qui parviennent à combiner le flair créatif de Londres à la grandeur historique de la France. Né en 1972 à Paris et d'origine franco-argentine, Yurkievich étudie au Studio Berçot de 1991 à 1993. En 1992, il fait un stage chez Thierry Mugler avant de partir travailler pour Jean Paul Gaultier en 1993, puis comme assistant chez Jean Colonna un an plus tard. Cette expérience au sein d'une griffe indépendante lui est extrêmement précieuse dans la mesure où elle lui permet d'intégrer chaque aspect de la création et de la production de mode. En 1997, il lance sa propre griffe pour femme, qui lui vaut la même année le prix prestigieux de Meilleur Styliste pour Femme au Festival de Hyères. En 1998, il présente à Paris une première collection financée par l'ANDAM, organisation de soutien aux jeunes créateurs fondée par le Ministère de la Culture. Le travail de Yurkievich explore la sexualité féminine et l'élégance moderne en les associant à des références historiques très explicites dans ses défilés, notamment pour sa collection Printemps-Eté 2002, présentée sur des danseuses professionnelles au légendaire cabaret du Crazy Horse. Sa prédilection pour des formes souvent longues, élancées et sévères rappelle le travail de Mugler, tandis que sa traduction de la mode de la rue trouve en partie sa source chez Gaultier et Colonna. Pourtant, Yurkievich se distingue par son style unique et énergique, son utilisation des tissus les plus somptueux et sa brillante interprétation des grands classiques. Aujourd'hui, Yurkievich est l'un des meilleurs représentants de cette nouvelle génération de créateurs français qui marient sans effort glamour et avant-garde.

"Sometimes I feel I have touched a moment of grace"

PORTRAIT BY CONSTANT ANÉE

GASPARD YURKIEVICH

What are your signature designs? I work a lot with shapes **What's your ultimate goal?** I will always try to keep my freedom **What inspires you?** Sweetness and people who are very free **Can fashion still have a political ambition?** When you use fashion you express the way you live, so, in a way, yes **What do you have in mind when you design?** I always have the collection on my mind. I present 40 outfits and sometimes I feel I have touched a moment of grace. I try to use this energy to create more and more. It's quite abstract **Is the idea of creative collaboration important to you?** For me it's the first moment of my work – the first collaboration is with my pattern-maker and that is when we discover the collection. It is a very intimate moment. To make collaborations with people is very exciting for me, and also for them **Who has been the greatest influence on your career?** My older sister. When I was a child she always used clothes to express herself. I was fascinated by it **Which is more important in your work: the process or the product?** What excites me is the process. I like the mechanism of creation **Is designing difficult for you and, if so, what drives you to continue?** It's difficult because it's a lot of work, it takes time and a lot of energy **Have you ever been influenced or moved by the reaction to your designs?** I think yes and no. You always have to see the context. At the moment, I haven't met any people that really impressed me, who have said things about my work **What's your definition of beauty?** The beauty that I like is not material **What's your philosophy?** I like chance – but you have to think **What is the most important lesson you've learned?** You can do anything in this world, but it has a price

536

ALBERTA FERRETTI

BLUMARINE

ANTONIO MARRAS

JIL SANDER

DOLCE & GABBANA

ROBERTO CAVALLI

FENDI

MOSCHINO

AEFFE SPA

CHAIRMAN: MASSIMO FERRETTI. DEPUTY CHAIRMAN: ALBERTA FERRETTI

CEO: GIOVANNI COCCODRILLI

BRANDS OWNED BY AEFFE SPA:

ALBERTA FERRETTI; **PHILOSOPHY DI ALBERTA FERRETTI**; **MOSCHINO** Franco Moschino started his own label in 1983, after working for Gianni Versace. Moschino became well-known for the visual puns that often decorated his expertly tailored clothes. After his his death in 1994, Moschino was succeeded by his right-hand woman, Rossella Jardini. Also: **NARCISO RODRIGUEZ**; **POLLINI** Shoemaker; **VELMAR** Beachwear and lingerie

CHANEL SA

OWNERS: WERTHEIMER FAMILY

BRANDS OWNED BY AND ASSOCIATED WITH CHANEL SA:

CHANEL The fashion house founded by Gabrielle 'Coco' Chanel in 1913 is now a name synonymous with the Parisian fashion establishment. Her little black dresses and wool boucle suits, her perfumes and her taste for suntans, camellias and costume jewellery are all chapters of a legend. Chanel re-opened her house in 1954 and fashion critics were dismayed to observe that she was proposing clothes that were hardly changed from her pre-war designs. Nonetheless, a neat Chanel suit and quilted, gilt-handled handbag for some time remained the international uniform of chic ladies. In 1983, Karl Lagerfeld took over design duties at the house. Also: **ERES** (from 1996) Beachwear and lingerie; **HOLLAND & HOLLAND** (from 1989)

FRANCE LUXURY GROUP

CEO: MOUNIR MOUFARRIGE

BRANDS OWNED BY FRANCE LUXURY GROUP:

JACQUES FATH Jacques Fath opened his haute couture salon in 1937, achieving fame in the late 1940s for his curvaceous evening gowns. In 1948 he started a ready-to-wear collection and his simplicity of line found him great popularity in the USA. In 2002, British designer Lizzy Disney was appointed chief designer for the house. **JEAN-LOUIS SCHERRER** Jean-Louis Scherrer worked at Christian Dior alongside Yves Saint Laurent until the latter succeeded Dior in 1957. Scherrer eventually established his own salon in 1962 and was known for his extravagant eveningwear. Indian designer Ritu Beri was appointed in 2002 to shine up the Scherrer brand.

GUCCI GROUP NV

PRESIDENT AND CEO: DOMENICO DE SOLE. CREATIVE DIRECTOR: TOM FORD

BRANDS OWNED BY GUCCI GROUP:

GUCCI A luggage and saddlery company started by Guccio Gucci in Florence in 1921. The Gucci name had a particular cachet in the '50s and '60s. Many of Gucci's leather goods have become 20th century fashion icons: the bamboo handle handbag, moccasins decorated with a metal bit and bags trimmed with the green and red striped webbing, taken from the girth of a horse's saddle. Gucci family disputes and mass licensing saw the brand hit a low in the 1980s, until new management appointed Tom Ford as womenswear designer in 1990. His debut collection in March 1995 marked the beginning of a revitalised image for Gucci, which has become a byword for hedonistic, aspirational fashion. **YVES SAINT LAURENT** (from 1999) Yves Saint Laurent and business partner Pierre Bergé founded his house in

1962 and, over decades, Saint Laurent produced a series of brilliant and, at times, revolutionary fashion collections. Tuxedo suits for women, sheer blouses and safari jackets are just a few among the house's greatest hits. The first couturier to launch a ready-to-wear line (1966), Saint Laurent christened his new venture Rive Gauche. He retired from fashion in 2002, and since the Gucci Group acquired the brand in 1999, Tom Ford has designed both the menswear and womenswear Rive Gauche collections. **BALENCIAGA** (from 2001) Founded in San Sebastian, Spain in 1916 by couturier Cristobal Balenciaga, described by Christian Dior as 'the master of us all'. His technical genius found expression in austere, sculptural forms; the 'sack' dress and the voluminous 'melon' sleeve are among his most influential creations. He was at the peak of his fame in the 1950s and 1960s, retiring and closing his Paris salon in 1968. In 1997 Nicolas Ghesquière was hired to design a ready-to-wear line, which has returned the house to its former glory. Also: **SERGIO ROSSI** (from 1999); **ALEXANDER MCQUEEN** (from 2000); **STELLA MCCARTNEY** (from 2001); **BOTTEGA VENETA** (from 2001)

HERMÈS GROUP

CHAIRMAN AND CEO: JEAN-LOUIS DUMAS

BRANDS OWNED BY HERMES GROUP:

HERMES Thierry Hermès, a harness-maker, set up business in 1837, and five generations of the Hermès family have since established a prestigious saddlery and leather goods company. During the 1920s, Hermès extended its business to 'saddle-stitched' leather handbags, which are now the brand's most famous product: the Hermès 'Kelly' and 'Birkin' bags being among the most desirable (and expensive) in fashion. Since March 1998, Belgian designer Martin Margiela has designed the ready-to-wear womenswear line for Hermès. Also: **JOHN LOBB** Shoemaker; **JEAN PAUL GAULTIER**

LVMH (LOUIS VUITTON MOËT HENNESSY)

CHAIRMAN AND CEO: BERNARD ARNAULT

BRANDS OWNED BY AND ASSOCIATED WITH LVMH:

CHRISTIAN DIOR Christian Dior's debut collection of 1947 – featuring the wasp-waisted jacket and long, full skirt that was known as the New Look – reinstated post-war Paris at the pinnacle of the fashion world and made Dior an overnight success. Christian Dior delighted in the quick change of fashions; unusually for the time, each collection would promote a dramatically different hemline or silhouette, making it very easy to date a dress and earning Dior a reputation as a 'dictator' of fashion. Dior enjoyed ten years of critical acclaim and international success, dying of a heart attack at 52. The successors to his house have included Yves Saint Laurent, Gianfranco Ferré and, since 1996, John Galliano. **LOUIS VUITTON** Louis Vuitton started out packing dresses for the French Empress Eugénie – he must have enjoyed it, because he went on to design luggage, opening his first store in 1854. Vuitton designed flat trunks that could be safely stacked in the first class compartments of his wealthy clients. The original status symbol, the 'LV' monogram canvas was introduced in 1896 and, by the beginning of World War I, Louis Vuitton owned the biggest travel goods store in the world. Marc Jacobs now designs the house's ready-to-wear collections. **GIVENCHY** (from 1988) Hubert de Givenchy, like his mentor Cristobal Balenciaga, favoured clean, sculptural lines over fussy decoration; the ballooning sleeves of the Bettina blouse is one of Givenchy's many innovations. In Audrey Hepburn, Givenchy

FASHION GROUPS

had one of the most successful designer-muse relationships in fashion history. Givenchy founded his salon in 1952, aged just 25, and retired in 1996, leaving his womenswear collections to be directed by a succession of young British designers: John Galliano, Alexander McQueen and, most recently, Julien Macdonald. **CÉLINE** (from 1996) Céline started life as a children's shoe store back in 1945, expanding into grown-up leather goods in 1963. A ready-to-wear collection followed soon after, and Céline became known for luxurious casual clothes. American sportswear designer Michael Kors took over design duties at the house in 1997. **EMILIO PUCCI** (from 2000) Emilio Pucci, the Marchese di Barsento, fell into fashion; a member of the Italian Olympic skiing team, he was photographed by 'Harper's Bazaar' on the slopes wearing ski-pants that he had designed himself. With encouragement from the magazine, Pucci went on to design similar clothes for women and during the 1950s his floppy, casual daywear - usually silk jersey, printed with signature swirling, multicoloured patterns – became incredibly popular, particularly among the Hollywood divas of the day. Parisian designer Christian Lacroix was appointed designer for the house in 2002. **KENZO** (from 1993) Kenzo Takada's fashion label began with his 1970 debut at his boutique, Jungle Jap. He made his name with exuberant colours, knitwear and new versions of the traditional Japanese kimono. Gilles Rosier has been Artistic Director for all of Kenzo women's lines since 1999. **LOEWE** Enrique Loewe founded his leather company in Madrid in 1846, and the house has become known not only for baggage and leather goods, but for fine leather clothes that fall with the fluidity of fabric. Past designers have included Karl Lagerfeld. In 1997, American designer Narciso Rodriguez was appointed to design the fashion collection, followed by José Enrique Oña Selfa in 2002. Also: **CHRISTIAN LACROIX** (1993); **DONNA KARAN** (2001); **FENDI** (2002); **MARC JACOBS**

MARZOTTO GROUP

CHAIRMAN: INNOCENZO CIPOLLETTA. CEO: ANTONIO FAVRIN

BRANDS OWNED BY MARZOTTO GROUP:

VALENTINO (from 2002) Valentino Garavani opened his own couture house in Rome in 1959, having spent ten years in Paris studying and working for established houses. Dramatic tomato-red evening dresses and neat skirt suits for lunching ladies are typical of Valentino's work. **HUGO BOSS** Founded in Germany in 1923 as a company producing workwear, Hugo Boss shifted their focus in the late 1960s, designing a slick brand of menswear. Womenswear collections were added in 1998.

PRADA GROUP

CEO: PATRIZIO BERTELLI

BRANDS OWNED BY AND ASSOCIATED WITH PRADA GROUP:

PRADA The Milanese leather goods company was established in 1913 by Mario Prada, selling high-quality leather bags, trunks and accessories. Mario's granddaughter, Miuccia, joined the family company in 1970 and gradually revived its fortunes, particularly with the introduction of her black nylon handbags and backpacks. An alliance in 1978 with Patrizio Bertelli, now Miuccia Prada's husband, created Prada Industrial and formed the basis for the worldwide distribution of Prada products. The first shoe collection was launched in 1982, with ready-to-wear following in 1989. The following years have seen the brand make a spectacular rise to prominence in the fashion industry. Also: **MIU MIU**; **HELMUT LANG** (from 1999); **JIL SANDER** (from 1999); **CHURCH'S** (from 2000); **CAR SHOE** (from 2001); **AZZEDINE ALAÏA** (from 2000); **GENNY** (from 2001)

RICHEMONT GROUP

CEO: JOHANN RUPERT

BRANDS OWNED BY RICHEMONT GROUP:

CHLOÉ (from 1985) Established in 1952 as a luxurious prêt-à-porter house by Jacques Lenoir and Gaby Aghion, Chloé represented a romantic aesthetic, favouring gauzy, fluid dressing. Martine Sitbon, Karl Lagerfeld and Stella McCartney are among the designers who have preceded the current Creative Director, Phoebe Philo. Also: **CARTIER**; **DUNHILL**; **HACKETT**

SALVATORE FERRAGAMO GROUP

CEO: LEONARDO FERRAGAMO

BRANDS OWNED BY SALVATORE FERRAGAMO GROUP:

SALVATORE FERRAGAMO Salvatore Ferragamo was first apprenticed to a shoemaker at the age of nine. In 1927 he founded a workshop in Florence and Hollywood stars clamoured to be shoed in Ferragamo. Ferragamo offered his clients invention as well as glamour: wedges, cork heels and unusual materials – anything from lace to snail-shells – all made famous Ferragamo shoes. **EMANUEL UNGARO** (since 1996) Emanuel Ungaro received a formidable training, under the tutelage of Cristobal Balenciaga and André Courrèges; in 1968 he formed his own fashion house, known for Space Age A-line dresses and tailoring. He later softened his lines and bold, colourful prints – especially florals and polka dots – are now his most recognisable signature, seen at their most exuberant in his haute couture collections. Giambattista Valli was appointed Head Designer for the label in 1996.

AEFFE SPA

CHAIRMAN: MASSIMO FERRETTI. STELLVERTRETENDER CHAIRMAN: ALBERTA FERRETTI
CEO: GIOVANNI COCCODRILLI
MARKEN, DIE AEFFE SPA GEHÖREN:
ALBERTA FERRETTI; PHILOSOPHY DI ALBERTA FERRETTI; MOSCHINO Franco Moschino gründete 1983 sein eigenes Label, nachdem er zuvor für Gianni Versace gearbeitet hatte. Berühmt wurde der Designer für die dekorativen Hingucker auf seinen handwerklich perfekten Kreationen. Nach Moschinos Tod 1994 übernahm Rossella Jardini, bis dahin die rechte Hand des Couturiers, seine Funktion. Außerdem: **NARCISO RODRIGUEZ; POLLINI** Schuhhersteller; **VELMAR** Beachwear und Lingerie

CHANEL SA

EIGENTÜMER: FAMILIE WERTHEIMER
MARKEN, DIE CHANEL GEHÖREN ODER AN DAS UNTERNEHMEN ANGEGLIEDERT SIND:
CHANEL Das 1913 von Gabrielle 'Coco' Chanel gegründete Couture-Haus gilt heute als Synonym für das Pariser Modeestablishment. Ihre kleinen Schwarzen und ihre Kostüme aus Wollbouclé, ihre Parfums und ihre Vorliebe für sonnengebräunte Haut, Kamelien und Modeschmuck sind allesamt Teil ihrer Legende. Als Chanel ihr Haus 1954 wieder eröffnete, waren die Modekritiker entsetzt, weil die neuen Kreationen sich kaum von ihren Entwürfen aus der Vorkriegszeit unterschieden. Dennoch blieben das adrette Chanelkostüm und die gesteppte Handtasche mit Goldkette noch für einige Zeit die Uniform schicker Damen in aller Welt. 1983 übernahm Karl Lagerfeld die Verantwortung für das Design bei Chanel. Außerdem: **ERES** (seit 1996) Beachwear und Lingerie; **HOLLAND & HOLLAND** (seit 1989)

FRANCE LUXURY GROUP

CEO: MOUNIR MOUFARRIGE
MARKEN, DIE ZUR FRANCE LUXURY GROUP GEHÖREN:
JACQUES FATH Jacques Fath eröffnete seinen Haute-Couture-Salon 1937 und war in den späten 1940er Jahren für seine figurbetonenden Abendroben berühmt. 1948 brachte er eine Prêt-à-Porter-Kollektion heraus, deren schlichte Silhouetten vor allem in den USA große Begeisterung auslösten. 2002 wurde die Britin Lizzy Disney Chefdesignerin des Hauses. **JEAN-LOUIS SCHERRER** Jean-Louis Scherrer arbeitete mit Yves Saint Laurent bei Christian Dior, bis Saint Laurent 1957 die Nachfolge Diors antrat. 1962 gründete Scherrer schließlich einen eigenen Salon und wurde rasch für seine extravagante Abendmode berühmt. Um der Marke Scherrer neuen Glanz zu verleihen, verpflichtete man 2002 die indische Designerin Ritu Beri.

GUCCI GROUP NV

PRÄSIDENT UND CEO: DOMENICO DE SOLE. CREATIVE DIRECTOR: TOM FORD
MARKEN, DIE ZUR GUCCI-GRUPPE GEHÖREN:
GUCCI 1921 eröffnete Guccio Gucci in Florenz ein Geschäft für Reisegepäck und eine Sattlerei. Der Name Gucci besaß vor allem in den 1950er und 1960er Jahren große Anziehungskraft. Und viele Lederwaren aus dem Hause Gucci wurden zu Markenzeichen der Mode des 20. Jahrhunderts: etwa die Handtasche mit dem Bambusgriff, die Mokassins mit Metallverzierung und die Taschen mit grün-rot gestreiftem Muster, das ursprünglich von einem Sattelgurt stammt. Familienstreitigkeiten und Massenlizenzen sorgten in den 1980er Jahren für einen Imageverlust der Marke. Die Situation änderte sich jedoch, als das neue Management 1990 Tom Ford zum Designer der Damen-

mode berief. Seine Debütkollektion im März 1995 markierte den Wendepunkt. Heute ist Gucci wieder ein Synonym für hedonistische, ambitionierte Mode. **YVES SAINT LAURENT** (seit 1999) Yves Saint Laurent und sein Geschäftspartner Pierre Bergé gründeten das Modehaus 1962. In den folgenden Jahrzehnten entwarf Saint Laurent eine Reihe von brillanten und gelegentlich revolutionären Kollektionen. Smokings für Damen, durchsichtige Blusen und Safarijacken sind nur einige Beispiele für die größten Erfolge des Hauses. 1966 stellte Saint Laurent unter dem Namen Rive Gauche als erster Couturier eine Prêt-à-Porter-Linie vor. Der Designer zog sich 2002 aus dem Modegeschäft zurück. Seit der Gucci-Konzern die Marke 1999 gekauft hat, entwirft Tom Ford sowohl die Damen- wie auch die Herrenkollektionen für Rive Gauche. **BALENCIAGA** (seit 2001) Christian Dior nannte den Couturier Cristobal Balenciaga, der 1916 im spanischen San Sebastian sein eigenes Modehaus gründete, einmal 'unser aller Meister'. Sein geniales handwerkliches Geschick kam in nüchternen skulpturalen Silhouetten zum Ausdruck. Die sogenannte Sackkleid und die voluminösen Melonenärmel zählen zu seinen einflussreichsten Kreationen. Den Gipfel seines Ruhmes erreichte der Designer in den 1950er und 1960er Jahren. 1968 zog er sich in den Ruhestand zurück und schloss seinen Pariser Modesalon. 1997 gewann man Nicolas Ghesquière dafür, eine Prêt-à-Porter-Linie zu entwerfen, die an den früheren Triumph des Hauses anknüpfen konnte. Außerdem: **SERGIO ROSSI** (seit 1999); **ALEXANDER MCQUEEN** (seit 2000); **STELLA MCCARTNEY** (seit 2001); **BOTTEGA VENETA** (seit 2001)

HERMÈS GROUP

CHAIRMAN UND CEO: JEAN-LOUIS DUMAS
MARKEN, DIE ZUR HERMES GROUP GEHÖREN:
HERMÈS 1837 gründete der Sattlermeister Thierry Hermès sein Geschäft, aus dem fünf Generationen seiner Familie eine angesehene Sattlerei und Lederwarenfirma gemacht haben. Seit den 1920er Jahren hat Hermès sein Sortiment um Handtaschen aus Leder erweitert, die heute zu den berühmtesten Produkten der Marke zählen: Die Kelly- und die Birkin-Bag gehören bis heute zum Begehrtesten (und Teuersten), was die Mode zu bieten hat. Seit März 1998 entwirft der belgische Designer Martin Margiela die Prêt-à-Porter-Linie von Hermès für Damen. Außerdem: **JEAN PAUL GAULTIER; JOHN LOBB** Schuhhersteller

LVMH (LOUIS VUITTON MOËT HENNESSY)

CHAIRMAN UND CEO: BERNARD ARNAULT
MARKEN, DIE LVMH GEHÖREN ODER DEM KONZERN ANGEGLIEDERT SIND:
CHRISTIAN DIOR Christian Diors Debütkollektion von 1947 – die durch Jacken mit Wespentaille und weit schwingende lange Röcke als New Look bekannt wurde – brachte Paris nach dem Krieg wieder an die Spitze der Modewelt und bescherte Dior über Nacht einen Riesenerfolg. Christian Dior schöpfte die Möglichkeiten des raschen Wandels in der Mode voll aus. Untypisch für seine Zeit präsentierte er mit jeder Kollektion eine total neue Saumlänge oder Silhouette. Das machte es leicht, seine Kreationen zu datieren, und brachte dem Designer den Ruf eines Diktators ein. Zehn Jahre lang genoss Dior den Beifall der Kritiker und internationalen Erfolg, dann starb er mit nur 52 Jahren an einem Herzanfall. Zu den Nachfolgern in seinem Haus zählten Yves Saint Laurent, Gianfranco Ferré und, seit 1996, John Galliano. **LOUIS VUITTON** Louis Vuitton begann seine Karriere damit, dass er die Kleider der französischen Kaiserin Eugénie einpackte. Das muss ihn inspiriert

MODEFIRMENGRUPPEN

haben, weil er sich fortan dem Entwerfen von Reisegepäck widmete und 1854 seinen ersten Laden eröffnete. Vuitton erfand flache Truhen, die sich bequem in den Erste-Klasse-Abteilen seiner reichen Kundschaft stapeln ließen. Das wahre Statussymbol, die auf Packleinwand gedruckten Initialen 'LV', wurde 1896 eingeführt. Zu Beginn des Ersten Weltkriegs besaß Louis Vuitton weltweit das größte Geschäft für Reiseartikel. Heute entwirft Marc Jacobs die Prêt-à-Porter-Kollektionen des Hauses. **GIVENCHY** (seit 1988) Hubert de Givenchy gab wie sein Mentor Cristobal Balenciaga klaren, skulpturalen Linien den Vorzug vor kleinteiligem Dekor. Die Ballonärmel der sogenannten Bettinabluse sind eine seiner zahlreichen Erfindungen. Das Verhältnis von Muse und Meister, das den Designer mit Audrey Hepburn verband, war eines der fruchtbarsten der Modegeschichte. Givenchy gründete seinen Modesalon 1952 mit nur 25 Jahren und zog sich 1996 aus dem Geschäft zurück. Seine Damenkollektionen verantwortete nacheinander eine Reihe von jungen britischen Designern: John Galliano, Alexander McQueen und zuletzt Julien Macdonald. **CÉLINE** (seit 1996) Céline begann 1945 als Geschäft für Kinderschuhe. Mit Lederwaren für Erwachsene befasst man sich dort seit 1963. Bald darauf folgte eine Prêt-à-Porter-Kollektion, die Céline für luxuriöse Freizeitkleidung berühmt machte. Der amerikanische Sportswear-Designer Michael Kors ist seit 1997 für das Design zuständig. **EMILIO PUCCI** (seit 2000) Emilio Pucci, der Marchese di Barsento, geriet per Zufall in die Modebranche. Als Mitglied des italienischen Skiteams bei der Olympiade wurde er von 'Harper's Bazaar' auf der Piste in einer Skihose fotografiert, die er selbst entworfen hatte. Durch das Modemagazin ermutigt begann Pucci, ähnliche Kleidung auch für Damen zu entwerfen. In den 1950er Jahren war seine locker sitzende, legere Mode – meist aus Seidenjersey und mit den typischen verwirbelten bunten Mustern bedruckt – unglaublich beliebt, insbesondere bei den Hollywooddiven der damaligen Zeit. 2002 wurde Christian Lacroix Chefsigner des Hauses. **KENZO** (seit 1993) Kenzo Takada gab sein Debüt 1970 in seiner eigenen Boutique Jungle Jap. Berühmt wurde er durch reichlich Farbe, Strickwaren und Neuinterpretationen des traditionellen japanischen Kimonos. Seit 1999 ist Gilles Rosier als Artistic Diector für alle Damenlinien von Kenzo zuständig. **LOEWE** Enrique Loewe gründete 1846 in Madrid eine Lederwarenfabrik. Seither ist dieses Haus nicht nur für Reisegepäck und andere Lederartikel berühmt, sondern auch für elegante Lederkleidung aus unglaublich weich fließendem Material. Zu den Designern, die bereits für Loewe gearbeitet haben, zählt auch Karl Lagerfeld. 1997 erhielt der Amerikaner Narciso Rodriguez den Auftrag, die Modekollektion zu entwerfen. Ihm folgte 2002 José Enrique Oña Selfa. Außerdem: **CHRISTIAN LACROIX** (1993); **DONNA KARAN** (2001); **FENDI** (2002); **MARC JACOBS**

MARZOTTO GROUP

CHAIRMAN: INNOCENZO CIPOLLETTA. CEO: ANTONIO FAVRIN

MARKEN, DIE ZUR MARZOTTO GROUP GEHÖREN:

VALENTINO (seit 2002) Valentino Garavani gründete sein eigenes Couture-Haus 1959 in Rom, nachdem er zehn Jahre lang in Paris studiert und bei etablierten Modehäusern gearbeitet hatte. Dramatische Abendroben in Tomatenrot und adrette Kostüme für Verabredungen zum Lunch gehören zu Valentinos Markenzeichen. **HUGO BOSS** Die 1923 gegründete deutsche Firma stellte zunächst Arbeitskleidung her. Erst in den späten 1960er Jahren änderte Hugo Boss die Ausrichtung und entwarf fortan schicke Herrenkleidung. Damenkollektionen aus dem Hause Boss gibt es seit 1998.

PRADA GROUP

CEO: PATRIZIO BERTELLI

MARKEN, DIE ZUR PRADA-GRUPPE GEHÖREN ODER ANGEGLIEDERT SIND:

PRADA Die Mailänder Lederwarenfirma, die hochwertige Taschen, Koffer und Accessoires aus Leder herstellte, wurde 1913 von Mario Prada gegründet. Marios Enkelin, Miuccia, trat 1970 in den Familienbetrieb ein und führte diesen schrittweise zu großem Erfolg, insbesondere durch ihre Handtaschen und Rucksäcke aus schwarzem Nylon. In Zusammenarbeit mit Patrizio Bertelli, der inzwischen Miuccia Pradas Ehemann ist, wurde 1978 mit Prada Industrial die Grundlage für den weltweiten Vertrieb von Prada-Artikeln geschaffen. Die erste Schuhkollektion stellte man 1982 vor; die Prêt-à-Porter-Modelinie folgte 1989. In den nächsten Jahren gewann die Marke eine ungeheure Prominenz innerhalb der Branche. Außerdem: **MIU MIU; HELMUT LANG** (seit 1999); **JIL SANDER** (seit 1999); **CHURCH'S** (seit 2000); **CAR SHOE** (seit 2001); **AZZEDINE ALAÏA** (seit 2000); **GENNY** (seit 2001)

RICHEMONT GROUP

CEO: JOHANN RUPERT

MARKEN, DIE ZUR RICHEMONT GROUP GEHÖREN:

CHLOÉ (seit 1985) Das 1952 von Jacques Lenoir und Gaby Aghion gegründete Haus für luxuriöse Prêt-à-Porter-Mode stand lange für die romantische Ästhetik von hauchzarten, fließenden Kreationen. Vorgänger von Phoebe Philo in der Position des Creative Director waren u.a. Martine Sitbon, Karl Lagerfeld und Stella McCartney. Außerdem: **CARTIER; DUNHILL; HACKETT**

SALVATORE FERRAGAMO GROUP

CEO DES KONZERNS: LEONARDO FERRAGAMO

MARKEN, DIE ZUR SALVATORE FERRAGAMO GROUP GEHÖREN:

SALVATORE FERRAGAMO Salvatore Ferragamo begann mit neun Jahren eine Lehre als Schuster. 1927 eröffnete er sein Atelier in Florenz, und fortan rissen sich die Hollywoodstars um sein Schuhwerk. Ferragamo bot seinen Kunden neue Erfindungen und Glamour: Keil- und Korkabsätze, ungewöhnliche Materialien wie Spitze oder Schneckenhäuser – Ferragamo kreierte aus allem berühmte Schuhe.

EMANUEL UNGARO (seit 1996) Emanuel Ungaro genoss eine großartige Ausbildung unter den Fittichen von Cristobal Balenciaga und André Courrèges. 1968 gründete er sein eigenes Modehaus, das bald für seine Space-Age-Kleider mit A-förmiger Silhouette und seine Maßarbeiten bekannt wurde. Später wurden die Konturen seiner Entwürfe weicher, und inzwischen sind kräftige, bunte Muster – insbesondere florale Motive und Punktmuster – sein Markenzeichen, das vor allem in den Haute-Couture-Kollektionen zum Ausdruck kommt. 1996 wurde Giambattista Valli zum Chefdesigner des Labels ernannt.

AEFFE SPA

PRÉSIDENT: MASSIMO FERRETTI. PRÉSIDENT SUPPLÉANT: ALBERTA FERRETTI

P-DG: GIOVANNI COCCODRILLI

MARQUES APPARTENANT À AEFFE SPA:

ALBERTA FERRETTI; PHILOSOPHY DI ALBERTA FERRETTI; MOSCHINO Après avoir travaillé pour Gianni Versace, Franco Moschino monte sa propre griffe en 1983. Il devient célèbre pour les effets visuels humoristiques qui ornent fréquemment ses vêtements à la coupe experte. A sa mort en 1994, c'est son bras droit Rossella Jardini qui prend la succession de la maison. Et aussi: **NARCISO RODRIGUEZ; POLLINI** Chausseur; **VELMAR** Maillots de bain et lingerie

CHANEL SA

PROPRIÉTAIRES: FAMILLE WERTHEIMER

MARQUES APPARTENANT EN TOTALITÉ OU EN PARTIE À CHANEL SA:

CHANEL Aujourd'hui, la maison fondée par Gabrielle «Coco» Chanel en 1913 fait indiscutablement partie de l'establishment de la mode parisienne. Ses petites robes noires, ses ensembles en laine bouclée, ses parfums et sa prédilection pour les teints bronzés, les camélias et les bijoux fantaisie ont écrit les chapitres d'une véritable légende. Lorsque Chanel rouvre sa maison en 1954, les critiques sont consternés de voir qu'elle propose des vêtements à peine différents de ses créations d'avant-guerre. Pourtant, tailleur Chanel et sac à main matelassé à chaîne dorée sont longtemps restés l'uniforme international des dames chic. En 1983, Karl Lagerfeld a repris la direction de la création de la maison. Et aussi: **ERES** (depuis 1996) Maillots de bain et lingerie; **HOLLAND & HOLLAND** (depuis 1989)

FRANCE LUXURY GROUP

P-DG: MOUNIR MOUFARRIGE

MARQUES APPARTENANT À FRANCE LUXURY GROUP:

JACQUES FATH Jacques Fath ouvre son salon de haute couture en 1937. Il devient célèbre à la fin des années 1940 pour ses robes du soir aux formes voluptueuses. En 1948, il lance une collection de prêt-à-porter dont les lignes simples lui valent un grand succès aux Etats-Unis. En 2002, la créatrice britannique Lizzy Disney a été nommée styliste principale de la maison. **JEAN-LOUIS SCHERRER** Jean-Louis Scherrer a travaillé chez Christian Dior aux côtés d'Yves Saint Laurent jusqu'à ce que ce dernier prenne la succession de Dior en 1957. Scherrer finit par lancer sa propre griffe en 1962 et se fait connaître pour ses tenues de soirée extravagantes. En 2002, la marque Sherrer a fait appel à la créatrice indienne Ritu Beri pour redorer son blason.

GROUPE GUCCI NV

P-DG: DOMENICO DE SOLE. DIRECTEUR DE LA CRÉATION: TOM FORD

MARQUES APPARTENANT AU GROUPE GUCCI:

GUCCI En 1921, Guccio Gucci crée sa compagnie de bagages et de sellerie à Florence. Dans les années 1950 et 1960, le nom Gucci revêt un cachet particulier et la plupart des articles de maroquinerie Gucci sont devenus des symboles de la mode du XXe siècle, tels que le sac à main avec poignées en bambou, les mocassins décorés d'une pièce de métal et les sacs doublés du filet rayé vert et rouge inspiré des sangles de la sellerie. Dans les années 1980, les disputes de la famille Gucci et les multiples accords de licence entraînent le déclin de l'entreprise, et ce jusqu'à ce que la nouvelle équipe de direction nomme Tom Ford au poste de styliste des lignes pour femme en 1990. En mars 1995, sa première collection marque le début de la nouvelle ère Gucci, un nom devenu depuis synonyme d'une mode hédoniste et des plus désirables. **YVES SAINT LAURENT** (depuis 1999) Yves Saint Laurent et son partenaire en affaires Pierre Bergé ont fondé la maison Saint Laurent en 1962 et, au fil des décennies, le couturier a produit une série de collections brillantes et parfois révolutionnaires. Smokings pour femme, chemisiers transparents et vestes safari ne sont que quelques exemples des plus grands hits de la griffe. Premier couturier à lancer une ligne de prêt-à-porter (1966), Saint Laurent baptise cette nouvelle activité Rive Gauche. Il a pris sa retraite en 2002, et après le rachat de la marque par le Groupe Gucci en 1999, c'est Tom Ford qui dessine les collections Rive Gauche pour homme et pour femme. **BALENCIAGA** (depuis 2001) Maison fondée en 1916 à Saint-Sébastien en Espagne par le couturier Cristobal Balenciaga, décrit par Christian Dior comme «notre maître à tous». Son génie technique s'exprime à travers des formes austères et sculpturales; la robe sac et les volumineuses manches melon comptent parmi ses créations les plus influentes. Au sommet de sa gloire dans les années 1950 et 1960, Balenciaga prend sa retraite et ferme son salon parisien en 1968. En 1997, Nicolas Ghesquière a été embauché pour dessiner une ligne de prêt-à-porter qui a depuis redonné ses titres de noblesse à la maison. Et aussi: **SERGIO ROSSI** (depuis 1999); **ALEXANDER MCQUEEN** (depuis 2000); **STELLA MCCARTNEY** (depuis 2001); **BOTTEGA VENETA** (depuis 2001)

GROUPE HERMÈS

P-DG: JEAN-LOUIS DUMAS

MARQUES APPARTENANT AU GROUPE HERMES:

HERMES Thierry Hermès, fabricant de harnais, monte son entreprise en 1837. Depuis, cinq générations de la famille Hermès se sont succédées pour faire de cette maison un sellier et un maroquinier de prestige. Dans les années 1920, Hermès diversifie ses activités de fabrication de sacs à main en cuir «piqûre sellier», le produit le plus célèbre de la marque: les sacs Kelly et Birkin comptent parmi les «must-have» les plus recherchés (et les plus chers). Depuis mars 1998, le styliste belge Martin Margiela dessine la ligne de prêt-à-porter féminin de Hermès. Et aussi: **JEAN PAUL GAULTIER; JOHN LOBB** Chausseur

LVMH (LOUIS VUITTON MOËT HENNESSY)

P-DG: BERNARD ARNAULT

MARQUES APPARTENANT EN TOTALITÉ OU EN PARTIE AU GROUPE LVMH:

CHRISTIAN DIOR En 1947, le New Look de Christian Dior réinstalle le Paris d'après-guerre à l'avant-garde de la mode mondiale avec les vestes ultra-cintrées et les longues jupes amples d'une première collection qui rend le couturier célèbre dès le jour au lendemain. Christian Dior adorait le changement; chose inhabituelle à l'époque, chaque collection met en avant une coupe ou une silhouette radicalement différente, ce qui permet de dater très facilement ses robes et assoit sa réputation de «dictateur» de la mode. Pendant dix ans, Dior ravit la critique et remporte un succès international avant de disparaître à 52 ans des suites d'une attaque. Parmi ses successeurs à la tête de la maison, on compte Yves Saint Laurent, Gianfranco Ferré et, depuis 1996, John Galliano. **LOUIS VUITTON** Louis Vuitton a débuté sa carrière comme malletier de l'Impératrice Eugénie, une expérience concluante qui l'incite à continuer dans la création de bagages et à ouvrir sa première boutique en 1854. Vuitton créait des malles plates parfaitement

GRANDS GROUPES DE LUXE

adaptées aux compartiments de première classe de ses clients fortunés. Véritable symbole de la maison, la toile au monogramme « LV » est lancée en 1896 et, au début de la première guerre mondiale, Louis Vuitton possède le plus grand magasin d'articles de voyage au monde. Aujourd'hui, c'est Marc Jacobs qui dessine les collections de prêt-à-porter de Vuitton. **GIVENCHY** (depuis 1988) Hubert de Givenchy, à l'instar de son mentor Cristobal Balenciaga, préférait les lignes nettes et sculpturales à la surcharge décorative ; il a lancé de nombreuses tendances, comme les manches ballon de son chemisier Bettina. Le créateur Givenchy avait trouvé sa muse en la personne d'Audrey Hepburn, avec qui il a noué l'une des plus belles relations de l'histoire de la mode. Givenchy a ouvert son salon en 1952, à peine âgé de 25 ans. Il a pris sa retraite en 1996 et depuis, ses collections pour femme ont été confiées à divers jeunes créateurs britanniques : John Galliano, Alexander McQueen et, plus récemment, Julien Macdonald. **CÉLINE** (depuis 1996) La maison Céline a ouvert ses portes en 1945 en tant que chausseur pour enfants, avant de devenir maroquinier en 1963. Une collection de prêt-à-porter suit rapidement et la griffe Céline devient célèbre pour ses vêtements au luxe décontracté. Le styliste américain de sportswear Michael Kors a repris la direction de la création de la maison en 1997. **EMILIO PUCCI** (depuis 2000) Emilio Pucci, le Marchese di Barsento, a débarqué dans la mode complètement par hasard ; membre de l'équipe italienne de ski olympique, Harper's Bazaar le photographie sur les pentes enneigées vêtu d'un pantalon de ski qu'il avait dessiné lui-même. Encouragé par le magazine, Pucci poursuit dans cette voie en créant des vêtements d'inspiration similaire pour les femmes. Dans les années 1950, ses tenues de jour fluides et décontractées – généralement coupées dans un jersey de soie imprimé de motifs multicolores et tourbillonnants très caractéristiques – remportent un succès foudroyant, notamment auprès des divas hollywoodiennes du moment. En 2002, la direction de la création a été confiée au couturier parisien Christian Lacroix. **KENZO** (depuis 1993) Kenzo Takada a lancé sa griffe en 1970 lors d'un premier défilé dans sa boutique Jungle Jap. Il s'est forgé un nom grâce à ses couleurs exubérantes, ses pièces en maille et son interprétation originale du kimono japonais traditionnel. Depuis 1999, Gilles Rosier est le directeur artistique de toutes les lignes Kenzo pour femme. **LOEWE** Enrique Loewe a fondé sa compagnie de maroquinerie à Madrid en 1846. La maison doit sa célébrité à ses bagages et articles en cuir, mais également à ses superbes vêtements de cuir qui tombent sur le corps avec la fluidité d'un tissu. Outre Karl Lagerfeld, la création des collections de vêtements a été confiée au styliste américain Narciso Rodriguez (1997), puis à José Enrique Oña Selfa (2002). Et aussi : **CHRISTIAN LACROIX** (1993) ; **DONNA KARAN** (2001) ; **FENDI** (2002) ; **MARC JACOBS**

GROUPE MARZOTTO

PRÉSIDENT : INNOCENZO CIPOLLETTA. P-DG : ANTONIO FAVRIN

MARQUES APPARTENANT AU GROUPE MARZOTTO :

VALENTINO (depuis 2002) Valentino Garavani a ouvert sa propre maison de haute couture à Rome en 1959, après s'être formé au métier pendant plusieurs années dans des maisons parisiennes de renom. Ses spectaculaires robes du soir rouge tomate et ses ensembles de cocktail impeccables comptent parmi ses pièces les plus célèbres.
HUGO BOSS Fondée en Allemagne en 1923 pour produire des uniformes de travail, la griffe Hugo Boss change d'orientation à la fin des années 1960 et produit une collection masculine des plus élégantes. Hugo Boss s'est lancé dans la mode pour femme en 1998.

GROUPE PRADA

P-DG : PATRIZIO BERTELLI

MARQUES APPARTENANT EN TOTALITÉ OU EN PARTIE AU GROUPE PRADA :

PRADA C'est en 1913 que Mario Prada fonde sa compagnie de maroquinerie à Milan pour vendre des sacs, des malles et des accessoires en cuir de qualité supérieure. La petite-fille de Mario, Miuccia, rejoint l'entreprise familiale en 1970 et insuffle progressivement une nouvelle vie à la maison, notamment en lançant ses sacs à main et sacs à dos en nylon noir. En 1978, Prada Industrial voit le jour grâce à une alliance avec Patrizio Bertelli, aujourd'hui marié à Miuccia Prada. Cette entité constitue la base de distribution mondiale des produits Prada. La première collection de chaussures est lancée en 1982, suivie par une ligne de prêt-à-porter en 1989. Depuis, la marque s'est développée de façon spectaculaire et occupe aujourd'hui une place très enviée au sein de l'industrie de la mode. Et aussi : **MIU MIU** ; **HELMUT LANG** (depuis 1999) ; **JIL SANDER** (depuis 1999) ; **CHURCH'S** (depuis 2000) ; **CAR SHOE** (depuis 2001) ; **AZZEDINE ALAÏA** (depuis 2000) ; **GENNY** (depuis 2001)

GROUPE RICHEMONT

P-DG : JOHANN RUPERT

MARQUES APPARTENANT AU GROUPE RICHEMONT :

CHLOÉ (depuis 1985) Fondée en 1952 par Jacques Lenoir et Gaby Aghion pour produire un prêt-à-porter de luxe, la maison Chloé se distingue par une esthétique romantique qui privilégie les vêtements vaporeux et fluides. Martine Sitbon, Karl Lagerfeld et Stella McCartney figurent parmi les stylistes qui ont précédé l'actuelle directrice de la création, Phoebe Philo. Et aussi : **CARTIER** ; **DUNHILL** ; **HACKETT**

GROUPE SALVATORE FERRAGAMO

P-DG DU GROUPE : LEONARDO FERRAGAMO

MARQUES APPARTENANT AU GROUPE SALVATORE FERRAGAMO :

SALVATORE FERRAGAMO Salvatore Ferragamo a débuté sa carrière à l'âge de neuf ans comme apprenti-chausseur. En 1927, il ouvre un atelier à Florence et rapidement, les stars de Hollywood ne jurent plus que par ses chaussures. Ferragamo offrait innovation et glamour à ses clientes : semelles compensées, talons en liège et matières inhabituelles, de la dentelle aux coquilles d'escargots... autant d'inventions qui l'ont rendu célèbre dans le monde entier. **EMANUEL UNGARO** (depuis 1996) Emanuel Ungaro a bénéficié d'une formation prestigieuse sous l'égide de Cristobal Balenciaga et d'André Courrèges ; en 1968, il crée sa propre maison et se fait connaître pour ses robes et sa coupe trapèze « Space Age ». Par la suite, il atténue ses lignes et deviendra surtout reconnaissable à ses imprimés colorés et audacieux – en particulier les motifs floraux et les pois – d'une exubérance frappante dans ses collections haute couture. Giambattista Valli a été nommé styliste principal de la griffe en 1996.

A BATHING APE
Bape Exclusive Aoyama
5-5-8 1F Minami Aoyama, Minato-ku
Tokyo, Japan

HAIDER ACKERMANN
Van Schoonbekestraat 73
2018 Antwerp, Belgium
T. +33 (0)1 49 23 79 79
F. +33 (0)1 49 23 79 90
nicolas@totemfashion.com
www.totemfashion.com

MIGUEL ADROVER
131 Chrystie Street, 4th floor
New York, NY 10002, USA
T. +1 212 941 6819

AF VANDEVORST
Indienstraat 8
2000 Antwerp, Belgium
T. +33 (0)1 49 23 79 79
F. +33 (0)1 49 23 79 90
corinna@totemfashion.com
www.totemfashion.com

AGENT PROVOCATEUR
Europe: T. +44 (0)20 7235 0229
America: T. +1 323 653 0229
enquiries@agentprovocateur.com
www.agentprovocateur.com

AZZEDINE ALAÏA
T. +33 (0)1 40 27 85 58

APC
39, rue Madame
75006 Paris, France
Europe: T. +33 (0)1 44 39 05 11
America: T. +1 212 966 0069
Asia: T. +81 (0)3 5459 6502
info@apc.fr
www.apc.fr

A-POC
Miyake Design Studio
1-23 Ohyama-Cho, Shibuya-ku
Tokyo 151-8554, Japan
T. +33 (0)1 44 54 07 05
www.isseymiyake.com

GIORGIO ARMANI
Via Borgonuovo, 11
20121 Milan, Italy
Italy: T. +39 02 72 31 81
France: T. +33 (0)1 58 05 43 00
UK: T. +44 (0)20 7808 8100
Belgium: T. +32 (0)2 51 38 11
Spain: T. +34 91 43 51 008
America: T. +1 212 366 9720
Japan: T. +81 (0)3 32 63 30 89
Hong Kong: T. +85 2 25 06 20 18
www.giorgioarmani.com
www.armanipress.com
www.emporioarmaniwatches.com
www.armaniexchange.com

AS FOUR
86 Forsyth Street, 4th Floor
New York, NY 10002, USA
T. +1 212 343 9777
asfour@asfour.net
www.asfour.net

BALENCIAGA
11, avenue d'Iéna
75016 Paris, France
T. +33 (0)1 47 20 21 11
www.balenciaga.com

NEIL BARRETT
Via Savona, 97
20144 Milan, Italy
T. +39 02 42 41 111
F. +39 02 42 41 11 260
commercial@neilbarrett.com

JOHN BARTLETT
John Bartlett Studio
415 West 23rd Street, Suite 15b
New York, NY 10011, USA
T. +1 212 647 9702
F. +1 212 647 9409
jbartlettstudio@aol.com

ANTONIO BERARDI
Jasbir Uppal PR
St Martins House
59 St. Martins Lane
London WC2N 4JS, UK
T. +44 (0)20 7836 4265
F. +44 (0)20 7836 6535
jasbir.uppal@btconnect.com
www.jasbiruppalpr.com

DIRK BIKKEMBERGS
Dirk Bikkembergs Showroom
59, rue de Turenne
75003 Paris, France
Europe: T. +33 (0)1 40 27 07 37
F. +33 (0)1 42 77 57 61
America: T. +1 212 966 8994
Asia: T. +81 (0)3 3267 3638
dirkbikkembergs_paris@bikkembergs.com
www.bikkembergs.com

MANOLO BLAHNIK
297 King's Road
London SW3 5EP, UK
Europe: T. +44 (0)20 7352 8622
America: T. +1 212 582 1583
Asia: +85 2870 3436

BLESS
Bless Kaag/Heiss GBR
Rosa Luxemburgstr. 17
10178 Berlin, Germany
T. +33 (0)1 48 01 67 43
blessberlin@csi.com
blessparis@wanadoo.fr
www.bless-service.de

BLUMARINE
Blufin
via G. Ferraris, 13.15/a
42012 Carpi (MO), Italy
Europe: T. +39 02 784 340
America: T. +1 212 319 2222
blufin@tin.it
www.blufin.it

BOUDICCA
16d King's Yard, Carpenter's Road
London E15 2HD, UK
T. +44 (0)20 8510 9868
F. +44 (0)20 8533 5183
www.platform13.com

VÉRONIQUE BRANQUINHO
James NV
Nationalestraat 123
2000 Antwerp, Belgium
T. +33 (0)1 49 23 79.79
F. +33 (0)1 49 23 79 90
samantha@totemfashion.com
www.totemfashion.com

BARBARA BUI
43, rue des Francs-Bourgeois
75004 Paris, France
Europe: T. +33 (0)1 44 59 94 06
America: T. +1 212 625 1938
info@barbarabui.fr
www.barbarabui.com

BURBERRY
18-22 Haymarket
London SW1Y 4SQ, UK
T. +44 (0)20 7968 0000
T. 07000 785 676 (UK only)
www.burberry.com

CACHAREL
36, rue Tronchet
75009 Paris, France
T. +33 (0)4 66 28 66 28

JOE CASELY-HAYFORD
Europe & USA: T. +44 (0)20 7729 0990
F. +44 (0)20 7729 8700
Asia: T. +81 (0)45 910 6360
joe.caselyhayford@btinternet.com

ROBERTO CAVALLI
Via Del Cantone, 29
50019 Oshannano, Sesto Fiorentino (FI), Italy
T. +39 05 53 24 21
F. +39 05 53 19 471
centralino@robertocavalli.it
www.robertocavalli.it

CÉLINE
23-25, rue du Pont-Neuf
75001 Paris, France
France: T. +33 (0)1 55 80 12 12
UK: T. +44 (0)20 7297 4999
www.celine.com

HUSSEIN CHALAYAN
109-123 Clifton Street
London EC2A 4LD, UK
Europe: T. +33 (0)1 42 61 99 80
America: T. +1 212 997 3600
Asia: T. +39 02 33 61 47 21

CHANEL
29-31, rue Cambon
75001 Paris, France
France: T. +33 (0)1 42 86 28 00
UK: T. +44 (0)20 7493 3836
USA: T. +1 212 715 4750
Singapore: T. +65 838 02 28
Hong Kong: T. +85 2 2526 6461
www.chanel.com

CHLOÉ
54/56, rue du Faubourg Saint-Honoré
75008 Paris, France
Europe: T. +33 (0)1 44 94 33 33
America: +1 212 957 1100
Asia: +81 (0)3 5575 5324
www.chloe.com

BENJAMIN CHO
427 West 14th Street, Suite 3R
New York, NY 10014, USA
T. +1 917 606 0683

SUSAN CIANCIOLO
T. +1 401 284 0384
susancianciolo@hotmail.com

CLEMENTS RIBEIRO
413-419 Harrow Road
London W9 3QJ, UK
T. +44 (0)20 8962 3060
F. +44 (0)20 8962 3061
clementsribeiro@btconnect.com

JEAN COLONNA
104, rue des Couronnes
75002 Paris, France
T. +33 (0)1 47 97 11 64
F. +33 (0)1 47 97 11 39

COMME DES GARÇONS
5-11-5 Minamni Aoyama, Minato-ku
Tokyo 107, Japan
Europe: T. +33 (0)1 47 03 60 81
America: +1 212 604 0013
Asia: +81 (0)3 407 2684

EMMA COOK
18 Shackleweli Lane
London E8 2E2, UK
T. +44 (0)20 7242 5483
www.emmacook.co.uk

COSTUME NATIONAL
Via Fusetti, 12
20143 Milan, Italy
T. +39 02 83 84 41
F. +39 02 83 84 42 51
www.costumenational.com

C.P. COMPANY
SPW Company
Via Confine, 2161
41017 Ravarino (MO), Italy
T. +39 02 42 20 141
F. +39 02 42 20 14 50
info@cpcompany.com
www.cpcompany.com

DAKS
10 Old Bond Street
London W1, UK
T. +44 (0)20 7409 4000
F. +44 (0)20 7409 4135
webmaster@london.daks.com
www.daks.com

ANN DEMEULEMEESTER
Populierenlaan 34
2020 Antwerp, Belgium
T. +32 (0)3 830 5272
F. +32 (0)3 830 0504

DESIGNER CONTACTS

DIESEL
Via Dell'Industria, 7
36060 Molvena (VI), Italy
Europe: T. +39 04 24 47 75 55
F. +39 04 24 70 83 33
America: +1 212 755 9200
info@diesel.com
www.diesel.com
www.dieselstylelab.com

CHRISTIAN DIOR
30, avenue Montaigne
75008 Paris, France
T. +33 (0)1 40 73 54 44
F. +33 (0)1 47 20 00 60

DIOR HOMME
40, rue François 1er
75008 Paris, France
T. +33 (0)1 40 73 55 70
F. +33 (0)1 40 73 57 46
www.dior.com

DKNY
550 7th Avenue
New York, NY 10018, USA
www.dkny.com

DOLCE & GABBANA
Via Goldoni, 10
20129 Milan, Italy
T. +39 03 31 40 92 11
www.dolcegabbana.it

E2
15, rue Martel
75010 Paris, France
T/F. +33 (0)1 47 70 15 14

ELEY KISHIMOTO
215 Lyham Road
London SW2 5PY, UK
mark@eleykishimoto.com
eleykishimoto.com (password recuired)

TIMOTHY EVEREST
32 Elder Street
London E1 6BT, UK
T. +44 (0)20 7377 5770
F. +44 (0)20 7377 5990
rtw@timothyeverest.co.uk

FENDI
Via Flaminia, 1063
Rome, Italy
Europe: T. +33 (0)1 49 52 84 52
America: T. +1 212 262 7344
www.lvmh.com

ALBERTA FERRETTI
Aeffe SpA
Via Donizetti, 48
20122 Milan, Italy
Europe: T. +39 05 41 96 53 79
America: T. +1 212 632 9300
Asia: T. +39 02 76 05 91
info@aeffe.com
www.philosophy.it
www.albertaferretti.it

ANGELO FIGUS
Pier srl
Via Verdi, 10
30121 Mogliano Veneto (TV), Italy
T. +33 (0)1 53 41 41 70
F. +33 (0)1 53 41 41 71
susanna@piersrl.it

JOHN GALLIANO
60, rue d'Avron
75020 Paris, France
T. +33 (0)1 55 25 11 11
F. +33 (0)1 55 25 11 14
www.johngalliano.com

JEAN PAUL GAULTIER
30, rue du Faubourg Saint-Antoine
75012 Paris, France
T. +33 (0)1 44 78 55 00
www.jeanpaulgaultier.com

GHOST
The Chapel, 263 Kensal Road
London W10 5DB, UK
T. +44 (0)20 8960 3121
info@ghost.co.uk
www.ghost.co.uk

MARITHÉ + FRANÇOIS GIRBAUD
5, place André-Malraux
75001 Paris, France
Europe: T. +39 02 54 11 60 77
F. +39 02 55 19 11 32
America: T. +1 212 563 0761
F. +1 212 563 0769
Japan: T. +81 (0)6 6241 4031
F. +81 (0)6 6241 4005
Philippines: T. +632 633 2895
F. +632 636 0059
www.girbaud.com

GIVENCHY COUTURE
3, avenue Georges V
75008 Paris, France
T. +33 (0)8 25 82 55 90
www.givenchy.com

GRIFFIN
297 Portobello Road
London W10 5TD, UK
UK: T. +44 (0)1380 831 053
F. +44 (0)1380 830 731
Italy: T. +39 02 54 12 24 49
Asia: T. +81 3 5772 2401
karina@griffin-studio.com
www.griffin-studio.com

GUCCI
173-176 Sloane Street
London SW1 9Q, UK
www.gucci.com

KATHARINE HAMNETT
T. +44 (0)20 7352 2400

ALEXANDRE HERCHCOVITCH
Rua Haddock Lobo, 1151
São Paulo 01414-003, Brazil
T. +33 (0)1 49 23 79 79
F. +33 (0)1 49 23 79 90
virginie@totemfashion.com
www.herchcovitch.com
www.totemfashion.com

HERMÈS
24, rue du Faubourg Saint-Honoré
75008 Paris, France
France: T. +33 (0)1 40 17 46 00
UK: T. +44 (0)20 7823 1014
America: T. +1 212 835 6444
Asia: T. +81 (0)3 3289 6811

TOMMY HILFIGER
11/F, Novel Industrial Building
850-870 Lai Chi Kok Road,
Cheung Sha Wan, Kowloon
Hong Kong, China
Europe: T. +31 20 58 99 888
America: T. +1 800 866 6922
Hong Kong & Taiwan: T. +852 2721 2668
F. +852 2312 1368
Japan: T. +81 (0)3 3407 6580
F. +81 (0)3 3407 5392/90

IMITATION OF CHRIST
498 Seventh Avenue, 24th floor
New York, NY 10018, USA
T. +1 212 643 4810 Ext.135
F. +1 212 971 6066
mandie_erickson@hotmail.com

MARC JACOBS
72 Spring Street
New York, NY 10012, USA
T. +1 212 343 0222
www.marcjacobs.com

STEPHEN JONES MILLINERY
36 Great Queen Street
London WC2B 5AA, UK
Europe & America: T. +44 (0)20 7242 0770
F. +44 (0)20 7242 0796
Asia: T. +81 (0)3 3225 2471
www.shop@stephenjonesmillinery.com
www.stephenjonesmillinery.com

DONNA KARAN
550 7th Avenue
New York, NY 10018, USA
T. +1 212 789 1500
www.donnakaran.com

KENZO
54, rue Etienne-Marcel
75002 Paris, France
Womenswear:
T. +33 (0)1 40 39 72 53
F. +33 (0)1 40 39 72 67
Menswear:
T. +33 (0)1 49 29 37 07
F. +33 (0)1 49 29 37 00
www.kenzo.com

CALVIN KLEIN
205 West 39th Street
New York, NY 10018, USA
Calvin Klein stores:
New York: T. +1 212 292 9000
Dallas: T. +1 214 520 9222
Paris: T. +33 (0)1 56 88 12 12
Tokyo: T. +81 (0)3 3470 3451
Seoul: T. +82 2 3444 3300
Singapore: T. +65 735 5790
Taipei: T. +88 62 2731 0020

SOPHIA KOKOSALAKI
3/138 Long Acre
London WC2E 2AD, UK
T/F. +44 (0)20 7836 7584
sophiakokosalaki@aol.com

MICHAEL KORS
550 7th Avenue, 6th Floor
New York, NY 10018, USA
T. +39 02 65 56 98 41
F. +39 02 29 01 45 10
www.michaelkors.com

LACOSTE
58 Broadwick Street
London W1F 7AL, UK
T. +33 (0)1 44 82 69 00
F. +33 (0)1 44 82 69 45
infoconso@devanlay.fr
www.lacoste.com

CHRISTIAN LACROIX
73, rue du Faubourg Saint-Honoré
75008 Paris, France
Europe: T. +33 (0)1 42 68 79 00
America: T. +1 212 931 2000
info@c-lacroix.com
www.christian-lacroix.com

LAGERFELD GALLERY
12, rue Vivienne
75002 Paris, France
T. +33 (0)1 44 50 22 00
F. +33 (0)1 44 50 22 05
caroline.fragner@lagerfeldgallery.fr

HELMUT LANG
80 Greene Street, 2nd floor
New York, NY 10012, USA
T. +1 212 334 1014
F. +1 212 334 1950
www.helmutlang.com

LANVIN
15-22, rue du Faubourg Saint-Honoré
75008 Paris, France
T. +33 (0)1 55 90 52 92

CHRISTOPHE LEMAIRE
CLFF S.A.
6, rue Grande
77430 Champagne s/Seine, France
T/F. +33 (0)1 43 55 58 27
clemaireCLFF@aol.com

LÉONARD
36, avenue Pierre-1er-de-Serbie
75008 Paris, France
Europe: T. +33 (0)1 53 67 87 87
America: T. +1 212 869 3601
Asia: T. +33 (0)1 5367 8787
jpgoddet@leonardparis.com

VÉRONIQUE LEROY
T. +33 (0)1 44 87 90 90
F. +33 (0)1 44 87 90 91
vleroy@veroniqueleroy.com

LEVI STRAUSS & CO.
Levi's Plaza
1155 Battery Street
San Francisco, CA 94111, USA
Europe: T. +32 (0)2 64 16 011
USA: T. +1 415 501 6000
Asia: T. +65 6735 9303
www.levi.com

LOEWE
Palacio de Miraflores
Carrera de San Jeronimo 15
28014 Madrid, Spain
Europe: T. +34 91 36 06 100
F. +34 91 20 40 426
America: T. +1 212 931 2000
Asia: +852 2968 5300
www.loewe.com

LOUIS VUITTON MALLETIER
2, rue du Pont-Neuf
75001 Paris, France
www.vuitton.com

MARKUS LUPFER
86 Greenfield Road
London E1 1EJ, UK
Europe: T. +44 (0)20 7377 9323
America: T. +1 212 226 5507
Asia: T. +81 (0)7 8845 9833

LUTZ
POLUX-Lutz
108, rue de Rivoli
75001 Paris, France
T. +33 (0)1 42 33 18 03
F. +33 (0)1 42 33 18 02
lutz.mail@wanadoo.fr

JULIEN MACDONALD
6B Golborne Road
London W10 5NP, UK
T. +44 (0)20 8968 9988

MAHARISHI
19a Floral Street
London WC2E 9HL, UK
T. +44 (0)20 7749 2290
F. +44 (0)20 7749 2270
wholesale@emaharishi.com
retail@emaharishi.com
store@emaharishi.com
www.emaharishi.com
www.emhi.co.uk

MAISON MARTIN MARGIELA
Bureau de Presse
175, rue du Faubourg-Poissonnière
75009 Paris, France
N. Europe: T. +33 (0)1 44 53 43 26
S. Europe: T. +33 (0)1 44 53 43 63
America: T. +33 (0)1 44 53 43 13
Asia: T. +81 (0)3 57 25 24 27
maison@martinmargiela.net

MARNI
Via Sismondi, 70/b
20133 Milan, Italy
T. +39 02 70 00 54 79
F. +39 02 70 10 19 77
verde@marni.it

ANTONIO MARRAS
Circolo Marras
Via Manzoni, 73
07041 Alghero (SS), Italy
T. +39 05 15 36 904
F. +39 05 15 36 096
enricoaccardo@tiscali.it

STELLA MCCARTNEY
13, rue de Turbigo
75002 Paris, France
Europe & Asia: T. +39 02 88 00 51
F. +39 02 88 00 54 96
America: T. +1 212 379 8412
F. +1 212 379 8649
agotti@stellamccartney.com
www.stellamccartney.com

ALEXANDER MCQUEEN
10 Amwell Street
London EC1R 1VQ, UK
T. +44 (0)20 7278 4333
www.alexandermcqueen.com

YVAN MISPELAERE
T. +33 (0)1 42 33 93 05
mail@2e-bureau.com

MISSONI
Via Luigi Rossi, 52
21040 Sumirago (VA), Italy
T. +39 03 31 98 80 00
F. +39 03 31 90 99 55
www.missoni.it

MIU MIU
Europe: T. +39 02 76 00 17 99
America: T. +1 212 334 5156
Asia: T. +852 2523 7833

ISSEY MIYAKE
1-12-20 Tomigaya, Shibuya-ku
Tokyo 151-8554, Japan
Europe: T. +33 (0)1 44 54 56 00
America: T. +1 212 226 1334
Asia: T. +81 (0)3 5454 1705
www.isseymiyake.com

ANNA MOLINARI
Blufin
Via G. Ferraris, 13.15/a
42012 Carpi (MO), Italy
Europe: +39 02 78 43 40
America: +1 212 319 2222
blufin@tin.it
www.blufin.it

HAMISH MORROW
T. +44 (0)20 7377 9444
F. +44 (0)20 7377 5398
hamishmorrow@hotmail.com

MOSCHINO
Via G. Ceradini, 11/a
20129 Milan, Italy
Europe: T. +39 02 75 41 31
F. +39 02 71 91 79
USA: T. +1 212 632 9300
info@moschino.it
www.moschino.it

ROLAND MOURET
The Courtyard, 250 King's Road
London SW3 5UE, UK
Europe: T. +44 (0)20 7376 5762
F. +44 (0)20 7351 9935
USA: T. +1 323 465 8700
sales@rolandmouret.co.uk
www.net-a-porter.com

NEW YORK INDUSTRIE
Via Del Progresso,10
36025 Noventa, Vicentina (VI), Italy
Italy: T. +39 04 44 78 45 00
UK: T. +44 (0)20 7841 6000
France: T. +33 (0)1 47 03 16 70
Spain: T. +34 93 36 33 633
USA: T. +1 646 613 8457
Japan: T. +81 (0)6 6241 4040
sales@staffinternational.it
www.newyorkindustrie.com
www.staffinternational.com

NINA DONIS
Sadovaya-Chernogriazskaya 11/2 #57
105064 Moscow, Russia
T. +7 095 207 8412
donis@aha.ru

JESSICA OGDEN
Jessica Ogden Studio
7 Peacock Yard, Iliffe Street
London SE17 3LH, UK
T. +44 (0)20 7701 6552
F. +44 (0)20 7701 6513
jessicaogdenstudio@hotmail.com

JOSÉ ENRIQUE OÑA SELFA
30, rue de la Longue Haie
1050 Brussels, Belgium
T. +32 (0)2 502 4308
F. +32 (0)2 502 4438

RICK OWENS
1638/1639 North Las Palmas
Los Angeles, CA 90028, USA
T. +1 323 465 8700 / 323 461 8620
F. +1 323 465 8710
owensslab@aol.com
noellelippman@aol.com

MARJAN PEJOSKI
Studio 2, 12 Chippenham Mews
London W9 2AW, UK
T. +33 (0)1 49 23 79 79
F. +33 (0)1 49 23 79 90
samantha@totemfashion.com

JURGI PERSOONS
RUFF nv
Kleine Kauwenberg 4-10
B 2000 Antwerp, Belgium
Europe & Asia: T. +32 (0)3 227 1267
America: T. +1 212 925 9700
jurgipersoons@freegates.be

PIERROT
PR Consulting
42 Bond Street, 6th Floor
New York, NY 10012, USA
T. +1 212 997 3600
F. +1 212 997 5515
shay@onwardusa.com

CAROL CHRISTIAN POELL
Via G. Watt, 5
20143 Milan, Italy
T. +39 02 81 35 004
ccp@carolchristianpoell.com
www.carolchristianpoell.com

POLO RALPH LAUREN
650 Madison Avenue
New York, NY 10022, USA
Europe: T. +44 (0)20 7535 4600
America: T. +1 212 318 7000
www.polo.com

ZAC POSEN
13-17 Laight Street
New York, NY 10013, USA
T. +1 212 925 1263
F. +1 212 925 1264
info@zacposen.com
www.zacposen.com

PRADA
PRADA Holding NV
Dam 3-7
1012 JS Amsterdam, The Netherlands
T. +41 91 986 6100
F. +41 91 986 6101

EMILIO PUCCI
Palazzo Pucci
Via de'Pucci, 6
50122 Florence, Italy
T. +39 05 52 61 841

RICHARD EDWARDS
145 Spring Street, 2nd floor
New York, NY 10012, USA
T. +1 212 334 4280
www.richardedwardsnyc.com

JOHN RICHMOND
Unit 1, 9 Park Hill
London SW4 9NS, UK
T. +39 02 77 33 15 00
info@johnrichmond.com
www.johnrichmond.com

NARCISO RODRIGUEZ
Aeffe SpA
Via delle Querce, 51
47842 S. Giovanni in Marignano (RN), Italy
Europe & Asia: T. +39 02 76 05 91
America: T. +1 212 632 9300
info@aeffe.com
www.aeffe.com

GILLES ROSIER
4/6, rue de Braque
75003 Paris, France
T. +33 (0)1 49 96 44 44
F. +33 (0)1 49 96 44 39
gillesrosier@club-internet.fr
info@gillesrosier.com

RUFFO
Ruffo Press Office
T. +39 02 70 06 61
F. +39 02 70 06 621
ruffo.milan@ruffo.it

SONIA RYKIEL
175, boulevard Saint-Germain
75006 Paris, France
France: T. +33 (0)1 49 54 60 60
Italy: T. +39 02 33 13 179
America: T. +1 212 223 2701
Asia: T. +81 (0)3 3423 9434
www.soniarykiel.com

JIL SANDER
Osterfeldstraße 32-34
D-22529 Hamburg, Germany
Europe: T. +49 40 55 30 20
F. +49 40 55 30 21 68
America: T. +1 212 447 9200
Asia: T. + 41 919 8660

STEPHAN SCHNEIDER
Reyndersstraat 53
2000 Antwerp, Belgium
T. +32 (0)3 226 2614
F. +32 (0)3 231 8443
interchic.bvba@pandora.be

JEREMY SCOTT
667 N Berendo
Los Angeles, CA 90004, USA
T. +1 323 662 8990
F. +1 323 662 8978

RAF SIMONS
DETLEF
Rosier 32/34
2000 Antwerp, Belgium
T. +33 (0)1 49 23 79 79
F. +33 (0)1 49 23 79 90
samantha@totemfashion.com
www.rafsimons.be

MARTINE SITBON
6, rue de Braque
75003 Paris, France
T. +33 (0)1 44 39 84 44
F. +33 (0)1 44 39 84 45

PAUL SMITH
Riverside Building, Riverside Way
Nottingham NG2 1DP, UK
UK: T. +44 (0)20 7836 7828
France: T. +33 (0)1 53 63 13 19
Italy: T. +39 02 58 31 65 02
America: T. +1 212 229 2471
Asia: T. +81 (0)3 3486 1500
www.paulsmith.co.uk

STEPHEN SPROUSE
KCD
450 W 15th Street no.604
New York, NY 10011, USA
T. +1 212 590 5117
F. +1 212 590 5101

LAWRENCE STEELE
Via Seprio, 2
20149 Milan, Italy
T. +39 02 48 19 51 28
F. +39 02 48 00 56 01
info@lawrencesteele.com
www.lawrencesteele.com

STONE ISLAND
SPW Company
Via Confine, 2161
41017 Ravarino, (MO), Italy
T. +39 02 42 20 141
F. +39 02 42 20 14 50
info@stoneisland.com
www.stoneisland.com

STÜSSY
17426 Daimler Street
Irvine, CA 92614, USA
www.stussystore.co.uk
www.stussy.com

ANNA SUI
275 West 39th Street, 6th floor
New York, NY 10018, USA
T. +1 212 768 1951
F. +1 212 768 8824
contactus@annasui.com
www.annasui.com

ATSURO TAYAMA
40, rue de Sévigné
75003 Paris, France
Europe: T. +33 (0)1 40 29 15 15
America: T. +33 (0)1 40 29 15 00
Asia: T. +81 (0)3 54 7869 2500
atparis@atsuro.fr

OLIVIER THEYSKENS
This be
52, rue de la Concorde
Brussels, Belgium
T. +33 (0)1 49 23 79 79
F. +33 (0)1 49 23 79 90
nicolas@totemfashion.com
www.totemfashion.com

PHILIP TREACY
Mount Barrow House
12 Elizabeth Street
London SW1 W9R, UK
T. +44 (0)20 7824 8787
F. +44 (0)20 7824 8262
sales-pr@philiptreacy.co.uk
www.philiptreacy.co.uk

UNDERCOVER
UNIMAT Bleu Cinq Point #C
5-3-18 Minami Aoyama, Minato-ku
Tokyo 107-0062, Japan
Europe: T. +33 (0)1 42 21 34 89
Asia: T. +81 (0)3 3407 1232
F. +81 (0)3 3407 1232

EMANUEL UNGARO
2, avenue Montaigne
75008 Paris, France
France: T. +33 (0)1 53 57 00 00
UK: T. +44 (0)20 7629 0550
America: +1 212 221 9011
www.emanuelungaro.com

WALTER VAN BEIRENDONCK
Henri Van Heuckstraat 5
2000 Antwerp, Belgium
T. +32 (0)3 231 7732

DRIES VAN NOTEN
Godefriduskaai 36
2000 Antwerp, Belgium
T. +33 (0)1 42 74 44 07
F. +33 (0)1 42 74 45 22
driesvannoten@compaqnet.fr

DIRK VAN SAENE
Henri van Heurckstraat 3
2000 Antwerp, Belgium
T. +39 04 14 53 640
F. +39 04 15 90 22 19

VERSACE
Via Gesu, 12
20121 Milan, Italy
Europe: T. +39 02 76 09 31
America: T. +1 212 753 8595
Asia: T. +81 (0)3 3261 3371
www.versace.com

VIKTOR & ROLF
Daniele Ghiselli Diffusione
Via Sidoli,19
20129 Milan, Italy
Europe: T. +39 02 70 10 08 03
F. +39 02 70 00 13 50
USA: T. +1 212 997 3600
F. +1 212 997 5515
Asia: T. +81 (0)3 3770 6911
F. +81 (0)3 3770 6912
office@viktor-rolf.com

JUNYA WATANABE
Comme des Garçons Co. Ltd
5-11-5 Minami Aoyama, Minato-ku
Tokyo 107, Japan
Europe: T. +33 (0)1 47 03 60 80
America: T. +1 212 604 0013
Asia: T. +81 (0)3 3407 2684

VIVIENNE WESTWOOD
44 Conduit Street
London W1S 2YL, UK
Europe: T. +44 (0)20 7439 1109
F +44 (0)20 7734 6074
America: T. +1 212 334 1500
Asia: T. +81 (0)3 3501 2770
www.viviennewestwood.com

BERNHARD WILLHELM
Begijnenvest 39
2000 Antwerp, Belgium
T. +33 (0)1 49 23 79 79
F. +33 (0)1 49 23 79 90
nicolas@totemfashion.com
www.totemfashion.com

MATTHEW WILLIAMSON
37 Percy Street
London W1T 2DJ, UK
T. +44 (0)20 7637 4600
F. +44 (0)20 7637 4681
joseph@matthewwilliamson.co.uk
www.matthewwilliamson.co.uk

WINK
166 Geary Street, Suite 307
San Francisco, CA 94108, USA
T. +1 212 925 9700
F. +1 212 925 1550

YOHJI YAMAMOTO
2-2-43 Higashi Shinagawa
Shinagawa-ku, Tokyo 140, Japan
Europe: T. +33 (0)1 42 78 94 11
America: T. +1 212 966 9066
Asia: T. +81 (0)3 5463 1500

GASPARD YURKIEVICH
38, rue Charlot
75003 Paris, France
T. + 33 (0)1 42 77 42 46
F. + 33 (0)1 42 77 42 47
gaspard.yurkievich@wanadoo.fr

YVES SAINT LAURENT RIVE GAUCHE
7, avenue George V
75008 Paris, France
Europe: T. +33 (0)1 56 62 64 00
F. +33 (0)1 56 62 65 00
America: T. +1 212 988 3821
Asia: T. +81 (0)3 5464 9960
www.ysl.com

ZERO
225 Mott Street
New York, NY 10012, USA
T. +1 212 997 3600
F. +1 212 997 5515
shay@onwardusa.com

KIM WESTON ARNOLD
T. +44 (0)7801 817 497
kweston_arnold@hotmail.com

ANETTE AURELL
M.S. Logan
T. +1 212 995 9079
info@mslogan.net
www.mslogan.net

KENT BAKER
Terrie Tanaka
T. +44 (0)20 7792 3500
www.terrietanaka.com

BARNABY & SCOTT
Barnaby Roper
barnaby.roper@virgin.net
Scott Lyon
me@scottlyon.com

ORION BEST
Penny Rich
T. +44 (0)20 7613 3886
www.pennyrich.co.uk

**ANUSCHKA BLOMMERS
& NIELS SCHUMM**
Walter Schupfer Management
NY: T. +1 212 366 4675
Paris: T. +33 (0)1 44 54 81 10
mail@wschupfer.com
www.wschupfer.com

MARK BORTHWICK
PMI
T. +1 212 965 1870
www.pmionline.net

RICHARD BURBRIDGE
Richard Burbridge Inc.
T. +1 212 989 0750

RICHARD BUSH
Untitled Management
T.+44 (0)20 7434 3202
www.untitled.uk.com

GIOVANNI CALEMMA
zowie77@hotmail.com

MARTHA CAMARILLO
T. +1 212 571 6192
martha.camarillo@verizon.net

DAVIDE CERNUSCHI
dcernuschi@aol.com
www.davidecernuschi.com

DONALD CHRISTIE
Z Photographic
T. +44 (0)20 8968 7700
www.zphotographic.com

JIM COCHRANE
T. +44 (0)7715 169 650
jimcochrane@compuserve.com

CRICCHI AND FERRANTE
Close-up
T. +39 02 89 42 09 08
close-up@libero.it
www.closeupmilano.it

SEAN CUNNINGHAM
T. +44 (0)7768 890 395

KEVIN DAVIES
T. +44 (0)20 8563 2349
kevinpdavies@hotmail.com

CORINNE DAY
Susan Babchick Agency
T. +44 (0)20 7287 1497

SOPHIE DELAPORTE
Michele Filomeno
T. +33 (0)1 55 35 35 00
www.mfilomeno.com

CLAUDIO DELL'OLIO
claudiodellolio@aol.com

JAN-WILLEM DIKKERS
Issue Management
T. +1 212 598 4130
www.issuemanagement.net

ANDREW DOSUNMU
T. +1 212 962 7615

PETE DRINKELL
Nicola Prior
T. +44 (0)20 7241 3379

LARRY DUNSTAN
Press Counsel Photography
T. +44 (0)20 7313 9100
www.pcp-agency.com

SEAN ELLIS
Sean Ellis Ltd.
T.+44 (0)20 7288 2333

GLEN ERLER
MAP
London: T. +44 (0)20 7424 9144
NY: T. +1 212 677 2690
info@mapltd.com
www.mapltd.com

JASON EVANS
WIB
T. +44 (0)1273 326 676

FABRIZIO FERRI
MAREK & Associates
T. +1 212 924 6760
www.marekandassociates.com

SIMON FLAMIGNI
7.11
T. +39 335 397236
7.11@libero.it

HUGER FOOTE
Maconochie Photography
T. +44 (0)20 7439 3159

GAUTHIER GALLET
Jaja Deffe
T. +33 (0)1 46 37 03 85
jajadeffe@yahoo.fr

KATE GARNER
kate@kategarner.com

TIERNEY GEARON
Management + Artists
NY: T. +1 212 931 9311
mao@managementartists.com
Paris: T. +33 (0)1 42 71 60 60
daniel@managementartists.fr
www.managementartists.com

JOHNNY GIUNTA
Clare Agency
T. +1 212 968 7185
clare@clareagency.com
www.clareagency.com

NATHANIEL GOLDBERG
The Katy Barker Agency
London: T. +44 (0)20 7493 3933
NY: T. +1 212 627 2558
Paris: T. +33 (0)142 97 90 31
www.katybarker.com

ALEX HOERNER
T. +1 310 459 2868
alexhoerner@hotmail.com

RAINER HOSCH
Walter Schupfer Management
NY: T. +1 212 366 4675
Paris: T. +33 (0)1 44 54 81 10
mail@wschupfer.com
www.wschupfer.com

KAYT JONES
Julian Meijer Associés
T. +33 (0)1 42 74 30 35
julianmeijer.com
Izzy King
T. +44 (0)20 8968 6718
izzy@izzyking.co.uk
www.izzyking.co.uk

MATT JONES
Management + Artists
NY: T. +1 212 931 9311
mao@managementartists.com
Paris: T. +33 (0)1 42 71 60 60
daniel@managementartists.fr
www.managementartists.com

GREG KADEL
MAREK & Associates
T. +1 212 924 6760
www.marekandassociates.com

RICHARD KERN
Vue Represents
T. +1 212 431 5780
rockstarvue@mindsprind.com

STEVEN KLEIN
Management + Artists
NY: T. +1 212 931 9311
mao@managementartists.com
Paris: T. +33 (0)1 42 71 60 60
daniel@managementartists.fr
www.managementartists.com

KIRBY KOH
T. +44 (0)7957 422 392

GLEB KOSORUKOV
T. +33 (0)6 64 25 36 20

HIROSHI KUTOMI
CLM
London: T. +44 (0)20 7750 2999
NY: T. +1 212 941 1660
www.clmuk.com

DAVID LACHAPELLE
Creative Exchange Agency
T. +1 212 414 4100
www.creativeexchangeagency.com

MARK LEBON
T. +44 (0)20 8968 8778
marklebon@lineone.net

DUC LIAO
Françoise Okala Agency
T. +33 (0)1 45 23 14 69
www.francoiseokala.com

ARMIN LINKE
T. +39 02 47 27 03
www.arminlinke.com

GREG LOTUS
Art Department
T. +1 212 925 4222
info@art-dept.com
www.art-dept.com

CYRUS MARSHALL
www.cyrusmarshall.com

CRAIG MCDEAN
Craig McDean Studio
T. + 1 212 431 0911

ALASDAIR MCLELLAN
MAP
London: T. +44 (0)20 7424 9144
NY: T. +1 212 677 2690
info@mapltd.com
www.mapltd.com

DONALD MILNE
MAP, NY
T. +1 212 677 2690
www.mapltd.com

MICHEL MOMY
Paris: 'art.
T. +33 (0)1 42 71 07 43
London: LEJ
T. +44 (0)20 7734 1110
lej@dircon.co.uk

EDDIE MONSOON
Monsoon Photographic
T.+44 (0)20 7286 0262
monsoonphoto@compuserve.com

STEFANO MORO
Close-up
T. +39 02 89 42 09 08
close-up@libero.it
www.closeupmilano.it

PHOTOGRAPHER CONTACTS

SHAWN MORTENSEN
T. +1 917 701 3925
doctorcornelius@yahoo.com

JEREMY MURCH
Webber
T. +44 (0)20 7439 0678
www.webberrepresents.com
Art Department
T. +1 212 925 4222
info@art-dept.com
www.art-dept.com

LAURENCE PASSERA
T. +44 (0)7773 800 236
lensi_@excite.com

BIANCA PILET
Chantal Hoogvliet Agency
T. +33 (0)1 42 72 78 99
www.chantal.tv

MARC QUINN
White Cube Gallery
T. +44 (0)20 7930 5373
www.whitecube.com

TERRY RICHARDSON
The Katy Barker Agency
London: T. +44 (0)20 7493 3933
NY: T. +1 212 627 2558
Paris: T. +33 (0)142 97 90 31
www.katybarker.com

MISCHA RICHTER
Izzy King
T. +44 (0)20 8968 6718
izzy@izzyking.co.uk
www.izzyking.co.uk

CHRISTOPHE RIHET
CLM
London: T. +44 (0)20 7750 2999
NY: +1 212 941 1660
www.clmuk.com

PAOLO ROVERSI
Streeters
T. +44 (0)20 7253 3330

AMBER ROWLANDS
Bird Productions
T. +33 (0)1 42 76 88 62

ALESSANDRO RUSSINO
T. +39 380 258 2646
F. +39 02 700 401 866
photo@alessandrorussino.com
www.alessandrorussino.com

MITCHELL SAMS
T. +44 (0)7788 750 517

THOMAS SCHENK
CLM
London: T. +44 (0)20 7750 2999
NY: +1 212 941 1660
www.clmuk.com

DENNIS SCHOENBERG
T. + 44 (0)7974 778 926
d-schoenberg@hotmail.com

SCHOHAJA
T. +33 (0)6 85 84 07 07
schohaja@yahoo.de

COLLIER SCHORR
Art + Commerce
NY: T. +1 212 886 0566
agents@artandcommerce.com
Paris: T. +33 (0)1 44 76 07 07
vsimonet@paris.artandcommerce.com
www.artandcommerce.com

ELFIE SEMOTAN
Walter Schupfer Management
NY: T. +1 212 366 4675
Paris: T. +33 (0)1 44 54 81 10
mail@wschupfer.com
www.wschupfer.com

WING SHYA
Cathy Yu
T. +85 293 771 670
cathy@atworkshop.com

DAVID SIMS
MAP
London: T. +44 (0)20 7424 9144
NY: T. +1 212 677 2690
info@mapltd.com
www.mapltd.com

JULIE SLEAFORD
T. +44 (0)1621 816 347

DAVID SLIJPER
CLM
London: T. +44 (0)20 7750 2999
NY: +1 212 941 1660
www.clmuk.com

FRANCESCA SORRENTI
Webber
T. +44 (0)20 7439 0678
www.webberrepresents.com

MARIO SORRENTI
Smile
T. +44 (0)20 7792 5566
www.smilemanagement.com

VANINA SORRENTI
MAP
London: T. +44 (0)20 7424 9144
NY: T. +1 212 677 2690
info@mapltd.com
www.mapltd.com

EWEN SPENCER
Marco Santucci
T.+44 (0)20 7226 7705
email@marcosantucci.com
www.marcosantucci.com

JOHN SPINKS
East Photographic
T. +44 (0)20 7729 9002
www.eastphotographic.com

ELLEN STAGG
Vue Represents
T. +1 212 431 5780
rockstarvue@mindsprind.com

RONALD STOOPS
ronaldstoops@hotmail.com

STEEN SUNDLAND
MAP
London: T. +44 (0)20 7424 9144
NY: T. +1 212 677 2690
info@mapltd.com
www.mapltd.com

SOLVE SUNDSBO
Clare Powell
T. +44 (0)20 7613 2020

TAKAY
ESP
London: T. +44 (0)20 7209 1626
NY: T. +1 212 431 8090
info@esp-agency.com
www.esp-agency.com

JUERGEN TELLER
Katy Baggott
T. +44 (0)20 8964 1109

GUSTAVO TEN HOEVER
Andre WETHER & Associes
T. +33 (0)1 45 23 93 93
www.andrewether.fr

TESH
Streeters
T. +44 (0)20 7253 3330
rachel@streetersuk.co.uk

WOLFGANG TILLMANS
Interim Art
T. +44 (0)20 7729 4112

MARCUS TOMLINSON
Art Department
T. +1 212 925 4222
info@art-dept.com
www.art-dept.com

NICOLE TREVILLIAN
T. +44 (0)7766 412 366
mail@nicoletrevillian.com
www.nicoletrevillian.com

TERRY TSIOLIS
Management + Artists
NY: T. +1 212 931 9311
mao@managementartists.com
Paris: T. +33 (0)1 42 71 60 60
daniel@managementartists.fr
www.managementartists.com

RUSSELL UNDERWOOD
T. +44 (0)207 354 2987
russunderwood@blueyonder.co.uk

MAX VADUKUL
Max Vadukul Inc.
T. +1 212 683 6160
office@maxvadukul.com

WILLY VANDERPERRE
Management + Artists
NY: T. +1 212 931 9311
mao@managementartists.com
Paris: T. +33 (0)1 42 71 60 60
daniel@managementartists.fr
www.managementartists.com

ELLEN VON UNWERTH
Smile
T. +44 (0)20 7792 5588
www.smilemanagement.com

JAN WELTERS
Management + Artists
NY: T. +1 212 931 9311
mao@managementartists.com
Paris: T. +33 (0)1 42 71 60 60
daniel@managementartists.fr
www.managementartists.com

PAUL WETHERELL
MAP
London: T. +44 (0)20 7424 9144
NY: T. +1 212 677 2690
info@mapltd.com
www.mapltd.com

ROBERT WYATT
The Katy Barker Agency
London: T. +44 (0)20 7493 3933
NY: T. +1 212 627 2558
Paris: T. +33 (0)142 97 90 31
www.katybarker.com

INDEX

C.P.
COMPANY

protest, support and act at www.diesel.com

GIORGIO ARMANI

GIORGIO ARMANI

I don't get married men anymore.

One man said it's because his wife is taking all his money.

a Harvey Nichols Fashion Victim

PAUL
SMITH

Prada Tel +44 207 399 2030

PR

Y's YOHJI YAMAMOTO

M·A·C

MAKE-UP ART COSMETICS

Lifestyle

Angelika Taschen / a.taschen@taschen.com

"A backbreaking photographic survey of African interiors."
—*Icon,* London, on *Inside Africa*

INSIDE AFRICA
Ed. Angelika Taschen / Deidi von Schaewen / Hardcover,
2 volumes, format: 24 x 31.6 cm (9.4 x 12.4 in.), 912 pp.
€ 99.99 / $ 125 / £ 69.99 / ¥ 15.000

"Tout est dit dans ces images qui nous font visiter l'Afrique dans sa splendeur et sa pluralité."
—*Le Figaro,* Paris, on *Inside Africa*

INSIDE ASIA
Photos: Reto Guntli / Ed. Angelika Taschen / Sunil Sethi /
Hardcover, 2 volumes, format: 24 x 31.6 cm (9.4 x 12.4 in.),
880 pp.
€ 99.99 / $ 125 / £ 69.99 / ¥ 15.000

Charlotte & Peter Fiell
Charlotte.Fiell@btopenworld.com
Julius Wiedemann
j.wiedemann@taschen.com

ANIMATION NOW!
Ed. Julius Wiedemann / Flexi-cover, book
+ DVD, format: 19.6 x 24.9 cm
(7.7 x 9.8 in.), 576 pp.
**€ 29.99 / $ 39.99 / £ 19.99 /
¥ 5.900**

DESIGNING THE 21st CENTURY
Ed. Charlotte & Peter Fiell / Flexi-cover,
format: 19.6 x 24.9 cm (7.7 x 9.8 in.),
576 pp.
**€ 29.99 / $ 39.99 / £ 19.99 /
¥ 5.900**

FASHION
The Collection of the Kyoto Costume
Institute / Ed. The Kyoto Costume Institute /
Flexi-cover, format: 19.6 x 27.3 cm
(7.7 x 10.7 in.), 736 pp.
**€ 29.99 / $ 39.99 / £ 19.99 /
¥ 5.900**

FASHION NOW
Ed. Terry Jones, Avril Mair / Flexi-cover,
format: 19.5 x 25 cm (7.7 x 9.8 in.),
640 pp.
**€ 29.99 / $ 39.99 / £ 19.99 /
¥ 5.900**

GRAPHIC DESIGN
FOR THE 21st CENTURY
Charlotte & Peter Fiell / Flexi-cover,
format: 19.6 x 24.9 cm (7.7 x 9.8 in.),
640 pp.
**€ 29.99 / $ 39.99 / £ 19.99 /
¥ 5.900**

JAPANESE GRAPHICS NOW!
Ed. Gisela Kozak, Julius Wiedemann /
Flexi-cover, book + DVD, format:
19,6 x 24,9 cm (7.7 x 9.8 in.),
608 pp.
**€ 29.99 / $ 39.99 / £ 19.99 /
¥ 5.900**

SCANDINAVIAN DESIGN
Charlotte & Peter Fiell / Flexi-cover,
format: 19.6 x 25.2 cm (7.7 x 9.9 in.),
704 pp.
**€ 29.99 / $ 39.99 / £ 19.99 /
¥ 5.900**

STARCK
Texts: Ed Mae Cooper, Pierre Doze,
Elisabeth Laville / Flexi-cover, format:
19.6 x 25.8 cm (7.7 x 10.1 in.), 576 pp.
**€ 29.99 / $ 39.99 / £ 19.99 /
¥ 5.900**

1000 LIGHTS.
VOL. 1: 1878 TO 1959
Ed. Charlotte & Peter Fiell / Flexi-cover,
format: 19.6 x 26.7 cm (7.7 x 10.5 in.),
576 pp.
**€ 29.99 / $ 39.99 / £ 19.99 /
¥ 5.900**

1000 LIGHTS.
VOL. 2: 1960 TO PRESENT
Ed. Charlotte & Peter Fiell / Flexi-cover,
format: 19.6 x 26.7 cm (7.7 x 10.5 in.),
576 pp.
**€ 29.99 / $ 39.99 / £ 19.99 /
¥ 5.900**

TASCHEN'S 1000 FAVORITE WEBSITES
Ed. Julius Wiedemann / Flexi-cover,
book + DVD, format: 19.6 x 24.9 cm
(7.7 x 9.8 in.), 608 pp.
**€ 29.99 / $ 39.99 / £ 19.99 /
¥ 5.900**

1000 CHAIRS
Charlotte & Peter Fiell / Flexi-cover, Klotz,
format: 14 x 19.5 cm (5.5 x 7.7 in.),
768 pp.
**€ 19.99 / $ 29.99 / £ 14.99 /
¥ 3.900**

ART NOUVEAU
Klaus-Jürgen Sembach / Flexi-cover,
format: 19.6 x 24.5 cm (7.7 x 9.6 in.),
240 pp.
**€ 14.99 / $ 19.99 / £ 9.99 /
¥ 2.900**

JAPANESE GARDENS
Günter Nitschke / Flexi-cover, format:
19.6 x 24.5 cm (7.7 x 9.6 in.), 240 pp.
**€ 14.99 / $ 19.99 / £ 9.99 /
¥ 2.900**

SIXTIES DESIGN
Philippe Garner / Flexi-cover, format:
18.4 x 24.5 cm (7.2 x 9.6 in.), 176 pp.
**€ 14.99 / $ 19.99 / £ 9.99 /
¥ 2.900**

© 2005 TASCHEN GmbH
Hohenzollernring 53, D–50672 Köln
www.taschen.com

Original edition: © 2003 TASCHEN GmbH
Editors: Terry Jones & Avril Mair
Creative Co-ordinator: Matthew Hawker
Managing Editor: Eloise Alemany
Production Manager: Jane Peverley
Fashion Editors: Edward Enninful, Marcus Ross, David Lamb, Fiona Dallanegra
Editorial Assistance: Mark Hooper & Glenn Waldron
Executive Director: Tricia Jones

Writers: James Anderson, Terry Burgess, Lee Carter, Nick Compton, Teddy Czopp, Nicole Fall, Jo-Ann Furniss, Mark Hooper, Jamie Huckbody, Dan Jones, Hellin Kay, Jörg Koch, David Lamb, Gianluca Longo, Avril Mair, Laurie Pike, Peter De Potter, Marcus Ross, Susie Rushton, Lucy Ryder-Richardson, Josh Sims, Glenn Waldron

Photographers: Linda Aldredge, Constant Anée, David Armstrong, Kim Weston Arnold, Anette Aurell, Christian Badger, David Bailey, Kent Baker, Barnaby & Scott, Orion Best, Anuschka Blommers, Mark Borthwick, Elisabeth Broekaert, Hamish Brown, Richard Burbridge, Richard Bush, Sergio Calatroni, Giovanni Calemma, Martha Camarillo, Davide Cernuschi, Donald Christie, James Cochrane, Cricchi and Ferrante, Sean Cunningham, Kevin Davies, Corinne Day, Sophie Delaporte, Claudio dell'Olio, Jan-Willem Dikkers, David Dorcich, Andrew Dosunmu, Pete Drinkell, Larry Dunstan, Sean Ellis, Glen Erler, Jason Evans, Fabrizio Ferri, Simon Flamigni, Huger Foote, Roberto Franckenberg, Gauthier Gallet, Kate Garner, Tierney Gearon, Johnny Giunta, Nathaniel Goldberg, Stefano Guindani, Andrew Hobbs, Alex Hoerner, Rainer Hosch, Kayt Jones, Matt Jones, Terry Jones, Greg Kadel, Richard Kern, Steven Klein, Kirby Koh, Flo Kolmer, Gleb Kosorukov, Hiroshi Kutomi, David LaChapelle, Karl Lagerfeld, Serge Leblon, Mark Lebon, Duc Liao, Armin Linke, Greg Lotus, Cyrus Marshall Craig McDean, Alasdair McLellan, Donald Milne, Michel Momy, Eddie Monsoon, Stefano Moro, Shawn Mortensen, Jeremy Murch, Helmut Newton, Ellen Nolan, Laurence Passera, Bianca Pilet, Marc Quinn, Terry Richardson, Mischa Richter, Christophe Rihet, Paolo Roversi, Amber Rowlands, Alessandro Russino, Mitchell Sams, Thomas Schenk, Dennis Schoenberg, Schohaja, Collier Schorr, Niels Schumm, Elfie Semotan, Wing Shya, Shari Simonsen, David Sims, Julie Sleaford, David Slijper, Francesca Sorrenti, Mario Sorrenti, Vanina Sorrenti, John Spinks, Ellen Stagg, Ronald Stoops, Steen Sundland, Solve Sundsbo, Takay, Juergen Teller, Gustavo Ten Hoever, Tesh, Tetsu, Luke Thomas, Wolfgang Tillmans, Marcus Tomlinson, Tony Torres, Nicole Trevillian, Terry Tsiolis, Russell Underwood, Ellen Von Unwerth, Max Vadukul, Willy Vanderperre, Camille Vivier, Anthony Ward, Jan Welters, Paul Wetherell, Robert Wyatt

Stylists: Mark Anthony, Catherine Ayme, William Baker, Victoria Bartlett, Rushka Bergman, Joanna Blades, Tal Brener, Terry Burgess, Belen Casadevall, Tamara Cincik, Anna Cockburn, Giannie Couji, Fiona Dallanegra, Soraya Dayani, Cathy Dixon, Claire Durbridge, Edward Enninful, Yasmine Eslami, Lucy Ewing, Jason Farrer, Christine Fortune, Simon Foxton, Avena Gallagher, Lynette Garland, Karina Givargisoff, Carisa Glucksman, Lawrence Green, Nick Griffiths, Gareth Griffiths, Sarah Hackett, Jane How, Jamie Huckbody, John Hullum, Hellin Kay, Jonathan Kaye, Geriada Kefford, Kanako B Koga, Havana Laffitte, David Lamb, Merryn Leslie, Hortense Manga, Loic Masi, Alastair McKimm, Annett Monheim, Thom Murphy, Samira Nasr, Diana Oberlander, Mel Ottenburg, Rebecca Oura, Antonio Picardie, Lucy Pinter, Karl Plewka, Katja Rahlwes, Timothy Reukauf, Sarah Richardson, Olivier Rizzo, Marcus Ross, Nicoletta Santoro, Sabina Schreder, Nadine Shaw, Yoshiyuki Shimazu, Richard Simpson, Simonez, James Sleaford, Sean Spellman, Neil Stuart, Toshio Takeda, Miranda Warburton, Patti Wilson, Brana Wolf, Stephanie Wolf, Kate Young, Rachael Zilli

Hair and make-up: Chuck Amos, Marion Anee, Frank B, Philipe Baligan, Michael Boadi, James Brown, Adam Bryant, Sam Bryant, Lisa Butler, AlexSandra Byrne, Jonathan Connelly, Liz Daxauer, Aaron De May, Max Delorme, Hina Dohi, Sharon Dowsett, Julien D'ys, Lisa Eastwood, Malcolm Edwards, Lisa Eldridge, Eric Farrell, Eric Foreman, Mary-Jane Frost, Val Garland, Peter Gray, Charlie Green, Andrew GN, Guido, Inge Grognard, HB, Rick Haylor, J Hallam, Sally Herschberger, Julie Jacobs, Nicholas Jurnjak, James Kaliardos, Diane Kendall, Gemma Kidd, Devra Kinery, Stephen Lacey, Ayo Laguda, Maxine Leonard, Emma Lovell, Siobhan Luckie, Mandy Lyons, Christian McCulloch, Pat McGrath, Sam McKnight, Liz Martins, Ed Moelands, Kay Montana, Neil Moodie, Matt Mulhall, Luigi Murena, Jimmy Paul, Frankie Payne, Petros Petrohilos, Peter Philips, Alain Pichon, Lucia Pieroni, Orlando Pita, Liz Pugh, Stacey Ross, Wendy Rowe, Rudi, Kevin Ryan, Raphael Salley, Samantha, Johnnie Sapong, Sebastian, Earl Simms, Romy Soleimani, Eugene Souleiman, Collier Strong, Debbie Stone, Taku, Bernadette Thompson, Charlotte Tilbury, Fernando Torrent, Francisco Vallera, Ward, Ashley Ward, Eli Wakamatsu, Gucci Westman, Oliver Woods and all the others who contributed.

Assistants: Karen Leong, Jenny Moore, Thomas Persson, Oriana Reich, Gordon Shettle, Adele Smith, Lesley Syme, Stephen Toal

Editorial co-ordination: Simone Philippi, Bonn
Production co-ordination: Ute Wachendorf, Cologne
Cover design: Sense/Net, Andy Disl and Birgit Reber, Cologne
German translation: Henriette Zeltner, Munich; Clara Drechsler, Cologne
French translation: Claire Le Breton, Paris; Jacques Bosser, Paris

Printed in China
ISBN 3-8228-4075-0